Sir David Nairne

Studies in the History and Culture of Scotland

Volume 8

PETER LANG
Oxford · Bern · Berlin · Bruxelles · Frankfurt am Main · New York · Wien

Edward Corp

Sir David Nairne

The Life of a Scottish Jacobite at the Court of the Exiled Stuarts

PETER LANG

Oxford · Bern · Berlin · Bruxelles · Frankfurt am Main · New York · Wien

Bibliographic information published by Die Deutsche Nationalbibliothek.
Die Deutsche Nationalbibliothek lists this publication in the Deutsche National-
bibliografie; detailed bibliographic data is available on the Internet at
http://dnb.d-nb.de.

A catalogue record for this book is available from the British Library.

Library of Congress Control Number: 2017957943

Cover design by Peter Lang Ltd.

ISSN 1661-6863
ISBN 978-1-78707-934-2 (print) • ISBN 978-1-78707-935-9 (ePDF)
ISBN 978-1-78874-297-9 (ePub) • ISBN 978-1-78874-298-6 (mobi)

© Peter Lang AG 2018

Published by Peter Lang Ltd, International Academic Publishers,
52 St Giles, Oxford, OX1 3LU, United Kingdom
oxford@peterlang.com, www.peterlang.com

This publication has been peer reviewed.

Printed in Germany

Sir David Nairne

Marie-Elisabeth Nairne

*The decision to write this biography was taken in 1992,
and the necessary research mainly carried out between that year and 2005.
The book was then written between 2013 and 2016.
The preparation of any book, particularly one produced over a
period of a quarter of a century, involves considerable personal sacrifice.
If this is true for the author, it is even more true for the author's
wife and family. This biography of Sir David Nairne could not possibly
have been written without the constant patience and generous
support of my wife Elizabeth, who not only put up with the presence of
Nairne in our lives, but also read, criticized and even copy-edited
each part of the book as it was written, as well as making all the
many translations from French into English. The biography is therefore
dedicated to her, with endless love and limitless gratitude.*

Contents

Illustrations

A Note on Translations

Although David Nairne was Scottish, he lived most of his life in France. For this reason his surviving papers (his diary and his letters) are written in French as well as English. For example, the diary of his visit to Italy in 1689–91 is entirely written in French. So too are both his copious correspondence with Cardinal Gualterio from 1713 to 1719, and the surviving letters written by his daughters. For the convenience of the reader, all quotations in the main text from these and other French sources have been translated into English. This is regrettable, because the flavour of Nairne's French cannot therefore be compared with that of his English. However all quotations in the endnotes have been left in the original language, for any readers who wish to study the subject beyond the basic text.

The many translations, which run throughout the entire book, have been made by my wife Elizabeth. In doing them, she has preferred the clarity of modern English rather than a recreation of the late seventeenth- or early eighteenth-century style which Nairne uses in his English letters. To this extent, the contrast between what Nairne wrote in French and what he wrote in English may have been maintained.

Nairne's Unique Position at the Court and in Jacobite Historiography

For nearly forty years, David Nairne was actively involved in the administration of Jacobite politics. A member of the exiled courts of the Stuart kings James II and James III, he worked for and with a succession of Jacobite secretaries of state: the Earl of Melfort; John, Lord Caryll; the Earl of Middleton; the Duke of Mar; the Earl of Dunbar; and the Earl of Inverness. Although his social status was unquestionably lower than that of these titled aristocrats, he was nevertheless just as involved in conducting Jacobite correspondence, deciding on Jacobite policies, and negotiating with the courts of Versailles, Lunéville and Rome. Moreover he enjoyed particularly close relations for most of the period with both of the exiled kings. Despite this, his name is not well known to most historians of the period, and one purpose of the present biography is to restore him to the relatively prominent and influential position which he occupied at the time.

It is unusual to be able to produce a comprehensive biography of a subordinate official. After all, most political biographies of the seventeenth and eighteenth centuries concentrate on the activities of monarchs, statesmen, diplomatists, aristocrats and other influential figures at the top level of society. They were not only the people who were responsible for the policies which they themselves formulated, they were also the people who preserved the archives on which most biographical studies are based. Yet political administration and diplomacy have always involved lesser individuals – often described as clerks or secretaries – who carried out subordinate duties like drafting, copying, translating and filing, and who might also, as was the case with David Nairne, have been asked to give advice and help formulate policy. All too often, we know little or nothing about these people beyond their names, their official positions, and perhaps their salaries, for the simple reason that the information concerning their private and even their public lives has regrettably not survived. David Nairne was both an observer and a participant in the struggle of the exiled Stuart monarchs to regain their kingdoms between 1689 and the end of the 1720s. It is therefore particularly fortunate that the chance survival of many of his papers has made it possible to reconstruct a full account of his life from his birth in Scotland in 1655 until his death in Paris in 1740.

Nairne wrote well in excess of 100,000 letters during his life. Even though only a small proportion of these has survived, it is nevertheless sufficient to give us the main outlines of most of his life. In addition to these letters, we have Nairne's own autobiography, covering the years from his birth until 1689, and the private diary that he then kept from 1689 until 1708. We also have a large collection of papers which he assembled and which cover most of his official career. The survival of these various documents has made it possible to write the present biography, which provides an account of Nairne's private as well as his official life. And it should be stressed that this is the only biography which could be written about any of the hundreds of Jacobites who lived and worked at the exiled courts. We know virtually nothing about the private lives in exile of even the secretaries of state or the most senior household officials. If it were not for Nairne, we would know very little about the life of the court itself.

It is very convenient that David Nairne should be the one exception, because he occupied a unique position at that court. He was not, as the others were, a reluctant political exile, but rather a voluntary ex-patriate. All the other Jacobites at the court in France, then Italy, had chosen to follow their king into exile, and were hoping to be able to return to their homes when he was restored. Nairne was already living in France by choice when the king first arrived, and had no desire to return to Scotland. He had a French wife, a stake in a French country estate, and children who were brought up to be more French than Scottish, all of which adds an extra dimension to his biography. In addition to giving an idea of what life at the exiled court was really like for the many Jacobites who lived there, Nairne's biography provides us with a fascinating account of the social conditions experienced by a Scottish ex-patriate gentleman, dividing his time between his home in Saint-Germain and his country estate near the river Yonne, and with no obvious personal stake in helping to achieve a Stuart restoration.

There is another respect in which Nairne occupied a unique position at the exiled court. He was the only servant of his seniority at Saint-Germain who was still with the court when it moved to Rome, and thus the only person other than the king through whose eyes we can learn about the gradual evolution of the court, and discover the contrast between what the court had been like in France and what it became in Italy. Moreover when the court did move to Rome, Nairne was the only courtier who had previously lived there.

These are not the only reasons why Nairne is such an ideal subject for a biography. As a young man in Paris he became particularly keen on playing and listening to music, and was acquainted if not friendly with some of the leading French composers living in the city. His diary and his letters give us precious information about the musical life of the exiled court. A little later, under the tutelage of Lord Melfort, himself a great connoisseur of painting, Nairne was introduced to many of the painters and dealers in Rome and became in his turn very experienced in commissioning portraits, particularly of the Stuart royal family. Our knowledge of the cultural life of the court, both musical and artistic, would be very considerably diminished if we did not have the testimony of David Nairne.

It is, however, his involvement in politics which is the most important theme in this biography. Nairne accompanied James II to Ireland in 1689, and to both La Hougue in 1692 and Calais in 1696 when the king was hoping to invade England with a Franco-Irish army. By the end of James II's life, Nairne had perhaps become the king's most trusted servant (his confessor excluded): he was entrusted with all the king's personal papers, and used them to write James II's first biography. Nairne was then closely involved in the negotiations with the French court leading up to the Franco-Jacobite attempt to invade Scotland in 1708. On that occasion, he sailed to Scotland in the same ship as James III. From 1711 to 1714, Nairne played a crucial role in the negotiations between James III and the Tory ministers in London aimed at repealing the Act of Settlement and preventing the Hanoverian Succession. Indeed, from 1714 to 1715, Nairne was the exiled king's principal adviser. He was with the king in Scotland during the

'Fifteen' rising, and again sailed back with him to France in the same ship. A little later he was accredited as James III's minister at the papal court when the king was in Spain planning yet another unsuccessful attempt to invade Great Britain. He made the arrangements at the court for the birth in Rome of Prince Charles Stuart ('Bonnie Prince Charlie') and, as an old man, remained a shrewd observer of the unfortunate developments at the court during the 1720s.

It is only by examining the testimony of Nairne that we can fully appreciate this gradual change in the nature of the exiled court, which had a significant impact on the prospects of the Jacobite movement as a whole. James II has a bad reputation among most British historians, but it is clear that he was dearly loved and respected by his servants at Saint-Germain. So too at first was his son, as Prince of Wales and then as James III. But the Hanoverian Succession in 1714, followed by the failure of the 'Fifteen', had a profound effect on the latter's personality. The young king, treated as an equal by Louis XIV at Versailles and Marly, and assuming that he would one day succeed his half-sister Anne as *de facto* King of Great Britain and Ireland, was embittered by the unexpected events of 1714–16, which completely undermined his prospects and his self-confidence. Through the correspondence of Nairne we can watch as the exiled Catholic king, now forced to live in the Papal States, gradually came under the influence of a small group of Protestants who gave him bad advice and deliberately alienated him from the people who had served him until then. We can see how Nairne in particular, having been the king's principal adviser, was gradually supplanted by these new favourites who succeeded in dominating James III and persuading him to follow their advice. As this even extended to the unkind way in which he treated his wife, Queen Clementina, and the ill-judged way in which he brought up their elder son Prince Charles, Nairne's letters permit us to understand how the king's personality hardened, and how it developed an unpleasant streak which had serious long-term consequences for Jacobitism. Nairne served the king in Italy through loyalty and obedience, whereas he had also served him in France with profound affection. And in this respect Nairne's experience was representative of the court as a whole. Through his testimony, we are able to appreciate the extent to which James III, obliged to live as the guest of an unpredictable papacy, and with little immediate prospect of a restoration, ceased to be the attractive young prince that he had once been, and alienated the leading Jacobites who might otherwise have chosen to live at his court.

Although he was an ex-patriate, and although his primary loyalty was to the Jacobite king, Nairne remained very conscious of his Scottish origins. He enjoyed very close relations with the members of the Collège des Ecossais in Paris, whom he visited whenever he could, and with whom he often corresponded on a daily basis. He also took a particular interest both in the Catholic mission to Scotland and in the general history of the country.

One important aspect of the history of Scotland concerns the development of Freemasonry. This subject is so shrouded in mystery that it is not surprising that Nairne's own links with the Craft remain obscure. But Nairne occupies a significant place in the history of Freemasonry because he was extremely friendly with the Chevalier Ramsay, another voluntary Scottish ex-patriate living in France. Ramsay was not only the author of one of the most important and influential texts in the entire history of Freemasonry, but was also married to one of Nairne's daughters. Masonic historians have known virtually nothing about Ramsay's wife, let alone the father-in-law with whom the couple was living when he (Ramsay) wrote his celebrated *Discours*. An account of Nairne's private life (his marriage, and the lives of his children) therefore adds considerably to our knowledge and understanding of this aspect of masonic history. Despite the differences in their ages, Nairne and Ramsay quickly established a close relationship when they first met, and indeed it was because the two men were already on such good terms that Ramsay chose to marry Nairne's daughter. Like so many other people who met him, Ramsay appreciated Nairne's intellect, and his modest and engaging personality.

We know what Nairne looked like in middle age, because we have his portrait, painted when he was fifty-nine years old.[1] He had brown eyes, and a prominent scar on the left side of his chin. We also know that he was of below average height for his generation, so perhaps little more than five feet tall.[2] He was a good linguist, fluent in both French and Italian as well as his native English, and able to read and translate Latin without difficulty. He had the capacity to work for very long periods of time, and had beautiful regular handwriting, though his eyesight inevitably suffered from too much secretarial work, and he had to wear glasses for reading. He seems to have been unusually honest, but unquestionably too reserved and self-effacing. If he had been more ambitious, and a more skilful courtier, he might well have been able to advance his career and achieve a more elevated status at the court. He might also have been able to counter the unfortunate influence of the king's new Protestant favourites.

Nairne, in fact, tended towards Quietism, which had been defended by Ramsay in the biography he wrote of his spiritual mentor, Archbishop Fénelon. Nairne was a convert to Catholicism, and was exceptionally pious, even by the standards of his time. In particular, he had a profound faith in Divine Providence, which inclined him to accept all adversity as God's will, and which inspired him to be optimistic about the eventual prospects of a Jacobite restoration. To a great extent this originated in the events of 1688–9. He had remained unemployed in Paris, despite all his attempts to obtain a position, so that he had been available to serve James II and Lord Melfort when they had been forced into exile. If anything good happened, such as when he and James III were not captured or shipwrecked when returning to France from Scotland in 1708 or 1716, then their lives had been preserved by Divine Providence. If one of his children recovered from an illness, or when his daughter remained a spinster so that the Chevalier Ramsay could propose marriage to her, this was also due to Divine Providence. But this calm acceptance of God's will, whereby the expected Jacobite restoration was merely delayed for reasons known to Him, could not be sustained indefinitely, and it seems that in his old age Nairne came to accept that God did not intend there to be an eventual triumph for the Jacobite cause.

For most of his career, however, Nairne's Quietism and essential goodness made him an agreeable companion. He was a good husband and a loving father, though he completely failed to establish good relations with his son and heir. He was sociable and never let his piety interfere with his enjoyment. He liked entertaining with his wife, he liked dancing, and he loved music and the visual arts (particularly painting and decorated baroque churches). He was also charitable. His greatest virtue, however, lay in his ability to bring people together and act as a peacemaker. When a succession dispute arose over his wife's family estate he was able to bring the two sides together and effect a compromise. If there was sometimes tension at the exiled court between the three British nationalities (English, Irish and Scottish), he was noted for maintaining good relations with all three, and for inviting all three to his home. If there was friction at the court, he did his best to remain neutral, though by the 1720s, when the king's favourites were badly treating the queen, he was no longer able to achieve this.

In fact, his entire career was only made possible because he was able to establish and maintain good relations with virtually all the people with whom he worked, and this is particularly evident in his dealings with the secretaries of state at Saint-Germain. He first worked for the Earl of Melfort, who was also Scottish and with whom he became a personal friend. Yet when Melfort was forced to resign and was replaced by John Caryll, an Englishman, Nairne established equally good relations with his new superior. Melfort was a bitter rival, if not enemy, of the Earl of Middleton, yet Nairne then began to work for Middleton as well as Caryll and established equally good relations with him. All the while, Nairne maintained his friendship with Melfort, so that eventually he was able to effect a reconciliation between the latter and Middleton. It was this sort of thing which made Nairne so popular at the exiled court. He was respected for his moderation and his relative lack of ambition, his desire to avoid conflict and confrontation, and his wish to preserve harmony among the courtiers who served the exiled kings. It was his failure to achieve this in his later years when the court was in Rome, and when the treatment of Queen Clementina was in such marked contrast to the respect shown to Mary of Modena at Saint-Germain, that made him keen to retire and live peacefully in Paris.

In one typical letter, sent from Cadiz in 1723, the king's former legal adviser, an Irishman who had decided to return to Ireland, and who had not seen Nairne for over ten years, wrote: 'My dear and most beloved friend, ... according to my hart you know I can't but love you, and believe I do above all Gentlemen this side of the water.'[3] It is in part his ability to inspire sentiments like this that makes Nairne an ideal subject for an extended biography. His honesty and relative detachment, combined with the chance survival of his diary and of so much of his private and official correspondence, mean that we are able to view the evolution of the exiled court at Saint-Germain-en-Laye, Bar-le-Duc, Avignon, Pesaro, Urbino, Rome and Bologna through his eyes.

Endnotes

1. It was painted by Alexis-Simon Belle at Bar-le-Duc in 1714. See p. 218
2. In one of his letters, Nairne told Cardinal Gualterio that 'le Comte de Douglas est un petit homme un peu pres de ma hauteur' (BL. Add MSS 31260, f.124, 26 August 1717). In a letter written a few months later, the Earl of Southesk referred to 'little Nairne' (HMC *Stuart* V, p. 204, to Paterson, 13 November 1717).
3. RA. SP 68/101, Power to Nairne, 23 August 1723. For Robert Power, see p. 144 and p. 195, note 21.

CHAPTER I

The Making of a Jacobite: From Scotland to France and Ireland, 1655–1689

David Nairne left Scotland at the age of eighteen, and lived most of his life abroad, but he remained conscious and proud of his Scottish origins. His family possessed the estate of Sandford in Fife, where it had been established for as long as anyone could remember, and he would himself have become the Laird of Sandford if the estate had not been confiscated by the government of William III.

In December 1716, when he was living in Avignon, Nairne received a bundle of papers concerning what he described as the family's 'antient little estate'. 'The oldest paper', he noted with some pride, 'is I think in 14th age [i.e. century] signd by one George Nairne of St foord which itself is I think a proof of pretty old standing of that Estates being in the name, about 400 years ago.'[1] A little later, by which time he was living in Urbino, he described the Nairnes as 'an old Scottish family whose title dates back more than 400 years and whose lands remained in their possession until the Revolution.'[2]

This statement was not entirely correct: the Nairnes had actually lost their estates temporarily during the upheavals of the 1650s. David's father, Sir Thomas, was captured during the Anglo-Scottish war of 1650–1 and imprisoned in London.[3] By the time he was released, in 1653 or 1654, the Cromwellian government had leased and then sold the estate to one Alexander Walker, and it was not recovered until the restoration of Charles II in 1660.[4] It was during that period, when the family was dispossessed, that David Nairne was born – 'about ye end of August' 1655.[5]

The family had presumably taken up temporary residence in St Andrews, because David was baptized near there, in St Fillan's Church, on 7 September. The identity of his godmother is unknown, but his two godfathers came

from the family of his mother Margaret. One was his grandfather, Sir David
Barclay of Collarnie; the other was his grandmother's brother, David Leslie.[6]
The latter had been commander-in-chief of the Scottish forces at both
Dunbar and Worcester, and was to be given a peerage as Baron Newark in
1661. It was no doubt partly through his influence that the Nairnes were
able to recover their estates in the general land settlement of 1660.

David Nairne matriculated at St Salvator's College in nearby
St Andrews in 1669, and remained there for four years. It is not known
what he studied. At that time the students of the university paid their fees
at one of three rates: the sons of peers the highest, the sons of landed or
professional men the middle, and the sons of artisans the lowest. Nairne
was predictably placed in the second category, but at his graduation in
1673, when a student's social status gave way to his academic performance,
he was placed top of his entire year. He then paid for his BA degree[7] and
returned to Sandford to decide on his future career.

During the previous year various members of the Nairne family had
registered their arms with the Lord Lyon. Apart from David himself, the
surviving list includes his grandfather Alexander, but not his father Sir
Thomas, who had died in July 1664. It also includes his elder brother, called
Alexander like his grandfather and described as the Master of Sandford.[8]
He had two younger brothers (not included in the list) and one sister, all
of whom are mentioned in his diary. One brother is referred to as Sam,
but neither of the other two names is ever given.

As his elder brother would in due course inherit the family estates,
David was destined to become a lawyer. It is not clear how he occupied
himself from 1673 to 1674. We may assume that he began some legal studies, perhaps at St Andrews, where he also paid for his MA degree.[9] At that
time, it was traditional for Scots to study the law at Dutch universities,[10]
so it might have been necessary to enter into correspondence with contacts
in the United Provinces to make the arrangements. David was to study
at the University of Leyden for six months and then at the University of
Francker for a further five, before specializing in civil law at the University
of Utrecht. He left Sandford in July 1674[11] and was probably expected to
return at the end of 1676 or during 1677. In fact, he never did return, and
saw neither his mother nor his elder brother ever again.

Nairne's diary contains plenty of information about his time as a student in the United Provinces, but does not adequately explain why he remained abroad. What was it that made him a permanent ex-patriate? He had been brought up in the Episcopalian Church of Scotland, and later converted to Catholicism. At one point, he suggested that he remained abroad because of his religion,[12] but (as we shall see) that is not a convincing explanation. His long-term plans, if he had any when he embarked at Leith in a merchant ship bound for Holland on 16 July 1674, cannot be discovered.

David Nairne's diary tells us nothing about studying law, concentrating rather on his travels and the people that he met. Thus we know that the sea voyage from Scotland to the United Provinces took ten days, during which 'wee had storme', and that in his first year he visited both Amsterdam and Haarlem. He was at Leyden from August 1674 to February 1675, and then at Francker until July. When he was at Utrecht, from July 1675 until October 1676, he fell into bad company, drank too much and even fought two duels. The first was with a fellow student called John Cockburn: 'ther was no hurt done on either side, and wee were made all friends again.'[13] The second was more serious. The Dutch were fighting a major war against France, and although England was neutral there were many English volunteers serving with the Dutch forces. Sir John Fenwick's regiment 'was in garison there that winter', and Nairne spent his free time with the younger officers. He recorded that with Lieutenant Cunningham 'I was ingagd in a duell wherein after I had given him a slight hurt in ye face he closd upon me, and in ye closing his sword or mine gave me ye cutt I bear ye mark of on my chinne, wch I did not feel nor perceive till ye blood discovered it to me after ye seconds ... had parted us.'[14] Nairne was probably lucky to escape without a more serious injury, but he was left with the scar which is clearly visible in his only known portrait.[15] Twenty years later, when looking back on these years, he referred to the 'follies of imprudent youth' and the 'effects of bad company and drinking'.[16]

In the autumn of 1676, there then occurred a turning point in Nairne's life. The United Provinces and France were still locked in war, but he decided to travel overland from Utrecht to visit Paris. It is true that the campaigning season had finished and that the frontiers between belligerent powers were not regarded in those days as uncrossable, particularly by a neutral foreigner. But still it was an unexpected decision. Was he discontented with his legal studies and reluctant to go back to Scotland? Or was he merely keen to see a little more of continental Europe before returning to Fife? There is no means of knowing, though his diary implies the latter. In any event, Nairne left Utrecht in October 1676 and travelled for eight days through Holland, Zealand and the Spanish Netherlands, until he reached Calais. There he boarded 'ye Calais coach for Paris', which cost him 18 *livres*. After another seven days, he reached Paris in the evening of 5 November.[17] He was to live there for the next twelve years.

There was already a Scottish community in Paris, centred around the Collège des Ecossais in the rue des Fossés-Saint-Victor, and it is possible that Nairne contacted his fellow countrymen. But he does not say so. He began by finding temporary lodgings in the rue Saint-Denis on the *rive droite*, near where the Calais coach entered Paris from the north. He then moved to the *rive gauche* near the Scots College and 'lodgd by St Etienne[-du-Mont]'.[18] Presumably he behaved like any tourist, and perhaps he intended to leave in the spring of 1677 when the weather improved. His reticence in the diary is frustrating. All he says is that after about a month he moved closer to the Seine, to what is now the Latin Quarter, and took a 'chambre garnie, rue de la Harpe, wher I fell acquainted with Mr l'abbé Jossier whose friendship induced and enabled me to stay in France longer than I intended'.[19]

It was Jossier who introduced Nairne to French society, and made him feel at home in Paris. The two men soon became the best of friends, and Nairne later recalled that 'when I was a day without seeing him he was uneasy, and when he had any treate to give or to receive, he had no plaisure unless I was of ye company, and his friends yt knew it did commonly invite me as his inseparable friend and camarad every time they invited him'.[20] All this while Nairne received an allowance from his elder brother Alexander in Scotland, supplemented by money from 'ye patrimony my father left me by his testament'.[21]

Nairne was now twenty-one years old, and in the first half of 1677 he applied himself 'wholly to learn ye French tongue', immersing himself in French history and literature, and 'conversing with French people'. He seems to have dropped the idea of studying or practising the law in Scotland. On the contrary, he began to try to obtain some employment in Paris. Jossier's father Louis had an important and influential post in the French war secretariat, responsible for payments as *trésorier extraordinaire des guerres*, and Nairne's friend promised him that he could be found a well-paid post. Nothing came of this, however, because Louis Jossier was obliged to resign. Nairne does not explain why, merely stating that 'unfortunately his affaires went wrong and he was forced to absent and could never recover his credit again nor his place ... so all my prospect of making my fortune by that means ceased.'[22]

This failure placed Nairne in a difficult position, as his family in Scotland was becoming concerned at his delayed return. In an attempt to persuade him to return to Sandford, his mother and brother cut off his allowance and refused even to send him the rest of the money he had inherited from his father. This was counter-productive. In July 1678, a few weeks short of his twenty-third birthday, Nairne informed them that he had decided 'to try to seek my fortune amongst strangers in France, since my relations did in a manner abandon me, as I termd it'.[23] He even told them that they could keep the rest of the money from his father. At this early stage in his life, Nairne seemed to be drifting towards disaster. Scarred by duelling in Utrecht, he now faced an unpromising future in a foreign country, without any income and with little prospect of gaining respectable employment. Moreover, he was a Protestant in a Catholic country where religious toleration was gradually being eroded.

What was it that motivated Nairne during these years, and how did he pass his time? It is impossible to say, but music might provide a clue. Evidence from the later years of his life shows that he not only had a profound love of music but also the ability to play several instruments to a high standard. It is possible to speculate that he was attracted by the rich and exciting musical life to be experienced in the French capital. Two of his cousins had settled in Paris in 1677 and were to stay there until 1684. These were James and Harry Maule (later 4th and 5th Earls of Panmure), who were enthusiastic musicians. The Maule brothers took lessons on the viol from the celebrated Sainte-Colombe, and were well acquainted with the latter's pupil Marin Marais. Nairne probably benefited from these contacts. It is also possible, as has been explained in detail elsewhere, that he earned a small amount of money by copying musical manuscripts.[24]

Nevertheless Nairne's decision to sever his links with his family in Scotland made him totally dependent on his friend the abbé Jossier. In August 1678 he left his 'chambre garnie' in the rue de la Harpe and accompanied Jossier to Arquenay, 'a prieury of his near Laval wher we stayd about 3 months'.[25] Back in Paris in the autumn of that year, he needed to find new and cheaper accommodation, so he moved temporarily to the rue des 'Fossés de Mr le Prince' near the Palais de Luxembourg, while looking for something permanent. The following April he moved back to the *rive droite* and 'lodged chez Mr Passanant rue St Anthoine au Griffon d'Or where I lived 7 years'.[26] It seems clear that his rent and his living expenses were now all being paid for him by Jossier.

We are not told why Nairne moved to the rue Saint-Antoine and remained there for such a long time, but it was an attractive area for someone who appreciated music. The organist in his own parish church of Saint-Paul was Henri Du Mont, one of the *sous-maîtres* of the *Chapelle Royale*, while the organist and musical director of the adjacent church of Saint-Louis des Jésuites was Michel-Richard Delalande, the most talented of the young composers living in Paris. The nearby parish church of Saint-Gervais had until very recently employed as its organist Charles Couperin, who had been training his son François (later known as Couperin *le grand*) eventually to inherit the post. Charles Couperin had died at the beginning of 1679 when his son was still only a boy, obliging the church wardens to find a replacement. Louis Jossier, despite his earlier problems, was one of the two church wardens at the time, and he persuaded Delalande to accept the post at Saint-Gervais on a temporary basis, and promise to evacuate it once François Couperin was old enough to take over.[27] Given Nairne's intimacy with the Jossier family and his strong interest in music it is likely that he was aware of this arrangement, which was made less than two months before his move to the rue Saint-Antoine. It is more than probable that he soon became acquainted with the ten-year-old François Couperin.

Nairne, however, was not a Catholic and showed no signs of becoming one – despite his dependence on the abbé Jossier. Shortly after moving to the rue Saint-Antoine, he became acquainted with Father Bruzeau, one of the priests in the church of Saint-Gervais. What followed is worth quoting at length from Nairne's diary:

> Mr Bruzeau prêtre de St Gervais ... engaged me in reading some books of controversy which gave me ye first douts of my religion. A sickness yt happened me this summer [1679] augmented my apprehensions and occasioned my applying myself seriously when ever I was recovered to instruct myself in ye controverted points of religion. To this end I had frequent disputes with Mr Bruzeau and one Mr Talon a learnd controversiste. I read ye Perpetuité de la Foy, I went twice or thrice to Mr Claude with whom I had long conferences as well as with another [Protestant] Minister of Charenton then at Paris, but got no solid satisfaction from any of them upon ye difficultys I proposd to them. I saw also ye Abbot of St Genevieve, Mr Beuvrier, with whom and with another Canon Regular of that Church I had severall conferences, and last of all I saw Mr Bossuet l'Eveque de Meaux at Paris and once at St Germains. This lasted about a 12 month before I could fully determine myself, so hard it is to change ye sentiments of religion in which one has been educated, even tho' never so erroneous. Ye 1st impression does generally so prevent people yt nothing but a particular providence and grace of God can remove that obstacle which blinds them to that degree sometimes, yt tho they have arguments layd before them as clear as demonstration they are insensible of them, and do not perceive ye convincing strength of them, till it pleases God to open their eyes afterwards, and then they wonder how they could have been so destitute of sense and reason as not to feel and see what was so plain and palpable. This was my case.[28]

Although he does not say so, Nairne's conversion seems to have gone beyond simply a question of religion. His eventual rejection of Protestantism also involved the adoption of a more sober and serious, even devout, attitude to life – a general acceptance of 'sense and reason'. Thenceforth he developed the attractive personality that would endear him to so many of his friends and acquaintances, combining modesty and reliability with an active appreciation of the fine arts. The days of duelling and excessive drinking had gone for good.

Although his own parish church was Saint-Paul, Nairne chose to be received into the Catholic faith by Father Bruzeau at Saint-Gervais. The ceremony took place privately on the Tuesday before Easter in 1680. Thereafter he regularly went to mass and took communion at Saint-Paul,[29] but he delayed his confirmation for another eighteen years. It was not until 25 May 1698, when he was living at Saint-Germain-en-Laye, that he went to Paris to be confirmed in the Cathedral of Notre Dame.[30] In his diary, he offers no explanation for this delay.

Nairne's activities during the years from 1680 to 1684 have unfortunately left no trace, and he himself made only the briefest of comments about them. In the rue Saint-Antoine, he wrote, 'I livd so retird from all my countrymen for some years yt I had almost quite forgot my english'.[31] This is surprising, because his conversion to Catholicism might then have brought him closer to the priests who ran the Collège des Ecossais. On the other hand, he remained friendly with, but also dependent on, his friend Jossier. 'I was still kept up with ye expectation of some imployment in France by ye means of my friend, who in ye mean time did very generously entertain me, and shard what he had with me like a brother'.[32]

Then, in September 1684, Nairne went to Arquenay (south-east of Laval) and 'regulated some affaires' for Jossier. He remained there until the beginning of February and it seems that while he was there he fell in love. His diary comments cryptically that 'I recd much cruelety ther from Mlle de Placé'.[33] Whatever the circumstances, Nairne cannot have seemed at that time a very good match for a young French noblewoman. Nevertheless, he was now twenty-nine years old and would benefit from making a good marriage. It seems also that Jossier was reluctant to go on financing him indefinitely, and indeed that he too was 'thinking to quitt his benefices' and get married.[34] During 1685, their friendship became increasingly strained, and Nairne realized that he would have to find some alternative arrangement before Jossier told him to provide for himself.

Matters came to a head in August and September 1685 when Nairne and Jossier visited Provins (north-east of Fontainebleau). While they were there, Nairne met and fell in love with another French noblewoman, Marie-Elisabeth de Compigny. She was then twenty-five or twenty-six years old, and her father had estates several miles to the south of Provins at Compigny and Bordes (between the Seine and the Yonne). This time his feelings were reciprocated, and his comment that 'we had some kindnes one for another'[35] is delightfully understated. Whether or not this precipitated the breach is unclear, but Nairne recalled:

> After our return from Provins, upon my refusing to signe a paper wch concerned a project he had, wch I could not as I thought with a free conscience comply with, hee grew cold and wee had some words and reproches and in fine an outfalling; I resolvd

I would be no more a charge to him, ye moment I found I was not so acceptable to him as I had been, and therefor thinking he had taken occasion of ye obligation I had to him to use me cavalierly of late, and seeing him quite changed from ye fondness and ye exces of civility he had always had for me before ... I thought it best to prevent his telling me to provide for myself, wch I did and cast myself upon providence.

Providence, of course, was Mlle de Compigny: 'I told her my circumstances, she imployed her friends for me, I petitioned ye King of France, she got Mr de Villacerf [*Contrôleur-Général des Bâtiments*] to befriend me with Mr de Louvois [*Surintendant des Bâtiments*], and I spoke myself to P. La Chaise [the king's Jesuit confessor], all wch produced me but a pension of 300 *livres* wch was payd me for ye first time in March 1686'.[36]

In the months immediately following the revocation of the Edict of Nantes (October 1685), Nairne no doubt qualified as a *nouveau converti*, but he was extraordinarily lucky to find a permanent source of income at precisely the time that he needed it, even if relatively small. In April 1686, he moved to a new home in the rue Sainte-Croix on the Ile de la Cité, and set about courting his benefactress. He does not say when he proposed and was accepted, but he spent May, June and July meeting various members of her family and visiting Compigny. On 17 September 1686, he recorded, 'I marrid Mlle de Compigny at her father's house, and we went that night to Fleurigny', the nearby château of her sister's husband. After a honeymoon of two weeks, they returned to Paris and temporarily lodged in the rue Saint-Avoye (in the *quartier* Sainte-Avoye), 'paying 57 *livres* 10 *soldes* a quarter' until they could find a more permanent home.[37]

Nairne did not mention his wife's dowry, but it cannot have been large, and as a married man he needed to supplement his small pension of 300 *livres*. 'I was everyday promised some employment', he recalled, 'and put off from time to time by Mr Malet gros fermier, by Mr de Torigny, by young Marquis de Villacerf and severall others, who had all given my wife and me reiterated promises of doing something for me.'[38] It is unlikely that any help was forthcoming from Jossier, with whom Nairne had no further contact until the summer of 1695.[39] But the newly married couple had other friends, and with their help and the money they were able to borrow because of his wife's connections, they continued to live in Paris with 'great hardships and difficultys'.[40] Their rents give some indication of their financial difficulties. After briefly living in the rue Tournon (near the

Luxembourg) from January to April 1687, they paid 62 *livres* 10 *soldes* each quarter until April 1688 for a home in the rue Neuve Saint-Méry (*quartier Saint-Martin*),[41] and then 70 *livres* for an entire year for lodgings in the nearby rue des Vieilles Etuves.[42]

Nairne determined to petition Louis XIV to augment his pension, but realized that this was unlikely to succeed unless he could produce documentary proof of his noble status in Scotland. This resulted in the creation of his birth brieve (also called borbrief), an official certificate produced in Edinburgh giving his sixteen quarterings, and occasionally granted to Scots living abroad. To obtain this parchment, of which very few examples have survived to this day, Nairne not only had to obtain the co-operation of his family in Scotland, but also had to pay the very large fees involved, which amounted to £671 17/-.[43] Nairne specifically states in his diary that he never received any money from Scotland after 1678,[44] so he presumably had to borrow a large sum in France or use his wife's dowry.

The birth brieve begins with a large family tree showing Nairne's parents, grandparents, great-grandparents and great-great-grandparents, and even gives an indication of the parents of most of those great-great-grandparents. This is endorsed by Nairne's elder brother Alexander. It continues with a written description of this 'Genealogie or pedigree', signed by the 'Representees and nearest relations of the respective families' concerned. It concludes with a lengthy document in Latin (and therefore readily understood in France), written on parchment and measuring four square feet, in which Nairne's genealogy was formally recognized in the name of the king (James VII/II) and the Lord Chancellor (the Earl of Perth). The accompanying documents, signed by the clerk of the Privy Council, state that Nairne had lived in France 'these severall years' and was 'now resolved to settle yr'. The petition is dated 24 February 1687, a little over five months after his marriage. It was formally accepted by the Scottish Privy Council on 4 March.[45]

Obtaining this valuable document must have involved both the transfer of a large amount of money and the patronage of people with influence. It must therefore have been at this time that Nairne obtained the support of the Collège des Ecossais in Paris, which was accustomed to transferring money between France and Scotland. The principal of the college was Father

Lewis Innes, who would become one of Nairne's closest friends. Innes had himself recently met and obtained the patronage of both the Secretary of State for Scotland, the Earl of Melfort, and his brother the Earl of Perth,[46] both of whom were recent converts to Catholicism.[47]

Once the birth brieve had been obtained, it had to be safely transported to France. This was done by Nairne's youngest brother, who arrived in May. Nairne then 'spoke to ye K. of France' in July and handed in a petition asking for his pension to be augmented. Within eight days, he was told that it had been increased to 400 *livres*, and he received that amount the following September.[48] He would continue to receive this French pension at about the same time every year for the rest of his life,[49] making the heavy expense he had incurred in obtaining his birth brieve a worthwhile investment.

During the following year, 1688, while events in England were moving towards the invasion by William of Orange, Nairne became increasingly friendly with the priests at the Collège des Ecossais. In addition to Lewis Innes, Nairne's new friends included Father Charles Whiteford (the procurator and prefect of studies), Father John Abercromby, a Father Muray, and John Wallace. The latter was an Episcopalian clergyman from Fife who, like Nairne himself, had converted to Catholicism and was then living in the college as a gentleman boarder.[50] Wallace would later be ordained a priest, and become the first Catholic Bishop of Edinburgh.[51]

Nairne and his wife were now looking after his youngest brother who had remained in Paris since his arrival aged twenty-three in May 1687, and who was studying medicine. Nairne recorded that his brother was 'a man free from any vice, full of good qualities, especially that of being a good friend, who had made no enemies',[52] and that his wife Marie-Elisabeth loved him 'like a brother'.[53] Like his older brother, back in 1679, the young man was questioning the Episcopalian faith in which he had been educated in Fife, so Nairne introduced him to Father Bruzeau at the church of Saint-Gervais, hoping that he also would be converted. Nairne recorded in his diary how he was reluctant to put any pressure on his younger brother:

> having had several discussions with Mr Bruz, read several books and agreed with many points taught by the Church he was raised in, gradually he began to recognise the true way but I left him completely free, however much I wanted him to become a Catholic and whatever joy I felt when he began to lean towards the Catholic religion

and to have doubts about his own. I never dared to put pressure on him, wanting his conversion to come entirely through his own will and the grace of God.[54]

In addition to regularly seeing his friends at the Collège des Ecossais and looking after his brother, Nairne was increasingly drawn into the family of his wife. Marie-Elisabeth's grandfather, called Nicolas Le Fèvre, had inherited the estates of Compigny and Les Bordes from his mother, an heiress named Marguerite de Guilly. In May 1625, he had changed his name from Le Fèvre to Compigny, and then acquired two further estates nearby, at Baby and Briottes. When he died in 1649, he had left Baby and Briottes to his elder son Henri de Compigny, and Compigny and Les Bordes to his younger son Louis de Compigny. Nairne's wife was a daughter of the latter. Her mother was dead, but she had one unmarried brother and one married sister. Her uncle Henri was also dead, but the estates at Baby and Briottes had been inherited by her first cousin Barthélemy, so Nairne had a father-in-law, a brother-in-law, a sister-in-law and a cousin by marriage.[55] It was not long before he also had a son.

Marie-Elisabeth's first pregnancy occurred within a few weeks of their marriage, but she miscarried in January 1687.[56] By the following summer she was pregnant again, and on 3 April 1688, in Paris, 'she was brought to bed of a son who was ondoié the 4th in the Church of St Mederie by the vicaire' and named Louis after his grandfather Louis de Compigny, who was also his godfather. The boy lived for only forty-three days, and was buried at Saint-Nicolas-des-Champs in the middle of May.[57] Nairne did not record his feelings at this loss, and was no doubt overjoyed when he discovered that his wife had become pregnant again in July.

They spent that summer at Compigny, and returned there again in the autumn, this time with Nairne's brother. There was apparently no château de Compigny, but rather a *gentilhommière*, parts of which still exist. It is now a farm on the north side of the village, 'entourée d'un étang et d'une mare',[58] in an otherwise open rolling countryside with vineyards as well as wheat fields. By 10 December, they were back in Paris,[59] where Nairne continued his fruitless search for some employment to supplement his modest French pension. It was then that his life was totally and permanently changed by the dramatic events in England. On the 21st, Mary of Modena arrived at

Calais with the baby Prince of Wales. By 7 January 1689, King James II had joined her in exile at Saint-Germain-en-Laye. They were accompanied by the Earl of Melfort, the Secretary of State, who needed to recruit a chief clerk fluent in French.

On 18 January 1689, Nairne travelled to Saint-Germain 'to kiss ye King's hand', hoping that while there he might obtain some employment. He was introduced by Lewis Innes to Lord Melfort, and by the latter to James II. Melfort was in negotiation with the ministers at Versailles, and urgently needed to have a paper translated into French, so Nairne seized his opportunity. The latter recalled that, 'being told I had been long in France, and had ye French tongue perfectly well, and knowing my family, that very night he [Melfort] sent for me and imployd me to translate a paper in French which I sat up all night to do and carryd it to him next morning'. Melfort was impressed and immediately appointed Nairne his *premier commis* or chief clerk.[60] This meant that he had to leave Paris and find himself somewhere to live in Saint-Germain.

There seems to have been no mention at this point of what salary Nairne would receive or how he was to pay for his new lodgings. His wife was over six months pregnant, and acquiring a second home outside Paris was bound to involve major expense as well as a great upheaval. Moreover, he needed to buy himself new clothes so that he could appear respectably at court. But of course the opportunity was much too good to be missed, and he readily plunged deeper into debt in order to take advantage of it. Within a short time he had used the credit he gained from his new post to borrow 2,000 *livres* from a banker in Paris.[61]

James II and Melfort, however, were preparing to leave Saint-Germain and sail to Ireland with a French army. Nairne was invited to accompany them, but was expected to make his own way to the coast, so had to face that expense as well. Fortunately James II intervened and (as Nairne recalled) 'orderd me 13 louis d'ors for ye home I had secured at St Germains and 10 louis to ride post to Brest'. Melfort obtained 'an order from M. de Louvois to furnish me with post horses on the road', and Nairne set out on 27 February. He travelled via Paris to Orléans, Angers, Nantes and southern Brittany. He reached Brest on 6 March, one day after Melfort and the king.[62]

Nairne was accompanied by a friend called Etienne du Mirail de Monnot, a Frenchman he had known in Paris during the 1680s, and whom Melfort agreed to employ as his junior clerk.[63] Nairne's wife had to remain behind as she was now eight months pregnant and in no fit state to travel, particularly to a country soon to become a major theatre of war. Though Nairne was delighted to have obtained such an important and respectable post, it is clear that he was very much upset at having to leave his wife. In his letters from Ireland he worried about her safety, her forthcoming delivery and, above all, the enormous debts she would be left with if he were to be killed at sea or in Ireland.

Nairne's work during the six months that he spent in Ireland is not of biographical importance. He spent all his time copying and translating the correspondence of Lord Melfort, who was almost continually in attendance on the king. It is more instructive to focus on the attitude he showed to his new employment, his efficiency, and the impression that he made on the secretary of state. It was these which were to have long term consequences and provide him with a career for the next forty years.

Nairne sailed to Ireland with Lord and Lady Melfort on the *Furieux*, a French warship carrying sixty guns and 350 men.[64] They left Brest on 17 March, St Patrick's Day, having been on board for ten long days 'waiting for a fair wind', and arrived safely at Kinsale on 12/22 March. From there they travelled due north to Cork, where they met the Viceroy, the Earl of Tyrconnell. James II decided to give Tyrconnell a *duke*dom and sent Nairne to ask him what title he would take. More importantly, he instructed him to prepare the warrant.[65] He had to be shown how to do this by Lord Melfort, but thereafter Nairne was given responsibility for producing and later recording royal warrants.

From Cork, Nairne travelled north-east via Kilkenny Castle to Dublin, which he reached on 28 March/7 April. During the three weeks that he was there, he re-established contact with his elder brother, now the Laird of Sandford, who had declared his support for the Jacobite forces under Lord Dundee. Nairne accompanied Melfort and the king to the siege of Derry, where they arrived on 28 April/7 May, and then returned with them to Dublin, where they remained until the second half of August.[66]

There are two journals among Nairne's papers which give details of the enormous amount of clerical work which he performed for Lord Melfort in Dublin from the middle of May to the end of July.[67] He seems to have dedicated himself to it completely, determined to impress his new master. In a private letter to Lewis Innes he referred to 'the hurry and multitude of things I have to writt by My Lords commands' and claimed to be 'allways ye first and last in ye Office', frequently having to work throughout the night.[68]

Nairne had the advantage of beautiful and very legible handwriting, a methodical approach to work, and the ability to keep papers in an orderly fashion. On 6/16 May, for example, he started keeping a 'Book of Entrys of Warrants Certificats and other Papers', recording every Household and other appointment with which he dealt.[69] It is clear that Melfort appreciated his chief clerk's hard work and efficiency. He soon came to value his loyalty as well.

By the summer of 1689 Melfort had developed a serious disagreement over strategy with the Duke of Tyrconnell, who was actively supported by the comte d'Avaux, the French ambassador attached to James II. Nairne could not help noticing and resenting the way these two men and others intrigued against Melfort. He observed that his master concentrated on his work to satisfy the king, while others concentrated on 'their divertissements to satisfy themselves':

> if an irreprochable conduct and an infatiguable labour in ye success of causes be what's required with a most excellent penetrating spirit and ye sweetest of humours, never minister of State I'm sure had more store of all those qualities yn Our Dear Lord whom I hope to see triomphe over all his ennemies.

Nairne claimed to have developed 'a real love of his person with a disinteressed attachement to all his concerns'.[70] Absolute loyalty to his masters, whether the secretaries of state or the Stuart royal family, was one of Nairne's principal characteristics.

He was clearly worried that the campaign in Ireland was not going well. 'I hope we shall meet in Englande er it be long', he informed Innes in July, while admitting that 'it's ye confidence I have in his Majesty's just cause yt makes me hope so in spite of all oppositions'.[71] As the chances of a quick military success seemed to recede, he became increasingly concerned about his wife. She had given birth in Paris to another boy, called Barthélemy, on 30 March,[72] but was extremely short of money. He entrusted his worries to Lewis Innes:

Pray see my poor wife some time, it will comfort her very much, and if you have any
occasion of getting her some little place at St Germans with ye Queen let me have
yt obligation to you with all ye others. She is a person yt you may very safely recommend – for as to vertue and discretion I know few of her sex but she may debate with,
and in ye circumstances I am in, it would be a great discharge to me who as profits
goes here am noways in a condition to maintain a family in France.[73]

He also spoke to Admiral Sir Roger Strickland, whose brother Robert
was vice-chamberlain to the queen at Saint-Germain, and persuaded him
to send a letter of recommendation.[74] However, the vacant posts in the
Household of the queen at Saint-Germain were understandably reserved
for English Jacobites who had gone into exile, and Nairne's efforts on behalf
of his wife were bound to fail.

He was right to be worried about the increasing debts his wife now
faced. In August, he obtained a credit note from Lord Melfort and hastened to send it to her. But it had to be done secretly, so that she would not
be importuned by her creditors. Once again, he asked Innes to intervene:

I desire you'l do me favour to send for her and give it her your self and desire her to
speake to nobody of ye little bill I send her because I know she may be engadged by
some persons to employ it otherways yn my designe which is that she may keep it
for her owne necessary occasions; or if you see any appearance yt she may succeed
to have some place about ye Queen, this which I have got upon credit may serve to
put her in equipage ... It will be a great comfort for me to know her settled and out
of fear of misery whatever may befall me. Pray doe not let her suspect yt wee are in
any danger here but yt all is well.[75]

Two days after Nairne wrote this letter, his baby son Barthélemy died in
Paris, having lived for only four months and twelve days. He was buried
with his brother Louis at Saint-Nicolas-des-Champs.[76]

Nairne's inability to send enough money to his wife may seem surprising, because he had an important position which gave him plenty of
opportunity to supplement his income. In part, the problem was that
James II had little money in Ireland and was not in a position to pay the
salaries of his servants, but there was more to it than that. Nairne's own
explanation reveals much about his personality and also helps us understand why he had failed to obtain any employment in Paris during the

1680s. He was willing to write with remarkable candour and had few illusions about himself:

> ye caractere of my spirit was never boldness nor presomption so I never had ye confidence to intrude myself upon any imployement, and tho' I see yt ye methods most contrary to modesty and submission are those yt commonly succeeds best at Court yet they shall never be mine let my fortune goe as it will. I thank God I can say what from ye first to ye meanest under clerk in ye Office I believe few but myself can that I never took a farthing from any man in Ireland, never touched no fees, never had a farthings profit, have refused even some very considerable bribes with disdain, and have since ever I came here lived upon what I was forced in my necessity to ask from My Lord and which he had ye goodness to advance me upon my sallery ... I envie no man's profit, I am poor, I have a family to care for and some depts to pay, but all yt can not make me a slave to interest. I have had such particular proofs of God's providence towards me yt as I never wanted hithertill, I hope I shall not want hereafter or if I doe yt same providence yt orders it for my well will certainly give me the grace to support it.[77]

His reluctance to play the courtier and his resignation to God's will would remain with him throughout his life, and become more pronounced as he grew older.

Providence intervened in the second half of August, when William III sent an army to Ireland under Marshal Schomberg and James II decided to send Melfort back to France to report on the situation to Louis XIV and Mary of Modena. Leaving Dublin on 26 August/5 September, Lord and Lady Melfort took Nairne and Monnot with them and returned via Kilkenny to Cork and thence to Kinsale. After a week 'waiting for a fair wind', they 'embarkd in a small French corvette and having a quick passage wee landed at Brest' after only two days. Melfort immediately left for Saint-Germain, and Nairne would no doubt have liked to accompany him, but he was ordered to remain with Lady Melfort, who was three and a half months pregnant, and escort her back more slowly. They left Brest on 25 September and reached Rennes on 1 October, whence Nairne wrote to Lewis Innes:

> My first visite in Paris shall be to pay my respects to you wch I hope shall be Saturday next at furthest ... I am most impatient to know ye success of My Lord's voyage and his reception in ye two courts so I long mightily to have a free and particular conversation wth you as ye only person I shall allways think it my duty to have nothing

hid from neither in My Lords nor my owne concerns, if I had any other way to show you yt I am incapable to forget ye infinit obligations I have to your kindness I should certainly make use of it.[78]

Four days later, they reached Alençon, where they rested for a day and 'visited Madame de Guise'.[79] They finally arrived in Paris on 8 October.[80]

It was not a happy homecoming. He arrived to be told that his son, whom he had never seen, had died while he was in Dublin. He also discovered that his wife's sister, Madame de Fleurigny, at whose home he had spent his honeymoon, had died.[81] Moreover he now faced an uncertain future, because it seemed unlikely that Melfort would be sent back to Ireland after reporting to Versailles and Saint-Germain, and that he in his turn would lose his post as chief clerk. On the other hand he did have the very important consolation both of living again with his wife and of being reunited with his brother, who was still studying medicine.

That, however, was to be only temporary, because Louis XIV and Mary of Modena soon decided to send Melfort to be James II's ambassador at Rome,[82] and Melfort invited Nairne to go with him as his first secretary. On 6 November, by which time his wife was pregnant once more, Nairne set off with Melfort for Rome,[83] leaving her behind again.

Endnotes

1.　SCA. BL 2/210/12, Nairne to T. Innes, 29 December 1716. There is some confusion concerning the spelling, if not even the name, of the family estate. It was actually 'Sandford', but was sometimes written as 'Sandfuird' and 'Samfoord', or variants on these. Nairne writes 'St Ford' in his diary, and the Ordnance Survey map shows that there is today a 'St Fort Home Farm' beside 'Sandford Hill'. The *Scots Peerage* says that the spellings 'St Ford' and 'St Fort' are ridiculous (letter from Slains Pursuivant to the author, 6 February 1998).

2.　BL. Add MSS 31261, f.72, Nairne to Gualterio, 20 March 1718. Little is known about the Nairnes of Sandford before the seventeenth century, but it may be noted that 'Alexander Nairne de Sandforde armiger' served as Comptroller of the Household to King James II of Scotland (1430–60) and is included in various safe conducts to England between 1446 and 1452 (Grant, Sir Francis J., ed., *Court of the Lord Lyon. List of His Majesty's Officers of Arms* (Scottish Record Society, Old Series 77, 1945), p. 25). The Nairnes of Sandford were related to the Nairnes of Kirkhill and of Strathord, both of whom had similar arms and shared the same family mottoes 'Spes Ultra' and 'Le Esperance Me Comfort' (Balfour Paul, Sir James, *An Ordinary of Arms* (Edinburgh, 1903), pp. 306–7).

3. Diary, 1658: 'My father Sr Tho Nairne of St ford and my unkle Colarnie [*sic*] were both taken prisoners at Dunbar in 1650 or Worcester in 1651 and carryd to London wher they sufferd very much for yr loyalty' to Charles II. 'Colarnie' was David Barclay, the brother of Nairne's mother Margaret.

4. The precise details of what happened to the Nairne property remain obscure. In addition to Sandford, the family seems to have possessed an estate at Wormit beside the Firth of Tay, and another at Inverdovat, a few miles to the north-east. By the 1680s, and perhaps also in the 1650s, it also had estates to the south-west, at Easter Kisleith and Langside (Douglas, Sir Robert, The *Baronage of Scotland* (Edinburgh, 1798), quoted in Slains Pursuivant to the author, 6 February 1998, for the 1650s; *Calendar of State Papers Domestic: William III, 1700–02* (London, 1937), p. 379, and *Calendar of State Papers Domestic: Queen Anne, 1703–04* (London, 1924), p. 433 for the 1680s). Hereafter *CSPD*.

5. Diary, 1655.

6. Ibid. St Fillan's Church at Forgan, sometimes called Forgan Church, is near Kirkton Barns and Leuchars, south-west of Tayport. It fell out of use in 1841, and is now a ruin. The earliest extant register of baptisms only starts in 1695. See di Falco, John, 'St Fillan's Church, Forgan, Fife', *Proceedings of the Society of Antiquaries of Scotland*, vol. 107 (1975–6), pp. 324–9; and Registrar General of Births, Deaths and Marriages, *Detailed List of Parochial Registers of Scotland* (Edinburgh, 1872), pp. 62–3.

7. Diary, 1669 and 1673; letter from the Keeper of the University of St Andrews Muniments to the author, 22 January 1993.

8. Balfour Paul, *An Ordinary of Arms*, pp. 306–7. Many years later, when living in France, Nairne carefully reproduced his arms at the back of his diary. The published list from the archives of the Lord Lyon gives the arms as 'parted per pale argent and sable On ane chaplet four mollets all Counterchanged', and the crest as 'ane Coelestial sphaere Or and azur standing on a foot gules' (ibid. p. 306). In his diary, he wrote 'Nairne of Sandford bears argent and sable parted per pale in a chaplet Or four mullets all counterchangd, insignd with a helmet answerable to his degrees mantelld gulles double argent, and for a crest on a terce of the coulours of his coat, a celestial sphere or and azure standing on a foot gueulles, and for his motto is an escrole above the same *Spes ultra*, and in a

compartment underneath his shield this other motto *l'Esperance me comforte*. He also recorded that 'upon this coat of armes Mr Weburn made these following verses impromptu

> Argento et nigro dirimit sua scuta resecta
> In palum, quinque queis stellas fulgere cernas
> Alternis vicibus, niveas nigrante colore,
> Albentique nigras.'

(Mr Weburn was Edward Weybourne, employed as Latin Secretary at Saint-Germain until his death in February 1698. See p. 96, note 248).

9. Letter from the Keeper of the University of St Andrews Muniments to the author, 22 January 1993.
10. Black, Jeremy, *The British Abroad* (Stroud, 1992), p. 289.
11. Diary, 1674.
12. He wrote in 1696: 'having had the happiness to become Cath I thought no more of going home. English are forbid to hear mass in Engld [*sic*]' (Diary, 1676).
13. Diary, 1675.
14. Ibid.
15. For this portrait, by Alexis-Simon Belle, see below, p. 218.
16. Diary, 1675.
17. Diary, 1676.
18. Diary, 1676.
19. Ibid.
20. Diary, 1680.
21. Diary, 1678.
22. Diary, 1677.
23. Diary, 1678.
24. Corp, Edward, 'The Musical Manuscripts of "Copiste Z": David Nairne, François Couperin, and the Stuart Court at Saint-Germain-en-Laye', *Revue de Musicologie*, tome 84, 1998, no. 1, pp. 37–62 (38–9).
25. Diary, 1678.
26. Diary, 1679.
27. Corp, 'Musical Manuscripts of "Copiste Z"', p. 51.
28. Diary, 1679.
29. Diary, 1680.
30. Diary, 25 May 1698.
31. Diary, 1680.
32. Ibid.
33. Diary, 1684.

34. Diary, 1680.
35. Ibid.
36. Ibid.
37. Diary, 1686.
38. Diary, 1680.
39. Diary, 22 and 28 August 1695.
40. Diary, 1680.
41. Diary, 1687. They lodged in the rue Neuve Saint-Méry with a Mlle de Fabre, with whom Nairne's wife continued to correspond after they had left (Diary, 12 June 1690, 28 May 1691, 14 July 1691). See below, p. 135, note 147.
42. Diary, 1688.
43. *The Scottish Antiquary*, ix (1895), pp. 118–24, 'Birth Brieve of Mr David Nairne, 1687'.
44. Diary, 1678.
45. Nairne's eight grandparents were George Nairne of Sandford and Beatrix Martine of Lathones; Edward Mathew of London and Penelopie Harvie of an unknown place in England; Sir David Barclay of Collarnie [*sic*: Collairnie] and Margaret Balfour of Mount Whannie and Burlay; and Patrick Lesly, Lord Lindores (son of the Earl of Rothes) and Lady Jean Stewart (daughter of the Earl of Orkney, a bastard son of King James V). His mother was therefore a third cousin of King James II, as he himself was a fourth cousin of the Prince of Wales (future James III).
46. Halloran, Brian M., *The Scots College Paris, 1603–1792* (Edinburgh, 1997). Innes had paid two recent visits to Scotland, during which he had met both Melfort and Perth, and the latter had agreed to send his son Lord Drummond to be educated at the college (ibid. pp. 58–9).
47. See the articles on Melfort and Perth by Edward Corp in the *Oxford Dictionary of National Biography* (*ODNB*) (2004), vol. 16, pp. 961–3 and pp. 968–71.
48. Diary, 1680 and 1687.
49. The pension was eventually inherited by one of his daughters: see Compigny des Bordes de Villiers de l'Isle-Adam, Alfred de, *Les Entretiens de Cambrai* (Paris, 1929), p. 62.
50. Nairne wrote very regularly to these people when he was living in Ireland and in Rome during 1689–91. He described Innes as his 'greatest friend' and Whiteford as his 'good friend' (SCA. BL 1/124/10, Nairne to L. Innes, 10/20 July 1689).
51. Halloran, *The Scots College Paris*, p. 211. The students in the college at that time included Thomas Innes (younger brother of Lewis Innes), James Gordon (later a bishop), Lord Drummond and Charles Fleming (son of the 5th Earl of Wigton), with all of whom Nairne would remain in contact in the years to come (ibid. pp. 201–11).

52. Diary, 15 February 1690:

> il etoit d'une chasteté et d'un temperance dans son manger qui etoit extra ord.
> re po.r une personne de son age, il etoit fort charitable, ne se soucioit point du
> bien, et n'avoit point d'ambition, ne s'emportoit jamais, ni ne juroit, et s'il buvoit
> quelquefois avec ses amis c'etoit rarem.t et quand cela arivoit c'etoit po.r la com-
> panie et jamais po.r le vin dont il etoit si indifferent comme de toutes les autres
> choses qui sont ordinairem.t les objets de la sensualité que mille fois je l'ai crû
> preferer l'eau au vin. Avec cela il avoit de bons sentimens de fidelité pour son roy.

53. Ibid.

54. Diary, 7 February 1690:

> ayant conversé plusieurs fois avec Mr Bruz, lu plusieurs livres, et approuvé beau-
> coup de points de l'Eglise ou il avoit eté instruit, et peu a peu il reconnoissoit
> la verité mais je lui avois laissé la liberté si entiere que quelque envie que j'eus
> de le voir Cathol. et quelque joye que je me sentois de ce qu'il commençoit
> a favorizer un peu la rel. Cathol et a douter de la sienne, je n'osois jamais l'en
> presser, voulant que sa conversion vint entierem.t de sa propre volonté et de
> la grace de Dieu,

55. *Inscriptions de l'Ancien Diocèse de Sens*, 4 vols, ed. Quevers, P. and Stein, H. (Paris, 1897–1904), vol. 2 (1900), pp. 169–76. Henri de Compigny had been a *capitaine de Régiment-Infanterie du Plessis* and had died in 1682. His son Barthélemy was a *capitaine au Régiment de Monberon*. Marie-Elisabeth's mother was Jacqueline (née Moreau). She (Marie-Elisabeth) actually had two brothers but one of them, named Antoine, had been disinherited many years earlier and is never mentioned in Nairne's diary. He was a *maître d'hotel du roi, capitaine de la marine du ponant and lieutenant au gouverneur de Senlis*, but he had converted to become a Huguenot, probably at the time of his marriage to Louise du Crost in about 1672, and lived in the Forez mountains, west of Lyon. He died in April 1696, and had a son Michel (1673–1694) who predeceased him. It is unlikely that Nairne ever met them. (These facts about Antoine de Compigny were discovered early in the twentieth century by Alfred de Compigny, and published in *Les Entretiens de Cambrai*, p. 60). (It might be added that Les Bordes is now called La Borde, and that Briottes is now called Briotte).

56. Diary, 1687. They moved to the rue Tournon on 8 January 1687, and on the following day his wife 'miscarried of her first child being about 3 months gone'.

57. Diary, 1688, with additional information from the list of Nairne's children written at the back of the volume.

58. Notes made by Monsieur Rondeau, former *Maire* de Compigny (then eighty years old) and enclosed in a letter from the *Mairie* de Compigny to the author, 28 January 1993.
59. Diary, 1687.
60. Diary, 1680 and 1689.
61. Diary, 1689.
62. Ibid.
63. HMC *Stuart* VII, p. 129, Monnot to Mar, 8 August 1718; RA. SP 43/117, Nairne to James III, 17 June 1719. Monnot was a 'natif de Bordeaux' (Dulon, J., *Jacques II Stuart à Saint-Germain-en-Laye* (Saint-Germain-en,-Laye, 1897), p. 123). His brother Pierre was a goldsmith in Paris who lived on the Quai de l'Horloge. See Bimbenet-Privat, Michèle, *Les Orfèvres et l'Orfèvrerie de Paris au XVIIIe Siècle* (Paris, 2002), p. 320.
64. Nairne recorded that 'we had in all 12 ships from 40 to 60 guns, 7 frigates, and 5 fire ships' (Diary, 1689).
65. Diary, 1689.
66. Diary, 1680 and 1689. Nairne noted that while he was with the king 'on ye hill before Derry ... severall persons going down to view ye town nearer I went down also ... within musket of the walls and I brought back one of ye Rebbels horses wth me'.
67. Bod. Carte MSS 181, ff.64–74, 18 May to 20 June 1689; ff.97–123, 1 June to 18 July 1689.
68. SCA. BL 1/124/10, Nairne to L. Innes, 10/20 July 1689. Nairne also wrote two other journals 'of what passed in Ireland, from his Majestie's arrival on the 12th of March, Old Stile, to the 18th of July 1689, when he prorogued the Parliament' (Bod. Carte MSS 181, f.134ff) and 'of what passed in Ireland, from the 19th of July to the 10th of August, O. S. 1689' (Macpherson, James, *Original Papers Concerning the Secret History of Great Britain from the Restoration to the Accession of the House of Hanover* (2 vols, London, 1775), vol. 1, pp. 216–21). These two journals were possibly written to be sent to Lewis Innes.
69. RA. SP Misc 18.
70. SCA. BL 1/124/10, Nairne to L. Innes, 10/20 July 1689. Nairne also referred in this letter to Melfort's 'generous heart', 'his candour and his equity'.
71. Ibid.
72. Diary, 1689, and the list of Nairne's children. He was named Barthélemy after his mother's first cousin Barthélemy de Compigny, Seigneur de Baby and Briottes, who was his godfather. The godmother was the latter's sister Marie-Jacqueline, who later married Captain John Ryan from County Clare, who was appointed a gentleman of the king's Privy Chamber at the exiled court in 1704.

73. SCA. BL 1/124/10, Nairne to L. Innes, 10/20 July 1689.
74. SCA. BL 1/124/12, Nairne to L. Innes, 31 July/10 August 1689.
75. Ibid.
76. Diary, 1689, and the list of Nairne's children.
77. SCA. BL 1/124/10, Nairne to L. Innes, 10/20 July 1689.
78. SCA. BL 1/124/13, Nairne to L. Innes, 1 October 1689. He continued:

> What time may produce I can not tel, but I confess yt hithertill I have been
> but a very bad improver of ye good fortune I owe you, since all ye gratitude my
> circumstances can permitt me to pretend to is an unfruitfull good will, but for
> such as it is, it's ye production of a heart yt's wholly yours and yt is not yet so
> discouraged but yt I hope yet by your means to be in a capacity to give you mor
> solid and reall proofs of my ressentments.

79. Madame de Guise was Marie de Lorraine, duchesse de Guise, who lived in the
     Palais de Luxembourg, and it is possible that Nairne had already met her because
     she patronized Marin Marais, Marc-Antoine Charpentier and Michel-Richard
     Delalande (Corp, *A Court in Exile*, p. 213).
80. Diary, 1680 and 1689.
81. Diary, 1689.
82. Macpherson, *Original Papers*, vol. 1, p. 330, Melfort to James II, 25 October 1689.
83. Diary, 1680 and 1689.

Chief Clerk at Rome and Saint-Germain, 1689–1701

When Nairne left Paris with Lord and Lady Melfort in November 1689, he began to keep a detailed diary in French, which he entitled 'Journal du Voyage d'Italie'. This diary, which he maintained with relatively few gaps until his return two years later in November 1691, is of particular biographical interest because it contains information about Nairne which we do not obtain from any other source. In addition to recording what he did and where he went each day, for and with Lord Melfort, the diary allows us to discover how he chose to occupy his free time and the pattern of his attendance at church services: we may reasonably assume these to have been similar in Paris during the 1680s and at Saint-Germain during the 1690s. The diary is also useful because Nairne would return to Rome in 1717, and live there for most of the time from the end of 1718 until 1734. It shows how well he already knew the city, and which places he particularly liked and frequented. Moreover, it provides evidence that he had already met several of the important people that he would encounter in later years. Two general impressions emerge: in Rome, Nairne's position with Lord and Lady Melfort changed from being that of a servant to that of a trusted friend; and also that the time he spent there was one of the happiest periods of his life.

In addition to Nairne, Melfort had recruited three other men to join his embassy. Monnot was to continue as junior clerk, John Hay, whose father was one of the clerks of Council and Session in Edinburgh, was to be a gentleman in attendance, and another Scot, John Constable, was to be in charge of the household. Hay was to be accompanied by his sister Mary, who was to serve and provide company for Lady Melfort and her seven-year-old son Lord Forth. Whereas Monnot and Constable, like Nairne, were Catholics, Hay and his sister were both Protestants.[2]

Nairne's diary records the details of their journey from Paris to Rome, mentioning all the places at which they dined at midday and spent each night, the distances they travelled, and how much everything cost. The group travelled by what was then the normal route, taking a coach for six days from Paris to Lyon, a 'grand bateau' for three days down the Rhône from Lyon to Avignon, and then a coach again for three days from Avignon to Toulon. There a frigate had been ordered by Louis XIV to take them to Leghorn (Livorno), though they had to wait six days for a favourable wind. The journey by sea then took another four days. Nairne noted that 'the port of Leghorn is very fine'. This was his first glimpse of Italy, and he observed that 'the houses are all painted' and that 'the large square in front of the church is extremely beautiful'.[3] They passed through Pisa, 'a large city with a small population', where they spent two days, and where Nairne particularly admired the famous bronze door of the 'great church' and the leaning tower: 'there is a tower ... which leans over to one side and looks as if it might fall'.[4] From Pisa they went to see Mary of Modena's uncle, Cardinal Rinaldo d'Este, at San Quirico d'Orcia (near Siena), after which they continued south by coach for five days via Montefiascone and Viterbo to Rome, where they arrived on 10 December. The entire journey took one month and four days.

Cardinal d'Este had arranged for 'a fully furnished house, near the Jesu', to be rented for Melfort to use as his embassy. It was in the parish of San Marco, at the south end of the Corso and conveniently close to the home of the French ambassador, Charles d'Albert, duc de Chaulnes, with whom Melfort was expected to collaborate. During the rest of December 1689 Nairne met the members of the French embassy, and also Cardinal Philip Howard, a brother of the 5th and 6th Dukes of Norfolk and Cardinal Protector of England.

The aim of Melfort's embassy was to obtain for James II the diplomatic and financial support of the papal court. He eventually failed to achieve this, though not through any lack of effort. The Papacy was anti-French, and James II was allied to and dependent on Louis XIV. Melfort was not technically an ambassador, having decided to save money by appearing *incognito*. Nairne recorded on 12 December, two days after their arrival, that Lord and Lady Melfort were treated as Excellencies, 'receiving the full honours of the Princes of Rome, because he was an English [*sic*] peer and Secretary to H. B. M., since although My Lord acted as Minister he did not adopt the title, because he was more than an envoy yet it was not appropriate to give him the title of ambassador'.[5] Melfort's first audience with Pope Alexander VIII (Ottoboni) took place a week later when he travelled in two coaches and was accompanied by a train of eight gentlemen. Nairne, who was one of them, noted that 'he was given the same privilege as the Italian Ambassadors and Princes of entering the Pope's Chamber wearing his hat and sword'.[6]

Their arrival coincided with the carnival season in Rome, and Nairne's diary mentions a series of ceremonial visits and the exchange of diplomatic presents. There were balls, including some masked ones, and regular visits to see the operas being performed that winter. Nairne had meanwhile arranged for his wife to join him, escorted by his younger brother, who had been studying medicine in France since bringing the birth brieve two and a half years earlier. While Nairne himself was enjoying the Roman carnival, his wife and brother were travelling in the middle of winter along the route which he had himself recently taken.

On 6 February, Nairne heard that they had reached Viterbo, about forty-five miles north of Rome, and was given leave by Melfort to join them there and escort them on the last part of their journey. He arrived on the following day to find that his brother was seriously ill, and wanting to convert to Catholicism. Nairne's diary contains details of both the doctors who attended him and the priests who received him into the Catholic Church. He commented:

> seeing that this time he was dying, I judged there was no time to lose, especially since it looked as if he might die during the journey to Rome. It was by God's good grace that he had had the strength to come so far to die close to me, that I could give him all necessary assistance, and have the consolation of paying him my last respects.[7]

His brother's formal conversion took place on 8 February, after which he became progressively weaker and died on the 15th: 'he had a malign fever, with a kind of internal rash.' Nairne poured out his grief in a very long passage in his diary, which clearly reveals his resignation to and acceptance of Divine Providence:

God who has designs for his own glory and for the good of his chosen ones in all things ... by his grace permitted him to recognise the truth and to die in the bosom of the Church, which was the only thing he lacked to become a truly good man.[8]

Throughout these final days the dying man was nursed by Nairne's wife Marie-Elisabeth, who was four months pregnant. 'Although she was pregnant', Nairne recorded, 'she never left his bedside by night or day, and became so tired and upset it was a wonder she did not fall ill herself, but God helped her.'[9]

Nairne arranged for his brother to be buried in the Cathedral of Viterbo, in front of the altar of the Holy Sacrament and opposite a recently built chapel dedicated to St Philip Neri. He and Marie-Elisabeth then remained in Viterbo for three more days 'so that we did not carry any bad air to Rome'.[10]

There then followed a short episode during which Nairne once again revealed that 'ye caractere of my spirit was never boldness nor presomption', something which would remain the case throughout his life and eventually hamper his career. He decided that it would not be right to bring his wife to eat in the embassy at Lord Melfort's expense, so he rented a room in the 'Ecu de France' *hosteria* in the Piazza di Spagna, where he intended to live with her thenceforth and walk each day to the embassy. After three days, Lady Melfort sent a message asking him to return to live in the embassy and bring his wife with him. He held out for one more day, but then Lady Melfort 'told me that that she would view it badly if she [my wife] did not come to eat her meals at the embassy table, begging my wife and myself not to make difficulties about it'.[11] So Nairne finally gave way: 'Je ne pûs plus honestem.t me dispenser de faire manger ma f a la table a moins de chagriner Mil.d et M.e'.[12] It was a good thing that he did, because the diary then records that Lady Melfort and Mrs Nairne quickly became firm friends, and that the latter became the former's constant companion, regularly accompanying her on her outings and her visits to mass – something, of course, which the Protestant Mary Hay, who was anyway primarily a servant, could never have done. Moreover the two women were both pregnant, Lady Melfort expecting her sixth child in March, and Marie-Elisabeth Nairne her third child in July, and this seems to have drawn them even closer together.

From a political point of view, Lord Melfort's embassy can be divided into three phases. During the first, from his arrival in December 1689 until the end of January 1691, he was unable to persuade Pope Alexander VIII to declare his support for James II and Louis XIV in their war against William III and Emperor Leopold I. Then, following the death of the Pope on 1 February 1691, the conclave took nearly five and a half months to elect his successor, and Melfort worked closely with Cardinal Howard, the duc de Chaulnes and the French cardinals in an unsuccessful attempt to secure the election of a new Pope favourable to French interests. Cardinal Pignatelli was eventually elected as Pope Innocent XII on 12 July 1691, and the following month both Melfort and Chaulnes received letters recalling them to Saint-Germain and Versailles.[13] This short third phase lasted until 4 September, when the Melforts and their staff of six people (including Nairne and his wife) all left Rome.

Throughout these three phases, Nairne worked very closely with Lord Melfort, copying and translating all his correspondence and his memorials. There are four extant letter books (out of an original six), beautifully kept by Nairne, which contain copies of Melfort's correspondence and record the progress of his mission.[14] Nairne also accompanied Melfort on nearly all his visits to the French embassy and to the many cardinals and princes resident in Rome. During the course of 1690, he went with him on twenty-one occasions to have audiences with Alexander VIII. Then, in the summer of 1691, he accompanied him on four more occasions to have audiences with Innocent XII. By the time he left Rome to return to France, Nairne was not only a very experienced senior clerk but also extremely well acquainted with Roman society and the Papal Curia. This would be enormously helpful to him when conducting the Roman correspondence at Saint-Germain, and especially when he returned to Rome many years later.

When he was not actually working for Melfort, Nairne explored the city and its surroundings as though he were a Grand Tourist. He visited the celebrated antiquities of Rome, notably the Coliseum, the Pantheon, the baths of Diocletian,[15] the catacombs, the Capitole[16] and the Castel Sant' Angelo. He also regularly went to the Piazza di Spagna and the Corso, and witnessed and took part in all sorts of processions and cavalcades, particularly during the carnival seasons.[17] He noted that he saw buffaloes for the first time,[18] and on summer evenings complained of 'blood sucking flies'.[19] He also mentioned the drinks which he had not previously experienced, such as tea,[20] 'a drink called Sillobub',[21] and wine 'de Montepulciano'.[22] On one occasion, he was invited to climb to the top of St Peter's, where 'telescopes' had been positioned. He noted that 'we could see Frascati, and make out the windows of the Belvedere 12 miles from Rome, we could read the time on the Trinita di Monte and the marble virgin on the Montecavallo Gate'.[23]

During the twenty-one months that he was in Rome, Nairne visited every church, several of them many times, notably Santa Maria della Pace, west of the Piazza Navona (ten times), San Lorenzo in Lucina, just off the Corso (nine times), Santa Maria Maggiore (eight), Sant' Andrea della Vale, south of the Piazza Navona (seven), the Chiesa Nuova, between the Piazza Navona and the Tiber (seven), Santa Maria sopra Minerva, near the Pantheon (six), San Giovanni in Laterano (six), San Stefano Rotondo, south west of Laterano (six), Sant' Agnese in Agone, in the Piazza Navona (five) and Santa Maria in Aracoeli, beside the Capitole (five). In most cases, he also attended mass in these churches, but they were not the ones which he mainly frequented. His five favourite churches included his parish church of San Marco, where he went on forty-five occasions, San Pietro in Vaticano, which he visited twenty-eight times, and above all the Jesu, where he attended mass on 123 different days. He first went to the church of San Carlo on the Corso in April 1690 and had been there twenty-one times before he left. His first visit to Santi Apostoli in the piazza of that name, and immediately beside the Palazzo Muti, was not until September 1690, but he liked it so much that he went back on thirty-nine subsequent occasions. The number of these visits combined, together with forty-four to the thirty-one other churches mentioned in his diary, make a grand total of 369 visits, and testify to the fact that Nairne attended mass approximately every other day, sometimes several times, normally with Lord Melfort, frequently with his wife and Lady Melfort, often by himself. No account of the life of David Nairne would be complete if it did not emphasize his strong Catholic faith, which motivated both his deep loyalty to the Jacobite cause and his devotion to duty, as well as his resignation in the face of adversity and to the workings of Divine Providence. Nairne's natural goodness, his reserve and his humility sprang from profound religious convictions.

Under different circumstances, Nairne might have taken holy orders, but he was happily married and keen to have children. It is noticeable, however, that in Rome, as in Paris, he established particularly good friendships with Catholic priests, both British and French. His special friends in Rome included the priests at the English and Scots Colleges,[24] the agents of the English and Scottish Catholic clergy,[25] and several French priests[26] whom he also encountered in the city.

Nairne established particularly good relations with the members of the French embassy,[27] and it seems from his diary (which of course was written in French) that he probably still regarded himself as more French than Scottish. He had lived in Paris for more than twelve years, he had a French wife, and he had no intention of ever returning to live in Scotland or England. So a successful Jacobite restoration, which he obviously expected, would have left him once again without employment. His new friendships with the members of the French embassy, and his regular attendance on the French cardinals (de Bouillon, Le Camus, d'Estrées and Fourbin) and on the other important visiting priests (including the future Cardinals de Fleury, de Janson and de Polignac) must in part have been designed to enhance his future prospects in France. Although working at the Jacobite embassy and being salaried by Lord Melfort, Nairne was nevertheless still receiving a pension from Louis XIV[28] – as he would continue to do at Saint-Germain.

The French embassy, which he visited very regularly, was at that time situated in the Palazzo Farnese,[29] but through his position with Lord Melfort he gained access to most of the other most important palazzi and villas of Rome. The former included those of the Altieri, Barberini, Borghese, Colonna, Giustiniani, Pamphili and Salviati families, as well as the Pope's Quirinale palace on Montecavallo and the one until recently occupied by Queen Christina of Sweden in Trastevere (later the Palazzo Corsini).[30] The villas included those of the Borghese, Chigi, Farnese, Ludovisi, Medici and Pamphili. Nairne left short descriptions of some of these buildings in his diary, noting in particular some of the paintings and sculpture which they contained.[31]

He also visited some of the famous places outside Rome, including Albano, Castel Gandolfo, Frascati, Marini and Tivoli.[32] His curiosity and appreciation of all these places, which included the architecture and interior decoration, as well as the painting and sculpture, and which extended to both the ancient and the modern, provided Nairne with an impressive artistic education to complement what he had already experienced in and around Paris. When he returned to Saint-Germain, he was not only among the very few Jacobite courtiers who had travelled beyond the British Isles and the north of France, but was also one of the even smaller number who had met the important people surrounding the Pope. In addition to many princes and princesses, Nairne's diary mentions his having met thirty-seven cardinals, in addition to the English and French ones already mentioned. These included Cardinal Albani, whom he met fifteen times between September 1690 and September 1691, a point of significance because Albani would be elected as Pope Clement XI in 1700 and would still be in office when Nairne returned to Italy with the Jacobite court in 1717. He also met Cardinal Conti, the future Pope Innocent XIII, who would succeed Albani in 1721, on at least three occasions in 1691. The time he spent in Rome with Lord Melfort would remain of inestimable value to Nairne for the rest of his career.

Nairne was also indebted to Melfort for introducing him to several of the leading painters working in Rome. Melfort himself was a connoisseur of painting and had assembled a very large collection which he had had to leave behind in London when he followed James II into exile.[33] At first, Melfort took Nairne with him to examine the many collections in Rome,[34] but he then began to assemble a new collection to replace the one he had lost, and Nairne noted on 12 January 1691 that 'My Lord did not go out but put all his pictures in one of the rooms'. Melfort continued to purchase both paintings and drawings until he left Rome eight months later, and always took Nairne with him when he went to visit the painters and dealers whom he patronized. There are various entries in Nairne's diary referring to visiting 'a painter'[35] or 'the painters',[36] but several painters are identified by name. They include Carlo Maratta, whom Nairne visited nine times and from whom Melfort commissioned portraits of himself and his wife,[37] Francesco Trevisani, whom Nairne visited nineteen times and whom Melfort also commissioned to paint a portrait of his wife,[38] Giuseppe Montani, Giovanni Maria Morandi, and Giovanni Odazzi.[39]

Nairne helped Melfort negotiate with these painters, two of whom also acted as dealers,[40] and it was Nairne who arranged all the payments.[41] By the time he returned to France, Nairne had acquired an exceptional knowledge of art, and of painting in particular, which would prove extremely useful when called upon to negotiate with the painters employed by the Stuart court at Saint-Germain and, much later, in Rome itself.

Nairne's years in Rome with Melfort also extended his knowledge of music, which had previously been restricted to the repertoire available in Paris during the 1680s, notably the works of Lully, Charpentier, Du Mont, Marais and Delalande (to name only the most famous). He was now exposed to the Italian, or to be more accurate the Roman, repertoire, which he heard during his very frequent visits to the churches and palazzi already mentioned. There are numerous references in his diary to the music he enjoyed, both religious and secular. The former included, for example, works by Carissimi at the church of Sant' Apolinare,[42] 'beautiful music' at the Irish church of St Isidore,[43] 'great music' in the Chiesa Nuova[44] and 'a great mass' in San Giovanni in Laterano,[45] as well as the singing of the nuns of both the Casa Santa Maria (opposite the Collegio Romano) and Sant' Ambrogio (beside the church of San Carlo)[46], and an oratorio by an unnamed composer in San Laurent in Lucina.[47] The secular concerts included a vocal one given by a singer whom he called 'le petit portugais'[48] and another by a singer named 'Mariane',[49] as well as music at the French embassy,[50] and 'the music ... of the Cardinals at Montecavallo'.[51] He presumably also heard the early trio sonatas of Corelli, and some of the cantatas of Alessandro Scarlatti. Later on, the music of both Corelli and Scarlatti would be directed at Saint-Germain by Innocenzo Fede, a Roman who had previously worked at the Spanish church in the Piazza Navona,[52] and Nairne (though perhaps also Monnot) would then be the only courtier who already had an extensive knowledge of both the Parisian and Roman repertoires.

In addition to all the music to be heard throughout each year, there were also short seasons of opera organized during the carnival. Nairne experienced two of these, in January and February 1690 (before he joined his wife and brother at Viterbo) and in the winter of 1690–1 (though that season was abruptly terminated by the illness and death of Pope Alexander

VIII). It was these seasons which provided Nairne with his introduction to Italian opera, so different from the French style created by Lully, and which he would not experience again until after his return to the Papal States in 1717. By chance, these were the first two seasons for many years during which the Pope permitted a public opera house to be opened in Rome, and the only ones between 1683 and 1719 when operas by Alessandro Scarlatti were performed there in public.[53] In January 1690, his *La Statira* was performed at the recently re-opened Teatro Tordinona, and Nairne went to see and hear it at least four times.[54] In December 1690 and January 1691, the same composer's *Gli equivoci in amore, overo La Rosauro* was put on by Cardinal Ottoboni (nephew of Alexander VIII) in the Palazzo della Cancelleria, and Nairne went to see at least three performances.[55] He also attended three performances of an opera by Pasquini in the Palazzo Rospigliosi,[56] and a second one by Pasquini in the Palazzo Colonna,[57] both of them in January 1690, as well as an unnamed opera in the Collegio Romano in February 1690.[58] In the following season, he attended two performances of a *pastorale* in the Cancelleria in November,[59] and at least one performance of Pasquini's *Il Colombo, overo L'India scoperta* at the Teatro Tordinona.[60]

While he was in Rome Nairne made two useful musical contacts. In December he met John Abel, who was on the Grand Tour with his brother-in-law the 4th Earl of Banbury. Abel and Banbury had arrived in Rome the previous day, and Nairne met them and Lord Kennedy at the oratorio in the church of San Lorenzo in Lucina already mentioned.[61] Abel and Banbury then visited Naples, but returned to Rome for two weeks in May 1691.[62] Abel, who was Scottish, was an exceptionally talented counter-tenor who had served in the Chapel Royal at Whitehall and was a groom of Queen Mary of Modena's privy chamber. After leaving Rome he joined the court at Saint-Germain where he remained until 1695.[63] The other contact Nairne made in Rome was the composer Francesco Gasparini, who was studying there with Corelli and Pasquini.[64] Gasparini later moved to Venice where he became the teacher and early patron of Antonio Vivaldi, and both his and Vivaldi's music would be popular at the Stuart court, perhaps in part due to Nairne's influence, when the latter arrived in 1717.

In addition to studying painting and enjoying music, Nairne occupied his days with more straightforward pursuits, including frequent walks both inside and outside the walls of Rome, sometimes along the river Tiber or along the walls themselves, and on at least two occasions in the Forum (Campo Vacchino). Most of these walks or 'promenades' took place between April and October, although in December 1690 Nairne explored both the Campo Marzio (west of the Corso) and the gardens of the English College on the Palatine.[65] Another outdoor activity that he enjoyed was playing bocce.[66] His indoor activities included cards ('la bassette', a popular game of chance)[67] and especially chess, which he played very regularly with his French friends.[68] Another sedentary pursuit was reading, and he noted the titles of some of the books which he read. In January 1691, for example, he read the celebrated contemporary *Life of Queen Margaret of Scotland* (died 1093), followed by an account of the differences between the Barberini family and Pope Innocent X (Pamphili), *Les Lettres Galantes du Monsieur le Chevalier d'Her**** (published anonymously by Bernard de Fontenelle in 1685) and an 'histoire de l'Empire'.[69] Shortly afterwards he was given 'a little book on the thought and meditations of Christ' by one of the priests at the Jesu,[70] and a few days after receiving it he wrote what he described as 'my little writing'.[71] He showed it to one of his friends at the French embassy,[72] but unfortunately he did not describe its contents in his diary and it has not survived among his papers.[73]

Nairne's interests were not only sedentary, however. He regularly played the 'jeu de paume' with Lord Melfort,[74] and he very much enjoyed dancing and going to balls. For example, on four consecutive days in November 1690, he records that he and his wife danced with the other members of the embassy and some French friends. On one evening, they occupied themselves with 'English dances', and on another they were joined by some Italians who danced 'la sauterelle'.[75] We are not told who provided the music, though on one occasion Nairne did record that his French friend abbé Fossé 'played the guitar and we danced'.[76] In May 1691, he bought Marie-Elisabeth a new gown, and he noted: 'My wife put on her new taffeta dress, and we danced.'[77] During the carnival season of 1691 he and his wife attended various balls. On two consecutive days at the end of February, he noted:

> We made up a party to go to the ball in the evening ... my wife came with us to the ball at Constable Colonna's where I led the dancing.

In the evening we went to Prince Carpegna's ball where my wife danced with the Constable and the Prince and we were very well received.[78]

By this time, both Lady Melfort and Marie-Elisabeth Nairne had safely given birth to the babies they had been expecting when they first arrived in Rome,[79] and the former was about to have another, her seventh. On 12 May 1690, Nairne noted in his diary that his wife 'went to the Piazza Navona to buy clothes and linen for her baby', and on 3 June that he took her to St Peter's and that 'my wife managed the climb even though she was 8 months pregnant'. A little over a month later, on 9 July, she had a baby girl:

> My wife felt so well in the morning that she went to mass but suddenly after dinner she became unwell and after an hour's labour she gave birth at half past ten Italian time to a baby girl ... Cardinal Barbarini came to visit My Lord and My Lady and it was midnight when he left. Then My Lady came up and spent nearly half an hour with my wife, cuddling the baby and seeing to it that Miss Hay, who had been present at the birth with the midwife and two servants and myself, gave her some violet syrup.[80]

On the following day, the little girl was baptized by one of Nairne's friends:

> My daughter was baptized by Father Magy, the Rector of the Scots College, assisted by Dom Francesco the vicar of St Mark's who had been called to My Lord's palazzo to do so. I had asked My Lady the Countess of Melfort to be godmother and she held the baby in her arms and gave her the name Euphemia in the presence of the English gentlemen and nearly all My Lord's household.[81]

The child, however, could only be legally baptized in the parish church, so on the following day 'My lady's nurse and the midwife took my daughter to the parish church of St Mark where the ceremonies which have to be done in church were performed'.[82]

From time to time, Nairne continued to refer to his daughter Euphemia in his diary, recording little intimate family details. For example, his wife brought some material and made the child a dress in January 1691 when she was six months old.[83] Then, at the beginning of March, Euphemia's 'first teeth appeared'.[84] She was still being breast fed by her mother, because later that month Nairne recorded that his wife also had to feed Lady Melfort's new baby, born on 20 February:[85] 'This evening and all night my wife breastfed My Lady's baby because the wet nurse's milk had dried up.'[86] Euphemia was finally weaned when she was one year old, and Nairne noted on 11 July that she was then given a christening present by her godmother: 'I went to mass with My Lady ... and she gave my daughter a silver bowl and spoon.'[87]

These final months in Rome were evidently a very happy time for Nairne. He had interesting work, which he was doing for a man whom he admired and was beginning to regard as a friend. He was living once again with his wife, who was on intimate terms with Lady Melfort and who had given him a healthy child to replace the first two who had died. He was visiting on an almost daily basis the churches of Rome,[88] and fairly regularly some of the city's palazzi and villas. He had an extremely stimulating social life and plenty of opportunities to satisfy his appreciation of both music and painting. Finally he had the satisfaction of serving a cause, Jacobitism, which he regarded as morally justified and enjoying divine approval, and which he had reason to hope would earn him employment whenever Lord Melfort was recalled from Rome.

We can catch a glimpe of Nairne's interests at this time because in the spring of 1691 Lord and Lady Melfort decided to visit Castel Gandolfo, and left Nairne in Rome as *chargé d'affaires* while the conclave was deliberating the election of a new Pope. It was the only time that Nairne was not in attendance on Lord Melfort for at least part of each day, and thus the only time when he was completely free to pursue his own interests. During the six days that they were away,[89] he visited the painter Trevisani three times and his friend abbé Fossé (who played the guitar) twice, and he was virtually every day with his other French friends: the other priests whom he knew, and the members of the French embassy including the duc de Chaulnes. Moreover, every day he heard mass with his wife in either the parish church of San Marco or at the Jesu.

On 22 August 1691, Lord Melfort received his *lettre de congé* recalling him to Saint-Germain, where James II had settled since leaving Ireland after the Battle of the Boyne. Nairne and the other members of the embassy were then given only two weeks to prepare their departure.[90] Apart from saying goodbye and taking his leave from all the people with whom he was acquainted – his French friends, the priests at the English and Scots

Colleges, the priests at the churches he frequented, most of the cardinals in Rome, the Superior General of the Jesuits (Thyrsus Gonzàlez de Santalla) and the Master-General of the Dominicans (Antonin Cloche) at the Minerva – Nairne's preparations included copying some Italian arias to take back with him,[91] buying some violin strings[92] and purchasing a painting for one hundred *scudi* when seeing Trevisani for the last time.[93] He also obtained some unspecified relics for his wife from one of the Jesuit priests[94] and bought some rosaries for himself which he arranged to have blessed by the Pope.[95] On the evening of 24 August, he and his wife went to the *Scala Santa* (beside San Giovanni in Laterano) and ascended it on their knees. Four days later the Superior General of the Jesuits gave Nairne 'a relic of the True Cross',[96] and on the 31st Lord Melfort asked him to deliver in person a letter from King James II to Innocent XII, so that he could take his leave of the Pope. Nairne meanwhile packed up all his possessions and arranged to have them, and all the 'bollets' of the Melforts and the other members of the embassy, weighed and despatched to France.[97]

The members of the Jacobite embassy were to sail from Leghorn with both the Cardinal de Bouillon and the duc de Chaulnes, but Melfort was keen to make a tour of the Papal States and Tuscany before he had to leave Italy. He therefore divided his staff into two groups. John Constable, Marie-Elisabeth Nairne and the four children (Euphemia Nairne and Melfort's own three sons) would travel directly by coach from Rome to Livorno with Bouillon and Chaulnes. Meanwhile he himself would travel with Lady Melfort, Nairne, Monnot and the Hays to Loreto, and thence up the Adriatic coast to Rimini, and along the Via Emilia to Bologna. They would then travel south-west over the mountains to Florence, and on to Leghorn to rendezvous with the others. This meant that Nairne was able greatly to extend his knowledge of Italy and thus complete his Grand Tour. As it turned out, this trip took him along the same roads and to the same places to which he would return twenty-five years later.

Nairne's diary records the main outlines of the journey, giving the names of the places where they stopped for dinner and where they spent each night, the distances travelled, and the money disbursed. The party left Rome on 4 September 1691 and travelled in three coaches up the Via Flaminia,[98] and then turned east via Macerata to Loreto, where they arrived

at midday on the 7th, and where they remained until the following afternoon. They visited the 'Santa Casa' and 'the chapel and said our prayers
there'. They then travelled north via Ancona, Fano, Pesaro and Rimini to
Cisena, and Nairne noted that 'we crossed the Rubicon between Rimini
and Cisena'.[99] They reached Bologna on the 10th, 'where we spent the
night at the residence of marquis d'Orsi'.[100] On the following day, Melfort
took Nairne and Monnot with him to Modena, leaving his wife and the
Hays behind. This gave Nairne the opportunity to meet Queen Mary of
Modena's family and to see where she had been brought up – an added
advantage when he had returned to Saint-Germain. He noted: 'We dined
there, and My Lord saw the Duke and Prince Cesare. We were shown all
the apartments of the castle, and returned to Bologna in the evening.'[101]

From Bologna the party travelled to Florence, 'My lord and My Lady
in a litter belonging to the Grand Duke' and 'the rest of the company on
horseback'.[102] It took them two days to get there, and they remained at
Florence for four more to see the sights: 'we visited all the churches and
went to see the Grand Duke's palace with its gallery and chapel'.[103] They
then travelled west to Leghorn where they met the others as planned and
Nairne was reunited with his wife.

The journey by sea was determined, as usual, by the weather. They had
to wait a whole week for a favourable wind,[104] but only got as far as Genoa
before storms obliged them to stop and wait for another eight days. This,
however, was an opportunity for more sight-seeing: 'During the 8 days
we visited the churches and other places of interest in the town, including
a priceless emerald cup.'[105] When they were finally able to continue their
journey, they remained close to the coast, stopping at Saint-Rémo to hear
mass, at Monaco to sleep the night in the château, and at Toulon. They
finally reached Marseille on 11 October, after a sea journey of two and a
half weeks.

Lord Melfort had arranged to meet his nephew Lord Drummond
at Marseille, so that the latter, who was on his Grand Tour, could travel
in the Grand Duke's galley when it returned to Leghorn. Nairne already
knew Drummond (the eldest son of the Earl of Perth) because the latter
had been a student at the Collège des Ecossais in Paris. But Nairne had not
previously met Drummond's travelling companion. This was William Hay,

6th Earl of Kinnoul. Many years later, Lord Kinnoul's son John (born in Scotland earlier that same year) would be created Jacobite Earl of Inverness and would cause Nairne considerable distress during the end of his career at the exiled court.

Melfort and his party left Marseille on 14 October and took the usual route up the Rhone valley to Lyon, overland this time because against the flow of the river. It took them a week to get there, and they remained in Lyon for eight days before continuing their journey to Paris.[106] They had reached Nevers, where they intended to take a boat along the river Loire, by 2 November. But now the weather broke and travelling became very difficult. Leaving the Melforts and the others at Nevers, in part because Lady Melfort was ill,[107] Nairne and his wife continued their journey with 'the children by boat'.[108] But now they came up against the reality of travel in those days. They had only journied a short way from Nevers when, 'the bad weather preventing us from travelling by river', they were obliged to remain two long days 'in a wretched village'[109] – probably Fourchambault. When the weather improved they continued as far as Sancerre, but then they encountered another problem: 'the river had become so ice bound that we had to leave the boat and take what transport we could find.' This turned out to be no more than 'a covered wagon',[110] and it was in that that they continued their journey to Paris, travelling via Gien, Nemours and Fontainebleau.

They arrived in Paris on 11 November, and spent that night at an inn in the rue Saint-Antoine ('La Bannière de France'), near where Nairne had lived for seven years as an unemployed bachelor. On the following day, they went to join the court at Saint-Germain, and hand over the three Melfort children to their parents, who had meanwhile travelled more quickly from Nevers. The whole journey from Rome to Saint-Germain had taken two months and eight days. It had been a difficult and trying time, but the memory of his Grand Tour to Italy, and his extraordinarily rich experiences in Rome, would remain with Nairne for the rest of his life.

***

While Melfort and Nairne were in Rome James II had returned from Ireland and entrusted the correspondence of the exiled court at Saint-Germain to a small group of secretaries, who divided between them the affairs of England, Scotland and Ireland. When, however, Melfort returned to Saint-Germain 'the management of all affairs was put in his hands' as sole secretary of state and chief minister.[111] Melfort had no hesitation in retaining Nairne and Monnot as his chief and assistant clerks.

Nairne spent the first few weeks after returning from Rome arranging his new life at Saint-Germain. He rented an apartment beside the Château-Vieux in the rue de la Salle, and purchased furniture in Paris.[112] He then equipped his new office in the château with some writing desks, a register book in which to keep copies of Melfort's letters, and other things he needed.[113] He also resumed issuing warrants and recording them in the book which he had started in Ireland.[114] He recruited a new clerk named Nicholas Dempster (from Muresk in Scotland) to work alongside Monnot, and during January he was informed that he would himself receive an annual pension of 1,000 *livres* from the king.[115]

Most of Nairne's time was again spent copying and translating Lord Melfort's correspondence. There was a great deal of work to be done, and at the beginning of December he confided to a friend that 'I believe I shall allways be in haste'.[116] On 1 January 1692, he noted in his diary that he stayed 'in ye castle till 12 of ye clock at night'. Immediately afterwards, however, his work was interrupted by a family tragedy.

His daughter became unwell after the New Year and by the 8th she was so ill that Nairne received a panic call to his office asking him to return home immediately 'to see my daughter dye'. He and his wife sat up all night with her, and by the next morning she seemed to have improved. Then there was a relapse and Nairne was told that 'she was past recovery'. He wrote: 'I watched her myself all night holding her in my arms when I thought several times she would have expired.' She died on the following day, the 12th: 'Eufemia after 9 or 10 days sickness dyed at 3 in ye afternoon betwixt her mother and me who received her last breath with an inexpressible affliction.'[117] When she was buried in the cemetery of Saint-Germain, he added that 'she was ye lovlyest child yt ever was seen'.[118]

Nairne's grief was very great. He and his wife had had three children, and all three of them had died. The death of babies and infants in those days was so frequent that it is easy to underestimate the feelings of the bereaved parents, and Nairne's diary contains nothing to indicate any great sense of loss after the deaths of his first two. The first had only lived for six weeks, and the second (whom he had never seen) for only four and a half months. It is clear that the loss of this third child affected him very deeply. She had lived for eighteen months and three days, long enough to develop some personality and to inspire the tenderest feelings in her parents. Nairne's brief comment in his diary gives a clear indication of his grief, but one of his private letters goes much further:

> my poor daughter ... dyed of a feaver ye 12th of ye month after 9 days sickness wch was such ane extraordinary grief to my poor wife and me and is still, yt wee are almost uncomfortable and I doe not think wee shall ever be able to forgett yt child ... you knew how lovely and sweet a child it was, and you know what fathers sentiments are in these occasions ... my deerest Eufemia [was] in my eyes the lovlyest child yt ever was borne and ... I shall never see [her] any more again while I live.

For consolation, Nairne turned to his Catholic faith, which helped to sustain him now and which would become ever more important to him in the future. He continued the same letter, written to one of his friends in Rome:

> O my deer Mr Lesly, this is hard, but after all wee must submitt to Gods will, and it is no small comfort to think yt the child is in heaven happier now yn ever she could have been on earth, and I hope she'l pray for me and all others her good friends yt lovd her here yt wee may be so happy as to see her hereafter and enjoy our share of yt eternall happiness she now enjoys like a little Angel singing ye praises of God almighty. I hope you'l pardon this digression to my excessive grief and ... pray for my wife and me yt wee may make a good use of our Cross.[119]

His wife's position must have been difficult to endure,[120] but Nairne himself could at least turn his mind to other things by returning to his work. He wrote in the same letter that 'I am still so presst ... yt I have hardly a moments time'.

The court at Saint-Germain was mainly English, and as a Scot it took some time for Nairne to be accepted in it. This was particularly the case as his master, Lord Melfort, was disliked by many of the English. In the first few months, Nairne naturally looked to the few Scots at the court for friendship and patronage. By the beginning of 1692 it was known that the queen was pregnant,[11] and Nairne set about trying to get a post for his wife among the women to be employed looking after the new prince or princess. This would provide her with an occupation, but the position would also carry with it an apartment in the château and a salary. He did everything he could during January and February to lobby the queen's ladies.

The Governess of the Prince of Wales was the Countess of Erroll, whose daughter-in-law was the sister of Lord Melfort. She had been joined at Saint-Germain by Lady Largo, whose estates were in Fife. As all the other ladies of the queen were English or Italian, Nairne naturally turned to these two for support.[12] By the end of January, he had introduced his wife to both of them, and Lady Erroll had introduced Marie-Elisabeth to the queen.[123] He showed his appreciation by giving each of them 'a present of Roman gloves and beads',[124] a significant gesture from a man who admitted to not being a good courtier.

By the middle of February, Nairne seemed optimistic, and recorded the progress they had made:

> My wife ... went at night to ye Nursrie wher she saw My La[dy] Governess ... and was noticed by ye Queen. (18th)

> My wife spoke to My La [Melfort] about her business and My La spoke yt same night to My La Govern about her. (19th)

> I thanked My La Governess, My La [Melfort] and La Largo for their interesting so kindly for my wife and I engaged Mr Inese to speak to My La Gov to fortify her. (21st)

After these positive entries, there occurs a gap of two months in Nairne's diary and it is impossible to trace the progress of his negotiation. He perhaps remained optimistic, because in April he drew up a detailed list of all the people occupying the apartments in the château,[125] presumably in an attempt to identify someone who should move out and create a vacancy for his wife and himself. However, Nairne's attempts were unlikely to succeed, partly because the Scots were in such a small minority at the court, but mainly because his wife was French. When the queen gave birth to a baby on 28 June, a princess named Louise-Marie, the women appointed to look after her were all English.[126] Having noted that 'the Queen was brought to bed of the Princess',[127] Nairne then abruptly stopped writing his diary for the next nine months. All that we are told is that his wife went to Compigny for two weeks at the end of August[128] and that she had been pregnant since January, shortly after the death of Euphemia. On 28 October, she gave birth at Saint-Germain to her fourth child, another boy. He was named Jean after his godfather, Lord Melfort. His godmother was the Countess of Erroll.[129]

Apart from these details, we know relatively little about Nairne's personal life at Saint-Germain between his arrival there in November 1691 and the summer of 1694. This is not just because he allowed his diary to lapse: we only have entries covering 1 January to 21 February 1692 and 1 April to 9 May 1693. It is also because the entries we do have are concerned almost exclusively with his official life, which was very busy, and no longer contain the more personal information which he had recorded in his 'Journal du Voyage d'Italie'. It is reasonable to assume that he regularly attended mass and other services both in the Chapel Royal and in the parish church facing the west wing of the château.[130] He no doubt took an active part in the musical life of the court, and appreciated with Melfort the many paintings which were displayed there, including the new portraits of the king, the queen and the prince by Benedetto Gennari and Nicolas de Largillière.[131] But none of these subjects is any longer referred to in his diary. We know that Nairne and his wife remained on extremely good terms with the Melforts,[132] who had an apartment immediately below that of the queen,[133] and that the four of them spent a few days together in Paris at the end of January 1692.[134] We also know that he continued to see the other friends he had made in the Rome embassy, notably his assistant Monnot and John Constable, still in charge of Melfort's personal servants and household. In both January and February of that year, Nairne invited Monnot and Constable, with other new friends, to join him and his wife for a meal in their new home in the rue de la Salle.[135] But this is all we are told. There are no references, for example, to his old friends at the Collège des Ecossais, not even to Lewis Innes who had been appointed junior almoner to the queen.

Nairne's diary does, however, tell us about his involvement in the attempts to restore James II to his thrones. During the early months of 1692 it was agreed that a French fleet should be assembled off the Cherbourg peninsula to transport an army, consisting primarily of James II's Irish regiments, to invade the south coast of England. Nairne was a witness to the administrative preparations, on one occasion visiting Versailles with Melfort and the Duke of Berwick and returning with the comte de Lauzun,[136] and on others having long discussions with the French secretaries of state, the comte de Pontchartrain (*marine*), the marquis de Barbezieux (*guerre*) and the marquis de Croissy (*affaires étrangères*).[137] His role, however, was primarily clerical, and it is unlikely that his advice was sought. On 20 April, James II issued a relatively uncompromising declaration to the English people, calling upon them not to resist his invasion. This declaration has been attributed to Lord Melfort, to whom the king had given the Garter earlier the same month.[138]

Nairne left Saint-Germain on 22 April and joined James II and Melfort six days later at the little village of Sainte-Marie (between Bayeux and Cherbourg). He then travelled with them up the coast to Quinéville.[139] Being attached to a small group of civilian advisers brought Nairne closer to the attention of the king than had been possible at Saint-Germain, and he took advantage of the situation to obtain a commission for his elder brother Alexander to be a captain of a troop of horse.[140] But it was never used.[141] On 1 and 2 June, Nairne was among the group of people with the king who stood on the cliffs watching the English fleet under Admiral Russell defeat the French under Tourville. He briefly commented that 'the English burnt ye French ships at La Hogue',[142] but this French defeat was a disaster for the Jacobite cause. The whole invasion had to be called off, and Lord Melfort was given the unenviable task of informing the King of France of the disaster.

Louis XIV was besieging Namur in the Spanish Netherlands. Nairne accompanied Melfort to Saint-Germain and thence to Namur, where they arrived on 9 June. He does not say whether he was present when Melfort informed Louis of the greatest military defeat suffered by the French for over half a century. In his diary he merely states that 'I went out a horseback with My Lord and vieud the siege of ye Castle, for ye town was taken before we came'. Melfort and Nairne 'lay at Mr de Croissy's tent 2 nights' and then 'got a lodging in a convent by ye means of Mr de Lauzun'.[143] They

Figure 1. *John Drummond, Earl of Melfort*, c.1692 (miniature),
by an unknown artist (Belton House)
This anonymous miniature shows Melfort with the Garter, which he received in 1692.

left on the 12th, reported to the queen at Saint-Germain and then rejoined James II at the military camp. 'Wee arived about midy at Peintrerie', Nairne noted on the 18th, '2 or 3 days after which ye K. returned to St Germ and I followd by soft journys a horseback and arrivd in St Germains .... some few days before ye birth of ye Princesse' on the 28th.[144]

By the end of June, therefore, Nairne's career had suffered two reverses. Politically speaking there was now no hope of a Jacobite restoration in the foreseeable future. And on a personal level his wife had failed to obtain a post in attendance on the princess. The future did not seem promising. Moreover, Lord Melfort's position was now considerably weaker, because the declaration was blamed for strengthening the resistance of the English fleet, and Nairne was so closely identified with Melfort that it seemed unlikely that he could survive his master's fall.

Given the situation it is particularly unfortunate that Nairne did not continue his diary at this time. For the two years from the end of June 1692 to the middle of June 1694 all that we have are the entries for April and the first half of May 1693. When the diary resumes in June 1694, we are immediately informed that Lord Melfort had been forced to resign and had left Saint-Germain. We have to fall back on the few other available sources.

Melfort's position began to be undermined in the spring of 1693 when James II was persuaded to adopt a more conciliatory line, and issue a new declaration promising to submit his suspending and dispensing powers to parliamentary limitation. It was agreed that if the king would do this he would be joined at Saint-Germain by Lord Middleton, a popular and respected politician who had been secretary of state for England from 1684 to 1688.

Middleton arrived at Saint-Germain on 13 April and the new declaration was published four days later.[145] On the 23rd, he was appointed joint secretary of state with Melfort, and given responsibility for the correspondence with England and the French court.[146] Middleton had his own under-secretary,[147] and Nairne's work was immediately diminished in quantity and importance. There are two brief references in his diary which indicate how worried he must have been at this time. On 3 May, he noted that Lord Melfort, during a visit to Versailles with James II and Lord Middleton, had given 'my borbrief to Mr de Croissy'. And two days later, he added that he had himself spoken to Clair Adam (Croissy's *premier commis*) 'concerning my déclaration de naturalité and lettres de noblesse'.[148] This subject is never referred to again, but the entry suggests that Nairne was having to envisage a possible future in France without employment at the Jacobite court.

Nothing, however, happened for the time being, partly because both James II and Mary of Modena retained their high opinion of the Melforts. In September 1693, they accompanied the king and queen during their annual visit to Fontainebleau, and Nairne went with them, but the evidence that he did so is in a letter announcing the death of the Countess of Erroll,[149] a loss which would further weaken his position.

By the end of 1693, James II was coming under considerable pressure from England to dismiss Melfort. In part this pressure came from the Jesuits who regarded Melfort as weak for having accepted the declaration of 1693. In part, it came from the supporters of Lord Middleton who regarded Melfort as intransigent for having advocated the declaration of 1692. It was argued by the latter that the leading politicians in England would be reluctant to support a Jacobite restoration so long as Melfort was employed at the exiled court, and consequently that Louis XIV would be unlikely to invest his resources in another restoration attempt unless it were supported by those politicians. Despite handing over to Middleton, Melfort continued to receive plenty of secret service information from England showing that this was not in fact the case, so he and Nairne set themselves the task of passing the information on to Croissy and the other ministers at Versailles. Between 1 December 1693 and May 1694, they sent to the French court various secret reports which they had received from England indicating that several of the most influential people there, including Lord Sunderland, one of the secretaries of state, were willing to come out in support of another attempt to restore James II now that he had issued his declaration of 1693.

At the beginning of May 1694, a particularly important report was received in cypher at Saint-Germain from Major-General Edward Sackville, who was one of their agents. It contained a letter from Lord Churchill (later the 1st Duke of Marlborough) indicating that he secretly supported James II, and demonstrating this by informing the king that the English fleet was planning a surprise amphibious attack on the remaining ships of the French Channel fleet at Brest in Camaret Bay. Sackville specifically requested that no one should be informed of the source of the information other than the queen and Melfort. Nairne decyphered both the message and Churchill's letter, and then translated them into French so that the warning could be passed on to Louis XIV. As a result the French were fully prepared, and an English landing in Camaret Bay was repulsed with heavy losses.

Neither the original message and letter in cypher, nor the decyphered versions in English, have survived, but Nairne kept among his papers a copy of his translation of both of them,[150] and these were discovered and published (translated back into English) in 1775.[151] The implication that the great Duke of Marlborough, by then one of the most admired men in British history, had in the mid-1690s been a secret Jacobite supporter, and had actually betrayed an important military secret to the French, came as a profound shock, and various historians attempted to defend the reputation of their hero. They did this by trying to discredit both Melfort and Nairne, even though they knew nothing of the latter. The most important defence came in an article in *The English Historical Review* of 1896 by Arthur Parnell, who was determined to establish that the documents, known collectively as the Camaret Bay letter, were a forgery.[152] Uncertain whether to blame the man who published the letter in 1775 (James Macpherson) or the man in whose handwriting the letter was preserved (David Nairne), he decided to blame them both. The former, he claimed, had 'ample opportunities for garbling, suppressing, concocting, or forging' the documents among Nairne's papers,[153] so he forged the Camaret Bay letter in Nairne's handwriting.[154] The latter, Nairne, was however equally to blame. 'I submit', he wrote:

> that this Camaret Bay draft, written by Nairne and corrected by Melfort, was simply, if ever presented at Versailles and *not a later forgery*, a cunning design of that most unscrupulous statesman [Melfort], partly to mislead Louis XIV into a false idea of the zeal of Marlborough on behalf of James, and partly to show his own importance. I submit also ... that the [other] accusatory documents are all of the same deceptive nature, and are of no more historical value than so much waste paper.[155]

Twenty-four years later, another article was published in *The English Historical Review* which conclusively demonstrated that the Camaret Bay letter was in existence, and had been seen by at least three reliable witnesses, before any of Nairne's papers had come into the hands of James

Macpherson, the man who published it many years later.[156] This implied, in the opinion of Marlborough's admirers, that if the Camaret Bay letter had not been forged by Macpherson, then it had to be a forgery by Nairne, so Winston Churchill devoted an entire chapter of his biography of the Duke of Marlborough to an attempt to persuade his readers that this was in fact the case.[157] Churchill, who knew nothing about Nairne, or even about the exiled court at Saint-Germain, began by suggesting that the papers preserved by Nairne were all forgeries. 'Nairne and Melfort concocted them together in Paris [sic]',[158] he wrote. He then specifically referred to the Camaret Bay letter:

> There is nothing in this letter which could not have been set down by Nairne and Melfort and presented by them to Mary of Modena, James and Louis. What was needed was not information but authority, something that would ... show to all how vigilant and irreplaceable were Melfort and Nairne, and how exclusive were the connexions they had established across the Channel.
>
> We cannot convict Nairne and Melfort of inventing and fabricating the Camaret Bay letter ... All we know is that they were capable of such conduct. Men who do not stop at murder for a cause will not stop at forgery.[159]

This extraordinary comment, accusing without any explanation both Nairne and Melfort of murder as well as forgery, can easily be dismissed by anyone who has studied Nairne's diary, his private correspondence, the handwriting and paper of the Camaret Bay letter, and the workings of the Stuart court at Saint-Germain. But it is an indication of how much the politics of the 1690s still mattered to many people in the early twentieth century. And Nairne, through his close association with Lord Melfort, became posthumously involved with this important debate about the secret sympathies of the leading politicians in London.

Two weeks after receiving the Camaret Bay letter, Lord Melfort wrote a lengthy 'Memoire justificatif'. It is dated 17 May 1694, is also preserved among Nairne's papers in French translation,[160] and was published in précis by Macpherson:

> Melfort was recalled from Rome, where he acquitted himself to the satisfaction of the French ministry, to act again as secretary of state. He carried on the correspondence with England. James's friends increased. The King of France was induced to attempt an invasion, and communicated his intentions to Melfort alone. James, from

thenceforward, never called to his council five Roman Catholic servants, with whom
he used to consult while Melfort was at Rome. This step, which Melfort opposed, in
vain, created him many enemies [particularly among the Jesuits].[161]

At the French court, it was a combination of these two groups, the
Jesuits and those like Croissy who now preferred Lord Middleton, who
succeeded in persuading Louis XIV that the time had come – despite the
Camaret Bay letter – for Melfort to be replaced. At the end of May, Louis
XIV asked James II to dismiss him, on the grounds that he was not trusted
by the majority of Jacobites in England, and James reluctantly agreed. Here
was the crisis that Nairne had feared and which threatened to terminate
his employment.

His position remained in the balance throughout June and July. It was
normal for secretaries of state to appoint their own under-secretaries and
clerks, and to regard them as personal rather than royal servants. The new
secretaries of state did not wish to employ men associated with and loyal to
their predecessors. But James II had different ideas. According to him, the
under-secretaries should be 'named by the King and ... have Warrants to be
so, and salarys, and [should] remain in their places tho the Secretary shall
chance to dy or be removed, that books of entrys remaine in the Office'.[162]
Nairne's fate was therefore to be determined by the extent of his association
with Melfort and by his perceived ability to transfer his loyalty to the new
secretary of state. In addition, Melfort and Middleton disliked each other,
so the latter's opinion was also to be taken into account. In the meantime,
all the correspondence was temporarily entrusted to Lord Middleton and
his under-secretary, David Lindsay.

Nairne's predicament is clearly revealed in a letter that he wrote to
Lewis Innes on 14 June. Some people had accused Innes, a secular priest,
of disloyalty to Melfort, and Nairne was anxious that there should be no
rift between his two patrons:

> I hope you found him a little altered as to ye impressions some people (whom God
> forgive) had given him of you.[163] I am sure I did my part to lett him know yt it
> was his true interest to take your councill, and depend upon your friendship as ye
> only means I saw left to support him against ye persecution of his enemys in his
> absence ... as I can not but love him my zeal for his good makes me unquiet till I
> know if I have been so happy in ye endeavours I have made to make you friends.

But he was mainly concerned with his own position:

> If you spoke anything together of me or my concerne and how I am to be left here, I
> should be glad to know it, for I was with My Ld Midleton yesterday who was civill
> to me, and told me I was secure for he knew ye King had a good opinion of me, but
> he said he had said nothing to him in particular of me, so I askt his protection and
> he promist it me, which was but very generall. And yesternight My Ld [Melfort]
> calld for ye chyffers and gave them to ye King, and I know not if ye King has spoke
> to him to leave his books and English intelligence in my hands or not. If you know
> any thing of it I hope you'l be so kind as to tell me and send me your councill what
> further step it is fitt for me to do, for I find there's no time to be lost.[164]

Five days later, Melfort and his wife, who was again pregnant, left Saint-
Germain for Paris.[165] Innes had also withdrawn temporarily to Paris,[166] and
Nairne was left to fend for himself.

During July, the king and queen decided that the Roman correspondence should temporarily be entrusted to John Caryll, the queen's Catholic
private secretary, rather than to Lord Middleton, who was a Protestant.
Nairne's letters suggest that he was allowed to work with Caryll on a trial
basis.[167] Melfort, meanwhile, was told to leave Paris and live in the provinces. The strain was too much for Lady Melfort, who miscarried *en route*
to Moulins.[168]

At the end of July, James finally made up his mind that Caryll should
be appointed joint secretary of state. This, for Nairne, was the moment
of decision. On 1 August, he noted in his diary that 'I gave to Mr Caryll a
memoriall I had drawn for the Queen representing my case to her, which he
promised to give her'. This petition was successful, and on the following day
'Mr Caryll was declared Secretary of State and got the seals. Immediately
after dinner the K was pleased to call me and tell me yt I was to continue
my employment under Mr Caryll.'[169] Nairne had survived. Because Caryll
continued to act as the queen's private secretary, Nairne was to serve him in
two separate capacities: as under-secretary dealing with the Roman correspondence and, in effect, as assistant private secretary to the queen. He also
persuaded Caryll to let him retain both Monnot and Dempster.[170] A few
days later, Nairne obtained all the letter books of Roman correspondence
from Middleton and Lindsay,[171] and settled down to his new work. He was
now a servant of the king and a permanent member of the Jacobite court.

***

For the next nine years, Nairne was employed as chief clerk to John Caryll. It was during this period that he became one of the most important, and certainly most trusted, members of the court. Nairne was thirty years younger than Caryll, and always remained his subordinate, but as the years went by the two men developed closer relations and eventually became friends as well as colleagues. At the same time, and thanks to the support of Caryll as well as to his own loyalty and capacity for hard work, he increasingly obtained the favour and the confidence of the king and the queen. In 1696 he was given additional responsibilities as clerk of the queen's council, in 1699 he was entrusted by James II with the task of converting the latter's memoirs into a lengthy biography, and in 1701 he was appointed clerk of the council of the new King James III.

Nairne was extremely lucky that it was Caryll who was appointed to replace Melfort. Caryll had been James II's agent in Rome from 1685 to 1686, so that both he and Nairne could speak and write Italian, while both of them had personal knowledge and experience of Rome, its churches and the papal court. Both men were also very keen on music and able to perform to a high standard.[172] John Caryll was a poet, with a significant literary reputation. Two of his plays had been performed on the London stage,[173] and his publications included two poems condemning Lord Shaftesbury[174] and two translations from the Latin of Ovid and Virgil.[175] Nairne and Caryll would spend many hours together translating other works from Latin into English, an activity which would cement their growing friendship.

Of more immediate significance was the fact that Caryll had been, and remained, private secretary to the queen, responsible for her extensive correspondence with her relations and friends in Italy, with many of the princes and cardinals, and also with the Pope. It made good sense to place the Roman correspondence of the king (handled by the secretary of state) and the correspondence of the queen (handled by her private secretary) in the hands of the same man and his chief clerk. In this way Nairne came increasingly to the attention of the queen. Yet Caryll was not only responsible for the Roman correspondence. He also inherited the highly secret correspondence which Melfort had been conducting with people in England and Scotland, such as the Earl of Ailesbury, the Earl of Arran and the non-juring Bishop of Norwich. It was in large part Nairne's clerical role in drafting, cyphering and decyphering this correspondence which increasingly brought him to the notice of the king as well as the queen. Despite working so closely and successfully with Caryll, Nairne continued to enjoy excellent relations with both Lord and Lady Melfort. He corresponded with them very regularly,[176] managed their finances and their household affairs at Saint-Germain, and even lent them money.[177] This showed courage as well as loyalty, because the Melforts had many enemies at Saint-Germain. On one occasion, Melfort wrote to Nairne:

> I am sorry that you have any reason to fear ye ennemys and I conjure you to doe nothing on my account to irritate any body and indeed if any thing of my interest hurt you I will certainly turn off all sort of correspondence with you.[178]

Lord Middleton, who had been Melfort's chief rival, initially viewed Nairne with some suspicion, and as late as April of the following year the latter noted that Caryll 'advertised me yt E.M[iddleto]n had still some jealousy of me'.[179] In addition, some of the Scottish Jacobites – though fortunately not Lewis Innes – distrusted Caryll because he was English. In September 1694, Nairne informed one of them:

> I must tell you yt Mr Caryll is a very honest man, a zealous good Christian and a good friend of Mr Innes. He has great credit with K and Q and yrfor you must have all ye trust in and esteem of him yt one ought ... He is my superior and ye K's minister.

He added that 'Mr Inese ... is a wise man of very good councill usefull to ye King and beloved by all'. As for Lord and Lady Melfort, Nairne told his correspondent that 'I look upon them as very happy to be out of ye embaras of a court wher they had ye ill luck to have so many enemys'.[180]

In September 1694, James II ordered Melfort to hand over all the papers he had kept concerning the attempted invasion of England in 1692, and particularly the copies of the memorials 'given in last year to the French ministers'. As Melfort was no longer in Paris Caryll wrote to ask him if Nairne might go to his house there and look for the papers.[181] Melfort agreed,[182] but he told Nairne privately that he was surprised the king had needed to ask for the memorials, because Middleton already had copies of everything, and he reassured Nairne that he should 'not fancy that I think you capable of being less my friend' for doing this.[183] Nairne replied that, although he had handed over all the official papers to the king, he had left behind the various drafts which Melfort had made in his own handwriting.[184]

By September 1694, Nairne's wife Marie-Elisabeth was eight months pregnant, and the letters he received from the Melforts contain frequent references both to her and to his son Jean (called Johnie by Melfort, who was his godfather).[185] At the end of that month, James II and Queen Mary went to join Louis XIV at Fontainebleau, and Nairne accompanied them there for five days, but he was back at Saint-Germain in good time for Marie-Elisabeth to give birth to a baby daughter on 17 October. The child was called Françoise, and was baptized four days later by Lewis Innes in the Chapel Royal of the château. Her godfather was the Prince of Wales, and her godmother one of the queen's ladies of the bedchamber (Lady Sophia Bulkeley).[186]

Shortly after the birth, Nairne's wife became seriously ill, and for two weeks there was a danger that she might die. On 31 October, she 'receaved ye viatique'.[187] Lady Melfort, who had just returned to Paris,[188] sent Mary Hay to help look after her, and by the end of the first week of November she was on the way to recovery.[189] Nairne was now the father of two little children, but he had lived through a difficult period of two weeks when he feared that he might lose his wife.

In the following years, the Nairnes and the Melforts continued to correspond, and Nairne himself continued to look after Melfort's financial affairs and other interests.[190] But none of their correspondence has survived, and our information comes exclusively from Nairne's diary which mentions the letters which he and his wife sent and received. It should be added that, with one or two exceptions, none of Nairne's voluminous correspondence with other people from the years 1695 to 1708 has survived either, so we have to rely almost exclusively on his diary to provide information for these years. For example, it tells us that he wrote several private letters each day, particularly to Charles Whiteford at the Collège des Ecossais and to Lewis Innes when the latter was absent from the court, and these letters must have contained personal opinions and reflections on his life at the court. By contrast, Nairne's diary during the mid-1690s is little more than a record of his work for Caryll, so our information is limited, but as the years went by he began to include more and more personal observations. It is these which enable us to follow the development of his life and career during the next thirteen years.

During 1695, Nairne established ever closer relations with Caryll and also came increasingly to the attention of the king and queen. On 21 January, for example, Nairne recorded how James II spoke to him at the levée, and 'bid me wait on him when he went in' to his closet to deal with some very secret correspondence in cypher. He noted in his diary: 'I told him how kind Mr C was to me and he said he was a just man.' A few months later he wrote to Melfort's brother Lord Perth, the Jacobite ambassador in Rome, and 'told him what obligations I had to Mr Car[yll]'.[191] In November Lady Melfort, who was again pregnant, obtained permission from the king and queen to come to Paris temporarily for the delivery of her baby, and Nairne noted that when she arrived he and his wife 'went to see her at night'.[192] When, however, Melfort also arrived in Paris a few weeks later Caryll advised Nairne that 'it was not fitt for me to go to see him, considering ye trust I had of ye K's affaires'.[193]

In addition to handling Caryll's correspondence for the king and queen, assisted by Monnot and Dempster, he also began to deal with Caryll's private affairs. For example, when Caryll wrote two new poems 'upon ye plot', it was Nairne who copied them out neatly and wrote a preface for their publication at Saint-Germain.[194] Nairne also began to manage Caryll's private investments, on one occasion being entrusted with 589 *louis d'ors* (8,249 *livres*) in cash to be taken to the Hôtel de Ville in Paris.[195] Shortly afterwards he helped Caryll draw up the latter's last will and testament.[196]

Nairne's diary entries allow us to observe his growing intimacy with the king. James liked to conduct his business in the château de Saint-Germain in one or other of the two rooms which lay beyond his bedchamber: his closet in the north-east pavilion, and the so-called little bedchamber which he shared with his wife, situated at the angle of the château between his own bedchamber in the north wing and the queen's bedchamber in the east wing. There are repeated references to Nairne's being called to work with the king in these two places,[197] and to his being shown public signs of favour. The king might stop and talk to him when processing from the chapel royal to take his dinner in the queen's privy chamber,[198] or he might single him out at his levée by making him 'a little bow and a smile',[199] or

Figure 2. *King James II*, 1691 (miniature), by Nicolas de Largillière (private collection)
This miniature is copied from the lost family portrait by Largillière, showing the Stuart
royal family at Saint-Germain-en-Laye in 1691.

by ordering him to come back to his apartment after dinner.[200] In January
1695, Nairne noted that Lewis Innes 'told me ye K had spoke very kindly of
me.'[201] When the king and queen paid their Easter visit to Paris in 1695 they
asked Nairne to join the small group to accompany them. One day, they

'heard tenebres' together at Sainte-Geneviève and then took communion at the Jesuit church in the rue Saint-Antoine. On the following day, they went to Saint-Roch beside the Louvre and then again to 'ye great Jesuites'.[202] During another visit to Paris, the king invited Nairne to dine with him at the Collège des Ecossais.[203] When James wanted Norbert Roettiers to make some new touch pieces, it was Nairne whom he entrusted with the necessary negotiations and with whom he discussed what the new puncheons should look like.[204]

Nairne seems also to have been appreciated by the queen, who was responsible for the young Prince of Wales until 1695, when the seven year-old-boy was handed over to be brought up by men. In October 1694, as we have seen, the queen agreed that the prince should be godfather to Nairne's daughter Françoise. Then, in May 1695, it was Nairne who was instructed to draft, under the supervision of Caryll, 'ye Rules for ye P.ces family'. They were written in two days, accepted by the king and queen with only one small amendment and one 'little addition', and dated 31 May.[205] At first, the upbringing of the prince was entrusted to two under-governors (Francis Plowden and Edmund Perkins), but the following year, when the prince was eight years old, he was given a governor, the Earl of Perth, who had returned from Rome. Nairne therefore amended the Rules and gave them to Perth to show to the king. The latter approved them and Perth 'told me ye K spoke very kindly of them'.[206]

Nairne was also entrusted by the queen with the commissioning of new portraits of the prince and princess. Taking advantage of the extensive experience he had gained in Rome, he negotiated with Nicolas de Largillière for various copies of a portrait of the prince in the summer of 1694,[207] for the celebrated double portrait of the prince and the princess at the end of 1694,[208] for some more portraits of the prince in the summer of 1695,[209] and several of the princess during the autumn of that year.[210] He also managed the distribution of an engraving of one of the portraits of the prince by Largillière which Lewis Innes had commissioned from Etienne Gantrel, ensuring that many copies of it were sent safely to England and Scotland.[211]

Another development which brought Nairne closer to the king was James II's decision, with the agreement of Caryll,[212] to employ him as the agent and adviser to Lord Henry FitzJames, created Duke of Albemarle in January 1696. FitzJames, like his elder brother the Duke of Berwick, was one of the king's two illegitimate sons, and was then serving with the French navy in the Mediterranean. Nairne was entrusted with soliciting on his behalf at Versailles and with receiving his money at Saint-Germain, and he conducted a regular correspondence with FitzJames. He showed the letters to the king and the queen, who then used him as a channel of communication in reply.

Throughout the year, Nairne continued to live with his wife and two children in the house he had rented in the rue de la Salle, but he still hoped to be given an apartment in the château, with an allocation of wood and candles. At the end of October, hoping to benefit from his regular contact with James II, he wrote 'a Memoriall for myself to give to ye K concerning lodging, fire and candle'.[213] He showed it to both Innes and Caryll,[214] and he probably obtained their support, but he noted in his diary that 'it was not given'.[215]

Caryll, however, obtained for him by way of compensation a promotion at the court. In January 1696, Nairne recorded in his diary that 'Mr Caryll proposed to me of his own motion to obtaine for me ye place of Clark of ye Q's Councill, being a place of his donation'.[216] It took a few weeks to be settled, but the following month Nairne noted:

> after ye Queen's supper she called me in and in presence of Mr Caryll ... told me yt she accepted very willingly of what Mr Caryll had proposed for me in her service, upon wch she gave me her hand to kiss and said she knew I was an honest man.[217]

By 1696, therefore, Nairne had established very good relations with both the king and the queen, as well as with his immediate superior, John Caryll, and this was demonstrated by a new development in February 1696.

At that time a French army was being assembled at the Channel ports in preparation for another attempt to restore James II to his thrones. It was agreed that the king would join the army at Calais and await a favourable moment to cross the sea, so he needed to decide whom he would take with him and whom he would leave behind with the queen at Saint-Germain. As regards the political secretariat, would he be accompanied by John Caryll or by Lord Middleton as Secretary of State? Nairne, of course, was Caryll's chief clerk; Middleton's chief clerk was called David Lindsay, a Protestant who had recently arrived at the court. On 26 February, Nairne made the following entry in his diary:

> The King gave me two letters of his ... to copie – in one of wch he writt wth his own hand yt Lind was not trusted wth any secret thing, but yt I was and yt he was assured of my faithfulness and secrecy by a long experience.[218]

On the following day, James II made his decision:

> The King of France came and then it was publickly declared yt ye King was to goe ye morrow to Calais. The K bid me prepare my self because he intended to send me ... to Calais.

James was to be accompanied by Middleton and Nairne, leaving Lindsay and Caryll behind with the queen. The king departed on the 28th, and Nairne left Saint-Germain two days later. When the latter took his leave of the queen she 'said she knew I was an honest man and was glad yt I was going to ye King'.[219] This was to be a turning point in Nairne's career.

Nairne left Saint-Germain on 1 March with Sir William Ellis and travelled via Luzarches (near Ecouen) and Abbeville to Calais, where he joined the king on the 3rd.[220] The two months which followed were a frustrating time. The Jacobites in England would not rise up against William III until the French had actually invaded; Louis XIV would not risk another invasion attempt and possible naval defeat until he knew the Jacobites had already made the first move. The result was stalemate, with James II and his entourage obliged to await developments. If this was politically disappointing, for Nairne as much as for everyone else, it nevertheless resulted in a growing intimacy between him and the king.

Nairne remained at Calais for nine days until the 12th.[221] He quickly established a daily routine, writing every day to Caryll, Innes and his wife, and most days to Monnot and Dempster. He saw the king very regularly, and was entrusted with sending and receiving the letters which James II exchanged with Queen Mary. On the 8th, 'wee saw a great many ships upon ye English coast towards ye Downs', so the king decided that if they came towards Calais and launched an attack he would withdraw to Dunkirk. At the levée that morning, he told Nairne that if he went to Dunkirk 'he

would take care yt I should go wth him', and added three days later that
he had given orders that Nairne should be provided with one of his own
horses. The party set out on the 12th, Nairne riding 'ye Berwick one of ye
K's horses', and travelled via Gravelines to Dunkirk, where John Caryll's
sister was the Abbess of the English Benedictine convent.[222] While James
II went to see the site of the Battle of the Dunes, in which he had fought in
1658, Nairne joined Lord Middleton in examining the fortifications of the
town. But Nairne also accompanied the king to mass 'at ye English nuns'
and added that 'wee went in and saw ye monastry [*sic*]'[223] – something
that the Protestant Middleton could not do. On the 15th, they returned
to Calais, dining at the convent of the English Poor Clares at Gravelines
on the way.

    Nairne remained with the king at Calais for eight days until 23 March,
continuing to write his daily letters to Caryll, Innes, his wife and others.
He then travelled with the king, and on another of the king's horses, to
Boulogne, where they remained for six weeks until 3 May.[224] Nairne now
regularly attended services with the king at the various churches, monaster-
ies and convents in the town, but he had very little else to do, complaining
in one of his letters to Innes 'about my having no imploym.t etc, Mr Sec.
ry [Caryll] charging me wth no comission to ye K',[225] and apologizing in
another for 'writing so oft wthout matter'.[226]

    Although these weeks at the coast brought Nairne much closer to
the king, it is clear that he found the time spent at Calais and Boulogne
particularly depressing. On 20 April, he confided to Innes that he felt very
melancholy because the 'wicked [were] prospering' against the 'just',[227]
and a few days later commented that 'ye K. of Fr should make an effort
to send us over' and thereby encourage the English Jacobites to rise up
against William III.[228]

    Faced with these weeks of inactivity, Nairne decided to write an
account of his life in Scotland, the United Provinces, France and Ireland
from his birth in 1655 until his departure for Rome with Lord Melfort at
the end of 1689. His aim was to provide an introduction to the detailed
diary that he had kept in Rome, to the diaries he had kept at Saint-Germain
in 1692 and 1693, and to the one which he had been keeping consistently
since the fall of Melfort in 1694. He entitled the new connected work

'Journal. 1 Tome', and later had it bound up into a single volume with his diaries. The volume contained 200 blank pages at the end, and by recording his experiences in ever smaller handwriting, he was able to continue adding to the volume for another twelve years, until 1708, when he finally filled up the last page.

Two other things concerned Nairne while he was at Boulogne, the first of which was an attempt to obtain financial compensation for his failure to obtain an apartment in the château at Saint-Germain. On 2 April, he wrote to Innes 'about my having dyet allowd me', by which he meant either becoming entitled to join the courtiers who dined at the king's expense in the château, or being given an addition to his salary instead. Innes spoke to the queen, who consulted the king, but Nairne's request was not granted.[229]

Of more pressing importance was the fact that Nairne's wife was pregnant again. She had had a miscarriage the previous year, in March 1695,[230] but was expecting to give birth to another child – her sixth – at the end of April. The timing was unfortunate because, if the attempted invasion of England had succeeded, Nairne would have followed the king across the Channel. By the beginning of April, however, when the chances of success were diminishing, Nairne was keen to rejoin his wife. In the meantime, he corresponded with her about the name to be given the child and about the choice of godparents. On the 14th, he noted that he had written to both John Caryll and Mary Stafford (governess of Princess Louise-Marie) asking them if they would agree to be the godfather and godmother. On the 30th, while he was still at Boulogne, his wife 'was brought to bed of a son, who was christend after my return to St Germ, Mr Sec.ry [Caryll] and Mrs Stafford standing [as godparents]'. The child was named Jean-Baptiste. When he initially received the news of the birth, he told his wife 'to christen ye child w.thout waiting for me',[231] but she refused and Nairne was present at the christening on 9 May 'at 4 a clock in ye afternoon in ye parish church'. He and his wife now had three children. Jean, the eldest, was three and a half years old, and Françoise was one and a half.

The decision to return to Saint-Germain was taken by James II on 30 April, the day on which Nairne's son Jean-Baptiste was born. The king left on 3 May with Lord Middleton and arrived at Saint-Germain two days later. Before he left, he told Nairne 'he had orderd one of his horses for me to go to St Germ. wch he believd would be ye convenientest way for me'.[232] It was the same horse (the Berwick) which Nairne had ridden when he went to Dunkirk. This time he went in company with eleven other courtiers and servants. The journey took five days, and involved spending each night at an inn, at Montreuil, Abbeville, Poix and Beauvais. They arrived 'about 9 a clock at night', and Nairne immediately went to see Caryll and Innes, before returning home to see his new baby son and family. The following day, he noted that 'at ye levé ye K spoke to me' and that 'at dinner I saw ye Queen who saluted me wth a smile and a bow'.[233]

The two months he spent with the king beside the Channel in the spring of 1696 had brought Nairne much closer to James II. His diary tells us that he was now called to attend the king in his closet after his levée,[234] and there he was employed to copy papers[235] and write letters,[236] acting on these occasions directly for the king rather than as usual through Caryll. In June we find Nairne walking in the gardens of Saint-Germain with both the king and Lord Perth,[237] and the following month Perth told him that the king 'had comended me [Nairne] pticularly for secrecy and fidelity'.[238] In June 1697, Nairne noted:

> The K called me in after ye levée to ye little bedchamber and gave me 5 or 6 smal phioles of water to write with in white, wch he bid me keep till yr should be use of them.[239]

Nairne continued to attend mass with the king, not just in the chapel royal with all the other courtiers, but also in the privacy of the little chapel, situated in the south wing between the apartment of the queen and the rooms occupied by the Prince of Wales and his sister princess Louise-Marie,[240] as well as in the queen's bedchamber.[241] In addition, Nairne went hunting with the king, and was with him when news was received of the Treaty of Ryswick: 'I ... went a stag hunting wth ye K Q and K of Fr in Marly forest where we had ye news yt ye peace was synd with ye Emp.r.'[242]

During 1696 and 1697, Nairne had been kept particularly busy during the negotiations leading up to the peace treaty. For example, he conducted a regular correspondence with the maréchal de Tessé, whom he had known since the 1680s. Tessé commanded the French army against the Duke of Savoy, and at the beginning of 1696 was charged by Louis XIV with negotiating a separate peace whereby Savoy would desert the League of Augsburg. The negotiations were secret, but Tessé kept Nairne informed about their progress. For example, on 25 January 1696, the latter wrote to Tessé 'to thank him in ye K's name for his kindness to his subjects and telling him I had shewd his letter to ye K'.[243] The peace treaty with Savoy was signed at Turin in June 1696, after which negotiations for a general peace treaty were opened at Ryswick. Nairne's role was purely clerical, but it involved a great deal of work drafting and copying papers for Caryll concerning Queen Mary's joynture, the payment of which was eventually made a condition of peace by Louis XIV. He was also involved in drawing up the Protestation which James II sent to the sovereign princes of Europe in June 1697 announcing that he would regard as null and void any settlement prejudicial to his interests.

Encouraged by all these developments, Nairne made another attempt to obtain 'lodging mony, wood and candle'. In December 1697, he gave 'a memoire' on the subject to Innes,[244] and in January 1698 he discussed his request with Caryll 'who said he would speak to ye K'.[245] Caryll did speak to the king,[246] but when nothing had happened by March, Innes urged Caryll to speak to the king again 'to help me with some consideration for my family'.[247] This time Nairne finally obtained what he wanted. He noted on 31 March 1698:

> Mr Caryl sent for me in ye afternoon ... and told me the K was pleasd to grant me an addition of 500# to my pension, and yt ye Q had been very forward in it and very much my friend.[248]

A few days later, Nairne took advantage of one of his private meetings with James II to thank him:

> being in his closet in his own side I took occasion to thank him for ye augmentation of my pension. He told me he had done it to shew ye consideration he had for my long and faithfull services but that he would have nobody know it but Mr Car and myself.[249]

At first, the money was given by the king to Caryll, to be handed on to Nairne,[250] but the following year James decided to change the arrangement: the king 'payd me my augmentation for ye month ... out of his own hand,

and said he would hereafter pay it me himself.'[251] As Nairne's salary had been 89*l* 7*s* 6*d per mensem* (or 1,072*l* 10*s* 0*d per annum*), this augmentation of 500 *livres per annum* brought him an additional 41*l* 13*s* 4*d per mensem*, an increase of nearly a half.[252] Later that same year, however, when he tried again to obtain an apartment in the château, he was unsuccessful.[253]

Although Nairne was now held in high regard by the king and the queen, he owed both the augmentation of his income and the security of his position to the support of his immediate superior, John Caryll. By the end of 1697, the two men had become so close that they began to dine together on a regular basis in Caryll's apartment, normally with Lewis Innes when the latter was at Saint-Germain. At the end of December 1696, Caryll asked Nairne to help him translate all the Psalms from the Vulgate into English.[254] The latter's diary records their progress during the first months of 1697, noting on 14 March that 'I finished ye transl of ye psalmes in ye morning'. Nairne then made a fair copy of the entire translation, which he had bound up in two volumes in Paris at the end of May so that he and Caryll could make any necessary corrections. Meanwhile, Nairne also wrote 'ye Preface to ye Psalmes'.[255]

During the summer of 1697, the two men made some more corrections and then put their work on one side for two and a half years. Eventually, in December 1699, they revised their work again, and Nairne wrote a new preface. Their translation was published under Caryll's name at Saint-Germain in 1700 as *The Psalmes of David, translated from the Vulgat*, 'intended only for the privat devotions of Lay persons'. Nairne's preface was included, but published anonymously.[256]

By then Nairne and Caryll had also translated the entire New Testament, starting with the Epistles (August 1697 to April 1698), and continuing with the Acts of the Apostles (August to October 1698), the Apocalypse (November 1698) and the four Gospels (February to June 1700). Nairne made fair copies of all their translations, and added titles for each section. The whole work, entitled *New Testament, translated from the Vulgat*, was eventually bound up in two manuscript volumes and sent to England in 1702 'to be left there for ye [Catholic] B[ishop]s to be examind, and printed with their approbation'.[257] Shortly afterwards, Nairne wrote a preface,[258] but in the event the work was never printed or published.

No copy seems to have survived, and it is not known what became of the two volumes sent to England. What concerns us, however, is that during a period of three and a half years, from the beginning of 1697 until the summer of 1700, Nairne spent many hours with John Caryll making these biblical translations from Latin into English. Nairne remained Caryll's chief clerk, but in fact he was now the older man's friend and confidante. He continued to manage Caryll's investments at the Hôtel de Ville in Paris, on several occasions being entrusted with very large sums of money.[259] He arranged for masses to be said in Saint-Germain for the deceased members of Caryll's family,[260] and he entertained and looked after Caryll's nephew, also called John (and well known to students of English literature as the intimate friend of Alexander Pope). A few weeks after the completion of the translation of the New Testament, in the summer of 1700, Caryll asked Nairne as a personal favour to accompany his nephew to Dunkirk where he was to meet his aunt, the abbess of the English Benedictine convent.[261]

The translations from the Bible, Nairne's very close relations with Caryll, and James's personal knowledge of Nairne's loyalty, secrecy and long service, persuaded the king that he should entrust Nairne with his personal papers and that he should ask Nairne to use them to compose his biography.[262] This was the origin of what would become *The Life of James II*. On 8 January 1699 Nairne noted in his diary that he 'began to write out the Kings Memoires', by which he meant a biography of the king based on the latter's manuscript memoirs. He then took a period of leave, and when he returned he recorded on 19 March that 'I began to write out ye history of ye K's Life drawn out of his memoires.'

It is not clear how much progress was made during the spring of 1699, but Nairne's diary records that he concentrated on producing a fair copy of what he had himself so far written between 17 July and 23 August of that year. On 15 August, he recorded that he had reached 'ye end of his first campagne in France in yr 1652' in 219 pages. By the 23rd, he had reached 1660. This part of the biography was then submitted to Caryll and to the king, both of whom presumably made various amendments but gave their approval before the end of the year. On 12 January 1700, Nairne began to make the fair copy in folio which is now in the Scottish Catholic Archives.

Nairne recorded on 1 May: 'I ended ye year 1660 of ye Ks memoires [*sic*: life], containing 497 pages from ye K's birth in ... [*sic*] to the late K's restoration in 1660'.[263] It is clear from his journal that Nairne was the principal author of this part of *The Life* and was not, as has been claimed, merely Caryll's 'amanuensis'.[264]

By the end of 1699, it was evident that James II was in poor health and not expected to live for very much longer. On 13 December, Nairne recorded in his diary that 'I saw ye K at dinner he was carryd to ye table in a rouling chaire'. During his last years, James II increasingly relied on Nairne to perform essential but everyday tasks. Whether it was getting his spectacles mended[265] or having his clock repaired,[266] it was Nairne to whom he turned. When he wanted to give a new penknife to the queen, he asked Nairne to purchase one for him.[267] When he wanted to get 'his sundyall' repaired, he entrusted it to Nairne.[268] In March 1700, he asked Nairne to make the necessary arrangements to have one of his teeth removed. The latter's diary entry for 18 March records that Nairne himself had one tooth pulled out 'by ye famous toothdrawer an Italian who [also] drew one of ye K's one of ye Q's and 3 or 4 of ye P.cesses'. When one of the women of the court wanted a cutting of the king's hair, it was Nairne who obtained it for her.[269] Other personal services included copying out some passages from the Jesuit Jean Croiset's *Retraite spirituelle pour un jour chaque mois* (Lyon, 1694) 'wch he had markd',[270] and copying 'a letter from ye K to ... [*sic*] in a counterfeit hand'.[271] It is not surprising that on one occasion Caryll emphasized to Nairne that 'ye K had a good estime' of him,[272] nor that Nairne later recorded an incident in which James II showed both his kindness and his 'bonne opinion de moy':

> he had sent me to fetch some things from his closet on the evening before a feast day, and after talking to me about other things he was going to ask me to write something for him the following day, when he remembered that the next day was a religious festival, and suddenly changed his mind and was kind enough to say to me 'that can wait, Nairne, for another day; because tomorrow you will want to concentrate on your religious devotions'.

Nairne testified that 'I was so struck by this that I have never been able to forget it'.[273]

The most important service which Nairne performed for the king was assembling and looking after his private papers. In September 1700, James II entrusted to him not only his correspondence with Armand-Jean Le Bouthillier de Rancé, 'ye Antient Abbé de la Trappe', but also some papers of Charles II ('ye late Kings papers') 'to seal up and send to La Trappe'.[274] A few days later, he gave Nairne some of his papers ('ye K's papers') to be deposited, possibly at Nairne's suggestion, in the Collège des Ecossais in Paris.[275] Then, on 29 March 1701, he gave Nairne the advice he had written for his son the prince of Wales in 1692.[276] Nairne recorded:

> At night ye K sent for me and gave me his memoires [sic] to his son to copie, telling me yt he wd trust them to no other body, ther being secret advices in them of great concern, and upon this occasion he commended me very much for my discretion and my fidelity, and told me how satisfied he was with me.

It was immediately after copying this long document that work was resumed on the king's biography.

The second volume was started on 14 April 1701, and was again written by Nairne himself though with some amendments by Caryll. Nairne noted on 31 May: 'We finishd ye 5th quarternione of ye 2d part of ye K's memoires [sic: life] being 248 pages – from ye year 60 to ye year 77'. However, this volume, which is also in the Scottish Catholic Archives, was put on one side. On 27 June 1701, James II, who was now seriously ill, told Nairne to stop, but thanked him for all that he had written by giving him a second increase to his pension. The diary entry for that day reads:

> The K sent for me in the morning and told me he was well satisfied wth my service and particularly wth ye pains I had taken in his memoires with Mr Caryll, yt he could not do for me at p.snt what he would, but he thought it just to put me a little more at ease and was resolved for that effect to augment my salary, and would speak to ye Q and Mr Caryll about it and regulate it with them.[277]

The new augmentation was of 500 *livres per annum*, bringing Nairne's total annual income to 2072*l* 10*s* 0*d*. His monthly salary was 89*l* 7*s* 6*d*, and his two additional pensions now gave him an additional 83*l* 13*s* 4*d*.[278] To preserve secrecy, the money appeared in the court accounts as an additional payment to Caryll.[279]

Nairne's diary does not tell us why the king told him to stop working on the biography, but we may assume it was because James II's life was at last drawing to an end, and that he was worried about the security of his papers after his death. In March he had had 'a fainting fitt at Mass',[280] followed a few days later by another collapse during his levée.[281] He had another 'fainting fitt just before Mass at 12 a clock' on 10 July. A few days later Nairne arranged to have the king's memoirs covering the years 1667 to the 1690s bound up into five quarto volumes[282] and wrote an 'abstract' describing their contents.[283] He then 'carryd ye 5 tomes of ye K's orig: memoires' to Paris, to be kept safely in the Collège des Ecossais.[284]

The event which provoked James II's collapse in March 1701, and which hastened his final illness and death later that year, was of particular significance for Nairne. It concerned Lord Melfort, with whom he had remained on very good terms despite becoming so close to Caryll, and despite undertaking so many duties for the king.

Back in 1694, James II had told Melfort that he did not wish him to live in Paris,[285] so Melfort and his wife had gone into provincial exile, at first at Orléans and then (since the beginning of 1696) at Rouen. In May 1697, Lady Melfort visited Saint-Germain for three weeks in an attempt to persuade the king to change his mind and let her husband return to Paris.[286] Her aim was to obtain the support of Caryll, so she asked Nairne to speak to his superior on her behalf, which Nairne did.[287] This seems to have been successful, because Lady Melfort returned to Saint-Germain shortly afterwards for a month.[288] Nairne noted that he visited her several times, and on one occasion walked with her in the garden outside the king's apartment.[289] When she left one month later he noted that 'I was up at 4 a clock to see her part',[290] making very plain his continued loyalty to the man who had first employed him at the court. Caryll meanwhile had persuaded the king to let Melfort return, and he gave Nairne the news informally at the end of July so that the latter could pass it on to Rouen. Nairne felt that he should not himself inform Melfort, so he had his wife write 'a long letter to My La. Melf. in my name' giving her the good news.[291] In the middle of August, Lord and Lady Melfort left Rouen and returned to Paris.[292]

Nairne was keen to see Melfort, but he did nothing for two months. Then, in October, he asked Caryll if he might go to Paris in order to do so.

He noted in his diary that Caryll 'did not approve it'.[293] Shortly afterwards, however, Lewis Innes went to see Melfort, accompanied by Lord Perth,[294] and this perhaps made Caryll change his mind. At any rate, on 29 October, Nairne noted that 'I went to Paris wth Mr In to see My Ld and La Melf', the first time he had seen Melfort for over three years.

For the next three years, during which he was translating the New Testament with Caryll and writing the Life of James II from the latter's memoirs, Nairne saw the Melforts regularly. His diary records that the Melforts visited Saint-Germain on fifteen occasions between November 1697 and December 1700, and each time Nairne went to see them, normally several times and sometimes with his wife. During the same period the diary mentions eight visits by Nairne to Paris during which he also saw the Melforts, sometimes with his wife. It says a great deal for Nairne's tact and popularity that he was able to do this so openly without ever losing the confidence of either Caryll or the king. Not even Lord Middleton, who was Melfort's old rival, seemed to object, and there are frequent references in the diary to Nairne's working with Middleton himself or visiting Lady Middleton.

The only occasions when Nairne had divided loyalties were when Melfort criticized Innes or Caryll. In August 1698, Melfort had a disagreement with Innes, and Nairne seems to have supported the latter.[295] In October 1699, when Melfort criticized Caryll in the presence of Nairne and his wife during one of his visits to Saint-Germain, Nairne noted that 'I did not open my mouth', but sent a message 'afterward to let them know yt if they woud speak any more of Mr Car in that manner I woud look on it as forbidding me their house'.[296] Given the regularity with which Nairne continued thereafter to see the Melforts, we must assume that this was an isolated incident.

And so we come to the events of 1701, which had such an unfortunate effect on the king and which were profoundly disturbing for Nairne himself. In February of that year, Lord Melfort sent Nairne a letter 'wth a copie of the filiation of his son [Lord Forth] wch he desir'd to have signd by ye King'.[297] This must have been the equivalent of the birth brieve which Nairne had himself obtained back in 1687.[298] With Caryll's agreement,[299] Nairne then copied out 'Ld Melforts pedigree ingrossd in parchment' and had it 'signd by the King having get directions for it from ye K and Q in presence of My Ld Perth'.[300] On the following day, Melfort came from Paris to Saint-Germain to thank Nairne, and presumably also the king.[301] All seemed well. Nairne could feel satisfied that the Melforts had returned to favour, and that he had made a significant contribution towards achieving this. And then the situation abruptly changed.

At the beginning of that month, Melfort sent a letter addressed to his brother, Lord Perth, at 'La Cour d'Angleterre', by which of course he meant the Château de Saint-Germain. For reasons which are not clear, but which were only possible because England and France were at peace, the letter was sent to the English court in London where it was quickly opened and shown to the secretary of state and to King William III. On the latter's orders, the letter was communicated to both Houses of Parliament on 17 February 1701.

Melfort had written to inform Perth that he had discovered from Madame de Maintenon that Louis XIV was preparing a great fleet which would put to sea during the summer with a view to controlling the English Channel. This, Melfort felt, would provide an ideal opportunity for the French to invade England, if only there was someone at Saint-Germain capable of drawing up the necessary plans with the Jacobites in England. The Catholics could be relied on to rise up, but Melfort argued that there was no one at the exiled court willing or able to conduct the necessary correspondence to prepare the High Anglicans: Middleton was 'lazy in his temper [and] an enemy to France', and Caryll was 'in society' with Middleton. Melfort argued that there was no time to be lost, because the English army had been disbanded since the peace treaty, so an invasion should be attempted before Parliament could pass a resolution in favour of war. As an expression of Melfort's personal opinion, included in a private letter to his brother, there was nothing exceptional in this. But once it was made public and communicated to Parliament it quickly caused a scandal.

The timing of the letter was particularly unfortunate because it was published at a time of acute international tension. In November 1700, Louis XIV had agreed that his grandson Philippe, duc d'Anjou should accept the succession to the entire Spanish Empire, left him by the terms of the will drawn up at his death by King Charles II of Spain. This involved renouncing the (Second) Partition Treaty which Louis had concluded with the Emperor and William III. The latter was therefore likely to want to renew war with France to achieve a partition of the Spanish Empire – if only he could persuade Parliament that war would be in England's interests. Any renewal of war between England and France would obviously be in the interests of the Jacobites, so people wondered if Melfort had deliberately sent the letter to the wrong court in order to provide William III with an argument in favour of war with which to persuade Parliament. Louis XIV, who was extremely keen to maintain peace with England, was bound to be very angry indeed.[302]

On 4 March, Nairne noted that 'the Engl letters came with ye news of a letter of My Ld Melf. to E. of P[erth] communicated by ye P. of O[range, i.e. William III] to both houses of Parl.t'. The reaction of the members of Parliament had been immediate: all Catholics in England 'were orderd to be disarmd' and the anti-Catholic penal laws 'to be put in execution'. It was this news which caused James II to faint in the middle of mass in the Chapel Royal.[303] Four days later, Nairne wrote to his friend Whiteford at the Collège des Ecossais 'concerning ye misfortune of E. M. letter, and ye noise it made and ye prejudice was feard from it'.[304] For Nairne it was especially painful that Lord Melfort's criticisms of Middleton, and particularly of Caryll, should receive such publicity.

It was not until 11 March that a copy of Melfort's letter, as published by Parliament, was received at Saint-Germain. When James II read it he was again 'taken ill'. Melfort, meanwhile had been summoned to Saint-Germain where he was interviewed by the marquis de Croissy, the French foreign secretary.[305] Once it was established that the letter was genuine Louis XIV ordered Melfort by *lettre de cachet* to leave Paris and go 'to Angers ther to be confin'd to the town'.[306] On the 15th, Melfort left Paris for a second provincial exile, his return this time dependent on the agreement of Louis XIV rather than James II, and Nairne was obliged to cut off all communication with him, at least for the time being.

On the following day, it was agreed that James II should go with Queen Mary to take the waters at Bourbon, in the hope that he might recover there.[307] They left on 5 April, did not return until 7 June, and it was three weeks afterwards that James gave Nairne his second augmentation. But the king's health did not improve, and on 10 July he had his second 'fainting fitt', after which (as we have seen) Nairne had the king's memoirs bound up and taken to be kept safely in the Collège des Ecossais.

It was shortly after that, on 2 September, that 'the King fell ill in ye Chapelle and went out in middle of ye mass'. It was now clear that he was dying, so James instructed Nairne to draw up his last will and testament.[308] It was finished on 4 September, and Nairne recorded in his diary that night:

> The King grew worse and vomited blood, he recd ye viaticum and ye holy oyles wch last sacrament I saw him receive wth great constancy and devotion, all ye company about him being in tears.

By the 7th, the king's condition had deteriorated and Nairne wrote to Whiteford 'and gave him no good hopes of ye King'. The new will was read to James II on the following day and signed for him by Lord Middleton before seven witnesses,[309] after which Nairne 'applyd the seal to it and dated it' 8 September.[310] The king lived for another eight days, during which he received numerous visits from his French cousins and was attended by his doctors, his confessor and his chaplains. On 12 September, the grief-stricken Nairne noted in his diary that 'I sat up in ye K's bed chamber all night, he being so very ill yt the Doctors concluded he could not live till day.' But he did survive the night, and it was on the following day that Louis XIV came to Saint-Germain and announced that he would recognize the Prince of Wales as the *de jure* King James III, just as he had continued since the Treaty of Ryswick to recognize his father.

On the 15th, when 'the King continued very ill' and there were 'no hopes left of his recovery', Nairne went to 'the chamber in ye morning and brought in my wife to see him'. Thereafter Nairne remained with his master all the time until he died in the early afternoon of the 16th, when the king 'rendered his last breath with a sorte of a smile' and 'I was present'. Nairne then wrote 'a full account of ye Ks good death, and his exemplary piety, patience and resignation, [and] his charity in pardoning [the] P[rince of] O[range]', to be sent to England and Scotland. By then the Prince of Wales had been proclaimed King James III and Nairne, with all the other courtiers, had 'kissd the young King's hand'.

Endnotes

1. SCA. BL 1/130/9, declaration by J. Hay, 13 September 1690.
2. SCA. BL 1/122/14, L. Innes to Leslie, 7 November 1689. Mary Hay converted to Catholicism after her return to France and married Monnot in September 1700 (Diary, 16 September 1700).
3. Diary, 29 November 1689.
4. Diary, 30 November 1689.
5. Diary, 12 December 1689. See also SCA. BL 1/124/14, L. Innes to Leslie, 7 November 1689: 'the Earle of Melfort ... is my speciall friend and patron. It has been thought fit he have no other character than that of Principal Secretary of State wch gives him as much trust as that of Ambassadr Extraordr and doth not oblige him to make so great expense wch would not be proper in his master's circumstances.'
6. Diary, 19 December 1689. The additional gentlemen included Sir John Lidcott (James II's previous agent in Rome), William Leslie (the agent of the Scottish Catholic clergy) and the latter's brother Walter.
7. Diary, 7 February 1690.
8. Diary, 15 February 1690.
9. Ibid.
10. Diary, 18–19 February 1690. See also BL. Add MSS 37660, p. 233, Melfort to Maxwell, 21 February 1690: 'Mr Nairne his wife followed him hither and brought his Protestant brother alongst who fell mortally sick at Viterbo, and in his sickness was happiely converted and died a good Catholique, as wee have good hopes of ye rest yt came with us.' Nairne arranged for masses for his brother to be said in Rome on 15 May 1690 and 15 February 1691, and he remained in contact with the priests who had helped him at Viterbo (Diary, 17 November 1690, 13 March 1691). Nothing has survived in the cathedral of Viterbo to indicate where Nairne's brother was buried. In 1901, Anne ffoulkes, whose nephew then owned Nairne's diary, visited Viterbo and spoke to an Italian lady. She wrote to a friend:

> My young acquaintance possesses an uncle there a Canon of the Cathedral, and he very kindly found the mention of the death in the registers. The dates *exactly* correspond ... but curiously the name is different ... Sir David mentions the exact place where he is buried in the Cathedral, but there seems to be no tablet or memorial now existing ... I have copied it as the Canon gives it
> Harlney
> The y might originally be an Italian flourish !
> (NLS. MS 14269, p. 46, Anne ffoulkes to Alys [name unknown], 10 July 1901).

11. Diary, 24 February 1690.

12. Diary, 25 February 1690. Shortly after his wife's arrival at the embassy, Nairne noted that he began to rent furniture from a Jew: 'le juif meuble notre apparte-ment' (Diary, 9 March 1690). In November he told 'le juif' to take away 'la moitié de ses meubles' (16 November 1690), and when he left Rome 'je vendit quelq hardes aux Juifs' (22 August 1691).

13. Diary, 22 August 1691.

14. BL. Add MSS 37660; BL. Lansdowne MSS 1163 A-C; Corp, Edward, 'An Inventory of the Archives of the Stuart Court at Saint-Germain-en-Laye, 1689–1718', *Archives* XXIII, no. 99, October 1998, pp. 118–46, at pp. 136–7.

15. Diary, 30 April 1690. Nairne referred to the baths as the 'Termini de l'Emp. Ant'.

16. Diary, 10 May 1690. Nairne noted: 'nous entrames par tout il y a des peintures fort antiques et des belles statues. Celles de Cesar et d'Auguste faites de leurs temps. Marc Aurele a cheval dans la cour.'

17. Nairne took part in the *cortèges* of the French ambassador (20 December 1689, 22 October, 13 December 1690, 5 February 1691), and also those of the Venetian ambassador (3 October, 10 December 1690, 19 March 1691).

18. Diary, 1 May 1690.

19. Diary, 8 June 1690.

20. Diary, 26 December 1690.

21. Diary, 24 November 1690.

22. Diary, 31 January 1691.

23. Diary, 3 November 1690.

24. He was particularly friendly with Father Andrew Maghie, the Rector of the Scots College, and another priest named Father Douglas.

25. The agents of the English and Scots clergy in Rome were Father Smith and Father Leslie.

26. The French priests with whom he was particularly friendly were the abbé Fossé, père Lucas and père Peiras.

27. His friends at the French embassy included M. Le Comte, M. de la Garde and M. Montaigu.

28. Nairne sent his *placets* on 25 April 1690 to the Collège des Ecossais, to be presented to the French Treasury on his behalf by one of his friends, and was told on 10 November that the pension had been paid. The money reached him via the Scots College in Rome (Diary, 14 November, 1 December 1690). The following year he sent his *placets* on 28 May and 4 June, but the money had still not been paid when he left Rome. He negotiated the payment of the money in person with the French Treasury after his return to Saint-Germain (Diary, 14, 21, 23 January, 10, 12 February 1692).

29. On 2 October 1690, after a visit to the Palazzo Farnese, Nairne noted that 'il y a les travaux de Hercule depeint par hanib. Caraccio [Annibale Caracci] dans une Galerie une tableau d'Alabastro et pieces rappartées d'agate et estime 100000 Ec. La statue d'Alex Farnese et celle de Tauran le dernier une chose inestimable, comme aussi celle d'Hercule dans la cour; Et quantité d'ouvrages de Michel angelo Buona roti. Le Palais est bati des pierres apportées de le Colisseo.'

30. Queen Christina of Sweden had died in April 1689 while Nairne was in Ireland.

31. Nairne noted that the Palazzo Borghese contained 'une enfilade de 12 chambres de plein pied remplie de beaux tableaux, des statues et tables riches, quantité de jets d'eaux, et un petit jardin' (10 May 1690), and that in the Palazzo Giustiniani 'il y a 1867 statues, beaux tableaux et 10 pieces de plein pied' (13 June 1691). At the Palazzo Quirinale ('la mais. et jard. di Montecavallo') he particularly admired the 'beau basin de poissons' (5 April 1691). In the Villa Farnesina, he singled out 'le tableau de Galatée' by Raphael (29 September 1690), and he wrote of the Villa Pamphili that 'il y a un grand parque des jets d'eau, une belle maison et quantité de belles statues et de peintures. C'est une des meilleurs qui soit autour de Rome' (20 May 1690).

32. At Frascati Nairne noted that 'nous vimes le palais Ludovisio [now the Villa Aldobrandini] ou il y a une tres belle girandole d'eau et Belvidere fait par Card. Aldobrandini et apartenant present.t a Pamphilio, il y a la girandole une cascade d'eau qui tourne au tour de 2 piliers, une comme une orge qui jout tout avec l'eau' (21 November 1690). At the Villa d'Este at Tivoli, he commented that 'le jardin est beau il y a une girandole admirable, une allée toute de jets d'eaux une orgue qui peut avec l'eau'. He also visited the nearby Villa Hadrian, still only partly excavated, which he described as 'une petite endroit qui represent l'ancien Rome et tous ses temples', and both the famous cascade and the temple of Sibyl: 'dans la ville on voit une cascade furieuse de la riviere et proche de là dans une situation affreuse les ruines du temple de Sibille. Il y a une eau proche de la qui forment de petites choses blanches comme des bonbon. On passe aussi en y allant une rivière [the Aniene] de souffre d'une puanteur horible' (7 June 1690). On 20 November 1690, he visited the Palazzo Savelli at Albano, which in 1721 would be given to James III for his summer residence, and where Nairne would stay on several occasions.

33. For Melfort's collection in England, see Corp, *A Court in Exile*, p. 197.

34. In addition to the collections in the palazzi and villas already mentioned, Melfort took Nairne to study the paintings belonging to 'un Monsignore' (31 January 1691), the Monte della Pieta (14 March 1691), 'Falconieri et Ragi' (27 April 1691), the late Queen Christina (3 and 7 May 1691), Constable Colonna (15 May 1691), and the abbé Sforza (10 July 1691). In addition to these, Melfort took Nairne to

examine paintings by Francesco Albano (15 December 1690, 19 April 1691) and Salvator Rosa (12 March 1691).

35. Diary, 16 February, 14 March, 19 April 1691.

36. Diary, 28 February, 2 March, 31 May, 1 June 1691, 23 July 1691.

37. For these portraits, which have been lost, see the diary, 28 May 1691. Nairne noted on 14 January 1692 that 'my L.ds picture was stollen' from the Château de Saint-Germain, a comment that might have referred to Maratta's portrait of Lord Melfort.

38. For this portrait, which has also been lost, see the diary, 16 and 19 January 1691.

39. The other painters, whom I have not identified, included 'Scylla' (or 'Schella'), 'de Domichino' (also 'Dom'), 'Grapponi', and 'le Venetiano'.

40. Melfort bought a painting from Trevisani which was believed at the time to be by Van Dyck. The other dealers from whom he bought paintings included Buoncore, 'Carlo Ant.', abbé Remode, and Montagne (or Montani). For information about the paintings purchased by Melfort in Rome, see Corp, *A Court in Exile*, p. 198.

41. Nairne paid an unspecified amount for a painting by Francesco Albano, and 50 *scudi* for one by Guido Reni, on 10 January 1691; 80 *scudi* for a 'Venus de Cintobrand' on 31 May 1691; 100 *scudi* for two paintings by Pietro da Cortona, 'une teste' by Annibale Caracci and a landscape by Francesco Mola on 1 June 1691; and 100 *scudi* for another painting by Albano on 14 June 1691. Other payments for unspecified paintings were recorded on 12 and 20 June 1691.

42. Diary, 24 March 1690.

43. Diary, 15 May 1690.

44. Diary, 26 May 1690.

45. Diary, 13 December 1690.

46. Diary, 8 May, 6 and 7 December 1690. The church of San Carlo is also called Santi Ambrogio e Carlo al Corso.

47. Diary, 21 December 1690.

48. Diary, 18 January 1690.

49. Diary, 26 June 1690.

50. Diary, 26 September 1690.

51. Diary, 24 December 1690.

52. Fede had directed the music at the church of San Giacomo degli Spagnoli, opposite the Palazzo della Sapienza which was then the University of Rome (Corp, Edward, 'Innocenzo Fede, 1661–1732', *ODNB*, vol. 19, p. 232; and *Court in Exile*, pp. 202–3). The church is now called Nostra Signora del Sacro Cuore and has been rearranged to open on to the Piazza Navona.

53. *The New Grove, Italian Baroque Masters* (London, 1983), pp. 244–7.

54. Diary, 8, 19, 22, 28 January 1690. The first performance was on 5 January.

55. Diary, 31 December 1690; 2, 7 January 1691.

56. Diary, 21, 27, 29 January 1690. The opera was *Alessio*. The performances were commissioned by Maria Camilla Rospigliosi (née Palavicini), duchesse de Zagarolo.

57. Diary, 23 January 1690. The opera was *La caduta del regno dell'Amazoni*. The performances, of which the first was on 15 January, were commissioned by the Spanish ambassador.

58. Diary, 3 February 1690. This was probably *Il martirio di S. Eustachio* by Flavio Carlo Lanciani, subsequently performed for Cardinal Ottoboni in the Cancelleria later that month. The Piazza Sant' Eustachio is a very short walk to the west from the Collegio Romano.

59. Diary, 5, 14 November 1690. The *pastorale* was *Amore e Gratitudine* by Flavio Carlo Lanciani.

60. Diary, 4 January 1691. He would probably have attended at least one performance of *L'Agrippina* by Giovanni Lorenzo Lulier in February, but the opera was cancelled because of the death of Pope Alexander VIII.

61. Diary, 21 December 1690. Abel was married to Lady Frances Knollys, sister of Charles Knollys, 4th Earl of Banbury. John, Lord Kennedy was the son and heir of the 7th Earl of Cassilis.

62. Diary, 2, 4, 9, 13, 14 May 1691. The other Grand Tourist whom Nairne met was Sir Robert Throckmorton, 3rd Bart. (or possibly his younger brother George), who was in Rome from April to June 1691 (Diary, 2 April, 8 June 1691).

63. Corp, *A Court in Exile*, p. 204. While he was at Saint-Germain he was introduced to Nairne's acquaintance François Couperin, who composed a motet for his voice. It was a setting of Psalm 13: 'Usquequo Domine' (Corp, Edward, 'François Couperin and the Stuart court at Saint-Germain-en,-Laye, 1691–1712: a new interpretation', *Early Music* XXVIII/3, August 2000, pp. 445–53, at p. 448).

64. Diary, 13 August 1691. In this diary entry Nairne referred to Gasparini as 'Gasp', which might imply that he had already met him and did not feel the need to write out his name in full.

65. Diary, 5 and 8 December 1690. Nairne also specified walking along the Tiber (26 April 1690), at Ripa Grande, the old port of Rome in modern Trastevere (20 September, 4 October 1690), along Lungotevere from Trastevere to St Peter's (4 and 18 March 1691), from St Peter's to Ponte Mole, three miles north of Rome (3 June, 17 September, 18 October 1690), at Porta Maggiore, east of Laterano (22 October 1690), and outside the Porta del Popolo (21 July 1691). His visits to the Forum were on 26 October 1690 and 3 July 1691.

66. Diary, 21, 24 November, 5 December 1690, 16 March 1691.

67. Diary, 16 January 1690, 11 May 1691.

68. There are sixteen references in the diary to playing 'echets' between 9 January and 5 August 1691. He played in particular with Monsieur Montaigu of the French embassy.

69. Diary, 12, 13, 14, 17 25 January 1691.
70. Diary, 1 April 1691.
71. Diary, 11 April 1691.
72. Diary, 4 May 1691. It was returned on 31 May 1691.
73. On 16 August 1691 Nairne noted that 'je fus reprendre mon petit livre chez le Libraire'.
74. Nairne referred to playing with Melfort on nine occasions from 19 December 1690 to 12 February 1691, with two more games in March (16th) and May (9th).
75. Diary, 21–24 November 1690. See also 2 January and 22 February 1691.
76. Diary, 17 December 1690. Nairne had noted on 17 January 1690 that on that day Lady Melfort 'commence a apprendre a jouer de la gitare'.
77. Diary, 6 May 1691. One month later Nairne also bought his wife 'un habit d'Eté' which cost him 20 *scudi* (12 June 1691). He had previously bought himself a new 'habit', some 'soulier' (13, 14 December 1691) and some 'foul. gris neufs' (6 May 1691). He makes no mention in his diary of buying or possessing a wig or a sword.
78. Diary, 26, 27 February 1691.
79. Lady Melfort gave birth to a baby boy on 16 March 1690. He was named Andrew.
80. Nairne had noted the progress of his wife's pregnancy during the preceeding days. On 30 June, 'ma f. acheta le reste des hardes qu'il falloit po.r ses couches'. On 3 July, she decided not to go out any more except 'po.r aller a la messe', and on the 4th she felt 'fort incomodée'. On the 7th 'elle commenca la nuit a se trouver mal pour accoucher et envoya querir la sage femme, mais ce ne fut rien'. On the 8th 'elle ne sortit pas de sa chambre. Elle sentit de temps en temps quelques petites douleurs mais ce ne fut encore rien.' It was on the next day that she decided to go to mass, and then began to give birth after dinner.
81. Diary, 16 July 1690. The 'mess Anglois' were the priests and students at the English College.
82. Diary, 17 July 1690.
83. Diary, 9 January, 4 February 1691.
84. Diary, 2 March 1691.
85. She had another boy, this one called Philip. Although he was born on 20 February, he was not baptized until 1 March (Diary). The date of his birth is recorded in the register of *Battesimi* of the parish of San Marco, p. 316. (I am grateful to Dottore Domenico Rocciolo for giving me a photocopy of the entry in the register of baptisms, now in the Archivio Storico Vicariato di Roma).
86. Diary, 16 March 1691.
87. Other entries in Nairne's diary refer to the general state of her health, and especially to the fact that she was 'fort malade' during that summer (30 June, 1 July, 4–5 and 13 August 1691).

88. The churches which Nairne mainly visited were nearly all relatively close together, and within a short walk from the palazzo occupied by Lord Melfort in the parish of San Marco.

89. 16–19 and 20–24 May 1691.

90. Although the *lettre de congé* only arrived on 22 August, Melfort and Nairne had in fact been expecting it ever since the election of Pope Innocent XII. Nairne had already spoken to the agent of the Grand Duke of Tuscany to arrange for a 'galers' to transport them from Leghorn to Marseille (11, 24 August 1691), and had obtained passports from the secretary of Cardinal d'Este (18 August 1691).

91. Diary, 13 August 1691.

92. Diary, 24 August 1691.

93. Diary, 1 September 1691.

94. Diary, 18, 21 August 1691.

95. Diary, 21, 22, 24, 27 August 1691.

96. Nairne put the relic in a box, with the following inscription in copper on the outside: 'Dans cette boête est une Croix de verre qui renferme un Relique en philigrame d'argent contenant une Parcelle de la Vraie Croix de N. S. raporté de Rome' (Compigny des Bordes de Villiers de l'Isle Adam, Alfred de, *Au Declin de l'Ancien Régime* (Paris, 1924), p. 27 with photograph).

97. Diary, 3 September 1691.

98. Nairne recorded in his diary that 'nous partimes de Rome sur le soir, et traversames la campagna de Rome cette nuit là. Mil[or]d et M[adam]e en caleche, Mr Hay et Mlle Hay dans un autre, et Mr Monnot et moy a cheval'. They went straight to Civita Vecchia where 'M.r Mon et moy primes une caleche'.

99. Diary, 9 September 1691.

100. The Melforts had met the marquis d'Orsi in Rome (Diary, 28 October 1690).

101. Diary, 11 September 1691. The Duke of Modena was Francesco II, the brother of Queen Mary. 'Prince César' was Cesare d'Este, marchese di Montecchio, a first cousin of Francesco II's grandfather, and at that time the effective ruler of the Duchy of Modena. Nairne had already met the Duchess of Modena (Margherita Maria née Farnese), the wife of Francesco II. On 19 April 1690, he went with her and Lady Melfort to visit 'la maison des Jesuites a l'Jesu, ou nous vimes la bibliotheque qui est assés belle et le sacristie qui est la plus riche de Rome. Et on nous expose le bras droit de St François Xavier sur son autel. Nous vimes aussi la statue de St Ignace fait sur son corps mort'. Two days later he, the Duchess and Lady Melfort had visited 'la maison des Peres de l'Oratoire de la Chiesa Nuova, nous y entrames tous avec elle et vimes le tout la chaise le confessional l'oratoire et le corps entiere de St Philipe de Neri fondateur du Orat.'.

102. Diary, 12 September 1691.

103. Diary, 14 September 1691.

104. Diary, 25 September 1691: 'Wee imbarkd in one of ye Gr. Dukes gallys, il y en avoit 3, une pr le Duc de Chaunes, une pour le Card de Bouillon, et l'autre pour Milord.'

105. Diary, 26 September 1691. Nairne added: 'Ma femme etant malade dans la galère, je le fis mettre a terre et nous logeames chéz Ralliff taileur Anglois a Genes.' This was possibly William Radcliffe, younger brother of the 2nd Earl of Derwentwater, a merchant in Italy whom Nairne would meet again many years later in Rome.

106. One reason why they remained so long at Lyon was that Lady Melfort felt ill.

107. Melfort had originally left the party at Lyon to get to Saint-Germain as quickly as possible, but had had to return when he received the news of his wife's illness.

108. Diary, 2 November 1691.

109. Diary, 4 November 1691.

110. Diary, 6 November 1691.

111. RA. SP Misc 7, 'Political Reflexions on the history and Government of England, the late Revolution and other State affairs written by an impartial hand in 1709', an anonymous manuscript (by Thomas Sheridan), p. 94.

112. Diary, 12 November 1691.

113. Diary, 30 November 1691.

114. RA. SP Misc 18. If anyone else recorded the warrants while Nairne was away in Rome his book did not survive, so we know nothing about the household appointments at the Stuart court in exile between June 1689 and December 1691.

115. Diary, 20 January 1692. Monnot's annual pension was 877 *livres*, and Dempster's was 585 *livres*.

116. SCA. BL 1/140/7, postscript by Nairne to Melfort to Leslie, 3 December 1691.

117. Diary, 11, 12 January 1692.

118. Diary, 13 and 14 January 1692. She died on Saturday afternoon, but was not buried on the Sunday 'night but Monday morning' (Diary; parish records of Saint-Germain-en-Laye).

119. SCA. BL 1/154/1, Nairne to Leslie, 21 January 1692.

120. Two weeks later Nairne wrote that 'my wife is ye same but still strangely afflicted for ye death of our poor child wch wee can not forgett' (SCA. BL 1/153/4, Nairne to Leslie, 4 February 1692).

121. James II formally announced that Mary of Modena was pregnant on 10 February 1692 (Diary), but Nairne had already mentioned the fact in a letter of 4 February (SCA. BL 1/153/4, to Leslie).

122. Diary, 3 and 10 January 1692.

123. Diary, 26 January 1692. On 28 January, Nairne noted that 'my wife saw ye K in ye nurserie again', and on 2 February that 'my wife spoke to My La [Melfort] for a place about ye prince to come'. He asked Lord Melfort 'to think of my wifes case' on 12 February.

124. 3 February 1692. He had brought 'des chapelets et des gands' in Rome on 24 August 1691 (Diary).

125. Bod. Carte MSS 208, ff.287–8, 'A Liste of such as Lodge in ye Castle' by Nairne, undated but April 1692. He had already inspected an apartment on 28 January and persuaded Lord Melfort to write in his favour to the Clerk Controller of the Green Cloth, Sir John Sparrow (Diary).

126. RA. SP 1/79, the salaries of the queen's Household, December 1693.

127. Diary, 28 June 1692.

128. Diary, 27 August 1692.

129. Diary, 28 October 1692, and the list of Nairne's children; parish records of Saint-Germain-en-Laye.

130. See SCA. BL 1/181/4, Nairne to Leslie, 5 April 1694. Nairne terminated this letter with the comment: 'Adieu I must go to church.'

131. For the portraits of the king, the queen and the prince painted between 1689 and 1694, see Corp, *King over the Water*, pp. 33–8; Corp, *A Court in Exile*, pp. 182–3; and Corp, 'The Lost Portrait of James II and his Family by Nicolas de Largillierre', *The Journal of the Northumbrian Jacobite Society* no.12, February 2012, pp. 57–62.

132. See, e.g., Bod. Carte MSS 209, Melfort to Nairne, 20 August 1694: 'I am still mor and mor obliged to yr friendship of which I will assur you neither I nor my wife has the least imaginatione that it will change and you may depend on our true and unalterable friendship and so may Mrs Nairne.'

133. Corp, *A Court in Exile*, p. 198.

134. Diary, 30 January to 1 February 1692.

135. Diary, 20 January and 6 February 1692. Three days before the first of these parties he noted that 'our tables were covered'. The other guests included James Nihell (the king's and Melfort's solicitor), Dr Daniel Day (the king's physician) and George Middleton (the king's apothecary).

136. Diary, 11 February 1692.

137. Diary, 1, 2 January, 12 February 1692.

138. *The Life of James II*, ed. Clarke, J. S. (London, 1816), vol. 2, pp. 479–88; Ruvigny and Raineval, Melville Henry Massue, Marquis of, *The Jacobite Peerage*, Edinburgh, 1904, p. 193. (Melfort was given the Garter on 10 April).

139. Diary, 22 to 28 April 1692.

140. The commission was dated 19 May but signed on the 20th (RA. SP Misc 18, published in Ruvigny, *The Jacobite Peerage*, p. 239; Diary, 20 May 1692).

141. Nairne sent the commission via Dunkirk to Scotland on the 23rd. He had previously written to his brother and mother on 17 February 1692 (Diary).

142. His diary outlines the main events at sea visible from the French coast from 29 May to 2 June.

143. Diary, 10 and 11 June 1692; also summarized in the Diary of 1680.

144. Diary, 12–18 June 1692.

145. Diary, 13 April 1693; *The Life of James II*, vol. 2, pp. 502–5.

146. Dangeau, Philippe de Courcillon, marquis de, *Journal*, ed. Soulié, E., and Dussieux, L., 19 vols (Paris, 1854–60), iv, p. 271, 23 April 1693.

147. Middleton's secretary was David Lindsay. Nairne noted in his diary on 7 May 1693 that 'I gave a supper to M. Lindsay'.

148. Diary, 5 May 1693. Nairne wrote to Adam on the same subject the following day. For Adam's position in the French foreign ministry, see Rule, John C., 'Colbert de Torcy, an Emergent Bureaucracy, and the Formulation of French Foreign Policy, 1698–1715', pp. 261–88 (265), in Hatton, Ragnhild, ed., *Louis XIV and Europe* (London, 1976).

149. SCA. BL 1/166/19, Nairne to Leslie, 4 October 1693.

150. Bod Carte MSS 181, f.572, 'Traduction d'une lettre en Cyffre du Sr Sackfield Mareshal des Camps de Sa M. B. au Comte de Milford, Ce 3 May 1694', and 'Traduction de la lettre de Milord Churchill au Roy d'Angleterre de meme date'.

151. Macpherson, *Original Papers*, vol. 1, p. 487. See the Appendix for the circumstances surrounding the publication of Nairne's papers.

152. Parnell, Arthur, 'Macpherson and the Nairne Papers', *The English Historical Review* XII, 1896, pp. 254–84. This article was provoked by another article by E. M. Lloyd which had accepted Churchill's guilt but defended him by claiming that he had 'only revealed what was common knowledge in England, and ... orders to fortify Brest had been given before the arrival of this communication' ('Marlborough and the Brest Expedition, *The English Historical Review* IX, 1894, pp. 130–2).

153. Parnell, 'Macpherson and the Nairne Papers', p. 279. The documents to which he was referring were published in Macpherson, *Original Papers*, vol. 1, pp. 458–87, from Bod. Carte MSS 181 and 209.

154. Parnell, 'Macpherson and the Nairne Papers', p. 282.

155. Ibid. pp. 273–4. See also p. 267, in which Parnell referred to 'the absurdity of treating these Nairne papers as authentic materials of English history', because they contained 'preposterous stories ... made up for the edification of the French monarch'.

156. Davies, Godfrey, 'Macpherson and the Nairne Papers', *The English Historical Review* XXXV, 1920, pp. 367–6 (368–9). The three men were Lord Hardwicke, Sir James Dalrymple and one of the librarians at the Bodleian (Thomas Monkhouse).

157. Churchill, Winston S., *Marlborough: His Life and Times* (London, 1933), vol. 1, chapter 25. The Camaret Bay letter in Nairne's handwriting is reproduced within this chapter, between pp. 436 and 437.

158. Ibid. p. 440. See also p. 449: 'we assert as the basis for the future that ... the Nairne Papers are without exception untrustworthy or mendacious documents fabricated out of the secret service reports to Saint-Germains.'

159. Ibid. pp. 440–1.

160. Bod. Carte MSS 209, ff.150–61, 'Memoire justificatif du comte de Melfort', 17 May 1694.

161. Macpherson, *Original Papers*, vol. 2, pp. 674–6.

162. 'For my Son, the Prince of Wales, 1692', published in *The Life of James II*, vol. 2, pp. 619–42 (641).

163. Melfort wrote to Nairne shortly afterwards: 'as for Mr Innes I am glad that you concurr with me in thinking him so sincere' (Bod. Carte MSS 209, f.246, 16 September 1694).

164. SCA. BL 1/181/8, Nairne to L. Innes, 14 June 1694.

165. Diary, 19 June 1694. Since returning from Rome Lady Melfort had given birth to two daughters (in March 1692 and April 1693).

166. SCA. BL 1/181/8, Nairne to L. Innes, 14 June 1694.

167. SCA. BL 1/181/9, Nairne to Leslie, 19 and 26 July 1694. Caryll's letters give the same impression: HMC *Stuart* I, pp. 88, 89, to Ellis, 28 June and 19 July 1694.

168. Diary, 21 July 1694; SCA. BL 1/181/12, Nairne to Leslie, 9 August 1694. The Melforts left Paris on 21 July and travelled via La Charité to Moulins, where they arrived in early August. They then went to take the waters at Bourbon in September, before returning via Moulins and Orléans to Paris in October. They stayed in Paris for about a month, and then went to live in Orléans (Bod. Carte MSS 209, ff.200–93, letters from Melfort and Lady Melfort to Nairne, 20 June to 31 December 1694).

169. Diary, 2 August 1694; SCA. BL 1/181/12, Nairne to Leslie, 9 August 1694.

170. SCA. BL 1/181/12 and 14, Nairne to Leslie, 9 and 23 August 1694.

171. Diary, 14 and 27 August 1694.

172. It was Caryll who had recruited Innocenzo Fede to become the Master of the King's Music at Whitehall, and now at Saint-Germain (Corp, *A Court in Exile*, p. 202).

173. *The English Princess, or the Death of Richard III* in 1666; and *Sir Salomon Single, or the Cautious Coxcomb* in 1671 (an imitation of Molière's *Ecole des Femmes* of 1662).

174. *The Hypocrite*, 1678; and *Naboth's Vineyard* (1679), which inspired Dryden's *Absalom and Achitophel* (1681).

175. Ovid's *Epistles*, 1680; and Virgil's *First Eclogue*, 1683.
176. The letters which Nairne received from the Melforts from June to December 1694 are in Bod. Carte MSS 209.
177. Bod. Carte MSS 209, f.250, Melfort to Nairne, 29 September 1694.
178. Bod. Carte MSS 209, f.221, Melfort to Nairne, 20 August 1694.
179. Diary, 16 April 1695.
180. SCA. BL 1/181/15, Nairne to Leslie, 16 September 1694. See also SCA. BL 1/181/16, Nairne to Leslie, 13 December 1694: 'I confess I cannot be a friend to one who speaks ... ill of E. M.' (i.e. the Earl of Melfort).
181. Bod. Carte MSS 181, Caryll to Melfort, 6 September 1694.
182. Bod. Carte MSS 209, f.238, Melfort to Caryll, 13 September 1694; Bod. Carte MSS 209, f.239, Melfort to Nairne, 14 September 1694.
183. Bod. Carte MSS 209, f.246, Melfort to Nairne, 16 September 1694.
184. Bod. Carte MSS 209, f.248, Melfort to Nairne, 23 September 1694.
185. It is clear from these letters that Lady Melfort and Mrs Nairne had remained on friendly terms. The former wrote to Nairne on 20 June: 'Remember me kindly to your wife. I could not speak to her at partin my hart was so ful to see her tears' (Bod. Carte MSS 209, f.203).
186. Diary, 21 October 1694.
187. Diary, 31 October 1694. Melfort sent worried letters to Nairne on 23 and 30 October 1694 (Bod. Carte MSS 209, ff.260, 264), and Lady Melfort wrote to Mrs Nairne on 25 October: 'I wish you joy with all my hert of your doghtr ... I wish you a hapy recvery and I give you a thousand thanks for all your obligasions I oue you which I shall never forget ... I desir you to kiss dear jony and litl miss frances for me' (Bod. Carte MSS 209, f.262).
188. The Melforts were in Paris from 30 October to 20 November 1694.
189. Bod. Carte MSS 209, ff.278, 266, 272, Melfort to Nairne, 1, 5 and 11 November 1694. (NB The letter of 5 November is undated).
190. There are frequent references to his doing this during 1695 when the Melforts lived at Orléans, but not thereafter.
191. Diary, 13 June 1695.
192. Diary, 21 November 1695.
193. Diary, 19 December 1695. Melfort remained in Paris until 21 January 1696, and on the 17th Nairne asked Charles Whiteford 'to make my complim.ts' to him. Lady Melfort did not leave until 24 February.
194. Diary, 4 and 14 February, 29 May, and 7 September 1695. This is a reference to *The Hypocrite* and *Naboth's Vineyard* (see above, note 174). They were published by William Weston.
195. Diary, 1, 20, 25 and 28 July 1695.

196. Diary, 20 January 1696. He made 'a copie of Mr Caryls testament' on 1 July 1699.
197. For the closet: 27 December 1694, 6 June 1695, 4 December 1696. For the little bedchamber: 1 September 1694, 6 June and 8 July 1695, 23 January 1696. For the position of the royal apartments, see Corp, *A Court in Exile*, pp. 82–3.
198. Diary, 31 December 1694, 21 January 1695.
199. Diary, 13 October 1695.
200. Diary, 19 February 1695.
201. Diary, 27 January 1695.
202. Diary, 31 March and 1 April 1695.
203. Diary, 20 November 1695.
204. Diary, 9 and 28 November; 11, 15 and 18 December 1695. Norbert Roettiers had left England in 1695 to join his uncle Joseph at the Paris Mint. For the new touch pieces, see Woolf, Noel, *The Medallic Record of the Jacobite Movement* (London, 1988), p. 39.
205. Diary, 10–12, 14, 18 and 20 May and 1 June 1695.
206. 18–19 July 1696. Entitled 'Rules for the Family of the Prince of Wales', the new document of 1696 has survived in RA. SP misc 18, pp. 83–7, published in HMC *Stuart* I, pp. 114–17. It contains 28 articles and, given the reality of living in exile and the architecture of the Château-Vieux de Saint-Germain, is very sensible as regards both the daily routine and the general security of the prince.
207. Diary, 23 June, 8 July, 13 August and 1 September 1694. For the portrait of the prince, see Corp, *The King over the Water*, p. 38 (Largillière 5).
208. Diary, 5 and 6 December 1694. For the double portrait, see Corp, *The King over the Water*, p. 38 (Largillière 6).
209. Diary, 29 and 30 June, 7 and 12 July, and 20 September 1695. These portraits of the prince were copied from the double portrait. See Corp, *A Court in Exile*, pp. 183–4.
210. Diary, 20 November 1695. These portraits of the princess were also copied from the double portrait.
211. Diary, 19 October, 2 and 12 November 1695; 9 and 12 January 1696. For this engraving, see Corp, *The King over the Water*, p. 38; and Sharp, Richard, *The Engraved Record of the Jacobite Movement* (Aldershot, 1996), pp. 89–90, no. 116.
212. Diary, 22 March 1695.
213. Diary, 29 October 1695.
214. Diary, 30 October 1695; 14 February 1696.
215. Diary, 29 October 1695. This comment was inserted at a later date.
216. Diary, 22 January 1696. Later that year Nairne wrote to John Wallace and told him 'what oblig. I had to Mr Sec.ry and of ye place he had given me' (Diary, 1 October 1696).

217. Diary, 29 February 1696. The warrant was signed and dated 20 June 1696 (Diary, 13, 20, 23 June 1696), and stated that Nairne was 'to be Clerk of her Council, of her Revenue, and of the Registrar of her Court, commonly called the Queen's Court, and of Keeper of the Seal of her Council'. It is wrongly dated 20 July in HMC *Stuart* I, p. 114. In fact Nairne had to wait a few years before he was given access to the queen's financial accounts (Diary, 17 March, 29 September 1697; 31 January, 28 December 1698; 18 November 1699).

218. It is not possible to say why the king trusted Nairne more than Lindsay, other than the fact that the latter was Protestant.

219. Diary, 29 February 1696.

220. Sir William Ellis was James II's Commissioner and Comptroller-General of the Revenue from Prizes. Nairne noted that they travelled by horse from Saint-Germain to Ecouen 'where no horses [were] to be had' so they had to go 'on foot' the three leagues to Luzarches (Diary, 1 March 1696).

221. Nairne did not record where he stayed at Calais. He merely wrote that on arrival 'I went to my lodging' (Diary, 3 March 1696).

222. 'Ye abesse ... orderd a lodging for me chez Mr Dawry' (Diary, 12 March 1696).

223. Diary, 12 March 1696.

224. 'I lodgd at one Mlle Camus de Moulineaux' (Diary, 23 March 1696).

225. Diary, 6 April 1696.

226. Diary, 12 April 1696.

227. Diary, 20 April 1696.

228. Diary, 26 April 1696.

229. Diary, 4, 6, 8, 11, 12 and 15 April 1696.

230. Nairne noted that his wife 'was brought to bed of a son' on 11 March 1695.

231. Diary, 1 May 1696.

232. Diary, 1 May 1696.

233. Diary, 8 May 1696.

234. Diary, 9 August and 5 December 1696; 25 March and 28 June 1698.

235. Diary, 9 Aug. 1696; 26 February and 16–18 March 1697.

236. Diary, 30 June and 13 November 1698.

237. Diary, 16 June 1696.

238. Diary, 18 July 1696.

239. Diary, 26 June 1697. See the entry for 30 June 1699: 'I carryd a Cypher writt in white to Mr Juxon to carry to Berry.' And 18 April 1702: 'I writt in white ink a paper of proposals to Gourney and Gilb. wch was sent by ye post to Berry, wth a sham letter of accts.' (Berry was the secret agent in England with whom Caryll regularly corresponded).

240. Diary, 1 January 1697; 25 December 1700.

241. Diary, 4 and 8 May 1698. For the position of these rooms, see Corp, *A Court in Exile*, pp. 82–3.

242. Diary, 3 November 1697.
243. Diary, 25 January 1696. Some of James II's Irish regiments were serving under Tessé's command in northern Italy.
244. Diary, 5 December 1697.
245. Diary, 25 January 1698.
246. Diary, 13 February 1698.
247. Diary, 8 March 1698.
248. Nairne's augmentation was occasioned by the death of Edward Weybourne, who had been Caryll's Latin secretary (Diary, 27, 29 and 31 March 1698). Nairne remembered Weybourne on the last page of his diary, where he recorded some verses in Latin made impromptu by Weybourne on the Nairne of Sandford coat of arms (see p. 28, note 8).
249. Diary, 10 April 1698.
250. Diary, 18 and 21 April, 13 and 15 July 1698.
251. Diary, 13 April 1699. See also 17 May, 19 July and 23 August 1699.
252. During 1699 the new pension was increased from 41*l* 13*s* 4*d per mensem* to 42*l* 0*s* 0*d* (Diary, 14 September and 14 December 1699).
253. See the diary entries for 5 and 6 November 1698: 'The Chancellor of Engl Herbert dyd at 6 in ye morning in his lodging in ye Castle.' 'Mr In. spoke to Mr Caryl for ye Chancellor's lodging to me, and I spoke to him in ye coach my self.' The Lord Chancellor of England was Sir Edward Herbert, created Jacobite Earl of Portland.
254. Diary, 31 December 1696.
255. Diary, 27 July 1697.
256. The book was printed and published at Saint-Germain-en-Laye by William Weston. It begins with 'A Table of the Psalms, Reduced under severall heads, according to the different matters principally contained in each of them; that so they may be more usefull for the privat devotion of every Christian, as his occasions shall require'. This is followed by Nairne's Preface, which occupies four pages, comments that the Psalms 'alone containe the whole substance of the old Testament', and explains the general policy adopted by Caryll and Nairne in making their translation. Each psalm is then introduced by a short paragraph explaining its content and purpose. A second edition, 'review'd and corrected' was published in 1704 as *The Psalms of David* instead of *The Psalmes of David*. Twelve more editions had been published by 1986.
257. Diary, 31 July 1702. Nairne and Caryll examined the entire translation between 16 and 31 May 1702, and made some last minute corrections.
258. Diary, 29 November 1702. The preface was sent to the Catholic bishops in England on 12 February 1703.
259. For example, on 27 November 1697 Caryll entrusted Nairne with 14,168 *livres*, and on 5 October 1701 with 18,000 *livres*. Other large amounts of money in cash are mentioned on 15 June 1699, 22 February 1700 and 22 September 1700.

260. For an example, see Diary, 22 May 1701. These masses, which Nairne arranged and paid for, were in the chapel of the Recollets at Saint-Germain.

261. Diary, 23 July 1700: 'Mr Sec.ry desird me if it were not troublesom to me, that I would go along with his nephew to Dunk..' They left Saint-Germain on 27 July, and Nairne recorded the details of their journey which lasted six days. He remained at Dunkirk from 3 to 13 August, regularly seeing Caryll's sister and the other nuns, attending mass in the convent and other churches, walking beside the sea and along the fortifications, and listening to music (including two recitals of Italian arias by Father William Pordage). During the return journey, which lasted nine days, and which is also recorded in detail, Nairne and Caryll were accompanied by Richard Waldegrave and two of Secretary Caryll's nieces, who were to be touched by James II three times to cure them of the King's Evil (Diary, 27 July to 20 August 1700). (Richard Waldegrave's brother Sir William was James II's First Physician. Father Pordage was a celebrated singer who had trained in Rome. For the concert which he gave in London on 27 January 1685, accompanied by Sir William Waldegrave on the lute, see the diary of John Evelyn, Everyman Edition, vol. 2, p. 207).

262. They also earned Nairne the respect of the queen. For example, he noted on 11 December 1699 that 'I heard 2 masses at ye chapelle with ye Q', and on 26 May 1700 that he was called into the queen's 'closette'.

263. He had finished 1653 on 18 January, 1654 on 6 March, and 1658 on 29 April. The last pages were amended on 3 May.

264. Corp, Edward, 'James II and David Nairne: The Exiled King and his First biographer', *English Historical Review* CXXIX, no.541, December 2014, pp. 1383–411 (1399).

265. Diary, 2 November 1698. James II's spectacles are now in the Victoria and Albert Museum (W. 5. 1970), and have a focal length of 30.5 cm.

266. Diary, 29 and 30 March, 26 May 1700.

267. Diary, 16 September 1700.

268. Diary, 25 June and 7 July 1701.

269. Diary, 28 August 1700: 'I got of ye Kings hair for Mrs Waldegrave.' Mrs Waldegrave (daughter of one of the king's equerries) was Elizabeth (née Buckingham), wife of Richard Waldegrave who was appointed a gentleman of the king's Privy Chamber in March 1702.

270. Diary, 18 February 1701.

271. Diary, 23 June 1701.

272. Diary, 8 March 1700.

273. Bod. Carte MSS 208, f.369, 'attestation du Chevalier Nairne', 3 July 1734: 'il m'avoit envoyé querir dans son cabinet pour quelque affaire la veille d'une bonne feste, et après m'avoir parlé d'autre chose il alloit m'ordonner quelque ecriture pour le lendemain, lorsque faisant reflexion que le lendemain etoit feste, il se

reprit tout d'un coup, et eut la bonté de me dire "il faut remettre cela Nairne a un autre jour; car vous avés demain vos devotions a faire". Cela me frappa tellement que je ne l'ay jamais pû oublier depuis'.

274. Diary, 20 September 1700. These papers had already been published for James II in 1690 in a pamphlet containing 'des écrits du Feu Roy de Grande-Bretagne'. At the end of each paper, James had added: 'C'est la veritable copie du papier écrit de la propre main du feu Roy mon Frere, que j'ay trouvé dans son cabinet.' The English version was published in 1694 as *Eikon Basilike Deutera. The Pourtraicture of His Sacred Majesty King Charles II. With his Reasons for turning Roman Catholick: published by K. James. Found in the strong box.* On 30 September 1696 Nairne wrote in his diary: 'The King gave me ye paper to copie wherein was ye acct of what passd at K. Ch: 2ᵈ reconciliation to ye church and receiving ye sacraments from fr. Hudleston on his death bed.' Later, on 12 March 1702, he recorded that 'I ... copied out a paper of ye Kings concerning K. Ch: 2ˢ conversion'. See the manuscript by James II entitled 'A true copy of the Relation of the King my brothers death and reconciliation to the Church of Rome' (RA. SP 1/14, 15), published in HMC *Stuart* I, pp. 3–5.

275. Diary, 30 September 1700.

276. James II's advice was contained in a quarto volume of fifty-four pages, in the king's own handwriting (Corp, 'Inventory of the Archives of the Stuart Court', p. 129).

277. Caryll had recommended this increase the previous year: 'Mr Car told me yt when ye K's memoires [*sic*] were done I should get a good gratification from ye K and that I deservd it' (Diary, 22 April 1700).

278. Diary, 2 July 1701, 14 February 1702.

279. Diary, 11 July 1701. This second augmentation was in part given to Nairne because he had not been given an apartment in the château. On 8 March 1700, 'Mr Car told me I had a better right to lodgings in ye Castle yn a great many who askt'. At the end of that year Nairne wrote a petition for the king and queen (28 November) which he discussed with Innes and Caryll (6, 8, 9 December; 19 January 1701). The three of them agreed that Innes would present the petition to the king and queen, and that Caryll would then support it (24, 26, 27 January). Innes did this on 28 March and told Nairne that 'the K. had spoke very kindly of' him. James II then 'sent for' Nairne and 'calld me in to him, while he was in bed' and spoke to Nairne about his request for lodging. It was later that day that he entrusted to Nairne 'his memoires to his son' and told him 'how satisfied he was with me' (29 March). Several weeks later Innes again 'spoke for me to ye K and Q' about having an apartment in the château (8 June) and it was partly this which prompted James II to give Nairne his second augmentation on 27 June

1701. Both augmentations were continued by Mary of Modena after the king's death (Diary, 11 and 12 March, 7 October 1702).

280. Diary, 4 March 1701.

281. Diary, 11 March 1701.

282. 23 and 26 July 1701. For the details of these five volumes, see Corp, 'James II and David Nairne', p. 1401.

283. Diary, 11 August 1701.

284. Diary, 12 August 1701. See also 22 August 1701. On 9 October Nairne gave Lewis Innes 'his warrant for keeping the K's papers'. The warrant was actually dated 24 March 1701 (HMC *Stuart* I, p. 159). A copy, dated 2 August 1702, is in SCA. CA 1/9/1, with a French translation by Nairne in SCA. CA 1/9/2.

285. Bod. Carte MSS 181, f.596, Caryll to Melfort, 6 September 1694.

286. Diary, 26 May to 12 June 1697.

287. Diary, 7, 8 June 1697.

288. Diary, 20 June to 23 July 1697.

289. Diary, 29 June 1697.

290. Diary, 23 July 1697.

291. Diary, 29 July 1697.

292. Diary, 11, 17 August 1697.

293. Diary, 15 October 1697.

294. Diary, 21 October 1697.

295. Diary, 2, 9, 21 and 25 June 1698.

296. Diary, 27 October 1699.

297. Diary, 7 February 1701.

298. See Chapter 1, p.

299. Diary, 9 February 1701.

300. Diary, 26 February 1701. Nairne noted that it was sealed with the 'Scots seal' on 7 March 1701.

301. Diary, 27 February 1701.

302. Most of Lord Melfort's letter was printed in Oldmixon, John, *The History of England, during the Reigns of King William and Queen Mary* (London, 1735), p. 218.

303. Nairne made a copy on 5 March of the letter that gave the news for the king.

304. Diary, 9 March 1701.

305. Diary, 8 and 9 March 1701.

306. Diary, 12 March 1701.

307. Diary, 16 March 1701.

308. The new will replaced an earlier one of March 1699. See Corp, 'James II and David Nairne', pp. 1398, 1402.

309. The seven witnesses were Caryll, Father Sanders, the two most senior grooms of the bedchamber (David Floyd and Richard Biddulph), the queen's vice-chamberlain (John Stafford), one of the gentlemen ushers of her privy chamber (Captain Hatcher) and Lord Perth.

310. Diary, 8 September 1701. The will is in RA. SP Add 1/45. Nairne translated it into French on 23 September 1701, and copies of his translation in his handwriting are in BL. Add MSS 20311, f.4; Archivio Segreto Vaticano, Segretario di Stato: Inghilterra 25, pp. 118–20; and Paris, Archives Diplomatiques, Correspondence Politique: Angleterre 211.

CHAPTER 3

An Ex-Patriate at the Exiled Court, 1691–1708

When James II died in September 1701, David Nairne had been employed at the exiled court for nearly ten years. He had made many friends among the courtiers, and had achieved a special position of trust with the royal family. Despite this he remained a voluntary or self-inflicted ex-patriate rather than a political exile, and this set him apart from the other servants and pensioners at Saint-Germain. If there had been a successful restoration in 1692 or 1696, then all the English, Irish and Scottish Jacobites would have crossed the Channel and rejoined the king in triumph, able at last to reclaim their estates and their property, and many of them to resume their employment with the royal family in England. Even the many Italians and French employed at the court, except for the locally recruited ones, would probably have followed Queen Mary back to London. What, however, would Nairne have done?

Because Nairne was with James II at La Hougue in 1692 and at Calais in 1696, he would certainly have crossed over to England and accompanied the king to London if either of those restoration attempts had been successful. It is possible, however, that he would then have returned to Paris to live with his French wife and children. This is not definite, because Nairne's feelings, if ever recorded, have not survived. But it is possible, perhaps even probable, that he would have done so. And in order to understand this we need to keep in mind Nairne's unique status at the Jacobite court. He was the only courtier at Saint-Germain who had 'gone native' with no overriding personal interest in achieving a Stuart restoration. It is most unlikely that he had any wish to return to Scotland, and perhaps even more unlikely that he would have wanted to live in Protestant England. So this chapter will seek to shed light on Nairne's life outside and beyond the court in which he was employed.

Nairne's father-in-law, Louis de Compigny, had four children, two sons and two daughters. One of the sons had been disinherited many years before,[1] and one of the daughters (Mme de Fleurigny) had died in 1689,[2] so he had only one son and one daughter left to inherit his property. When the remaining son died at the siege of Namur in 1692,[3] Marie-Elisabeth was, by the terms of her marriage settlement, left as the sole heiress of the family estates at Compigny and Les Bordes. Louis de Compigny was by then a relatively old man (at least sixty years old, perhaps much more),[4] and was not expected to live for very much longer, so Nairne had every reason to anticipate that he and his wife would inherit the estates, thus providing them with an income and financial security in the event of a Jacobite restoration.

It seems, however, that Louis de Compigny was reluctant to see his estates pass to the family of his Scottish son-in-law, though we do not know why. In 1692, and despite his relatively advanced age, he took a second wife. She was called Anne Gouère and was about twenty-five years old. They were married in Paris in the church of Saint-Etienne du Mont.[5]

This marriage is not mentioned in Nairne's diary because it took place during the period when the diary was not being kept.[6] For Nairne and his wife Marie-Elisabeth it meant that any children born to the new Madame de Compigny would threaten their anticipated inheritance, particularly if the children were to be sons. And their worst fears were soon realized. In June 1693 a son was born, named Jean-Louis. In 1695 a second son was born, named Sébastien.[7] Neither of these births is mentioned in the diary,[8] though Nairne did mention sending letters to his father-in-law in October 1694 and May 1695, as well as letters to his wife's first cousin, Monsieur de Baby, in October 1694.[9] The latter, who was the son of Louis de Compigny's deceased elder brother, and thus the head of the family, visited the Nairnes at Saint-Germain in June 1695,[10] and we may speculate that the future of the Compigny estates was likely to have been discussed. So long, however, as Louis de Compigny remained alive the future of his estates remained in abeyance.

During the years 1692 to 1697, Nairne used his position at the Stuart court to help both his father-in-law and the peasants on the Compigny estates. Every year from 1693 to 1697, he persuaded the French secretary of state for war, the marquis de Barbezieux, to dispense Louis de Compigny from having to pay money in lieu of performing military service.[11] In 1697 he also persuaded the local *intendant* to exempt both Compigny himself from having to pay the *capitation* tax and the latter's peasants from having to pay the *taille*.[12] It is likely, therefore, that he expected his wife would still inherit part of her father's estates, despite the births of her two half-brothers. And during these years he continued to receive some of the produce of the estate, such as corn, wine, hares and partridges.[13] Then, in February 1698, Nairne received the news that his father-in-law had died,[14] and shortly afterwards that Compigny had left all his property to his two little sons, thereby disinheriting his daughter Marie-Elisabeth.[15]

The result was an extended legal battle which lasted for the rest of 1698 and which involved Nairne and his wife in an enormous amount of correspondence – all of it mentioned in his diary. In April, Marie-Elisabeth left Saint-Germain and went to Compigny with her two older children and a signed procuration from her husband 'impowering her to act in all things relating to ye succession of her father'.[16] During May, she attempted unsuccessfully to persuade her young step-mother Anne de Compigny and the latter's *notaire*[17] to accept that her late father's will could not invalidate her marriage contract with David Nairne, and therefore that she should still inherit part of the estate. When this failed, Nairne consulted two *notaires* in Paris, sending them in June a long letter containing the six relevant documents: 'my Contract of mariage, Mr de Compigny's will, his marriage contract with his first wife, the request to the Paris official, the certificate of remarriage at St Estienne du Mont, and the contract with the second wife.'[18] There then followed several weeks of discussions and correspondence, during which Nairne and his chief *notaire* consulted two *avocats*, only one of whom agreed with Nairne's contention that the will could not overrule the marriage contract.[19] Eventually, in September, having exchanged numerous letters with his wife, Nairne decided that he would himself have to go to Compigny in order to reach an amicable settlement.

With permission from Caryll, Nairne left Saint-Germain on 23 September, consulted the *avocat* in Paris who supported him, and travelled on to Compigny where he arrived on the 27th. While he was there, he saw Monsieur de Baby and many old family friends, and eventually

proposed a compromise settlement (a 'plan d'accomodement')[20] whereby
his wife would inherit one third of the property, thereby renouncing the
other two thirds to the five year old Jean-Louis de Compigny, the elder of
her two half-brothers. When this had been agreed Nairne left to return
to Saint-Germain on 27 October, leaving his wife and two older children
behind. The compromise needed to be formally settled and officially registered with the *notaires* and *avocats* in Paris, and then sent to the *notaire*
who was representing Madame de Compigny, which involved yet more
meetings and correspondence which extended through November and
December. All was finally ready just before Christmas.

On 10 January 1699, Nairne left the court at Saint-Germain for a second
time and travelled to join his wife at Compigny. This time he remained there
for three weeks and 'regulated ye affaires of ye succession' with Madame
de Compigny's lawyer, 'regulated ye acc[oun]ts' with Anne de Compigny
herself, and 'divided ye household goods whereof m.w. got a third'.[21] The
evidence suggests that this was done relatively amicably, as the Nairnes
seem to have enjoyed good relations with Madame de Compigny and her
sons thereafter. On 4 February, Nairne and his wife finally left Compigny,
taking all their household goods with them, and reached Saint-Germain
four days later. The Nairnes were now the owners of one third of a country estate, with a substantially increased income and with new household
goods to furnish and equip their home at Saint-Germain. Nairne's unique
status as a voluntary ex-patriate at the court with property in France was
thereby enhanced. And thus the possibility of his remaining in France in
the event of a Stuart restoration was consequently increased.

During the summer of 1698, while the negotiations over the Compigny
estates were proceeding, Nairne attempted to obtain an increase to the
French pension of 400 *livres per annum* which he had been receiving from
the war secretariat since 1687. Each year it was his practice to send a *placet*
to one of his friends in the secretariat at Versailles during July or August,
in return for which he received an *ordonnance* for payment at the *Trésor
Royal* in Paris in August or September. In 1698, however, he 'drew a petition for augmentation of my pension to ye K of Fr'.[22] He explained his
request to his French friends, and obtained the support of the comte de
Tessé (younger brother of the *maréchal*).[23] He then showed his petition

to Caryll and Innes. The former, as Nairne recorded, 'took my petition and letter [addressed] to M. Barbez[ieux] and said he would speak to ye K [James II] of it'.[24] The latter (Innes) promised 'to speak to Mr Car yt he might get ye K to give it to ye K of Fr and recommend it'.[25] James II preferred not to get personally involved, but he obliged Nairne by instructing Lord Middleton to sign 'a letter of recommendation to Mr de Barbezieux to accompany my petition'.[26] On 13 August, Nairne was presented in the *grande galerie des glaces* at Versailles by the comte de Tessé to Barbezieux 'to whom I deliverd E.M[iddleton's] letter of recomendation of my placet'. Barbezieux replied: 'Mons[ieu]r je ferai de mon mieux.'

Whether or not Barbezieux was willing to speak to Louis XIV in Nairne's favour cannot be said. The French probably thought that Nairne was adequately provided for at the Stuart court, and did not need an augmentation. At any rate, four days later, Nairne recorded that his request had not been granted: 'my pension was answerd *bon pour 400# seulement*.' The incident is interesting because it provides further evidence that Nairne probably expected to remain in France in the event of a restoration.

By the end of the 1690s, however, no restoration was anticipated in the immediate future, so Nairne and his wife began to consider how best to benefit from their one third share of the estates at Compigny and Les Bordes. It was not easy to help manage the farms when obliged to live at Saint-Germain, nor to transport one third of their annual produce to their home so far away. In the autumn of 1699, therefore, they decided that it might be best to lease their share to Madame de Compigny and her elder son in return for a cash payment. They explained their intention to the lawyers on both sides[27] and in July Marie-Elisabeth went with her children to stay at Compigny and discuss the matter with her young step-mother.[28] We do not know how the negotiations progressed, except that Nairne and his wife exchanged numerous letters during the rest of July, throughout August and into September. Eventually, on 22 September, Nairne again left Saint-Germain to conclude the arrangement.

Nairne was at Compigny from 25 September to 18 October. Immediately after his arrival, as he recorded, 'wee began ye vintage',[29] but much of his time there was spent discussing his plans with Monsieur de Baby, and then with Madame de Compigny's lawyers. It says much for Nairne's tact that once again he brought matters to a successful and amicable conclusion, and he noted in his diary that 'my wife let her part of ye house to Mr de Compigny for 9 years'.[30] In other words, the Nairnes agreed to withdraw from the management of the family estates and the sharing of their produce until the autumn of 1708, by which time there might have been a Stuart restoration, and by when Jean-Louis de Compigny would be fifteen years old.

When the day came to leave Compigny and return to Saint-Germain, Nairne noted that 'I parted with my wife and 2 children ..., carrying wth us a muid and a half of win, 4 flies of corn, a great chest, and other goods and cloths'.[31] The wine was stored in the cellar of his home at Saint-Germain and lasted until the end of the following year, when Nairne noted that he 'drew out the rest of the Compigny wine, 10 bottels'.[32] The corn was sent 'to be milled at Poissy'.[33] And the great chest and other goods joined all the household goods which had been brought back to Saint-Germain earlier that year. As we shall see, Nairne then started to redecorate his home, using both the extra money received from James II and the money he had obtained from granting the nine-year lease. Having failed to obtain accommodation in the Château de Saint-Germain, he now seemed intent on furnishing his home in the town in a style befitting his new status.

At the beginning of 1698, when he received the news of his father-in-law's death, David and Marie-Elisabeth Nairne had four children. They were Jean (born in October 1692),[34] Françoise (born in October 1694),[35] Jean-Baptiste (born in April 1696)[36] and Jacques. The latter was born on 24 October 1697, which was James II's birthday, when Nairne noted that 'my w was brought to bed of a son at 11 in ye fornoon wanting 2 or 3 minutes'. The child was baptized four days later by Lewis Innes in the Chapel Royal, and Nairne proudly recorded that 'the King of England was his godfather'. The godmother was the Countess of Almond, the queen's Italian lady of the bedchamber.

By this time Marie-Elisabeth had stopped breast feeding her children, preferring to employ a local wet nurse,[37] so Jacques was sent to live with the latter. One day after receiving the news in March 1698 that Louis de Compigny's will had disinherited Marie-Elisabeth, Nairne noted that his wife 'was advertised that Jamé [sic: Jacques] was sick' and that 'she went and brought him from his nurse home'.[38] Nairne consulted Sir William Waldegrave, the king's physician, who 'order'd plasters and julip for him', but the boy 'continued very ill'[39] and 'dyd about 4 in ye afternoon' of the 15th. On the following day he was 'bury'd in ye church yard' aged four months and ten days.[40] Nairne did not record his feelings about this loss, but we must assume that he and his wife were deeply upset. It was not until six weeks later that Marie-Elisabeth left for Compigny with her husband's procuration to negotiate the succession to her father.

Apart from the one month that Nairne also spent at Compigny (September to October 1698), he and his wife were separated for eight months until January 1699. Then the family was hit by a major tragedy. On the afternoon of 5 January, Marie-Elisabeth was travelling with her six-year-old son Jean in an open *calleche* from Compigny to Baby to celebrate twelfth night when the horses bolted. Nairne described what happened next:

> ye horses having taken ye mord aux dents throwen ye coachman off his seat, and almost killd him, my wife being frighted but ye child fallen who sat before her in an open calleche fell down she did not remember how, and was kill'd upon ye spot, ye caleche which having run over his head, ye mother transported wth grief and fear threw herself out of ye caleche, and had ye collar bone of her right arme broke and both her hands disjoynted, so yt she was caryd home in ye caleche almost dead and her poor son lying dead at her feet, by a farmer of hers yt chanced to pass by.[41]

It was this which prompted Nairne to return to Compigny in January 1699. When he arrived on the 11th, six days after the accident, he was told by Monsieur de Baby that his wife 'had been made believe all this time yt he [Jean] was alive and had only a leg broke'. It was therefore left to Nairne himself to give her the bad news. He recorded that 'I stayd wth m.w. to comfort her and take care of her, and did not leave her till she was in a condition to be brought back to St Germ'. It was during these four weeks that he regulated the succession to his father-in-law's estates, but it is clear that he still regarded his elder son as the true heir to Louis de Compigny. He noted that 'I went every day to mass and kneeld upon my sons grave who was buryd by his grandfather in ye quire of Compigny in ye place wher ye seign.r of ye parish's seat is'.[42] Meanwhile Lewis Innes wrote to tell him that both James II and Queen Mary 'had expressd a great concern for us, and yt never anything was so universally regretted in Court'.[43]

Nairne returned to Saint-Germain during the first week of February
with his wife and daughter Françoise, breaking the journey in Paris to give
Marie-Elisabeth a rest. It was during the following month that their next
child was conceived at Saint-Germain.

When Marie-Elisabeth returned to Compigny in July to negotiate the
lease of her share of the estates she was four months pregnant. As we have
seen, Nairne joined her there in September to finalize the arrangement,[44]
and they returned to Saint-Germain in October. Two months later, on
Christmas eve, Marie-Elisabeth gave birth to another son:

> My wife ... had found some pains ye day before ... and at night within less yn a quarter
> of ten a clock she brought a Son into ye world whilst ye matines of Christmas eve
> were singing before midnight mass. It was ten a clock before she was quite deliverd.

Two days later, the boy was 'christend after salut in ye parish church by ye
Curet'. The godfather was Lewis Innes, the godmother was Lady Audly
(wife of James Porter, the king's vice-chamberlain), 'and ye child was namd
Louis'. So once again the Nairnes had two sons and one daughter. Françoise
and Jean-Baptiste were living at home with them, but Louis was sent to
live with a wet nurse until he was over a year old.[45]

Three and a half months after the birth of Louis, Marie-Elisabeth
conceived her ninth and last child. The intervening period was worrying
because Jean-Baptiste contracted smallpox in January 1700,[46] 'upon which',
Nairne recorded, 'I was obligd to quitt the house' and sleep elsewhere for
three weeks 'till my son was recoverd, and the danger of ye air was over'.[47]
As Marie-Elisabeth remained with her son, we must assume that she, unlike
her husband, had previously contracted smallpox. On 9 February, Nairne
'returnd home after having had leave from Mr Caryll wth whom I dind
everyday'.[48]

Nairne and his wife spent the spring and summer of 1700 together at
Saint-Germain, but in September Marie-Elisabeth returned to Compigny
with her two elder children.[49] She remained there for two months, and did
not come back to Saint-Germain until 11 December, by which time she was
eight months pregnant. Her last child was born on 15 January 1701. Nairne
recorded that his wife's labour started the previous evening, and that 'at
3 a clock and a quarter past, and near 3 and a half in ye morning my wife

was brought to bed of a girle, none being present but ... the midwife, my girles nurse, and Me Monnots maid, and myself'. On the following day, 'at 5 a clock in ye afternoon', the child 'was christened in the Chapel Royal by Doctor [John] Ingleton almoner to ye Queen, ye Q. being godmother she held ye child and gave her name Mary'. For reasons left unexplained there was no godfather.[50]

Marie-Elisabeth's extended visits to Compigny, leaving her husband by himself at Saint-Germain, require some comment, especially as she would continue to spend long periods there without him in the following years. The most obvious explanation seems to be that she felt a very strong attachment to the family home where she had been brought up, and that she had established a good relationship with Anne de Compigny and the latter's two sons, who were approximately the same age as her own two older children. There is no evidence that she felt excluded from the Jacobite court where she had failed to find employment. Nairne often took her to the château with him,[51] and as a couple they had plenty of friends among the international group of courtiers there. Nor is there any hint of strained relations between her and her husband. On the contrary, whenever the couple were separated they wrote to each other very regularly, sometimes every day. Unfortunately none of their letters has survived. The only hint in Nairne's diary of what these letters might have contained comes in an entry dated 26 October 1700, when he had not recently received a letter from her and was feeling lonely without her: 'I writt to m.w. for whom I was in peine and had a letter from her at night.'

It was during his wife's first visit to Compigny, following the death of her father in January 1698, that Nairne began to receive the first augmentation to his salary from James II. He used part of it to purchase various items to improve the appearance of his dinner and supper table. During the second half of 1698, he recorded that he bought a salt, four spoons, forks and knives, two small spoons for his children and two cups, all of them in silver. He also bought a set of pewter plates, and a table on which they could all be set.[52] For his kitchen, he bought a dresser, some shelves, and some 'utensiles ... viz marmite, chaudron, visselle d'etain, table, dressoir, faillance, vers, tournebroche etc to ye value of 100#'.[53] After his wife returned to Saint-Germain in February 1699, having acquired one third of

Figure 3. *Marie-Elisabeth Nairne, née de Compigny*, 1700 (97 × 62.5 cm),
by François de Troy (private collection)
The painter recorded on the back of the canvas that the picture was 'Peint à Paris en
1700'. It was probably commissioned by Lord Caryll as a present to thank Nairne for
escorting his nephew to Dunkirk.

her father's estate, he bought several more spoons, forks and knives, but this time some of them were in gold or gilt and the most important items were engraved with his coat of arms.[54] By April 1699, he was able to entertain his family and his friends in a much grander style than he had previously been able to do. By then he had also set about enhancing the furnishing and decoration of his home.

We cannot be sure where the Nairnes were living by this time, as there is no reference in his diary to their moving from their apartment in the rue de La Salle to a larger home. It is possible that they moved into one of the vacant *hôtels* in Saint-Germain at a time when the diary was not being kept – either between June 1692 and March 1693 after the failure of the 1692 invasion attempt, or between May 1693 and June 1694 when for the first time they had two children living with them. In December 1698, Nairne paid a mason to create a new balustrade for his staircase,[55] which suggests that he and his family were by then living in a house rather than an apartment.

During 1699 and the first half of 1700, Nairne bought himself a new bureau and had it covered in green serge, and also both a portrait of the Prince of Wales and a tapestry for his *salle*, where he paid a mason to install a new chimney.[56] But it was his bedchamber (which he described as his wife's chamber) on which he mainly concentrated. He paid about 1,300 *livres* to three of the local tradesmen to build him a new bed with an Imperial and curtains, together with a set of chairs, a tapestry, a looking glass and a new chimney.[57] He noted on 16 January 1700 that 'wee lay ye first night in our new bed and new furnishd chamber'. It took him the rest of 1700 to discharge his debt,[58] and by then he had himself set up a new bed with green curtains in what he described as his 'little chamber'.[59]

These, and other details recorded in his diary, provide evidence of how Nairne lived at this time, and by extension of the relatively high standard of living enjoyed in exile by the Jacobites at Saint-Germain who had salaries or pensions higher than his. We are given details of many of the things which Nairne and his family ate and drank, together with some of the prices paid. When, for example, he had bottled and drunk the last of his Compigny wine he brought barrels of the local wine from Verneuil, then Triel, then Conflans.[60] For cider he went to Le Pecq,[61] whereas his beer was brewed in Saint-Germain itself.[62] He acquired *ratafiat* from a man who worked in the *Bouche du Roi* at Versailles,[63] but he made his own black cherry brandy, and also added the 'mar of grapes' to put into his wine to distil his own marc brandy.[64] We are also given details of the candles he bought to light his home, and of the charcoal and wood he purchased to heat it and for cooking. For example, he burned four *cordes* of wood each year, which cost him about 105 *livres*.[65]

We are also told about his hobbies and pastimes. He continued to play chess[66] and *boules*,[67] as he had in Rome, but now he also played ombre,[68] the card game which had recently become very popular throughout Europe. During the summer of 1699, while his wife was at Compigny, he recorded that he made a study of mid-seventeenth-century French history. After studying Pascal's *Pensées* (published posthumously in 1670), he read a biography of the *maréchal de* Turenne, then one of the *Prince de* Condé (the *Grand Condé*) and then one of Cardinal Mazarin.[69] His main hobby, however, continued to be music. He attended both the concerts in the château[70] and the sung services in the parish church.[71] He also began to take music lessons from Abraham Baumeister, one of the musicians employed at the court.[72] In 1697, he had bought himself a bass viol and a flute,[73] and he was now able to perform with his friends both at home and in the château,[74] something he could share with John Caryll who also performed on the viol in the court concerts.[75]

More important than all these things, however, was Nairne's growing piety, which he shared with his wife, and which was influenced by the example set by King James II. He very regularly attended the services held in the chapel royal of the château, the parish church and the chapel of the Récollets in the town.[76] In 1697 his diary records his attendance at high mass, vespers, sermons and *salut*, sometimes in the same place, sometimes in all three, as on 14 July 1697 when he was in the chapel royal for 'sermon', in the parish church for vespers, and at the Récollets for *salut*. During 1698, however, when he was negotiating the Compigny inheritance and beginning to buy new items for his table and kitchen, his diary records a very significant increase in his religious devotions and attendance at services. Perhaps his growing piety was partly stimulated by the death of his son Jacques in March of that year. Perhaps also it was the result of the extended absence of Marie-Elisabeth at Compigny during that spring and summer. It must certainly have been influenced by the translations he was making with John Caryll of the Psalms and the Epistles, which they finished in April. In any event, in May 1698, he took two important steps which testify to the extent of his total commitment to Catholicism as the moral justification for the Jacobite cause.

On 23 May, Nairne joined the Confraternity of the 'Bona Morte' or 'Bona Mors' (Happy Death), a Jesuit inspired confraternity which had been established in the chapel royal by the king and the queen, and which involved regular attendance to meditate on the human suffering of Christ. The special services, which took place every Friday and included 'prieres et benediction du St Sacrament', were designed to prepare the confraternity's members against any sudden or unexpected death, as it was believed that such an unprovided-for death would lead to hell. From this point onwards there are regular entries in Nairne's diary mentioning his attendance at 'Bona Morte' on Fridays.[77]

Two days later, having confessed his sins to Father Bartolomeo Ruga (the queen's chaplain) he went to Paris to be confirmed in the Cathedral of Notre Dame. He recorded in his diary that day:

> I recd ye sacrament of Confirmation from ye bishop of Frezius [*sic*: Fréjus] Mr Daquin dans la chapelle de l'Archeveché, and took ye name of Louis together wth my name of baptisme David. From thence I went to ye great church and recd before ye altar of our Lady.

Following his confirmation, Nairne continued to translate the books of the New Testament with Caryll, started to compose the biography of James II, and copied the Advice which the king had written for his son.

The years 1699 to 1702, during which he attended the services in the Chapel Royal, the parish church and the chapel of the Récollets with ever greater frequency, further strengthened Nairne's piety and his deep religious convictions. There were various reasons for this. The sudden death of his son Jean in January 1699, followed by another death in the family in July 1701,[78] and then the exemplary and saintly death of his master James II in September 1701, reinforced his total acceptance of God's will and his resignation in the face of Divine Providence. Another factor was his realization that for the time being the Jacobite cause, which he knew to be just, was encountering little success against its enemies. Two other important influences, as we shall see in the next chapter, were his study of James II's Papers of Devotion, and a series of miraculous cures which began to take place and which were attributed to the intercession of the late king.

Nairne's profound piety culminated in his joining the Confraternity of the Holy or Blessed Sacrament, which was instituted at Saint-Germain by the *curé* in July 1702. The members of the confraternity, or *société*, committed themselves to remaining for an agreed length of time before the Blessed Sacrament, which would be exposed in the parish church, a practice known as the 'adoration perpétuelle du Saint-Sacrement'.[79] Nairne noted that on 13 and 20 August he was 'an hour before ye b. Sacram.t'. Then, on the 25th, he recorded that 'my wife and I took billets in ye Sacristie and enterd ourselves in the Society of ye adoration perpetuelle du St Sacram.t'. They both agreed that they would fulfil their duty 'from 4 to 5' in the afternoon. Two days later, 'I went wth my wife to the King's tomb where Fr. Jonson was taking ye Deposition of a woman that was curd by ye intercession of ye King'. Thereafter Nairne recorded that he passed 'an hour before ye B. S. between 4 and 5' once or twice, sometimes three times each week, whenever he was at Saint-Germain.[80]

Between 1702 and 1708, Nairne attended the services in the parish church, at the Récollets and in the Chapel Royal of the château with ever greater regularity – and probably with greater regularity than the other members of the court. The offices performed each day by the priests at Saint-Germain included prone, high mass, several low masses, vespers and *salut*.[81] In addition to these, there were several daily sermons, the king's mass in the Chapel Royal, compline, *matines* (particularly at All Saints and All Souls), and *ténèbres* at Easter.[82] On Fridays, the Bona Morte services were held in the chapel, and on every day of the week the Blessed Sacrament was exposed in the parish church for the *adoration perpétuelle*. Nairne recorded in his diary that when he did his devotions, which was on most days, he normally attended at least three or four of these. If he was very busy he went to the evening services of vespers and *salut* with a sermon, but on other days he would attend – and sometimes assist at – several services spread throughout the day. No account of Nairne's life would be complete if it did not recognize the full extent of his piety during these years. The following examples, chosen at random, indicate the extent to which he was committed to his Catholic faith:

> I did my devotions. I heard high mass, prone, King's mass, vespers, salut, and was an hour before ye B. S. (6 May 1703)

> Having confessd ye night before I recd in ye parish church and heard high mass, prone, 2 sermons and salut and was an hour before ye B. S. (1 March 1705)

> I went to comunion, heard high mass, vespers, salut and 4 sermons and an hour before ye B. S. (7 March 1706)

> I heard 4 sermons, 2 masses and vespers and salut. (21 March 1706)

> I heard all ye office. (28 March 1706)

> I confessd and receivd in the parish, and was about 9 hours in ye Church. (6 February 1707)

> I comunicated at ye Recolets, heard there 3 masses, sermon and vespers and at ye parish high mass, prone and salut. (13 March 1707)

> I communicate at ye parish and was 8 hours in ye Church. (17 July 1707)

He went to confession and took communion approximately once a month, though sometimes much more frequently, and went to the Bona Morte services on most Fridays. His attendance at church was at its most intense from the Wednesday before Easter until Easter Monday. On the first three of these six days he listened to the singing of the *leçons de ténèbres* as well as several other services, he then fasted from Thursday midday until nine o' clock on Friday evening when he ate a small piece of bread, he visited all the churches, he sat up all of one night before the Blessed Sacrament, and he assisted at all the offices – high mass, several low masses, *matines*, vespers, *salut* and numerous sermons. During these days, he normally went to confession and took communion on two occasions, and for most of the time he was accompanied by his wife who shared with him the lengthy fast.[83]

These deep religious convictions did not, however, prevent Nairne's enjoying himself in the company of his friends, and his diary refers to the many occasions when he invited people to have dinner or supper in his house, or when he was himself invited out. He very regularly dined with Caryll, and with his friends from the Collège des Ecossais (Lewis Innes, Charles Whiteford and John Wallace) when they were at court. The people with whom he most regularly ate at home during the 1690s were his colleagues Monnot and Dempster, an Irish lawyer named Nihill, a Scottish colonel named Brown,[84] and the wives of these four. For example, in February 1698, three months before he joined the Confraternity of the 'Bona Morte', he noted that 'wee had a great supper at my house, and dancing afterwards, till 4 in ye morning'.[85] In August 1702, five days before he and his wife joined the Confraternity of the Blessed Sacrament, he 'gave a dinner and supper to Mr Caryll and Mr Waters and Mr Gally, and had musick till 11 at night'.[86] There are a great many other references to large dinner or supper parties given by the Nairnes. Normally they invited no more than six guests at a time,[87] though on one occasion he recorded that 'we were 15 mouths at 2 tables' and 'after dinner they sent for violins and danced till 11 at night'.[88]

As the years went by, Nairne's dinner and supper companions gradually changed. He continued to dine with Caryll and to eat regularly with Monnot and his wife, but Dempster, Nihill and Brown were invited less frequently. What is worth noticing, however, is that the people who replaced them were English, Irish, Scottish and French, a significant point because it is often assumed that the different nationalities at the exiled court were hostile towards each other.[89] That was certainly not true in Nairne's case. In addition to the members of the court, Nairne invited the French and Irish priests of the parish church, notably Father Thomas Geoghagan.[90] He was also on good terms with two other Frenchmen at Saint-Germain. The first was Joseph Du Mont, a musician who was probably a relation of the composer Henri Du Mont.[91] The second was the portrait-painter Alexis-Simon Belle, with whom Nairne and his wife became particularly friendly in 1706 and 1707.[92] In March 1707, for example, Nairne noted that 'I dind wth my wife and daughter at Mr Bel's'.[93] These dinners and suppers evidently remained enjoyable occasions, and on one of them another guest was Marie Chappe, the most celebrated soprano among the singers of the *Chapelle Royale* at Versailles and noted for her singing of the motets of François Couperin.[94] In August 1707, Nairne noted that 'I dind at Mr Monnots with Mlle Chape and heard her sing'.[95]

On the occasions when Nairne visited Compigny, he also enjoyed the normal pursuits of a country gentleman. When he was there in October 1698, for example, he went hunting five times. He specified that the first time he 'went a shooting' and 'killd 2 hairs and a patridge', and that on the second he went 'a coursing on horseback with greyhounds, and wee killd 2 hairs'. He occupied some of his other days by travelling out from Compigny on horseback to visit his relations and friends at Baby, and further afield on the river Seine at Bray, Villenauxe, Passy and Nogent, all of them several miles away.[96] In order to get to Compigny from Paris he took either 'ye coche de Sens'[97] or 'ye coche d'Auxerre'[98] as far as Serbonnes on the river Yonne, where he was met by a *calleche*, but on at least one occasion he returned by boat along the Yonne and the Seine.[99] Nairne also enjoyed walking. When he went to Compigny in September 1698 he began the journey from Saint-Germain by going 'in ye morning to Paris afoot',[100] and the following year he also went on one occasion the six miles from Compigny to Bray 'on foot'.[101]

By June 1701, when James II gave him the second augmentation to his salary, Nairne could be very satisfied with his life at Saint-Germain. While working very hard for the king and Caryll in the court, he was obtaining considerable spiritual satisfaction from his 'devotions' and living comfortably with his wife and children at home. Françoise was six years old, Jean-Baptiste was five, and Louis was one and a half. Marie was only five months and still with her wet nurse. There was no immediate prospect of a Stuart restoration, so Nairne had no pressing worries about his future, and meanwhile he had established a degree of financial independence for himself and his family in France. All seemed well in his private life. And then he and his wife were confronted by yet another personal tragedy: Jean-Baptiste died after a prolonged and agonizing illness.

The problem began in May 1701 when the little boy contracted measles. He remained at home in bed, but after only four days was judged to be well enough to get up,[102] Nairne noting that 'my son was purgd wth a pouder in ye morning, and went out a little in ye afternoon.[103] The boy had obviously not properly recovered from his measles, but he went back to his day school[104] and on 2 June was taken for a walk in the gardens of the château. On the following day he 'fell ill, had convulsions and was speechless for 6 hours', which 'happened to him about 7 a clock after coming from school'. He seemed to get better, but four days later it happened again. Nairne noted that 'when I was set down to dinner wth Mr Caryll I was sent for to my son who was fallen ill again and could not speak'.[105]

For the rest of June and into early July, Jean-Baptiste remained gravely ill, and his father recorded in detail the various treatments he was given and how he reacted to them – thereby providing a unique testimony to the reality of medical conditions at the exiled court. Because Sir William Waldegrave was dying, Nairne summoned two other Jacobite doctors,[106] as well as a French surgeon and an apothecary.[107] The child was given a 'vomiter', he was 'blooded in ye Jugular veine', he was 'purged wth manna', and was repeatedly given a 'clyster' with 'a potion for his cholique'. None of these treatments did him any good. More 'clysters' and purges were prescribed, supported by 'Julip' and 'an emulsion', but the boy continued to vomit what little food he could eat, getting weaker and weaker as each day went by.[108] By the 22nd, it was felt necessary to apply 'a plaister to his belly, and let nature work', but this was no more successful, and on the following day Nairne noted that his son 'was exceeding weak and could take no rest at night': it 'was ye 21st day from his first falling ill, and he was thought to be in great danger'. And so the days went by: more 'clysters', more 'manna' and more 'pouder'. Meanwhile the boy remained unable to speak and 'his eyes were turnd'.[109]

On the 27th, the doctors 'concluded from these symptoms and ye obstinacy of ye distemper against all remedys that the disease was in the head', and again 'concluded him in great danger'.[110] So the little boy's 'head was shaved and a plaister put on it',[111] but still he 'continued feverish', 'his eyes [were] turned and squinting a little', and he had 'a difficulty in his speech'.[112] By the beginning of July, he was having repeated convulsions,[113] so 'a vasicatory plaister' was applied 'to his neck' which 'made a very good suppuration'.[114]

By this point Nairne had decided that these remedies needed to be supplemented by prayer. He and his wife had three special masses said for their son in the parish church,[115] and they sought the assistance of one of the local saints as a last resort. On 2 July, Nairne noted that he had 'a shirt and nightcap of my sons touchd by ye relicts of Ste Genevieve de Nanterre, wch wee put upon him, and a mass was said for him next morning at Nanterre'. This brought some temporary improvement, and that morning 'my son ... recoverd his sight and knowledge for a little while and seeing me calld to me mon cher pere'. But the convulsions returned, so that evening Nairne 'gave him a spoonful of water of St Genevieves well wch he took'.[116]

This time it was the end, and Jean-Baptiste 'fell very ill, had a burning heat in all his body and his face and his respiration very much oppressd'. He survived throughout the night and eventually died the following morning, 5 July. Nairne noted in his diary:

> My poor son John baptiste dyd at 9 a clock, about ye same hour yt he was born, on Munday 30 April 1696, being 5 years 2 months and 5 days old, exactly two and a half years after ye death of his elder brother John wch happened on Munday 5th Jan 1699. He passt wthout any grimace immediately after he had got a priests benediction, his mother and I went and heard mass for him one after another while he was in agony and wee were both present when he expired, after having been from ye fryday 3 June yt he first fell ill of a sort of apoplecie (after his being recoverd of ye misles wch he took 30 May) 4 weeks and 5 days sick in wch time he sufferd like a poor martyre especially from the time yt his collick began wch was ye 17th June.

He was buried in the parish church on the following day 'at 7 a clock at night',[117] leaving both his parents deeply distressed and his mother temporarily 'ill of a collick in her stomach, with vomitings and looseness'.[118]

The death of Jean-Baptiste coincided with the final illness of James II. It was when the king heard about the boy's condition that he granted Nairne the second augmentation to his salary on 27 June. And it was on 10 July, four days after Jean-Baptiste's death, that James had his second 'fainting fitt'. A little over two months later the king would also be dead. The long drawn out drama of his son's death clearly had a profound impact on both Nairne and his wife, as is suggested by the exceptional detail with which he described it in his diary, and strengthened still more his resignation in the face of Divine Providence. Six of their nine children had now died, leaving them with Françoise and the two youngest, Louis and Marie, and they must have wondered how long these would remain with them.

For the time being, however, Nairne was keen to provide his remaining children with a good education. Françoise began dancing lessons when she was seven and a half,[119] and was taught to play the spinet when she was eight.[120] One year later, Nairne noted that 'Mr Ardlet began to teach my daughter musique',[121] which presumably involved music theory as well as performance. But most of her education was entrusted to the English Augustinian nuns in Paris. Their convent was situated beside the Collège des Ecossais, and Nairne first sent her to be a boarder there from June to August 1704 when she was nine and a half.[122] She spent the rest of that year at Compigny with her mother,[123] but was then at the convent for most of the time until the summer of 1707 when she was again taken to Compigny.[124] This meant that when he visited or stayed with his friends at the college he was able to see her. Her board, lodging and education cost 50 *livres* each quarter.[125]

Nairne recorded his daughter's progress in his diary, and the occasions when he saw her or wrote to her. She made her first communion at the convent when she was twelve,[126] and shortly afterwards was taken to court wearing a new set of clothes bought specially for the purpose.[127] In fact, Françoise was being brought up to become an eligible and accomplished bride, and Nairne might well have also hoped to secure for her a position at the court in the service of Princess Louise-Marie, who was two years her senior.[128]

Louis Nairne suffered from ill health as a little boy, and had to be taken to Paris to see a surgeon on more than one occasion,[129] but he survived smallpox when he contracted it in 1706 at six and a half years old.[130] There is no mention in the diary of his being given any dancing or music lessons, but as the diary stops in April 1708 when he was still only seven that is not surprising. Nairne did, however, record that he sent his son to a local schoolmaster when he was just six years old.[131]

Marie, the youngest, contracted and survived smallpox when she was five.[132] We know from later documents that she, like her sister, was educated as a boarder by the English Augustinian nuns in Paris, so presumably she went there in about 1710 when she was nine years old, having already started dancing and music lessons at Saint-Germain.

At the end of May 1702, Nairne began to write his testament. He seems to have put it aside, because he did not finish it until April 1706.[133] It must have been a relatively long document because he felt the need to write a 'table of my testam[en]t' shortly afterwards.[134] It was finally signed and witnessed in January 1708.[135] We do not know what this testament contained, though it must have made provision for his three children, and perhaps also for his wife. Shortly before he signed it Nairne also bought two *rentes* on the Hôtel de Ville in Paris 'of 1200# each au denier 10 in my name, and ye viag. Rents one on my son Louis Life, and ye other on my Daughter Francese [*sic*] her Life'.[136] He presumably intended to buy a third one to benefit Marie, then still only six years old, when he had saved enough money to do so.

There are frequent references in the diary to Nairne's growing prosperity during the first decade of the new century. In addition to the new clothes he bought from a tailor in Saint-Germain for himself, his wife and his children,[137] he noted that he bought a new wig for 54 *livres* in 1702 to replace one had bought in 1697.[138] He had acquired a sword in 1699,[139] but he replaced it three years later. In October 1702, when he bought a new suit with brass buttons and a *pinchinat* coat, he noted that 'I put on my new suite wth my new sword wch I bought ye day before 58# 14s and my old sword'.[140] Shortly afterwards he noted how he and Marie-Elisabeth 'bought 16 ells of damas at 9# for a manteau and peticoat for my wife'.[141] Some of Marie-Elisabeth's new clothes can be seen in her portrait which was painted by François de Troy in 1700.[142]

There are also references in the diary to the nurses who were employed by the Nairnes to look after their children when they were old enough to live at home, and to the maids who served Marie-Elisabeth. Most if not all of these women were recruited at Compigny,[143] where she continued to pass some of her summers,[144] and where Nairne himself joined her in October 1704 and October 1707.[145]

Nairne and his wife were very sociable people and had many French friends outside the Jacobite court: the diary mentions the names of about thirty people with whom they socialized at Saint-Germain, whom they visited in Paris or who visited them at Saint-Germain. These included Nairne's original patron and friend the Abbé Jossier, with whom he had resumed his correspondence in 1694,[146] and Mlle Fabre with whom he and his wife had lodged in Paris in 1687.[147] They even included Mlle de Placé, from whom he had received 'much cruelty' in 1684–5.[148] But their closest French friends seem to have been their relations in the country, Marie-Elisabeth's first cousin M. de Baby and his wife, the second wife of her brother-in-law M. de Fleurigny, a widow since January 1696, and

Mme de Compigny and her two sons. They saw them whenever they were
at Compigny, and the diary refers to visits by the Babys to Saint-Germain
in both 1703 and 1704.[149]

As the years went by, and the end of the nine year lease in 1708 drew
closer, Nairne took an increasing interest in the affairs of the Compigny,
Baby and Fleurigny families. There are frequent references in the diary to
correspondence with the lawyers who had drawn up the lease,[150] and also
to Nairne's using his influence at the Stuart court to help his wife's relations. In 1707 he wrote a *placet* for Mme de Compigny requesting that her
tenants should be exempt from having to pay the *taille*, and sent it for her
to the French court.[151] When his wife's nephew, a knight of the Order of
Malta known as the Commandeur de Fleurigny, wanted one of his friends
to be given a priory, Nairne wrote to the agent of the order on his behalf
and even asked Caryll to help.[152]

Nairne also helped one of his Compigny relations in another way.
Monsieur de Baby had a sister named Marie-Jacqueline, and in November
1698 she married an Irishman named Captain John Ryan,[153] who was serving
in the French army. Marie-Jacqueline is never again referred to in Nairne's
diary, but her Irish husband is. On 20 July 1701, two weeks after the death
of his son Jean-Baptiste, Nairne noted that 'I gave a certificat for Cap.
Ryan to Mr Caryll to get signed by the K'. This was a *déclaration de noblesse*
recording that 'John Ryan, Captain in Lee's Irish Regiment, is a gentleman
descended from the Ryans of Glanogaha, Tiperrary, a family that has always
been Catholic and loyal'.[154] Then, in February 1704, Nairne noted that he
drew a warrant for Captain Ryan to be appointed a gentleman of the king's
privy chamber.[155] As this was a somewhat unusual appointment, it is probable that it was obtained by Caryll at Nairne's request. No more is known
at present about the Ryans, but according to the parish registers they were
at Saint-Germain in 1710, when Ryan's wife described herself as 'Marie
Jacqueline de Compigny, épouse de Jean de Ryan, colonel d'infanterie' and
signed her name as the 'comtesse de Ryan'.[156]

In addition to his wife's relations in and near Compigny, Nairne also
kept in touch with his own family. One of his cousins, Mary Nairne, was
living at Saint-Germain with her husband, a Jacobite named Cornelius
Collins. The latter was not a salaried servant at the court, nor was he in
receipt of a pension from the king or queen, so he probably worked as

an occasional servant of one of the Jacobite courtiers. Between 1694 and 1699, Mary Collins gave birth to four children, of whom the first two died in childhood.[157] The third child was a girl, named Marie Elisabeth after Nairne's wife who was her godmother,[158] and it was during her short life that Nairne took an active interest in the Collins family.

In April 1700 Nairne noted that he went to visit 'poor Colins and his wife that were sick' and asked Lewis Innes, the queen's almoner, to give them some charity money.[159] Shortly afterwards Collins was arrested and 'put in prison for a false lotry ticket'.[160] The circumstances of this case are unclear, but Nairne immediately did what he could to help his cousin. He 'writt a long letter to Mr Innes about Colins business',[161] and persuaded Caryll to write to the queen.[162] As a result the king and queen intervened to rescue Collins from prison. Nairne noted on 29 May that 'the K and Q stopt on going to mass to order me to desire the Prevost to come to speak to them about Colins after dinner'. The queen then gave Collins twenty *livres* so that 'the poor man should [not] suffer want',[163] to which Caryll added a crown.[164]

Three months later, at the end of September 1700, the four year old Marie-Elisabeth Collins died of smallpox.[165] Nairne responded by sending her father 'half a crown of charity and procurd 2 crowns more for him at Paris from Mr Caryl and Mr In'.[166] Two weeks later he gave Collins another crown,[167] and on a later occasion he recorded that he obtained more charity money from Innes for his cousin Mary Collins.[168] Collins himself died at the Hôpital de la Charité in Saint-Germain at the end of December 1706, when Nairne repeatedly visited him during his last illness,[169] but there are no further references in the diary to Nairne's cousin Mary, who predeceased her husband.[170]

Apart from identifying that one of Nairne's Scottish cousins was also living at Saint-Germain, these details are useful because they provide evidence of Nairne's willingness to help others. There are references in the diary both to his giving charity and to his wife's raising money to help the poor, such as in 1706 when 'my wife began to beg and make a purse for a poor family of Montagu who had their house and cattle all burnt and nothing left them but 6 smal children and what they had on their backs'.[171]

One of Nairne's other cousins, Mary Gordon, had also come to live at Saint-Germain. She was much younger than him and is not mentioned in his diary, but information about her can be gleaned from other sources. Her father was Alexander Gordon, described in the parish records of Saint-Germain as a 'gentilhomme écossais', and her widowed mother Frances was said to have worked as a housekeeper at Saint-Germain since 1692. Her younger sister Isabella was born in 1691,[172] so Mary was possibly born in about 1690. She married the king's barber and surgeon, Gerald Fitzgerald, in 1710 when she was perhaps about twenty.[173] In later years, when both sisters and their younger brother served at the court in Rome, Nairne would be on very good terms with them, but their precise family relationship is unclear.

During the 1690s Nairne kept in contact with the members of his family who had remained in Scotland, either by correspondence or by sending messages via people making clandestine visits to Saint-Germain. For example, he noted on 25 July 1695 that he sent a reply to a letter from his mother Margaret, dated 3 July of that year, and a few months later that he sent a letter to his elder brother Alexander to be taken by Major Buchan.[174] In June 1697, a Jacobite agent named Kelly arrived from Scotland,[175] and Nairne wrote to John Wallace at the Collège des Ecossais 'to tell Kelly to see my brother' when he returned.[176]

The conclusion of the peace treaty at Ryswick later that year made it easier to send letters between France and Scotland, and Nairne took full advantage of this. By then his elder brother Alexander had one son and two daughters (Magdalene and Christian).[177] His younger brother Samuel had three sons and three daughters.[178] Alexander was living with his mother on the family estate at Sandford, whereas Samuel was the Episcopalian minister at Moonzie, a few miles away to the south-west.[179] There is no evidence that Nairne corresponded with Samuel, but there are many references to the letters and messages which he exchanged with his mother and Alexander.

Between January 1698 and March 1702, when war was resumed between France and both England and Scotland, Nairne sent eight letters to his mother and seven to his brother. He also sent one letter to his 'sister', though it is not clear if this really referred to an unnamed sister or to one of his sisters-in-law.

Nairne opened the correspondence with a long letter to his brother in which he told him the number of his own children and suggested that he,

Alexander, by then a widower, might like to send his son to visit France and even live with him and Marie-Elisabeth at Saint-Germain.[180] The offer was not taken up, and in September Nairne was told by a friend arrived from Scotland that his brother had recently re-married.[181] If this was one reason for not sending Alexander's son to be brought up in France, then another was the obvious fact that Nairne's family in Scotland was Episcopalian whereas he himself and his wife were Catholic.

In March 1699, Nairne received two letters, one from his mother, the other from his brother.[182] Although these letters have not survived it seems that the one from his mother contained criticisms of Catholicism. Nairne sent an extract from this letter to his friends at the Collège des Ecossais, and then set about drafting a lengthy reply in which he would refute his mother's arguments. He worked on the letter for nearly two months (April and May) and gave what he had written to be examined by his friends at the college and by Father Bartolomeo Ruga, one of the queen's chaplains.[183] When the letter was finished it ran to twenty-two pages, and was accompanied by a two-page explanatory letter to his brother.[184] Nairne sent it away via London on 3 June.

Margaret Nairne was probably exasperated if not offended by what her son himself described as 'my long letter of controversy to my mother'.[185] In any event she declined to answer it, and it was not until the end of December that she eventually sent a reply. This was not, however, to discuss religion, but rather to convey some very important family news. As Nairne himself put it, his mother's letter gave 'me acct of my brother Sams wife's death, and my nephews death young St foord [*sic*]'.[186] The death of his nephew, Alexander's only son, left Nairne himself (or his son Jean-Baptiste, then Louis) as the heir to the Sandford estate in Fife.

Nairne waited one month after receiving his mother's letter before sending a reply. He noted in his diary on 1 June 1700:

> I sent ... my letter to my mother dated ye 31 May, in answer to hers of Xber condoling wth her and my brothers upon ye death of my neveu and sister in law, and in ye end of ye letter I told her I hopd she would not deprive me of her correspondence for that I resolvd to importune her no more upon the subject of religion since she eluded answering upon that head tho it was she herself yt first put me upon it, wch I thought indeed was an odd way of proceeding in those who were her advisers, and a shame to her ministers to refuse the defy given them by so weak an adversary as I was, shewing plainly in that the distrust they had of their cause.

Although Nairne sent further letters to his mother and brother in 1701 and early 1702[187] their correspondence was then abruptly terminated by the renewal of war.

At some point during 1701, before the war started, the government in Scotland decided to take action against Nairne's family at Sandford. It was well known that David Nairne himself was employed at the exiled Stuart court, which rendered him in their eyes guilty of treason and therefore liable to forfeit any property he had in Scotland. His brother Alexander, who had accepted a captain's commission from James II in 1692,[188] was probably known to be a Jacobite, and some of his correspondence might have been intercepted. For whatever specific reason, the Scottish privy council issued a warrant on 24 June 'giving to Capt. James Coult, in the Castle of Edinburgh, the lands of ... Sandford, and of Wormett ... in the sheriffdom of Fife'.[189] Whether or not this warrant was actually acted upon remains unclear, but if it was then Nairne's brother, his nieces and his mother would have been forced to leave their family home.

In July 1703, Nairne's niece Magdalene, the elder daughter of his brother Alexander, married Patrick Gordon of Myrinton, with whom she would have one son and one daughter.[190] It is unlikely that he (Nairne) was made aware of this at the time, but this marriage resulted in an appeal to the privy council which then reversed its earlier decision. On 2 November 1703, a new warrant was issued granting the 'lands and barony of Sandfuird, of Innerdovat, Langside and Easter Kinsleiff ... to Patrick Gordon of Myrinton and his heirs'.[191] Thus the family property was secured in the possession of Alexander Nairne's son-in-law.

Two and a half years later, in May 1706, Lewis Innes told Nairne that news had been received at the college that Alexander had died.[192] The death of his elder brother, following that of his nephew a few years earlier, left David Nairne as the legitimate owner of the estate at Sandford. His family continued to live there and manage the estate for the time being, and there does not appear to have been any conflict between Nairne himself and his niece Magdalene or her husband over the real ownership of the property. But his position at the exiled court was now changed. For the first time, he had a personal stake in helping secure the restoration of King James.

Nairne, however, did not want the estate at Sandford for himself, but rather for his son Louis, particularly as the nine-year lease on the estates at Compigny would expire in 1708 and he and his wife could expect to live there after a restoration. By the autumn of 1707, plans were being made for a French fleet to carry James III and a small army to Scotland. Nairne was to accompany the king, as he would have in 1692 and 1696, so once again he was obliged to consider his future – to remain with the king in Scotland or England, or to return to France. As evidence that the latter was still the more likely, we find in his diary that, having received the *ordonnance* for his French pension as usual at the end of August 1707,[193] he took a letter of recommendation signed by Lord Middleton to the war secretariat at Versailles asking for an augmentation.[149] Nairne did not record what happened, and it is very unlikely that he obtained what he wanted. But there seems no reason to doubt that in 1708, as in 1692 and 1696, he continued to regard himself as primarily an ex-patriate, hoping to be able to live comfortably in France on his French income.

Endnotes

1. Antoine de Compigny (d. 1696) and his son Michel (1673–1694). See p. 30, note 55; and Compigny, *Au Déclin de l'Ancien Régime*, pp. 15–16.
2. See above, p. 26.
3. *Inscriptions de l'Ancien Diocèse de Sens*, vol. 2, pp. 169–76 for the Compigny family.
4. His parents married in July 1601, and his mother died in 1641. Assuming that his mother was no younger than eighteen in 1601, and that she experienced the menopause at the usual time, then Louis de Compigny was probably born no later than the 1620s, possibly well before that (Compigny, Alfred de, *Autour d'un Grenier à Sel* (Paris, 1924), p. 163; Morenas, H. J. de, *Grand Armorial de France* (5 vols, Paris, 1935), vol. 3, p. xx).
5. Diary, 9 June 1698.
6. Nairne's last entry in his diary for 1692 is 17 June, except for an isolated entry on 27 August: 'My wife went to Compigny and stayd till ye 13 Sep.' The marriage possibly took place immediately before or after that visit.

7. *Inscriptions de l'Ancien Diocèse de Sens*, vol. 2, pp. 169–76.

8. Nairne was not keeping his diary in June 1693, but he *was* throughout 1695.

9. Diary, 19, 27 October, 1 November 1694, 4, 11 May 1695.

10. Diary, 2 June 1695. Nairne wrote again to M. de Baby on 22 July and 10 October 1695.

11. This is a reference to the feudal practice of summoning the vassals of the King of France to perform military service, known as the *arrière-ban*. See Diary, May 1693, March and May 1695, February 1696 and May 1697. Nairne was not keeping his diary in the spring of 1694.

12. Diary, 15 June 1697.

13. Diary, 16, 17 November, 13 December 1696.

14. Diary. He died on 18 February 1698, and Nairne received the news four days later. M. de Baby visited the Nairnes shortly afterwards, from 2 to 5 March.

15. Diary, 12 March 1698: 'I had a letter from Mr Ripar telling me yt Mr de Compigny had left [only] two sons.'

16. Diary, 29 April 1698. She was accompanied by her two older children, Jean and Françoise, leaving Jean-Baptiste behind at Saint-Germain.

17. M. de Ripar, or Ripart, was a *notaire* at Bray, and was a partner of M. Fortier, both of whom worked for Madame de Compigny.

18. Diary, 9 June 1698.

19. Nairne's *notaires* were M. Chennant and M. L'Enfant. The *avocats* were M. Doriaux and M. Dinet. It was the latter who told Nairne that his argument 'was not good' (Diary, 8 September 1698).

20. Diary, 20 November 1698.

21. Diary, 11 January to 4 February 1699.

22. Diary, 15 May 1698.

23. Nairne had corresponded regularly with the *maréchal de* Tessé in 1695 and 1696. When he met him at Fontainebleau in 1703 he noted that Tessé 'spoke very kindly to me as being his old acquaintance and correspond.t' (Diary, 11 October 1703).

24. Diary, 5 August 1698.

25. Diary, 8 August 1698.

26. Diary, 9 August 1698.

27. Diary, 1 June, 13 July 1699.

28. Diary, 15 July 1699.

29. Then as now the vintage was very dependent on the weather. Nairne noted two days earlier that 'ther fell a violent hail wch did at least a third of a loss to ye vintage of Compigny' (Diary, 24 September 1699).

30. Diary, 1 to 18 October 1699.

31. Diary, 18 October 1699. A muid is a large barrel with a capacity of 159 gallons or 600 litres. Among the other goods were the 'Compigny books' that he had

wanted (Diary, 24 August 1699). Nairne also brought some partridges which
he presented to Caryll (Diary, 27 October 1699). In the spring he had received
some hares sent to him from Compigny (Diary, 5, 7, 18 May 1699).

32. Diary, 26 October 1700.

33. Diary, 27 October 1699.

34. See p. 52.

35. See p. 63.

36. See p. 70.

37. Nairne did not record whether or not his wife breastfed Jean in 1692 or Françoise
in 1694. Jean-Baptiste was perhaps the first to have a wet nurse. Nairne recorded
that the nurse was changed on 6 September 1696, and that the child was weaned
on 4 June 1697 when he was just over thirteen months old.

38. Diary, 13 March 1698.

39. Diary, 14 March 1698.

40. Nairne noted that 'he had allways had a vomiting wch was thought to have been
at last ye cause of his death (Diary, 15 March 1698).

41. Diary, 9 January 1699.

42. Diary, 11 January 1699.

43. Diary, 11 January 1699.

44. Nairne took his son Jean-Baptiste with him, and recorded that the latter had a
serious accident when mounting the *coche* in Paris: 'My sons fingers hurt by ye
rope that drew ye locke, and he escapd narrowly being killd or lamd at least of a
hand, but one Me Judin gave me plaisters wch curd his fingers in a months time'
(Diary, 23 September 1699).

45. Diary, 25 September 1700, 12 February 1701. He was weaned when he was thirteen and a half months old.

46. Diary, 15 to 17 January 1700.

47. Diary, 18 January 1700.

48. Diary, 18 January 1700. Nairne contracted smallpox in 1712: see p. 189 and
p. 212, note 300.

49. Diary, 21 September 1700.

50. No godfather is mentioned either in Nairne's diary or in the Saint-Germain
parish registers (Lart, C. E., *The Paerochial Records of Saint-Germain-en-Laye:
Jacobite Extracts* (2 vols, London, 1910, 1912), vol. 1, p. 107). Nairne recorded that
his wife was churched on 30 January 1701, fifteen days after giving birth, and that
she 'began to bath' four months later, on 28 May.

51. Apart from Caryll and Innes, Marie-Elisabeth particularly visited the queen's
ladies in their apartments in the château, including Lady Perth, Mary Stafford,
Lady Almond, Lady Sophia Bulkeley, Lady Middleton, the Duchess of Berwick
and the Duchess of Albemarle (Diary, 26 December 1696, 24 May, 12 July, 20

December 1699, 25 April 1700, 10 April 1701). To quote just one example, 'I carryd my wife to visite Mr Caryl, Mr Inese, Me d'Almond, My La. Perth and Lady Buckly' (8 November 1699). Marie-Elisabeth also attended the royal family's dinners and suppers. On 16 May 1700, for example, 'my wife went wth her children to the K and Qs dinner. The Q commended her children, and asked severall questions about her family, and spoke very kindly to her.' On 7 August 1701, 'my wife and daughter went to ye Ks dinner. Ye Q gave a platefull of sweet-meats to my daughter.'

52. Diary, 4, 14, 17, 23 June, 5 July, 26 August, 24 September, 19, 25 November, 3, 18 December 1698.

53. Diary, 25, 28 November 1698.

54. Diary, 9, 17 February, 13, 14, 18 March, 2, 23 April 1699. He bought further items in 1700 and 1702: 25 May, 22 June 1700, 30 September 1702). On 13 November 1699, 'Mr Caryl gave me a present for my wife of a silver sugar box wth Ld Dumbartons arms.'

55. Diary, 13 December 1698.

56. Diary, 17, 18, 24 December 1698, 30 July 1701, 20 September, 15, 27 November 1702. The portrait of the Prince of Wales is not itself mentioned in Nairne's diary, but he noted on 23 November 1699 that he 'bought a frame for ye Prince's picture'. Given the date it was probably painted by François de Troy (Corp, *A Court in Exile*, p. 186; Corp, *The King over the Water*, p. 40).

57. Diary, 17 November, 4, 9, 16, 22 December 1699, 4, 12, 14 15, 16 January 1700.

58. Diary, 13, 15 February, 19 May, 20 October, 4, 15 November 1700.

59. Diary, 16 February 1700.

60. Diary, 22 February, 15, 16 December 1701, 1 January, 20 November 1702. Verneuil, Triel and Conflans are on the river Seine, north-west and north of Saint-Germain-en-Laye. In 1705 he bought his wine from Héricy, also on the river Seine, but north-east of Fontainebleau (Diary, 7 September 1705).

61. Diary, 19 August 1698, 18 November 1702.

62. Diary, 22 September 1695, 27 June, 5 July, 22 August 1698, 27 February 1701, 28 November 1702.

63. Diary, 12 August 1698. The man was Jacques Gourlade, described several times in the parish registers as 'officier de la bouche du Roi' de France. In the following year Nairne made his own *ratafiat* (Diary, 9 September 1699).

64. Diary, 1, 11 August 1699, 9 October 1702. Nairne also made his own *confitures* (Diary, 24 July 1699).

65. Diary, 17, 18, 19, 20, 21 September 1704, 10 January 1705.

66. Diary, 23 April 1697.

67. Diary, 9 April, 11 June 1698, 9 July 1702.

68. Diary, 3 September 1698, 18 February, 18 July 1700.

69. Diary, 1 July, 27, 28, 29 August 1699. Four years later he read *L'Histoire du Cardinal Ximenes* in two volumes (Paris, 1693) by Esprit Fléchier, the Bishop of Nîmes (Diary, 25 June 1703).

70. Diary, 28 April, 5, 12 May, 11 August 1697, 20 June 1698.

71. Diary, 22 November 1698, 28 May, 9 June 1700, 6 February, 18 June 1701.

72. Diary, 19 November 1696.

73. Diary, 7, 11, 22, 26 June 1697.

74. Diary, 24, 26 October 1696, 23 December 1697, 29 January 1698.

75. Diary, 15, 16 October 1696, 16 June 1697.

76. During the 1690s, Nairne also went to mass and confession at the Augustinian monastery built in a clearing in the forest of Saint-Germain and known as *Les Loges*. It was dedicated to Saint-Fiacre, and the *curé* of Saint-Germain said mass there every year on Saint-Fiacre's day (31 August). Nairne attended the service in 1697, 1698 and 1699, but thereafter there are no references in his diary to the monastery. For the *Loges*, see Forteau-Venet, Nathalie and Fournel, Isabelle, *Saint-Germain-en-Laye: Histoire d'un millénaire* (Saint-Germain-en-Laye, 2004), pp. 72, 74.

77. The establishment of the Confraternity of the 'Bona Morte' at Saint-Germain was probably inspired by the arrival of a new *curé* in the parish church. The old *curé* (François Converset) died on 29 April 1698. His successor (Jean-François de Benoist de Chasel) took possession of the parish on 21 May, and the Confraternity was established two days later (Diary). For the list of the *curés*, see the manuscript 'Martyrologe de l'Eglise Royalle et paroissiale de St Germain en Laye', pp. 43–8, written by Jean Antoine and still preserved in the parish church. For the Confraternity of the 'Bona Mors' see also the appendix to this chapter.

78. See pp. 117–19.

79. Diary, 23 July 1702.

80. Diary, 3, 5, 8, 17, 24 September, 1, 8, 15 October 1702, and many references thereafter.

81. Prone was an exhortation or homily read out or delivered in church. Vespers was the sung evening office. *Salut*, short for *Domine, salvum fac regem* (God save the King), was a motet sung in honour of the King of France at the end of each day in the parish church and chapel royal at Saint-Germain, and elsewhere. The music would have been by Lully, Charpentier, Delalande, Couperin or Marais. There are nine settings of the motet by Delalande and twenty-four by Charpentier. The other three composers set the motet once each.

82. Compline was the last office of the day. *Matines* was the first office of the day, performed in the middle of the night or before sunrise. The *leçons de ténèbres* were a setting of the lamentations of Jeremiah, performed in the afternoon or evening

of the Wednesdays, Thursdays and Fridays of Holy Week, in which candles lit at the beginning of the service were gradually extinguished one by one in memory of the darkness of the crucifixion. The music would have been by Charpentier (who set the *leçons* several times), Delalande or Couperin (who both set them once each).

83. Diary, 7–12 April 1700, 23–28 March 1701, 12–17 April 1702, 4–9 April 1703, 19–24 March 1704, 8–13 April 1705, 31 March to 5 April 1706, 20–25 April 1707.

84. James Nihill was the king's *avocat*, having been appointed Solicitor to the Commissioner of the Revenue in 1689. Colonel Brown commanded the Scots company formed at Saint-Germain in 1692 by a group of Scottish officers and cadets (Ruvigny, *The Jacobite Peerage*, pp. 240, 246).

85. Diary, 5 February 1698. The food was ordered from Henry Parry, the Clerk of the King's Kitchen. See Diary, Saturday 1 February 1698: 'I met at Mr Parys chamber in ye morning, and wee orderd a supper for wedensd. following.'

86. Diary, 20 August 1702. John Caryll was the nephew of the secretary of state; George Waters was an Irish banker; Marco Antonio Galli, a Jesuit, was the queen's confessor.

87. For example, Diary, 17 February 1700: 'I had Mr Nihell and his wife to dinner, after wch we playd at umber, and Mrs Nihell wonn 2 Crowns for her and me from Mr Mon. and Coll. Brown, then wee suppd wee were 8 at table, viz. ye fores.d persons wth Mrs Brown, Mr Demster and my wife, it cost me in all about 20#.'

88. Diary, 8 January 1704.

89. The English included Dr Lawrence Wood and an apothecary named George Middleton; the Irish included Sir Randal MacDonnell (groom of the bedchamber) and Father Nicholas Farelly; and the Scots included Captain James Murray (gentleman usher of the king's privy chamber) and Sir John Forester (a colonel in the Irish brigade).

90. Nairne invited '2 Irish priests of the parish church' (26 April 1701), various unnamed priests (1 July 1706, 12 May 1707), his confessor (12 February, 5 September 1703, 22 October 1704), and both Geoghagan and the *vicaire* (1 September 1705, 16 February, 7 March, 28 December 1706, 20 July 1707), but never the *curé*.

91. Joseph Du Mont was the king's kettledrummer.

92. For example, Diary, 7, 16 February 1706.

93. Diary, 3 March 1707.

94. Beaussant, P., *François Couperin* (Paris, 1980), p. 148; Tunley, D., *Couperin* (London, 1982), pp. 41–2.

95. Diary, 29 August 1707. See also 29 July 1707: 'Mlle Rebel dind wth us.' (Mlle Rebel was a daughter of the composer Jean-Ferry Rebel and niece of Michel-Richard Delalande).

96. Diary, 30 September to 27 October 1698.

97. Diary, 25 September 1698.
98. Diary, 23 September 1699.
99. Diary, 19, 20, 21 October 1699.
100. Diary, 23 September 1698.
101. Diary, 1–18 October 1699.
102. Diary, 23, 27, 28 May 1701.
103. Diary, 29 May 1701.
104. Diary, 30 May, 1 June 1701.
105. Diary, 7 June 1701.
106. Dr Lawrence Wood and Dr Calahan Garwan were later given warrants to be James III's physicians in ordinary (Ruvigny, *The Jacobite Peerage*, p. 222). Sir William Waldegrave died on 8 July 1701 (Diary).
107. The French surgeon was Dr Caron; the Jacobite apothecary was Mr Paply.
108. Diary, 14 to 21 June 1701.
109. Diary, 23 to 27 June 1701.
110. Diary, 28 June 1701.
111. Diary, 29 June 1701.
112. Diary, 30 June 1701.
113. Diary, 1 to 4 July 1701.
114. Diary, 3 July 1701.
115. Diary, 23, 24 June, 2 July 1701.
116. Diary, 4 July 1701.
117. Diary, 6 July 1701: 'Sr Mungo Muray, Mr Nevill, Mr Nihil and Macarty 4 children about his age carrying ye 4 corners of ye cloth, ye Curet and all ye parish priests attending ye convoy wth some few of our friends. I had his head and belly opend by Mr Beaulieu in presence of Dr Garwan and Dr Wood, who found all his entralls as well as his head perfectly sound and wthout appearance of any thing yt could have been ye cause of his distemper and death unless it was that they found a little more blood and water in the brain than commonly ther uses to be; his buriall cost 29# 10s.' (François de Gassis de Beaulieu was the king's principal surgeon).
118. Diary, 8 July 1701. She was given 'a purge of rubarbe in pouder, and then ye vin emetick, and at night a potion cordial', and recovered after a few days.
119. Diary, 8 June 1702.
120. Diary, 18 January 1703.
121. Diary, 11 February 1704. Antoine Hardelet was a member of the 'petits violons' of the King of France at Versailles, but he lived in the rue de la Salle at Saint-Germain-en-Laye (Corp, 'The Musical Manuscripts of "Copiste Z"', p. 52).
122. Diary, 14, 15, 16, 17, 18 June 1704. For this convent, and the Jacobite families which patronized it, see Corp, *A Court in Exile*, p. 149.

123. Diary, 22 August, 11 December 1704.
124. She came home for two and a half months in the summer of 1705, when her parents bought her a new damask gown and various other clothes (Diary, 28 June, 7 July, 18 September 1705), and again at the end of 1706 and during the summer of 1707, but otherwise she seems to have remained permanently at the convent (Diary, 20 November 1706, 28 June, 11 July 1707).
125. Diary, 12 June 1705.
126. Diary, 8 May 1707.
127. Diary, 28 June 1707.
128. Marie-Elisabeth took Françoise to 'make her court' to the princess on several occasions (Diary, 9, 28 October 1701, 28 June 1702, 21 June 1703, 28 June 1705, 28 June 1707).
129. In August 1702, Nairne and his wife took Louis, then two and a half years old and suffering from an inflammation of his neck, to Paris to see a woman named Mlle de Veaux, who sold them 'a little pot of ointment' to be applied to his body as a 'plaister'. However they also took Louis 'to another surgeon Mr Arnauld' who told them that the boy 'had nothing but serosités' [*sic*: serositis] and forbad them 'to make use of Mlle de Veaux plaister'. Arnauld then saw Louis a second time and changed his diagnosis: he 'confirmd us yt his disease was only scrofulé and yt he wanted only to be purgd' (Diary, 27, 28, 29, 30 August 1702). Rather surprisingly there is no mention in Nairne's diary of his son being then touched by the king for scrofula, perhaps because James III, then only fourteen years old, had not yet started the practice of touching for the King's Evil (scrofula). Nairne noted that he took his son Louis to see Arnauld again in both 1704 and 1705 (Diary, 14 June 1704, 29 September, 10 November 1705), when the king was sixteen and seventeen years old. Nairne's son Jean-Baptiste, by contrast, *had* been touched by James II for the King's Evil (Diary, 5 January 1698).
130. Diary, 18, 19, 20 August, 14 October 1706.
131. Diary, 3 February 1706. This may be contrasted with the experience of Jean-Baptiste who had been sent to school when he was only four and a half (Diary, 4 January 1701).
132. Diary, 30, 31 August, 1 September, 14 October 1706.
133. Diary, 16 April 1706: 'I finishd the faire copie of my Testament wch I had writt for the first time in ye year 1702 having begun it a little after the grand Jubilé wch was closd Sunday ye 28 May.'
134. Diary, 14 May 1706.
135. Diary, 16 January 1708: 'This day I signed my testament in presence of Mr Geoghagan.' Thomas Geoghagan was an Irish priest employed at the parish church of Saint-Germain-en-Laye.

136. Diary, 22 December 1707: 'Mr Whiteford writt me word yt he had that morning carryd ye mony to Ledegive Notary and been with him at the Tresor and that he had consumated ye business.' Nairne paid for the *rentes* by taking an advance on his salary of 600 *livres* (Diary, 13 December 1707).

137. His tailor was called L'Epine. See Diary, 28 November 1697, 30 August 1698, 18 September, 6 November 1699, 14 September 1702, 15 September 1703, 17 September 1704.

138. Diary, 25 January 1697, 6 January 1702. The first wig cost 52 *livres*, and the second cost 54 *livres*.

139. Diary, 23 March 1699.

140. Diary, 19, 24, 29 October 1702.

141. Diary, 6 December 1702.

142. The portrait of Marie-Elisabeth was painted in Paris by François de Troy in 1700. (It measures 97 × 62.5 cm). As the portrait is not mentioned in his diary, it must have been painted when Nairne was at Dunkirk from 27 July to 19 August. Perhaps it was commissioned by Caryll to thank Nairne for accompanying his nephew to the coast.

143. For example, there was a nurse called Madelon from Bray (12, 22 September 1699, 20 March 1700), and a maid called Babé from Compigny who died in November 1701 (13, 14, 15, 16, 21 November, 19 December 1701). See also 20 November 1702, 6 March 1703, 20 July, 17 December 1704.

144. Marie-Elisabeth stayed at Compigny with Françoise and Louis during September, October and November 1702, leaving Marie behind with her wet nurse (Diary, 31 August, 17 September, 5 December 1702); and again with all her three children from August to December 1704 (22 August, 11 December 1704). She went to Compigny again with the three children in August 1707 and remained there with them until April 1708 (Diary, 24 August 1707, 25 April 1708).

145. Nairne was at Compigny from 6 to 14 October 1704, and from 16 to 17 October 1707.

146. Nairne wrote to Jossier twenty-one times between 13 August 1694 and 11 February 1701, with a further three letters in 1706–7. Jossier was living at Mauberge in Flanders, and in 1695 he sent Nairne useful information concerning the siege of Namur (Diary, seven letters, 28 August to 9 September 1695).

147. Mlle Fabre seems to have been a relation of the Fleurigny family and lived at Provins as well as in Paris. Nairne and his wife saw her at Compigny and Paris, and she visited them at Saint-Germain in 1699, 1703 and 1706 (Diary, 20–21 April 1699, 30 May to 1 June 1703, 5–11 August 1706).

148. See above, p. 16. Nairne's diary records contact with Mlle de Placé in 1702 (27 April, 4 and 7 June).

149. Diary, 25–27 March 1703, 19–24 December 1704.
150. Diary, 5 January, 14 April 1703, 19, 23 January, 3 September 1706, 30 July, 17 August 1707.
151. Diary, 8, 17 December 1707. On 17 October Nairne noted that 'my wife and daughter went to Nogent to speak to the Intendant', and it was when that failed that he offered to prepare the *placet* to be given to King Louis XIV. Marie-Elisabeth had previously made the same request to the *intendant* in 1698 (Diary, 30 September to 27 October 1698).
152. Diary, 3, 5, 7, 12, 16, 20 November 1706, 5 March, 25 April, 26 October 1707.
153. Nairne noted on 24 November 1698 that 'Marie was maried'.
154. Ruvigny, *The Jacobite Peerage*, p. 200.
155. Diary, 17 February 1704.
156. Lart, *Jacobite Extracts*, vol. 2, p. 97, 12 February 1710. Ryan signed the parish register on 30 May 1713 (ibid. p. 16).
157. Lart, *Jacobite Extracts*, vol. 1, pp. 59–60.
158. Diary, 18 August 1696; Lart, *Jacobite Extracts*, vol. 1, p. 60. The godfather was Francesco Riva, the master of the queen's robes, who might perhaps have employed Collins or his wife as a servant.
159. Diary, 23 April 1700.
160. Diary, 17 May 1700.
161. Diary, 19 May 1700.
162. Diary, 20 May 1700.
163. Diary, 21 June 1700.
164. Diary, 20 June 1700.
165. She died on 30 September 1700 (Diary). Because she died somewhere else, probably in Paris, her death was not recorded in the Saint-Germain parish register.
166. Diary, 30 September 1700.
167. Diary, 12 October 1700.
168. Diary, 4 October 1700.
169. 19 to 22, 31 December 1706.
170. When he died Collins was described as 'veuf' (Lart, *Jacobite Extracts*, vol. 2, p. 50).
171. Diary, 19 March 1706. To take another example, on 9 January 1707, a few days after the death of Cornelius Collins, 'my wife and daughter' raised money 'in ye parish for the sick of ye charity'.
172. Hooke, Nathaniel, *Correspondance, 1703–1707*, ed. W. D. Macray (2 vols, Roxburgh Club, 1870), vol. 2, p. 534, memorandum by Father Connell, 22 December 1707: 'Isabelle Gordon, of the age of sixteen years, desires a pass from Ireland, to come here to her mother, where she is these fifteen years a housekeeper; the

pass must be in form for six months; 'tis usual in such passes to have leave for a governant and a footman.'

173. Lart, *Jacobite Extracts*, vol. 2, p. 10, 6 November 1710. The marriage was witnessed by David Nairne and Father Connell.

174. Diary, 9 November 1695. Major James Buchan was a Scottish officer who travelled secretly between Saint-Germain and Scotland.

175. Diary, 28 June 1697.

176. Diary, 24 July 1697.

177. Alexander Nairne had married Elizabeth Hay (daughter of Peter Hay of Naughton) on 1 June 1678. Naughton (or Norton) is in Fife, very close to Sandford. (These and other details concerning Nairne's family in Scotland are taken from Stirnet, the genealogical internet site).

178. Samuel Nairne had married Margaret Bruce (daughter of Andrew Bruce of Earlshall Castle, Leuchars, Fife). Earlshall Castle is a few miles to the south-east of Sandford.

179. He was subsequently the Episcopalian minister at Errol in the Carse of Gowrie, six miles east of Perth, and on the opposite side of the Firth of Tay.

180. Diary, 21 January 1698.

181. He married Elizabeth Hamilton (daughter of Gavin Hamilton of Reploch, now part of Stirling) on 27 April 1698.

182. Diary, 29 March 1699.

183. Diary, 31 March, 29 April, 20, 22, 23, 27, 28 May, 2 June 1699.

184. Diary, 2 June 1699. Nairne's letter to his mother was dated 20 May and the one to his brother 28 May.

185. Diary, 31 August 1699.

186. Diary, 20 April 1700.

187. Diary, 29 March, 11 June, 16 July 1701, 4 January 1702.

188. See p. 22.

189. *CSPD: William III, 1700–1702*, p. 379. Wormit is adjacent to Sandford, to the west.

190. They married on 19 July 1703. It was perhaps in anticipation of this that Nairne sent a letter via a secret agent to his brother Alexander on 25 April 1703.

191. *CSPD: Queen Anne, 1703–1704*, p. 433. Inverdovat is adjacent to Sandford, to the north-east. Easter Kinsleith is a few miles to the south-west, beside Moonzie. Langside is further south, near Kennoway and the Firth of Forth.

192. Diary, 21, 23 May 1706. This was one month after Nairne had finished his testament in April 1706, and might explain why he did not have it signed and witnessed until January 1708 (see above, notes 133–5).

193. Diary, 28 August 1707.

194. Diary, 3 October 1707.

Appendix to Chapter 3
Nairne's Commitment as a Member of the Confraternity of the 'Bona Morte' or Happy Death

According to Ralph Benet Weldon, a monk at the English Benedictine convent in Paris, membership of the confraternity involved attendance at a daily service, which included a *Stabat Mater dolorosa* 'sung in musick'. In the Chapel Royal at Saint-Germain 'the hour was usually three in ye afternoon'; elsewhere it was often at four o'clock in the afternoon. At Saint-Germain it involved 'the Devotion of ye king every Friday in ye afternoon before ye Most Holy Sacrament of ye Altar exposed in his Chapel by his Chaplains in order to obtain a happy Death'.[1]

When Nairne had his name 'enterd into ye Catalogue of ye Confraternity by ye Father Director' he committed himself to obeying the 'Rules to be observed by those who shall desire to joyn in this H. Exercise of Devotion to ye Passion of our Lord for obtaining a Happy Death'. There were five 'Directions' which he resolved 'to perform':

> They are to keep by 'em a Picture or Image of our Savior Crucified, and of his B. Mother in her Agony of Grief; so to raise frequent and lively representations in yr minds of his bitter Passion and Death, whereby they may more sensibly aprehend ye enormity of sin, ye Ransom whereof did cost so dear, and also ye infinity of his mercy in ye work of our redemption, and let ym say every day 3 Paters and Aves in Memory of ye 3 hours in wch our B. Saviour hung upon ye Cross, to ye intention of obtaining for themselves and all those of ye Confraternity a happy Death.
>
> With ye same Intention, and in honor of ye sacred Pains and Death of our Lord they must daily assist at ye H. Sacrifice of ye Masse, and in case of any lawful impedim.t, let them at least say 5 Paters and Aves to ye Intention above named.
>
> They are to frequent ye holy Sacraments of Confession and Communion at least once a month; It were very commendable to do it oftner, but with ye Advice of their Spiritual Directors.
>
> 'Every Friday they must be present at this pious Exercise, wch will be performed in ye Chapel from Four till Five in the Afternoon; But upon any lawful hinderance,

let 'em say in private at yr leasure, ye Prayers above set down, or at least let 'em say 5 Paters and Aves with Devotion, and to ye same Intention already specified.

'They must excite yr Domesticks, and those in whom they have any Interest to this pious and wholesome Exercise, and to a tender affection towards our Crucified Lord, and his most holy, and most sorrowful Mother.[2]

These were the rules by which Nairne lived his daily life.

Endnotes to the Appendix

1. BL. Add MSS 10118, R. B. Weldon, 'Collections for a Life of James II', p. 716.
2. Ibid. pp. 722–3.

CHAPTER 4

Clerk of the King's Council and Under-Secretary at Saint-Germain, 1701–1713

For six and a half years, from the accession of James III in September 1701 until the spring of 1708, when the French attempted to invade Scotland, Nairne consolidated and strengthened his position at the exiled court. In 1701 he was appointed clerk of the new royal council. In 1703 he was appointed chief clerk to Lord Middleton while still working for Lord Caryll, thus becoming under-secretary of state. And in 1706 he was retained as clerk of the king's council when James III achieved his majority. Caryll, who had been born in 1625, celebrated his eightieth birthday in 1705 and gradually delegated more work to Nairne, who meanwhile established an excellent working relationship with Middleton. By 1708, as a result of his hard work and unquestioned loyalty, Nairne had emerged as one of the most important and influential members of the exiled court.

Under the terms of James II's will, Queen Mary was declared the guardian of her thirteen-year-old son James III. She was not to be regent, so she presided over what was referred to as the new king's council. The position of clerk of the council was to be given either to Caryll's chief clerk (Nairne) or to Middleton's chief clerk (Lindsay). On 23 September, one week after the late king's death, Nairne noted that 'after dinner Mr Sec.y told me he had spoke to ye Q to have me to be Clerk of the Kings Councill, and yt the Queen had granted it'. On the following day 'ther was a Councill held at night at 6 a clock in the Queen's Chamber':

> My Ld Perth was declard Duke of Perth in Scotld, My Ld Middleton E. of Monmouth and Mid in Engld, and Mr Secretary Lord Caryll of Dunford. The Queen was pleasd likewise to declare me Clark of the Kings Councill.

Lord Middleton, who continued to use his Scottish title, congratulated Nairne on his appointment[1] and began to work with him in drafting the minutes of each meeting.[2] One consequence of his new appointment was that the two augmentations to Nairne's salary which had been granted by James II were now placed formally 'upon ye Qs establishment'.[3] His salary remained at 89*l* 7*s* 6*d* each month, but his combined pensions were now guaranteed to bring him the additional 83*l* 13*s* 3*d*, thus giving him a combined monthly income of 173*l* 0*s* 9*d*.[4]

Immediately after his appointment as clerk of the king's council Queen Mary entrusted Nairne with the management of James II's posthumous reputation, though under the general supervision of Lord Caryll and responsible to herself. Nairne had already made considerable progress in the organization of the king's papers, but there was still a great deal of work to be done. He had sent many documents to the Abbaye de La Trappe and to the Collège des Ecossais in Paris for safekeeping, he had written an abstract of some of their contents, he had made a copy of the king's advice 'For my Son the Prince of Wales', and he had written a lengthy (but incomplete) biography of the king up to the year 1677, based on James II's memoirs and other papers. In effect he now became James's literary executor.

His first task was to prepare a short biography of the king which would concentrate on the latter's final years, and which could be published in the near future – unlike the full-length work which could not be finished for a long time. On 27 September, he wrote 'an abregé of ye K's life in 4 sheets in folio', on both sides of the paper and in very small handwriting. He then asked Father Sanders, James II's confessor, to give him a 'paper concerning ye K's christian life and death' which he could use to expand his 'abrégé'.[5] He discussed it with Lord Caryll and produced the new short biography, which he finished on 11 January 1702. There then followed a series of meetings in March with Lord Caryll, Lord Middleton, Father Sanders and Lewis Innes, after which Nairne amended his work in the light of their suggestions.[6]

For political reasons, the new book needed to be published under a well-known name, because Nairne's was unknown and would carry no weight. Nairne therefore translated his book into French[7] and sent it to Père François Bretonneau, a Jesuit celebrated for the quality of his sermons, who agreed to pretend to be its author.[8] The final drafting sessions took place in July. Nairne noted:

> I read ye Life and sentiments of ye late King in presence of My Ld Middleton and My Ld Caryl and writt down some few objections of My Ld Mid wch were shewn to ye Q. This was done at 3 severall sittings, in three days.[9]

The book was eventually published in the summer of 1703 and entitled *Abrégé de la vie de Jacques II ... tiré d'un écris anglois du R. P. François Sanders ... Confesseur de S. M.*[10] This, the first posthumous biography of James II, may now be seen to have been written by Nairne, who wrote the first part of the king's *Life*, rather than Bretonneau.

The writing of Nairne's biography of James II was facilitated by the discovery in the late king's closet of his papers of devotion.[11] Nairne began to copy them on 12 October and finished on 5 November:

> I finished ye collection of ye K's papers of devotion wch I had copied out of ye originals, in all 35 pages, and made a Table of ye contents of them.

Other papers were then discovered, some of which were written in French, so Nairne made two complete sets by translating the English ones into French and the French ones into English.[12] He gave each paper a title,[13] and wrote a preface to introduce the entire collection.[14] In July 1702, he 'writt a sheet of ye K's sentiments wch were sent to Rome writt in 4 sheets as ye life was'.[15] The papers including Nairne's English translation were then published in London as *The Pious Sentiments of the Late King James II of Blessed Memory upon Divers Subjects of Piety.*[16] Thus Nairne was the editor of the king's papers of devotion as well as his first biographer.

In addition to the papers of devotion, Nairne also used the advice which James II had given to the Prince of Wales (now James III) in 1692. He finished a new copy on 19 December 1701, 'being 46 pages in folio', and on the following day 'writt with My Lord [Caryll] an extract' for the guidance of the new king.[17] He also used James II's correspondence with Rancé, which had been returned to the queen mother by the present abbé de La Trappe.[18] On 10 January 1702, Nairne noted that Lord Caryll 'gave me ye Ks letters to ye Ab of La Trappe, to copie out wth ye Abots answers'. Three days later he added:

> My Ld ... told me ye Q was pressd to have them so I went on with them so assiduously yt I finishd them the Thursday night following [19 January] and deliverd them

bound up together the next morning [20 January]. There was 240 pages in little 4°
wch I writt in between 5 and 6 days time.

Shortly after the publication of the biography Nairne gathered together
all the papers he had used[19] and sent them to be added to the collection
of James II's papers at the Collège des Ecossais in Paris. He noted on 12
December 1703 that 'I seald the 2 inventorys of papers of the late Ks deposited in the Scotch College'.

Nairne was also involved in producing the inventory of James II's personal possessions. The original draft of 'ye Inventory of ye late Ks goods'
was produced in May 1703 and given to Nairne 'to write out fair by the Q's
order',[20] which he did on 1 and 2 June. He was then asked to check all the
contents of the inventory[21] and produce two final copies, both of which
were attached to copies of James II's testament,[22] and signed and dated
22 July 'in ye Ks presence by ye Q D.Perth EM Ld C and Mr Power'. On
the following day, he 'put ye Qs signet to ye 2 Inventorys'.[23] When James
III came of age three years later, these documents were required to bring
the queen's guardianship formally to a conclusion. Nairne recorded on
26 July 1706:

> I was calld for the 1st time to [the King's] Council, where I read the Inventory of
> the late kings effects annexed to his Will, and ye K having declard in Council that
> he was satisfied of all the articles containd therein, and yt he approvd everything
> the Q. had done relating thereunto, his Ma: wth advice of his Council orderd that
> a discharge should be given to the Q. in due forme of all the effects mentiond in ye
> sd Inventory, and I had orders to appoint Mr Power his Ma: Council at law to draw
> the discharge, and to communicate the Inventory to him for that effect if need was.[24]

There was one other task which Nairne carried out concerning the posthumous reputation of the king. Shortly after James II's death it was reported
that various miracles had taken place. Nairne noted on 3 January 1702 that
'I writt out some attest.n of miraculous cures of sick people by ye intercession of ye late K'. Other miracles were reported during 1702 and 1703,
including two at the king's tomb in the chapel of the English Benedictines
in Paris.[25] The political implications of these miracles were quickly grasped
by the Jacobites, who hoped that any beatification or even canonization
of the late king might have a profound influence in the Catholic states

which had so far supported William III and the Protestant succession in England. In August 1703, Nairne 'put ye papers of ye Ks miracles in order to be copied',[26] made a list of them and wrote a 'Relation of ye late Ks miracles'.[27] He also sent the eight most important attestations of the miracles to Cardinal Caprara in Rome, with a view to the beatification of the king.[28] Three years later, by which time the series of miraculous cures had come to an end, Nairne produced a revised list and Relation.[29]

Nairne's work on the papers and biography of James II had a significant influence on Lord Middleton and his son Lord Clermont, both of whom were Anglicans. At the beginning of August 1702 Nairne noted in his diary that Lord Clermont had been converted to Catholicism by Dr Thomas Witham, the superior of the English College of St Gregory at Paris.[30] Three weeks later, on 21 August, he received the much more important information that Lord Middleton had also been converted: 'I had ye news airly yt My Ld Middleton was converted and yt he had been recd and reconcild to ye Cath. Church in Paris ye day before, by Dr Witham.'

This was a significant development in the history of the Jacobite court because there was no longer a Protestant secretary of state to correspond with the Protestant Jacobites in England and Scotland, and for three months Middleton argued that he should be replaced.[31] At the end of November, he finally agreed to resume his work,[32] though he was now distrusted by many Jacobite Tories. Middleton's relations with Nairne, however, became very much closer as thenceforth they shared the same religious faith. For example, a few years later Middleton joined Nairne as a member of the Confraternity for the 'adoration perpétuelle du Saint-Sacrament'.[33]

The impact on David Lindsay, Middleton's Protestant chief clerk, was very different. Passed over by Nairne to be the clerk of the king's council, even though Middleton was the senior secretary of state, he now found himself the only Protestant in the political secretariat and out of sympathy with the man for whom he was working. In May 1703, he announced that he intended to leave the court and return to live in Scotland.

This unexpected development, provoked by Middleton's conversion to Catholicism, provided Nairne with an ideal opportunity to further his career at the court. He began by speaking to Lady Middleton and letting her know that he would like to work for her husband as Lindsay's replacement.[34] One week later he spoke to Lord Middleton himself: 'I waited on my Ld Middleton and offered my services to him in Mr Lindsays place who was going away, and he ... accepted of ye offer.'[35] But everything depended on the reaction of Lord Caryll. Nairne spoke to him on the following day and told him 'yt My Ld Middle. was disposd to imploy me if he approvd of it'. To Nairne's relief 'he consented'.[36] Now everything depended on Queen Mary.

The queen had such a high opinion of Nairne that it is not surprising that she agreed, and Lady Middleton later told him that 'it was ye Q herself that I had the obligation to of my new imploym.t under My Ld'.[37] But Nairne was also fortunate in the timing of Lindsay's departure. The correspondence of both Lord Caryll and Lord Middleton had considerably reduced since the renewal of war in 1702, while the courts at Saint-Germain and Versailles awaited the outcome of the military campaigns in Flanders, northern Italy and Spain. During 1704 and 1705, by contrast, their correspondence greatly increased. Nairne could persuasively argue in May 1703 that he was fully capable of working for both the secretaries of state, thus co-ordinating all the work of the political secretariat as under-secretary. When the work increased he was able to cope with it because by then he was no longer engaged in translations with Caryll and no longer occupied dealing with the papers of James II. Nevertheless Nairne's increased work load meant that he could not complete the full-length biography of James II which he had written up to the year 1677. When James III decided that work on the biography should be resumed[38] the task was entrusted to William Dicconson.[39] Nairne was consulted, but he was not responsible for the continuation of *The Life* from 1678 to 1701.[40]

The decision to employ Nairne as under-secretary was taken by Queen Mary on 11 June, and we have two accounts of what happened. Hitherto Nairne had written one entry in his diary for each day, but he now decided to keep two diaries, one for his work with Caryll, the other for his work with Middleton. The entry in the Caryll diary is much shorter:

> I enterd in possession of the Imployment of Sec.ry to My Ld Middleton who told me at ye Kings dinner yt the Queen had consented to it, and bid me come to him at 5 a clock wch I did and he gave me a key to his Closet, and ye key of the seals and papers ... I lookd over My Ld Midletons papers.

The Middleton diary is much more useful:

> This day My Lord Middleton was pleasd to tell me that he had acquainted the Queen with his resolution of imploying me as his Secretary in the room of Mr Lindsay, and that her Maty had approvd of it. Upon which he appointed me to wait on him in the afternoon in his Closette, which I did, and there his Lp gave me a key of his closette, with the keys of a bureau and two armoires in which were his papers entry books, and seals, viz 3 signets, of the late King and of his p.nt Maty, and his Lps own seal. And so he put me in possession of the employment of being his Secretary, which I was to exerce without discontinuing to be in the same station and imployment under My Ld Caryll ... I put the French ministers letters by themselves, and the memorials apart and lockd all up in the bureau, where I found only 3 entry books, viz one of Memorials and 2 of letters.

Although he did not actually say so, Nairne was surprised that Lindsay had not preserved a better record of Middleton's correspondence.[41]

Nairne continued to write two diaries for a little over two weeks until 27 June, when he reverted to recording a single entry for each day. His entries both before and after 27 June make it clear that the new arrangement was a complete success. Nairne continued to dine with Caryll on a regular basis, but he now established excellent relations with Lord and Lady Middleton. On 21 June, for example, he recorded that Lady Middleton made him 'a complim.t' about his work. Later entries record Nairne's going for a walk at night with Lord Middleton, drinking coffee with him and Lady Middleton in their apartment, and accompanying Lord Middleton to Versailles.[42]

It was particularly during Middleton's visits to the French court that the success of the new arrangement was apparent, because Nairne already knew the senior officials in the French ministries and could converse with them with much greater ease than Lindsay had been able to do. There are frequent references in Nairne's diary to his contacts with the members of the foreign and war secretariats.[43] In July, for example, 'I went wth My Ld M to Vers, he dind wth Mr de Torcy [the French foreign secretary] and I spoke wth Mr Adam [the *premier commis*]'.[44] A few weeks later: 'I dind wth Mr Adam at Mr Labadies'.[45]

The most important aspect of Nairne's work for Lord Middleton concerned the negotiations with the Scottish Jacobites, and with the court at Versailles, with a view to preparing a Franco-Jacobite invasion of Scotland.

Figure 4. *Charles, 2nd Earl of Middleton*, c.1683 (73.6 × 60.9 cm),
attributed to Sir Godfrey Kneller (private collection)
This portrait was painted when Middleton was Secretary for Scotland, about ten years
before he in went into exile at Saint-Germain-en-Laye.

Before examining Nairne's role in these negotiations, however, it will be
convenient to concentrate on his work for the queen and Lord Caryll. In
his work for Middleton, Nairne was assisted by Monnot, whereas in his
work for Caryll he was assisted by Dempster.

Nairne's work on her late husband's papers convinced Queen Mary that she could entrust to him the management of her accounts. It was Nairne who drafted the letters for Caryll to send to Michel Chamillart, the *contrôleur-général des finances* at Versailles, concerning her income from the salts of Brouage,[46] and he formally witnessed a secret arrangement whereby the queen's *rentes* were registered in the name of William Dicconson, her treasurer.[47] Also, and in anticipation of an eventual restoration, Nairne compiled a list of all the debts which the queen had left behind in England when forced to flee to France at short notice in December 1688.[48]

The queen also employed Nairne to commission new portraits of James III and his sister Princess Louise-Marie from Alexis-Simon Belle.[49] In May 1705, for example, Nairne obtained a portrait of the king to be sent to Scotland,[50] and in May 1706 he obtained one of the princess.[51] In September 1706 Nairne noted that he sent 'a picture of ye Ks from him for My Ld Strathmore, and orderd 3 more at Mr Bels to be sent to Scotld'.[52] They were ready nine days later when they were taken by Nairne's friend John Wallace.[53] It was these commissions which resulted in the growing friendship between Nairne and Belle. In January 1704 Nairne 'went to see Mr Bel draw Mr Carylls picture',[54] and by February 1706 they were dining with their wives in each other's houses,[55] as already noted.

In March 1705, it was decided that the Jacobite court should send an ambassador to represent its interests at the court of King Philip V of Spain, whom James III had known as the duc d'Anjou before his (Philip's) accession to the throne. The choice fell on Sir Tobie Bourke, an Irishman who had lived in both Italy and Spain.[56] The correspondence with Spain, like the correspondence with Rome, was the responsibility of Lord Caryll, and Bourke's appointment resulted in a considerable increase in the former's workload. A despatch was sent to Madrid every week from July 1705 onwards, in reply to the regular despatches which were received from Bourke.[57] At first Nairne drafted the letters for Caryll to sign, but by November 1705 he was conducting the correspondence himself. No doubt he discussed the content of his letters with Caryll, but it is clear from his diary that the responsibility for conducting the correspondence was delegated to him.

At the end of 1705, Lord Caryll composed a new poem denouncing the influence over Queen Anne in London of her two leading Whig ministers, Sidney Godolphin (lord treasurer) and the Duke of Marlborough (commander-in-chief and victor of the Battle of Blenheim). The poem was entitled *The Duumvirate.*[58] Nairne noted that, despite his new responsibilities with Lord Middleton, he was still employed by Caryll in a personal capacity. In December 1705, he wrote that 'I dind wth My Ld Car and writt out his verses the Duumvirate'.[59] On five more occasions during the next year he either 'copied ye Duumvirate' or 'writt out My Ld Caryls new amendment to his Duumvirate'.[60] The poem was eventually printed but it does not seem to have been distributed.[61]

An achievement which gave Nairne particular satisfaction was the rehabilitation of Lord Melfort, who was still living in internal exile at Angers after the unfortunate publication in London of his letter to Lord Perth. Now that war had been resumed between France and England there seemed no reason why Melfort should continue to be punished because his letter had gone to London rather than to Saint-Germain, so Lady Melfort came to Paris in July 1702 hoping for Nairne's support.[62] He and his wife went to visit her,[63] and Nairne then approached Lord Caryll who agreed to see Lady Melfort in Saint-Germain to discuss her request that her husband should be allowed to return.[64] Caryll told her to be patient and wait a little longer, so she rejoined her husband at Angers.[65]

A year and a half later, she tried again and Nairne noted that 'My Ld Car told me that he had got a letter from My La Melf about her Lds being called back and that he had spoke to ye Q of it'.[66] The queen felt that his return was still premature, and anyway that it depended on the agreement of the King of France,[67] but she spoke to Louis XIV and eventually persuaded him to allow Melfort to live once again in Paris.[68] Five months later, in December, 1704, Nairne noted that Lady Melfort arrived at Saint-Germain[69] and that he and Marie-Elisabeth invited her to dinner in January to discuss how best to proceed.[70]

Permission was eventually granted by the queen for the Melforts to return to the Jacobite court. Lord Melfort himself arrived discreetly at Saint-Germain 'at one in the morning' on 15 February 1705,[71] and four days later Nairne spoke about him to Lord Middleton. On the following day, 20 February, he spoke to both Middleton and Caryll and recorded: 'I spoke again to E. M. and Ld C about E. Melf and did all I could to dispose things for a reconciliation.' He advised Melfort to send a conciliatory message to Middleton which 'was well recd',[72] and on 14 March Nairne eventually brought about the reconciliation that he had so dearly wanted between the Melforts (his original patrons) and the two secretaries of state for whom he now worked. He wrote on 14 March that 'My Ld Middleton visited My Ld and La Melf, Ld Melf kissed ye K and Qs hand and their title was declard', by which he meant that the Melforts were raised in the Jacobite peerage to the rank of duke and duchess. It is difficult to see how this rehabilitation could have taken place without the active encouragement of Nairne, itself made possible by the continued good relations which the latter enjoyed with Lord Caryll and the respect and trust he had inspired in Lord Middleton.

Given what Melfort had written about Middleton in the letter to his brother Perth – Middleton was 'lazy in his temper [and] an enemy to France'[73] – Nairne had healed a serious breach among the Jacobites in France, with significant political implications. Three months after Lord Melfort's return to Saint-Germain, Queen Mary commented on the attitudes of Perth, Caryll and Middleton concerning the planned invasion of Scotland. Perth, she said, 'wanted to go too fast'; Caryll 'wanted to do nothing ... which stemmed from his great age' (and perhaps also because he was English, not Scottish); and Middleton was 'the most moderate', though very cautious.[74] Given that Melfort and Perth shared the same attitude, what Nairne had done was to bring together the leaders of the two opposing groups at the exiled court and encourage them to develop a common approach.

During the rest of 1705, and until the end of 1707, Nairne continued to see the Melforts whenever he could without ever undermining the confidential relations which he had established with Caryll and Middleton.[75] In July 1705, to give one example, Nairne 'went to Paris' and 'visited My Ld and La Melf', adding that that night he 'lay at My Ld Midletons house' in the city.[76]

James III, meanwhile, was approaching his age of majority, when Queen Mary's guardianship would come to an end and he would begin to reign and make political decisions in his own right. In May 1706, one month before the king's eighteenth birthday, Nairne became concerned lest the young king should wish to appoint someone else to be the clerk of his council. He wrote a memorial in which he argued his case and asked to be confirmed in his post. Having persuaded Lewis Innes to plead his case with Lord Middleton,[77] he then 'gave my Memorial to E. M. to give to the Q'.[78] Nine days later, and four days before James III's birthday on 21 June, he obtained what he wanted: 'Ld Mid told me to prepare a Warrant for myself to be Clerk of the Ks council, and told me ye Q. had granted it very cheerfully.'[79] Nairne did as instructed[80] and his warrant was signed by the king 'at ye levé'.[81] Four days later, James III presided over his first council meeting:

> There was a Council at 4 in ye afternoon at ye end of wch I was called in and kissd ye K and Q's hand upon my place of Clerk of ye Council and at night I kissd ye P.sses.[82]

This appointment brought Nairne an augmentation to his salary and pension. In February 1703, all the salaries and pensions paid at Saint-Germain, including Nairne's, had been retrenched by seven and a half per cent.[83] Thus his combined monthly income had been reduced from 173*l* 0s 9d to 159*l* 19s 7d.[84] In 1704 he had failed to obtain 'a lodging' in the château when he again asked for one.[85] Now, in June 1706, when told to prepare the warrant appointing him clerk of the new king's council, Lord Middleton told him 'yt I should have lodging mony and yt she [the queen] would make up my retrenchm.t some way'.[86] When nothing had happened for nearly a month, Nairne 'gave a memor.l to My Ld Mid to speak to ye Q about my lodging mony etc'.[87] Two and a half weeks later, Lord Caryll told him that the queen had decided to give him a monthly increase of 15*l* 4s 7d, bringing his income back up to 175*l* 3s 2d. As Nairne noted in his diary, 'I recd from My Ld Car 6 louis d'ors wch ye Q. gave me for a quarter lodging mony and compensat.n of retrenchment to be continued privatly'.[88]

During the summer of 1707, Nairne discovered that the Hôtel de Bouillon at Saint-Germain was to be vacated and allocated by Queen Mary to one of the Jacobites. Lord Caryll spoke to the queen on his behalf, but was told that 'she had been spoken to before' and had already granted it to someone else.[89] Thus Nairne continued to live in the house that he and his family already occupied. Despite this failure, however, he was now being paid more money than he had received before the general retrenchment, and was held in very high regard by the queen and the two secretaries of state for whom he worked.

In addition to his political work for Caryll and Middleton, Nairne had various administrative duties to perform. One of these concerned the drafting of certificates or *déclarations de noblesse*. Given the system of primogeniture throughout the British kingdoms, it was not always apparent that the younger sons and grandsons of Jacobite peers and gentlemen enjoyed the same status as the *noblesse* in France. They would be styled 'Mr', and regarded in parliamentary terms as commoners, whereas the younger sons of French and other continental nobles would be styled in such a way as to make their social status clear. During the late 1690s, therefore, there was a growing demand among the exiled Jacobite community, in Spain as well as in France, for these certificates declaring that the bearer was, in continental terms, a nobleman.[90]

It was Nairne's responsibility, as Caryll's chief clerk, to draft these certificates for the secretary of state to submit to the king for signature. And according to the normal practice at the time, it was expected that the applicant would pay a fee to the chief clerk for his work, ranging from about one *louis d'or* to as much as four *louis d'ors*. As Nairne could not be expected in every case to know who was and who was not really of noble status, the applications were normally sponsored and presented to him by a member of the royal household whose recommendation could be trusted.

There were many Irish Jacobites, however, who were not known to the members of the royal household and who needed to be sponsored by someone else. They obtained letters of support from the officers of the Irish regiments in the French army, and then asked for an attestation of their heraldry from the Irish pursuivant of arms, known as the Athlone Herald. This was a man named James Therry.[91] In 1700 James II had regulated that Therry's fee for each of his attestations should be four *louis d'ors*.[92]

An Irishman who was not known personally to someone at the court would therefore pay one fee to Therry to persuade him to present a formal request to the office of the secretary of state. If the latter agreed to prepare a certificate for the king, then the Irishman would pay a second fee to Nairne, the amount left to the discretion of the applicant, though it was normally less than four *louis d'ors*. Once the certificate had been signed by the king it would be sent directly by Nairne to the applicant, or to the applicant's sponsor.

The system seemed to work perfectly satisfactorily, and Nairne's diary mentions both types of application – from members of the royal household,[93] and from Therry.[94] In the summer of 1700, however, Therry complained that when the certificates based on his attestations had been signed by the king they should be given back to him rather than to Nairne for despatch to the applicants. It seems that he was hoping to be able to demand a second fee – the first for the attestation, the second for the signed certificate – and felt that Nairne was depriving him of an opportunity to increase his income. At the beginning of September, Nairne sent a very firm letter to Therry informing him that 'I can not comply with your desire as to the new Certificats'. As Nairne's letters to Therry are virtually the only ones among the thousands that he wrote during this period that have survived, it is worth examining them at some length.

Nairne began by reminding Therry how the system should be operated, and categorically refused to hand over to him the signed certificates:

> I am to tell you from Mr Secretary that you are to meddle only henceforth with what belongs to your Imployment as herald, which is to give your own Certificat [i.e. attestation] and take the fees the King has permitted you to have for them but his Ma.ties Certificat which is not a thing that's granted of course to attend the arms or genealogies which you give out to people for mony, is what I am orderd hereafter not to deliver to you, but to the person directly concern'd and this to prevent the abuse of putting the Kings Certificat into the bargain of your genealogies. As for the offer you make me of mony, I am obligd to you, but if the offer were 50 louis d'ors as well as five, I would refuse it, for thank God I never had a farthing of your mony, and I am resolvd never to take any; but this shall not hinder me from doing you what service I can, as long as you keep within the bounds of your Imployment, and do the duty thereof.

He offered to help Therry receive the four *louis d'ors* which were his due, but in doing so reiterated his refusal to hand over the signed certificates:

> I suppose you never give [your certificats, i.e. attestations] without being payd your 4 louis d'ors, but if you be not payd them all I can do for your service is that when application is made here ..., in case it be thought fitt to grant them, they shall not be deliverd out of this office till you be satisfied of what is your right, but whether they will be granted or not is no more your business to inquire into, since even when

granted they are not to be deliverd to you, and ther neither is nor will be any step made for the procuring them upon your account, so if you make arms or genealogies for them you may take your own methods to secure the payment of your own labour, which has nothing in common with the Secretary's office, the expeditions whereof are neither to be granted nor stopd upon that motive.

Nairne concluded by making very clear how he regarded his own position at the court as Caryll's chief clerk:

Mr Secretary receives the Kings pleasure in these things, and he is my rule, and I do nothing but what I am authorisd by him to do, and am not accountable to you or any other but the king and him who is my superiour for my actions and conduct in the station I am in.... wrong you I never will, but on the contrary I'll be allways ready to help you in any thing yt depends on me, as far as it is just and reasonable only remember this as a rule to govern yourself by and wch I am authorisd by Mr Sec.ry to intimate to you, that you must not meddle in any manner of way with the Kings certificats.[95]

Nairne noted in his diary that evening that 'I writt to Mr Therry in answer to his letter, and read it to Mr Sec.ry'.[96]

A few days later, Nairne discussed the matter with Lewis Innes.[97] Because it seemed clear that what Therry really wanted was to be able to charge a second fee, over and above the four *louis d'ors* granted him by the king for each attestation, it was felt that the best person to resolve the question was James II himself. Nairne noted on 13 September that 'the K called Therry at ye levé and rejected his request, after which he [Therry] ... spoke with Mr Caryll who rebuked him calling him an ungrat troublesom fellow'.

The matter seemed to be settled, but in July 1701 Therry made a second attempt to accuse Nairne of depriving him money which rightfully belonged to him.[98] He prepared a petition to be presented to the king,[99] and in August, one month before James II's death, Therry gave it to him. Nairne noted that James 'was angry with him and took it to be rid of him'.[100] James Porter, the vice-chamberlain of the household, was told to examine the petition, and Nairne recorded that he 'went to Porter's where, in the presence of Terry, I justified myself'.[101]

This should have been the end of the matter, and shortly afterwards Nairne even gave four *louis d'ors* to a poor Irish woman who would not

otherwise have been able to pay Therry his fee.[102] But the latter was not
prepared to give up, and in March 1702, through an act of kindness, Nairne
provided him with an opportunity to return to the attack. Someone who
had already been given a certificate signed by James II asked Therry to
obtain an authenticated copy signed by the secretary of state. Presumably
he intended to give Therry a fee for doing this, but there was some doubt
as to whether he intended to pay Nairne as well. Out of generosity Nairne
decided to give the authenticated copy directly to Therry rather than as
was normal practice directly to the applicant:

> I could adress myself to him by another hand, but to show you that I can both forgive
> and forget, I will not deprive you of any benefit you may have by handing this paper
> to [the applicant]. When it is procurd I shall send it to you and you shall have the
> delivering of it, being resolved to make a tryall how far you'l be just to me when you
> may see by this instance how far I am from desiring to wrong you. I'l take no mony
> from you, you know I have told you that, long ago, and having never done it yet, I will
> not begin now, but I hope when you are satisfied yourself of all you have to pretend,
> you will not grudge nor hinder the partys giving me a gratification for what I deliver
> out of the Secretarys office in things of this nature, in which you know very well
> by experience that I do nothing but what I have my superiors approbation for ...
> I am very confident that that gentleman who wants this certificat and values it so
> much will be generous enough of himself if the thing be but rightly represented to
> him, wch I could get done by another (as I have told you already) but for this time I
> chuse rather to leave it to you, hoping after so many faire promises made me ... that
> you will not be sorry I give you this occasion to shew your sincerity and gratitude.'[103]

Far from showing any gratitude, Therry used this letter to complain
to the Duke of Perth (the king's governor) that Nairne and Caryll were
attempting to charge fees which belonged by right to the heralds, and
that Nairne in particular was trying to deprive him (Therry) of half of
the money due to him from the man who had asked for the copy.[104] In a
letter which he sent to Perth in August 1702, Therry referred to Nairne's
'craving desires' and argued that 'any fees he pretends to ... were never yet
known, or heard of', and were 'no better than extortion'. He even alleged
that Nairne had forced him to give him money before handing over any
certificates to the people who had applied for them.[105]

Perth was impressed and arranged for Therry to have an audience
with Queen Mary, before whom he repeated these accusations and even

swore an oath that Nairne had extorted money from him. This accusation overstepped the limit, and Lord Caryll advised Nairne to accept no more applications for certificates from Therry unless he would recant. Nairne wrote in his diary on 12 August:

> I got Terry to signe under his hand yt I never askt nor took a farthing mony from him, wch he declard also before Mr Inese, notwthstanding wch, against his own handwritt, he [had] averred the contrary upon oath before ye Queen not to commit himself wth My Lord Perth to whom he had said the thing.

On the following day, Nairne 'dind with my Ld Caryll and discoursd him further about Terry's business, and he did me all ye justice I could desire'. Perth, however, was not prepared to take sides. On 14 August Nairne noted that, having dined again with Lord Caryll,

> I went to my Ld D. of Perth and spoke to him of Terrys affaire and mine, and begd him yt he would call Terry before me, and I did not doubt but by ye questions I would put to him I would get him to own yt if not all at least a great part of what was in the paper was true, tho' he had sworn it to be all false, but My Ld wd not do me that favour.

Nairne explained that 'I made this step in order to remove any grudge I found in my heart and to endeavour to be in charity wth everybody, as also to justify myself'.

Nairne had to be content with knowing he had the full support of both Caryll and Innes,[106] so he continued to obtain the certificates which Therry requested.[107] But there are two more entries in Nairne's diary which shed an interesting light on this dispute. On 2 November 1702, he noted that Therry 'begd me pardon and ownd ye obligations he had to My Ld and me, [and] promised he wd make me reparation'. And on 11 April 1703: 'Ye business between Terry and Dr Kennedy was tryd before Coll. Porter and Mr Plowden, and Terry was cast, and ye deed he produced provd to be false.'[108]

This whole episode had created considerable ill feeling, but it sheds light on Nairne's character, his attitude to his work and the relations between Queen Mary's leading ministers. Nairne enjoyed the total support of Caryll and Innes, as well as James II, because they all trusted him completely. But Perth, who was well aware of Nairne's close relations with his brother Melfort, was reluctant to support Lord Caryll, whom he distrusted as an Englishman and whose cautious attitude towards Scotland he resented.[109] So he declined to support Caryll's chief clerk.

The last that we hear of Therry comes in June 1703, immediately after Nairne began to work for Lord Middleton as well as Lord Caryll. Therry wrote to both secretaries of state and asked them 'to speak to the Queen to get a competency settled upon him to support his family'.[110] The queen declined to give Therry a pension,[111] so he continued to live off the fees that he could charge for providing the Irish with attestations of their heraldry. Meanwhile Nairne continued to prepare numerous certificates, some applications from members of the royal household, some from Therry, for the king to sign.[112]

Although Nairne took advantage of what he, Lord Caryll and the king all regarded as a legitimate perquisite of his office, he was not intent on securing financial advantage whenever he could. A case in point concerns Lady Sophia Bulkeley, one of the queen's ladies of the bedchamber. In 1703 she was pursuing a legal action in Rome to claim some money there under the will of Sir William Godolphin,[113] and wanted to obtain Nairne's support to persuade Lord Caryll to write to Rome on her behalf. To this end she sent a present for Nairne's daughter Françoise (her god-daughter), but Nairne sent it back. He noted:

> I writt a tre to La Sophia in answer to hers and sent her back ye note she had sent me of a gift for my daughter ye night before, wch I would not so much as satisfy my curiosity to look upon the paper to know what it containd. I had a long conversation wth her after dinner.[114]

She tried again a little later, and Nairne noted this time that 'My La. Bukly writt to my wife and sent her a seald paper, wch I obliged my wife to send back to her again'.[115] The point, of course, was that Nairne was willing to help her without being offered any financial incentive.

Another example of Nairne's willingness to help members of the court concerned the Duchess of Tyrconnell, who was also one of the queen's ladies of the bedchamber. In 1702 the duchess had left the court and returned to England,[116] but she came back in 1707 to sell the houses she owned in

Saint-Germain and recover the goods she had left in her lodging in the château. No other Jacobite would have been able to travel freely between France and England, particularly when the two countries were at war, but she was the sister of the Duchess of Marlborough, who was married to the commander-in-chief of the allied armies in Flanders, so her personal safety was guaranteed. Nevertheless she needed an agent to handle her affairs at Saint-Germain. In March 1707 Nairne dined with her in Paris[117] and agreed to act on her behalf. During the spring and summer of 1707 he 'retird La Tyr's goods out of her lodging',[118] drew up an inventory 'of ye goods',[119] sold her houses,[120] and wrote her numerous letters to keep her informed.[121] There is no mention in the diary of Nairne's receiving any fee for doing this.

It was not only the wealthy and influential whom Nairne was willing to help. In September 1701, a Quaker named William Bromfield was imprisoned in the Bastille on the orders of Louis XIV for falsely accusing the Anglicans at Saint-Germain of holding unauthorized services.[122] One year later, Nairne persuaded Lord Caryll to write to the marquis de Torcy asking that Bromfield should be released or at least given better treatment in prison.[123] He also obtained charity money from the queen for Bromfield's wife,[124] and had her added to the list of people receiving a pension.[125] After his appointment as chief clerk to Lord Middleton, he persuaded the latter to ask Torcy 'to have leave for her' to visit her husband in prison.[126] He regularly wrote letters of encouragement to both Bromfield himself[127] and his wife,[128] and in January 1706 was instrumental in having Bromfield transferred from the Bastille to house arrest at Charenton.[129] If Nairne perhaps obliged Lady Sophia Bulkeley and the Duchess of Tyrconnell because they were both Catholic and important courtiers, no such factors could have influenced the help he gave to the Bromfields, who were Protestant dissenters of no distinction whatsoever, and not even members of the royal household.[130]

The available evidence certainly suggests that, despite the allegations of Therry, Nairne attempted to put into practice his strongly held Catholic convictions of piety and charity. Indeed the years following his appointment as under-secretary in 1703 must have been among the most satisfying that he ever experienced. Happily married, he had three children, a large circle of friends, and a well-appointed home. He had stimulating and important work for two men (Caryll and Middleton) whom he both liked and admired, and he had the immense personal comfort of his regular attendance at the chapel royal, the parish church and the church of the Récollets. Finally, he took an active part in the musical and social life of the court, which became ever more important as James III and his sister Louise-Marie grew up.

During 1702 and the first three months of 1703, Nairne attended thirty-three concerts given in the châteaux de Saint-Germain, several of them in the apartment of Lord Caryll.[131] He also practised playing the violin[132] so that he could himself perform in some of the court concerts. In November 1702 he bought himself a new violin,[133] and two days later made his first appearance in one of the concerts.[134] Between November 1702 and March 1703, he performed in public on ten occasions,[135] bringing the total number of concerts he attended or played in to forty-three. He normally played on the violin, but on one occasion he specified that the instrument on which he performed was the flute.[136]

This intense musical activity came to an end in June 1703 when Nairne replaced Lindsay as Middleton's chief clerk and acquired a greatly increased workload. Thereafter there is no reference to his performing in public. Nevertheless he continued to attend the court concerts from time to time,[137] as well as the *grands motets* in the parish church.[138] In August 1707 he recorded that he took the celebrated soprano Marie Chape to sing before James III and his sister.[139]

We have no means of knowing what music Nairne heard or performed during these concerts, though we have enough information to know that it would have included works by both Italian and French composers.[140] There must have been sonatas, arias and cantatas by Innocenzo Fede, Alessandro Scarlatti and Archangelo Corelli. There were probably vocal and instrumental extracts from the ballets and operas of Jean-Baptiste de Lully and his successors. There is no evidence, however, that Nairne ever attended an opera at Saint-Germain or even in Paris throughout the period from 1692 to 1708 – and this in striking contrast to his experience in Rome when he had attended several operas in a short period of time. The only reference in his diary to an opera comes during his visit to the French court at

Fontainebleau in October 1703 when he says that he attended 'a repetition of a new opera of Destouches'.[141] He must have attended other musical performances at the French court, but he does not mention them. Three years later, however, he did record that he was admitted to the intimate circle of people who 'heard musique at Me de Maintenons' apartment at Fontainebleau.[142] This music would almost certainly have been performed, if not composed, by François Couperin, whom Nairne had known in Paris when he had first arrived there as a young man. And it is possible, if not probable, that by then Couperin had begun to work for part of the year at the Jacobite court.[143]

Concerts were not, however the only occasions when secular music could be heard at the court. There were also the balls which were organized in the château de Saint-Germain during each carnival season and to celebrate the birthdays of the king and the princess.[144] The season at the beginning of 1708, when Nairne was preparing to accompany James III on the Franco-Jacobite expedition to Scotland, was the most brilliant. His diary mentions six balls, of which he attended two, between 2 January and 20 February,[145] all of which would have been accompanied by a sizeable ensemble of instrumentalists playing music from French ballets and operas. It was eight days after attending the last of these that Nairne left Saint-Germain to join the expedition to Scotland.

***

The expedition was the culmination of more than five years of negotiations between the court of Saint-Germain, the court of Versailles and the Scottish Jacobites. In his role as Lord Middleton's under-secretary Nairne made a significant contribution to these negotiations, drafting important papers at Saint-Germain and corresponding with the Jacobites in Scotland. To understand his contribution, however, we need to consider the main outlines of these negotiations throughout the five years.

The background to the negotiations was the Act of Settlement, passed by the English parliament in 1701, followed by the accession of Princess Anne as Queen of England and Scotland in 1702. The act stated that the throne of England would pass, on the death of Queen Anne, to Sophia, the Dowager-Electress of Hanover, and then her son George. But the

Hanoverian Succession, as it was called, did not apply to Scotland. Unless, therefore, the Scottish parliament were to pass a similar act, there was a possibility that the regal union between the two kingdoms might be broken. Although he was a Catholic, and for the moment debarred by the Scottish Claim of Right, James III might become king of a separate Scotland as a stepping stone to a restoration in England.

The possibility was increased when the government in London declared war against France, thus forcing Scotland into another expensive and unpopular conflict with the country which many Scots regarded as their 'auld' ally. Queen Mary and her ministers at Saint-Germain needed to give encouragement to the Jacobites in Scotland, and make sure that no Scottish Protestant with a distant claim to the throne would be given priority over her (Queen Mary's) Catholic son James.

The only Scottish nobleman with a viable claim to the throne was James Douglas, the 4th Duke of Hamilton, referred to at Saint-Germain as the Earl of Arran.[146] Nairne had corresponded with him in 1695, and now, in the summer of 1702, he renewed his correspondence.[147] Arran was very heavily in debt and said he would be willing to support James in return for receiving a French subsidy.[148]

The situation was then suddenly changed when Lord Lovat, another impoverished Scottish nobleman, arrived in Paris. Lovat was a Protestant, but he was accompanied by Sir John Maclean of Duart, a Catholic who had been educated at the Scots College in Paris and who was acquainted with the Duke of Perth. Maclean arranged for Lovat to see Perth, who in turn persuaded Queen Mary to give Lovat an audience.[149]

Lovat was in fact a dishonest intriguer who was merely hoping to deceive the court at Saint-Germain into giving him some money to pay his debts. However, he pretended that he had been sent to France by the Highland clan chiefs and many of the Lowland nobles, whom he claimed were ready to rise in revolt against Queen Anne if they were given the help of a small French expeditionary force. Lovat specifically claimed that he had enrolled the support of the 12th Earl of Erroll, who was Perth's nephew, and of the 9th Earl Marischal, who was Perth's son-in-law.[150]

Lovat's arguments, coming immediately after the renewal of war and at a time when the Scottish succession was still undecided, divided opinion at the Stuart court. Perth supported Lovat, but the queen, Middleton and Caryll distrusted him and were highly sceptical of his claims. Middleton, moreover, thought that the English would never accept a king in a separate Scotland who had been put there by the French. Despite this, the queen arranged for Lovat to have an audience with Louis XIV at Versailles. How much credence Louis gave Lovat is not clear, but the war was in its early stages and Louis saw no reason why he needed to divert valuable resources from Flanders and Italy to Scotland.[151] This audience, however, emphasized to the French that one way of restoring James III and defeating the English might be by sending an expeditionary force to Scotland.

Nairne's diary makes no mention of Lovat's arrival in the summer of 1702, or of his audience with the King of France. But there seems no doubt that he would have discussed the credibility of Lovat's claims both with Lord Caryll and with Lord Middleton and David Lindsay. What followed suggests very strongly that he came to regard Lovat as completely untrustworthy, because he advised Middleton to send an agent to Scotland to verify Lovat's claims.

Nairne was on very good terms with Captain James Murray, a younger brother of Sir David Murray of Stanhope and an officer in the French army.[152] For example, when Murray was at Saint-Germain Nairne mentions dining with him in company with Lindsay and the two assistant clerks, Monnot and Dempster.[153] In the winter of 1702–3, while Lovat was still in Paris, Nairne suggested that Murray should be sent secretly to Scotland to interview the Jacobites whose support for a rising Lovat claimed he had recruited.

Nairne drafted some 'Instructions' for Murray in January 1703 and showed them to Lord Middleton as well as Lord Caryll.[154] His paper was then considered by Middleton who 'after some alterations bid me write them [the 'Instructions'] out faire both in French and English wch I did'.[155] The French copy was to keep the ministers at Versailles informed; the English copy was to be taken by Murray to Scotland. Two days later Nairne noted that 'I writt a letter to my brother to go with C[aptain] Murray',[156] his hope being that Alexander Nairne would help Murray interview the Fife and Perthshire nobles. Finally, on 18 April, 'Cap.n Muray got all his tres and Instructions and kised ye K and Q's hands', and was given money for his journey. Nairne noted that night that 'I supd wth him in Mr Lindsays chamber'. Murray then left the following day.

Middleton, meanwhile, had decided to call Lovat's bluff by sending him back to Scotland to secure positive pledges of support from the Jacobite nobles there. Only then could he hope for money and the possibility of French support. Suspecting that Lovat could not be trusted Middleton insisted that he should be accompanied by Captain John Moray of Abercairny, a naturalized Frenchman who was also an officer in the French army. Moray's task, like Murray's before him, was to assess the situation and find out how much support there really was for a Jacobite rising.[157] Nairne noted at the beginning of May that 'I recd My Ld Mid. orders about Ld Lovets Instructions and a comission for him', and that he made a fair copy of them for the king to sign. He added that Middleton also asked him to prepare 'C[aptain] Jo[hn] Murays Instr[uctions]'.[158]

By the late spring of 1703, therefore, two men had been sent to Scotland, in part at Nairne's suggestion, to check whether or not Lord Lovat was telling the truth. Captain James Murray had left in February;[159] he did not return to Saint-Germain until February 1704.[160] Captain John Moray left with Lovat in May. Lovat returned by himself in January 1704,[161] followed by Moray in May.[162] What is striking about all this is that Nairne had already started working for Middleton before he formally replaced Lindsay as Middleton's chief clerk in June 1703. Indeed it seems likely that Nairne's role in testing the veracity of Lovat's claims, and thereby working for Middleton, partly provoked Lindsay's decision to resign his office and return to Scotland.

It was while Lovat was back in Scotland, and Queen Mary and her ministers were waiting for Murray and Moray to report, that Middleton and Nairne's worst suspicions were confirmed. What Lovat really wanted was to obtain money for himself rather than to restore James III. He visited the pro-Jacobites in Scotland and used his credentials from James to try to get them to promise to rise in revolt against Queen Anne in the event of a French invasion. But his real aim now was to obtain as much incriminating evidence as he could so that he could give their names to the Scottish government in return for money. During the summer of 1703 he betrayed both the Jacobite nobles and Captain John Moray to the Duke of Queensberry, Queen Anne's commissioner in Scotland, and offered to return to Saint-Germain as a spy for the Whig government.[163]

Nairne, meanwhile, kept in close contact and discussed Scottish affairs with Adam, his opposite number in the French foreign secretariat. This was facilitated when Middleton accompanied the king and queen to Fontainebleau, and asked Nairne to go with him.[164] Nairne was at Fontainebleau from 2 to 16 October, 'lodgd a la perle, rue basse, by billet' and eating all his meals 'at the table de l'ancien grand maitre [in the] Cour des Cuisines' of the château. He wrote virtually every day to Lord Caryll, Lewis Innes and his wife, enjoyed a walk along the canal, and attended the rehearsal of a new opera by Destouches.[165] But most of the time he was kept busy translating papers about Scotland for Torcy and the papal nuncio, Filippo Antonio Gualterio, and discussing their contents with Adam.[166]

In January 1704, Lovat arrived back at the court of Saint-Germain and reported that his mission to Scotland had been a success. In fact, the Highland clan chiefs and Lowland Jacobite nobles had not definitely promised to rise up in support of a French invasion,[167] even if their expressions of sympathy had given Lovat the opportunity to denounce them to Queensberry. Lovat, however, claimed that they *had* definitely promised to rise in rebellion in the event of a French landing.

Meanwhile the news of Lovat's treachery had already begun to to leak out: on 12 January Nairne noted that 'I was all day at My Ld C. translating Eng. tres giving acct of Ld Lovat and a plot'. In particular, Gualterio received positive information from his contacts in London that Lovat had betrayed the Scottish Jacobites to the Whig government.[168] When, therefore, Nairne received Lovat's account of his voyage, he translated it into French for both Torcy and Gualterio, and prepared 'Interogatorys to be made to My Ld Lovat'.[169] On 12 February, Nairne 'drew a Mermoire Reflexions sur la Relat.n de Mild. Lovat' in which he denounced Lovat as a traitor, and which he 'read at night to ye 2 Lds and Mr Inese'.

Opinion at Saint-Germain, however, was divided. Middleton, Caryll and the queen agreed with Nairne that it was unlikely that the Scottish Jacobites would necessarily rise up against Queen Anne at this point. Perth, on the other hand, was willing to believe in Lovat and urged Queen Mary to adopt a more positive attitude.[170] He was encouraged by recent events in Scotland and, as the queen put it, wanted 'to go too fast'.[171] But there were reasons for his attitude. The Scottish parliament had passed three acts in 1703 which indicated considerable dissatisfaction with the government in London. The Act anent Peace and War stated that all foreign policy decisions after Anne's death would have to be approved by the Scottish parliament. The Wine Act and the Wool Act allowed trade in those two commodities between Scotland and France despite the war embargoes in force in England. In particular, a Bill for the Security of the Kingdom threatened to bar the Hanoverians from the Scottish throne 'unless ... there be such conditions for government settled aand enacted as may secure the honour and sovereignty of this crown and kingdom, the freedom, frequency and power of Parliaments, the religion, liberty and trade of the nation from English or any foreign influence'.[172] Although the bill had been vetoed by Queen Anne, it was reintroduced in the next session of parliament. So, even if Lovat was indeed a traitor, it was still possible to argue that a French invasion of Scotland might provoke a Jacobite rebellion.

It was at this point, on 15 February, that Captain Murray returned to Saint-Germain and reported that Lovat had not really obtained positive pledges from the Scottish Jacobites, though the latter had expressed their willingness to support a French invasion. Nairne translated Murray's paper into French for Torcy and Gualterio,[173] and used it to interrogate Lovat. His 'Remarques on Lovats answers' were then given to Middleton and the queen.[174] But a balance had to be struck, because the court at Saint-Germain wanted to encourage Louis XIV to send an expeditionary force to Scotland. While, therefore, Lovat was exposed as a traitor and Whig spy, the French were told about the strong support which James III enjoyed in Scotland. On 29 February, Nairne 'drew a paper concerning Lovat wch ye Q carryd to Vers to give to ye K. of Fr'.[175]

On 19 May, Captain Moray arrived at Saint-Germain. His return had been delayed because he had been forced to go into hiding to avoid capture. Although he confirmed that many of the Scots Jacobites were willing to rise up if they had French support,[176] his testimony provided yet more evidence against Lovat.[177] The latter was arrested, imprisoned in the Bastille[178] and then sent to be confined in the Château d'Angoulême.[179] Nairne rounded off the whole episode by writing 'a short acct of Ld Lovats history and caracter'.[180]

Although Lovat was now totally discredited, the reports of Murray and Moray had both indicated that there would be support in Scotland for a French invasion. Nothing could be done in 1704 as the French military plans and troop deployments had already been made. Louis XIV intended to join with the Elector of Bavaria and invade Austria.[181] But the reports had stimulated the differences between Perth and the two secretaries of state, and they came to a head when news reached Saint-Germain that David Lindsay had been arrested for returning without authorization to England.[182] He was interrogated by the Privy Council, then put on trial for high treason, and when questioned about the attitude of the ministers at Saint-Germain concerning a French invasion of Scotland he criticized the Duke of Perth, though without mentioning his name:

> That there are restless, inconsiderate and mad people among them, I am as far from justifying as any man, and to muzzle and bridle these fools is a task too hard for any man to get the better of. Follies from this kind have happened, and they have been quashed by my Lord Middleton as much as it was in his Power to do.[183]

When the published details of his trial were received at Saint-Germain the Duke of Perth was furious, and Nairne noted on 25 July that 'My Ld Perth had a dispute about Lindsay', presumably with Middleton and Caryll (though he did not specify). Then, on 3 August, Queen Mary 'made a short speech after dinner by way of reprimande upon ye occasion of the dispute and heat that happened upon ye occasion of Mr Lindsay's words in the Narative and breaking of the laws'. Two weeks later, and unaware that the French and Bavarians had just been defeated at Blenheim, Queen Anne felt obliged to give her assent to the Act for the Security of the Kingdom. The prospect of an eventual Jacobite restoration in Scotland therefore seemed to be significantly increased. And despite their differences, both Middleton and Caryll, as well as Nairne, now came to agree with Perth that a French invasion of Scotland might be the best way of achieving this.[184]

Nothing could be done during the rest of the 1704 campaigning season, and when Middleton and Nairne accompanied the king and queen to Fontainebleau that autumn it was still premature to press for a Scottish expedition. This time Nairne was at Fontainebleau from 23 September to 6 October, after which he went to Compigny and nearby Baby for nine days. While at Fontainebleau he was lodged 'au Mouton blanc' in the town and spent most of his time corresponding with Lord Caryll, Innes, his wife and various other people, including Captain James Murray.[185] He also saw his opposite numbers in the French war secretariat to discuss the careers of some Jacobite officers in the French army. On one day, he recorded that he went to Louis XIV's dinner and then visited the Duchess of Perth and Lady Sophia Bulkeley. But his diary makes no mention of Scotland.[186]

During the autumn and winter of 1704–5, Queen Mary and Lord Middleton tried to persuade the French government to plan an invasion of Scotland for the coming campaigning season. An expedition to England had been considered and rejected,[187] so in January 1705 Middleton pressured Torcy and the other French ministers to give priority to Scotland in their military planning. He was supported by James III's bastard half-brother, the Duke of Berwick, and by Colonel Nathaniel Hooke, an Irishman who had caught the attention of Torcy by arguing that an expedition to Scotland would be the best way of defeating the English.[188] Realizing that, despite their differences of temperament, both Middleton and Perth were now in favour of a Scottish expedition, it was at this time that Nairne succeeded in effecting the reconciliation between Middleton and Perth's brother Melfort.[189]

The political situation became more urgent in March 1705 because the English parliament passed the Aliens Act, which was designed to force the Scots to negotiate a union of the two kingdoms. The act threatened that, if the Scottish crown was not settled as the English crown had been settled (i.e. the Hanoverian Succession) by 25 December 1705, the import of all Scottish staple products into England would be banned and all Scots would be treated in law as aliens, and therefore all Scottish property in England would be endangered. That summer the Scottish parliament, guided by the nobles and merchants with a vested interest, agreed to the appointment of commissioners to negotiate for a union with England. As the choice of commissioners was left to Queen Anne, the Scottish commissioners, as well as the English, were strongly in favour of union.

The draft treaty was not signed until the following year, but the prospect of a union made it absolutely urgent that the opposition of the Scottish Jacobites should receive every encouragement from France. To this end Colonel Hooke was ordered in June 1705 by the courts of Saint-Germain and Versailles to go to Scotland to see as many as possible of the notable Jacobites. His instructions were to sound them out, and to try to persuade them if possible to rise up without French help.[190]

While Hooke was in Scotland he discussed with seven peers the possibility of a French invasion, and these named twenty-six others whom they were sure would support a rising.[191] His return to France with this positive news coincided with the next annual visit of James III to Fontainebleau – though this time without the Queen Mary who was unwell.[192] As usual James was accompanied by Middleton and Nairne, as well as Perth, so Hooke was able to report to them as well as Louis XIV and his ministers. Nairne, who went to Fontainebleau on 1 October, refers in his diary to his usual occupations: writing every day to Caryll and most days to his wife, as well as to various other people, negotiating on behalf of Jacobite officers in the French army,[193] going to services in the chapel royal and attending Louis XIV's dinners. Then, on the 12th, the day before he returned to Saint-Germain, he had a conference 'wth My Ld M at M. de Cham[illart]s and Mr de Torcys' to discuss the news from Scotland with 'Coll Hook'.[194]

Hooke and Middleton, supported by Nairne, did all they could to persuade the French ministers to advocate an invasion of Scotland in 1706. Hooke then wrote a detailed report explaining what he had done and whom he had seen in Scotland. In November Nairne was given the task of copying Hooke's report, which he finished in three days, commenting that 'Hooks relation of Scotld' was '58 pages long'.[195] The plan to invade Scotland in 1706 was then formally discussed by Louis XIV and his ministers in the *conseil d'en haut* at Versailles in December. Believing that the verbal assurances brought back by Hooke were insufficient, Louis eventually decided that the Scottish invasion should be postponed, and that the French army would concentrate on Spain during the campaigning season of 1706.[196] This meant, of course, that no invasion had yet been planned when the English and Scottish commissioners concluded the draft Treaty of Union on 1 August 1706 (22 July OS).

One reason for Louis' reluctance to commit his troops to Scotland was because Hooke had not been able to give him written evidence that the Scottish Jacobites would definitely rise up in support of a French invasion. In fact, they had subsequently sent an agent, Charles Fleming (brother of the Earl of Wigton), with the necessary documentation, but he did not set off until November, and did not reach Saint-Germain until January,[197] by which time Louis had made his decision.[198] To make matters worse, Fleming's ship had been intercepted at sea by a Flemish privateer which he thought might really be an English or Dutch ship. Fearing that his incriminating documents might be captured, Fleming had thrown them all overboard into the sea. He therefore arrived empty handed and had to send to Scotland for papers to verify his *bona fides*.[199] But in the days after his arrival he reconstructed as much as he could of the specific proposals of the Scottish Jacobites, including the amount of French support they would need.[200] Nairne noted on 12 February that 'I copied Ch. Flemings Memoire of Scotld 3 sheets of paper'.

No more could be done until later in the year when the French would begin to make their strategic decisions for 1707. But contact was maintained between Saint-Germain and Scotland because the Wine Act and the Wool Act permitted Scottish merchant ships to trade freely with France. One of Nairne's tasks was to obtain passes from the French foreign secretariat to permit these Scottish ships to enter and leave French ports. For his correspondence with Scotland he particularly used a merchant captain named Taite, who had transported Fleming, and there are frequent references in Nairne's diary to his obtaining passes for Taite between 1703 and 1706. In 1705 Nairne invited Taite to Saint-Germain, arranged for him to have audience with the queen,[201] and gave him a portrait of the king by Belle.[202] In February 1706, he invited him again, and arranged for him to see the queen, Lord Middleton and the Duke of Perth.[203] Taite showed his appreciation for the passes and audiences by giving Nairne some money, but the latter noted that 'I returnd ye 4 louis he gave me'.[204]

In August 1706, the news reached Saint-Germain that the draft Treaty of Union had been concluded by the English and Scottish commissioners. It would not come into effect unless and until it had been accepted by the parliaments of the two kingdoms, but this made it even more urgent for the queen and Middleton, with Hooke and Fleming, to persuade Louis XIV and his ministers to agree to invade Scotland in 1707. They were helped in their arguments when the French army was heavily defeated at Ramillies, as an expedition to Scotland would oblige the English to withdraw some of their troops from the continent.[205]

Shortly afterwards, still in August, a Scottish merchant captain named Henry Stratton arrived in France with renewed messages from the Scottish Jacobites requesting a French invasion. Nairne, who had arranged the pass for the ship,[206] noted on 20 August that 'H. Str arrivd here, and sent for me'. Stratton had brought oral messages from various Scottish Jacobites, including Middleton's nephew Lord Strathmore, but no written pledges. Nairne took him to see Middleton[207] and then told him to produce a paper which could be shown both to the queen and to the French ministers. Two days later, Nairne made a fair copy: 'I writt Cap.n Stratons relation.'[208]

In the days which followed, Nairne arranged for Stratton to see both James III and Queen Mary, as well as Middleton and Perth.[209] He also introduced him to some of the other Jacobite courtiers[210] and arranged for him to be rewarded with a portrait of the king by Belle.[211] Nairne's most important task, however, was to encourage Stratton to expand his 'relation' into a much longer document for the French. It was eventually ready on 23 September when Nairne noted that 'I finishd H. St.s acct of the p[rese]nt state of Scotld of 40 pages'. This paper was then given to the French ministers who, with Louis XIV, were making their strategic decisions for 1707. But it was to no avail. Louis decided that, in view of the recent French defeat outside Turin, he would concentrate on Provence and Spain rather than Scotland.[212]

Nairne, however, was not to be put off. He wrote to Stratton, who had now returned to Scotland, urging him to provide more positive evidence of the willingness of the Scottish Jacobites to rise in support of a French invasion.[213] Stratton agreed to do this, and sent a letter in cypher assuring the exiled court that many of the Scottish nobles were ready to rise in rebellion against the Treaty of Union, even without a French invasion.[214]

This was the kind of document which the court needed. On 30 December, Nairne recorded that 'a Council was held about Str. letter, and I put E. M. ans.r to St tre in cypher and I writt to him my self'. On the following day Nairne translated Stratton's letter into French and sent it to Torcy. It seemed that Louis XIV might after all change his mind and sanction an invasion of Scotland in 1707. But then the news arrived that the Scottish parliament had unexpectedly voted in favour of the Treaty of Union on 13 January (2 January OS) and that no Jacobite rising had resulted. Louis stuck to his original plan and postponed the invasion yet again.[215]

Nevertheless the French defeats in Flanders and northern Italy had made the idea of invading Scotland, and thus diverting English troops away from Flanders, ever more appealing. Louis XIV therefore decided that Colonel Hooke should be sent back to Scotland to make sure that a French invasion really would be supported. Middleton protested that this was unnecessary, as both Hooke's previous visit and Fleming's report had established that the Scots would indeed rise with French support.[216] But of course the court at Saint-Germain had no choice but to agree.

In February 1707, Nairne and Middleton drafted a 'Declaration of Warr' to be signed by James III and taken to Scotland by Hooke.[217] The declaration referred specifically to the Act of Security, because James stated in it his 'unalterable resolution of securing to them [the Scots] their religion, laws, liberties and independency'. It also gave the Scottish Jacobites a free hand to draft a resolution concerning a constitutional settlement which the king would sign and publish whenever he landed.[218] The two men then drafted 'Instructions to Hook',[219] which Nairne converted into 'Demands to be answerd' by the Scottish Jacobite nobles.[220] Hooke then left in March, taking with him the declaration, the demands and some letters to the leading nobles from the king.[221] Nairne, meanwhile, wrote to one of his contacts in Scotland to make it clear that Hooke's mission was to obtain assurances of support and that no French invasion could be expected that year.[222]

Hooke met the Jacobite leaders in Scotland during May[223] and assured them that James III and Louis XIV would support their constitutional and religious demands, notably concerning the security of the Protestant religion.[224] He then returned to France, bringing with him details of the amount of French help the Scots would need in order to rise up. He reached Saint-Germain at the end of June,[225] and prepared a report on his mission. Nairne 'copied ye Scots proposals to ye K. of Fr brought by Mr H',[226] and noted at the beginning of August that 'I got Mr Hooks relation of his 2d voyage into Scotld. to copie out for ye Q'.[227] The paper was long, but Nairne typically rose to the challenge. On the following day he noted:

> I finishd H. Rel. wch was 108 pages of large paper and in my hand 92. I began it fryd at 9 in ye morn. and ended saturd a little after 7 at night.[228]

Hooke's report named nine peers whom he had met in Scotland and with whom he had discussed the proposed French invasion, and twenty other 'seigneurs' who were sympathetic. It also outlined the help that they would need from France. But the most important point was that, in return for James's guaranteeing the security of the protestant religion and various constitutional concessions, the Scottish Jacobites made a definite commitment to rise up in support of a French invasion.[229]

They went even further. Just as they had sent Charles Fleming to France after Hooke's first mission, so the Scottish Jacobites now sent James Ogilvie (son of Lord Boyne) to confirm what they had promised Hooke, and with full powers to negotiate with James III and Louis XIV. He arrived in August[230] and saw James at Saint-Germain. It was agreed that, in the event of a Stuart restoration, the union of the two kingdoms, which had come into force on 12 May (1 May OS), would be terminated and that the king would accept all the laws passed by the Scottish parliament since 1689 which his first parliament wished to keep.[231] On 10 September, Boyne went to Versailles and had a private audience with Louis in which he confirmed all that Hooke had reported and emphasized the willingness of the Scots Jacobites to rise up.[232] The moment for decision had arrived.

On 22 September, Nairne left Saint-Germain with the king, the queen, Middleton, Perth and the other senior members of the Stuart court to go to Fontainebleau for their annual visit. His diary makes no mention of Scotland, concentrating on the many letters that he wrote. He was again 'lodgd au mouton blanc rue basse' and he mentions speaking with Adam of the French foreign secretariat. He 'rid out to ye Cavalcade about ye Canal on one of ye K. of Fr horses', and it was during this visit that he was invited to hear music in Madame de Maintenon's apartment.[233] The queen and Middleton were meanwhile doing everything they could to persuade Louis XIV to order an invasion for 1708.

At the end of September, Louis XIV and his ministers in the *conseil d'en haut* agreed that the invasion of Scotland would definitely go ahead in the spring of 1708.[234] The winter of 1707–8 was therefore to be spent making the necessary preparations. This decision to mount the invasion had important implications for Nairne himself, as he knew he would be expected to accompany the king. His wife and their three children had been staying at Compigny since August, and would probably have soon returned to Saint-Germain. But Nairne had other ideas. On 6 October he left Fontainebleau and went to join them. 'I stayd at Compigny ten free days', he wrote, and 'I went 2 or 3 times a hunting'. The main purpose of his visit was to persuade his wife to remain with the children at Compigny for the winter and not to return to Saint-Germain until the following year. He wanted them to be with their family and friends in the country rather than at the court when he would be absent for an extended period. As he briefly put it, 'I regulated my wife's accts and left her some mony'.[235] For the next five months, and until he left on the expedition to Scotland, he wrote to her virtually every day, knowing that he would not see her again for a long time, and fearing that, if the invasion went badly, he might never see her again.

Nairne returned to Saint-Germain on 19 October, but does not seem to have been involved in any of the preparations until the following February. This was partly because the planned invasion was a tightly kept secret, and partly because the preparations were primarily military and naval. When, however, Middleton drafted a new declaration for Scotland to replace the one he and Nairne had produced the previous year, he needed the latter's help. On 11 February, Nairne wrote in his diary that 'My Ld Mid. sent for me and gave me ye Decl. to be writt out faire and to be printed, and told me I shd have known it sooner, yt it was a nicety and no distrust'.

In the following days, Nairne made a copy of the declaration, had it printed, corrected the proofs, engrossed the manuscript[236] and took it 'to ye Qs closette at night wher ye great seal was put to it in the K, Q, D of Perths and E. Mid presences and ye K signd it'.[237] James III's 'Declaration to his good people of his Ancient Kingdom of Scotland' was dated 1 March and included all the promises that Ogilvie had asked for on behalf of the Scottish Jacobites.[238] Nairne 'bought a trunk and put up' all the printed copies of the declaration into it, together with 'ye great seals and signets' to be used once the king had landed in Scotland.[239]

Meanwhile, it had been decided that Charles Fleming should be sent to Scotland in a fast ship to inform the Jacobite nobles that an invasion was imminent, so they could make their preparations.[240] Nairne therefore 'drew Instructions for M. Flem',[241] made nine copies[242] and 'dated and seald' them.[243] Fleming sailed from Dunkirk at the beginning of March, and landed at Slains Castle (about thirty miles north of Aberdeen) where he saw Perth's nephew Lord Erroll and his mother (Perth's sister). Erroll then alerted the Earl Marischal (Perth's son-in-law), while Fleming himself travelled south to warn Middleton's nephew Lord Strathmore at Glamis Castle and then the other Jacobite nobles.[244] It was not known where the French troops would be disembarked, but Erroll, Marischal and Strathmore prepared pilots in case the landing was to be somewhere on the east coast beside their estates. In France, meanwhile, Middleton and Hooke[245] were discussing with Claude, comte de Forbin, who had been appointed to command the French fleet, as to where the landing should take place. Middleton favoured Burntisland on the north side of the Firth of Forth, immediately opposite Edinburgh, and his arguments prevailed.[246]

During February, James III decided which of his household servants and other courtiers would accompany him to Scotland, and which would be left behind at Saint-Germain.[247] In making his selection the king naturally gave priority to the ones who had military or naval experience. From his bedchamber, he took Perth and the other gentleman (who was a Lt General), three of his thirteen grooms (all of whom had been captains in the Royal Navy) and his master of the robes (another Lt General), as well as four of his valets.[248] From his Chamber, he took only his vice-chamberlain, his confessor, his surgeon, his two physicians and Captain James Murray.[249] There was no need to take anyone from the Stables, as equerries and grooms would be available in Scotland, but he took the comptroller of the household and one of his cooks to form the nucleus of a new Household Below Stairs.[250] Finally he took his former under-governor (another Lt General).[251] These were the men with whom Middleton and Nairne were to travel, leaving Lord Caryll, Monnot and Dempster to provide secretarial support for the queen at Saint-Germain.

On 3 March, Nairne noted that 'I prepard myself for my departure for Dunk[irk] in order to [*sic*] the exped. of Scotland'. Two days later he wrote again to his wife at Compigny, 'and told her for the first time yt I was going a journy wher my duty calld me, and wch the Curet [of Saint-Germain] would explaine to her to whom I gave my letter to be sent to her after my departure'. On the following morning, Tuesday 6 March, 'after having heard mass and taken leave of My Ld Car, Mr In and other friends', Nairne left Saint-Germain with Lord Middleton's two sons, whom the king had exceptionally allowed to join the expedition. They were joined by Middleton himself at Saint-Denis, and then the four men made their way north. They reached Saint-Omer on Friday 9th, spent the night at the English Jesuit college, and on the following day 'came in the Kings boat by water to Dunk, where we arived about 3 in ye afternoon'. James III, who had travelled separately, was already there. Nairne noted that 'the K lodgd at ye Intendants. I lodged at Mr Spickits rue des Minimes.'²⁵²

The plan had been to set sail on the following day, Sunday 11th, but then two serious problems arose. Nairne recorded laconically in his diary that 'the Kings sickness, and ye English fleet appearing, made us lose a whole week at Dunk, so we did not embarke till saturday 17'. In fact the *entreprise d'Ecosse*, as it was called, was very nearly cancelled at the last moment. On 9 March, the very day that James III had arrived at Dunkirk, a squadron of twenty-six English ships commanded by Admiral Byng was seen cruising outside the port. Then, on 10 March, James was diagnosed with measles.²⁵³

We do not how Nairne mainly occupied himself during these six tense days at Dunkirk, though he presumably wrote numerous letters, and he spent some time in both the parish church and the chapel of the Capuchins. The tides at Dunkirk meant that, having failed to sail on 11 March, the French ships could not leave the port until the 17th, when the water would again be deep enough. Fortunately for the French and the Jacobites, Admiral Byng withdrew his squadron from Dunkirk to the Downs on the 13th, leaving only a few ships to observe the port. And by the 17th, James III had recovered sufficiently from his measles.²⁵⁴ So the fleet was able to set sail 'in the afternoon' of that day and leave without being observed under cover of dark.

The French expeditionary force consisted of a squadron of thirty ships (five *vaisseaux de guerre*, twenty-one *frégates* and four *corsaires*) under the overall command of the comte de Forbin, transporting a small army commanded by the comte de Gacé.²⁵⁵ In addition to the French troops, there were nearly 200 officers seconded from the Irish regiments, who were expected to muster and lead the men (approximately 30,000) whom the Scottish Jacobite nobles said they could raise.²⁵⁶ Forbin and Gacé sailed with James III, Middleton, Nairne, Hooke and the members of the royal household in the *Mars*, one of the *vaiseaux de guerre*. Lord Middleton's two sons sailed with two other volunteers (Edward, Lord Griffin and Thomas Sackville) and with Colonel Francis Wauchope of the Irish brigade in the

Salisbury (an English *vaisseau de guerre* captured by the French). James Ogilvie of Boyne, who had been sent from Scotland to Saint-Germain the previous year, was on one of frigates, the *Espérance*, with a Scottish colonel named Canon.

The details of the expedition, which failed to effect a landing and had to return to Dunkirk, have been fully described by Professor Szechi[257] and can only be summarized here. Forbin's task was to sail up the North Sea as quickly as possible, to enter the Firth of Forth, and disembark the troops at Burntisland. It would not take long before the English ships outside Dunkirk would discover that the French ships had sailed, so Admiral Byng would be alerted, would sail to Dunkirk to check, and then follow Forbin's squadron as quickly as he could – though he would not know their precise destination. Speed was therefore of the essence, as Byng would only be two or three days behind, and might guess that the French would go to the Firth of Forth. The troops had to be disembarked before he arrived.

The expedition's timetable went wrong from the start, because the French ships immediately ran into very bad weather and had to ride out the storm behind the Nieuport Banks (between Dunkirk and Ostende) until 20 March. Having lost two valuable days, and three frigates dispersed in the storm, the French then overshot the Firth of Forth and first sighted the Scottish coast near Stonehaven, about fifteen miles from Aberdeen and a hundred miles north of the Forth, on the night of the 22nd. Instead of landing at Stonehaven or Montrose, which he ought then to have done, Forbin ordered his ships to go all the way back south to the Forth, thus losing another day. It was not until the evening of 23 March that the French arrived at the mouth of the Firth of Forth on the south-east side of the Fife coast. Pilots were called for and a rapid disembarkation was planned for the following morning after the squadron had sailed further west into the firth.

Byng, however, who had not been delayed by the storm outside Dunkirk and had decided to go straight to the Firth of Forth, had been able to catch up. The English fleet of twenty-eight warships arrived at the entrance to the firth late at night on the same day as the French (the 23rd), spotted the twenty-seven French ships the following morning and prepared to attack. The French squadron had no option but to escape out of the firth and sail back north, with the English in hot pursuit.

Nairne wrote two accounts of his experiences on the *Mars* with James III. The longer one, which he wrote day by day for Lord Caryll while on board ship, has not survived.²⁵⁸ The shorter account, which he included in his diary after his return, refers very briefly to these developments:

> contrary winds and mistakes of pilotes keeping us 8 days a going to Scotld, gave the enemy time to come up to us the saturday after our embarking ye 25th [*sic*: 24th]. We were then anchord in ye mouth of ye Forth where we had lyen all night when at break of day we perceivd ye English fleet: so instead of going up the river to land we were forced to saile to ye north.

What Nairne did not say was that this was the first time he had seen Scotland since he had sailed away as a young man thirty four years before in 1674. We may only guess at his feelings as he looked out at St Andrews, where he had gone to university, knowing that his mother and family were only a few miles away. Presumably he had felt sea sick during at least part of the journey, and perhaps afraid during the storm which the *Mars* had had to weather. But he did not say so.²⁵⁹

After leaving the Firth of Forth and returning up the coast, the French squadron made its way north to the Moray Firth, where it arrived on the 25th with the intention of landing at Inverness. The English fleet pursued it as far as Montrose before giving up the chase, but succeeded in overtaking and capturing the *Salisbury*. Nairne described this part of the voyage in his diary:

> the Enemy followd us, and some of their best sailers gaind upon us, and one fought desperately with 3 or 4 of our ships, from 4 in ye afternoon till night, ye Salsbery had a close fight wth this ship, and was taken next morning, and in her My Ld Clerm[ont] and his brother [the two sons of Lord Middleton], Ld Griffin, Coll. Wachop and Mr Sackville. In ye night our fleet changd its course, putting out their lights, so next morning the enemy lost sight of us, and we had 7 or 8 of our ships dispersd. Yet we endeavourd all sunday [26th] and the following night to get towards Enverness to land there having sent Boyne and Canon in ye Esperance before us to get pilots.²⁶⁰

Then bad weather intervened again. A gale set in from the north and on 26 March Forbin's squadron struggled all day to make any headway. Eventually it was agreed to call off the planned disembarkation and return to Dunkirk. But the return journey back was dreadful and took twelve days, with further storms lashing the ships all the way. Nairne described this part of the voyage in more detail:

violent contrary winds hinderd us to advance. Our fleet was dispersed, and having reason to believe ye Enemy would keep along the coast and be upon us before we could land all our troops and amunition, the french to whom ye King left to do what they thought most for their masters service and his, did advise and even press his Maty to return back to Dunk the wind being very faire then. And accordingly Mr Fourbin gave ye signal and orders, and changd his Course. But ye winds did so often change and were so often high and contrary that what with this and other faults of pilotes, as we were 8 days a going to Scotland we were a fortnight a coming back and it was a great providence we escaped all the dangers of the sea and of ye enemy who had time enough to follow us, besides yt we were very near falling in upon ye banks of ye Texel [off the Dutch coast in north Holland] in a fogy evening, if by providence ye fog had not cleard up and made us discover the fanal on the land wthin a league and a half of us. This was tuesday 3 April.

It must have been with enormous relief that Nairne wrote in his diary on Saturday, 7 April: 'After 3 weeks being at sea we landed safe at Dunk, about 4 in ye afternoon being the eve of Easter.'[261]

For a man like Nairne with little experience of the sea, it was a terrifying experience, being battered by violent March winds for over three weeks in the North Sea, within sight of land but never able to disembark, and facing a serious risk of being shipwrecked on the return journey. Given his strong Catholic faith, we may assume that he spent much of the time in prayer, and placed his life in the hands of Divine Providence. When he finally arrived back at Saint-Germain he noted that 'I did my devotions at ye parish church in thanksgiving for his divine goodness in preserving me during my journy and bringing me safe back againe'.[262]

If the *Mars*, like the *Salisbury*, had been captured we may only guess what might have happened to King James III. But Nairne, who was still Scottish despite being an ex-patriate in France, would certainly have been indicted for high treason along with Middleton and the household servants of the king. Imprisonment or execution were all that he and they could have expected. In the event, Lord Middleton's two sons were imprisoned in England for several years, whereas Lord Griffin (also on the *Salisbury*) was sentenced to be executed.[263]

Nairne and the others remained in Dunkirk for nine days recovering from their ordeal, before travelling back to Saint-Germain. He spent much of his time writing letters to Lord Caryll,[264] Lady Middleton, Lewis Innes, his assistants Monnot and Dempster, and of course to his wife. He was 'lodgd at Mr Geraldins' (the merchant captain whom he had known for several years), but was able to renew his old friendship with Jossier, the man who had supported him in Paris between 1676 and 1685, and who was now by chance living in Dunkirk.[265] On the 16th, he sent away his 'trunks by St Omers to St Germ',[266] and on the following day 'parted post wth Cap.n Murray an hour or two after ye K'. The journey took three and a half days, with overnight stops at Boulogne, Abbeville and Beauvais, and the two men reached Saint-Gerrmain at 'about 5 or 6 a clock at night' on the 20th. The first thing Nairne did was to ask his wife to come to join him as soon as possible: 'I writt that night to my wife from whom I had a letter and sent her 2 louis d'ors.'

That weekend, Nairne gave another *louis d'or* to the parish church 'for masses and for ye poor' and did his devotions, but he was now longing to see his wife and children again. The family was finally reunited on the 25th after a separation of six and a half months. Nairne merely commented in his diary that 'my wife arrived from Compigny. I went to see her in Paris where I stayd two or three days.' We may assume that this was a particularly happy reunion, but it raises the question as to what Nairne had actually expected or hoped for.

If the *entreprise d'Ecosse* had been successful, the French troops had landed at Burntisland and James III had been restored at least to the Scottish throne, what would Nairne have done? Lord Middleton and the Duke of Perth would have recovered their Scottish estates, and the other household servants (who were English, Irish, Italian and French, but not Scottish) would also have remained in the service of the king. We can confidently say that Nairne would have visited his family and recovered his own estate at Sandford in Fife. But would he also have remained in Scotland? Would he have invited his wife and children to join him there? We can only speculate.

The final pages of Nairne's diary, the book into which he had been recording his daily activities since the 1690s, were filled up with his account of the voyage to Scotland and the family reunion in April 1708. He was then fifty-four and a half years old, at an age when he might have decided to retire and return to live in Paris and at Compigny. It would have been appropriate to have concluded both his diary and his service at the Jacobite court at the same time, and it is interesting to observe that Nairne testified that 'the following years of my life' were recorded 'in another Tome of my Journal' in French, not English.[267] Nevertheless, we cannot know for sure what Nairne would have done if James III had been restored in 1708, and his diary does not enlighten us. All it contains is a brief comment on 21 February 1708, two weeks before he left Saint-Germain for Dunkirk, that 'I sent a mem: I drew concerning myself to My Ld Mid'. Whatever that memorandum might have contained, it seems that Nairne had been very conscious that a successful restoration would have had a profound impact on his future life. Its failure meant that he had little option but to continue working for Lord Middleton and Lord Caryll in the service of James III at the exiled Stuart court.

***

The five and a half years following his return from Scotland present a challenge for Nairne's biographer. The journal which Nairne had kept since 1689 comes to an abrupt end, and relatively few of the private letters which he wrote between the end of May 1708 and the end of December 1713 have survived.[268] There are plenty of documents from this period in his handwriting, but the difficulty is to establish which of them represent his own thoughts and initiatives, and which were merely drafted or copied on the orders of the king, Lord Middleton or Lord Caryll.

In both the summer of 1708 and the summer of 1709 James III served as a volunteer with the French army fighting in Flanders, and on both occasions he took with him (among others) Lord Middleton and David Nairne. This means that Nairne was present at both the Battle of Oudenarde in July 1708 and the Battle of Malplaquet in September 1709. Yet we know nothing about his experiences during these two campaigns. This is not because he did not record them, but simply because what he wrote has not survived. At the end of his journal which *has* survived he made the following entry:

> The Journall of the Campagne of 1708 is here after in French, as also that of 1709 and the following years of my life in another Tome of my Journal.

Without these two campaign journals, there is very little that we can say about either 1708 or 1709.[269]

At the end of April and the beginning of May 1708, Nairne made two visits to Paris to buy what he needed 'for the camp', which he described as 'a field bed and other things'. He noted:

The rest of this month of April, and to the 27 of May I stayd in St Germains, the
King and those that were to attend him to the Camp being all the time preparing
their equipage.[270]

James III left for Flanders on 18 May with Lord Middleton, and Nairne
followed him nine days later with 'the Controller [Francis Plowden] and
ye rest of ye equipage'.[271]

While he was with the king in Flanders Nairne wrote two letters, both
dated 23 June, to a close Scottish friend who had recently taken service with
the King of Prussia. The originals of the letters have not been discovered,
but copies were sent by the King of Prussia to the Duke of Marlborough
and have survived among the latter's papers.[272] The letters reveal that Nairne
was instrumental in helping to foil a plot to assassinate the Duke of Savoy.[273]

Nairne explained to his friend that he had been told in confidence
that six of the officers attached to the king were planning to travel to Turin
and assassinate the duke on 14 October Old Style (i.e. 25 October), which
was the birthday of James II. They regarded the duke as 'the author of all
of France's and thus of their Prince's [i.e. James III's] ills'. Nairne hoped
that his friend would be able to 'make the plan fail' by informing the King
of Prussia and asking permission himself to go to Turin to expose the six
assassins whom he knew and would be able to identify.[274] This was mainly
because he (Nairne) regarded the planned assassination as morally wrong
and against the teachings of the Church, but also because he hoped it
would benefit his friend at the Prussian court. Nairne explained that he
had been told of the plot in the greatest confidence and that he had been
made to swear 'on the Bible not to speak to anyone about about it in this
country'. He explained to his friend:

> You know how careful I am about swearing oaths, such that had you not been in a
> foreign country it would seem very likely that that the plan to be carried out would
> not have been discovered.

Nairne asked his friend to be very careful to keep the secret and to speak
only to the King of Prussia and his ministers, 'because you can see that I
am risking much for you', and urged him to keep him informed by writing
'confidentially'.

No evidence has come to light to explain exactly what happened next. Nairne's friend must have spoken to the King of Prussia because the latter wrote to the Duke of Savoy in September to inform him of the planned assassination and sent him copies of Nairne's two letters, which he described as written to a 'certain Gentilhomme Ecossais demeurant à Berlin nommé Aikenhead, lequel est prest aussi de se rendre luy même aupres de V. A. R. si Elle le souhaite'.[275] The incident, however, is interesting because it shows both Nairne's revulsion from the use of political assassination, even of one's enemies in wartime, and his attitude to the strict wording of the oath that he swore to persuade the plotters to inform him of their plan.[276] It is the first occasion when we have evidence of Nairne's taking an independent political initiative.

The first letter also contains an interesting comment by Nairne concerning the possibility of his visiting Scotland now that his elder brother had died and he had inherited the family estate at Sandford. The reference is oblique: Nairne hoped that his friend would be able to take advantage of the information he was giving him to procure 'that for which you have been hoping for so long', and he added: 'and for which I too would hope if my Family did not keep me here'.

Nairne returned to Saint-Germain at the end of the campaign, probably in September 1708, and remained there until the following June, when he again accompanied the king and Lord Middleton to 'the camp'.[277] He was with them 'pres de Mens' on 8 July,[278] and otherwise followed the army of the Maréchal de Villars until the Battle of Malplaquet in September, when James III returned to Saint-Germain. It is regrettable that this very significant experience has left no record.

Nairne remained at Saint-Germain during the winter of 1709–10, working as usual for both Lord Middleton and Lord Caryll. In February 1710, he agreed to be a witness at the wedding in the parish church of one of the king's footmen,[279] but that is all that we know. When, however, James III decided to join the French army in Flanders for the third successive year he told Middleton and Nairne that they should remain with the queen because it was 'more necessary' that they should be with her than with him.[280] As the queen decided to spend the entire summer at the *couvent de la visitation* at Chaillot, both Middleton and Nairne had to follow her there and live in what James described in a letter to Middleton as 'your hermitage'.[281] The king was with the French army from the middle of May to the end of the first week of September,[282] so Nairne remained in the 'hermitage' at Chaillot for most of that period.

It was while Nairne was at Chaillot in the summer of 1710 that he began to keep a letter book which he himself entitled 'Entries of some letters writt to England ..., some by E. Mid[dleton] and most by N[airne]'.[283] The book covers the period from May 1710 to December 1713, and includes both the letters which Nairne was instructed to send to the Jacobite agents in England and Scotland by Middleton and those which he sent on his own initiative. A chance reference in a letter of 7 August tells us that Nairne was given permission to leave Chaillot and visit his family estate at Compigny during that summer.[284]

Apart from the letters in this book, the only information about Nairne's activities during the winter of 1710–11 again comes from the registers of the parish church. On 6 November, he was a witness at the wedding of one of the king's *valets de chambre* named Gerald Fitzgerald. The bride was Mary Gordon, daughter of the late Alexander Gordon, and is described in the register as Nairne's cousin.[285] Mary Fitzgerald, as she now became, would become one of Nairne's closest friends in later years.

Shortly before this wedding, the political situation in Great Britain, and consequently the prospects of a Jacobite restoration, were dramatically altered by the change of ministry in London. Queen Anne dismissed both her Whig ministers and her Whig military commander-in-chief (Marlborough) and replaced them with Tories, who were determined to bring the war to an end and were suspected by the Whigs of having Jacobite sympathies. The general election of October 1710 provided the new Tory ministry with a significant majority in the House of Commons. With the political situation thus completely transformed, Nairne now found himself increasingly involved in the negotiations with the Tory ministers under Robert Harley, created Earl of Oxford in May 1711. In the first place, these negotiations involved making peace between France and the British government, despite the opposition of the United Provinces and the Holy Roman Emperor. They then concerned the possibility of repealing the Act of Settlement of 1701 and preventing the Hanoverian succession on the death of Queen Anne, despite the opposition of the Whigs and some (pro-Hanoverian) Tories. Underpinning all the negotiations was the desire of the pro-Jacobite Tories to persuade James III to make a timely conversion to Anglicanism, which might keep the Tory party united and facilitate the repeal of the act. These developments had a direct impact on Nairne because Lord Middleton had converted from Anglicanism to Catholicism in 1703 and was consequently distrusted by the Tory leaders in London. Nairne's letter book makes it clear that he was steadily entrusted with more responsibility, particularly during 1712 and 1713, and that Middleton deliberately became less involved in the correspondence with the Jacobite agents in England and Scotland.

During the spring of 1711, Nairne composed a long paper which he entitled 'Letter to a Friend'. It was written in the style of a printed pamphlet, and was presumably intended to become one, though there is no evidence that it was actually printed. Its aim was to overcome the doubts or fears of any Tories who were worried about the prospect of Anne's being succeeded by a Catholic Stuart rather than a Protestant Hanoverian, and for the purposes of the 'Letter' Nairne wrote as though he were loyal to Queen Anne and himself an Anglican.[286]

The document, which covers five folio pages in small handwriting, begins by arguing that only a Stuart restoration could safeguard the Church of England and the Tory party against the Hanoverians, the Dutch and the Whigs, and warns that England and Scotland would face a civil war if the issue was not settled before the death of Queen Anne. James III, therefore, should be invited to come to London once peace had been signed, because Anne was not in good health and might die at any time. It would take too long to repeal the Act of Settlement and *then* invite him, so he should be invited during the recess of Parliament and introduced to the Tory ministers, with whom he could make arrangements for the future. Parliament could then be recalled, the Act of Settlement quickly repealed, and (as Nairne put it) 'all the rights and privileges of the Church and State, Crown, Parliament and People settled again upon the solid foundation of the antient laws and Constitution of the Kingdom'. The 'Letter' stresses that James III should be invited to go to London, to overcome there any opposition from the Hanoverians or Whigs. If, however, he were not invited to London James would feel obliged to go to Edinburgh instead which, Nairne warns, might create difficulties, because in that event he might be asked by the Scots to end the Union 'which I have good reason to believe he is resolvd not to do'.

Nairne's 'Letter' is the first document we have which clearly states a political opinion. It ends with a significant passage in which he confronts the problem of James III's Catholicism, and argues that the king's sincere belief in religious toleration was the best guarantee of the future security of the Church of England. This would remain his opinion throughout the negotiations during the coming years:

Anything that tends towards Jacobitisme (as I own this letter dos) sounds ill in the ears of those who are allways usd to tack popery slavery and arbitary Government together and have no other notion of a Popish King but that of a Bigot Tyran, But I who know from unquestionable hands that the Pretender (as we call him here) besides his other great and good qualitys, is too wise and too just a Prince to think of persecuting any body for his religion, that on the contrary all those of our Church that are about him at present, have distinguishd marks of his bounty shewd to them, with assurance that it shall not be his fault if they have not the full exercice of their religion wherever they go with him: I who know also that he has sent particular directions to his friends here, to joyn themselves unanimously to vote for and support the measurs of the Court and present Ministery, with all the interest they have; am not only fully perswaded of his true affection for his sister, and love for his Country, but am also convinced in my conscience that our establishd Religion as well as our Libertys Estats and employments and everything els that is dear to us, will be infinitly more secure under his Government than under a Lutheran foreign Prince influenced by German and Whig Councils: And therefore to you I am not ashamd to own my self so far a Jacobite as to wish a perfect good understanding between our gracious Queen and her brother, which I look upon to be the only means to make her Ma.ty happy easy and safe as long as she lives, our present Ministry out of danger of being ever oppressd by their enemies, our Church safe, and our Country happy. To be a Jacobite at this rate, is being in my opinion a true Patriot, and a faithfull subject, and I hope you do me the justice to have no other opinion of me.

Shortly after writing this 'Letter', Nairne drafted the two letters which James III sent to his half-sister Queen Anne in May 1711. If the sentiments were clearly dictated by James himself, and discussed with Lord Middleton, the precise wording seems to have been chosen by Nairne. In the first letter the king explained that 'plain dealing is best in all things especially in matters of religion':

> I am satisfyd of the truth of my own religion, yet I shall never look worse upon any persons because in this they chance to differ from me ..., but they must not take it ill if I use the same liberty, I allow to others ... I may reasonably expect that liberty of conscience for myself which I deny to none.'[287]

In the second letter, the draft of which covered six quarto pages, James asked his sister to send someone to Saint-Germain, or receive a negotiator from Saint-Germain, so that 'things can be adjusted to our mutual satisfaction'. Nairne's draft is eloquent:

> The voice of God and nature calls you to it; The promises you made to the King our Father enjoin it; The preservation of our family, the preventing of unnatural wars require it; and The publick good and wellfare of our Country recommend it to you, to rescue it from present and future evils ... in the meantime I can assure you, that it is my unalterable resolution to make the Law of the Land the rule of my Government, to preserve those of the Church of England in all their just rights and Priviledges as by law establish'd.'[288]

During the summer of 1711, peace negotiations were opened between the French court and the new Tory ministry in London, so James III felt it would be inappropriate for him to join the French army for a fourth campaign in Flanders. Instead he decided to make a tour of the eastern provinces of France, and he invited both Middleton and Nairne to accompany him. Unfortunately we know virtually nothing of Nairne's experiences and reactions during this trip. The king's party left Saint-Germain in June, and were at Saverne (between Lunéville and Strasbourg) by 9 July.[289] From Alsace they went south to Lyon, where they inspected both the hospital and the silk factory, and then continued to the Dauphiné to join the French army commanded by the Duke of Berwick.[290] At some point, Nairne fell ill during the journey, but he noted in his letter book on 27 September, by which time the king had returned to Saint-Germain: 'I writt a line to my mother to tell her of my recovery.'[291]

Nairne's correspondence with his family was sent secretly to the Jacobite agents in Scotland, and none of it has survived. The letter book, however, makes the occasional reference to these family letters. On 21 May 1711, for example, he noted about one of his political letters that he had enclosed '2 for my mother and sister'.[292] And another letter, of 29 June, indicates that he was now regularly sending money to his family. Nairne was then about to accompany the king on his tour of the eastern provinces, and knew that this would inevitably cause him additional expense, so he wrote to Captain Henry Stratton: 'I told him not to draw on me for his 600 liv. till Aug: and to tell my cosen not to draw for his 300 till Oct.'[293] Shortly after his return he sent his mother 100 *livres*.[294] These were large amounts of money, given that his combined monthly salary was 198*l* 18*s* 6*d*[295] and that he had a wife and three children to support, so it is not surprising to find this note from the following March:

> I sent him a letter to my mother wth one to my sister in answer to their last without date, and told them how sorry I was yt I could not comply with what they expected of me.[296]

While Nairne was away from Saint-Germain his friend Lord Caryll, for whom he had worked since 1694, became very seriously ill. Middleton wrote from the Dauphiné on 6 September that 'poor Lord Caryll has visited the frontier of the world'.[297] Caryll was eighty-six years old, and had actually died at Saint-Germain two days before Middleton wrote this letter. It was Caryll who had saved Nairne's career after the fall of Lord Melfort, and it was Caryll who had enabled Nairne to start working for Middleton in 1703. The two men had enjoyed a perfect working relationship, and Nairne must have been deeply saddened by his old master's death, at a time when he was unable to say goodbye. The death had little impact, however, on Nairne's work in the political secretariat, because the king decided not to replace Caryll as secretary of state, and gave Middleton the responsibility for the Roman correspondence which Caryll had been conducting. Nairne now worked solely for Middleton, 'one factor', as he put it, 'being enough for the little trade there is at present'.[298] He was assisted, as before, by Monnot and Dempster.

The winter of 1711–12 was the last that Nairne was destined to spend with his wife and children at Saint-Germain, and once again it is disappointing to record that no evidence concerning his life there has survived.

We do have evidence, however, of his growing political involvement. Peace preliminaries were agreed between the French and British governments in September 1711, much to the fury of the Whigs, the Dutch, the Emperor and the Elector of Hanover, all of whom wanted to continue the war and humble the French by advancing from Flanders to Paris and Versailles. From a Jacobite perspective it was essential that the peace preliminaries should be accepted by the Tory majority in Parliament, and we find Nairne in November 1711 instructing one of the Jacobite agents to 'get all the Scots Jacobites in Parliament, and the English Jacobites in Parliament also, to favour peace, as also to keep well with the ministry, to know all they could from it, and send account here'.[299]

In the spring of 1712, the Stuart court at Saint-Germain, like the French court at Versailles, suffered from a serious outbreak of smallpox. Nairne was one of the many people who contracted the disease, and for about four weeks from early April to early May he was unable to work.[300] By the time he had recovered several other members of the court, including most notably Princess Louise-Marie, had died.[301] James III himself was seriously ill but recovered. His death would have left the Jacobites without a viable claimant to the throne,[302] but Nairne was able to report to his correspondents in England and Scotland on 5 May that 'ye King was now intirely recoverd and ye Q. as well as her affliction could allow her to be'.[303]

One condition insisted on by the British government in the peace negotiations with the French at Utrecht was that James III should leave France and take his court to the Duchy of Lorraine, where Duke Léopold-Joseph eventually offered him the château at Bar-le-Duc. Queen Mary was to remain at Saint-Germain with most of the Jacobite courtiers, and James was to take with him only his own household servants. Nairne wrote to a Jacobite agent in England on 3 July that 'we are ready to remove at a days warning, but no day fixt yet'.[304] In other letters, he emphasized that 'ye King carryd no Jesuits wth him but yt he carryd all his protestant servants wth him',[305] and commented that 'it was hopd ye Ch. of Engl.d would see by this, the K's inclination towards them, he being resolvd on this as well as on all other occasions to be just and kind to them and to be an impartial common father'.[306] He also emphasized that the king would even be accompanied to Lorraine by an Anglican chaplain.[307]

James III, Middleton and Nairne left Saint-Germain on 18 August and moved temporarily to the château du Raincy, situated to the east of Paris.[308] After two short visits to Paris, at the end of August and in early September,[309] they then left on the 13th of that month to go to Châlons-sur-Marne,[310] on the French side of the border with Lorraine, to await the formal conclusion of peace at Utrecht. Nairne occupied part of this period sending engraved portraits of the king to stimulate support in England and Scotland.[311] He added his own commentary:

> [The king] is a tal proper well shapd young gentleman, ... he has an air of greatness mixd with mildness and good nature, and ... his countenance is not spoilt with the smal pox, but on the contrary ... he looks now more manly than he did, and is really healthier than he was before.[312]

With the peace negotiations at Utrecht reaching their conclusion, James III now came under increasing pressure from the Tory ministers, notably Lord Oxford and Lord Bolingbroke, to convert to the Church of England. Nairne therefore drafted a long paper in which he explained the king's reasons for not making an insincere conversion. In the event James decided not to use the draft, because he thought it 'fitter to say nothing at all upon that subject',[313] and Nairne commented privately to one of the agents in England:

> he'l promise and actually perform any thing his creditors can require of him for their satisfaction that is consistent with his honour and conscience, but beyond these bounds he never can nor will go, for he is a thorow honest man and will deceive nobody, and certainly his being of this character is a far greater security for all traders that deal with him than if he were a man of Swift's or Austin's principles.[314]

While Nairne was at Châlons, he again fell ill, though the available documents do not specify what was wrong with him. He wrote on 21 October that 'since my last of ye 12 Sep: I have been sick and not in a condition to write to you before now'.[315] Nairne's indisposition served to emphasize how important he had now become in the secretariat. Lord Caryll had been able to read Italian, but Lord Middleton, now handling the Roman correspondence, was unable to do so and had to depend on Nairne. There is a letter of 30 September 1712 sent by Middleton from Châlons to Cardinal

Gualterio in which he apologizes for not replying to one of his letters, the reason being 'the illness of my secretary who understands Italian'.[316]

Nairne's letter book contains the summaries of several letters which he wrote on 21 October, the day he resumed work. In one of them, written to his mother ('ye La of St ford'), he told her that he 'had sent directions to remitt 100 livres to her by ye same way I sent her ye like sum last year'.[317] If the loss of these family letters to Scotland is very regrettable from a biographical point of view, it is even more disappointing that we have none of the letters that Nairne sent to his wife. When James III left Saint-Germain, he gave orders that none of his servants was to be accompanied by his wife. As a result, though unknown to him at the time, Nairne was never to see his wife again. We may safely assume that they would have conducted a regular correspondence during their separation.

James III eventually left Châlons on 20 February 1713 and arrived at Bar-le-Duc on the following day.[318] At first he lived in the town in the rue des Tanneurs (now the rue Docteur Nève), in a house belonging to one of the town-councillors. Nairne might have been given a room in this house, but he was probably one of the majority who were provided with lodgings elsewhere. Then, in March, the court moved up to the château at the top of the hill overlooking the town, and Nairne was given accommodation in proximity to the king's apartment.[319]

At the beginning of May, the Duke of Lorraine invited James III to visit him at Lunéville[320] where he remained for about four weeks. He was accompanied by both Middleton and Nairne,[321] and the latter commented that James was received very 'kindly' and that 'he was esteemd and belovd here [Lunéville] by all even by the Germans who could not see him and know him without wishing well to him'.[322] Shortly after their return they stayed for ten days at the château de Commercy with the prince de Vaudémont,[323] with whom Nairne established cordial relations and began a correspondence.[324]

Apart from a short visit with the king to Plombières in August,[325] and another to see the Duke of Lorraine at Lunéville in early November,[326] Nairne remained at Bar-le-Duc for the rest of 1713. For most of that time he lived in the château at the top of the hill, but the king preferred to return to the house he had previously occupied in the town during the winter of

1713–14. As the house adjoining the king's was now also occupied by the court, Nairne was probably given lodgings there.[327]

By the end of 1713, it was a year and a half since he had seen either his wife or his three children. His elder daughter Françoise was nineteen years old, and of an age to help her mother. The younger children, however, Louis and Marie, were still only just fourteen and nearly thirteen respectively. The evidence of later years indicates that Louis was disturbed by the unexpected and prolonged separation of his parents. Nairne must have remitted money to his wife at Saint-Germain, and it is interesting to observe that this year he also sent to his mother in Scotland 200 *livres* instead of the 100 *livres* he had sent her in the two previous years.[328]

Now that Great Britain and France were at peace, and the Tories controlled both the ministry and the parliament in London, the time had come when James III hoped that the Act of Settlement would be repealed and that he would be invited to succeed peacefully to the throne after the death of his sister Queen Anne. Everything depended on the goodwill of the Tory ministers, notably Lord Oxford, and James III felt that he had to wait for the latter to take the initiative. The Scottish Jacobites became frustrated by this inaction and wanted to start a Jacobite rising, so Nairne had to write to explain the situation. In December 1712, for example, he wrote:

> As to advice or directions the K could give none to his friends in Scotland at present being advisd by his best friends to do nothing at present for fear of spoiling any good intentions some persons may have for him, that all depended on H[arley, i.e. Lord Oxford] who being a dark man, nobody knew well what to reckon upon and how to act therefore in the uncertainty, nothing seemed more prudent than to wait to see how things will turn.[329]

He wrote again in January 1713 that 'the King was bid ly quiet and say nor do nothing till he shall see clearer into the dark dopings of the chief director of trade [i.e. Oxford], least in clashing with them he shall ruine himself'.[330] It was still the same at the end of April:

> trade has beene of late such a mistery and is so still, that in the nice conjecture he is in, he can not with prudence give any directions either to Scotland or England, and has been positively advis'd by his best ministers to be quiet, and neither say not do any thing, least speaking and doing in the dark might do him more hurt than good.[331]

Nairne eventually had to reassure the Scots that 'in case the Princess of Denmark [i.e. Queen Anne] dies, and that nothing be done by her to secure the King's restoration, he is resolved to have immediat recourse to Scotland'.[332] One reason for the delay was the determination of many Tories that James III should announce his conversion to the Church of England as a necessary precondition for repealing the Act of Settlement. This, as we have seen, was the one thing that James was not willing to do. To show his good faith, he invited the Rev. Charles Leslie, a leading Tory Anglican, to open a Protestant chapel in the château de Bar-le-Duc,[333] and meanwhile Nairne did what he could to emphasize the king's genuine belief in religious tolera-tion. In a letter to one of the Jacobite agents, he doubted if Lord Oxford was himself insisting that the king should convert.[334] Professor Szechi, the leading authority on these negotiations, has commented:

> A spate of attempts to highlight James's natural toleration, and zealous compliance with a ministerial request to order the Jacobites to support Tory candidates in the general election, accompanied this. The Jacobite Court plainly hoped these measures would avert such a demand, or else soften the impact of James's inevitable refusal. But in the event, Oxford denied any such wish, in a letter in his own hand according to the relieved Nairne.[335]

The period of waiting dragged on through the autumn of 1713, which Nairne found 'very melancholy and disheartening'. He wrote in a letter of 24 October:

> the King continues still resolv'd to try what time patience and all good offices on his side will produce, leaving ... the event to God alm[ighty]: and to the Princess of Denmark's and Harley's consciences. But when Parliament comes to town we shall be better able to judge how matters will go, for tis raisonable to beleeve yt then or never some people will show themselves.[336]

In the event, they did not show themselves, but Lord Oxford now made a move which was to have a profound impact on Nairne's career. Oxford informed James III that an obstacle to the wished for restoration was his continued employment of the Catholic Lord Middleton as his secre-tary of state. Middleton, he argued, should be replaced by a Protestant.

No mention seems to have been made of Nairne, another Catholic, nor of the fact that Nairne had by then taken over most of the correspondence.[337] But the implication was clear. If the Jacobite Tories were only prepared to correspond with a Protestant at the exiled court, then both Nairne and Middleton would have to be replaced. In a letter of 2 December, James III informed the marquis de Torcy that with great reluctance, and knowing that Louis XIV believed this to be necessary, he had agreed to appoint an Anglican secretary of state.[338]

Endnotes

1. Diary, 25 September 1701.
2. Diary, 25 September 1701: 'I writt ye minutes of what had been orderd in Councill'; 1 October 1701: 'I waited on E. Middleton who dictated to me what had been orderd the day before in Councill.' It seems that several council meetings took place during October 1701 to which Nairne was not invited (17, 21 October 1701), but he was present at the meetings held to discuss the news that Princess Anne had succeeded William III (20, 29 March 1702), and at the few meetings held thereafter (12, 14, 29 June 1703).
3. Diary, 12, 14 March 1702.
4. Diary, 6, 7 October 1702.
5. Diary, 19 October 1701.
6. Diary, 14, 16, 17, 18 March 1702. Nairne had also incorporated some details from a memoire which he obtained from 'ye nuns of Chaillot containing some passages of ye late Kings holy life' (Diary, 11 February 1702).
7. Diary, 18 March 1702.
8. Diary, 30 June, 1 July 1702.
9. Diary, 13–15 July 1702. Nairne also sent a copy 'in a small hand in 4 sheets of paper to be sent by post to Rome to be put in Latin. In ye original manuscript there was 18 sheets, wch I contain in 4' (Diary, 1 and 16–23 July 1702). He had previously sent a copy to Cardinal de Noailles, the Archbishop of Paris, on 1 June 1702.
10. Nairne's original version in English (in eighteen sheets) was entitled 'A Short Relation of the Life and Death of James the Second King of England etc, written by his Ma.ties Confessor the Reverend Father Sanders', and the first pages

are in Bod. Carte MSS 180, ff. 51–9. It was shown to Sanders on 16 April 1703 and printed by Weston in May (Diary, 2 May 1703). A copy was sent to Cardinal Caprara in Rome on 28 August 1703, but Nairne had already given a proof copy to Monsieur de Baby on 27 March.

11. These papers were found in James II's closet shortly after his death 'lying in heaps on the floor, the papers of consequence confounded with Petitions, begging letters and other useless papers' (RA. SP 196/136, L. Innes to James III, 20 May 1737). The 'loose sheets and small pieces of paper' in the handwriting of the king were bound up into a quarto volume of 173 pages, which is now in the library of Trinity College, Dublin, MS 3529, and which was published in London in 1925 as *The Papers of Devotion of James II* (ed. G. Davies).

12. Diary, 9, 10 November 1701 ('I finishd ye Translation of some of ye K's papers of devotion writt at Anet wth 3 other papers of ye same nature 2 of wch were prayers'), 12, 13 December 1701, 11 January 1702. For the papers written at Anet in July 1698, see *The Papers of Devotion*, pp. 115–24.

13. Diary, 14 December 1701.

14. Diary, 12 January 1702.

15. Diary, 16–23 July 1702. Nairne recalled many years later that 'je scais qu'il a laissé ecrittes de sa propre main des preuves incontestables de sa pieté dans beaucoup de ses manuscrits dont j'ai vü, lü et copié grand nombre' (Bod. Carte MSS 208, f.371, 'attestation du Chevalier Nairne', 3 July 1734).

16. Nairne's French translation of all the papers (in Monnot's handwriting), with one which has never been published in English (in Nairne's own handwriting), is in in RA. SP 248/150. See also Corp, *A Court in Exile*, pp. 235–6.

17. Nairne's French translation of his 'extract' from the king's advice to his son is in RA. SP 248/150. Entitled 'Instructions au Prince de Galles', it contains a short introduction followed by eleven numbered sections.

18. Copies of thirty-eight of James II's letters to Rancé, and the originals of eighteen of Rancé's letters to James II, have survived, and are calendared in HMC *Stuart* I.

19. Diary, 25 November, 5 December 1703.

20. Diary, 31 May 1703. It was given him by Francis Plowden, the comptroller of the Household.

21. Diary, 6 July 1703. He did this with Plowden and Robert Power, the king's 'Counsillor at Law'.

22. Nairne finished making the two copies of James II's testament on 11 July 1703.

23. One copy of the inventory was eventually deposited in the Collège des Ecossais in Paris and was published by the Royal Society of Antiquaries in 1817 (*Archaeologia*, xviii, pp. 223–39). The other copy, which belonged to James III, is now in the Brotherton Library of the University of Leeds (MS Dep 1984/2/5), and was reproduced in *The Historian* n°.7, summer 1985, no pagination).

24. James III wrote a second discharge to the queen for her guardianship on 6 March 1708 before he sailed for Scotland (Corp, 'Inventory of the Archives of the Stuart Court', p. 133).

25. Diary, 15 May, 29 August 1702 ('I went wth my wife to the King's tomb where Fr Jonson was taking ye Deposition of a woman that was cured by ye Intercession of ye King'). On 15 June 1702, Cardinal de Noailles (Archbishop of Paris) appointed a commission 'to examine ye Truth of ye King's miracles ... to serve for his Canonisation at Rome' (Scott, Geoffrey, '"Sacredness of Majesty", the English Benedictines and the Cult of James II', *Royal Stuart Papers* XXIII (Huntingdon, 1984), p. 3).

26. Diary, 25 August 1703. See also 12 and 17 July 1703, when Nairne mentioned copying letters and papers concerning the miracles 'of ye late Kings to be sent to ye Q. at Chaillot'.

27. Diary, 27 August, 1 September 1703.

28. Diary, 28 August 1703. Caprara was the Jacobite minister in Rome and later became Cardinal Protector of England. The 'récit' of one of these miracles is now in Archivio Segreto Vaticano, Fondo Albani 164, p. 14.

29. Diary, 27 August 1706. The commission established by Cardinal de Noailles verified nineteen miracles out of a much larger number submitted to it (Scott, '"Sacredness of Majesty"', p. 3). Nairne's copies of the 'Relations of Miracles' are in Bod. Carte MSS 180, ff.4–29. He recalled many years later that 'il y a entre autres, une attestation comme quoy feüe mon Epouse fit dire ... une neuvaine dans l'Eglise [des Benedictins Anglois, au Faubourg St Jacques] pour mon fils [Louis, born on 24 December 1699], qui etoit agé alors d'environ 5 ans, et incommodé d'une rupture, dont il fut gueri peu après que la neuvaine fut achevée, et n'a jamais plus rien senti de cette incommodité du depuis' (Bod. Carte MSS 208, f.371, 'attestation du Chevalier Nairne', 3 July 1734).

30. Diary, 1 August 1702.

31. Diary, 5, 9, 10 September, 6, 16 October 1702.

32. Diary, 27, 30 November 1702.

33. Diary, 30 July 1706.

34. Diary, 24 May 1703.

35. Diary, 1 June 1703.

36. Diary, 2 June 1703.

37. Diary, 21 June 1703.

38. On 12 January 1707, James III signed a warrant 'to transport for some months to St Germains so many of the late King's memoirs and other papers in his own hand deposited in the archives of the Scots College as relate to the year 1678 and downwards, there to be inspected and perused by persons appointed for

that purpose' (HMC *Stuart* I, p. 209. See also ibid. p. 216, warrant by James III, 9 November 1707).

39. Dicconson's copy of the biography, which is in four folio volumes, is now in the Royal Library at Windsor Castle. He began by having everything that Nairne had already written copied into a new volume by Monnot, and then himself continued the story of the king's life from 1678 until his death in 1701, but gave it to Monnot to copy out fair. Dicconson's copy is therefore in a single handwriting throughout, and consequently has given the erroneous impression that it was all composed by him. It was finished before 1715, by which time Nairne had left Saint-Germain and accompanied James III to Lorraine. The queen then instructed Monnot to add to the copy started by Nairne (which finished in 1677) all that Dicconson had written (covering the years 1678–1701). Showing the handwriting of both men, it is now in the Scottish Catholic Archives, in five folio volumes (SCA. KJ).

40. Dicconson's contribution to *The Life of James II* draws on documents which were (and still are) among Nairne's personal collection of papers.

41. Corp, 'Archives of the Stuart Court', p. 135. In part, this was because Lindsay had had very little work. See BL. Add MSS 40733, Trant to Prior, 7 January 1699: 'Mr Lyndsay ... has no other employmt but to play at cards, and of post days to disperse ye publick Gazetts.'

42. Diary, 11, 16 September, 6 December 1703. See also 27 December 1704: 'I dind wth My Ld C ... and drunk caffé at My Ld Mid.'

43. Nairne's contacts at Versailles included Adam in the Foreign Secretariat, and Neuermeil, Villatte and Hyacinthe-Louis Jossigny in the War Secretariat.

44. Diary, 8 July 1703.

45. Diary 6 August 1703. Labadie was Jacques Delabadie, the senior page of the king's bedchamber.

46. Diary, 14 June, 22, 25 December 1703.

47. Diary, 11 January 1704.

48. Diary, 30 August, 25 October 1705. The list of the queen's unpaid bills in Nairne's handwriting is in Bod. Rawlinson MSS C.987, p. 146.

49. Diary, 7 August 1703 ('I writt to Belle'), 26 December 1703 ('I writt to Bel ye painter').

50. Diary, 9 May 1705.

51. Diary, 28 May 1706.

52. Diary, 11 September 1706. John Lyon, 5th Earl of Strathmore was Lord Middleton's nephew.

53. Diary, 20 September 1706. Another portrait of the king was sent on 11 September 1707.

54. Diary, 4 January 1704.
55. Diary, 7, 11, 16 February 1706.
56. For Bourke's earlier career, see Kerney-Walsh, M., 'Sir Tobie Bourke, ambassadeur de Jacques III à la Cour de Philippe V (1705–1713)', in Corp, Edward, ed., *L'autre exil: les Jacobites en France au début du XVIIIᵉ siècle* (Montpellier, 1993), p. 121–7.
57. Bourke's letters were preserved by Nairne and are in Bod. Carte MSS 180, ff.109–97 and Carte MSS 209, ff.489–577.
58. For a description of *The Duumvirate*, see H. Erskine-Hill, 'The Poetic Character of James II', in Corp, *A Court in Exile*, pp. 220–34, at pp. 231–3.
59. Diary, 18 December 1705.
60. Diary, 7 January, 3 March, 11 May, 29 December 1706, 11 January 1707.
61. The only surviving copy of *The Duumvirate* is in Nairne's papers, Bod. Carte MSS 208, ff.397–98.
62. Diary, 10, 18 July 1702.
63. Diary, 28 August 1702.
64. Diary, 29, 31 August, 1, 4, 5 September 1702.
65. Diary, 12 September 1702.
66. Diary, 12 March 1704.
67. Diary, 13 March 1704.
68. Diary, 15 July 1704.
69. Diary, 12 December 1704.
70. Diary, 17 January 1705.
71. He was given permission to come on 12 February 1705 (Diary).
72. Diary, 13 March 1705.
73. See p. 79.
74. Szechi, Daniel, *Britain's Lost Revolution? Jacobite Scotland and French grand strategy, 1701–8* (Manchester University Press, 2015), p. 81, quoting Hooke to Torcy, 10 June 1705.
75. The Melforts came to Saint-Germain on seven occasions and Nairne and Marie-Elisabeth made a point of visiting them. Nairne also visited them twice in Paris (Diary, 7 July 1705, 8 June 1707).
76. Diary, 7 July 1705.
77. Diary, 25 May 1706.
78. Diary, 8 June 1706.
79. Diary, 17 June 1706.
80. Diary, 18, 20 June 1706.
81. Diary, 21 June 1706; HMC *Stuart* I, p. 205.
82. Diary, 25 June 1706. Nairne refers to attending three council meetings in 1706 (26 July, 11 October, 31 December), but only one thereafter, on 3 January 1708.

He bought an 'Entry book for the minuts of Council' on 14 September 1706, but it has not survived.

83. Diary, 3 February 1703. See also Corp, *A Court in Exile*, p. 131.
84. 5, 6 February 1703. His salary was reduced from 89*l* 7*s* 6*d* to 81*l* 18*s* 7*d*, and his two pensions from 83*l* 13*s* 3*d* to 78*l* 1*s* 10*d*.
85. Diary, 5 September 1704.
86. Diary, 16 June 1706.
87. Diary, 15 July 1706.
88. Diary, 9 August 1706.
89. Diary, 18 June 1707. The *hôtel* was granted to Thady Meagher, an Irishman, whose wife Dorothy was the sister of Thomas, 4th Viscount Fitzwilliam (whose great-grandson founded the Fitzwilliam Museum in Cambridge).
90. Ruvigny, *The Jacobite Peerage*, pp. 195–204.
91. James Therry had been the Athlone Pursuivant of Arms in Dublin and had followed James II to Saint-Germain in 1690. His archives were published as *The Pedigrees and Papers of James Terry [sic], Athlone Herald at the Court of James II in France, 1690–1725*, ed. C. E. Lart (Exeter, 1938). See also Biblioteca Apostolica Vaticana, Vaticani Latini 14937, *The Variation of the Armes, and Badges of the Kings of England, from the Tyme of Brute until the present Yeare of our Lord, One Thousand Six Hundred Ninety and Seven*, an illuminated manuscript presented by Therry to the Prince of Wales.
92. Diary, 18 January 1700.
93. For example, John Kearney (under-secretary for Ireland) sponsored Nicholas Geraldin (Diary, 16, 18, 23 April, 8 May 1700; Ruvigny, p. 198); Edmund Barry (gentleman usher of the queen's presence chamber) sponsored another Edmund Barry (Diary, 24, 25 September 1700; Ruvigny, p. 200); Thomas Banckes (clerk to the treasurer and receiver-general) sponsored John Coyle (Diary, 2, 4, 5, 9 November 1700; Ruvigny, p. 200); John Bagot (gentleman usher of the king's privy chamber) sponsored Daniel O'Riordan (Diary, 26, 27 March 1700, 2 November 1703; Ruvigny, p. 200); and Theobald Bourke, Lord Brittas sponsored Thomas Grace (Diary, 28, 29 April 1702; Ruvigny, p. 201).
94. For example, Louis Matthias Becquet and Peter Thomas Becquet (Diary, 18 August 1699; Ruvigny, pp. 197–8); Catherine Fitzgerald, wife of the Sieur du Bourg (Diary, 9, 10, 13 July 1700; Ruvigny, p. 199); Paul and Stephen Leonard and Nicholas Aylward (Diary, 31 August, 1, 2 September 1700; Ruvigny, p. 199); Catherine Macarty and Cornelius O'Sullivan (Diary, 4 September 1700; Ruvigny, p. 199). See also Bibliothèque Nationale de France (hereafter BNF.) MSS Fd Fr Pièces Originales 2088, p. 13, Nairne to Therry, undated but 12 May 1700: 'I do assure you I have not been forgettfull of the Certificats you recommend to me, I have begd Mr Sec.ry to get them signd, I have told him the concern I

had in them, and have neglected no motif to prevail to get them dispatchd ... ye persons concernd must have a little patience, and with time I hope to serve them effectually'; BNF. MSS Fd Fr Pièces Originales 2088, p. 2, Therry to Nairne, 23 July 1700: 'There is none alive after my family I longe now to see for one halfe an ower ... [other than] you and if you please to allow it me may have a true understanding in these affayres.'

95.   BNF. MSS Fd Fr Pièces Originales 2088, p. 4, Nairne to Therry, 4 September 1700.

96.   Diary, 4 September 1700.

97.   Diary, 10 September 1700.

98.   Diary, 18, 20 July 1701.

99.   Diary, 30 July 1701.

100. Diary, 9 August 1701.

101. Diary, 15 August 1701.

102. Diary, 25, 27 August, 1 September 1701. For the certificate given to Mrs Roche, mother of Theobald Roche, see Ruvigny, *The Jacobite Peerage*, p. 201. See also Diary, 5 August 1702: 'Mrs Harvie got her Certificat and offerd me mony but I refusd it.'

103. BNF. MSS Fd Fr Pièces Originales 2088, p. 11, Nairne to Therry, 15 March 1702. The man who asked for the authenticated copy was Philip Francis Becquet, a cousin of the Becquets mentioned in note 94 (Ruvigny, *The Jacobite Peerage*, p. 202).

104. BNF. MSS Fd Fr Pièces Originales 2088, p. 11, minute by Therry on Nairne to Therry, 15 March 1702.

105. BNF. MSS Fd Fr Pièces Originales 2088, p. 15, Therry to Perth, undated but probably 12 August 1702.

106. Diary, 15, 16 August 1702.

107. Diary, 17 August, 30 October 1702, 2 April 1703.

108. Dr Matthew Kennedy was an Irish lawyer who had been appointed Master in Chancery in Dublin in 1689. He was the author of *Généalogie des Stuarts* (Paris, 1705), a history of the Stuart royal family which argued that the family had originated in Ireland.

109. In 1705 Perth wrote that 'I have not been kindly used ... Had I been an Englishman ... I had been more distinguish'd' (Nathaniel Hooke, *Correspondance, 1703–1707*, vol. 1, p. 236, Perth to Lady Erroll, 7 July 1705.

110. Diary, 12 June 1703.

111. Therry is not included in the surviving lists of salaries and pensions after 1703.

112. Nairne did not normally mention what fee he was paid, but on 10 December 1707 he noted that 'Mr Geraldin of Martinique sent me 8 louis d'ors by

Mr Monnot, and 3 for himself [Monnot] for his declaration de noblesse'. Nairne was well acquainted with the Geraldin family. Sir James Geraldin and his son Tobie were privateers operating from Dunkirk and Saint-Malo. In 1695 Nairne had invested money in the armament of one of their ships, 'ye Sauvage', and he noted that in return he received a share of 'ye prise mony' (Diary, 7 December 1695, 28 January, 15 March, 6 October 1696, 29 January 1698). See also above, note 93, for the *déclaration de noblesse* of their cousin Nicholas Geraldin (Ruvigny, *The Jacobite Peerage*, pp. 198, 203, 235). Mr Geraldin of Martinique was another cousin named Claude Francis Geraldin, sieur of Mont Gerald and a counsellor of the sovereign council of Martinique (Ruvigny, *The Jacobite Peerage*, p. 204).

113. Diary, 21 July 1703. Sir William Godolphin, a Catholic, had died in Madrid in 1696 leaving his property in England to his Protestant nephew and niece, and his investments on the Continent (mainly in Rome and Spain) to be distributed to charity. (See *DNB*, vol. 8, p. 46; and Venerable English College (hereafter VEC.), Rome, Scritture 11/12/1–8 (particularly 5), and Membrane M.405). Lady Sophia Bulkeley was Godolphin's second cousin and argued unsuccessfully that she should receive most of his charitable bequest. (See her correspondence of 1697 and 1698 in VEC. Scritture 17/2, unsorted Meredith Papers). When her sister, the Duchess of Richmond, died in 1702 Lady Sophia was unable to inherit her money because she was in exile at the Jacobite court, so she renewed her claims to inherit Godolphin's money, and asked for Nairne's help. (See her correspondence of 1703 and 1705 in Bod. Rawlinson MSS D.21 (sorted Meredith Papers) ff.27, 31).

114. Diary, 23 July 1703.

115. Diary, 21 November 1703. Nairne was prepared to accept '2 bottels of Esqueba' from her (2 January 1704), but made a point of sending her in return 'a box of tea' (12 July 1704). (I have not been able to identify Esqueba, though perhaps it was a Spanish wine).

116. Corp, *A Court in Exile*, p. 237.

117. Diary, 29 March 1707.

118. Diary, 2 April 1707.

119. Diary, 8 April 1707.

120. 18 April, 16 May 1707. For her houses, see Corp, *A Court in Exile*, p. 143.

121. He wrote nine letters to her between 3 April and 11 September 1707.

122. Diary, 26 September 1701; Corp, *A Court in Exile*, pp. 154–5.

123. Diary, 3 October 1702.

124. Diary, 3 July, 7 September, 15 November 1703.

125. Diary, 5, 10 June 1704.

126. Diary, 7 September 1703.

127. He wrote five letters to him between 20 March 1703 and 10 September 1704.

128. He wrote nineteen letters to her between 28 July 1703 and 3 December 1707.

129. Diary, 2 January, 7 March, 8 October 1706. Although originally a lunatic asylum, the prison at Charenton also housed prisoners who were perfectly sane and held under *lettres de cachet*. Bromfield was eventually released in 1711 (Corp, *A Court in Exile*, p. 157). For further information about him in 1712–14, see Strickland, Agnes, *Lives of the Queens of England: Vol. 10, Mary of Modena* (London, 1847), pp. 172–3.

130. See also p. 210, note 272 for the help that Nairne gave to Mr and Mrs Ocahan.

131. Most of the concerts took place (in the Château-Neuf as well as the Château-Vieux) in February, March and November 1702, and January, February and March 1703, but there were others during the summer of 1702. Nairne also went to some concerts at Le Pecq (Diary, 9 June, 23 July 1702).

132. Diary, 5 April 1702 ('I playd on ye violin wth his [Lord Caryll's] nephew after dinner'), 29 May 1702 ('I playd after dinner wth M. Caryl before My Ld').

133. Diary, 3 November 1702.

134. Diary, 5 November 1702 ('at night I playd at ye consort').

135. Diary, 5, 15 and 16, 18 and 19, 22, 26 November 1702, 14 January, 8, 16, 22 February, 22 March 1703. (The concerts on 15 and 18 November 1702 were actually rehearsals).

136. Diary, 16 February 1703. The last reference to music in his diary before his appointment as under-secretary was on 21 April 1703: 'I playd at night at My Lds wth Mr Caryl, Mr Foster and Mr Gally.' (Guy Forster was a gentleman usher of the queen's presence chamber).

137. Diary, 9, 22 July 1703, 12 July, 18, 22 September 1705, 1 January, 26 December 1707. There were probably other concerts which he did not mention in his diary.

138. For example, he attended performances of a *Te Deum* in the parish church on 26 and 27 June 1704.

139. Diary, 30 August 1707.

140. Corp, *A Court in Exile*, chapter 8.

141. Diary, 13 October 1703. The opera was *Le Mariage du Carnaval et de la Folie* (Corp, *A Court in Exile*, p. 210).

142. Diary, 30 September 1707.

143. The organist at the court of Saint-Germain was Gian-Battista Casale, who had previously been the organist of the king's chapel at Whitehall. Like most of the other musicians at the court he was not paid a salary as a household servant: in his case he must have been paid from the budget of the chapel royal. In 1696 Nairne, who referred to him as Mr Baptiste and was obviously a friend, persuaded both Innes and Caryll to ask the queen to give him a salaried household post as

page of the backstairs (also known as page of the queen's bedchamber) (Diary, 30 June, 28 November, 4 December, 9 December 1696). He was appointed in January 1697 (Diary, 6 January, 22 February 1697), and he and Nairne remained on good terms thereafter (Diary, 4 January 1698, 15 November 1699). When Casale was dying in 1706, Nairne accompanied the Blessed Sacrament to him, and then attended his funeral (Diary, 14, 17, 18 May 1706). It was after Casale's death that Couperin probably became the organist at the Stuart court, though he was only available from 1 April to 31 December of each year. He was not given a household post, so he does not appear in the lists of salaries and pensions (Corp, Edward, 'François Couperin and the Stuart Court at Saint-Germain-en-Laye, 1691–1712', p. 450; Corp, *A Court in Exile*, pp. 213–14).

144. Nairne attended the one on 2 January 1704, and the king's 'ball and mascarade' on 22 February and 8 March 1707. He also mentioned that there was music at James III's *levée* to celebrate his birthday on 21 June 1707.

145. Diary, 2, 10, 20, 27 January, 7, 20 February 1708. Nairne attended the balls on 27 January and 20 February.

146. The mother of James Douglas, Earl of Arran was the sole heiress of the 3rd Duke of Hamilton. When the duke died in 1698 William III allowed the title to be inherited by Arran as the 4th Duke. His title was not therefore recognized at the exiled court.

147. Diary, 13 June 1702: 'I had a … note in cypher from My Ld Arans own hand, wch I uncypherd and gave to My Ld [Caryll] who gave it to the Queen;' 23 July 1702: 'Mr In had a tre from Scotld telling … yt my letter to My Ld Aran had been safely deliverd.' See also 8 February, 16 March, 8 July 1703.

148. Szechi, *Britain's lost revolution*, p. 91.

149. Gibson, John S., *Playing the Scottish Card. The Franco-Jacobite Invasion of 1708* (Edinburgh University Press, 1988), p. 20. Sir John Maclean of Duart, born in 1670, had studied at the Collège des Ecossais in Paris from 1688 to 1690 and been converted to Catholicism by Lewis Innes (Nicholas Maclean-Bristol, *Castor and Pollux* (Society of West Highlands and Island Historical Research, 2012), p. 99; Halloran, *The Scots College Paris*, p. 104).

150. Perth's sister Anne married the 11th Earl of Erroll. His daughter Mary married the 9th Earl Marischal.

151. Szechi, *Britain's lost revolution*, pp. 119, 170; Gibson, *Playing the Scottish Card*, p. 21.

152. Diary, 25, 31 January, 16, 18 February, 10 September, 30 October, 9 December 1698, 2 June 1699, 8 January 1700. Captain James Murray was the younger brother of Sir David Murray, 3rd Bart of Stanhope (near Peebles, south of Edinburgh).

153. Diary, 20, 22 February 1702.

154. Szechi, *Britain's lost revolution*, p. 145.
155. Diary, 23 April 1703.
156. Diary, 25 April 1703.
157. Szechi, *Britain's lost revolution*, pp. 124, 145, 171.
158. Diary, 4, 5, May 1703.
159. Nairne sent at least one letter to Murray while he was in Scotland (Diary, 3 August 1703).
160. Diary, 14 February 1704.
161. Diary, 14 January 1704.
162. Diary, 19 May 1704.
163. Szechi, *Britain's lost revolution*, pp. 26, 119.
164. Diary, 8 September 1703.
165. He also went to a *Te Deum* in the parish church.
166. Diary, 1 to 17 October 1703. The other Jacobites at Fontainebleau, by contrast, were able to enjoy all the entertainments of the French court. See Haile, M., *Mary of Modena: Her Life and Letters* (London, 1905), p. 377, Rizzini to Duke Rinaldo of Modena, October 1703: 'the [English] Court ... [is] enjoying the Comedies, Music and the play' at Fontainebleau.
167. Gibson, *Playing the Scottish Card*, p. 25.
168. Szechi, *Britain's lost revolution*, p. 124; Gibson, *Playing the Scottish Card*, p. 33. Nairne received further information from Lord Ailesbury and Lord Drummond (Lord Perth's eldest son) on 3 and 5 March 1704.
169. Diary, 14, 15, 16, 18, 20, 23, 25 January 1704.
170. The abbé Renaudot wrote in January 1704 that Perth 'is now a little estranged by the dominant credit of the English faction, who have persuaded the Queen to enter into their views' (Haile, *Mary of Modena*, p. 383). Renaudot obviously regarded both Middleton and Nairne, like Caryll, as English.
171. See p. 151, note 107. See also the memoir de Leviston, February 1704: 'Je viens de Saint-Germain.... Le Conseil de la Reyne est Anglois, et par consequent ennemis jurez des Ecossois ...; de plus, le plupart sont beaucoup mieux icy qu'ils ne seroient chez eux ...; ce qui fait qu'ils n'ont aucun epressement pour le retablissement de leur Roy.' (Hooke, *Correspondance*, vol. 1, pp. 62–3). It is interesting to observe that Leviston also regarded Middleton and Nairne as though they were English.
172. Coward, Barry, *The Stuart Age: England, 1603–1714* (2nd edition, Harlow, 1994), p. 418. Nairne translated the bill into French while he was at Fontainebleau.
173. Diary, 16, 22, 23 February 1704.
174. Diary, 17, 19, 23 February, 11 March 1704.
175. Torcy brought Louis XIV's answer on 25 April 1704. See also Diary, 13, 15, 30 March, 14, 24 April 1704.

176. Szechi, *Britain's lost revolution*, p. 171.
177. Diary, 30 May, 2, 3 June 1704.
178. Szechi, *Britain's lost revolution*, p. 124.
179. Diary, 8 August 1704.
180. Diary, 20 November 1704. See also 17, 18, 22 July 1704. Nairne's papers concerning Lord Lovat are in Bod. Carte MSS 180, ff.358–447.
181. Szechi, *Britain's lost revolution*, p. 172.
182. The details of Lindsay's return to Scotland, and subsequent decision to visit England where he was arrested, are recorded in *CSPD, Queen Anne, 1703–04* (1924), pp. 204, 219, 472, 478–9, 511, 603.
183. Middleton, Dorothy, *The Life of Charles, 2nd Earl of Middleton* (London, 1957), p. 183. For Lindsay's interrogation by the Earl of Nottingham in December 1703, see BL. Add MSS 20311, ff.32, 34. Lindsay was tried for high treason and found guilty in April 1704, and sentenced to imprisonment in Newgate (Salmon, Thomas, *Tryals for High Treason, and other Crimes* (4 vols in 6, London, 1720), vi, pp. 411–25). He unsuccessfully petitioned Queen Anne to be removed from Newgate to another prison in November 1704 (*CSPD, Queen Anne, 1704–05* (2005), no. 807), and when he was eventually released in 1707 was banished for life (*CSPD, Queen Anne, 1705–06* (2006), no. 1322). Nairne resumed his correspondence with Lindsay in May 1707, and sent him eight letters between then and January 1708.
184. Hooke, *Correspondance*, vol. 1, p. 197, Hooke to Torcy, 10 June 1705: 'La Reyne me dit ... que My Lord Middleton ... a cependant approuvé le dessein don't il s'agit, comme l'unique ressource qui reste pour le Roy d'Angleterre, et comme un coup important pour la France.'
185. Although Captain Murray was serving with the French army, Nairne had recently used his influence with Caryll and Innes to have him appointed a gentleman usher of the king's privy chamber (Diary, 8, 9, 12 August 1704). Whenever Murray was at Saint-Germain he and Nairne regularly took supper together. When Murray was in Flanders during the campaigning seasons he and Nairne corresponded. Nairne recorded sending forty-three letters to him in 1705, twenty-nine letters in 1706, and thirty-one letters in 1707.
186. Diary, 20 September to 6 October 1704.
187. Szechi, *Britain's lost revolution*, p. 172.
188. Nairne was well acquainted with Hooke (Diary, 21 July 1703, 20 May, 31 August 1704).
189. See pp. 150–1.
190. Szechi, *Britain's lost revolution*, p. 173.
191. Ibid. p. 93.

192. Hooke, *Correspondance*, vol. 1, p. 345, Perth to Hooke, 28 September 1705: 'The King goes to Fontainebleau on Thursday, but the Queen's breast hinders her to make the journey, which I am sorry for upon her account and upon that of our affaires.'

193. Nairne wrote on 13 October 1705 that 'in eleven days I writt 55 letters besides mem: and placets at Fontbl'.

194. Diary, 1 to 13 October 1705.

195. Diary, 26, 29 November 1705.

196. Szechi, *Britain's lost revolution*, pp. 173–4.

197. Diary, 21 January 1706.

198. Szechi, pp. 127, 174.

199. Szechi, p. 76.

200. Szechi, pp. 127, 137.

201. Diary, 4, 5 May 1705.

202. Diary, 9 May 1705.

203. Diary, 18, 19 February 1706.

204. Diary, 8 March 1706. Taite, however, was not to be put off. A few days later he gave Nairne 'a present ... of 2 silver candlesticks' (Diary, 13 March 1706) and in September sent him '25£' (Diary, 18 September 1706).

205. Szechi, *Britain's lost revolution*, p. 174.

206. Diary, 27, 29 July 1706.

207. Diary, 21 August 1706.

208. Diary, 23 August 1706.

209. Diary, 27, 31 August, 3, 10 September 1706.

210. Diary, 12 September 1706.

211. Diary, 11 September 1706.

212. Szechi, *Britain's lost revolution*, pp. 174–5. It should be added that the English court did not go to Fontainebleau in 1706 because the French court did not go there (Corp, *A Court in Exile*, p. 169).

213. Diary, 10, 12 October, 21 November, 12 December 1706.

214. Szechi, *Britain's lost revolution*, p. 175.

215. Ibid. pp. 175, 177.

216. Diary, 22, 25 January 1707; Szechi, p. 177.

217. Diary, 11, 12 February 1707: 'I drew a draft of a declaration for Scotld', 'E. M. shewd me ye draft he had made of a Declar. of war.'

218. Szechi, *Britain's lost revolution*, p. 148.

219. Diary, 12, 14 February 1707.

220. Diary, 15 February 1707.

221. Diary, 11, 12 March 1707.

222. Hooke, *Correspondance*, vol. 2, p. 128, Nairne to Gideon Murray, referred to in a note by Hooke on Erroll to Lady Erroll (his mother), 6 February 1707.

223. Szechi, *Britain's lost revolution*, p. 179.

224. Ibid. p. 136.

225. Diary, 25 June 1707.

226. Diary, 29 July 1707.

227. Diary, 5 August 1707.

228. Diary, 6 August 1707.

229. Szechi, *Britain's lost revolution*, pp. 94, 180.

230. Ibid. p. 135.

231. Ibid. pp. 128, 135.

232. Diary, 10, 11 September 1707.

233. Diary, 22 September to 6 October 1707. See Chapter 8, p.

234. Szechi, *Britain's lost revolution*, pp. 14, 181.

235. Diary, 6 October 1707.

236. Diary, 12, 22, 24 February 1708.

237. Diary, 28 February 1708.

238. HMC *Stuart* I, pp. 218–20; Szechi, *Britain's lost revolution*, pp. 146, 148.

239. Diary, 29 February 1708.

240. Szechi, *Britain's lost revolution*, p. 28.

241. Diary, 20 February 1708.

242. Diary, 21 February 1708.

243. Diary, 24 February 1708. He 'writt another Instruction for Scotld.' on 2 March 1708. One of the original nine copies, in Nairne's handwriting, is referred to in Hooke, *Correspondance*, vol. 2, pp. 560–3.

244. Szechi, *Britain's lost revolution*, pp. 29–30.

245. Hooke had just been given a peerage by James III (Diary, 18 February 1708: 'I drew a warrant in blank for an Irish baron').

246. Szechi, p. 35. Hooke suggested either Inverkeithing, Burntisland or Blackness, then changed his mind to Inverness. Forbin agreed with Middleton that the best place would be Burntisland.

247. Szechi, *Britain's lost revolution*, p. 60.

248. The bedchamber servants were: Perth and Lt General the Earl of Newcastle (gentlemen), Captain Sir Randall MacDonnell, Captain Richard Trevanion and Captain Daniel MacDonnell (grooms), Lt General Richard Hamilton (master of the robes), and Balthassare Artema, Edmund Johnson, Styles (Christian name unknown) and Charles Oneal (valets).

249. The Chamber servants were: James Porter (vice-chamberlain), Francis Sanders (confessor), François Gassis de Beaulieu (surgeon), Calahan Garwan and

Lawrence Wood (physicians), and Captain James Murray (groom of the privy chamber).

250. The Household Below Stairs servants were: Francis Plowden (comptroller) and one of the five cooks.

251. Lt General Dominic Sheldon.

252. Diary, 10 March 1708.

253. Szechi, *Britain's lost revolution*, p. 25.

254. Ibid. pp. 25–8.

255. The *Mars*, the *Jersey* and the *Auguste* had sixty guns each; the *Blackwall* and the *Salisbury* had fifty. The army consisted of twelve battalions drawn from six French regiments (Gibson, *Playing the Scottish Card*, p. 115)

256. Szechi, *Britain's lost revolution*, pp. 33, 60.

257. Ibid. pp. 33–9. See also Gibson, *Playing the Scottish Card*, pp. 93–134. This account is also based on an anonymous 'Relation de l'arivée, de l'embarquement, du voyage, et du retour de S. M. Britannique à Dunkerque' written by a French officer on the *Mars* (Archives of the Scots College, Rome, vol. 3, Leslie Papers, 1643–1711, no. 82).

258. Diary, 7 April 1708: 'I sent a journal of ye Voyage to My Ld Caryl.'

259. According to Forbin there were '80 Domestiques de tout état' on the *Mars*, responsible for providing meals for sixty-seven 'seigneurs du premier ordre et à des Officiers Généraux'. There were three sittings for dinner each day: 'le Table du Roy de douze couverts ..., trois autres Tables de quinze couverts chacune, et la mienne de dix.' Nairne would probably have eaten on one of the tables laid for fifteen people (Claude, Comte de Forbin, *Mémoires* (Paris, 1729) vol. 2, p. 325).

260. The anonymous 'Relation' (see note 257) states:

le 24 au matin on reconnoit 28 vaisseaux Anglois c'etoient les memes qui avoient paru devant dunquerque les quels nous auroient infaillillent brulléz si nous eussions eté plus avant enferméz dans la riviere, ils nous suivirent toute la journée à veüe, et deux de leurs vaisseaux meilleurs voiliers liurent combat à deux des nôtres qui ne finit qu'à la nuit, le feu de canon, et de la mousqueterie fut terrible.

Comme nous n'avions que cinq vaisseaux arméz en guerre et que Mr le Conte de Forbin etoit chargé de la personne du Roy d'Angleterre il ne songea qu'a s'eloigner pendant que les autres avoient ordre de soutenir et d'arreter les Ennemis, nous craignions qu'il ne tombassent sur nos petits Batimens. Mais le 25 nous en aurions encore 20 et il ne nous en manquoit que cinq depuis le combat, et l'on iugera qu'ils etoient retournéz à dunquerque parce que nous avions fait fausse route, un des deux vaisseaux attaquéz etoit du nombre ...

... il ... nous manque ... par malheur le vaisseau de guerre qui est le Salisbury, comandé par Mr le Chevalier de Nangis et du nombre, et on croit pris, il y avoit sur ce vaisseau Mr le Marquis de Levi [*sic*: Lévis] Lieutenant general,

Mr Wachop Colonel Ecossois, Mr de Meuse Colonel du Regim.t d'agenois, et cinq compagnies du Regim.t de bearn, avec beaucoup de provisions et munitions.

The French account makes no mention of Lord Griffin or the sons of Lord Middleton.

261. The *Mars* reached Dunkirk with three other *vaisseaux de guerre* and five *frégates*. Sixteen other *frégates* had already arrived. The 'Relation states:

> Comme nous n'etions pas suivit des Ennemis malgré la diminution tant des 5 Batimens que de trois autres qui nous avoient quitéz dèz le 19 par l'incommodité de gros temps on ne laissa pas de vouloir faire une nouvelle tentative au nort d'ecosse aux port de Cromarty, et d'invernesse, que les ministres de Sa M. B. nous indiquerent, mais comme aucun de nos pilotes ne les connoissoit on envoya une fregate en chercher au Cap de Bomaness [*sic*: Whiteness Head?] qui fussent pratiques du pays, on en suivoit la route le 26. Lors qu'il seleva un vent si contraire qu'en un moment nos vaisseaux furent separéz les uns des autres, et comme il etoit à craindre à causé des Equinoxes que ce vent durat, que la fregate dessinée pour aller chercher des pilotes ne pouvoit continuer son chemin, que nous n'avions aucune certitude qu'en ces lieux aussi rudéz et aussi sauvages on trouvat des secours pour le debarquement qi'il etoit aussi à craindre que les Ennemis suivant toutes les apparences rangeroient les cotes, et nous y suivoient, que nos forces étoient afoiblies, que les batimens despeseréz courroient risque de manquer de viures toutes ces considerations determinerent Sa M. Brit. à profiter pour retourner en France du meme vent que l'empechoit d'aborder en Ecosse.
>
> On donna sur l'heure le signal à la flotte de prendre la route de dunquerque, et on laissa deux fregates en travers pour avertir les batimens qui séroient restéz dérriere, mais les calmes succederent au vent puis les Brunes qui nous aprocherent meme avec danger des terres du texel, et enfin nous ne sommes arrivéz à la rade de dunquerque que le Samedi 7ᵉ avril, veille de pacques avec quatre vaisseaux de guerre, et cinq fregates, nous y trouvames heureusem.t.

At the time of writing, the four *corsaires* were still at sea.

262. Diary, 22 April 1708.

263. Lord Middleton's two sons were imprisoned in the Tower of London until 1711 when they were released on bail. They were allowed to return to France in June 1713 (Middleton, *The Life of Charles,* 2nd *Earl of Middleton,* pp. 212, 229). Lord Griffin was sentenced to be executed, but was given several reprieves until he died of natural causes in 1711 (Szechi, *Britain's lost revolution,* pp. 48–50). Thomas Sackville was a groom of the king's bedchamber, but had joined the expedition as a volunteer. He escaped from England by pretending to be French (HMC *Stuart* VII, p. 602, Mrs Elizabeth Sackville to Mar, 4 December 1718). Colonel

Wauchope, like the other Jacobites in the French army, was treated as a prisoner of war (Szechi, *Britain's lost revolution*, p. 51).

264. For example, Diary 7, 8 April 1708: 'I sent a journal of ye Voyage to My Ld Caryl', 'I writt by the post to my Ld Car and ye letter came to ye Q before Mr hooks paquet who was sent express with it the evening before and in wch paquet I writt to My Ld Car'.

265. Nairne mentioned dining with Jossier on three occasions (Diary, 12, 15 April 1708).

266. Nairne's trunks arrived at Saint-Germain on the 25th. They had been taken by a servant called John Noel, alias Champagne, whom Nairne referred to as 'my man' (Diary, 16, 25 April 1708), so presumably Nairne had taken a servant with him. Noel later became one of the king's footmen, and seems to have died in Lorraine.

267. Diary, immediately after 27 May 1708.

268. According to his diary, Nairne wrote virtually every day to Charles Whiteford, and very regularly to Lewis Innes, in the years leading up to March 1708. He presumably continued to write to both men with similar frequency.

269. These two journals were deposited after his death in the Collège des Ecossais in Paris, where they remained until they were destroyed during the French Revolution. See Corp, 'An Inventory of the Archives of the Stuart Court at Saint-Germain', p. 139; and below, p. 496.

270. Diary, April to May 1708.

271. Diary, 18 and 27 May 1708.

272. It is clear from these letters that the man to whom they were written, apparently called Captain Thomas Aikenhead, was a very close friend. Nairne addresses him throughout both letters as 'tu' not 'vous', signs the first one 'je serai toujours, cher ami, entierement à toy', and signs the second one: 'aime moy toujours, et sois persuadé que je serai toute ma vie, Cher Amy, tout a toy'. Yet there is no mention in Nairne's diary of anyone called Aikenhead, so this cannot have been his real name. The man in question must actually have been Captain Ocahan, whose name was confused by a clerk working in Berlin. The confusion seems to run as follows: Oc/Aik; a/en; han/head. Ocahan/Aikenhead. There are numerous references in Nairne's diary to Captain Ocahan, who served in Limerick's Regiment until 1697 and then in Bourke's Regiment. Whenever Ocahan was at Saint-Germain, Nairne tried to further his career by recommending him to Colonel Wauchop, the Duke of Berwick and various other people, including Chamillart and the clerks in the French war secretariat. When Ocahan was with his regiment, Nairne wrote to him very regularly. For example, between April 1703 and February 1707, he sent him thirty-nine letters. Nairne and his wife also helped Mrs Ocahan. On thirteen occasions between December 1697

and October 1707, one or other of them gave her money or obtained money for her (including a regular pension) from the queen, Lady Almond, Innes and Caryll.

273. BL. Add MSS 61254, ff.88 and 89, Nairne to Aikenhead, both letters dated 23 June 1708.

274. Nairne named the six men as 'Holms, Nicholson, Stanford, Cavenach, Terrily et Campbel', of whom 'trois sont de ceux qui ont dejà leurs têtes mis a 1000 Sterl. en Angleterre et les autres trois de nos mangeurs de Saint Irlandois'.

275. BL. Add MSS 61254, f.87, King Frederick I to Duke Vittorio Amadeo II, 22 September 1708. It is to be noted that the name Aikenhead was included in a letter written by a man who did not speak English.

276. The two letters are both dated 23 June 1708, but this is perhaps a mistake by the copyist, as the second one was probably written a few days later. They are also both dated from Saint-Germain, despite the fact that Nairne was with the king in Flanders at the time (see, e.g., BL. Add MSS 20292, f.15, James III to Gualterio, 12 August 1708).

277. He was still at Saint-Germain on 27 May, and probably also on 4 June, so he presumably left for Flanders in the first half of June. See Macpherson, *Original Papers*, vol. 2, pp. 126–7, 130, Beauvilliers to Middleton, and Middleton to Beauvilliers, both 27 May 1709; and a memorial translated by Nairne, 4 June 1709.

278. BL. Add MSS 20292, f.19, James III to Gualterio, 8 July 1709.

279. Lart, *Jacobite Extracts*, vol. 2, p. 18. The footman was a Frenchman named Antoine Mitelet, who married Jeanne Françoise Taveau. The other witnesses were Etienne du Mirail de Monnot, another of the king's French footmen (Nicolas Prévot), and Simon Mitelet. Nairne signed the register as 'secrétaire du Conseil d'Etat de S. M. britanique'. Antoine Mitelet died the following year, in April 1711, aged thirty-two (ibid. p. 101).

280. Macpherson, *Original Papers*, vol. 2, p. 155, James III to Middleton, 4 July 1710: 'I am here alone, which is far from easy to me, upon many accounts. But necessity has no law; and that alone could have made me not carry you along with me.' See also ibid. p. 162, James III to Middleton, 2 August 1710, summarized as 'He wishes he had lord Middleton along with him, but his Lordship was more necessary where he was'.

281. Ibid. p. 152, James III to Middleton, 2 June 1710.

282. The king was accompanied by Charles Booth, one of his grooms of the bedchamber, who was instructed to send regular letters to Lord Middleton to substitute for the campaign journal which Nairne would otherwise have kept. They are in Bod. Carte MSS 210, ff.111–338, with a minute by Nairne: 'Mr Booths letters of the Kings 3d Campagne from the 16 May 1710 to the 8 Sep.ber.'

283. Bod. Carte MSS 212.

284. Bod. Carte MSS 212, f.9, Nairne's letter book, 7 August 1710: 'No copie kept of this letter. I was then in the country.'

285. Lart, *Jacobite Extracts*, vol. 2, p. 10. The other witnesses were Edmund Barry (gentleman usher of the queen's presence chamber), Thaddeus Connell (chaplain to the king), and Thomas Sackville (groom of the bedchamber). Nairne signed the register as 'Secrétaire du Conseil d'Etat ... et cousin de l'epouse'. See also Chapter 3, p. 145.

286. Bod. Carte MSS 180, ff.268–78, 'Letter to a Friend, 1711' (printed in Macpherson, *Original Papers*, vol. 2, pp. 218–23, as 'A Letter to a friend; with a state of affairs in England, 1711').

287. Bod. Carte MSS 210, f.409, James III to the Princess of Denmark, 2 May 1711.

288. Bod. Carte MSS 180, f.305, James III to the Princess of Denmark, 12 May 1711.

289. Bod. Carte MSS 238, f.218, Middleton to Torcy, 9 July 1711.

290. Bevan, B., *King James the Third of England* (London, 1967), p. 60; Middleton, *The Life of Charles, 2nd Earl of Middleton*, p. 223.

291. Bod. Carte MSS 212, f.21, Nairne's letter book, 27 September 1711.

292. Bod. Carte MSS 212, f.19, Nairne's letter book, 21 May 1711.

293. Bod. Carte MSS 212, f.19, Nairne's letter book, 29 June 1711.

294. Bod. Carte MSS 212, f.45, Nairne's letter book, 21 October and 30 October 1712.

295. For Nairne's salary, see pp. 109, 117, 119, 142, 152, 199.

296. Bod. Carte MSS 212, f.27, Nairne's letter book, 6 March 1712.

297. Bod. Carte MSS 212, f.20, Middleton to Menzies, 6 September 1711.

298. Bod. Carte MSS 212, f.21, Nairne's letter book, 10 October 1711. For Lord Caryll's will dated 9 November 1707, and the five codicils up to 9 July 1711, see BL. Add MSS 28250, ff.208–35.

299. Macpherson, *Original Papers*, vol. 2, p. 234 (quoted in Szechi, Daniel, *Jacobitism and Tory Politics, 1710–1714*, (Edinburgh, 1984), p. 13), 19 November 1711. See also Bod. Carte MSS 212, f.22, DN's letter book, 29 November 1711 (quoted in Szechi, p. 8): 'To Menzies. I told him again to get all the Scots Jacobite MPs and peers and the English Jacobite MPs and peers to favour peace.'

300. Bod. Carte MSS 212, f.32b, DN's letter book, 5 May 1712: 'To Berry. I ... told him my sickness was ye reason he had been for long without hearing from me'; and Bod. Carte MSS 212, f.32c, DN's letter book, 8 May 1712: 'To Menzies. I told him ... yt my sickness had hinderd my writing to him since ye 10 Ap.' For the fact that Nairne had not previously contracted smallpox, see p. 108 and p. 129, note 48.

301. Corp, *A Court in Exile*, p. 280.

302. For further details, see Corp, Edward, 'The Court of Turin and the English Succession, 1712–1720', in Bianchi, P., and Wolfe, K. (eds), *Turin and the British*

in the *Age of the Grand Tour (British School of Rome Studies)* (Cambridge, 2017), pp. 56–72.

303. Bod. Carte MSS 212, f.32b, Nairne's letter book, 5 May 1712.
304. Bod. Carte MSS 212, f.36, Nairne's letter book, 3 July 1712.
305. Bod. Carte MSS 212, f.32, Nairne's letter book, 12 May 1712.
306. Bod. Carte MSS 212, f.32c, Nairne's letter book, 12 May 1712.
307. Bod. Carte MSS 212, f.33, Nairne's letter book, 5 June 1712.
308. Bod. Carte MSS 212, f.39, Nairne's letter book, 18 and 25 August 1712; Corp, *A Court in Exile*, p. 282.
309. Corp, *A Court in Exile*, p. 282; Bod. Carte MSS 212, f.43, Nairne's letter book, 8 and 12 September 1712. It was during the former visit that the king attended a performance of *Le Ballet des saisons* by Collasse at the Opéra. It is not known whether or not Nairne accompanied him.
310. Bod. Carte MSS 212, f.44, Nairne's letter book, 12 September 1712.
311. Bod. Carte MSS 212, ff.27, 32, 37, 38a, 46, Nairne's letter book, 6 March, 12 May, 17 July, 28 July and 10 November 1712. The engravings were by François Chéreau, after the portrait of the king painted at Saint-Germain by Belle in 1712. See Corp, *A Court in Exile*, p. 195.
312. Bod. Carte MSS 212, f.40, Nairne's letter book, 1 September 1712.
313. Bod. Carte MSS 212, f.41, 'Draught [by Nairne] of an answer to Mr Anderson upon the article of religion, Sep:1712 not made use of, the King thought fitter to say nothing at all upon that subject', September 1712; Bod. Carte MSS 212, f.40, Nairne's letter book, f.40, 1 September 1712.
314. Bod. Carte MSS 212, f.40, Nairne's letter book, 1 September 1712. The reference was to Jonathan Swift and, perhaps, John Austin (1613–69).
315. Bod. Carte MSS 212, f.44, Nairne's letter book, 21 October 1712. See also Bod. Carte MSS 212, f.45, DN's letter book, 21 October 1712: 'To ye La of St ford. To tell her I had been ill but was recoverd again.' This was the third time that Nairne had been ill in only one year. See above notes 291 and 300.
316. BL. Add MSS 31257, f.133, Middleton to Gualterio, 30 September 1712.
317. Bod. Carte MSS 212, f.45, Nairne's letter book, 21 October 1712. The other letters of 21 October on ff.44–45. See also f.45, 30 October 1712.
318. Bod. Carte MSS 212, f.50, Nairne's letter book, 17 and 23 February 1713.
319. Corp, *A Court in Exile*, p. 284.
320. Macpherson, *Original Papers*, vol. 2, p. 408, Nairne to Scot and Berry, 27 April 1713. James III arrived at Lunéville on 2 May 1713 (Archives Départementales de Meurthe et Moselle 4.F.14, anonymous manuscript entitled 'Séjour du Roi d'Angleterre Jacques 2 [*sic*] en Lorraine 1713-14-15 et 16', p. 5 (I am grateful to Jérémy Filet for giving me this reference).
321. Bod. Carte MSS 212, f.54, Nairne's letter book, 18 May 1713; Bod. Carte MSS 211, f.177, L. Innes to Middleton, 23 May 1713.

322. Bod. Carte MSS 212, f.56, Nairne's letter book, 20 May 1713. According to the anonymous manuscript, James III, and therefore Nairne, was entertained with 'magnificence' and 'la splendeur des fêtes ... tant au chateau qu'à la campagne: les plaisirs de la Cour étaient entremêler de repas, de collations, de bals, de concerts, de comédie, de promenades, de chasse, de feux d'artifice etc, mais chaque jour tout était nouveau' (p. 5).

323. Macpherson, *Original Papers*, vol. 2, p. 417, Nairne to Menzies, 22 June 1713. The visit to Commercy started on 7 June. According to the anonymous manuscript, the Duke and Duchess of Lorraine were also present, and 'M. le Prince de Vaudémont' gave 'les deux cours ... chaque jour quelque fête d'une nouvelle imagination, et l'on estime que la dépense qu'il a fait à cette occasion, va à plus de quarante mille livres' (p. 6). This was spent on 'la chasse, aux festins, aux bals, aux concerts, et autres pareils divertissements' (p. 7).

324. See below, Chapter 5. Nairne had first met the prince de Vaudémont during the latter's visit to Saint-Germain in 1707 (Diary, 14 May 1707).

325. Bod. Carte MSS 212, f.59, Nairne's letter book, 16 August 1713.

326. Macpherson, *Original Papers*, vol. 2, p. 445, Nairne to Menzies, 24 October 1713.

327. Corp, *A Court in Exile*, p. 285.

328. Bod. Carte MSS 212, f.58, Nairne's letter book, 15 August 1713.

329. Bod. Carte MSS 212, f.46, Nairne's letter book, 10 December 1712 (quoted in Szechi, *Jacobitism and Tory Politics*, p. 8).

330. Bod. Carte MSS 212, f.48, Nairne's letter book, 25 January 1713 (quoted in Szechi, p. 10).

331. Bod. Carte MSS 212, f.53, Nairne's letter book, 27 April 1713 (quoted in Szechi, p. 13).

332. Bod. Carte MSS 212, f.55, Nairne's letter book, 30 April 1713 (quoted in Szechi, p. 18).

333. Bod. Carte MSS 212, f.57, Nairne's letter book, 3 August 1713.

334. Bod. Carte MSS 212, f.57, Nairne's letter book, 20 August 1713 (quoted in Szechi, p. 23).

335. Bod. Carte MSS 212, f.61, Nairne's letter book, 25 November 1713 (quoted in Szechi, p. 23).

336. Bod. Carte MSS 212, f.60, Nairne's letter book, 24 October 1713 (quoted in Szechi, p. 39).

337. Middleton was not even corresponding with the English Catholics. See Szechi, *Jacobitism and Tory Politics*, p. 26, James III to Torcy, 1 February 1713: 'I told him that no ground was given from hence for the English Roman Catholics' jealousy against him, Middleton having kept no correspondence with them since the advice Menzies gave of the proposal they intended to make concerning Religion.'

338. Szechi, *Jacobitism and Tory Politics*, p. 23, James III to Torcy, 2 December 1713.

Secretary of the King's Closet in Lorraine, Avignon and the Papal States, 1713–1717

During the autumn of 1713, James III came under pressure from Lord Oxford and various members of the Tory party in England to dismiss Lord Middleton and appoint a new secretary of state.[1] They argued that they were unwilling to negotiate the king's restoration after the death of Queen Anne with a man who had converted to Catholicism, and whom they did not trust. With great reluctance the king agreed to let Middleton resign his post and return to Saint-Germain, and then appointed a new Protestant secretary of state. There were in fact only four Protestants at the court in Lorraine, and none of them was suitable, but James had to select one from among them. He chose Thomas Higgons, who had been serving as a gentleman usher of the privy chamber.[2] On 29 November, Higgons, who did not speak French, was given a knighthood and told to prepare himself for his new role.

The king was not willing to dismiss Middleton, so it was agreed that the latter would resign voluntarily and take up a new post as master of the horse to the queen. James III explained to Cardinal Gualterio on 16 December:

> the changes recently made in my household by Lord Middleton's voluntary retire-
> ment and my choice of the Chevalier Higgins (an English Protestant, of good birth,
> always loyal to my interests, for which he was even imprisoned during the King my
> father's time) to underake the role. The reasons for such a choice will be obvious to
> you and the cause of Lord Middleton's retirement are not unknown to you ... I have
> made his son Lord Clermont first Gentleman of the Bedchamber to show my con-
> sideration for the long service and loyalty of his father whose loss of position means
> no lessening of my friendship and esteem, which are so well deserved.[3]

The appointment of Higgons as the new secretary of state had a significant impact on the position of David Nairne. Higgons, a protestant, could

not be entrusted with conducting the king's correspondence with Gualterio, with the other cardinals and especially with the Pope, so the retirement of Lord Middleton resulted in the promotion of Nairne to become in effect – though not in name – joint secretary of state. James told Gualterio:

> Since it would be inappropriate for a Protestant to be in charge of the Correspondence with Rome, I have given to Nairne who is known to you for being an old and faithful servant the post of Secretary of the Closet with responsibility for everything concerning the business of that Court. He will write to you in my name when I am not able to do so myself.[4]

Nairne's warrant was dated 29 November 1713. It appointed him to be:

> Secretary of our Closet for our privat letters and dispatches, by vertue of which place he is to receive immediately from us our orders and directions in all such affaires as we shall think fit to trust him with and employ him in, relating to our privat letters, cyphers and correspondence or entering the same.[5]

Nairne, in other words, was no longer to be subordinate to the secretary of state and was instead to work directly for the king. He noted on 14 December:

> After this, having left the Sec.rys office in wh I had been ... years [sic] undersecretary, during E. Melf, Ld Car and E. Middletons Ministery's the King was pleasd to make me Sec.ry of the Closette in wh station I writt only from time to time some letters to Eng.ld by his Ma.tys immediate orders of wh I kept no copie, only showd them allways to his Ma.ty before I sent them. But the roman correspondence being my separate province I kept entrys of all my letters to Rome in a book apart from that time.[6]

Two days later, he sent his first letter to Cardinal Gualterio:

> The King of England my master, having been obliged regretfully, for reasons known to Your Excellency, to allow Lord Middleton to resign his post of Secretary of State, has chosen an English Protestant gentleman named Sir Thomas Higgons to take on the position, pleased in doing so to be displaying to his Protestant subjects the confidence he has in them. But since it would be inappropriate for H. M.'s correspondence with Rome and with Y. E. to pass through the hands of a Protestant H. M. has done me the honour of entrusting me with the position of Secretary of the Closet.[7]

Although Middleton's retirement greatly benefited Nairne, the latter regretted his departure, especially as he (Nairne) was not allowed to correspond with his former superior.[8] He also had to explain to Gualterio that he was not even allowed to act as a go-between and pass on the latter's letters to Middleton.[9]

During the spring of 1714, James III came under renewed pressure from both Lord Oxford and Lord Bolingbroke to convert to Anglicanism, so that they could repeal the Act of Settlement. The king sent them a definitive refusal in March,[10] much to Nairne's relief, and the latter wrote to reassure Gualterio that 'I may assure Y. Ex that by the grace of God the King is unshakable upon this point'. Nairne, like James, believed that a restoration was possible without the king's having to make an obviously insincere conversion, commenting that 'I have absolutely no doubt that God in his good time will reward him by restoring him to the throne of his ancestors'.[11] The negotiations with Oxford and Bolingbroke were conducted by the abbé François Gaultier, and it seems probable that James turned to Nairne rather than Higgons for advice. It was at this time that Nairne wrote two long papers, the first entitled 'Walters Negotiations at the Courts of France and England' in twenty-three folio pages, and the second entitled 'Notes on the letters of Abbé Gaultier' in thirty-five pages.[12] Nairne remained equally optimistic in July, when he told Gualterio that the king 'still has many good friends [in England] and has good reason to hope that the justice of his cause will prevail and will succeed in the end'.[13]

In the spring of 1714, while continuing to negotiate with the Tories and waiting for Queen Anne to die, James III went to take the waters at Plombières, and returned via Commercy where he was entertained by the prince de Vaudémont. Nairne accompanied him on his trip and was back at Bar-le-Duc by the end of the first week of June.[14] A few days later, he decided to ask a favour of Cardinal Gualterio:

> I am taking the liberty, Monseigneur, of sending you the attached short memoire asking permission to read prohibited books. Several people are regularly granted this favour and I would, God willing, use the privilege with discretion and be most grateful to Y. Em.ce.[15]

Nairne's strong Catholic faith, like that of James III, was never in doubt, but at a time when many people were trying to persuade the king to convert he seems to have felt the need to acquaint himself with various heretical Protestant books. His memoire, however, was drafted in more general terms, indicating his genuine interest in theology and doctrinal debate, notably concerning Jansenism:

> Since I have occasionally read prohibited books without realising they were pro-scribed, and read others that I was told were in the Index and since most of the casu-ists in this country claim these works can be read without any scruples, even though there are others who claim the opposite; in order to alleviate such scruples, and to read with a clear conscience books of history, of controversy, and Translations and debates on both sides, I have always aimed to examine them objectively to discover heretical beliefs the more to detest and guard against them, to strengthen myself and confirm my ever-growing and unshakable attachment to the Holy Roman Catrholic Church in which by the grace of God I hope to live and to die. I very humbly beg Your Eminence to have the goodness to obtain for me permission to read prohibited books, which by the grace of God I will not put to bad use.
>
> If it is necessary to have an attestation to my honest and sober way of life, Father Innes and Father Ingleton, almoners to HBM, with whose approval I am asking for this permission, could bear witness to Y. Em.ce.[16]

Gualterio replied at the beginning of July that he had spoken to the Pope, but it is not clear whether or not permission was eventually granted. Nairne wrote back in September that 'if there is any difficulty about this I am happy to submit and no longer to hope for it'.[17]

It was probably at Bar-le-Duc in June or July 1714 that Nairne had his portrait painted by Alexis-Simon Belle, who had been invited to come from France to paint three new portraits of the king.[18] For the portrait of Nairne, Belle repeated a composition which he had previously used at Saint-Germain for a portrait of Charles Fleming, but he changed it to show Nairne holding a letter addressed 'Au Roi d'Angleterre'. The portrait is a bust and shows Nairne looking to his left, holding the letter in his left hand. He has the fashionable high wig which was typical of the period, and around his shoulders he is wearing a red cloak which hangs low at the front over his chest. The scar on the left side of his chin is clearly visible.[19] The painting was probably sent by Nairne to his wife whom he had not seen since he left Saint-Germain in September 1712,[20] but before it was sent away several miniature copies were made, perhaps by Belle, perhaps by someone else.[21]

In August 1714, the king decided to visit the duc de Lorraine at Lunéville and then go on once again to take the waters at Plombières,

Figure 5. *King James III*, 1714 (74 × 59.5 cm), by Alexis-Simon Belle (private collection)
This was one of three portraits of the king painted by Belle at Bar-le-Duc.

expecting to be away from Bar-le-Duc for about six weeks.[22] Shortly before
his planned departure he was informed that Queen Anne had died much
earlier than expected on the 12th. James's immediate reaction was to leave
Lorraine and travel through France to the Channel, hoping for a restoration

Figure 6. *David Nairne*, 1714 (76.2 × 63.5 cm), by Alexis-Simon Belle
(private collection)
This portrait was painted at Bar-le-Duc to commemorate Nairne's promotion to the
Secretary of the Closet for the King's private letters and despatches. Nairne is shown
holding a letter addressed 'Au Roy d'Angleterre'.

before George, the Elector of Hanover, could also arrive in England. He left Bar-le-Duc with Nairne and a small group of servants on 15 August and entered France in violation of the Treaty of Utrecht.[23] Leaving the other servants at Meaux, he and Nairne went to see the queen-mother at Chaillot, and James then asked Louis XIV to let him continue to the channel. The King of France sent the marquis de Torcy to say that he could offer no assistance, and in consequence obliged James to return to Lorraine.[24] Nairne gave Gualterio the news on 21 August, having arrived back at Bar-le-Duc the previous evening, and having been 'a la suitte' of the king for six days.[25]

James then reverted to his original plan and set off the next day with Nairne for Lunéville and Plombières, but the intervention of Louis XIV was a disaster for the Jacobite cause and enabled the Whigs to secure the Hanoverian succession. We cannot say with any certainty what would have happened if James III had been allowed to reach England or Scotland in August 1714, but it is perfectly possible that he would have been restored. Nairne sent the following comments from Lunéville on 29 August:

> the situation in which the king's affairs stand remains very depressing, and what he feels most is having been prevented from risking all with the few friends he has in his Kingdoms while they were able to join him, but each day is making things more difficult; not to say impossible after the measures his enemies have had time to adopt to prevent his followers joining him such that nothing can be done for him. I will not go into my thoughts on this depressing subject, it is useless to regret what is past; we must concentrate; on new plans for the future, not on the past lack of success, hoping that sooner or later God will make justice triumph. It remains a great consolation that H. M. is entirely blameless, having done everything that honour demanded.
>
> We are leaving tomorrow for Plombières where H. M. will wait to see what turn English events will take holding himself always ready ... at the slightest reasonable encouragement from that country or from Scotland to make another attempt to travel over there so secretly and so incognito, that there would be no way of stopping him.[26]

It was at Plombières in August 1714 that James III drafted his celebrated Protestation, accompanied by an engraved 'Genealogie de la Maison Royalle de la Grande Bretagne' which showed that there were fifty-seven people (all of them Catholics) who had a better claim to the throne than George of Hanover.[27] It is possible that part of the document was drafted by Higgons, but much more likely that Nairne was responsible for most if not all of the text. The wording of parts of the Protestation is almost identical to some of the sentences in his letters to Gualterio. Although James III himself refused to convert, he made it clear in his Protestation that he intended to leave the Church of England secure in all its rights and privileges, prompting Nairne to remind Gualterio that 'H. M. has made it abundantly clear through his conduct, his inviolable attachment to the Catholic faith, without its being necessary to overdo things by showing indiscreet and uncalled for zeal.' It is hard to know how optimistic Nairne really was at this time, particularly when the news was received that George had landed in England and had been proclaimed king, but he struck a positive note in his correspondence:

> All that now remains for him to do is to trust in Providence and wait for another suitable opportunity to pursue his just ambitions which he will never give up so long as he lives ... For the rest, things are not so desperate that they might not improve with time.[28]

There was no printing press at Plombières,[29] so the Protestation could not have been printed until the king returned to Lunéville. Nairne wrote while still at Plombières on 19 September:

> We will have to see the consequences. God is just and perhaps will not permit heresy injustice and disloyalty to triumph for ever.... He will not leave here until October 1st and will spend a few days at Luneville before returning to Bar.[30]

In fact, the king went from Lunéville to visit the marquis de Lunati at Frouard for a couple of days,[31] and he and Nairne only returned to Bar-le-Duc on 10 October.[32]

The king now decided to recall Lord Middleton from Saint-Germain. Sir Thomas Higgons was out of his depth as secretary of state so that Nairne, who was busy handling the Roman correspondence, also had to do some of the latter's work and write letters to England and Scotland. More particularly James III badly needed an experienced minister now that the Hanoverian Succession had been achieved. Nairne was delighted, and wrote on 2 November:

> Lord Middleton is expected to come back at any moment with the approval of the French Court to counsel him and give him his advice on all matters. The intelligence

and experience of this worthy Minister will be a great help and comfort to H. M. at the present time. He will be consulted on all things but will not take on any official position.[33]

In practice Middleton replaced Higgons as secretary of state, but did not put his signature to the letters sent to England and Scotland.

While waiting for Middleton to arrive James and Nairne went to see the duc de Lorraine at Lunéville,[34] and then returned to Bar-le-Duc on 21 November in time to greet him.[35] Nairne's pleasure at being reunited with his former chief is very obvious in his letters to Gualterio. For example he wrote on 29 December:

> Apart from the fact that justice demanded it, his return in the present circumstances was absolutely essential, both for H. M.'s satisfaction and for the good of his affairs in which his advice holds great weight.[36]

Another letter, of February 1715, demonstrates how Nairne had now also developed an admiration for Gualterio. The cardinal had written to Middleton, and the latter had asked Nairne to forward his reply:

> at the same time I have the satisfaction of seeing in this exchange of letters two great men, both of whom are held in esteem by my master the king showing their high regard for each other.[37]

James III and his court remained at Bar-le-Duc for Christmas and the New Year, after which they were invited to spend two months with the duc and duchesse de Lorraine at Nancy.[38] The duke had recently built a new opera house, designed in the Italian style by Francesco Galli-Bibiena, and had ordered Henri Desmarets (his *Surintendant de la Musique*) to produce a winter season of operas. In January and February, the repertory consisted of revivals of works by Lully, which Nairne already knew and loved, and the first performance of Desmarets' *Diane et Endymion*. One of the courtiers wrote privately that these 'great sports' were 'unseasonable' and that the king should be making another attempt to go to England rather than attending 'carnavals',[39] but it is unlikely that Nairne was of that opinion. The Jacobite court did not return to Bar-le-Duc until 12 March,[40] and it was while it was at Nancy that Nairne's wife became seriously ill at Compigny.

None of the letters written to each other by David and Marie-Elisabeth Nairne has survived, so we know very little about their relationship and nothing at all about what Mrs Nairne had done since being separated from her husband in September 1712. She might have remained at Saint-Germain, but it is much more probable that she returned to her family home at Compigny. Her daughter Françoise was twenty years old in 1714 and would have accompanied her. On the other hand, her son Louis and her daughter Marie were only fifteen and fourteen respectively, the former being educated by the English Benedictine monks at Douai and the latter by the English Augustinian nuns in Paris.

On 28 March 1715, Nairne wrote to Gualterio that he was with the king at Commercy visiting the prince de Vaudémont, and that they would return to Bar-le-Duc in four days' time.[41] It was that night that his wife died. Nairne later wrote at the back of his diary:

> Madame de Nairne died at Compigny during the night of Thursday to Friday 29 March 1715 at around one o'clock in the morning, after more than two months' illness. She was [*sic*: fifty-five] years old. She was attended at the end by her elder daughter Françoise and the priest of Compigny who administered the last sacraments and wrote a letter to her husband at Bar le Duc describing her admirable and exemplary death. She is buried in the church at Compigny close to her father and her son Jean.[42]

She was buried the following day, the 30th, as recorded in the parish register:

> buried in the choir of the church lies the body of Elisabeth de Compigny, wife of David Nairne, esquire, joint lord of this parish, Baron of St Fort in Scotland, and secretary of state to His Britannic Majesty. The said lady died yesterday at one o'clock in the morning having received the sacraments of the church with firm and complete faith and with exemplary piety; nothing can equal the total resignation she displayed to God's will amidst all the pain of a long and violent illness, bearing it with fortitude ... to the very last moment of her life which ended in the fifty-sixth year of her life to enter a better place ... in the presence of the venerable and discreet persons, Messires Charles Cotton, the incumbent licenced priest of the Sorbonne, the curé of Sergines ... of Barthélemy de Compigny, esquire, lord of Baby, Briotte and other places, of Jean-Louis de Compigny, chaplain at Sens cathedral, et of Sébastien de Compigny et des Bordes, esquire, lord of this place, the paternal brothers of the deceased lady.[43]

Nairne was not given the news until four days later, on 3 April, perhaps because the messenger originally went to Commercy rather than Bar-le-Duc. We can only guess at the pain which he felt when he learnt of the death of his wife, whom he had not seen for so long, and who left him with two young children, as well as a grown-up daughter. All we get is a brief reference in a letter to Cardinal Gualterio:

> That is all that the King ordered me to write to Y. Em in reply to your letters. I hope that Y. E. will forgive me if I do not write more today, having received the very sad news for me only two days ago of my wife's death.[44]

Françoise Nairne returned to Paris and lived with her young sister Marie at the English Augustinian convent, situated in the rue des Fossées Saint-Victor beside the Collège des Ecossais. The girls wrote affectionate letters to their father,[45] and would become his great consolation in the years to come. Their brother Louis, on the other hand, seems to have taken his mother's death particularly badly, and tried to run away from the English Benedictine monastery at Douai.

By chance, the letter book of Louis de Sabran, the rector of the English Jesuit college at Saint-Omer, has survived, and it contains information about the education of Nairne's son Louis.[46] Sabran had baptized the Prince of Wales (James III) at Whitehall in 1688 and had then been James II's almoner at Saint-Germain, but he had left the court and since 1712 had been rector at Saint-Omer.[47] Sabran noted on 17 June 1715:

> From Mr Nairne. To recommend his son he designes to send me from Douay where he is so discontented that he hath endeavourd to run away. Desires I say nothing of the concerns of his son att Douai. That he learn musick. Had sent him first hither butt for his special acquaintance with two masters there. Sends inclosed the following –
>   From Mr Charles Booth. Recommending Nairne's son as very acceptable to the King.

Sabran sent Nairne a 'civil acceptation', and told him that the 'pension' or fees would be of 315 *livres* each quarter.'[48] Louis Nairne joined the English Jesuit college on 10 July, and Sabran sent his father 'a full account of him', with a 'promiss of all care possible of him'.[49]

Within only two weeks, Nairne began to complain that his son had not written to him. Sabran noted on 26 July:

> To Mr Nairne. In answer to his. A fuller account of his son, and of the reasons why he differd to answer his letters.[50]

When the fifteen-year-old boy did eventually send his father a letter, it was not at all what the latter had expected or wanted. Sabran noted again on 9 August:

> From Mr Nairne. Discontented att his son's undutifull letter to which he incloses a sharp answer. Begs that I labour to reclaime him, if possible, by faire otherwise by whatever meanes.[51]

So Sabran spoke to Louis and wrote back to Nairne 'with a right letter inclosd from his son of whom I give him a good and full account'.[52]

These family problems coincided with another unsuccessful attempt by James III to leave Lorraine and travel through France to England, taking Nairne with him. As a result Sabran's letter went astray, and Nairne wrote angrily from Bar-le-Duc:

> From Mr Nairne. Againe about his son, having receivd, after 3 weekes, no answer from him. The same as other letters – to bend or break him.[53]

Sabran replied on 28 August giving 'an account of his son's submissive letter I sent him' and 'of my hopes of him'.[54]

Nairne, meanwhile, had consulted his old friend Lewis Innes at the Collège des Ecossais in Paris, to whom he now wrote at the end of August:

> I have writt as you advise me a kind letter to my son and another of thanks to the Rector desiring him to give him all the encouragement he can to make him easy, and have promisd the first that when he has finishd his humanitys at St Omer I shall bring him to Paris to study his philosophy wch I hope will please him.[55]

This letter is not dated, but his 'letter of thanks' to Sabran was received on 2 September, as the latter noted on that day:

> From Secretary Nairn. With an inclosd to his son. Great sense of thankfulness for my retrieving his son. Abandons all to my conduct. Willing to give him any thing for pocket money. Would have him goe up to Sintaxe. An ould father must seeke that his son bee soone in a condition to bee provided for.[56]

Louis XIV died on 1 September and seventeen days later the Earl of Mar began the Jacobite rising in Scotland. Nairne was therefore busy preparing with James III and Middleton for a third attempt to leave Lorraine and travel through France to a Channel port. Nevertheless he found time on 18 September to send another letter to Sabran (which took twelve days to reach Saint-Omer):

> From Mr Nairne. 18 September. Still dissatisfyed not to have had from his son an answer to his last kinde letter. Would have one, confident, acquainting him with his progress, etc, from his son every fortnight. So many pious books not necessary, one or two, etc. Would knowe by next quarter what his son expended on particulars, to repay it with the quarter. When he would have any extraordinary would have him ask it first of him by letter; so he will write oftener to him. Would have him goe on in musick and give him an account of his progress in it.[57]

By the autumn of 1715, Father Sabran's term as rector of the English Jesuit college at Saint-Omer was coming to an end. He was replaced on 28 October, at which point his letter book comes to an end. The last two entries which concern Nairne are both dated from that month. On the 1st, Sabran wrote back to Nairne:

> To Mr Nairne. With an inclosd from his son as he desires. I satisfye him why I gave his son those books, and assure him he need not feare that others, or other things of moment shall bee bought for his son.[58]

The last letter is Nairne's reply of the 18th, sent from Commercy:

> Large acknowledgement of obligations to me for his son's entire conversion to his duty. Will allowe him 10 livres a quarter (40 livres a year) that shall alwayes bee payd with the pension. Desires I make him satisfyed with it, and recommend him to the new Rector. Would knowe what place he hath, and would also know it from me. Is content so he heares from his son once a month. Once a quarter will trouble me with a letter to knowe how his son doth and how his masters are satisfyed with him.[59]

Louis Nairne remained at Saint-Omer until 1716, when he left the Jesuit college and was transferred to the Collège des Ecossais in Paris.[60] His relations with his father never recovered, and would remain bad throughout the rest of his education and indeed the rest of his life. We cannot say to what extent his behaviour was the result of losing his mother when he was only fifteen years old, because we have no information about his behaviour before this stage. Did he resent his father for some reason, perhaps for being obliged to follow the king and leave his wife and children behind in 1712? Did he refuse to write letters because he knew that that was what his father did every day at the court of James III? Did he dislike music, and resent his father's insistence that he be given music lessons? We cannot say. But from a biographical point of view we should note that this family problem exactly coincided with Nairne's participation in the great crisis of the Jacobite cause which took place in the second half of 1715 and the beginning of 1716.

In March 1715, the Whig government of George I opened impeachment proceedings against the leaders of the Tory party, including Oxford, Bolingbroke and the Duke of Ormonde, for their part in the secret peace negotiations leading to the Treaty of Utrecht. Oxford and Ormonde remained in England to defend themselves, but Bolingbroke fled to Paris where he contacted both the Duke of Berwick and Queen Mary and offered to work for James III.[61] It was agreed that Bolingbroke, who was appointed secretary of state in the place of Higgons, would remain in Paris and co-ordinate plans for an invasion of England, which was to coincide with a Jacobite rising in the West Country, while Middleton and Nairne would continue to advise the king at Bar-le-Duc. The rising was to be under the leadership of the Duke of Ormonde, supported by Lord Lansdowne and Sir William Wyndham.

In June 1715, Queen Mary came to see James III at Bar-le-Duc,[62] to report on her meetings with Bolingbroke and Berwick. She and the king then went together to visit the prince de Vaudémont at Commercy, and the duc and duchesse de Lorraine at Nancy, with Nairne in attendance on both occasions.[63] In the middle of July, they all returned via Commercy to Bar-le-Duc.[64] A few days later, on 21 July, James decided to make his second attempt to travel through France and sail for England to join the planned rising. As Nairne explained to Gualterio on that day, it would be wrong for the king to delay going to England or Scotland while George I and his Hanoverian entourage remained deeply unpopular in both kingdoms. 'I hope', he added, 'that God will bless such a noble and just plan, great things cannot be undertaken without risks, but with justice on our side, and by doing our duty we must for the rest put ourselves in the hands of providence.'[65]

The plan was that Nairne would travel by himself to Paris, carrying with him a sealed bag containing 1,000 old *Louis d'ors*, a second one containing 800,[66] and a 'strong box' or 'trunk' containing 'a suite of cloths, and 2 little bundels of body linen, and a little bottle' for the king, as well as clothes for himself.[67] He would then wait '8 ou 10 jours' at the Collège des Ecossais, after which he would be joined by the king and only two personal servants, and they would travel together to the coast and sail for England.[68] No one at Saint-Germain was told of these plans, but Nairne was meanwhile instructed by James III to tell the Duke of Perth 'to acquaint my family at St Germain that they may follow me when they please, but that not to be said till they know I am sett sail.'[69] The only people at Bar-le-Duc who were originally in the secret were the queen and Lord Middleton.[70]

Unfortunately for the Jacobites, the Whig government discovered their plans and took decisive action to prevent the rising. An arrest warrant was issued against the Duke of Ormonde, who fled to France on 1 August. Then Lansdowne was arrested, Wyndham went into hiding, the rising was cancelled, and the Jacobites in England advised James III that he should definitely not attempt to cross the sea to join them.[71] Nairne wrote disconsolately on 28 July:

> Since my arrival here there has been news ... which forces the king to delay his journey for a time, which he finds very hard to bear ...
> Instead of continuing my journey to the designated place I am expecting at any moment to be ordered to return to Bar.[72]

He was still in Paris six days later, on 3 August:

> I have learned from Bar that their Majesties are well. I await my orders to return there. Y. Em will have understood from my last letter why I came here expecting to make a longer journey. Thus I will say nothing more than that delays in this sort of journey are always disagreeable and even dangerous, but let us hope that what is postponed is not altogether cancelled and that nothing will be lost by waiting. God's will be done.[73]

Because Nairne stayed at the Collège des Ecossais he was able to see his daughters in the English Augustinian convent next door. He also had the opportunity to discuss his son Louis' behaviour both with his daughters and with the senior members of the college. He conferred with Lord Bolingbroke, and one day before he left to return to Bar-le-Duc he saw the Duke of Ormonde, who had just arrived. Both men reiterated their advice that James III should delay going to England. Nairne left both the sealed bags and the locked 'strong box' at the college, and told Gualterio on the 16th, when he had recently returned to Bar-le-Duc, that the king's voyage was only delayed.[74]

Events now took a new turn, because the news was received that Louis XIV was not only gravely ill at Versailles but was actually dying. Queen Mary hastily left Bar-le-Duc, feeling that she should be at Saint-Germain at such a time,[75] and Nairne sent the following very characteristic letter to Gualterio:

> We shall shortly see what effect this great change will produce in the King my master's fortunes, and since it is God who rules over the world and decides the fate of Princes and Kingdoms in the wisdom and justice of his Providence, we should not doubt that this same God can turn this loss, however catastrophic it may seem to us, into something for our good: Diligentibus Dominum omnia cooperantur in bonum [All things work together for the good to them that love God].[76]

During his stay in Paris, Nairne had been able to discuss the developing situation with Lewis Innes, and a letter that Nairne sent his friend at the end of August from Bar-le-Duc gives a much more detailed explanation of his point of view at this critical moment. Innes wanted James III to go immediately to England, but Nairne felt that the king had been right to accept the advice of Bolingbroke and Ormonde in favour of delay, as it would be useless to go 'without any probable prospect of either safety or success':

> Of the two evils, the irretrievable one is certainly the greatest. There is no doubt delays are dangerous, for some persons may suffer thereby, and many may despond, but prudent or timely methods may prevent or at least lessen a great deal of what is feard so much on that point, and when things are well layd and concerted after this in a proper time, when the Parl.t is up, the alarme over and the sea clearer, all that may be repard, but the loss of the King's person never can. Besides if the fact be true of han's [i.e. George I's] having the aversion of 3 parts of 4 of the nation such a general aversion dos not change so easily nor so quickly, and who knows but it may even increase. One would have thought a visionary who would have entertaind a year ago the least hope of seeing the surprising changes to the better wch have happened

since that time, and why should we have such a strong fancy that this instant must be the period, and that increase of changing to the better, and that the present <u>now</u> is precisely the <u>Nunc aut nunquam</u>? For my part I see no reason to despaire of a moderat delay's producing as favourable a <u>Nunc</u> some time hence as now. The 2 great men whom Providence has brought over ... [are of the same opinion] ... I hope you'l excuse ... this being only to yourself from whom I cannot in true friendship hide nor dissemble my poor opinion, tho in the present case it has the disadvantage to appear on the pusilanimous side ... contrary to the Kings inclination ... I cannot make my court at so dear a rate, tho when it comes to the duty part of sharing in the danger, I hope in God I shall as well as others have nothing to reproche myself on that head.[77]

Although the Jacobite rising in the West Country had been cancelled, plans were afoot for risings to take place elsewhere. These had originally been planned as diversionary moves, but now they assumed an enhanced importance. The Earl of Mar was travelling to Scotland to proclaim James as king in the Highlands, while the Earl of Derwentwater and Thomas Forster (an MP), hearing that they were about to be arrested as Jacobite supporters, planned to do the same in Northumberland. When, therefore, the news reached Bar-le-Duc on 6 September that Louis XIV had died on the 1st,[78] James III decided to make a third attempt to leave Lorraine and make his way secretly to the Channel.

Lord Mar raised the Jacobite standard at Braemar on 17 September, and twelve days later his brother-in-law John Hay captured Perth for the Jacobites. On 17 October, Derwentwater and Forster proclaimed James III king in Northumberland, and shortly afterwards Lowland Scots under Lord Kenmuir and William Macintosh of Borlum marched south to join them at Kelso. When James III was informed of Mar's declaration in his favour in Scotland, he determined to leave Lorraine as quickly as he could. In the middle of October he left Bar-le-Duc to stay with the prince de Vaudémont at Commercy, whence it would be much easier to make a secret departure and travel through France without being recognized.[79] Now that Louis XIV was dead he would pass through France without informing the French government, and would not be deterred from embarking by any pessimistic reports coming from his kingdoms. Only Middleton, Nairne and Higgons would be informed in advance of his plans.[80]

James III left Commercy on Monday 28 October without an escort and with only two servants,[81] and told Nairne that 'nothing but the necessity of keeping the secret could have oblig'd him to part as he did literally alone, without the comfort of having any body of confiance with him'. Before he left he gave detailed instructions[82] that Nairne was to explain the situation to the prince de Vaudémont[83] and 'to stay at Commercy from Munday to Saturday, and to write to Paris by the wensdays and frydays post as if the King were still in Loraine, and send by these 2 posts 2 blank paquets in 2 covers directed to the Queen in his Ma.ties own hand'. On Saturday, 2 November, Nairne returned with Lord Middleton, Sir Thomas Higgons and four others to Bar-le-Duc,[84] where he was told to remain until orders were received from the queen to proceed to Saint-Germain.

Nairne, Middleton and Higgons set off from Bar-le-Duc on Monday 4 November and reached Saint-Germain on Friday, 8th.[85] Middleton and Higgons went directly to report to the queen, but Nairne stopped at the Collège des Ecossais in Paris where he was to deliver James III's 'great seals' and collect the 'strong box' which he had left there during the summer. This he was now to deliver to the queen, along with 'all the King's papers and the 2 little boxes that were in the long black trunk in the Kings closette of which he had the key',[86] as well as 'a seald paquet of papers' in the king's 'own hand', 'a little golden heart on a chagrin case, and a copy of *La retraitte spirituelle*'.[87]

The king had again left instructions with the queen that no one was to follow him until the news arrived at Saint-Germain that he had managed to reach the Channel and sail for Scotland. 'In his directions to the Queen', Nairne noted, he 'particularly named Nairn[e] and My Ld Mid[dleton] to be sent to him at the first.' In 'the mean time' Nairne was told that he 'should wait upon the Queen, and receive and follow her orders in any thing he was to write or act in his [the king's] service'.[88] It was assumed that the king would soon send the news that he had embarked for Scotland, and Nairne wrote that 'I did not expect to remain here for even a week when I arrived, but every day the orders for our departure have been delayed'.[89]

In fact, it took James III six weeks to travel through France to Dunkirk, and he was not able to sail for Scotland until 27 December.[90] Throughout November and December, therefore, Nairne and Middleton remained with the queen at Saint-Germain, anxiously awaiting the news that they should follow him and sail to Scotland. On 17 November, he confided to

Gualterio that he was 'in a state of uncertainty ..., far from my master the King, anxious to receive news of him and waiting impatiently for orders to follow him.'[91]

What must Nairne's thoughts have been during November and December 1715 as he waited anxiously for news that James III had sailed to Scotland? The journey that he would then undertake, as autumn turned into winter, was not only hazardous in itself, but also ran the risk of interception by the British navy, in which case Nairne would be imprisoned on a charge of treason. If all went well and he successfully disembarked on the east coast of Scotland, then he would be returning to his native country for the first time since he had left it well over forty years ago, in 1674. Unlike all the other Jacobites, Nairne was a voluntary ex-patriate, not an involuntary political exile, so he must have viewed the possibility of a successful Stuart restoration with mixed feelings. There can be no doubting his loyalty to James III, nor his total commitment to achieving a restoration, yet the implications for him of a restoration were bound to be different from what they would be for all the other Jacobite courtiers. The others would happily return to their homes and their estates, whereas there is no indication that Nairne ever had any intention to leave France and return to live permanently in Scotland. As a Catholic, he was extremely unlikely to be retained by James III in his present position, while the king would inevitably employ people in his political secretariat who had recent experience of British politics and of actually living in England or Scotland. Nairne would no doubt follow the king to Edinburgh and even to London, but thereafter he would probably be pensioned off. He was now sixty years old, so perhaps that is what he actually hoped for. He could then return to live with his three surviving children and to supervise the education of the two younger ones. It is true that his wife was now dead, so he would not need to return for her sake, but it seems most likely that Nairne would have felt that his work was complete once James III had been restored. In the meantime, however, he had to face the prospect of a long voyage up the North Sea, followed by a military campaign in which he might well be captured or even killed.

If Nairne was seriously worried about the prospect of joining a military campaign being conducted in the depths of a Scottish winter he must also have been excited (or apprehensive) about seeing his Episcopalian family after such a long time. Margaret, his mother, was still living in the family home at Sandford in Fife, while his brother Samuel was living with his wife and six children to the west of Dundee at Errol, where he was the Presbyterian minister. Sandford was relatively inaccessible, between the Firth of Tay and the Firth of Forth, whereas Errol was between Dundee and Perth, on the actual road that Nairne was almost certain to take when travelling to join the king. In addition to his mother and brother, Nairne was likely to see, for the first time, his elder brother Alexander's two daughters, now grown up and married with their own children.

The strain of waiting at Saint-Germain, with some or all of these thoughts running through his head, seems to have been too much, and during the second half of November Nairne had an attack of gout which prevented his being able to walk or even go to mass until 29 December. He wrote to Gualterio on that day:

> about a month ago I had an attack of gout in one of my feet for the first time in my life, which was very painful and forced me to stay in my room and even in bed for a short time. And I was not able during this time to get out and only today have I had the honour of seeing the Queen ... Speaking confidentially to Y. Em our affairs appear to be in a very doubtful state, but since all is in God's hands, we must put our hope in Him and resign ouselves to His holy will ... All the King's officers and other servants who were on the List to follow him at a moment's notice have the same order as I have to stay here and await new orders. Thus for more than 6 weeks we have daily been expecting orders, forced to be ready to leave from one day to the next, which leaves us in a very troubling state of uncertainty.[92]

In another letter written on the same day he explained that when he went to see the queen 'I even had to go with an open shoe, my foot still being so swollen.'[93]

In fact, the king managed to embark at Dunkirk two days before Nairne wrote these letters, but the news that he had done so did not reach Saint-Germain until 1 January.[94] Other news about the Jacobite rising had, however, already arrived, notably that the Earl of Mar had failed to defeat the government army at Sheriffmuir on 24 November, and that the Northumberland and Lowland Scots Jacobites had surrendered at Preston on the following day. Among them was one of Nairne's relations who had been executed for treason.[95] As usual Nairne showed his faith in Divine Providence, this time in a letter to the prince de Vaudémont:

> the present state of affairs in Scotland is very doubtful and worrying, and let us not deceive ourselves, it appears there is more to fear than there is to hope for, but God is above all, and when a just cause is abandoned by men there is great consolation in putting one's hopes in Providence and resigning oneself to God's will.[96]

At last the news arrived that James III had sailed for Scotland, and the queen gave permission for Nairne, Middleton and the other courtiers on the list to follow him.[97] Nairne wrote to keep Gualterio informed on 5 January:

> after many problems and difficulties, and after actually putting to sea on one or two occasions only to be forced back by unfavourable winds, and having been obliged to change his point of departure and alter his itinerary which was very troublesome and tiring, the King at last found a way to set sail from near Dunkirk on the 27th of last month in the evening accompanied only by a single valet. The urgent letter bringing the news to the Queen arrived here on New Year's day, and it also reported that the ship had been seen the next morning with a fair wind near Ostend, such that we may have good reason to think that H. M. has arrived safely in Scotland, where we can now hope that his presence will encourage his party to continue fighting the opposition however superior in numbers they may be and in time that Providence will provide new means to support our just cause.[98]

Nairne added that 'God willing I shall leave one day this week'. In fact he and the others did not leave Saint-Germain for another eight days, until the 13th,[99] by which time news had been received that the king had landed safely at Buchan Ness, near Peterhead, on the 2nd. Before leaving Nairne wrote with renewed optimism to the prince de Vaudémont: 'I am hoping soon to be able to write to you from Scotland and to inform you of some successes won by H. M.'s army.'[100]

Nairne, Middleton and the other Jacobite courtiers, accompanied by 'sixty military officers', travelled from Saint-Germain to Calais. After a delay of several days, perhaps caused by bad weather or perhaps because of difficulty in chartering a suitable ship, they then sailed for Scotland and arrived safely at Aberdeen on 3 February.[101] By that time, James III was with Lord Mar, now the Duke of Mar, at Scone Palace near Perth.

Since landing at Buchan Ness the king had made his way south to Aberdeen, and then to Feteresso west of Stonehaven, a property belonging to the Dowager Countess Marischal, daughter of the Duke of Perth. It was here that he had met Mar, the Earl Marischal and the other Jacobite leaders. From there he had moved south-west to Brechin Castle, home of the Earl of Panmure, and Kinnaird Castle, home of the Earl of Southesk – both places to the west of Montrose. His next stop had been Glamis Castle, home of the Earl of Strathmore (Middleton's nephew), which he had reached on 14 January, one day after Nairne and his party had set out from Saint-Germain. From Glamis the king had continued to Scone, home of Viscount Stormont just north of Perth, where he had been joined by Mar's brother-in-law John Hay (a son of the Earl of Kinnoul).[102]

By the end of January, when Nairne was sailing up the North Sea, the military situation was very depressing. The Hanoverian army, which Mar had failed to defeat when it was still possible, had been steadily reinforced, and was marching north from Stirling to Perth, thus blocking any prospect of the Jacobites' advancing from Perth to Stirling and thence to Falkirk and Edinburgh. In addition, the Jacobite army was short of weapons and supplies, and had very little money because ships bringing gold given by the King of Spain had run aground and been lost on the Dundee sandbanks.[103] It was the middle of winter and the weather was freezing cold.

The Jacobites remained at Scone until 9 February, when James III held a council of war with the Scottish lords to discuss the rapidly deteriorating situation. Facing inevitable defeat if he remained where he was, James then decided to retreat to Montrose. Part of the army was to travel inland via Coupar Angus and Glamis, while the other part was to travel with the king and Mar along the coast road via Dundee and Arbroath. It was on that day, 9 February, when the king reached Dundee that he ran into Nairne and Middleton travelling south to join him. Looking back a little later to the twelve days that he spent in Scotland, Nairne recorded that he had 'the honour to join the King at Dundee, on the very day he was obliged to leave Perth [sic: Scone]'.[104] The disappointment must have been very considerable.

The king's retreat meant that it was no longer possible to see Margaret, his mother. Dundee is only sixteen miles from Nairne's family home at

Sandford in Fife, though in those days the first mile involved taking a ferry to cross the Firth of Tay. Mrs Nairne was by then over eighty years old and she died later that year without ever again seeing her son.[105] To make the situation even more disappointing, Nairne probably never saw his younger brother Samuel, who was living only six miles west of Dundee at Errol.[106] Samuel's wife Margaret and one of their six children would many years later be mentioned in Nairne's will,[107] so it is just possible that one or more of them might have come to see him during the short time that he was at Dundee. This, however, is unlikely.

James III, Nairne, Middleton and Mar reached Montrose (where Middleton had his estates) on 12 February. In the harbour there they found a French ship, the *Marie-Thérèse* of Saint-Malo, which offered the possibility of escape. By this time both parts of the army were rapidly disintegrating, the soldiers losing heart and thinking only of returning home. The king realized that he had no alternative but to leave while he still could.[108]

It was decided that the *Marie-Thérèse* would sail for France on the evening of 15 February. During that day, while the ship was being made ready, James III and Nairne drafted a letter to be sent to the Duke of Argyll, in command of the Hanoverian army. The letter has survived in Nairne's handwriting and is dated Montrose, 4 February 1716 (Old Style = 15 February New Style). The king informed Argyll that he had left money with some of the magistrates at Perth and elsewhere to be used to repair damages caused by the military operations and as compensation for supplies which had had to be commandeered. The key passages were as follows:

> It was the view of delivering this my antient Kingdom from the hardship it lay under, and restoring it to its former happiness and independency that brought me into this country, and all hopes of effectuating that at this time being taken from me, I have been reduced much against my inclination but by a cruell necessity to leave the Kingdom with as many of my faithfull subjects as were desirous to follow me or I able to carry with me, that so at least I might secure them from the utter destruction that threatens them, since that was the only way left me to shew them the regard I had for and sense I had of their unparalel'd loyalty ... I have neglected nothing to render them a free and prosperous people, and I fear they will feel yet more than I the smart of preferring a foreign yoak to that obedience they owd me ..., but however things turn or Providence is pleasd to dispose of things, I shall never abandon my just Right nor the pursuite of it but with my life.[109]

In addition to Nairne, the party which sailed with the king included Middleton, Dominic Sheldon and Roger Strickland, but also the Duke of Mar, and Lord Drummond (the eldest son of the Duke of Perth).[110] Sir Thomas Higgons, Lord Clermont, Lord Edward Drummond, Charles Booth and Dr Lawrence Wood were all left behind, because they were not in Montrose when the king made his decision and could not be summoned in time.[111] The Jacobite troops left Montrose on the day after the king's departure, retreated to Aberdeen and disbanded. In fact the king left just in time, as the Hanoverian army occupied Montrose on 17 February.[112] The rising was over.

Leaving on one side the military and political disaster experienced by the Jacobites, the return journey to France must have been especially depressing for Nairne. If he *had* hoped that a successful restoration would have led to his own retirement, then such a hope had obviously been dashed. More important, perhaps, was the fact that the king was now surrounded by a new group of advisers, all of whom were Protestant, headed by the Duke of Mar. These men had lived in England and Scotland throughout the reigns of William III and Anne, and their advice was bound to carry more weight with James than that of his old servants who had lived in exile for twenty years and even more. Mar in particular had served in London as secretary of state for Scotland for four years, and as the man who had raised the Jacobite standard at Braemar was bound to become the king's principal minister. These men had a low opinion even of Lord Middleton, let alone a lesser figure such as David Nairne.

The *Marie-Thérèse* reached Boulogne-sur-Mer on 23 February, after a voyage down the North Sea lasting eight days.[113] Roger Strickland was sent ahead to announce the news of the king's safe arrival to the queen at Saint-Germain, but James III, Middleton and Nairne took their time to travel south. This was partly because the Regent would not let the king stay at Saint-Germain, and partly because arrangements needed to be made to provide him with accommodation elsewhere. While the Duke of Mar, therefore, travelled directly to Paris, James and his servants moved slowly, finally arriving at the château on 26 February. The king remained for three days, but did not sleep there, instead going each evening a few miles away to Malmaison, and taking with him a small staff of servants from his bedchamber. Middleton and Nairne, meanwhile, remained with the queen.[114]

On 29 February, James III left Saint-Germain and Malmaison and hid for eight days in a house in the Bois de Boulogne, where he and Mar, joined by the Duke of Ormonde, discussed future plans with the Spanish ambassador. It is very unlikely that Nairne was present during these meetings, but during one of them James decided to dismiss Lord Bolingbroke from his position as secretary of state. The latter had revealed Jacobite secrets to a mistress whom he shared with the pro-Hanoverian abbé Dubois and could no longer be trusted. Moreover he had been half-hearted in organizing reinforcements and supplies to be sent to Scotland while the king was there.

James III then returned to Lorraine, where he hoped that he might be able to reside once again. He took with him Roger Strickland and a small group of servants, but neither Mar nor Ormonde who remained in Paris, nor Nairne who remained at Saint-Germain. He joined the prince de Vaudémont at Commercy on 9 March without either a minister or even a secretary.[115]

Nairne did not have to wait long before he was summoned to rejoin the king at Commercy. He wrote to the prince de Vaudémont from Saint-Germain on Sunday 8 March that 'I am intending ... to leave here on Tuesday and Paris on Wednesday taking the road to Soissons, as ordered by H. M.'.[116] James III, however, had meanwhile been told by the duc de Lorraine, who had received an ultimatum from the Regent, that he could not remain in the duchy, so Nairne probably never reached Commercy. Instead, having passed through Reims, he seems to have found the king near Châlons-sur-Marne in France (possibly at the Château de Sillery), where they then remained together for twelve days until 24 March.[117]

It was during this short period that James invited the Duke of Mar to join him and become his new secretary of state.[118] It was also during this period, advised by Mar and Nairne, that James was forced to accept that the only place to which he could now go was Avignon, the chief town in the Comtat Venaissin, the papal enclave in the south of France. On 22 March, the king sent a letter, drafted by Nairne, to inform Pope Clement XI,[119] and on the following day Nairne also wrote to inform Cardinal Gualterio – the first letter he had sent him since his departure for Scotland. He explained that he had had no time to write, 'even though I came back from Scotland some while ago, having had the honour to return to France on the King's ship', and that 'I have spent very little time in any one place since my return, and had little time to myself'. On the following day, 24 March, he set out for Avignon with the king and Mar, accompanied by Strickland and a few servants.[120] After a journey of ten days, which would have taken him very close to Compigny, and then involved sailing down the river Rhône from Lyon, they arrived at Avignon on 2 April.[121] It was the first time Nairne had been there since returning from Lord Melfort's Rome embassy in 1691.

When James III reached Avignon he moved into the Hôtel de Serre de la Marine, previously occupied and now vacated for him by the commanding officer of the papal guards.[122] So too did Nairne and the other servants who had accompanied him. The Duke of Mar, by contrast, preferred to live elsewhere in the city.[123]

In the days and weeks which followed the court gradually increased in size as more and more Jacobites began to join the king. There were the servants who had been with him in Lorraine, though excluding both his confessor and chaplain (Dr John Ingleton and Thaddeus Connell) who were left behind at Saint-Germain, there were the Scottish lords, and there were many other Scots, particularly Highlanders, who had preferred to follow him into exile rather than remain in Scotland.

The first person to arrive was the Duke of Ormonde on 6 April,[124] followed by the Earl of Panmure.[125] On 12 May, Nairne noted that 'the king has a ... larger court here than he had at St Germain',[126] and on the king's birthday on 21 June that 'more than a hundred gentlemen attended him in the morning, accompanying him to a solemn sung Mass with music in his parish church'.[127] In July, Nairne noted that more people kept arriving 'every day',[128] and that among them were those people the king had had to leave behind in Scotland, including Lord Clermont, Lord Edward Drummond, Charles Booth, Sir Thomas Higgons and Dr Lawrence Wood.[129] It was the same story in August when Nairne referred to 'those wretched officers and other refugees whose numbers increase daily since a vessel arrived recently in France from the north of Scotland carrying Lord Seaforth, General Gordon, and about fifty others who had fortunately escaped the hands of the enemy'.[130]

As most of the Jacobites who now joined the king were Protestants it was necessary to provide them with their own Protestant services in this papal enclave. Nairne informed Gualterio at the end of May that the court had been joined by two Protestant chaplains, specifically requested by Ormonde and Mar, and that their services were held discreetly in the apartment of Ormonde 'qui est logé chez le Roy'. The door to the room was always left open, and the services were held without causing any scandal, but the king was keen to ensure that the Pope was made aware of the situation.[131] Nairne assured Gualterio that the principal chaplain (Charles Leslie) was 'a very moderate and good old man'.[132] With the support of Alamanno Salviati, the papal vice-legate in Avignon, the Pope gave formal approval for these services to be held in the privacy of the king's residence.[133]

The arrival of all these new Jacobite exiles from Scotland inevitably placed a strain on James III's finances, because the military expedition had used up most of the king's money,[134] and because the pension received from the French court was now several months in arrears.[135] The king therefore became dependent on the new pension he received from the Pope for maintaining his court and for paying the salaries of Nairne and the other servants.[136]

It was many years since Nairne had lived in southern Europe, and he found Avignon uncomfortably hot, especially when the Mistral wind also blew down the Rhone valley. In May, we find him complaining of 'the heat and the disagreeable winds in this part of the country',[137] and in June of 'the excessive heat'.[138] Relief eventually came at the beginning of September when he referred both to the climate and to the fact that more and more Jacobites were still continuing to arrive: 'the heat thank God has begun to diminish. But the King's suite grows day by day.'[139]

For most of the time, Nairne was fully occupied, as usual, dealing with the king's correspondence, but during these months he also cultivated the friendship of Salviati,[140] the vice-legate, and of Salviati's private secretary, Eustachio Buglioni. He told Gualterio in November that by then he had come to know Buglioni really well: 'he is a very good man, a true and frank friend and always ready to be of service ... we see each other as often as we are able.' One place where they regularly met was in a beautiful garden which belonged to a friend of Gualterio named the Chevalier Lily. Nairne went there as often as he could, particulartly during the hot summer months, to escape the excessive heat.[141]

While he was establishing very good relations with Salviati, Buglioni and Lily, Nairne came to realize that he was viewed with distrust if not hostility by the Duke of Mar and some of the king's new Protestant courtiers. Confident that he enjoyed the trust and favour of the king, he wrote frankly about this to his friend Thomas Innes[142] in September:

> I have not [recently] met with D. of Mar ... His Grace lodges in town and I am so ill a courtier, that I never yet went to his lodgings but twice when the K. sent me. I believe his Grace cares little for my courtship and I am not sorry he should perceive that I am pretty indifferent upon that head, and that any body that seems shy dry or reservd for me, shall have as little occasion given him by me as possible to think me officiously fond of his friendship or confidence. I am too old to begin the world again, or to constrain my self to seek for new patrons, nor is it either suitable to my humour or consistent with my post to be a humble companion to any great man whatever but this en passant.[143]

In the months and years which were to follow, Nairne would be forced to recognize that it was now Mar and the new Protestant exiles (notably Mar's brother-in-law John Hay) who enjoyed the king's favour, and that he could not really afford to maintain this attitude of reserve. One sign of things to come could be seen in the dining arrangements at the court. Two tables were laid each day in the king's apartment, the first for James III himself, Mar as secretary of state, the most senior household servants, the Scottish lords, and anyone else whom the king chose to invite. The second table was for Nairne and the other senior members of the household. Nairne commented that 'I have never had the honour of being among those occasionally asked to sit at his table, whereas every day he invites the junior members and gentlemen of his suite'.[144]

Nairne, who did not have a servant,[145] was obliged to make his own arrangements for eating his other meals. It seems that he often ate in the town with Charles Booth, with whom he now became particularly friendly.[146] In one of his letters to Thomas Innes he wrote that he had met one of the latter's friends, the abbé Gassaud, and that 'Mr Booth was so kind as to order a very good dinner for us with a couple of bottels of burgundy ... and we had caffé after dinner'.[147]

Nairne kept in regular contact with Ingleton and Connell, whom the king had not invited to join him at Avignon, and tried unsuccessfully to obtain benefices for them in France.[148] He also corresponded with both Thomas and Lewis Innes at the Collège des Ecossais,[149] and persuaded the former to embark on writing a history of Scotland.[150] He had met Dr Patrick Abercrombie, the author of a history entitled *The Martial Achievements of the Scots Nation, being an Account of the Lives, Characters and Memorable Actions of such Scotsmen as have signalized themselves by the Sword, at Home and Abroad*, published at Edinburgh in two volumes in 1711 and 1715. Nairne told Innes that he had reservations about Abercrombie as an historian and found him lacking in modesty: 'The very title of his history shocks me and seems affected.'[151] He believed, rightly, that Innes was much better qualified to write an accurate and reliable history of their native country.

Nairne also kept in regular contact with the Innes brothers for family reasons. At the end of March 1716, Thomas Innes arranged for a memorial service to be held in the chapel of the Collège des Ecossais to mark the first anniversary of the death of Nairne's wife. When he heard about it Nairne wrote to thank his friend:

> I was sensibly touchd with what you writt to me about my dear wifes anniversary, and am glad my daughter [Françoise] performd her duty upon that occasion so as to deserve your approbation, the honour you was pleasd to do both her and me in celebrating the most essential part of that ceremony was truly kind and friendly for which I return you my hearty thanks, and I confess it is a great comfort to me that the holy sacrifice was offerd by one in whose fervent prayers for so deserving a subject I have a very great confidence. I hope the departed soul is in a state to return your charity wch is to me so feeling a satisfaction that I cannot think of it but with tears of joy. . Pray God you may render me the like good office one day and that your prayers may be as efficacious and as acceptable to God almighty in behalf of the greatest of sinners as I am confident they have been on this occasion for the happy soul in question.[152]

In the same letter, Nairne asked if he had given Innes his will before setting out for Scotland 'for I have it not with me'. Presumably the will contained provisions for his three children, Françoise, Louis and Marie, with perhaps some small legacies for other people. We do not know because the document has not survived. It would be interesting to know what it stated concerning the family estate at Sandford.[153]

Since his elder brother Alexander's death in 1706, the house at Sandford had continued to be occupied by his mother Margaret, but she died at some time during the summer or autumn of 1716. As Nairne himself was proscribed as a Jacobite, the estate had been inherited by the second husband of his niece Magdalene (Alexander's daughter) who had a son named Patrick. The latter also died in 1716, but in the previous year Magdalene had re-married John Palmer. The Palmers now decided that the estate would have to be sold 'for the benefit of the creditors', and arranged to sell it, as Nairne put it, to 'a fellow that was in my time a tennant of one our next door neighbours'. Palmer, however, arranged for all the surviving family papers to be sent down to Avignon for David Nairne, as the head of the family. They were 'but scraps of a great many more important papers wch were in the charter kist of St.ford, but all has been dispersd in so many hands'. When Nairne received these papers he decided to send them to his daughter Françoise, with instructions to pass them on to Thomas Innes who, as an historian, would be able to read the script and evaluate their worth. Surrounded by the Duke of Mar and the other Scottish lords claiming superiority based on the antiquity of their lineage, Nairne seems to have been keen to establish his own:

> I desire you'l be so kind at your leisure as to peruse them and give me your opinion of them whether you think them proofs I do not say uncontestable, but reasonable ones to satisfy the ancientness of my family of St.foord Nairne of which I am now the next heir male and representative. I am not so visionary as to expect that at my age and in the state things are in I can ever pretend to redeem that ancient little estat ..., but it is not impossible that my son may live to be in a condition to recover that ancient patrimony of his predecessors and therefore I put these old papers in your hands to keep for him ... The oldest paper that I found amongst those you have, is I think in the 14th age signd by one George Nairne of St.foord that itself is I think a proof of a pretty old standing of that estates being in the name, about 400 years ago. Pray send me if you please when you have leasure a little bordereau of these papers marking the dates of each, with your opinion upon the whole, which I'l keep by me as an authentick testimony and approbation thereof.[154]

Nairne maintained a regular correspondence with both his daughters,[155] though neither of them chose to tell him that Françoise was quite seriously ill during September, a fact which he only found out because he was told by Lewis and Thomas Innes, and also by Etienne du Mirail de Monnot.[156] His main concern, however, continued to be the education of his son who did not write to him.

Nairne was keen to transfer his son Louis from the English Jesuit college at Saint-Omer to the Collège des Ecossais in Paris, but Lewis Innes replied that he and his brother Thomas were not keen on the idea because of 'the boy's humour and indocility'. When Nairne urged them nevertheless to accept him they realized that they would have to give way. Lewis Innes wrote to his brother at the end of April that 'he [Nairne] seems very uneasy and takes it ill, and we must not disoblige the poor man'.[157]

During that summer, Lewis Innes wrote to tell Nairne that he was willing to accept Louis as a pupil at the college, but Françoise also wrote to her father to say that Lewis Innes 'did not seem to her to approve' of the idea. Nairne needed to give due notice to the Jesuits at Saint-Omer so he wrote to Thomas Innes to seek clarification. ''Tis under your care he must chiefly be', he wrote, 'and therefore I should be glad to hear from you upon that subject.' But he had no doubt that his son would receive a better education in Paris: 'I must be determind by what is most for my sons good and I own I think he would improve more under your direction than any where els.'[158]

Before he could receive a reply from Thomas Innes, Nairne had a letter from Father Sabran (head of the Jesuit community at Saint-Omer, though no longer rector of the college) who urged him to leave Louis where he was for another year, and then send him to 'a seminary at Lyons for his philosophy'. Nairne had no intention of doing this, commenting that Louis would 'never study heartily so as to profit in a place where he is disgusted'. But he wanted to know if Lewis and Thomas Innes would really accept him:

> do you think him fitt for your colledge, and can you hope that under your direction he'l improve as much in poetry, wisdom piety and good conduct in a years time, as he'l do where he is, if this be so and that you'l be so friendly and charitable as to undertake it and do your endeavours, I will not balance one moment giving the preference to your colledge for I make no comparison between the principles you'l educate him in, and those of the Society, and I do not dispair but with the help of God keeping him in obedience in managing his temper rightly with a prudent mixture of authority and affection, severity and mildness, you may gain him so as both to make a schollar and an honest man of him. You'l be pleasd Sir to consult your brother in this matter wch is a very important one for me, and let me have your answer as soon

as possible, that I may take my measurs accordingly and write in conformity to St Omers. I pray God direct you to advise me for the best.[159]

Thomas Innes replied that the Collège des Ecossais would accept him, and Nairne's acknowledgement indicates his fatherly love and his hopes for Louis as well as just how difficult he found the sixteen-year-old boy:

> As for my son I hope he'l be obedient and conforme himself as others to the rules of the colledge, I am only sorry there should be any grounds for thinking him less tractable in that point than all the other boys, he has his faults, no doubt but I hope he is not incorigible, and under your care I hope well of him, my orders to him shall not be wanting to contribute thereto.[160]

After some further correspondence, it was agreed that Louis Nairne would leave Saint-Omer and join the Collège des Ecossais in January 1717.[161]

Nairne's plan was that his son should study poetry and philosophy, and above all 'réthorique'. He had a high opinion of the rhetoric teacher and asked Thomas Innes to 'recommend him [Louis] particularly to Mr Morus for whom I have allways a great esteem, and shall be glad to ow the last and best part of my sons education to him'. This, he felt, should be enough, so that Louis could then embark on his future career when he was eighteen years old, commenting that 'I hope by taking right methods with him he may be able in two years time to give him enough of Colledge learning'.[162] As we shall see, Nairne's hopes for his son were to be disappointed.

Despite these family worries, Nairne was preoccupied for most of the time with his political work. Since the death of James III's sister in 1712 there had been no direct Jacobite heir to the thrones of England, Scotland and Ireland. The heiress presumptive was the Duchess of Savoy, now also the Queen of Sicily since 1713, and it was very unlikely that Vittorio Amadeo, her husband, would do anything to oppose or even offend George I. The future of the Jacobite cause therefore depended on James III alone, until the latter could get married and have children. Viewed in this light it was an enormous relief that James had been neither captured nor killed in Scotland, and that he had sailed safely back to France from Montrose. Nairne was acutely aware of this, and believed that Providence had protected the king, as can be seen from a letter he wrote shortly after ariving in Avignon in April 1716:

Despite all our misfortunes it is certain that we should praise and thank God for preserving our sacred King, as I am convinced that his preservation is a definite mark of the great designs of Providence for him, and that sooner or later we shall see him restored to the Throne which is his by right. He has justice on his side but also the almost general favour of his people who are being oppressed today by a faction for his sake yet continue to support him, indeed they are more aggrieved and their just resentment will explode all the more violently as soon as a favourable opportunity arises for their liberator to be able to join them.[163]

Following the king's hasty departure from Montrose, pro-Hanoverian propaganda had been arguing that James III was a coward who had been reluctant to join the Jacobites in Scotland in the first place and who had then deserted them as soon as he could, leaving them in the lurch to suffer the fate of rebels against the government of George I. To counter this the Duke of Mar arranged for a pamphlet to be sent to England and Scotland entitled *A Letter from an Officer in the King's Army after it had marched Northward from Aberdeen to his friend in London, February 1715/16*. Containing detailed information about the king's difficult journey from Commercy to Dunkirk in October to December 1715, and explaining what had really led up to his departure from Montrose in February 1716, the pamphlet which was printed in Avignon presented both James III and Mar himself in the most favourable light. Nairne then arranged for it to be translated into French so that it could be widely distributed in continental Europe. Sending two copies to the prince de Vaudémont in June he explained that 'it is a simple account of those facts of which H. M. has already for the most part informed Your Serene Highness at Commercy but since the letter is up to date concerning this unfortunate affair we felt it right to inform the public'. Nairne felt encouraged by the news which was reaching Avignon of pro-Jacobite manifestations in London: 'in spite of the severity with which the so-called rebels are every day persecuted to death, dying as true martyrs for justice', and 'in spite of the injustice of men and the desertion even of the Powers of Europe, we should not despair of a just cause'.[164]

While Nairne was at Avignon the French theologian Louis Ellies Dupin published two pamphlets in which he advocated a union of the Gallican church in France and the Anglican church in England to resist the claims of papal supremacy.[165] He was encouraged to do this because his old friend William Wake, whom he had first met in Paris in the 1680s, had just been appointed Archbishop of Canterbury, and also wanted to negotiate a union of the two churches.[166] Such a union, if it could have been achieved, would have had far-reaching theologicial and political consequences. Dupin was not himself a Jansenist, but by opposing the ultramontane arguments of the Jesuits his strong Gallicanism was bound to have an impact on the Jesuit-Jansenist controversy which had bitterly divided French opinion since the publication of the papal bull *Unigenitus* (which condemned Jansenism) in 1713. The idea of a Gallican-Anglican union also had implications for Jacobitism, because it was his refusal to convert which had prevented James III's restoration in 1714. If, however, the Gallican Catholic church in France could be reconciled to the Church of England, in a joint resistance to papal pretentions, then a way might be opened for a peaceful Jacobite restoration.

In June 1716, when he received the first of Dupin's pamphlets, Nairne was favourably impressed, writing that 'I must say I think he provd very strongly what ever he advanced either as to Gallican libertys or Roman usurpations.'[167] He was worried, however, that Dupin was too critical of the Jesuits and that as a result he would alienate many people, including both James III and Queen Mary. He commented to Thomas Innes in July that Dupin should 'adoucir the point of the Jesuites, without wch his authority with some persons (especially at Chaillot) will allways be suspected and rejected even in the solid essential points'.[168] The more Nairne examined Dupin's arguments the more critical of them he became, commenting in his next letter to Innes: 'as to Dupin, his paper when I considerd it seriously is but a poor production for a man like him'.[169]

Negotiating a union of the Gallican and Anglican churches was all very well as a theoretical proposition, but in practice there were major doctrinal differences between them which could not be ignored, and in the event of a Jacobite restoration King James III would have to decide how to treat the Church of England. Dupin argued that James should 'protect the Church of England', by which he meant that he should not attempt to alter the religion of England, and that to do so would be 'resisting Gods providence'. Nairne disagreed, and argued at length that the king ought to adopt a more positive attitude, on the grounds that it 'can never be lawfull' to 'protect maintain and encourage' a 'heretick church':

> my difficulty is whether it be not in effect and in reality supporting that heretical church as much by promising to maintain the members of it in the possession of their churches schools colledges as if the promise were made in Du pins terms. But you Churchmen are best judges of these matters for I do not pretend to understand much less to decide these nice distinctions. I think it were enough that the K. should promise to be passive and never go about by force ... to alter the settled constitution in church and state, this I am sure might be lawfully promisd and sincerely performd, and I think a church that is in possession, that has the laws of the Parliam.t on their side, should be contented wth such a promise, and fear nothing, if they believe (as they ought to do) that their religion is proof against all fair arguments of persuasions in friendly peaceable and christian conferences; but if we be all obliged (as certainly we are) to wish the propagation of the true religion and the salvation of our neighbour and to contribute to both in our general stations, by such prudent and lawfull means (violencies apart) as providence affords us, I think no Catholick Prince can make any promise derogatory to that obligation.[170]

For the time being there seemed very little prospect that such a union of churches could be achieved, so Nairne was more concerned with cultivating support at Rome than with opposing Roman pretentions. He tried to do this by stimulating support for James III among the cardinals, and by nurturing the Jacobite representation at the papal court.

In a letter of September 1716, Nairne asked Gualterio to approach Cardinals Aquaviva and Conti, the Protectors of Spain and Portugal, to obtain their support. The King of Spain was already James III's friend and virtual ally, but the King of Portugal should be reminded that James 'will one day be in a position to remember who were his benefactors and real friends'.[171]

The most important English priest in Rome was Lord Richard Howard, a brother of the Duke of Norfolk and a canon of St Peter's. Known as the *abbé* or *abate* Howard, the Jacobites hoped that he would one day become a cardinal, as one of his uncles had been, so Nairne tried to keep him informed of English politics.[172] It was also hoped that Lord William Drummond, a son of the 1st Duke of Melfort, might also become an influence at the papal court and eventually become a cardinal. Born in Rome during his father's embassy there, Lord William was now known as the abbé Melfort. He was sent to Rome in July 1716 with a letter of recommendation for Gualterio, to whom Nairne wrote: 'Because of his family I would be very pleased if Y. E.'s protection and reputation could help him get a benefice'.[173] In September, the abbé Melfort was given his first benefice, and Nairne wrote to inform his brother and mother that he owed it to Gualterio's influence.[174] In December he asked Gualterio to bring Melfort to the attention of the Pope and obtain a second benefice for him:

> He is young and sensible, and if he continues, as I hope, to behave well in Rome, he could one day see himself established there advantageously and held in respect like the Abbé Howard.[175]

James III, however, was concerned that Melfort was too demanding, because it transpired that the latter had himself approached Cardinal de Noailles and asked him to give him a valuable abbey in Brittany, while continuing to live in Rome.[176] In later years, Nairne would come to distrust and even dislike the abbé Melfort.

It was while Nairne was concentrating on these questions that James III began to suffer from piles, which by October had become sufficiently serious to necessitate a dangerous surgical operation.[177] With no Jacobite heir other than the Queen of Sicily, the consequences of the operation resulting in the king's death could hardly be overestimated, and Nairne was one of the very few people privy to the secret that an operation had to be performed. He wrote with relief to the prince de Vaudémont on 21 October:

> Mr Guerin a surgeon from Paris this morning performed the operation which the King endured with almost incredible fortitude. In consequence the danger and the worst eventuality being past, there is nothing left for us to do but thank God.[178]

Shortly before the king's operation the Regent of France informed Queen Mary at Saint-Germain that he was negotiating an alliance with the government of George I, and that one of its terms was that he would oblige James III to leave Avignon and transfer his court over the Alps to Italy.[179] It was understood that James would not be able to travel until he had recovered from his operation, but by the time the alliance was signed on 4 January 1717 preparations were already under way for the journey. The king hoped that the King of Sicily would let him reside somewhere in Piedmont, but when Vittorio Amadeo refused to allow this,[180] James realized he had no option but to go to the Papal States, where Pope Clement XI told him he could live wherever he wanted.[181]

***

The year 1717 was an important turning point both in the history of the Stuart court in exile and in the life of David Nairne. Despite the presence of so many new exiles, mainly Protestant and Scottish, the court at Avignon was similar to what it had been at Bar-le-Duc in Lorraine, consisting predominantly of the royal household brought by James III from Saint-Germain. When it moved to Italy, however, the court's structure and personnel began to be changed.[182] A similar alteration took place in the position of David Nairne at the court. Having gradually acquired a position of considerable influence at Saint-Germain, Nairne had become James III's most important councillor at Bar-le-Duc and had remained close to the king at Avignon. After the move to Italy, however, Nairne found himself gradually sidelined and supplanted by some of the new Protestant exiles who now became the king's favourites.

James III left Avignon in February 1717 and arrived in March at his new residence at Pesaro on the Adriatic coast after what Nairne described as 'a boring journey taking six weeks'.[183] The king remained at Pesaro for two months and then went with only a few servants, including Nairne, to visit Pope Clement XI in Rome. The visit lasted nine and a half weeks, after which James returned north, not to Pesaro but to Urbino in the hills nearby. The court then remained at Urbino from July 1717 to October 1718.

In order to understand how Nairne's position changed we have to examine briefly the Jacobite political secretariat, which had been divided into two parts at Bar-le-Duc in December 1713. Sir Thomas Higgons had then been appointed secretary of state, assisted by Nairne's friend Etienne du Mirail de Monnot as his chief clerk. Nairne as secretary of the king's closet had been entrusted with the Roman correspondence, without any clerical assistance, because Nicholas Dempster had been left behind at Saint-Germain with the queen. After the return from Scotland in February 1716 the Duke of Mar had become secretary of state and had selected his own assistants in preference to Monnot who remained at Saint-Germain. One of Mar's assistants was John Paterson, who had been his secretary during the rising of 1715–16, and who like Mar himself could not read or speak French. The other was Robert Creagh, an Irishman who had lived for many years in France and who was recommended by Nairne so that Mar's correspondence could be translated when necessary. The arrival of so many new Jacobite exiles, and the ongoing secret negotiations with leading Tory politicians in England and Scotland, considerably enhanced the importance of Mar as the secretary of state dealing with most of the Jacobite correspondence. Yet the establishment of the Jacobite court at Avignon, within the papal enclave in the south of France, gave a new importance to the Roman correspondence for which Nairne was responsible. As we have observed, the relations between Mar and Nairne soon became strained, but Nairne was able to hold his own at the court because he provided an essential service for the king and because, unlike Mar, he could converse with Alamanno Salviati and the other important ecclesiastical and secular dignitaries in the city.

Unknown to James III, who trusted him completely, the Duke of Mar was regretting his involvement in the Jacobite cause and hoping to obtain a pardon from George I. When, therefore, the time came for James III and his court to go to Italy, Mar said that he wished to visit his wife in Flanders and deserted the king shortly after they had left Avignon. In fact, he went to Paris and contacted the British ambassador (the one who had employed the assassin to kill James III at Nonancourt) and wrote to his other old friends in the government in London, in an unsuccessful attempt to obtain permission to return to England.[184] If he had succeeded, he would not have needed to rejoin the Jacobite court in Italy, but he left John Paterson with the king as an insurance, to keep him informed of developments in case he failed to obtain a pardon. He took his other assistant, Creagh, with him to act as his interpreter in France, though of course the latter, an Irish Catholic, was not informed of Mar's secret negotiations.

The sudden departure of Mar left James III without a secretary of state, and inevitably raised the question as to who should deal with his correspondence. Paterson, as Mar's under-secretary, had Mar's cyphers, so he needed to do the clerical work of deciphering the letters received, while James III himself had to become personally involved in drafting many of the replies to be put into cypher for despatch by Paterson. But James inevitably looked to Nairne, who had opened and dealt with the correspondence of successive secretaries of state over so many years, to help him in this task. And Nairne was naturally pleased to do this, if only because it confirmed his position as the most senior member of the secretariat.

In his correspondence Nairne simply informed Gualterio without comment that Mar 'has left us ... on some private matter',[185] but he must have had mixed feelings. On the one hand he was presumably shocked by Mar's decision to desert the king, if only temporarily. On the other hand, he was probably relieved to see the departure of such an influential courtier with whom his relations had become strained.

John Paterson, meanwhile, decided to write a 'Narrative of the Journey of James III' which he would eventually submit to the Duke of Mar. He noted two days after the latter's departure that 'Mr Nairne deliverd me a letter ... to the Duke of Mar, ... and ordered me to decipher it, which I did and gave it to the King, who kept it and gave me no orders about it'. He observed that the letter had already been opened 'when Mr Nairne gave it to me'. Although Paterson did not actually say so, it seems clear that he resented the fact that Nairne had opened Mar's correspondence and given him instructions, and also that he (Paterson) made no secret of these feelings, in part perhaps because he knew that Mar had little regard for Nairne.

That evening Dominic Sheldon, as vice-chamberlain of the court, summoned Paterson to his lodging and gave him a friendly warning. The latter reported to Mar:

> 'he ... made several kind promises of his friendship ... I made the best return I could, and begged him to give me his advice from time to time, and I would be very observant of it, on which he advised me to endeavour to gain Mr Nairne's friendship, which stunned me a little at first. I could not help thinking I had spent too much time and labour if after all I was to depend on Mr Nairne's patronage, but I believed Mr Sheldon meant it well, and remembered that the Duke of Mar had ordered me to follow his advice, and so I told him I should endeavour to be well with Mr Nairne, and every other servant the King had.[186]

Shortly after this incident Paterson was ordered to give copies of Mar's cyphers to Nairne.

When Mar heard about this incident he did what he could to undermine Nairne's position with the king. On 2 May, he wrote from Paris, in a letter to be showed to James III, that 'Nairne often mistakes the ciphers in the letters he writes for the King, so that there is nothing to be made out of them.[187] James defended Nairne and informed Mar that the mistakes were the result of a faulty copy of the cypher,[188] but Mar returned to the charge in June and accused Nairne of being indiscreet.[189] Once again the king defended Nairne,[190] but by the time the court reached Urbino it was clear that the arrival of the new Protestant exiles from Scotland had brought into the Jacobite court a group of people who disliked Nairne's influential position with the king and would be keen in future months to do what they could to reduce it. So long as Mar remained in Paris, attempting to betray James III, then Nairne's position continued to seem secure, but by the summer of 1717 it was apparent that the influence which Nairne had enjoyed since the court had been at Bar-le-Duc was now under threat.

When James III first realized that he would have to leave Avignon and move somewhere in the Papal States he hoped to be given a palace somewhere near Rome, but he then changed his mind and decided that it would be better to live in Bologna.[191] Nairne wrote to Gualterio from Avignon on 26 January 1717 that Bologna was 'the most agreeable, the most beautiful and the largest town on the Papal States after Rome'. As at Avignon, the court would need 'a commodious palazzo for the King where he could accommodate near him his most essential nobles and household servants, and the rest of his suite could be lodged in houses nearby'. By then, however, the Pope was having second thoughts, suggesting that James might like to go to Pesaro, and that Salviati might then be transferred from Avignon to become *Presidente* of the area, living nearby at Urbino. Nairne told Gualterio that this idea did not appeal to the king:

> since the decision had already been made to go to Bologna, which seems to the King's friends to be more suitable for his use at the present time than any other place he is convinced that His Holiness having allowed the King to choose, will not find this a bad choice, and His Majesty cannot at the present time change the measures he has taken to go to Bologna.[192]

James III realized that he could not take all the Jacobites at Avignon with him to Bologna, so he ordered some of them to remain in France and the Highlanders to go to Toulouse.[193] He then divided his servants and the remaining courtiers into two groups. James himself would travel north up the Rhône to Valence and then through the Dauphiné to Chambéry in Savoy, after which he would go over the Mont Cenis pass into Piedmont, while the 'gros equipage' would be sent down the Rhône and then by sea from Marseille to Livorno to rendezvous with him at Bologna.[194] Meanwhile the Duke of Ormonde's cousin, George Bagnall,[195] was to travel to Rome to explain to the Pope that the king would prefer to reside at Bologna rather than Pesaro.

James III left Avignon on 6 February accompanied by Ormonde, Mar, Nairne, Dominic Sheldon the vice-chamberlain, Dr Lawrence Wood the king's physician, Mar's under-secretaries Robert Creagh and John Paterson, and forty servants headed by his two equerries.[196] They had sixty-nine horses ('ventinove cavalli del re' and 'quaranta cavalli de traino' for pulling), three 'carrozze' (coaches), one 'lettiga' (litter) and four 'carri' (wagons).[197] Nairne commented that in 'la suitte du Roy il n'y a aucun Seigneur de distinction que Milord Duc d'Ormond [et] M. le Duc de Mar.[198]

The king, who was still extremely uncomfortable after his operation, travelled in short daily stages. The February weather was freezing cold, and his party did not reach Montmélian (near Chambéry) in Savoy until the 16th.[199] It was at this point, when they were about to climb the Alps towards the Mont Cenis pass, that the Duke of Mar announced that he intended to leave and return to Paris. On the 17th, the king's party left Montmélian and travelled to Aiguebelle, and from there went on the 18th to Saint-Jean de Maurienne, where they rested for one day. It was there that John Paterson began to write his 'Narrative' for Mar.

The next stages of the journey took them to Modane and to Lanslebourg, the last town before the Mont Cenis pass. They made the hazardous journey over the pass in deep snow on the 21st, but King Vittorio Amadeo had ordered that the road itself should be cleared. The Duke of Ormonde wrote to Salviati that 'a thousand men have been ordered to clear the snow along the road, and 400 horses to accompany him'.[200] Thanks to this snow-clearing Nairne and the other members of the king's party arrived safely at Nouvalaise in Piedmont, where they were met by some household servants sent by Vittorio Amadeo. That night they arrived at Susa, where they had another day of rest, and on the 23rd travelled on to Rivoli, whence Nairne wrote to inform Gualterio of their safe arrival:

We crossed the mountains last Sunday and came to spend the night and a day at
Susa where we were yesterday. Tomorrow H. M. will pass incognito through the
town of Turin, and see Their Majesties in secret and then sleep and spend a day at
Moncalieri. I am not exactly sure which route we will take next. But as soon as we
arrive in Bologna I will have the honour of writing more fully to Y. E..[201]

Bagnall, meanwhile, had arrived in Rome where he was greeted by
Gualterio and taken to see the Pope, with whom he had two audiences.
Gualterio noted in his diary that 'the Pope says that he does not mind at
all where H. B. M. chooses to live', but he believed that in reality the Pope
now wanted James to go to Pesaro.[202] Knowing that James was reluctant to
go there, Gualterio reverted to the original idea that the king should live
in one of the apostolic palaces near Rome, and went to inspect the one at
Albano (which would later, in 1721, be accepted by James for his *villeggia-
turi*).[203] Nairne, however, sent a negative reply, saying that the king felt
that it would be inconvenient to be so close to Rome and would prefer, if
necessary, to go to Pesaro.[204]

Having left Moncalieri on the morning of 25 February, Nairne travelled with the king that day to Villa Nuova d'Asti, where they remained for
two days,[205] and then to Alessàndria where they remained until 4 March.
On the following day, they reached Tortona, where they found Bagnall
on his return from Rome, and crossed into Lombardy. It was at this point
that James III decided that he would have to live at Pesaro rather than
Bologna. Nairne wrote to tell Gualterio of the king's decision, adding that
'he [His Majesty] proposes to travel there directly only stopping for one
night in Bologna', and that he was sending Bagnall to inform Cardinal
Agostino Cusani, the Papal Legate in Bologna, of his decision. James was
presumably influenced by what Bagnall reported, and said how pleased
he was that Salviati would be appointed *Presidente* of the area.[206] But
there was another reason why James changed his mind. Gualterio noted
in his diary that 'none of the Cardinals was prepared to give up his house
to S. B. M.',[207] whereas Cardinal Davia had offered to vacate for him the
palazzo apostolico at Pesaro which he had been using as papal legate of the
Romagna.[208] As the king now only needed temporary accommodation
in Bologna his banker, Giovanni Angelo Belloni, agreed to make his *casa*
available for a few days.

On 27 February, when James III was still in Piedmont, the Pope ordered marchese Bufalini to join the king and 'to serve him on the journey',[209] and his nephew Don Carlo Albani to travel to Bologna so that he could formally welcome the king when he crossed the river Panaro and entered the Papal States.[210] The Pope also gave orders that the *palazzo apostolico* at Pesaro should be fully furnished and made ready for the king's arrival there, and as this would take some time James decided that he would have to remain longer in Bologna than he had planned.

After leaving Tortona the king's party travelled via Broni, where they stayed for one day,[211] and Burgo San Domino, where they remained for two days.[212] From there the journey took them to Piacenza and then along the Via Emilia to Parma, Reggio and Modena. In the latter city, where James III stayed with his uncle, Duke Rinaldo, whom Nairne had met very regularly when he had been in Rome with Lord Melfort in 1689–91, Nairne also had the opportunity to see some of his old acquaintances from Saint-Germain.[213]

The river Panaro, which was then the frontier between the Duchy of Modena and the Papal States, is situated a few miles south-east of the city of Modena, and James III and his courtiers reached it on the morning of Saturday, 13 March. They were greeted there on behalf of the Pope, as planned, by Don Carlo Albani, who had brought with him from Bologna the painter Giuseppe Maria Crespi to record the encounter. The painting, now in the Narodni Gallery in Prague, shows Albani, Bufalini and some Bolognese senators on the right hand side of the canvas, welcoming James who is shown on the left with five of his courtiers. Two of them can be identified as the Duke of Ormonde and Dominic Sheldon, because the former has the Garter and the latter has a black wig. One of the three others must therefore by David Nairne, though it is not possible to specify which one he is, if only because the painter had no opportunity to prepare proper portraits of the newly arrived Jacobites.[214]

Nairne remained with the king for two nights in the Casa Belloni, which was illuminated and specially decorated for their arrival.[215] During this short visit he established good relations with both Giovanni Angelo Belloni himself[216] and conte Sicinio Pepoli,[217] and saw his old friend Sir Joseph Ronchi, who had returned to Bologna from Saint-Germain.[218] He

Figure 7. *The Meeting of James III and Don Carlo Albani on the Banks of the River
Panaro outside Bologna, 13 March 1717*, 1717 (149 × 225 cm, detail),
by Giuseppe Maria Crespi (Narodni Gallery, Prague)
In this painting, James III is shown with five of his courtiers, including the Duke of
Ormonde (second from left, with the Garter sash shown incorrectly over the right, not
the left, shoulder) and Dominic Sheldon (fifth from left, with the black wig). Nairne is
one of the other three Jacobite courtiers, possibly the one on the left behind Ormonde.

also sent a letter to Gualterio to tell him of the king's arrival and to say how very pleased the latter was with Don Carlo Albani.[219] Then, on the 15th, James III left Bologna and travelled to Imola, where he was greeted at the archbishop's palace by Cardinal Ulisse Giuseppe Gozzadini. This time the scene was recorded by Antonio Gionima, in a painting now in the Castel Sant'Angelo in Rome, and once again the king is shown on the left hand side of the canvas with five courtiers. Ormonde and Sheldon can easily be identified, so Nairne must again be one of the other three. It is possible that he is represented by the shorter Jacobite who stands on the left and is shown looking straight ahead out of the picture – though in this case also the painter had no opportunity to produce proper portraits of the Jacobites.[220]

From Imola the king's party travelled via Faenza to Forlì, Cesena and Rimini, and finally arrived at Pesaro on the 20th.[221] A few days later, the servants with the 'gros baggage' also arrived, presumably bringing Nairne's personal possessions with them. They were followed by the Scottish peers and other pensioners who had been given permission to follow the king to Italy.[222]

Nairne's opinion of Pesaro has not survived. He told Gualterio on 22 March that the king 'finds the countryside agreeable, and the palace spacious and comfortable',[223] but in fact he probably shared the rather negative opinions of others which *have* survived.[224] For example, Roger Strickland wrote to a friend in Avignon that

> although the stay in Pesaro is pleasant as far as the town and countryside go, the inhabitants are unfriendly and barbaric, the wine and bread are no good, and there are only two dilapidated carriages in the town.

He found the air unhealthy, and added that he 'did not believe one could stay there long before dying of some illness'.[225]

We know virtually nothing about Nairne's life in Pesaro, beyond his work for the king in the secretariat, but as the only Italian speaker at the Jacobite court and one of the relatively few important ones who spoke French he must have been involved in the reception of the numerous visitors who came to see the king.[226] In one of his letters, he refers to drinking chocolate with Belloni 'and the theological adviser of Cardinal Davia who is a man of learning'.[227] We may also assume that he attended performances

Figure 8. *James III being received by Cardinal Gozzadini at the Archbishop's Palace at Imola, 16 March 1717, 1717* (dimensions unknown, detail),
by Antonio Gionima (Castel Sant'Angelo, Rome)
In this painting James III is again shown with five of his courtiers, including the Duke of Ormonde (second from left, with the star of the Order of the Garter on the left side of his coat, but without the blue sash) and Dominic Sheldon (fifth from left, with the black wig). Nairne is probably the Jacobite on the left of the group, standing behind Ormonde.

of the three operas staged at the Teatro del Sole,[228] his first Italian operas since 1691.

In his correspondence with Cardinal Gualterio Nairne promised that the Protestant Jacobites would behave themselves properly in Pesaro, as they had at Avignon, and added that as none of them could speak Italian they would anyway not be able to discuss their religion with the local people.[229] He also sent Gualterio a list of all the Protestants who were with the king.[230] Another religious question which concerned Nairne was the appointment of a new confessor for the king, as John Ingleton had been left behind in France and as James had used a local priest while he was at Avignon. The Pope wanted to send Father Plunket, an Irish Dominican, from Rome, but Nairne told Gualterio that the king had already appointed Father John Brown, another Irish Dominican whom he had found in Fano.[231] It was eventually agreed that Plunket should remain where he was, and that the king would keep Brown, whom Nairne described as 'a good Religious who does not meddle'.[232]

The most important subject which occupied Nairne during his two months at Pesaro was the visit which James III was intending to make to see the Pope in Rome. In order to prepare the ground for this visit Nairne had to make arrangements for Gualterio to come from Rome to discuss the details, but Gualterio's visit to Pesaro (like the king's visit to Rome) had to be postponed until James had effected a full recovery from his operation.[233] This, of course, had been retarded by the discomfort of his six week journey from Avignon.

On 8 April, Nairne was able to tell Gualterio that the king's health was improving,[234] and ten days later he added that the king was once again able to eat in public, though he was still convalescing.[235] Finally, at the beginning of May he assured Gualterio that the king would be entirely recovered after three more weeks,[236] so that both visits (Gualterio's to Pesaro, then James III's to Rome) could take place as from the last week of that month.

James had originally decided that he would go to Rome while he was still at Avignon,[237] and Gualterio had at that time offered to let him use his own palazzo on the Corso when he was there.[238] It was not until May, however, when he was well on the way to recovery, that James decided to go to Rome 'avant les grands chaleurs'. Nairne told Gualterio that when he came to Pesaro he could choose between the apartments in the *palazzo apostolico* which had been allocated to Ormonde and Mar, both of which were available.[239] Then, just as everything seemed to have been arranged, the king's decision to go to Rome earlier than expected meant that Nairne had to tell Gualterio that James now wanted to meet him in Rome rather than Pesaro.[240] According to Gualterio's diary, the cardinal then discussed with the Principessa di Piombino, whom James had met in Avignon, how best to organize the king's visit[241] and began to prepare his palazzo on the Corso 'per il vienini del Re'.[242]

Apart from a general curiosity to see the city, and a natural desire to establish a personal relationship with the Pope, James III had two main reasons for wanting to visit Rome. He wanted to persuade Clement XI to appoint Gualterio to be the Cardinal Protector of England, something he had so far refused to do. He also wanted to persuade the Pope to allow him to leave Pesaro and move his court to the *palazzo apostolico* at Urbino.[243] This second aim had been encouraged by Don Carlo Albani.

Shortly after the arrival of the court at Pesaro, Don Carlo went to live in the Palazzo Albani at Urbino[244] and invited some of the Jacobite courtiers to visit him there.[245] The king himself was not well enough to travel, so it is unlikely that Nairne was one of the visitors, but the reports which came back convinced James that Urbino would be a much better place than Pesaro in which to live.[246] Don Carlo Albani therefore remained in Urbino[247] and began to prepare the large *palazzo apostolico*. In part this was for Alamanno Salviati, who was going to live there as *Presidente*, but it seems that it was also to make the building ready for the king. Nairne wrote to Gualterio on Thursday, 29 April: 'M. Don Carlo has just written to me to say that he will not be able to have the furnishing of the palace of Urbino finished before next Sunday or Monday after which he will come here'.[248] Albani returned to Pesaro on Wednesday, 5 May,[249] and then left to see his uncle in Rome to persuade him to agree to James III's request to move his court to Urbino.[250] Salviati, meanwhile, had gone to Rome to see the Pope and now arrived at Urbino at the beginning of May.[251] He wrote to Nairne:

> I wish you were here. You will see that his Holiness has forgotten nothing for fitting up this magnificent palace in a manner suitable to his Majesty, and I assure you that you will not suffer from the trying summer heats.[252]

By May 1717, Nairne's position at the Jacobite court still seemed secure. He was, as his friend John Ingleton put it, 'the only person of confidence the King has about him',[253] as well as the only one who could speak and read Italian. He had established an intimate correspondence with Cardinal Gualterio, he was on good terms with Cardinal Davia, and now his friends Alamanno Salviati and Eustachio Buglioni had arrived from Avignon. The Duke of Mar showed no sign of returning to the court from France, and meanwhile Nairne had good relations with at least one of the Scottish peers at the court. This was the Earl of Panmure whom he had known in Paris between 1678 and 1684, and whom he described as 'a worthy good sort of man'.[254]

There was, however, one indication of how vulnerable Nairne's position was with the king. The Duke of Mar's brother-in-law, John Hay, had been left behind in Avignon when the king decided who should accompany him to Italy. A few days after his arrival at Pesaro, however, James regretted this decision and summoned Hay to rejoin the court as soon as possible, commenting to Mar that 'you know the kindness I have for him'.[255] During the visit to Rome it would become apparent that the king, now nearly twenty-nine years old, wanted to surround himself with young men of his own age like Hay rather than older men like Nairne, who by May 1717 was approaching his sixty-second birthday.

James III decided that he would go to Rome with only four gentlemen and a few valets.[256] He told Mar that 'nobody goes with me but [Charles] Booth and John [Hay], and Nairne, that will meet me at Rome by another road'. He added that 'Paterson will stay here to forward all packets or expresses'.[257] In fact, Nairne was to travel with the king's physician, Dr Lawrence Wood, whom he (Nairne) regarded as 'un homme fort sage habile et prudent'.[258]

The king and his party left Pesaro on Saturday, 22 May, and travelled down the Adriatic coast to Loretto, before turning inland to join the Via Flaminia. They arrived in Rome on the evening of Wednesday, 26th.[259] Nairne and Dr Wood, joined at the last minute by the Duke of St Andrews, then left Pesaro on Monday, 24th,[260] travelled down the Via Flaminia, and arrived in Rome the same evening.[261] Nairne, Booth and Hay were each given a room in the Palazzo Gualterio with the king, while Dr Wood and the duke had to find lodgings elsewhere.[262] It was the first time that

Nairne had returned to Rome since he had left the city with Lord Melfort in September 1691.

On Friday, 28 May, two days after their arrival, James III had the first of five private audiences with Pope Clement XI, and on that occasion introduced Nairne, Booth, Hay, Wood and St Andrews.[263] Encouraged by their reception, Nairne confided to Paterson, with whom his relations seem to have improved:[264]

> I wish there was no objection against this place's being his séjour for good and all, till he could go where he ought to be [i.e. England], for I never could be of opinion it was his interest to choose such an exile as Pesaro or Urbino.[265]

Nairne believed that it would be much better for the king to be living in close proximity to the Pope and the cardinals rather than in such remote places as Pesaro and Urbino. However, he was also influenced by the rich cultural and social life which he and the others in the king's party now experienced. A lavish programme of visits and entertainments had been prepared, and, throughout the month of June, James and his courtiers were exposed to the many things which the city of Rome could offer. Charles Booth was apparently unimpressed, but Nairne was delighted. He wrote on 11 June:

> we have had fine music and seen fine pictures and statues, all which, as old as I am, I am not philosopher enough to despise, especially the music part, in which you will not condemn me quite so much as Mr Booth does. As for the ceremonial part, I cannot say I like it, for nobody does, but I can bear it more patiently than Mr Booth. The King keeps his health very well. Mine has been altered a little these two or three days.[266]

James III noticed the different reactions of Nairne and Booth, and commented that 'I believe Nairne will live a year longer and Booth as much shorter for this journey'. It was an indication of where the king's preference now lay that in the same letter he again referred to his new favourite Hay by his Christian name: 'our friend John is delighted with all he sees here.'[267]

The music which Nairne appreciated included secular concerts organized in their palazzi by the Albani, Colonna, Pamphili and Ruspoli families, as well as masses and other musical services in several of the churches. On 3 June, Nairne was present when Domenico Scarlatti, 'grand musicien, joua du clavessin et chanta' in the Palazzo Albani.[268]

Nairne regarded the grand gallery in the Palazzo Colonna as 'one of the finest things in Rome, which can be compared with the Gallery at Versailles'.[269] But perhaps the most impressive part of the visit was a trip to Castel Gandolfo overlooking Lake Albano, organized for the king on 15 June by Don Carlo Albani and involving magnificent illuminations and fireworks on and around the lake. In addition to visits to Frascati, Grotta Ferrata, Marino and Albano, there was a performance at Castel Gandolfo of a cantata specially composed by Domenico Scarlatti in the French style entitled *Il ritorno di Telemacho*. It was sung by the two most famous castrati in Rome at the time, supported by a large orchestra and a chorus.[270]

Nairne's weeks in Rome were practically useful as well as enjoyable, because he was able to make contacts which would be extremely important in the years to come, including with the painter Antonio David.[271] He now established excellent relations with Gualterio, with whom he had been corresponding for three and a half years, while Salviati sent him an account of 'who are my friends there and about my affairs' so that Nairne could be introduced both to his friends and to his patrons.[272] Nairne also renewed his acquaintance with Lord William Drummond (the *abbé* Melfort),[273] and struck up friendships with Lord Richard Howard (the *abate* Howard) and the agents of the English and the Scottish Catholic clergy in Rome.[274] The agents were Father Lawrence Mayes and Father William Stuart, both of whom would later become his very close friends. He wrote to Mayes shortly afterwards:

> Remember me kindly to good Mr Stuart ... I esteem him and shall allways be ready to serve him because he deserves it but without ceremonies or compliments, and I hope he'l favour me with the continuation of his friendship and good prayers. I beg of you also to give my most humble respects to Mr Chanon Howard for whom I have all the true respect and value his birth and good qualitys do so justly deserve.[275]

Another useful aspect of Nairne's time in Rome was a visit to the Collegio Clementino in the Piazza Nicosia. His son Louis was now studying at the Collège des Ecossais in Paris, but Nairne now decided that when he left there he might usefully finish his education in Rome. On 30 June, he noted that,

It is a College founded for the children of the nobility, who learn there not only academic subjects but also physical skills. The King watched them dancing, jumping, weapons training, and riding.[276]

He was probably particularly attracted to the college because of its emphasis on music. During this visit to the college there were performed 'symphonies and dances, by the Academy of letters and arms in honour of James III.'[277]

Shortly after his arrival in Rome James III gave permission for the Scottish peers at Pesaro to join him, and during the first week of June the Earls of Nithsdale, Panmure and Southesk arrived with Viscounts Kilsyth and Kingston.[278] Their presence in Rome prompted Clement XI to visit the Scots College. Nairne was present on 10 June when the Pope said mass in the college chapel in the presence of James III and his other courtiers.[279] One of the latter wrote to a friend in Avignon that 'the Pope came to the church of the Scots where the feast of St Margaret was celebrated: the King of England met him at the door and received communion from the Pontiff's hands.'[280]

Clement XI had already, on 5 June, agreed that James III should transfer his court from Pesaro to Urbino when he left Rome,[281] but had still not accepted Gualterio as Cardinal Protector of England when he gave the king his final audience on 3 July. On that occasion James III spoke to Clement XI for two hours and eventually persuaded him to agree to Gualterio's appointment, after which the Pope 'invited the Lords and a few other gentlemen' including Nairne to enter the room where 'they kissed his foot'.[282] Nairne commented that 'I think it is a great deal to the King's credit as well as satisfaction to have gaind that great point amongst other things by his journy to Rome'.[283]

When James III left Rome on 4 July, he instructed Nairne to remain behind until he had received Gualterio's formal letter of appointment from the Pope. This time the king invited only John Hay to travel with him in his coach, leaving Charles Booth to travel separately in another one, thereby indicating not only his displeasure at Booth's lack of enthusiasm for the entertainment they had received in Rome, but more particularly his new favouritism towards Hay.[284] Three days later, on 7 July, Nairne had an audience with the Pope during which he was given 'the letter for the Protection of England' for Gualterio.[285]

Before his departure on 8 July Nairne had a second audience with the Pope, to whom he gave 'a small memoire ... in Italian to recommend to him the Abbé Buglioni'.[286] During this audience Nairne also discussed various political questions, including the Spanish plans to invade Sardinia. As King Philip V of Spain was a friend and ally of James III, Nairne defended the Spanish point of view against the Pope's criticisms, and was concerned when he heard from Don Carlo Albani that Clement XI had not been pleased. He told Gualterio that he had spoken moderately and with respect to the Pope and that 'I did not deserve ... the reproaches which he [His Holiness] made', and that

> I am happy to maintain my innocence by writing to D. Carlo, and am not too worried about this knowing it to be but a small detail, so long as the Pope continues always to treat the King well.[287]

When Nairne received no reply from Don Carlo he wrote characteristically to Gualterio that 'M. D. Carlo ... was perhaps displeased, but we must be patient. I am not a good courtier.'[288]

On 8 July, Nairne left Rome and travelled as fast as he could up the Via Flaminia to catch up with the king, who had been making a deliberately slow progress.[289] He joined him at Foligno on the evening of the 9th,[290] and it was then decided that Nairne should travel on the next day directly to Urbino to get everything ready for the king's arrival one day later. On the last stage of his journey, however, between Fermigniano and Urbino, where the road was 'so very bad and hilly'[291] and very 'dangerous with a French chair',[292] Nairne had an accident. He described it as 'a fall which I had on the way here, my chair having overturned in the mountains of the last stage of the journey'.[293] His head was badly damaged and he arrived that evening at Urbino with concussion. By the time the king arrived on the following evening it looked as though Nairne might have suffered permanent injury.

The incident emphasized to James III how indispensable Nairne had become. Two days after his arrival the king wrote to Mar that 'Nairne is sick and I have not a soul that can write French, and cannot, I am sure, do all myself'.[294] Mar was therefore requested to send his under-secretary Robert Creagh to join the court as soon as possible, and Paterson, writing in the third person, explained: 'Nairne is out of order, Paterson, you know, writes but one language.'[295]

In fact, Nairne made an unexpectedly quick recovery. He wrote on Thursday, the 15th, that he had been 'bled' on Monday, the 12th, 'from his right arm for the second time' and that 'I can still feel the bruise on my head'. But, he added, 'since the pain has diminished and I no longer have a fever I am hoping there will be no serious consequences'.[296] Three days later he wrote that 'my health thanks to God is now better, and my head no longer hurts'.[297] By the end of the month, he had fully recovered,[298] but it was an inauspicious start to the fifteen and a half months that he would remain at Urbino.

Endnotes

1. Corp, *A Court in Exile*, p. 289; Szechi, *Jacobitism and Tory Politics*, p. 7, 22–3. See also BL. Add MSS 31259, f.85, Nairne to Gualterio, 2 November 1714:

    > V.Em. scait bien que l'eloignement de Milord Middleton a été l'effet d'une complaisance forcée que le Roy a eu pour une cabale et pour plaire a Mr Olive [i.e. Lord Oxford], dont on esperoit de grandes choses.

2. Corp, *A Court in Exile*, pp. 287–8, 291. The other Protestants were Sir William Ellis (Commissioner then Treasurer of the Household), a page of the bedchamber named Styles, and the Rev. Charles Leslie.
3. BL. Add MSS 31255, f.3, James III to Gualterio, 16 December 1713. See also the explanation given by the king's confessor: WDA. Epist Var 5/no. 42, Ingleton to Mayes, 25 January 1714:

    > I doubt not but you have heard ere this of the changes made in our Court since my last. The King's affairs and interest forcd him to part with my Lord Middleton, and he did it with all regret, and all the marks of honour and esteem imaginable. My Lord is now at S. Germans, and made Master of horse to the Queen. His son Lord Clermont is made Lord of the Bedchamber to the King. The Office of Secretary of State is given to Mr Higgins [*sic*], now Sir Thomas Higgins a Protestant, which might perhaps give occasion to an idle and ground-less report that the King was become Protestant.

4. BL. Add MSS 31255, f.3, James III to Gualterio, 16 December 1713. See also the explanation given by the king's confessor: WDA. Epist Var 5/no.42, Ingleton to Mayes, 25 January 1714: 'The Roman Correspondance is in the hands of Mr Nearn [*sic*], a pious good Catholick.'

5. RA. SP Misc 19, p. 97 (HMC *Stuart* I, p. 284), James III to Sheldon, signed by Middleton, 29 November 1713.

6. Bod. Carte MSS 212, f.62, note by Nairne on Middleton to Berry, 14 December 1713.

7. BL. Add MSS 31259, f.1, Nairne to Gualterio, 16 December 1713. See also SCA. BL 2/192/1, T. Innes to Stuart, 1 January 1714.

8. BL. Add MSS 31259, f.29, Nairne to Gualterio, 5 April 1714.

9. BL. Add MSS 31259, f.9, Nairne to Gualterio, 25 January 1714:

> En partant d'ici il [Middleton] a prié le Roy de trouver bon qu'il n'entretint plus aucune correspondence avec ceux qui sont chargeés des affaires de S. M. croyant qu'il était a propos pour le bien de son service (qui a toujours été l'unique but de ce digne ministre) de s'abstenir de tous ce qui pourroit donner le moindre ombrage a ceux qui ont souhaitté sa retraitte.

On the same day that Nairne wrote this letter, Lord Melfort died in Paris.

10. Nairne's abstract of James III's letter about not changing his religion, dated 13 March 1714, is in Bod. Carte MSS 210, f.409.

11. BL. Add MSS 31259, f.23, Nairne to Gualterio, 15 March 1714. This letter and at least two of Nairne's subsequent letters on the same subject were copied and sent to Pope Clement XI: ASV Albani 168, p. 49, 'Articolo di lettera del Seg.e del Gabinetto de Re in data di 15 marzo 1714' and both '22 di Marzo 1714' and '18 Marzo 1714'. In response the Pope gave James III 49,344 *livres* in March 1714 and another 141,935 in August 1714 (Corp, *A Court in Exile*, p. 291).

12. Both papers were dated 1714 and destroyed during the French Revolution. See Corp, 'Archives of the Stuart Court at Saint-Germain-en-Laye', p. 142.

13. BL. Add MSS 31259, f.55, Nairne to Gualterio, 12 July 1714.

14. BL. Add MSS 31259, ff.39, 41, 43, 45, Nairne to Gualterio, May (undated), 18 and 30 May, 7 June 1714. They went to Commercy again in July for two weeks: BL. Add MSS 31259, ff.55, 59, Nairne to Gualterio, 12 and 26 July 1714.

15. BL. Add MSS 31259, f.47, Nairne to Gualterio, 14 June 1714.

16. BL. Add MSS 20298, f.1, undated memoire in Nairne to Gualterio, 14 June 1714.

17. BL. Add MSS 31259, 75, Nairne to Gualterio, 26 September 1714.

18. Corp, *King over the Water*, p. 50; Corp, *A Court in Exile*, pp. 292–3. In one of the portraits James was shown in his robes as a Knight of the Order of the Garter.

19. See p. 11. Nairne had acquired the scar as a result of fighting a duel in 1675.
20. The portrait has survived and is illustrated as the frontispiece and on p. 220. See also pp. 481-2 for its provenance.
21. Three years later, in 1717, Nairne gave Gualterio a miniature copy of this portrait by Belle. See below Chapter 6, p. 218 and note 91.
22. BL. Add MSS 31259, f.63, Nairne to Gualterio, 10 August 1714.
23. See Macpherson, *Original Papers*, vol. 2, p. 527, Duke of Lorraine to James III, 15 August 1714: 'You have taken the only proper course, by going to Paris; and I hope that you will find at the court of France the succours which are necessary for securing the success of your enterprise.'
24. See BL. Add MSS 31254, f.443, Queen Mary to Gualterio, 20 August 1714: 'mon fils estoit resolu de tout hazarder et aller en Ecosse [*sic*], mais le Roy lui a fait entendre, que non seulement il ne vouloit (c'est a dire qu'il ne pouvoit) pas lui doner le moindre secours que mesme il seroit obligé de le faire avertir, si il alloit plus loing, et qu'il n'avoit pas d'autre part à prendre de s'en retournir à Bar'. See also Corp, *A Court in Exile*, p. 293.
25. BL. Add MSS 31259, f.65, Nairne to Gualterio, 21 August 1714.
26. BL. Add MSS 31259, f.67, Nairne to Gualterio, 29 August 1714.
27. HMC *Stuart* I, p. 333; RA. SP 3/101. The Protestation is dated 29 August 1714, and Nairne's copy (in French) is in Bod. Carte MSS 210, f.429.
28. BL. Add MSS 31259, f.71, Nairne to Gualterio, 12 September 1714.
29. I am grateful to Frédéric Richard-Maupillier for this information, presented in his paper during the Jacobite conference at the Collège des Irlandais, Paris, in July 2013.
30. BL. Add MSS 31259, f.73, Nairne to Gualterio, 19 September 1714. See also BL. Add MSS 31259, f.75, DN to Gualterio, 26 September 1714: 'Le Roy partira d'ici lundi prochain pour Luneville, et dans 8 ou 10 jours aprés il se propose d'etre a Bar.'
31. BL. Add MSS 31259, f.77, Nairne to Gualterio, 4 October 1714.
32. BL. Add MSS 31259, f.79, Nairne to Gualterio, 12 October 1714.
33. BL. Add MSS 31259, f.85, Nairne to Gualterio, 2 November 1714.
34. BL. Add MSS 31259, ff.90, 92, Nairne to Gualterio, 10 and 15 November 1714.
35. BL. Add MSS 31259, f.94, Nairne to Gualterio, 23 November 1714.
36. BL. Add MSS 31259, f.102, Nairne to Gualterio, 29 December 1714.
37. BL. Add MSS 31259, f.123, Nairne to Gualterio, 28 February 1715.
38. BL. Add MSS 31259, f.113, Nairne to Gualterio, 17 January 1715. They originally expected to be at Nancy for '8 ou 10 jours', but were persuaded to stay on for the entire winter season. Although he was at Nancy Nairne gave his address to

one of his correspondents in Portugal as follows: 'My direction is a Mr Nairne Secretaire du Cabinet du Roy d'Angleterre A Bar le Duc, under cover of a Mr Pajot de Villers Controlleur gen.l des Postes a Paris' (Bod. Carte MSS 211, f.314, Nairne to Fitzgerald, 22 February 1715).

39. Corp, *A Court in Exile*, p. 294.

40. BL. Add MSS 31259, ff.127, 128, Nairne to Gualterio, 8 and 15 March 1715.

41. BL. Add MSS 31259, f.136, Nairne to Gualterio, 28 March 1715.

42. NLS. MS 14266, a note at the end of the list of Nairne's children at the end of his diary.

43. Archives Départementales de l'Yonne 2.E.115, register of the parish church of Compigny, 30 March 1715. Barthélemy de Compigny was Marie-Elisabeth's first cousin (Monsieur de Baby); Jean-Louis and Sébastien de Compigny were her half-brothers, then only twenty-one and nineteen years old.

44. BL. Add MSS 31259, f.137, Nairne to Gualterio, 5 April 1715.

45. SCA. BL 2/210/2, Nairne to T. Innes, 4 June 1716; MSS d'Avignon 1725, f.37, Nairne to Gonteri, 27 February 1717 (quoted in Lart, *Jacobite Extracts*, vol. 2, p. 37).

46. *The Letter Book of Lewis Sabran, S. J., October 1713 to October 1715*, ed. G. Holt (Catholic Record Society, 1971).

47. Born in 1652, son of the marquis de Sabran, Louis de Sabran had been educated at Saint-Omer and joined the Society of Jesus in 1670. Since leaving the court at Saint-Germain he had travelled to Italy on various occasions to see the Pope on behalf of the queen, and was with the king during his campaign in 1710. He spent the last fifteen years of his life at the English College in Rome (*The English Jesuits, 1650–1829*, ed. G. Holt (Catholic Record Society, 1984), p. 217).

48. *The Letter Book of Lewis Sabran*, p. 273, 17 June 1715.

49. Ibid. p. 282, 11 July 1715.

50. Ibid. p. 287, 26 July 1715.

51. Ibid. p. 292, 9 August 1715.

52. Ibid. p. 294, 19 August 1715.

53. Ibid. p. 296, 27 August 1715.

54. Ibid. p. 296, 28 August 1715.

55. Bod Carte MSS 211, f.330, Nairne to L. Innes, August 1715.

56. *The Letter Book of Lewis Sabran*, p. 298, 2 September 1715.

57. Ibid. p. 310, 30 September 1715.

58. Ibid. p. 310, 1 October 1715.

59. Ibid. p. 317, 24 October 1715.

60. See Chapter 5, pp. 183–4. Nairne later described Sabran as 'an intriguing man', i.e. an intriguer (HMC *Stuart* VII, p. 513, Nairne to James III, 9 November 1718).

61. Szechi, *Jacobitism and Tory Politics*, p. 75.
62. BL. Add MSS 31259, ff.161, 163, Nairne to Gualterio, 21 and 27 June 1715.
63. BL. Add MSS 31259, ff.165, 167, Nairne to Gualterio, 4 and 11 July 1715.
64. BL. Add MSS 31259, f.169, Nairne to Gualterio, 18 July 1715. One year later, in July 1716, Nairne told the prince de Vaudémont how much he and Charles Booth missed the hunting in 'la belle foret de Commercy' (BL. Add MSS 38851, f.88, 23 July 1716).
65. BL. Add MSS 31259, f.171, Nairne to Gualterio, 21 July 1715.
66. HMC *Stuart* I, p. 376, receipt by Nairne, 21 July 1715.
67. Bod Carte MSS 211, f.332, James III's orders and commissions for Nairne, [28 October 1715], with Nairne's marginal notes.
68. BL. Add MSS 31259, f.171, Nairne to Gualterio, 21 July 1715.
69. Bod Carte MSS 211, f.329, James III to Perth, 21 July 1715.
70. Corp, *A Court in Exile*, p. 295.
71. Szechi, *Jacobitism and Tory Politics*, pp. 75–6; Corp, *A Court in Exile*, pp. 294–5.
72. BL. Add MSS 31259, f.171, Nairne to Gualterio, 21 July 1715, with postscript of 28 July.
73. BL Add MSS 31259, f.173, Nairne to Gualterio, 3 August 1715.
74. BL. Add MSS 31259, f.175, Nairne to Gualterio, 16 August 1715.
75. BL. Add MSS 31259, f.177, Nairne to Gualterio, 23 August 1715.
76. BL. Add MSS 31259, f.179, Nairne to Gualterio, 30 August 1715.
77. Bod Carte MSS 211, f.330, Nairne to L. Innes, August 1715.
78. BL. Add MSS 31259, f.181, Nairne to Gualterio, 6 September 1715.
79. BL. Add MSS 31259, f.196, Nairne to Gualterio, 18 October 1715.
80. Corp, *A Court in Exile*, p. 296.
81. BL. Add MSS 31259, ff.199, 201, Nairne to Gualterio, 1 and 17 November 1715. The servants were Baltassare Artema and Thomas Saint-Paul, respectively page of the bedchamber, and barber and valet.
82. Bod Carte MSS 211, f.332, James III's orders and commissions for Nairne, [28 October 1715], with Nairne's marginal notes.
83. He was also to send 'two circular letters to the D. of Lor and the El. of Treve' (see note 82).
84. The four others were 'the 2 Mr Stricklands; Dr Ingleton, [and] Mr Connel'. The Stricklands were Roger (groom of the bedchamber) and his brother Francis (page of honour in the stables), Dr John Ingleton was the king's confessor, and Mr Thaddeus Connell was the king's chaplain.
85. BL. Add MSS 31259, f.201, Nairne to Gualterio, 17 November 1715.
86. Nairne 'put them in a more convenient trunk for travelling' and was to tell the queen 'how the severall papers are sorted in bundels for the conveniency of finding them when there is occasion of having recourse to them' (see note 82).

87. *La retraitte spirituelle* was by Jean Croiset, S. J., and published at Lyon in 1694 (English editions as *Spritual Retreat*, 1698 and 1700). For the importance attached to this book by James III's father, see Corp, *A Court in Exile*, pp. 247, 251. Before leaving Bar-le-Duc Nairne had entrusted all the king's other books, including 'the 4 tomes of the late Kings Memoires which [he] had in his custody at Bar in a little box', to Sir William Ellis and Dr Ingleton. He kept for himself 'a little Diurnal ... wch I would willingly keep as a prayer book', and the king's 'old inkhorn and portefeuille' for which the king had 'no more use' and which he (Nairne) regarded as 'a proper perquisit of my place' (see note 82).

88. See note 82.

89. BL. Add MSS 38851, f.65, Nairne to Vaudémont, 29 December 1715.

90. BL. Add MSS 20298, f.2, Nairne to Gualterio, 5 January 1716. James III travelled to Nantes but was prevented from chartering a ship, so he headed instead for Normandy. On the way he was nearly captured and killed at Nonancourt by an assassin sent by Lord Stair, the British ambassador in Paris. He finally reached Saint-Malo, where he found the Duke of Ormonde and Lord Tynemouth (the eldest son of the Duke of Berwick), but the weather was too bad to let him sail. In desperation, and after waiting for several weeks, he rode across land with Tynemouth, Artema and Saint-Paul to Dunkirk, where he found a ship. He embarked with Artema and Saint-Paul, and a young highlander named Alan Cameron whom he had met at Dunkirk (Corp, *A Court in Exile*, p. 297. For a fuller description, see Bevan, *King James the Third*, pp. 81–4).

91. BL. Add MSS 31259, f.201, Nairne to Gualterio, 17 November 1715.

92. BL. Add MSS 31259, f.205, Nairne to Gualterio, 29 December 1715. It is interesting that Nairne described this attack of gout as the first he had experienced, because he seems to have had a previous one in 1699. He wrote in his diary on 30 May of that year that 'I fell ill of a sore foot'. Then, 'I was forced to ly in bed' (31 May), 'I kept my bed still' (1 June), 'I kept still my chamber wth a sore foot' (3 June), and 'I went abroad' (5 June).

93. BL. Add MSS 38851, f.65, Nairne to Vaudémont, 29 December 1715.

94. BL. Add MSS 20298, f.2, Nairne to Gualterio, 5 January 1716.

95. BL. Add MSS 38851, f.65, Nairne to Vaudémont, 29 December 1715:

> Il y a eu un de mes parens et de mon nom qui a eu un plus triste sort, il etoit Major d'un Regiment, mais toujours bien intentionné pour le Roy. Ainsi on l'avoit reformé et il etoit du nombre de ces officiers a la demi paÿe, qui s'etoit joint au parti du Roy a Preston, ou tout le parti fut obligé de se rendre a discretion, et ce pauvre officier avec 3 ou 4 autres fut condamné par un Conseil de guerre, et passé par les armes, parce qu'il etoit a la demie paye, quoiqu'il n'eut aucun poste actuelle. Au reste il a eu l'honneur de mourir pour son

Roy et pour la justice, quoique traitté par le Gouvernement comme deserteur et Rebele.

Major John Nairne was shot by firing squad at Preston on 2 December. He had visited Saint-Germain in December 1707 (Diary, 14–16 December 1707), and Nairne recorded sending him twelve letters between 26 November 1707 and 5 January 1708 (Diary).

96. Ibid.

97. They included Sir Thomas Higgons, Roger Strickland, Lord Clermont, Lord Edward Drummond, Charles Booth and Dr Lawrence Wood, but not Lord Bolingbroke or the Duke of Ormonde (Corp, *A Court in Exile*, p. 298). The 2nd Duke of Melfort was probably also with them (see below, note 110).

98. BL. Add MSS 20298, f.2, Nairne to Gualterio, 5 January 1716.

99. BL. Add MSS 31259, f.207, Nairne to Gualterio, 13 January 1716.

100. BL. Add MSS 38851, f.68, Nairne to Vaudémont, 10 January 1716.

101. BL. Add MSS 31259, f.215, Nairne to Gualterio, 13 April 1716. The date when they embarked from Calais does not seem to have been recorded, but it had taken James III and his party five days to sail from Dunkirk to Buchan Ness. The ship left Aberdeen to return to Calais on 11 February (ASV. Albani 165, p. 81, Dempster to Gualterio, 17 February 1716).

102. Corp, *A Court in Exile*, pp. 298–9. The king's itinerary is based on the dates and locations of his correspondence in HMC *Stuart* I.

103. Ibid. p. 299.

104. BL. Add MSS 31259, f.215, Nairne to Gualterio, 13 April 1716. See also Bod. Carte MSS 211, f.334, 'his Ma.ties reasons for the resolution taken of abandoning Perth the 23 January OS / 3 Feb.ry 1716', in Nairne's handwriting.

105. SCA. BL 2/210/12, Nairne to T. Innes, 29 December 1716.

106. This information is taken from the genealogical website entitled 'Stirnet'.

107. See below, p. 458.

108. Szechi, Daniel, *1715: The Great Jacobite Rebellion* (New Haven and London, 2006), p. 168; F. McLynn, *The Jacobites* (London, 1985), p. 102.

109. Drambuie Collection, reproduced as an illustration in Maxwell Stuart, Flora, *Lady Nithsdale and the Jacobites* (Traquair, 1995), pp. 69–70, James III to Argyll, 4/15 February 1716. The king minuted the letter, which is in Nairne's handwriting: 'I thought to write this in my own hand but had not time. James R.'

110. The 2nd Duke of Melfort was probably with them. In 1723 he was given a commission as a *maréchal de camp*, backdated to Montrose, 4 February 1716 Old Style (RA. SP 71/77, James III to Melfort, 20 December 1723; RA. SP 72/27, Melfort to James III, 9 January 1724) The commission was counter-signed by Nairne (*House of Lords Sessional Papers, 1852–53, vol. XXVI, Evidence before the*

Lords Committees for Privileges and Before the House, July 1846, April 1847, June 1847 and August 1848, p. 151, no. 38).

111. *A Letter from an Officer in the King's Army after it had marched Northward from Aberdeen to his friend in London, February 1715/16* (London, 1716), p. 5.

112. Szechi, *1715*, p. 168.

113. As the *Marie-Thérèse* was passing the coast of Zealand the weather was so bad that the captain, who was Irish, was forced to take temporary shelter in one of the Dutch ports, where the king and his party (including Nairne) might have been arrested by the Dutch authorities. Although the king was recognized by the woman who received him in her house, his presence in the United Provinces was not given away, so he was able to continue his voyage. See Tayler, A. and H., *The Stuart Papers at Windsor* (London, 1939), pp. 255–6, Anne Maria de Gausé to James III, 21 August 1747. For the nationality of the ship's captain, see BL. Add MSS 31261, f.193, Nairne to Gualterio, 11 August 1718.

114. Corp, *A Court in Exile*, pp. 299–300.

115. Ibid. p. 301.

116. BL. Add MSS 38851, f.71, Nairne to Vaudémont, 8 March 1716.

117. Corp, *A Court in Exile*, p. 301.

118. He brought with him as his chief clerk or under-secretary Robert Creagh, 'whom Mr Nairne recommended to me' (HMC *Stuart* II, p. 19, Mar to James III, 17 March 1716).

119. BL. Add MSS 20292, f.86, James III to Clement XI, 22 March 1716.

120. BL. Add MSS 31259, f.209, Nairne to Gualterio, 23 March 1716.

121. BL. Add MSS 31259, f.211, Nairne to Gualterio, 4 April 1716.

122. P. de Brion, 'Sur les Pas des Stuarts et des Ecossais qui vécurent à Avignon, 1716–1813', in G. Dickson, *Jacques III Stuart, un Roi sans couronne* (Paris, 1993), pp. 291–7 (295). The Hôtel de Serre de la Marine was not large enough for James III's court, so after a few days 'l'on agrandit donc d'une partie de l'hôtel d'Entraigues, qui la jouxtait et avec laquelle on la fit communiquer intérieurement'. Both buildings were destroyed during the nineteenth century. The king and Nairne had reached Lyon on 29 March, Vienne on 30 March and Pont Saint-Esprit on 1 April. From there they travelled down the west side of the river Rhône to avoid going through Orange. They then crossed the river from Villeneuve-les-Avignon and entered Avignon by the Porte de Maille (Bibliothèque de la Ville d'Avignon (BVA.) MS 3188, ff.172–3, the diary of Dr Brun, 29 March to 2 April 1717, printed in Twigge, R. W., 'Jacobite Papers at Avignon', *The Scottish Historical Review* X, 1913, pp. 60–75 (62)).

123. SCA. BL 2/210/7, Nairne to T. Innes, 6 September 1716. The Duke of Mar, the Marquess of Drummond (2nd Duke of Perth) and the Earl of Panmure were

given lodgings in his hôtel by the marquis de Villefranche (Brion, P. de, 'Sur les Pas des Stuarts', p. 297).

124. BL. Add MSS 31259, f.211, Nairne to Gualterio, 4 April 1716.

125. SCA. BL 2/210/1, Nairne to T. Innes, 16 April 1716. The Earl of Panmure had been the first Jacobite to leave Scotland, having been wounded at Sheriffmuir. He sailed from Arbroath, leaving the king to retreat without him to Montrose (*A Letter from an Officer in the King's Army after it had marched Northward from Aberdeen to his friend in London, February 1715/16*, (Avignon, 1716), p. 3).

126. BL. Add MSS 31259, f.225, Nairne to Gualterio, 12 May 1716.

127. BL. Add MSS 31259, f.242, Nairne to Gualterio, 23 June 1716. James III heard mass every day in the nearby church of Saint-Didier accompanied by Nairne and his other Catholic courtiers. On this occasion 'il y aura toute la musique de la Ville' (the diary of Dr Brun, 21 June 1716, in Dickson, *Jacques III Stuart*, p. 263).

128. BL. Add MSS 31259, f.245, Nairne to Gualterio, 7 July 1716.

129. BL. Add MSS 38851, f.288, Nairne to Vaudémont, 23 July 1716. Lord Edward Drummond arrived on 2 July followed by Lord Clermont on 21 July and Charles Booth a few days after that. Sir Thomas Higgons arrived in July but returned to Saint-Germain at the beginning of August, and Dr Lawrence Wood arrived on 28 September (HMC *Stuart* VII, pp. 128–9, Higgons to James III and Mar, 8 August 1716; RA. SP 41/38, Higgons to Mar, 9 January 1719; the diary of Dr Brun, in Dickson, *Jacques III Stuart*, pp. 266, 268, 276).

130. BL. Add MSS 31259, f.259, Nairne to Gualterio, 18 August 1716.

131. BL. Add MSS 31259, f.231, Nairne to Gualterio, 26 May 1716.

132. BL. Add MSS 31259, f.237, Nairne to Gualterio, 10 June 1716.

133. Corp, *A Court in Exile*, p. 305; Corp, *The Jacobites at Urbino*, p. 19. On the feast day of St Andrew (30 November), the Scottish Protestants joined the Scottish Catholics like Nairne for a celebration: 'Les Ecossais des deux religions ont célébré la fete de Saint André patron d'Ecosse, ils portoient tous à leurs chapeaux une croix de St André, l'ecusson de taffetas de la grandeur d'une ecu blanc avec la croix de fil d'argent' (the diary of Dr Brun, 30 November 1716, in Dickson, *Jacques III Stuart*, p. 279).

134. BL. Add MSS 31259, f.215, Nairne to Gualterio, 13 April 1716.

135. BL. Add MSS 31259, f.310, Nairne to Gualterio, 15 December 1716.

136. Corp, *A Court in Exile*, p. 305; Corp, *The Jacobites at Urbino*, p. 20.

137. BL. Add MSS 31259, f.225, Nairne to Gualterio, 12 May 1716.

138. BL. Add MSS 38851, f.78, Nairne to Vaudémont, 25 June 1716.

139. BL. Add MSS 31259, f.265, Nairne to Gualterio, 1 September 1716.

140. See Salviati's friendly letters to Nairne of February 1717 (HMC *Stuart* III, pp. 525, 542) and of March to June 1717 (HMC *Stuart* IV, pp. 151, 152, 224, 239, 282, 315).

141. BL. Add MSS 31259, f.297, Nairne to Gualterio, 24 November 1716; BL. Add MSS 31260, f.2, Nairne to Gualterio, 5 January 1717. I have been unable to locate this garden. Dr Brun refers in his diary also to a Jardin de Castelet (in Dickson, *Jacques III Stuart*, p. 276). The first reference in Nairne's diary to Thomas Innes ('young Mr In') was in January 1698 when the two men had supper together (12, 16 January 1698). They dined together on 17 June 1702, after which they began a regular correspondence. Between June 1702 and August 1707 Nairne sent twenty-nine letters to Thomas Innes, mainly in 1705 and 1707.

143. SCA. BL 2/210/7, Nairne to T. Innes, 6 September 1716.

144. BL. Add MSS 20298, f.67, Nairne to Gualterio, [?]August 1718.

145. SCA. BL 2/210/4, Nairne to T. Innes, 2 July 1716. It should be added that Nairne no longer had any clerical assistance, as both Monnot and Dempster had been left behind at Saint-Germain.

146. SCA. BL 2/210/11, Nairne to T. Innes, 20 October 1716.

147. SCA. BL 2/210/12, Nairne to T. Innes, 29 December 1716.

148. WDA. Epist Var 6/no. 29, Ingleton to Mayes, 23 October 1716; BL. Add MSS 31259, ff.297, 306, Nairne to Gualterio, 24 November and 8 December 1716; BL. Add MSS 31260, f.2, Nairne to Gualterio, 5 January 1717.

149. By 1716 Thomas Innes was the prefect of studies, and his brother Lewis was the former principal. Nairne also continued to correspond with Charles Whiteford, the actual principal (SCA. BL 2/210/2 and 12, Nairne to T. Innes, 4 June and 29 December 1716).

150. SCA. BL 2/210/10, Nairne to T. Innes, 1 October 1716. It was eventually published in London in 1729 as *A Critical Essay on the Ancient Inhabitants of the Northern Parts of Britain or Scotland*. See below, p. 436.

151. SCA. BL 2/210/11, Nairne to T. Innes, 20 October 1716. In the same letter he added:

> We are very good friends, and I would serve him in any thing, but I must own I was not edifyd wth his unkindness to Mr Semple while he was here, for he took all the pains in the world to perswad My Ld Mar that Mr Semple has no title to the Lordship, and by this means the poor man was refusd ye only favour he had ever askd of the K. of being ownd Ld Semple or at least permitted by connivance to take the title upon him in case it should prove to be of use for establishing his son.

The Sempill peerage had passed on the death of the 8th Baron to his sister Anne Abercrombie, despite the claim of their uncle Archibald as the surviving male heir. The 'Mr Semple' referred to here was Robert, the son of Archibald, who had been in French service since before the Glorious Revolution and was by 1716 a captain in Dillon's regiment.

152. SCA. BL 2/210/1, Nairne to T. Innes, 16 April 1716.
153. See above p. 120, for the signing of Nairne's will in January 1708.
154. SCA. BL 2/210/12, Nairne to T. Innes, 29 December 1716.
155. SCA. BL 2/210/2, Nairne to T. Innes, 4 June 1716.
156. SCA. BL 2/210/9, 10, Nairne to T. Innes, 20 September and 1 October 1716.
157. SCA. BL 2/207/18, L. Innes to T. Innes, 27 April 1716.
158. SCA. BL 2/210/7, Nairne to T. Innes, 6 September 1716.
159. SCA. BL 2/210/8, Nairne to T. Innes, 14 September 1716.
160. SCA. BL 2/210/9, Nairne to T. Innes, 20 September 1716.
161. SCA. BL 2/210/8, 10, 11, Nairne to T. Innes, 14 September, 1 and 20 October 1716.
162. SCA. BL 2/210/10, Nairne to T. Innes, 1 October 1716. See also SCA. BL 2/210/11, Nairne to T. Innes, 20 October 1716: 'I am very much obliged to you for recommending my son to Mr Morus.'
163. BL. Add MSS 31259, f.217, Nairne to Gualterio, 20 April 1716.
164. BL. Add MSS 38851, f.78, Nairne to Vaudémont, 25 June 1716. Nairne's printed copy of his French translation of *Lettre d'un officier de l'armée du Roy* is in Bod. Carte MSS 210, f.423.
165. Dupin's two pamphlets published in 1716 were *Méthode pour étudier la théologie, avec une table des principales questions à examiner et à discuter dans les études théologiques, et les principaux ouvrages sur chaque matière*, and *Défense de la Monarchie de Sicile contre les entreprises de la Cour de Rome*.
166. Wake had been chaplain to the English ambassador in Paris from 1682 to 1685. See J. H. Lupton, *Archbishop Wake and the Project of Union* (London, 1896).
167. SCA. BL 2/210/3, Nairne to T. Innes, 16 June 1716.
168. SCA. BL 2/210/4, Nairne to T. Innes, 2 July 1716.
169. SCA. BL 2/210/5, Nairne to T. Innes, 14 July 1716. Nairne added that he wished the Jesuit-Jansenist controversy could finally be settled: 'I wish you learn'd churchmen would decide that matter one way or other that we might know with certainty a quoy nous en tenir ... I find the Jesuits have still a strong party for them in France, and good pens on their side.'
170. SCA. BL 2/210/6, Nairne to T. Innes, 2 August 1716.
171. BL. Add MSS 31259, f.269, Nairne to Gualterio, 2 September 1716. See also WDA. Epist Var 6/no.29, Ingleton to Mayes, 27 October 1716; BL. Add MSS 31259, f.306, Nairne to Gualterio, 8 December 1716; and BL. Add MSS 31260, f.2, Nairne to Gualterio, 5 January 1717.
172. WDA. Epist Var 6/no. 29, 34, Ingleton to Mayes, 23 October and 6 December 1716.
173. BL. Add MSS 31259, f.245, Nairne to Gualterio, 7 July 1716.
174. BL. Add MSS 31259, f.273, Nairne to Gualterio, 29 September 1716. See also ibid. f.291, Nairne to Gualterio, 10 November 1716.

175. BL. Add MSS 31259, f.306, Nairne to Gualterio, 8 December 1716. Gualterio presented the abbé Melfort to the Pope on 9 November 1717 (BL. Add MSS 20577, f.154, Gualterio's diary).

176. BL. Add MSS 31260, f.2, Nairne to Gualterio, 5 January 1717.

177. SCA. BL 2/210/10, Nairne to T. Innes, 1 October 1716.

178. BL. Add MSS 38851, f.91, Nairne to Vaudémont, 21 October 1716. He informed Gualterio in his next weekly letter on 27 October 1716 (BL. Add MSS 31259, f.285).

179. Corp, *The Jacobites at Urbino*, p. 11; and p. 159, note 5.

180. Edward Corp, 'The Court of Turin and the English Succession, 1712–1720' p.64.

181. BL. Add MSS 31260, f.13, Nairne to Gualterio, 26 January 1717.

182. Corp, *The Jacobites at Urbino: An Exiled Court in Transition*.

183. BL. Add MSS 31260, f.33, Nairne to Gualterio, 22 March 1717. See also BVA. MS 1725, f.40, Nairne to Gonteri, 1 April 1717 (printed in Lart, *Jacobite Extracts*, vol. 2, p. 40).

184. Gregg, Edward, 'The Jacobite Career of John, Earl of Mar', in Eveline Cruickshanks (ed.), *Ideology and Conspiracy: Aspects of Jacobitism* (Edinburgh, 1982), pp. 179–200, at pp. 184–5.

185. BL. Add MSS 31260, f.24, Nairne to Gualterio, 6 March 1717.

186. HMC *Stuart* III, p. 540, Narrative by Paterson of the Journey of James III over Mont Cenis, February 1717.

187. HMC *Stuart* IV, p. 224, Mar to Hay, 2 May 1717.

188. Ibid. p. 280, James III to Mar, 28 May 1717.

189. Ibid. p. 349, Mar to James III, 14 June 1717.

190. Ibid. p. 393, James III to Mar, 1 July 1717.

191. BL. Add MSS 31260, f.20, Nairne to Gualterio, 23 February 1717: 'A l'egard de l'offre obligeant que le Pape a fait a V. E. d'une maison a luy près de Rome pour le Roy on verra dans la suitte suivant les conjonctures a prendre son parti la dessus, mais comme le Roy a marqué Boulogne dans sa lettre au Pape il commencera par aller là, et on songera quand il sera là a y rester ou a aller ailleurs comme il sera trouvé plus convenable.'

192. BL. Add MSS 31260, f.13, Nairne to Gualterio, 26 January 1717.

193. Corp, *The Jacobites at Urbino*, pp. 12–13; Corp, Edward, 'The Jacobite Presence in Toulouse during the Eighteenth Century', *Diasporas*, n°.5, Presses Universitaires de Toulouse – Le Mirail, pp. 124–45, at pp. 127–9.

194. BL. Add MSS 31260, f.17, Nairne to Gualterio, 2 February 1717.

195. George Bagnall was the son of Dudley Bagnall, who had been a groom of the bedchamber to both James II and James III from 1698 until his death in 1712.

196. Ormonde was accompanied by Colonel Richard Butler (brother of the Earl of Newcastle), his secretary David Kennedy and his equerry Captain Stoken.
197. BUB. MS 20(9i), Manzoli to the Senate of Bologna, 4 March 1717 (quoted in Marinelli, Giuseppe, 'Il palazzo Belloni di via de' Gombruti e i soggiorni dei reali Stuart', *Strenna Storica Bolognese* LXIII, 2013, pp. 267–302, at pp. 286–7, note 79).
198. BL. Add MSS 31260, f.24, Nairne to Gualterio, 6 March 1717.
199. Nairne travelled with the king via Chantilins, Orange, Pierrelatte, Montélimar and Valence, and then turned east to Romans and Grenoble. For the route through France, see BVA. MS 3188, ff.299–300, the diary of Dr Brun, 14 February 1717 (printed in Twigge, 'Jacobite Papers at Avignon', pp. 71–2); and for Salviati's letter to Nairne of 12 February thanking him for the letter he had sent from Romans, see HMC *Stuart* III, p. 525. Except where specified, the dates of the journey after Montmélian are taken from HMC *Stuart* III, pp. 539–41, Narrative by Paterson, February 1717.
200. BVA. MS 3188, f.302, the diary of Dr Brun, 19 February 1717, (printed in Twigge, 'Jacobite Papers at Avignon', p. 72): 'le Duc d'Ormond a écrit au Vice Légat ces nouvelles.'
201. BL. Add MSS 31260, f.20, Nairne to Gualterio, 23 February 1717.
202. BL. Add MSS 20577, ff.49–55, the diary of Cardinal Gualterio, 17 to 23 February 1717.
203. Corp, *The Stuarts in Italy*, pp. 20–1.
204. BL. Add MSS 31260, f.22, Nairne to Gualterio, 1 March 1717.
205. BVA. MS 1725, f.37, Nairne to Gonteri, 27 February 1717, (printed in Lart, *Jacobite Extracts*, vol. 2, p. 147); HMC *Stuart* IV, p. 111, L. Innes to Mar, 9 March 1717.
206. BL. Add MSS 31260, f.24, Nairne to Gualterio, 6 March 1717. On 24 March 'le Vice-legat Salviati a receu un courrier exprès du Pape pour partir incessement et aller joindre le Roy Jacques 3 à Urbino ou à Pesaro, ou il residera en qualité de Prelat-President aupres du Roy' (BVA. MS 3188, f.313, the diary of Dr Brun, 24 March 1717, printed in Twigge, 'Jacobite Papers at Avignon', p. 72).
207. BL. Add MSS 20577, f.92, the diary of Cardinal Gualterio, 1 April 1717. The list of accommodation which James III needed had been sent to Bologna by Senator Manzoli on 4 March 1717 (see above, note 197). See also ASB. Assunteria di Magistrati, Affari Diversi 118/19/683, which specified the accommodation which James III himself needed, and which included a closet for Nairne (summarized in Corp, *A Court in Exile*, pp. 308–9).
208. BL. Add MSS 20577, f.95, the diary of Cardinal Gualterio, 4 April 1717.
209. BVA. MS 3188, f.315, the diary of Dr Brun, 31 March 1717, (printed in Twigge, 'Jacobite Papers in Avignon', p. 73). Nairne informed Gualterio that the king was very pleased with Bufalini, who remained with the Jacobite court until May (BL. Add MSS 31260, ff.28, 33 and 71, 14 March, 22 March and 9 May 1717).

210. BL. Add MSS 20577, f.59, the diary of Cardinal Gualterio, 27 February 1717.

211. BL. Add MSS 31260, f.24, Nairne to Gualterio, 6 March 1717.

212. BL. add MSS 31260, f.26, Nairne to Gualterio, 7 March 1717.

213. One of the daughters of Lady Almond and four of the daughters of Contessa Molza were among the people who greeted the king at Modena (Corp, *The Jacobites at Urbino*, p. 13).

214. The painting is reproduced in Corp, *The Jacobites at Urbino*, p. 14; and Corp, *The King over the Water*, p. 111.

215. BUB. MS 770, vol. 88, 'Avisi Secreti dall' Abate Ant. Francesco Ghiselli', 20 March 1717.

216. BL. Add MSS 31260, f.60, Nairne to Gualterio, 29 April 1717.

217. BL. Add MSS 31260, ff.28, 37, Nairne to Gualterio, 14 and 29 March 1717. Pepoli was married to James III's cousin, Eleonora Colonna, and would later become the patron and friend of Farinelli (Edward Corp, ('Farinelli and the Circle of Sicinio Pepoli: A Link with the Stuart Court in Exile', *Eighteenth Century Music* 2/2, September 2005, pp. 311–19).

218. RA. SP 52/74, Ronchi to Nairne, 1 March 1721. See also Chapter 8, p. 305.

219. BL. Add MSS 31260, f.28, Nairne to Gualterio, 14 March 1717. In this letter Nairne also told Gualterio that the king had received an invitation from Perugia to settle there, and in another letter that he had also received an invitation from Viterbo (BL. Add MSS 31260, f.35, Nairne to Gualterio, 25 March 1717).

220. The painting is reproduced in Corp, *The Jacobites at Urbino*, p. 16; and Corp, *The King over the Water*, p. 110.

221. BL. Add MSS 31260, f.33, Nairne to Gualterio, 22 March 1717.

222. Corp, *The Jacobites at Urbino*, p. 15.

223. BL. Add MSS 31260, f.33, Nairne to Gualterio, 22 March 1717.

224. Corp, *The Jacobites at Urbino*, p. 15.

225. Strickland to Doni, 20 April 1717, quoted in the diary of Dr Brun (BVA. MS 3188, f.319, printed in Twigge, 'Jacobite Papers at Avignon', p. 73).

226. The visitors included Cardinals Davia, Pico and Paulucci, *abate* Domenico Passionei, Giovanni Antonio Belloni, the marquis de Villefranche from Avignon, and possibly Lord Richard Howard and Bishop Philip Ellis, the brother of Sir William (BL. Add MSS 31260, ff.60, 63, 68, 67 [*sic*], 73, Nairne to Gualterio, 29 April, 2, 6, 9 and 13 May 1717).

227. BL. Add MSS 31260, f.60, Nairne to Gualterio, 29 April 1717. In this letter Nairne asked Gualterio to forward a petition from Belloni to the Pope asking to be allowed to have a private chapel in his *casa*. Gualterio agreed to do this (BL. Add MSS 31260, f.67, Nairne to Gualterio, 9 May 1717).

228. Corp, *The Jacobites at Urbino*, p. 17; and p. 161, note 28.

229. BL. Add MSS 31260, f.24, Nairne to Gualterio, 6 March 1717.

230. BL. Add MSS 31260, f.33, Nairne to Gualterio, 22 March 1717.

231. BL. Add MSS 31260, ff.47, 58, Nairne to Gualterio, 11 and 25 April 1717.
232. BL. Add MSS 31260, f.88, Nairne to Gualterio, 25 July 1717.
233. BL. Add MSS 31260, ff.28, 33, Nairne to Gualterio, 14 and 22 March 1717.
234. BL. Add MSS 31260, f.45, Nairne to Gualterio, 8 April 1717.
235. BL. Add MSS 31260, f.51, Nairne to Gualterio, 18 April 1717.
236. BL. Add MSS 31260, ff.63, 68, Nairne to Gualterio, 2 and 6 May 1717.
237. BL. Add MSS 31260, f.17, Nairne to Gualterio, 2 February 1717.
238. BL. Add MSS 31260, f.22, Nairne to Gualterio, 1 March 1717. Don Carlo Albani also offered to lend his palazzo in Rome, but James III had already accepted Gualterio's (BL. Add MSS 31260, f.37, Nairne to Gualterio, 29 March 1717).
239. BL. Add MSS 31260, f.67, Nairne to Gualterio, 9 May 1717. Ormonde had left in April, at the king's request, to try to negotiate an alliance with Peter the Great who was visiting France (Corp, *The Jacobites at Urbino*, p. 17).
240. BL. Add MSS 31260, f.75, Nairne to Gualterio, 14 May 1717.
241. BL. Add MSS 20577, f.138, the diary of Cardinal Gualterio, 17 May 1717.
242. BL. Add MSS 20577, f.140, the diary of Cardinal Gualterio, 19 May 1717.
243. Corp, *The Jacobites at Urbino*, p. 22.
244. BL. Add MSS 31260, f.41, Nairne to Gualterio, 1 April 1717.
245. BL. Add MSS 31260, f.49, Nairne to Gualterio, 15 April 1717: 'M. Don Carlo est allé passer 8 ou 10 jours a Urbino, ou il a convié avec sa politesse ordinaire quelques uns de nos Messieurs, dont trois y sont allés aujourdhuy, a scavoir le Marquis de Tulebardine, Milord Edouard Drummond et Mr Bagnal.'
246. BVA. MS 3188, f.315, the diary of Dr Brun, 31 March 1717, (printed in Twigge, 'Jacobite Papers at Avignon', p. 73): 'Le roy est presentement à Pesaro ... et comme l'esté y est tres chaud, il habitera à Urbino ... Il sera comme souverain dans ces deux villes.' See also BUB. MS 770, vol. 88, 'avisi secreti' of Ghiselli, 3 April 1717, in which he recorded that the Duke of Perth and other 'Inglese' were visiting Bologna from Pesaro, and that the courtiers were hoping to move to Urbino.
247. BL. Add MSS 31260, ff.53, 58, Nairne to Gualterio, 22 and 25 April 1717.
248. BL. Add MSS 31260, f.60, Nairne to Gualterio, 29 April 1717.
249. BL. Add MSS 31260, f.68, Nairne to Gualterio, 6 May 1717.
250. BL. Add MSS 31260, f.67, Nairne to Gualterio, 9 May 1717.
251. Salviati had left Avignon on 5 April (BVA. 3188, f.317, the diary of Dr Brun, 5 April 1717, printed in Twigge, 'Jacobite Papers at Avignon', p. 73) and, according to his letters to Nairne, had gone straight to Rome before he travelled to Pesaro via his family home in Florence (HMC *Stuart* IV, pp. 239, 224, Salviati to Nairne, 12 April and 1 May 1717; BL. Add MSS 31260, f.51, Nairne to Gualterio, 18 April 1717).
252. HMC *Stuart* IV, p. 282, Salviati to Nairne, 28 May 1717.

253. WDA. Epist Var 6/no.52, Ingleton to Mayes, 2 July 1717.
254. SCA. BL 2/210/1, Nairne to T. Innes, 16 April 1716.
255. HMC *Stuart* IV, p. 140, James III to Mar, 27 March 1717.
256. BL. Add MSS 31260, f.75, Nairne to Gualterio, 14 May 1717.
257. HMC *Stuart* IV, p. 252, James III to Mar, 19 May 1717.
258. BL. Add MSS 31260, f.41, Nairne to Gualterio, 1 April 1717.
259. Corp, *The Jacobites at Urbino*, p. 22; BL. Add MSS 20577, f.244, the diary of Cardinal Gualterio, 26 May 1717.
260. It had originally been planned that Nairne would leave on Friday 21st, but he had to delay his departure because Dr Wood was 'un peu incommodé et hors d'etat de partir' (BL. Add MSS 31260, f.77, Nairne to Gualterio, 20 May 1717).
261. HMC *Stuart* IV, p. 289, Hay to Mar, 30 May 1717.
262. ASV. Albani 166, p. 25, James III to Gualterio, 24 May 1717.
263. ASV. Albani 166, pp. 25–34, 'Due Relazioni della venuta à Roma del Re d'Inghilterra Giacomo III', at p. 32, 28 May 1717.
264. HMC *Stuart* IV, p. 333, Nairne to Paterson, 9 June 1717; ibid. p. 336, Paterson to Nairne, 10 June 1717; ibid. p. 337, Nairne to Paterson, 11 June 1717.
265. Ibid. p. 289, Nairne to Paterson, 29 May 1717.
266. Ibid. p. 337, Nairne to Paterson, 11 June 1717.
267. Ibid. p. 317, James III to Mar, 5 June 1717.
268. Corp, *The Jacobites at Urbino*, pp. 25–6.
269. Ibid. p. 23.
270. Ibid. pp. 26–7.
271. Corp, *The Jacobites at Urbino*, pp. 23–4.
272. HMC *Stuart* IV, p. 315, Salviati to Nairne, 4 June 1717.
273. BL. Add MSS 20577, f.251, the diary of Cardinal Gualterio, 1 June 1717.
274. Bod. Carte MSS 208, ff.338–56 at f.343, 'Journal du Séjour de S. M. B. à Rome' by Nairne, 7 June 1717. Nairne had already met Lord Richard Howard when the latter had visited Bar-le-Duc at the beginning of 1713 (Bod. Carte MSS 211, f.295, Howard to James III, 4 February 1713).
275. WDA. Epist Var 6/no.54, Nairne to Mayes, 29 July 1717.
276. Bod. Carte MSS 208, ff.338–56 at f.353, 'Journal du Séjour de S. M. B. à Rome' by Nairne, 30 June 1717. The Collegio Clementino had been founded in 1601 as an élite school for young noblemen of every nation and the richest families in Rome.
277. Corp, *The Jacobites at Urbino*, p. 165, note 28. Alessandro Scarlatti wrote oratorios to be performed at the Collegio Clementino.
278. BL. Add MSS 20577, f.255, the diary of Cardinal Gualterio, 5 June 1717. Dominic Sheldon also joined the king in Rome (HMC *Stuart* IV, p. 337, Nairne to Paterson, 11 June 1717, postscript of 12 June).

279. Corp, *The Jacobites at Urbino*, p. 29.
280. BVA. MS 3188, f.340, the diary of Dr Brun, June 1717, (printed in Twigge, 'Jacobite Papers at Avignon', p. 74).
281. Corp, *The Jacobites at Urbino*, p. 28.
282. Ibid. p. 30. That evening the Pope sent James several presents, including 'un Corps Saint de ceux qui sont dans la Sacristie de la chapelle pontificalle du Quirinal, avec les sceaux d'or massifs d'une Croix cristal avec du Bois de la Ste Croix' (BVA. MS 3188, f.351, the diary of Dr Brun, July 1717, printed in Twigge, 'Jacobite Papers at Avignon', p. 74). The king entrusted these to Nairne and told him to ask Gualterio to send them to Queen Mary at Saint-Germain (BL. Add MSS 31260, f.79, Nairne to Gualterio, 9 July 1717).
283. WDA. Epist Var 6/no. 54, Nairne to Mayes, 29 July 1717.
284. Corp, *The Jacobites at Urbino*, p. 30.
285. ASV. Albani 166, p. 70, Gualterio to Clement XI, 7 July 1717.
286. BL. Add MSS 31260, f.86, Nairne to Gualterio, 22 July 1717, postscript of 23 July.
287. BL. Add MSS 31260, f.82, Nairne to Gualterio, 18 July 1717.
288. BL. Add MSS 20298, f.8, Nairne to Gualterio, 30 July 1717.
289. Corp, *The Jacobites at Urbino*, p. 30.
290. BL. Add MSS 31260, f.79, Nairne to Gualterio, 9 July 1717.
291. Corp, *The Jacobites at Urbino*, p. 31, the diary of Dr Blair, June 1717.
292. HMC *Stuart* VII, p. 428, Nairne to Mar, 23 October 1718.
293. BL. Add MSS 20298, f.6, Nairne to Gualterio, 15 July 1717.
294. HMC *Stuart* IV, p. 445, James III to Mar, 13 July 1717.
295. Ibid. p. 448, Paterson to Mar, 13 July 1717.
296. BL. Add MSS 20298, f.6, Nairne to Gualterio, 15 July 1717.
297. BL. Add MSS 31260, f.82, Nairne to Gualterio, 18 July 1717. See also BL. Add MSS 31260, f.86, Nairne to Gualterio, 22 July 1717: 'le petit accident qui m'etoit arrivé, et que Dieu mercy n'a point eu de suitte.'
298. WDA. Epist Var 6/no.54, Nairne to Mayes, 29 July 1717: 'The fall I got coming hither has had no ill consequence, for I thank God my head is quite well again.'

Personal Disappointments and Family Problems, 1717–1719

The fifteen months that Nairne spent at Urbino, from July 1717 to October 1718, brought him considerable distress and eventually made him extremely unhappy. There were several reasons for this, but most of them resulted from the excessive favouritism which the king showed towards three of the new Scottish Protestant exiles. They gave the king what Nairne considered to be bad political advice and contributed to what he regarded as the king's lack of judgment in negotiating with the Pope. They were allowed to dominate the organization of the court, thereby turning the king against all his old servants from Saint-Germain, and making Nairne aware that he himself was no longer appreciated and becoming increasingly marginalized. They also monopolized all the favours which the king was able to grant so that, for example, any future posts at the court would be reserved for them, their wives and their supporters. The present chapter will begin by concentrating on Nairne's position as clerk of the closet in charge of the Jacobite Roman correspondence. It will then examine Nairne's financial difficulties in maintaining and educating his children, and his realization that he could no longer hope for any support from the king.

Nairne's fifteen months at Urbino may for convenience be divided into five periods of unequal length. From July to November 1717, James III was increasingly influenced by John Hay in the management of the royal household (the bedchamber, the chamber, the household below stairs and the stables). Nairne in the secretariat was not directly affected by this, except that four of his old friends from Saint-Germain chose to leave the court rather than remain there with Hay.[1]

At the end of November 1717 the Duke of Mar rejoined the court, having been away in France since February. As secretary of state Mar began to influence the king's attitude towards the Pope, even though this was Nairne's special area of responsibility. In particular Mar went out of his way to turn the king against his whole Saint-Germain background, and thus against the people like Nairne who were associated with it. This second period culminated in March 1718 in the summary dismissal at Saint-Germain of Nairne's patron and friend Lewis Innes, on charges trumped up by Mar.

The third period brought a temporary relaxation, because Mar left the court to visit Rome from the end of March until the middle of May 1718. Yet this short period, during which Hay remained at the court, again saw the departure of four of Nairne's old friends, who returned to Saint-Germain,[2] thereby leaving him virtually isolated at the court as the only senior servant of his rank who had been with the king in France.[3] It was at this time that news reached the court that Queen Mary, whom Nairne had served for so many years and who had been forced to accept the dismissal of Lewis Innes, had died at Saint-Germain.

During the weeks following the return of Mar, in May and June 1718, Nairne's sense of dissatisfaction greatly increased, such that he too longed to leave the court. However he could not afford to do so, if only because he could not hope to maintain his children if he no longer received his salary from the king.

This brief fourth period was followed by the final one from June to October 1718, when all of Nairne's problems came to a head. His health deteriorated, he was snubbed by the king, he was disgusted by the favouritism shown towards Hay and Mar, and he was alienated from the court as a whole. Yet this was not all, because it was during this fifth period that the court was joined by Hay's wife and by the latter's brother James Murray (not to be confused with Captain James Murray who had been a good friend at Saint-Germain). Murray rapidly achieved an influence over the king which became as great as, if not greater than, that of Mar and which, in collaboration with the influence exerted by his sister and his brother-in-law Hay, achieved a virtual dominance over the king. By October 1718, it is clear that Nairne was very deeply depressed, was longing to escape from the court, and even had little desire to go on living.

We may assume, from the evidence contained in his Saint-Germain diary, that Nairne found what consolation he could in his profound religious faith. A branch of the Confraternity of the 'Bona Morte' was already established at Urbino, in a chapel beside the cathedral and only a minute's walk from the palazzo ducale,[4] and Nairne probably attended its weekly meetings (though we have no direct evidence of this). He certainly attended the services in the cathedral and perhaps elsewhere, commenting on one occasion that one of the priests in the town preached 'really extremely well' and that 'I hear his sermons as often as I can.'[5] When Urbino was struck by an earthquake he joined the local people in '3 days of prayers ... and salutation services and fasting.'[6] His letters also demonstrate that he continued to give considerable thought to his religious faith. In a long letter of August 1717, for example, he explained why he could not believe that 'the house of the Virgin Mary' had really been transported from Nazareth to Loretto, and that he regarded the cult as fraudulent and superstitious. 'I know', he added, 'that among the people of the Marche and perhaps in Rome too I would be seen as worse than a Jansenist (which says a lot) if I dared suggest the slightest doubt about such a fashionable and profitable devotion.'[7] When he heard that Gualterio's brother had died, he sent the cardinal a letter of condolence containing a long extract from St Augustine on the subject of death.[8]

In fact, it was his friendship with Gualterio which enabled Nairne to keep going in the face of so much adversity. Except when Gualterio was visiting Urbino, he and Nairne wrote to each other at least once a week. Many of their letters were official, and written in the knowledge that they would be seen by the king. But many others were confidential, to be seen neither by the king nor by Gualterio's private secretary. And from a biographical point of view this correspondence is extremely significant. Whereas the diary that Nairne had kept at Saint-Germain tells us what he did, but rarely tells us what he thought, the letters that he sent to Gualterio from Urbino have the opposite effect: they rarely tell us what he did, but they regularly inform us, and in very great detail, what he thought and how his attitude gradually evolved during the five periods identified above. It is these letters, preserved by Gualterio even though he was asked to burn them, which form the basis of the present chapter.[9]

Before, however, we examine Nairne's time at Urbino we must recognize that not everything was bad, particularly at first. Unlike many of the other courtiers, Nairne enjoyed living at Urbino, commenting in the summer of 1717 that 'the air here is good, the water is excellent, the heat is much tempered by the wind, and finally the palace is fine and comfortable,'[10] and in particular 'a lot more so than the one in Pesaro'.[11] Some people found Urbino much too cold in winter, but in both January and February Nairne commented that 'it is not excessively cold for the season',[12] and at the end of March he described the weather as 'the most perfect in the world'.[13] When the summer returned and many people, particularly the Scots, found the weather intolerably hot, he commented that in his opinion the heat was moderate and that 'this place in the Summer has an advantage over many others'.[14] But neither the king nor the Duke of Mar shared this opinion, and Nairne informed Gualterio that 'the King has not been feeling well here for some time, and the Duke of Mar and several others have found the heat very difficult'. As he explained, 'the air in this country ... suits some constitutions but not all'.[15] Nairne might not have regarded Urbino as a good residence from a political point of view, but at least he was personally comfortable living there.

Another positive aspect of the months spent at Urbino concerned music, performed both by talented amateurs among the courtiers and the noble families in the town, as well as by visiting professional singers and instrumentalists.[16] In a letter of January 1718, the Duke of Mar recorded that the concerts at the court were held three times each week, the ensemble consisting primarily of 'a voice tolerably good, an excellent violin, [and] one that plays well on the harpsichord', sometimes joined by a 'bass fiddle' and a flute.[17] Nairne might have taken part in one or more of these concerts (though he never mentions them), but perhaps he was much too busy to be able to devote time to rehearsals. Nevertheless we can deduce that he did attend them.

By contrast we know definitely that he went to the opera at Fano in February 1718, because he sent an enthusiastic report to Gualterio:

> a remaining taste for worldly pleasures which my old age has not yet cured led me first to the Opera, where I admit (perhaps to my shame) I stayed until nearly midnight without tiring of it, and since I intend to go there again this evening I am convinced that music will always have the same effect on me.[18]

The Duke of St Andrews (married to one of Melfort's daughters) wrote to Nairne that 'I am persuaded that after hearing the operas at Fano, you will not be able to bring yourself to hear the concerts of Urbino'.[19] We may assume, however, that Nairne did go on attending them.

Having experienced the operas at Fano, James III was keen to have some operas performed in the theatre of the palazzo ducale at Urbino, and Nairne entered into negotiations with Cardinal Albani to persuade the Pope to allow this.[20] Nairne, like the king, disliked the fact that the papal authorities would not permit women to appear on stage, and he commented that 'one must admit that the scruples and difficulties posed in this country appear somewhat excessive'. Women were not allowed to 'sing in an opera before the King, which they are allowed to do in Bologna'. And moreover,

> eunuchs everywhere are permitted to dress as women in the theatre, which is as little within the strict rules and moral discipline as women singing on stage.[21]

During the spring of 1718, various *castrati* came to sing at Urbino, both in concerts and in oratorios. But Nairne wanted to hear women. After one concert which he attended in the Palazzo Staccoli Nairne wrote that the hostess, Lucrezia Staccoli, 'herself sang extremely well'.[22] A little later a soprano named Innocenza Magnani arrived from Bologna and sang at a concert in the Palazzo Bonaventura. John Paterson (Mar's under-secretary) recorded that

> the king was present and all his subjects except Sir W. Ellis and myself, and lucky it was for us. Never any lady, I believe, made a more universal conquest. Not a single man escaped her, I mean of a subject ... Of the wounded Nairne and Creagh seem to be in the most desparate condition.[23]

Nairne showed his appreciation by trying to get Signor Magnani (Innocenza's father) appointed Governor of Faenza,[24] and when that failed he approached Gualterio:

> I am hoping with Y. E.'s support that we may be able to find him a more profitable position, of which he is said to be very worthy, and everyone speaks highly of the virtue and merit of his daughter the virtuosa Sig.ra Innocenza who has so earnestly requested this that I could not help but take an interest in the Father.[25]

Innocenza Magnani remained at Urbino until October, and provided Nairne with considerable musical pleasure at a time when he was otherwise very depressed. In one of his letters he wrote:

Signora Innocenza ... sang yesterday and played on the lute most charmingly to
Lady Nithsdale and had the applause, vivats and benissimos of all the company, of
which Mr Erskine was one and myself another, two lords, Mr Graham and his mistress, Mr Panton and an Italian, so you see we have here in your absence our little
diminutive pleasures.[26]

When not accompanying herself on the lute, Innocenza was accompanied
on the harpsichord by her singing teacher, named Agostino Tinazzoli.
Nairne commented that 'I wish you had heard her master ..., Tenazoli
[sic], who is reckoned one of the best players on the harpsichord and ablest
masters of music in Italy'.[27]

As these letters show, Nairne was not without friends at Urbino
although, as noted, the ones he had known at Saint-Germain gradually
departed. Among the Scottish pensioners he was probably also on good
terms with Charles Fleming, whom he had known both as a student in the
1680s[28] and when planning the *entreprise d'Ecosse* in 1706–8, and also with
Lord Winton, whom he had known for many years.[29] In February 1718, for
example, Winton gave a *régale* to Nairne and four of the latter's friends:
Dominic Sheldon (vice-chamberlain), Charles Booth (groom of the bedchamber), Sir William Ellis (treasurer) and James Delattre (equerry).[30] As
a young man Nairne had also known Lord Panmure, whom he described
as 'a worthy good sort of man',[31] though the latter left the court five days
before Winton gave his *régale*.[32]

Other old friends, or at least acquaintances, who were at Urbino for
some of the time included the Duke of Melfort's daughter Lady Mary, whom
Nairne had known since her birth at Saint-Germain in 1693, and who was
married to the Spanish Duke of St Andrews. She and her husband were at
Urbino from November 1717 to February 1718.[33] So also was the Duke of
Perth's eldest son, the 2nd Duke, whom Nairne had known as a student in
the 1680s[34] and who was appointed Lord Chamberlain in March 1718.[35]
But Nairne, one of the only two members of the court other than the king
who could speak Italian,[36] was on especially good terms with Alamanno
Salviati and his secretary Eustachio Buglioni.

Salviati lived in the former apartment of the Duke of Urbino, immediately beside that of the king, and Nairne told Gualterio that he himself
lived with Salviati 'as a friend'.[37] But he became even more friendly with
Buglioni, whom he esteemed[38] and for whom he admitted he had 'a soft

spot'.[39] He told Gualterio that 'I love him for his good heart and his loyalty and he is not at all lacking in ability'.[40] He could not help noticing, however, that Buglioni was badly treated by Salviati, and as time went by this made him modify his opinion of the latter. In August 1718, he confided to Gualterio that he thought that Salviati was mediocre and self-interested, and would persecute anyone who did not support the Jesuits.[41] And he added that 'I wish with all my heart that I could see him well provided for or employed as he deserves'.[42]

Another friend whom Nairne cultivated at this time was the astronomer Francesco Bianchini, whom he had met in Rome in June 1717, and whom he regarded as 'a very good man who is full of zeal and scientific learning'.[43] Bianchini visited the Stuart court at Urbino on three occasions. The first, in August 1717, was very short and lasted only three or four days,[44] but his second visit was much longer, and lasted from 27 August to 20 October 1717.[45] The main purpose of the visit was for James III and Bianchini, and presumably Nairne as well, to watch an eclipse of the moon from the roof of the palazzo.[46] Nairne commented that Bianchini had 'shown here a modesty to match his zeal and his affection' and that he was 'truly very good-hearted and a real *honnete homme*' who had not tried to interfere in any 'business'.[47]

Bianchini's third visit was not until August 1718, and in the meantime he and Nairne remained in regular correspondence.[48] Once again Nairne found him a 'very good man' with 'plenty of the zeal for the King', but felt that one had always to be on one's guard with him 'in conversation, because he is known to like writing letters and involving himself in politics'.[49] Nevertheless, whatever private reservations he might have felt about Bianchini, this was an important friendship with an influential and well-placed priest in Rome which would be particularly useful to Nairne in the months to come.

In the summer of 1717, when the court moved to Urbino, Nairne was sixty-two years old and beginning to feel his age. When Gualterio told him in March 1718 that he (Gualterio) had been suffering from gout, Nairne replied:

> I myself have never been much afflicted with it, but either through gout or old age I am no longer in the state I was, having a bad foot and bad eyesight and unfortunately my best spectacles have recently been broken.[50]

Unfortunately for Nairne, he also had a bad attack of gout in June:

> for the last 3 days the gout (which had remained quiet since the expedition to
> Scotland) has cruelly attacked me in both feet. I really do not wish to become a
> crippled old man with a life full of troubles rather than pleasures. I hope this gout
> will not last, but the state I am in makes it hard for me to write.[51]

Two days later, on 25 June, he wrote to another friend that 'I have got the
gout, and was vomited yesterday and purgd today ... My back is weary sitting up on my bed to write this and other letters I was obliged to write'.[52]

Nairne dictated some of his letters to his friend Buglioni,[53] though
he assured Gualterio that he only let him copy ordinary and unimportant
letters containing nothing of secrecy.[54] By the end of June he was able to
get out of bed and sit in a chair,[55] and a week later he began to walk 'a few
steps in my bedchamber'.[56] It was not until 10 July, after being confined to
his bedroom for nearly three weeks, that he was well enough to leave his
lodging on the second floor and go downstairs to the king's apartment.[57]

One particular problem facing Nairne, as this episode made clear,
is that he had no regular clerical assistance[58] – unlike Mar who had both
Paterson as his under-secretary and Creagh as his clerk. In April 1718, he
complained of having had to spend 'a good part of the day decyphering
long letters in which there was nothing important, which is a very tedious
occupation'.[59] On another occasion, in September 1718, he recorded that he
had that day written twenty-one letters in addition to all the ones he had
written for the king.[60] It was around this time that Nairne produced three
long memoranda – all in his own handwriting – for the king to send to
the Pope urging the latter to give him extra money, perhaps as a wedding
present.[61] And to make his life more difficult Nairne had been obliged to
lay off his personal servant because he could no longer afford to pay him.[62]

Another thing which distressed Nairne throughout the time that the
court was at Urbino was the dining arrangements. At Saint-Germain the
king had provided 'diet' for his household servants, of whom the most
important ate at the 'gentlemen's table'. Nairne, like the other members of
the secretariat, was not strictly speaking a household servant, so had made
his own arrangements for his dinners and suppers, eating at home or in
the lodgings of someone else, notably Lord Caryll. Then, at Bar-le-Duc
and Avignon, when none of the courtiers had his own home and all lived

at the court, Nairne had his meals provided by the king, and normally ate at the gentlemen's table.

The dining arrangements at Urbino were the same as they had been at Avignon. There were now two tables, the first of which was for James himself, the gentlemen and grooms of the bedchamber, the lord chamberlain, the vice-chamberlain, the secretary of state and anyone else whom the king chose to invite. The second was for the other senior members of the household, while the junior members were fed in the basements and given the food which remained at the end of each meal. The pensioners, when not invited by the king, were expected to feed themselves in their own rooms or in the town.[63]

Nairne felt that, in his capacity as secretary of the closet, he should be included among the select few who normally ate with the king, but in fact he was told to eat at the second table. This, he felt, detracted from the 'dignity' of his psition. He explained to Gualterio:

> apart from during a few journeys in France, and when the king was in Rome, I have never had the honour to be one of those whom he sometimes invites here to eat at his table whereas every day he invites junior officers and gentlemen of his suite who certainly have no more right to it than I do. In the minds of those people who judge by appearances, this puts me in a lower rank as if I were a kind of clerk, which displeases me greatly.

This, he said, was bad for the prestige of the office held by someone who had the honour of corresponding with Gualterio and the other cardinals.[64]

Restricted to the second table, Nairne normally ate with Sir William Ellis, James Delattre, Mar's two assistants (Paterson and Creagh), the king's doctor (Charles Maghie), and the king's confessor (Father John Brown). On one occasion, he tried to console himself by imagining that the king's reason for leaving him on the second table was so that he could eat with Ellis:

> Sir William Ellis eats with me, and the King has not done him the honour of inviting him to his table, whereas in France he did me that honour more than 30 times, and perhaps he does not want to mortify him.[65]

The only positive aspect of obliging Nairne to eat at the second table seems to have been an improvement in his relations with Paterson, as is suggested by a letter the former sent to the latter in October 1718. Delattre,

Paterson, Maghie and Brown were away from the court, leaving only Nairne, Ellis and Creagh eating on the second table. Nairne sent Paterson the following tongue-in-cheek comment in one of his letters:

> Our little grave table salute you and all three never miss a day drinking a health to the travellers but be not scandalized, for we never pass our couple of bottles a piece, which is short of the Doctor's 14.[66]

Yet despite this enforced jocularity, it is clear that the dining arrangements contributed to the feelings of disappointment and distress which Nairne increasingly felt throughout the time he remained at Urbino.

Between July and November 1717, there were several political matters to which Nairne had to attend, of which the most important was ensuring the security of the king. In addition to rebuilding the walls of the city, this involved increasing the number of Corsican and Swiss guards in attendance and evicting various local people who had been using parts of the palazzo ducale, all of which Nairne achieved with Salviati and in correspondence with Cardinals Gualterio and Albani.[67]

The most serious threat at the time appeared to be the arrival of Lord Peterborough at Bologna in September 1717, because it was rumoured that he had come to Italy with the intention of assassinating James III. Nairne had no doubt that Peterborough should be arrested and interrogated, though this should 'be done with as little éclat as possible'. He added:

> the essential thing is to get all his people, his trustees, his bravoes, and even his mistress, if it be thought convenient, secured. He may have had the weakness to discover his secret to her, and fear will make a woman squeak sooner than a man.[68]

Peterborough was duly imprisoned, but Dominic Sheldon, who was sent to speak to him, concluded that he was innocent and that the rumours about him were unfounded. He was eventually released in November, after the British government threatened naval action against the Papal States, but Nairne was in no doubt that the king had been right to have Peterborough arrested. He wrote to Gualterio:

> If Lord Peterborough is innocent of the intention imputed to him by many and supported by several strong indications then all the better for him and we would be delighted, but that would not prevent the fact that everything the King has done as

a result of opinions given and the indications has been done according to the rules of justice and prudence, because in such cases one cannot be too careful.[69]

In the absence of Mar, Nairne was satisfied that the relations between James III and the papacy were being conducted satisfactorily. This was not the case, however, as regards the management of the household.

When the court had been at Pesaro, the king had created the new post of *maggiordomo*. It had made sense to put one man in charge of both the household below stairs and the stables because the footmen in the stables were now employed to wait at the king's table, and the arrangement of the basements at Urbino (which contained the stables as well as the kitchens) facilitated this overall co-ordination. The *maggiordomo* was described as being in charge of 'the Household Below Stairs, the Table and the Stables', and the post was given to Charles Booth, until then a groom of the bedchamber.

One of the equerries in the stables, subordinate to Booth, was the king's new favourite John Hay. In July 1717, shortly after the court moved to Urbino, James III decided to promote Hay by demoting Booth. Hay would cease to be an equerry in the stables and would instead become a groom of the bedchamber. Hay would then take charge of the household below stairs and the table, but not the stables which he disliked. Booth would cease to be a groom of the bedchamber and would be in charge of the stables, thereby relinquishing to Hay the household below stairs, the table and the title of *maggiordomo*.

When the king saw Booth in the middle of July and told him what he had decided, Booth understandably refused to accept the change, and said he would like to take a temporary period of leave. This placed the king in a difficult position: Booth was not willing to look after the stables only, and Hay (who was evidently lazy) was not prepared to look after the stables as well as the household below stairs and the table. So James was obliged to appoint someone else to be *maggiordomo* in charge of the household below stairs, the table and the stables. Hay ceased to be an equerry and became a groom of the bedchamber, Booth returned to Saint-Germain at the beginning of August, and the post of *maggiordomo* was given to Lord Clermont, who was a gentleman of the bedchamber and therefore senior to both Hay and Booth. It was understood that when Booth returned from leave he would be subordinate to Clermont.[70] Nairne explained this development to Gualterio on 5 August:

> The King has ordered me to inform Y. E. that he has given to Lord Clermont the responsibility for all household matters, including his table and his stables in the absence of Mr Booth, who will have to serve on his return under My Lord who will continue to give the orders in general, and Mr Booth will give detailed orders answering to My Lord as to his senior officer. I am sure that Y. E. who knows the young lord, will approve this judicious choice made by H. M., and will be pleased also for his worthy father Lord Middleton, who deserves this consolation in his old age after a lifetime of service to H. M..[71]

What Nairne's letter did not indicate is how divisive the king's decision had been, because Booth was an old servant from Saint-Germain whereas Hay was one of the new exiles. Moreover, Booth was English and Catholic, and Hay was Scottish and Protestant, so the change was bound to create friction at the court. In a remarkably frank letter James III tried to justify what he had done:

> I ... have found by experience that my goodness to certain people [e.g. Booth] serves only to make them insolent, and that such as I am just to without being kind [e.g. Nairne] are those who give me less trouble.

James then followed this up with a sweeping condemnation of all his old servants from Saint-Germain – including, of course, Nairne:

> Ld Clermont ... is ye only untainted from St Germains principles I mean of St Germains people, for out of them there was a necessity of chusing at this time.[72]

It is against this background, and specifically the king's comment that he would be 'just' but would not be 'kind', that we can examine the confidential correspondence exchanged between Nairne and Gualterio during the summer of 1717.

On 30 July, Nairne thanked Gualterio for sending him a 'confidential letter', which he had not shown to the king, and then made the following comments about himself:

> to intervene of my own accord is not part of my character. I dislike officiousness in others such that I cannot and should not tolerate it in myself. I like modesty and it gives me great satisfaction that having no other merit at least I have that.

He then considered how he would behave if he, like Booth, were to be demoted or dismissed:

> And if (though I think it unlikely) he ever changed his mind and found it suitable to dismiss me I would give him all the reasons that I could to convince him of my incapacity ... There you are Monseigneur, I am using straight words and revealing to you my deepest thoughts ... You may find in them an excessive delicacy and a kind of interior vanity to which I admit I am not exempt ... I admit that I enjoy and desire the esteem of men to a certain extent, and perhaps more than Christian humility allows ... but I insist that it would be more glorious to merit that esteem, even without having it, than to have it without deserving it.[73]

However admirable Nairne's sentiments certainly were, they were not designed to maintain his position at the court against an unscrupulous and ambitious new favourite like Hay. But they earned him the respect of Gualterio, who replied on 4 August that 'your sentiments ... command universal respect, and especially mine', and that he felt for Nairne 'strong feelings of friendship'. He added that 'I well know your exceptional zeal, your discretion and your very great efficiency', but gently warned Nairne that 'it is necessary after all to take into account the interested party' (i.e. the king).[74] A little later Gualterio admitted that he also disapproved of what the king had done, and added:

> I opened my heart to you perhaps more than was wise. But I have not and never shall keep anything from you to whom I speak as if to myself; nothing can equal the respect and veneration in which nobody more than myself will honour you in life and death.[75]

These letters are worth quoting because they demonstrate very clearly what close relations Nairne had established with Gualterio, who was not only the Cardinal Protector of England but James III's minister at the papal court. Gualterio wrote again that 'I think it is a good thing that there should be a private correspondence between us when dealing with important matters', adding that 'one cannot tell the Master [James III] everything without being disrespectful'.[76]

Unfortunately for Nairne, he could not overcome his excessive modesty and reciprocate Gualterio's sentiments as an equal. He replied to these letters on 19 August:

I am the lowliest and most unworthy of the King's servants ... It is true I have nothing to reproach myself with in terms of work and willingness, when it concerns my
actual service ... in the small department for which I am responsible, since I would
be lying if I said I take things easy and do not push myself hard; but I do all that
only as my duty, and when I have done that, it is all so unimportant, that it has to
be admitted that I am truly a useless servant.[77]

This was really not the way to consolidate an equal relationship with
Gualterio. Even when the latter replied that 'you have complete authority
over me, and you can do what you will with everything concerning me,'[78]
Nairne undermined his own position by replying:

It is too much honour for me to be the unworthy channel of your correspondence
with the King. Provided I am fortunate enough for my small services to be useful to
both of you that is all that I ask, I am only doing my duty, and any trouble I take is
too trifling to be taken into account.[79]

Such self-effacement began to worry Nairne's friends, who could see
that he would not be able to maintain his position against Hay, or against
Mar when he returned. But Nairne was not to be persuaded. He wrote to
Thomas Innes:

I am sure it will be a greater pleasure to me to do you and yours a good office than
if it were for my self or mine, for I must own to you your chiding letter has not converted me upon that point, I speak wth pleasure when it is proper and when I can for
a friend, and think it my duty, but I cannot think it so proper nor so becoming my
place (little as it is) to speak for my self. If my services and modesty do not speak for
me I must ... have patience. I allways admird My Ld Mid.s disinterestedness in that
way, and if I cannot emulat him in all, I would endeavour to do it in this at least.[80]

For the time being, however, and with Mar still away in France, Nairne's
position in the secretariat seemed secure. In the autumn of 1717, James III
invited Gualterio to visit him at Urbino,[81] and Nairne wrote to tell his
friend how much he was looking forward to seeing him again.[82]
    Gualterio arrived at Urbino at the end of October and stayed with
James III in the palazzo ducale for about a week.[83] It is regrettable that we
have no description of this visit, but we may easily imagine the impact that
it must have made if Gualterio showed to Nairne the same friendship in
public that he had revealed in his confidential letters. The king, Gualterio,

Salviati and Nairne could have spoken to each other in Italian, whereas none of the other members of the court would have been able to understand what they were saying. Or they could have spoken to each other in French, in which case the old servants from Saint-Germain would have understood, but neither Hay nor any of the Scottish Protestant pensioners would have been able to. Nairne was fully conscious of how impressed some of the courtiers would be, and had even hoped that the Duke of Mar would have returned in time to see it himself.[84] The Earl of Southesk, however, was able to witness the visit, and he recorded his feelings of resentment at how unimportant he and the other Protestants were made to feel as they witnessed Nairne's easy relationship with the visiting cardinal:

> they now give themselves their great St Germains airs ... there is not an Italian but believes they are the only people who are favoured by the King, and the only ones worthy of his favour, and that is come to such a height that they think even little Nairne a greater man than any that followed the King in our late affair.[85]

From Nairne's point of view this must have been the high point of his time at Urbino – except, of course, that at each meal he would have been left on the second table while Gualterio and others ate with the king.

The Duke of Mar, who was travelling with Charles Booth, was expected to arrive at Urbino at the beginning of November 1717,[86] but delayed his arrival until the 22nd because he wanted to visit Venice, Verona, Padua and Bologna on his way.[87] Nairne cannot have looked forward to Mar's return to the court. He told a friend at the beginning of November that he had not been corresponding with Mar because the latter never wrote to him and did not treat him 'as I think I ought to be':

> I never writt a scrape of a pen to him all the time he has been absent tho I am not at all ignorant of his ex.ry favour, which shews you how ill a Courtier I am. I love old tryd friends, and cannot bring my self to admire some new great men so extraordinarily as I see a great many do. I believe there is a little pride in this wch I am sorry for but I cannot help it, and of the two I had rather have this fault and be sincere than be a flatterer.[88]

Within a very short time of his arrival Mar succeeded in completely poisoning the mind of the king against his old servants from Saint-Germain, whom James now regarded as 'without principles'. Mar and Hay were 'honest', whereas the old servants, including even Lord Clermont, were trying to impose on him.[89] The king explained on 7 March:

> though I never much admired St Germain's proceedings, I am now quite surprised of them, and ... I do not desire to have any more to do with them; their principles and notions and mine are very different ... so that I am not at all fond of the ways of those I have so long lived with.[90]

This inevitably had an impact on the position of Nairne in the secretariat, though as Mar could speak neither Italian nor even French he could not persuade the king that Nairne should be dismissed.

The period from late November 1717 to the end of March 1718 was therefore one of increasing difficulty and isolation for Nairne. He should have taken advantage of the excellent relations he enjoyed with Gualterio, but he remained much too diffident, preferring the relationship of a client towards his patron to one of equality. He sent Gualterio a miniature copy of his portrait by Belle,[91] but in a typical letter that he wrote on 26 December he told the cardinal:

> I am embarrassed by the ceremony that Y. E. has shown me by honouring me (unworthy as I am) with a letter of Christmas greetings. I can only reply by begging you to allow me to remain in the ranks of your humble and devoted servants, as I have never aspired to these marks of distinction which it is not my place to do. And to speak sincerely, the kindness you show me in so many ways is more than ample to fulfil my ambitions.[92]

It would not be surprising if Gualterio was beginning to be exasperated by such comments.

During this second period, Nairne was responsible for obtaining and distributing twelve bust copies from Antonio David of the three-quarter length portrait of the king which he (David) had painted in Rome.[93] Nairne was particularly pleased when David told him that he was painting an additional copy to give him as a present.[94] At the end of January 1718, Nairne had the original sent to Queen Mary at Saint-Germain, with 'the copy which Mr David did for me' included in the same package, 'marked and addressed to my daughter in the English convent on the fossés St Victor in Paris'.[95]

Figure 9. *King James III*, 1717/18 (44 × 33 cm), by Antonio David
(photo courtesy of the Weiss Gallery)
This is one of the many bust copies which David made in 1718 of the three-quarter-
length portrait of the king, which he had painted in 1717. He gave it as a present to
Nairne. It measures 44 × 33 cm, whereas the three other known copies are much larger
and measure 80 × 63 cm, 73.5 × 55.7 cm, and 72.4 × 55.9 cm.

These copies of the portrait of the king brought Nairne, who had considerable experience of dealing with painters, into a minor disagreement with Mar, who believed himself to be superior in all matters artistic. The king decided to reward Antonio David with a warrant appointing him to be his official portrait painter, and told Mar to produce the necessary document. But Mar disliked David's portrait of the king, and thought it was 'by no means a good picture',[96] so he deliberately delayed producing the document. Nairne reassured David 'that he can count on the warrant since H. M. has promised it',[97] but asked Gualterio to tell him to be patient: 'The Duke of Mar has recently been so occupied with other more important matters that he has had no time to think about it.'[98] When the warrant was finally ready it was given to Nairne for him to send to Gualterio, to be handed over to David. In his letter Nairne apologized for the poor quality of the Latin, saying that he had had nothing to do with it, and that he had merely reminded the king about it from time to time, 'without troubling to provide a model for the office of the Protestant Secretary of State, where I have never had any business, nor ever will, God willing (but I am only saying this in confidence to Y. E.)'.[99]

Another question which concerned Nairne in the winter of 1717–18 was the difference between France and the Papal States regarding the food to be eaten during Lent. He wanted Gualterio to obtain permission from the Pope for the king and his courtiers to eat milk, butter and eggs 'as they do in France' and for those of weaker constitutions to eat meat 'on certain days of the week'.[100] In the end, and with the help of Gualterio and the Archbishop of Urbino, he obtained a particularly generous dispensation, 'which involves eating meat 4 times a week, and eggs and dairy products on the other days apart from during Holy Week'.[101] In the event, the king, presumably influenced by the Protestant favourites with whom he ate, did not keep Lent at all except on the Wednesday of Easter week,[102] though Nairne himself, eating on the second table, probably restricted his diet as in France, and then fasted at the end of the week.

In February 1718, James III decided to visit Fano on the Adriatic coast for ten days so that he and Mar could attend some performances of the operas to be performed there in the Teatro della Fortuna. Nairne preferred to remain at Urbino and give himself 'the natural pleasure for an elderly man and one of my character of spending a few days resting quietly beside my fire'. But at the last moment the king ordered Nairne to join him at Fano, and the latter wrote that 'leaving the mountains of Urbino, Y. E. can imagine how very agreeable we found Fano and the entertainment around there'.[103] This visit was significant because it completed the king's 'conversion' (Mar's word)[104] to Italian rather than French music, another aspect of James's rejection of his Saint-Germain background. For Nairne, however, apart from musical pleasure, the visit to Fano was memorable because he met there and developed a friendship with the poet Cavaliere Pietro Paolo Carrara, who was then the *Gonfalonier* of the town.[105]

In March 1718, shortly after their return from Fano, Mar persuaded James III to send a letter abruptly dismissing Lewis Innes from his post as Lord Almoner to Queen Mary at Saint-Germain.[106] As Mar put it, he was determined that the old servants from and at Saint-Germain should have less influence 'than ever' and if possible 'next to none at all'.[107] The queen was not consulted, and was mortified at having to obey her son in such a humiliating manner.[108] Nairne, who had known Lewis Innes since the 1680s, and who regarded him as his patron as well as his friend, was disgusted. He wrote to Gualterio on 24 March:

> The attachment for Mr Matre [*sic*: Mar], and the high (to my mind excessively high) opinion in which he is held and the desire to do everything to please him has meant the letter he composed was signed too quickly. This has resulted in the letter being supported more warmly than might have been hoped and the devotion and sincerity of those who express their opinion have been taken badly. These are the facts which I relate to Y. E. in the strictest confidence and with real pain.[109]

In a postscript Nairne added that the letter which the king sent to his mother, obliging her to dismiss Innes, had been sent without either consultation or reflection, and that James knew that both he and Dominic Sheldon strongly disapproved. He described Innes as

> completely dedicated to the King and incapable of a single malicious thought, he has worked for so many years to give every service he could. This has pained me more than I can say, more with regard to the King than to my friend, whom I will still find very contented with the retirement he has been granted and very satisfied that his conscience is completely clear ...
>
> Would Y. E. have the goodness to burn this letter after reading it.[110]

Gualterio told Nairne that he agreed with him and that the king would soon realize he had made a mistake.[111] But Nairne could not overcome his feelings of disgust, as can be seen in a letter that he sent to Lewis Innes' younger brother Thomas:

> It is the greatest of happiness, to have the grace to bear with certain unaccountable changes that happen in this world, with the patience and resignation that becomes us. I own to you I am weaker than you, for I find it no easy matter in my self, and I cannot yet overcome the impression which the sudden resolution taken about your brother has made upon me, it sticks with me still, and many other things I have remarkd of late and do remark dayly make me wish heartily I had my quietus but my poor children stick with me. In fine Gods will be done.

Nairne added that he had said nothing to the king 'out of respect' but that the latter was well aware of what he thought:

> I believe I have not made my Court by it, but I cannot help that: I am perhaps a little usefull, and for that reason more than inclination I continue still to be trusted and imployd, but I shall not be surprisd if my turn comes as well as others. I am sure I expect nothing by staying but continuation of toyl and labour ... But enough of this which is only to your brother and your self.'[112]

Having persuaded the king to dismiss Lewis Innes, Mar then left the court (and therefore stopped conducting his correspondence as secretary of state) to have a holiday in Rome, and did not return until the middle of May. While he was away Nairne, who of course was unable to take time off and neglect *his* work, kept going as best he could. 'I hope in God', he wrote to Thomas Innes, that

> I shall still do my duty to the last and as I believe I may say without vanity I labour as much and as usefully in my post as the great man in his, and I see no great doings of his either as to advising or writing but what I could make a shift to compass perhaps as well as he if supported as he is, whilst what I do I am sure he could not do. Adieu shew this to no body but to your brother.[113]

While Mar was away in Rome, Hay persuaded the king that he should also dismiss Lord Clermont from his position as *maggiordomo*, so that he (Hay) could replace him, though with no direct responsibility for the

Figure 10. *John Erskine, 6th Earl and 1st Duke of Mar*, 1718 (70.5 × 57 cm), by
Francesco Trevisani (Alloa Tower)
This was painted during Mar's visit to Rome in April and May 1718. It is the only por-
trait of Mar which shows him with the insignia of both the Jacobite Garter and the
Jacobite Thistle on his chest.

stables. James III wrote to inform Mar that he had done this, describing Clermont as having 'no right sense of [his] duty', as being 'incapable of friendship, or personal attachment, and not very susceptible of shame'.[114] Nairne, who had 'great respect and gratitude' for Clermont's family,[115] was shocked and still further alienated. It is regrettable that none of his correspondence with Lord Middleton has survived, as we may assume that he wrote to express his feelings to Lord Clermont's father, just as he wrote to Lewis Innes' brother.

During the summer of 1718, Nairne's physical and mental condition deteriorated. It was in June that he experienced his attack of gout, as already noted. But more important than that, it was in June that the court was joined by Hay's wife Marjory, accompanied by the latter's arrogant brother James Murray. The scene was set for the final, and most disagreeable period of Nairne's life at Urbino.

By July 1718, James III was preoccupied with organizing his marriage to Princess Clementina Sobieska, and with negotiating the transfer of his court from Urbino to another location closer to Rome and with a milder winter climate.[116] Both of these necessitated the agreement and support of the Pope, and therefore the assistance of Cardinal Gualterio as the king's minister at the papal court. Nairne was responsible for conducting the necessary correspondence with Gualterio, but he found himself unable to influence the king, who became more and more keen to please Hay, Hay's wife, Mar and Murray. As a result Nairne became increasingly critical of the king and keen to retire.

On 24 June, shortly after Murray's arrival at Urbino, James III sent him to Ohlau (in Silesia) to negotiate the marriage contract with Prince James Sobieski. The contract was signed on 22 July, when it was agreed that Princess Clementina would travel with her mother to Ferrara, where the marriage would take place in October. Nairne thought that the marriage should be held at Urbino, which would not only be cheaper but would also please the Pope,[117] but he was overruled by the king's favourites. He supported the king in his desire to leave Urbino and spend the winter near Rome, and agreed that the *palazzo apostolico* at Castel Gandolfo would be the ideal location,[118] but when he realized that the Pope did not want the Jacobite court to go there[119] he argued that it would be better for James to ask for somewhere else. But again he was overruled, and he told Gualterio in September that he thought that the king managed the Pope very badly, persistently irritating him rather than flattering him and winning him over.[120] In October, shortly before the planned marriage, he agreed with Gualterio that 'it is certain that several letters were written and steps taken that were unlikely to have found favour with' the Pope, 'and this at a time when we have most need of him'. He complained that he was now obliged to do things of which he disapproved, and told Gualterio that he would like to retire.[121]

Part of Nairne's problem was that the Duke of Mar, as secretary of state, was increasingly interfering in the management of the Roman correspondence, and trying to get Nairne demoted to become his under-secretary or clerk. As early as July 1718, Nairne told Gualterio that

> As for the Duke of Mar, we are getting on fairly well at the moment, ... Having seen, as did the King, that I was not going to take orders from him, now when we work together he shows more civility towards me. So I have kept my independence and I think that the situation for the present is that neither he nor the king will treat me as a clerk.[122]

But Nairne was his own worst enemy, because he would not or could not bring himself to manage Mar more skilfully:

> I get on very well with the Duke of Mar and respect him as long as he does not put on his superior act with me, and I know that if I were a flatterer and toady I could even become a friend, but I neither expect nor wish for anything from him except to live in peace. The way I see things going, I admit, does not please me, though I hope I am wrong. I am speaking about true service and the wellbeing of the King. For myself my ambitions are small, I am obsolete and I would need to be blind not to see it, for confidence and honesty may be pleasing, but when one realises that over all these years it has not occurred to a master to do the least thing for a servant then where there are no words there can be no friendship. This is for Y. E. only.[123]

Under these circumstances, it is perhaps not surprising that James III was more influenced by Mar than by Nairne in his dealings with the Pope[124] and the Italian princes.[125]

It was not only Mar, however, with whom Nairne now had to deal, as the king showed an even greater favouritism towards Hay, Hay's wife and Murray, and this had serious political consequences, as Nairne explained in October:

The Pope ... has not acted in a noble and frank manner, but it must also be said that instead of pandering to him in all things as prudence would suggest in this state of affairs, several useless things have been done to annoy him, compromises are never offered, and actions are undertaken to please [the favourites] rather than him. It is to be feared that people are noticing this, as the nephew [Don Carlo Albani] has said to me more than once and to others too that the king if left to himself has the best sentiments and intentions in the world, but as soon as others (whom I shall not name) have spoken to him, he completely changes.[126]

In another letter, written after Murray had returned from Ohlau, Nairne expressed himself even more frankly. He began by referring to Mar and Hay, and the way Clermont and Booth had been treated:

The King continues to treat me with more confidence and consideration than I deserve, but by love and inclination he has put a deeper and exclusive trust in someone else. Mâtre [i.e. Mar] is the oracle and Mr Hays [sic], who is a young man of only average merit and capabilities, is all-powerful in the household with nothing concealed from him. Lord Clermont and poor Mr Booth have been pushed aside to make room for him, though he certainly has neither their experience nor their intelligence, but it is not always real merit that governs inclination.

He then continued by referring to the newly arrived favourites:

The wife of Mr Hays is already assured of being close to the queen when we have one, and the Duchess of Mar will be lady of the bedchamber when she decides to join the court. Mr Murray, who has real aptitude and genius for business but who is still very young, thinks himself more capable than he actually is and gives himself the airs of a Minister. He too enjoys full confidence, being brother-in-law of Mr Hays and also totally devoted to Lord Mar.

These comments were no doubt entirely justified but, as Nairne admitted, he was a 'mauvais Courtisan'. He then considered his own position in a long passage which he specifically asked Gualterio to burn after having read it:

This is how I see things, and since I am unable and have no wish to flatter these new favourites, I keep myself to myself and only go to the King when he asks for me, and get on with my own work, and deal without curiosity or affectation with what he wants to convey to me. It is true that in important matters he seems to be completely open with me, and has the kindness to ask my opinion often, and when Lord Mar (who is aware that I know everything or at least most of it) talks to me, we discuss things together with great ease but I never ask him to confide in me, in order to leave him entirely free to do what he wants, which certainly favours neither the Catholic nor the old servants' side, having got rid of a large part of the latter, and I do not know how I have not suffered the same fate before now. But I imagine my turn will come, because I certainly do not pretend to have the merit of Lord Middleton or Mr Inese [*sic*], who are overlooked in a manner I cannot approve because I do not believe it to be in the interests of the King. All in all, I may be mistaken but I cannot hide my feelings, and all that I do in many things which distress me, not for me but for the good of His Majesty's service, is to keep quiet. I only speak so openly to Y.E with whom I feel completely safe in divulging everything I can, including my own weaknesses.[127]

These letters to Gualterio, which are so revealing from a biographical point of view, make it very clear that during the summer of 1718 Nairne effectively transferred his loyalty away from the Stuart king whom he had served for so long to the Italian cardinal who had become his patron. At the beginning of July 1718, for example, he wrote:

I wholeheartedly declare that there is nobody in the world in whom I have more confidence, to whom I owe more, and for whom I have more respect and attachment.[128]

Gualterio, rather than James III, was now 'the person in the world for whom I have the most tender veneration and upon whose affection and good heart I depend the most'.[129]

In September, James III finalized the arrangements for his marriage to Princess Clementina. Hay had been sent to visit Prince Sobieski at Ohlau and to accompany the latter's wife and daughter over the Alps to Italy; Hay's wife was told to meet them at the frontier of the Papal States and accompany them to Ferrara; and Murray was given a warrant to marry the princess by proxy if for any reason that should prove necessary.[130] Nairne informed Gualterio:

the favourite has already been sent ahead with vital recommendations, his wife will go to the frontier and the brother-in-law as soon as he is well enough[131] will perform the marriage by proxy, and everything will be done as decided in order to satisfy people to whom everything is granted.

He hoped that 'the public will not perceive the glaring favouritism of which I am only too well aware',[132] because Murray in particular was given 'every honour imaginable'.[133] The king himself would be accompanied by Mar, Father Brown, Dr Maghie[134] and a few household servants to Bologna,

Figure 11. *Cardinal Filippo Antonio Gualterio*, c.1720 (90 × 70 cm),
by Antonio David (private collection)
This portrait was later included in the large painting by David of the Baptism
of Prince Charles in the Chapel Royal of the Palazzo del Re, 1725
(Scottish National Portrait Gallery).

where they would wait for news that Hay, his wife and the two princesses had arrived at Ferrara. The king's party would then also go to Ferrara where the wedding would take place. The fact that Nairne was excluded, when he had always in the past been one of the few selected to accompany the king, showed very clearly the extent to which he had lost favour.[135]

Nairne remained at Urbino waiting for the news of the king's marriage at Ferrara, and enjoying the singing of Innocenza Magnani and the harpsichord playing of Agostino Tinnazoli. It is interesting to note that he was invited on more than one occasion to dine with the Pope's nephew, Don Carlo Albani in his palazzo. Apart from Albani's wife, the other guests were the latter's mother-in-law (contessa Boromei), his sister-in-law (marchesa Bentivoglio) and the latter's husband.[136] The contrast between the way he was treated by Albani and the way he was treated by James III, who left him to eat on the second table, inevitably reinforced Nairne's sense of dissatisfaction with his position at the Jacobite court. On 20 October, he sent a remarkably frank letter to Gualterio, re-emphasizing how much he wished that his financial situation, and the expenses of maintaining his children, would permit him to retire, leave the court, and return to his previous life as an ex-patriate in France:

> I would serve with greater pleasure and possibly speak the truth more robustly on some occasions, but since that is not fitting for the lowliest and least wealthy of servants, I take the option of a *silence respectueux*, and if I do not choose to retire as well, it is not that I view it as a temptation or a wicked thought that should be driven away, on the contrary I believe nothing is more natural nor more pardonable at my age and after 30 years of work than wishing to leave troubles behind and to find a little peace and quiet, with all the little comforts and the satisfaction suitable for my chartacter. I am not so vain as to believe myself indispensable to the King, the young man [i.e. Murray] is perfectly capable of fulfilling my duties and he will then be rewarded and rejoice in every imaginable honour that I myself was only granted in part. It is therefore only my own situation that does not allow me to withdraw with dignity, and in this I must accept my fate and resign myself to Providence. And that Monseigneur is what I try to do as well as I can.[137]

Later the same day, shortly after writing this letter, Nairne and the other members of the court at Urbino received the dramatic news that Hay and the two Sobieski princesses had been arrested at Innsbruck on

the orders of the Emperor Charles VI, and that the planned marriage at
Ferrara had therefore to be postponed indefinitely.[138] With Hay under
arrest at Innsbruck, Murray waiting at Ferrara for Hay and the princesses
to arrive, and Mar waiting with the king at Bologna for the news that they
had arrived, James III had no one other than Nairne to whom he could
now turn. So the latter suddenly found that, after all, he was 'indispensable' the king. On the 22nd, he received a letter from James ordering him
to 'go immediately to Rome in the Duke of Mar's French chair' to obtain
the diplomatic support of the Pope against the Emperor.[139] From being the
increasingly marginalized secretary of the king's closet at Urbino, Nairne
now found himself transformed into the Jacobite minister to the papal
court in Rome.

***

Nairne's arrival at Rome in October 1718 coincided almost exactly with
the thirtieth anniversary of the revolution of 1688 and the exile of James
II, Queen Mary and their six-month-old son (the future James III) to
Saint-Germain. In January 1719, therefore, it was thirty years since David
Nairne had first been employed by Lord Melfort in the political secretariat
of the exiled court. For most of that time Nairne had been a voluntary
ex-patriate rather than a reluctant exile, and it is possible, if not probable,
that he would have remained in France had there been a successful Jacobite
restoration – in 1692, or 1696, or 1708 or 1716. The failure of the rising in
Scotland in 1715–16, however, changed Nairne's situation, because he was
obliged to leave France and follow James III to Italy, so that, just like all the
other members of the court, he was no longer living in the country of his
choice. In that sense he too was now a political exile, cut off from his family
and friends in France and totally dependent on the king for his livelihood.

Nairne's changed status was emphasized because he stopped receiving
the French pension of 400 *livres per annum* which he had been granted in
1686.[140] He wrote in January 1719 that '4 or 5 years ago a small pension I
had been receiving from the Royal Treasury in France for 32 years stopped
and I miss having it.'[141] This implies that the officials in the French treasury
stopped paying him his pension either after the death of Louis XIV in 1715
or after the departure of the Jacobite court to Avignon in 1716, and either
way this reinforced Nairne's total dependence on the king. In November

1717 one of the new Scottish exiles complained that Nairne and the other old servants from Saint-Germain 'esteem themselves the only sufferers for the King, while they have been growing rich by him these nine and twenty years, and are in better circumstances than they could ever hope for, had he been on his throne'.[142] Leaving on one side the fact that Nairne had always worked extremely hard in the secretariat to earn his salary, there was some truth in the last part of this comment, especially now that he was a political exile as well as an ex-patriate. But he had certainly not been 'growing rich'.

By 1717, when he first arrived at Urbino, Nairne had to consider how to provide for his three children, because the absence of his French pension was making it difficult to maintain them. Françoise and Marie had both been living at the English Augustinian convent in Paris since their mother's death in March 1715,[143] and Louis had been a boarder at the Collège des Ecossais next door since leaving the English Jesuit college at Saint-Omer in January 1717.[144] Both the English Augustinian convent and the Collège des Ecossais charged fees, which Nairne was finding it increasingly difficult to pay without getting into debt, so he needed to look for some relief. One possibility was to obtain positions for his children at the Jacobite court. Françoise was twenty-three in October 1717 and well qualified to join the household of the new queen. Moreover she was one of James III's god-daughters. Louis was eighteen in December 1717 and might also have obtained a post at the court, perhaps in the secretariat with his father. Marie, the youngest, was seventeen in January 1718, and also qualified to be given a position with the new queen, but in fact she wanted to become a nun. Having served both James II and James III for so long, Nairne reasonably hoped to obtain positions at the court for Françoise and Louis, and some financial assistance from the king towards paying the dowry which Marie would need to become a nun.

It soon became clear at Urbino, however, that James III was not willing to do anything to help. The king said he would be 'just' but not 'kind', unlike James II, who had been both just and kind. In fact, James III was not willing even to be kind to Nairne, and the latter came to realize that he would have to look elsewhere for assistance. As he became increasingly discontented at the Jacobite court, he turned more to Cardinal Gualterio to give him the help that he badly needed. By 1718 the only thing which stopped him leaving the court was his lack of independent financial means and his continuing duty to provide for his children. While he was at Urbino, he became more and more conscious that he was originally only an expatriate, and increasingly keen to revert to a life of retirement with his family and friends in France if only he could escape from the court in Italy.

By the beginning of May 1718, Nairne was seriously worried about his finances, and commented that 'I really cannot hold out any longer wth the charge I am at wth my children'.[145] His children had inherited their mother's one-third share of the family estate at Compigny, but Nairne for the time being had no hope of recovering his estate at Sandford for his son:

> I have nothing to leave to him, and in the present state of affairs if I died today, he and his two sisters would be reduced to begging: a sad fate for the poor children of a father who has served the King for 30 years.[146]

It was under these circumstances that he developed a plan for finishing Louis' education in Italy.

Nairne's annual salary from James III was 2,461 *livres* 18s 0d,[147] yet the cost of keeping Louis at the Collège des Ecossais was about 3,600 *livres per annum*,[148] and on top of that he had to maintain his daughters in the English Augustinian convent. Presumably the difference between his income and this expenditure had to some extent been covered by the income from any investments he had in Paris, as well as money from the Compigny estate, but it seems that those sources were insufficient and that Nairne was faced with the prospect of borrowing money and running up substantial debts. The idea of taking his son out of the Collège des Ecossais and bringing him to Italy was therefore attractive on financial grounds alone.[149]

Yet there was another reason for bringing Louis to Italy: he was behaving badly at the college. At first Nairne's friends were too tactful to tell him the truth, merely suggesting that at eighteen years of age the boy might benefit from seeing more of the world and learning Italian.[150] By May, however, the situation was becoming too difficult, and Nairne observed that 'as to my son I find he'l be lost in Paris if some new measures be not taken to keep him out of bad company and moderat his excessive inclinations to satisfy his own will'.[151] For Nairne, who was so pious and moderate in his own behaviour, this news was particularly worrying, and especially as it exactly coincided with his growing dissatisfaction at Urbino. When several of his friends urged him to get his son away from

Paris as soon as possible, he noted that 'I am afraid there are some strong reasons for that, wch not to chagrine me too much are not told me'. He added: 'I pray God I may be mistaken but I fear everything from youth and ill company'.[152]

On 20 March Nairne sent a confidential letter, to Gualterio in which he asked him to recommend Louis to Cosimo III, the Grand Duke of Tuscany, to be employed by him as a page. He also asked if he (Nairne) should try to get a second letter of recommendation from Cardinal Davia. Gualterio was bound to wonder why Nairne did not seek employment for his son at the Jacobite court, so he explained:

> an unconquerable distaste that I have even to give the appearance of wishing to introduce my son to the Court of the King without being asked to do so, still less to ask H. M. for a position for him in the household, knowing how many requests of this nature he receives and not wanting to increase the numbers of those bothering him, all of that makes me feel I must sacrifice my modesty, which I see as a duty and a matter of honour for a good and neutral servant. But as I am a father as well as a servant, I am obliged by my conscience to think of my son's future.[153]

Gualterio sent a positive reply and told Nairne he would give him two letters of recommendation to be sent to Florence: one for the Grand Duke himself and one for his *maestro di camera*, Tommaso Del Bene.[154] He also agreed that Nairne should try to get another letter of recommendation to the Grand Duke from Cardinal Davia.[155]

During April, therefore, Nairne wrote to Davia, who consented to give him a letter which he could send with the two from Gualterio.[156] They were despatched to Florence on the 22nd, and Nairne noted that if his request was refused by the Grand Duke he would not tell James III. If, on the other hand, it was accepted, 'then it will be my duty to speak to him about it and to have his agreement'.[157] In fact Nairne changed his mind and did tell the king, who remarked that he approved of what Nairne had done, because he would not have been willing to approach the Grand Duke himself.[158] While awaiting a reply from Florence, Nairne wrote to tell Thomas Innes at the Collège des Ecossais what he had done:

> As for the K's recommendation I did not ask it and I did well for he would not have given it. I have told him now what I have done, and he could not blame me for employing my friends, on such an occasion.

But Nairne resented the king's lack of interest:

> after what he has seen me forced to do about my son without making me [the] least
> offer of his taking care of him, or so much as a compliment for his not being in a
> condition to do it at present you may judge what I have to expect.[159]

Partly prompted by their correspondence with Nairne concerning these letters of recommendation, Cardinals Gualterio and Davia decided to visit James III at Urbino,[160] where they arrived on 10 May. Davia stayed for two days only,[161] whereas Gualterio remained at the Jacobite court until the beginning of June,[162] but they both brought with them the letters which they had received in reply from the Grand Duke of Tuscany.

It turned out that Louis at eighteen years of age was too old to start as a page, because that was the age at which pages ceased to be employed at the Tuscan court. But the Grand Duke offered to pay 'not only the accommodation but also the maintenance' for Louis to be educated for two years in a college[163] 'where he may finish his education and exercises'. Both cardinals recommended Nairne to accept the offer, which they regarded as better training than being a page, and proposed that Louis should be sent to the Collegio Clementino in Rome which Nairne already knew, and which he described as 'a sort of academy where they learn to ride and generally every thing els, and they are all gentlemen that are there'. As Gualterio's nephews were already at the college Nairne hastily accepted their suggestion, hoping that the patronage of the Grand Duke and the two cardinals would procure an employment for his son when he left the college. 'This is no settlement for my son', he wrote, 'but still it may be a way towards it by improving him farther in what may make him more capable to seek his own fortune hereafter since I have none to give him'.[164]

In addition to opening up employment prospects for his son, the Grand Duke's offer promised greatly to ease Nairne's pressing financial problems. As the latter put it, 'this Providential generosity has come just in time to rescue my poor family'.[165] But any pleasure that he felt was dented by the lack of interest which was shown by the king. In fact James III had forgotten that the two visiting cardinals were helping Nairne which, as the latter wrote, 'put me a little out of countenance'. When Cardinal Davia left Urbino Nairne got up early so that he could see him 'to his chair' at five o' clock in the morning in order to thank him for what he had done. Then, when Nairne saw the king later that day, he explained what had been decided about the Collegio Clementino in Rome, adding that 'by this means my son would learn Italian at least, and give me time to see to provide otherwise for him'. But James III remained indifferent:

> To all wch he made me no offer and so it passd, indifferently enough as I thought on both sides, thô the Card.ls had assurd me he had spoke extreme kindly of me to them yesterday wch costs nothing.... I have [reason] to think I have no real effects shewd of me of a hearty affection, and just sense of my modesty in my hard circumstances after so many years service.[166]

In the second half of May, Nairne asked Thomas and Lewis Innes to send his son to Italy as quickly, but also as cheaply, as possible. One possibility was that he might accompany Dominic Sheldon, who said that he might perhaps return to Urbino, but Nairne doubted that he really would, 'because I am sure in his place I would not'.[167] Sheldon did not return, so in the end Nairne's friends at the Collège des Ecossais arranged for Louis to leave Paris by himself in the middle of July and travel via Marseille, Livorno and Florence, where he was to be looked after by Salviati's family before finishing his journey to Urbino.[168] The whole journey would unavoidably cost a great deal of money, but Nairne felt that it was worth it:

> I know ... that his travel expenses are going to be a problem, but I can regret nothing for the education of my only son, and if I have to produce a supplement from my own funds to maintain him in Rome I will continue to cut almost everything to fulfil my duty towards him.[169]

Louis Nairne did not join his father at Urbino until 9 August,[170] and while awaiting his arrival Nairne came to realize that he had no hope of obtaining a post for Françoise in the household of the new queen. He explained the situation frankly to Gualterio in a letter of 1 July:

> I confess to Y. E., from whom I can keep nothing hidden, that I find it impossible to close my eyes to what I see distributed around me every day not only in compliments but in actual benefits to other new favourites. ... Y. E. will see that when we are fortunate enough to have a queen, these men's wives, relatives and friends will be put above everyone, and not even the smallest position will be given to my elder daughter, though she is the King's god-daughter.

Nairne felt that Françoise was well suited to be appointed a bedchamber woman, or a 'maid of honour' if it was decided that the bedchamber women should all be married.

> If one truly wanted to console an old and loyal servant, that would be the way. Everyone knows that I love my daughter very much and that she deserves it for her good qualities and sensible behaviour, added to which she is pleasing to look at. But Y. E. will see that it will not even be considered and I will not mention it, my modest nature being too proud to risk a refusal.

Apologizing for saying this to Gualterio, Nairne told the cardinal that he was 'the only person in the world to whom I know I can safely open my heart and who is kind enough to take an interest in my littles troubles, with more kindness than I merit.'[171]

Gualterio replied by urging Nairne to ask the king to give his daughter a post in the new queen's household, and even offered to write to the king himself on his behalf. But Nairne was not to be persuaded:

> As for my daughter, Y. E. will permit me to persist in my total determination not to ask H. M. either directly or indirectly for anything for myself or my family. He honours me with his confidence and that is enough for me. His tendency to distribute his other favours is turned in an entirely different direction.

He added that he did not want Gualterio to write on his behalf to the king, as he was convinced that it would not succeed:

> I especially beg you that I shall not be seen or suspected to be the one asking, as I declare sincerely to Y. E. that all I have written on the subject has been to impart in confidence what any good father would wish.

In conclusion he had 'very little hope of success', but would not try to stop Gualterio approaching the king if he wanted to do so.[172]

This general attitude of reserve was unlikely to help procure a post for his daughter, but nevertheless Gualterio renewed his offer to ask the king to give her one. Nairne replied by explaining that the wives of John Hay and Lord Nithsdale had already been offered positions:

> As for my daughter, Y. E. is too kind towards her and me and I am embarrassed. I admit that it would be a great comfort for me to have her near me and to see her provided for, but I have little hope of it ... he has not even thought of my daughter,

and thinks me philosophical enough not to care about my own and my family's concerns. Every day he distributes favours to others and he informs me of them, but that is all, and I say nothing, but think much. I shall see everyone rewarded and all the newcomers passing before me. Please God that this will never make me fail in my duty.[173]

Once again Gualterio offered to speak to the king on his behalf, and this time Nairne agreed – so long as the king would not think that he had asked Gualterio to do this:

> Where my daughter is concerned, however much I long to see her provided for before I die, I confess to Y. E. that I will never make up my mind to open my mouth myself to the King nor can I consent that others speak to him for me. I prefer to leave all that to Providence and retain the virtue of humility, avoiding at the same time the sorrow of a refusal. So that if the opportunity arises, and if the exceeding kindness Y. E. shows me ... ever brings you to speak about my daughter to the King, I beg that it should be with so much circumspection that H. M. cannot suspect that I asked you, as indeed I have not done so.

Nairne added that he loved Françoise 'tenderly' and that she was not 'unworthy', but that he had 'made a vow to depend entirely on the King's will in everything concerning myself and my family', and that he had resolved never to 'importune the King nor to have others intercede on my behalf'.[174] A few days later he complained that 'I have nothing to hope for' and that 'my fate is to continue to work, often without satisfaction, and always without expecting reward at least in this world'.[175] And in the end Gualterio was unable to speak to the king because a visit which he planned to make in September was cancelled.[176]

When Louis Nairne arrived at Urbino on 9 August, he and his father had not seen each other for nearly six years, since James III had left Saint-Germain in 1712, taking Nairne with him. The boy had then been only twelve years old. He had been sent as a boarder to the English Benedictine monastery at Douai, and thus separated from his mother and sisters, and while he was there (aged fifteen), in the spring of 1715, his mother had died at Compigny. Shortly afterwards he had been moved to the English Jesuit college at Saint-Omer, before being moved again to the Collège des Ecossais in Paris.[177] It was perhaps not to be expected that he and his father would get on well together when they were reunited after so long, but their relations quickly became worse than perhaps either of them expected. Louis

Nairne was extravagant and irresponsible, keen to enjoy himself to the full, and with absolutely no interest in academic or intellectual pursuits. Moreover, he almost certainly thought he was more mature and grown up than he actually was. These characteristics were bound to bring him into conflict with a father whose excessive modesty and self-effacement have been only too clearly revealed in the present chapter.

It did not take long for Nairne and his son to reach a fundamental disagreement, because the boy had never been told that, having left the Collège des Ecossais, he was to be sent to another college in Rome. It soon transpired that he wanted to be a soldier, had no interest in 'science or literature', and felt that at eighteen years of age he was too old to be sent back to any college. As Nairne put it, 'as soon as my son arrived I saw that he did not wish to go to the college'.[178] He hoped his son would change his mind once he had entered the Collegio Clementino,[179] but Louis told his father that he did not intend to go there. For five weeks there was an impasse, during which Nairne remained optimistic that Louis *would* go to the college and continued to correspond with Gualterio about various details.[180] These were mainly financial,[181] and Nairne was keen that when his son was at the college he should be able to go out into society properly dressed, as well as to buy books and mathematical instruments, and to have a music teacher.[182]

When he arrived at Urbino the boy had been well received by the king,[183] and on one occasion he had eaten at the second table with his father, but Nairne sensed that James was not pleased:

> As concerns dining with me, I have decided that he will not do so unless the King himself orders it, without which command I can suppose he does not wish it, and I believe in doing this I am acting for the best, though the company has urged him several times to eat with us but have no more right to do so than I have. If the King wished it he would tell me himself, and I myself am not in the mood to ask for such things and still less to do them without asking.

This meant that Nairne now had the additional expense of paying for his son's food at Urbino. He had already had to borrow money to pay for the journey from Paris, and knew he would have to borrow even more to send him on to Rome. Louis then told his father that he had not only spent all the money he had been given for his journey from Paris but had borrowed money when he was at Florence,[184] which of course increased his father's debts. All of this made Nairne keen to send his son to Rome as soon as possible, so that he could begin to be at the charge of the Grand Duke,[185] and he was extremely disappointed when Gualterio strongly advised him that it would be dangerous to expose his son to the 'challeurs' of Rome before the beginning of November.[186] This meant that he had to find somewhere for his son to live at Urbino, and he was relieved when his friend Eustachio Buglioni offered to provide accommodation for Louis without asking for any payment.[187] This arrangement, and the prospect of having his son eventually paid for by the Grand Duke, was a great help, as he explained to Gualterio:

> I am still delighted to have found through you this slight relief of my domestic problems for the present, although the outlay I made for my son's travel will continue to inconvenience me for some while, but I have the pleasant thought that he will receive a good education under Y. E.'s eye, after which Providence will provide. Thank God that for a long time now I feel perfectly resigned for myself and my concerns. All I ask of God is that He gives me grace to do my duty faithfully to the end, and that I obtain salvation. Apart from these He may do with me and mine as He pleases.[188]

But Nairne could not help noticing that the king made no effort to help him:

> I am very sensitive about seeming to be a man desirous of introducing his son here for personal gain. As he was not invited to come ... I think the less time he remains here the better.[189]

Shortly after this, when the king was preparing to leave Urbino to meet Princess Clementina at Ferrara, Louis Nairne decided to rebel against his father, by completely refusing to go to the Collegio Clementino in Rome. His father later recalled that,

> he declared that having no inclination to go into the Church or administration, and having studied enough philosophy and the humanities in France for the army career to which he was drawn, he could not accept, having seen and had some experience of the world, to return at his age to a College with children, and nobody had told him that that would be the case when he left France otherwise he would have spoken his mind earlier.[190]

The result was a terrible scene between father and son, at the end of which Nairne gave Louis an ultimatum: either go to the college, or leave and make his own way in life. Unfortunately the boy called his father's bluff, packed up to leave, and tried to get a horse from Buglioni. The latter warned Nairne who, in desperation, told the king what had happened. James III then summoned Louis and tried to reason with him, explaining that neither he (James) nor the boy's father would be able to procure him a commission in any regiment. The king also tried to persuade Louis to go to the Collegio Clementino, but the boy again refused, after which Nairne told Gualterio that his son had become violent, saying that life and death were all the same to him.[191]

Nairne decided that he would have to give way, particularly as the king told him that the boy was too old to be forced. So Nairne wondered if Louis might complete his education in Rome somewhere other than the Collegio Clementino, where he might have more liberty. This, however, raised the problem of finance, as the Grand Duke had offered to pay for Louis' education in a college, and had also agreed that the Collegio Clementino should be the one selected.

In any event, Nairne was now more than ever keen to get his son away from Urbino, because 'I was a little suspicious that certain young people at our court had encouraged his aversion to going to the College'.[192] Knowing that Gualterio was leaving Rome to spend the autumn at his country estate at Corgnolo (near Orvieto),[193] Nairne asked him if he would be prepared to receive his son and make one final attempt to make him see reason.[194] Gualterio agreed, and Louis left Urbino on 30 September. 'He is not leaving in disgrace', Nairne wrote, 'since he had the honour of kissing the King's hand yesterday evening, and H. M. spoke to him so graciously that I was quite flustered and very touched.'[195] He also told Gualterio that he had had a reconciliation with his son, who promised to be obedient in all other matters, and that he regretted having tried to force him to go to the college. After all, a military career would be respectable, even though he would have preferred his son to earn his living with 'the pen'. Moreover, if he went to the college the staff would soon have to complain about him, and the Grand Duke would hear about it. In conclusion, he lamented that his son had too much 'hauteur' and wanted too much liberty.[196]

By the beginning of October, when Louis Nairne joined Cardinal Gualterio at Corgnolo, James III was preparing to leave Urbino with the Duke of Mar and travel to Bologna. Before he left he sent the following letter to the cardinal:

> I am ashamed for poor Nairn [*sic*] that he sent you his son to bother you in the country, but I did not dare to prevent him because he is old and takes umbrage easily and ... is to be pitied for having such a son.

He added that he thought Nairne was 'too lenient with' his son.[197] Nairne himself, who was to remain at Urbino without either his son or the king, admitted to Gualterio that

> His obstinate refusal to attend the College causes me grief and anxiety. I expect little satisfaction from my post, nor a fortune for myself and my family, and I am too old to start a new life elsewhere.[198]

Nairne remained at Urbino for another three weeks, during which he kept in regular contact with Gualterio at Corgnolo. On 6 October, he hoped that the latter would write on his behalf to the Grand Duke:

> I am anxious to learn whether Y. E. has had the kindness to write to the Grand Duke to attempt to obtain his continuing favours for my son independently of the College. I am extremely annoyed that my son's lack of sense has forced me to make this change, for he has certainly chosen a wrong path for his own good, but I still flatter myself that he will conduct himself so well in Rome that his folly will be remedied ... Nevertheless if the G. Duke abandons me over this, I will be in a sad predicament.

Knowing his son's extravagance, he specifically asked Gualterio not to mention how much money might still be available from the Grand Duke:

> if I am fortunate enough to be given the 400 Scudi I would ask Y. E. to say nothing to my son as to the amount, because being open-handed as he is, it would encourage him to be extravagant, whereas believing it to be only half that amount, necessity would oblige him to be more economical.[199]

Three days later he sent Gualterio 'an enclosed letter concerning my son' which the cardinal could send on to the Grand Duke if he wanted. The letter summarized what had happened since Louis' arrival at Urbino, and emphasized that the boy had now promised to behave himself very well, and willingly study dancing, mathematics, fortification, history and music for two years in Rome, so long as he was not enclosed in a college.[200] In a covering letter for Gualterio, he hoped that he, as the boy's father, might be allowed to select what he now regarded as the most appropriate education for his son, and that the Grand Duke would not concern himself with the details, as 'the suggestion that he go to the college came from our side and not his'.[201]

Fortunately for Nairne, Cardinal Gualterio did agree to write on his behalf to the Grand Duke, though he did not use the 'enclosed letter'.[202] He also offered to pay for Louis to be accommodated temporarily in his palazzo at Orvieto, under the supervision of one of the canons of the cathedral, an offer which Nairne quickly accepted.[203] The latter commented that 'my son's lack of financial sense is incomprehensible', that his son 'is too caught up in gaming and other extravagant expenses', and is 'completely absorbed in his entertainments'.[204]

The Grand Duke's reply was not received for several weeks, and in the meantime Nairne was ordered by James III to leave Urbino and go to Rome to obtain the support of the Pope for having Princess Clementina released. He was given an apartment in the palazzo which Gualterio occupied on the Corso, and it was there, on 12 November, that he received the news from the cardinal that the Grand Duke had agreed to pay the money he had promised, even if Louis did not attend a college. The Grand Duke, however, did make it clear that his support would be limited to two years. Nairne commented that 'the fact of restricting the pension to two years is not ideal, because it seems to preclude any hope from that quarter of further favours or a position for my son'.[205] Nevertheless Nairne knew how lucky he was and wrote to Gualterio to express his gratitude.[206]

The Grand Duke had arranged for all the money (800 *scudi* for two years) to be paid to his agent in Rome, and then handed to Gualterio when the latter returned from his country estate at Cornolo.[207] Gualterio would then give Nairne 400 *scudi* to cover each year, the first when he returned to Rome, and the second one year later. But Nairne was now so much in debt that he hoped that Gualterio would give him the money for the first year immediately, and the money for the second year in May. His son had already cost him 1,000 *livres* during the six months since he left Paris, 'not counting the provisions made there for his journey', and Nairne explained that

> a thousand livres ... is about half a year's pension that has already been spent and the other half will scarcely cover all the expenses of his first 6 months of living in Rome.

Because the Grand Duke had originally agreed to pay the money for two years in May 1718 he hoped that the pension might be regarded as having started then, so that he could receive the money for the second year in May 1719. This meant that his son would only be able to study in Rome for one year, but Nairne hoped that during that period Louis might be able to obtain a post in the service of Spain, the Grand Duke or the Pope. 'I estimate', he wrote,

> half a year of his two years' pension to support him at first in his post, half a year already spent, and one year for his upkeep in Rome. That makes 2 years by my calculations.[208]

Gualterio did not rule out doing what Nairne had asked, but he made it clear that no money could be paid until he himself had returned to Rome and seen the Grand Duke's agent.[209] And a new development had taken place to delay his return. James III had arrived in Rome on 14 November, and moved in to the Palazzo Gualterio with his most important courtiers and essential household servants. This meant that for the moment there was no room for Gualterio in his own home, and that he would not be able to return to Rome until the Jacobite court had found another building and vacated his palazzo. Nairne's financial position became more and more desperate.

Louis had meanwhile left Orvieto and joined his father in Rome on 9 November, having already spent all the money he had been given and having had to borrow eighteen *scudi* from Gualterio to make the journey.[210] The cardinal had failed to persuade him to go to the Collegio Clementino, even as an *externe*,[211] so Nairne had to find lodgings for his son,[212] as well as clothes[213] and various teachers. By the end of November, Nairne had arranged for Louis to start riding lessons in the *manège* of Prince Rospigliosi, and had found 'two masters, one for dancing and one for weapons train-ing'.[214] In the following weeks, he employed additional teachers for math-ematics and music, but stopped the dancing lessons because of he could not afford them. Thus his son did riding and weapons training each morning, and mathematics and music each afternoon, with some recreation time in between.[215] After a few weeks, however, Nairne was obliged to stop the music lessons as well because he could not afford to pay the teacher.[216]

Despite all his father's efforts, Louis soon began to complain that he did not have enough 'liberté'[217] and refused to account for any of the money he was given.[218] When news reached Rome in November 1718 that war had broken out between Spain and the Emperor, Louis told his father that he wanted to join the campaign in Sicily immediately, despite having neither money nor a military commission, and added: 'I will manage it somehow or I will beat my brains out, life and death are the same to me.'[219] Nairne confided to Gualterio in December that he was finding it increasingly dif-ficult to stop his son from going to Sicily and that, despite all his efforts, he was unable to do anything to keep Louis contented in Rome.[220]

At first Nairne still hoped to keep his son in Rome for one year, feel-ing that Louis was too immature to behave sensibly in the army and that he would quickly run up debts.[221] But his son was increasingly arrogant[222] and immediately spent any money that he was given.[223] By the beginning of January 1719, therefore, Nairne's financial situation was so desperate that he braced himself to ask Gualterio to give him all the Grand Duke's money in one payment, without waiting until May to hand over the 400 scudi of the second year. On 5 January, he wrote two long letters, one an 'enclosed letter' which could be forwarded to the Grand Duke, the other a letter of explanation for Gualterio only.

In the former letter he explained that he had exhausted his credit and that he could no longer support his family. He enclosed a memoire show-ing how much money he had already had to spend on his son, and what he would now need to keep him in Rome for one year, which would be much more than if Louis had agreed to go to the Collegio Clementino. He asked Gualterio to give him all the money immediately, and stated that at the end of one year in Rome his son would start on a military career.[224]

In the second letter Nairne explained that he had been waiting for Gualterio to return to Rome so that he could explain his financial difficulties in person, but that the delay in finding a new building for the Jacobite court meant that he could wait no longer. Moreover, the difference in the exchange rate between Urbino and Rome had reduced his salary by 'about 20 *livres* a month', and in addition he now had to pay for his own 'board and lodging', all of which he had received at the king's expense in the palazzo ducale at Urbino, 'which comes to nearly 100 *livres* a month' on a salary of 205 *livres*. This, he explained, was why he could no longer sustain the expense of keeping his son, and why he had decided to send the enclosed letter. If he could receive all the money in one instalment, once Gualterio returned to Rome, then he might be able to keep his son properly for one year, during which he would do all he could to find some military employment for him.[225]

Nairne obviously felt very uncomfortable about making this request, because he sent another letter two days later, before he had received Gualterio's reply. In this one he apologized for the liberty he had taken in sending the previous ones, but said that the only thing that would now save him from dishonour, and give him time to find employment for his son in Spain or elsewhere, was to receive the Grand Duke's money in advance. He promised to keep strict accounts, including even the cost of washing clothes, and told Gualterio that he did not have a 'domestique' to keep him and his son decent. He added in conclusion that he was not willing to ask the king for help and would continue

> to show the reserve and silence that I am determined never to break before the King, however tempted I may be in the face of the easy and contented lives being enjoyed by the new favourites, who lack nothing. But as far as I can I try to reject such grumbling thoughts, as being unworthy of a Christian and a gentleman. But being neither blind nor insensitive I admit, to my shame, that it pains me.[226]

Not surprisingly, Gualterio wrote back to say that he did not feel able to give Nairne all the Grand Duke's money in one instalment, and that he would have to give him the second payment of 400 *scudi* one year after the first, so Nairne said he would have to sell his remaining *rente* in Paris. After all, he said, Louis *was* his son, and he had to carry out his paternal duty.[227] But Gualterio strongly advised him against selling his *rente*, except 'as a last resort', so Nairne agreed that he would do everything else possible in Rome – except of course to importune the king.[228] He was now so much in debt, he said, that when Gualterio arrived and gave him the money for the first year it would all be used to repay the money he had had to borrow. He added that he would force himself to live on bread and water only rather than to borrow money he could not repay.[229]

Nairne's remaining hope was that France might join the war on the side of the Emperor against Spain. In this event it might become easier for Louis to obtain a commission in the Spanish army. It was an indication of how desperate Nairne had become that he now felt that that would be a better option than keeping his son in Rome for one year.[230] It must also have been a personal sadness that the change in French foreign policy since the death of Louis XIV made such a thing necessary. Nairne's son had been born and brought up in France, with a French mother and an ex-patriate Scottish father who had chosen to make France his home. The boy was now keen to join the Spanish army and fight against his own country.

On 1 February, the news reached Rome that France had declared war on Spain.[231] A few days later James III left Rome with John Hay to travel to Spain, where he would join a Spanish invasion force destined for England. At the same time the Duke of Mar left Rome with John Paterson, his under-secretary, to travel overland to join the king in England. A palazzo had been selected in the piazza dei Santi Apostoli to be occupied by the Jacobite court, allowing Gualterio to return to Rome, and one of the last things James did before he left was to order that Nairne's son was 'to be lodged in the house in Mr Patersons lodging'.[232]

Gualterio did not return to Rome and give Nairne his first 400 *scudi* until the beginning of March,[233] but in the meantime he promised Nairne that once he was there he would do everything he could to secure a commission in the Spanish army for Louis.[234] In practice this meant speaking to Cardinal Francesco Aquaviva, the Spanish ambassador. For the rest of February, therefore, Nairne had to be patient. His credit had run out, he had to send most of the money he still had to settle a debt in France, and he now hoped that the second instalment of money from the Grand Duke, when eventually received, might be spent on maintaining his son in the Spanish army until the latter could be paid, rather than on educating him in Rome.[235]

Much to Nairne's relief, Cardinal Aquaviva, when approached by Gualterio, arranged for Louis to be given a commission as an ensign in a newly formed Spanish regiment.[236] His commission was even backdated by five months to 17 October 1718, so that he could be given money in advance to buy some of the things he needed: 'a dozen shirts ... with cravats and other suitable garments, a complete outfit with an overcoat and a cloak and all the rest, a silver cutlery set, and several other essentials, with a small camp bed.'[237]

Louis Nairne departed from Rome at the end of April, having thanked Cardinal Aquaviva,[238] and having been taken by his father to receive a blessing from the Pope.[239] He travelled to Livorno and thence to Porto Longone on the island of Elba, where his regiment was stationed.[240] This, however, was not the end of Nairne's financial worries, partly because Louis did not receive any more pay until the end of the year, and partly because his son immediately ran up considerable gambling debts. So Nairne had to go on sending him money which he could not afford.[241] Because his son had joined the Spanish army instead of continuing his education in Rome, Gualterio was uncertain about giving Nairne the second instalment of the Grand Duke's money when it eventually became due. By September Nairne was so desperately in debt that he asked Gualterio to obtain the Grand Duke's permission to make the second payment that autumn, without waiting any longer. Reminding the cardinal that 'it is now more than 14 months since my son arrived in Italy, and since he had the honour of being presented to H. R. H. [the Grand Duke], and that but for the great heat he would have arrived in Rome at the beginning of October when he went to Orvieto under the supervision of Y. E.', he admitted quite frankly:

> The reason for my haste (apart from the debts run up on behalf of my son) is that I am still afraid H. R. H., if he discovers that my son is in the service of Spain, will make changes, and it will be difficult to conceal the truth for long.[242]

It says a lot about Gualterio's warm feelings of friendship towards Nairne that he was prepared to do as requested, and that he persuaded the Grand Duke to authorize the payment of the second instalment of 400 *scudi* to Nairne without waiting for a year to elapse since the first. The letter in which Nairne thanked him for doing this is dated 4 November 1719, and is actually the last letter between the two men in which the problems caused by Louis Nairne are mentioned. The letter is intriguing because, instead of saying that he would use the money to maintain his son in the Spanish army until he was paid, or to pay for his son's gambling debts of

90 *scudi*, Nairne told Gualterio that he intended to send most of the money to help his daughter Marie in France![243] As we shall now see, the problems that Nairne had in maintaining his daughters in France had become even greater than the problems he had in maintaining his son in Italy.

In a letter dated January 1719 Nairne wrote that his younger daughter Marie 'for 5 years has been asking my permission to become a nun with such an inspiring perseverance that I cannot doubt her vocation any longer and have consented'. This suggests that Marie had wanted to become a nun since the winter of 1713–14 when she was only thirteen years old, and when her mother (who died in March 1715) was still alive. The problem was that 'the English Convent where she is in Paris' were asking for '1000 *livres* for accepting her' and that, as Nairne put it, 'I cannot affort it'.[244]

Fortunately for Nairne, his elder daughter Françoise had no wish to become a nun. 'She is very happy to be unmarried', he wrote, 'and thanks to God I have the consolation to see that she is loved and respected by all who know her for her sensible and modest conduct'.[245] Nevertheless Nairne had to pay for the board and lodging of both girls at the English Augustinian convent because there was no prospect of obtaining a post for Françoise at the Jacobite court, and this was becoming increasingly difficult because of the heavy expenses incurred by their brother Louis in Rome.

It was agreed that Marie would take the habit of a novice or postulant at the convent in May, and that she could be admitted as a nun or canoness one year later. Before that could happen, however, Nairne would have to pay 1,000 *livres* to the convent, which was the equivalent of nearly five months of his salary. Heavily in debt in Rome, even after Louis was given his Spanish commission, Nairne now had to find this additional money. And not surprisingly he turned to Gualterio for help.

In an undated letter which Nairne sent to Gualterio at the end of January 1719, he wrote that he had been advised that there was money available in Rome to pay the dowries of girls who wanted to become nuns, even if they were not from Roman families.[246] When Gualterio returned at the beginning of March he agreed that money was available, and he advised Nairne to prepare a petition which could eventually be presented to the Pope. Before that could be done, however, Marie would have to be already accepted as a novice.[247]

The ceremony was scheduled to take place at the English Augustinian convent in Paris on 2 May. Françoise wrote to tell Nairne how happy her sister was, and how the latter seemed more beautiful since he had given his permission.[248] Marie then began the necessary preliminary retreat of eight days in a cell before the ceremony.[249] Marie herself wrote from her cell to her father: promising to think of him and her brother during the ceremony, she asked for her father's blessing and assured him that, despite taking the habit, she would always love him.[250]

The ceremony on 2 May started at 10.30 in the morning and lasted for over three hours. It was attended by all the nuns of the convent[251] and by many Jacobite ladies and gentlemen, nearly all of whom Nairne knew personally. Among the former were daughters of the 1st and 2nd Dukes of Powis, Lady Dillon and one of her daughters, Dorothy Sheldon (who would later become a friend of Queen Clementina) and one of the daughters of John Stafford.[252] Among the latter were Lord Montgomery (son of the 2nd Duke of Powis), Lord Linton and Mr Panton (both of whom had recently been at Urbino), and some of Nairne's closest friends: Lewis Innes and Charles Whiteford from the Collège des Ecossais next door, John Ingleton (previously James III's confessor) and Abbot Thomas Southcott (President of the English Benedictines). It was evidently an important social event for the Jacobite communities of both Paris and Saint-Germain, and all the guests were invited by Françoise to a dinner afterwards. Lewis Innes and Thomas Southcott both sent Nairne glowing accounts of how Françoise had organized everything to perfection, though the former added that she had invited too many people and spent more of Nairne's money than she should have. Both men were also full of compliments for Marie herself, telling Nairne that he was lucky to have such a daughter and that she was well suited to become a nun.[253]

Nairne received these letters in Rome in the middle of May, together with a long one from Françoise describing for him the ceremony in detail and repeating how happy Marie was. But the dowry now had to be found, and Françoise ended her long letter with these words:

> I hope ... My dear Father that Providence, which has so clearly called her to this state, will help you find the means in the course of this year to pay the dowry, which is all that is lacking for her to be happily settled.[254]

So Nairne now had to find an additional 1,000 *livres*, on top of all the money that Louis was costing him in equipment and gambling debts.

In the first half of June, therefore, Nairne composed a memoire which could be presented by Cardinal Gualterio as a petition to the Pope.[255] The memoire itself was very long, and Nairne attached to it copies of both the letters he had received from his daughters and the ones he had received from Lewis Innes and Thomas Southcott. The work involved was very considerable, because Gualterio advised Nairne that he should give copies to the Pope's three nephews and to the Cardinal Protectors of Scotland and Ireland, as well as to himself and the Pope, making seven copies in total, all of them in Nairne's own beautiful handwriting. They were finished by the 22nd[256] and Gualterio said he would present the original to the Pope soon after.[257]

The memoire, which was written in French, explained that Marie had for a long time wanted to become a nun, that she needed a dowry of 1,000 *livres* to be accepted by the convent, and that he, her father, was 'absolutely incapable of paying her dowry' because he was one of the 'poor Catholic refugees who are suffering for their faith and for their loyalty to their legitimate Prince, himself so unjustly persecuted for his Religion'. Nairne therefore begged the Pope to order that some of the money available to be given in charity 'to poor girls' might be employed in favour of his daughter. By June 1719, it was known in Rome that the Spanish attempt to invade England had failed, so Nairne included the following paragraph:

> If the King of England was in a state for me to plead with him, and if the recent measures to help his restoration had succeeded as quickly as we assumed, this supplicant is convinced that after 30 years of service, he would not have needed to look elsewhere than the generosity of H. M. for the establishment of this young woman who has the honour of being the goddaughter of the late Queen, as her elder sister is of the King.[258]

It is possible that Nairne really believed this, particularly if James III had succeeded in invading England, but most of the evidence suggests otherwise. On the other hand, Nairne did refer to his children in a letter which he sent to the king on 20 June, two days before he gave Gualterio his memoire for the Pope. In that letter he referred to 'my poor children who are at present a very great charge upon me, one of them being now actually a Novice of whose portion I must within a twelve month find 1000*l* God knows how'. He added, perhaps in the belief that James III might help him, his 'hope that Divine Providence ... will put me in some way or other in a condition to finish this pious work as also to support my son in the expensive but honourable trade he has taken'.[259]

It seems that the king ignored these comments, as well as Nairne's reminder in a letter of 12 August about the 'charge I have in France of two daughters, for the maintaining and settling of whom I have nothing in the world but Providence and your Ma.tys charity and goodness to trust to'.[260] Cardinal Gualterio, by contrast, now offered to do what he could to persuade the French treasury to resume the payment of Nairne's annual pension of 400 *livres*. In August he gave Nairne a 'life certificate' and a letter of recommendation, which the latter sent on to Françoise in Paris to be given to one of the officials at the French treasury.[261] This seems to have been a success, though it is not known when the first payment was made,[262] and anyway it would not have been enough to cover Marie's dowry.

In the end, Nairne felt that he had no option but to sell his *rente* at the Hôtel de Ville. He wrote to Gualterio on 24 September:

Y. E. is doubtless aware that all the *rentes* at the Hôtel de Ville are either going to be sold or reduced in value to 3 per cent. I have so little invested there that my loss will be very small and the selling price will at least enable me to pay my daughter's dowry if I cannot find assistance elsewhere. It is annoying to use ones capital however small, but when it is urgent for establishing ones children or for other expenses one is obliged to use what one has.

Although Gualterio had advised him not to sell his *rente* back in January, Nairne added that he had prepared a procuration, authenticated by a *notaire*, which he intended to send to Françoise so that she could sell it.[263] This was finally done in May 1720, when Nairne received 1,100 *livres*, at which point the money for Marie's dowry became available, exactly one year after she had become a postulant.[264]

It seems, however, that Nairne made one final attempt to obtain the necessary money for the dowry without having to use the proceeds from the sale of his *rente*. In the letter of 4 November, already referred to, in which Nairne told Gualterio that when he received the second payment of 400 *scudi* from the Grand Duke, originally intended to cover Louis' education, he admitted that he would send most of the money to help his daughter Marie in France. This letter also tells us that by then his petition to the Pope had failed, mentioning 'my daughter whom I love dearly, and for whom I expect no further help from the Pope'. Nairne's *rente* had not yet been sold, and he added that he had written to ask the Grand Duke if he would provide the money for Marie's dowry as well as for Louis' education:

> At least I thought I must discreetly try this route, having tried those of this court to no avail, so that I will be able to say that I have done everything I can for the comfort and future salvation of my poor daughter and have nothing to reproach myself with in this matter ... Poverty is always hard to bear, especially when one is reduced to begging from those in high places and to bothering ones friends.[265]

It was a last desperate attempt to obtain the money without having to sell his *rente*, and it is surprising that Nairne thought that the Grand Duke would be willing to help.

During the summer of 1719, James III returned to Italy from Spain and married Princess Clementina at Montefiascone. Far from giving Nairne some money to provide for his children, one of the first things he did – as we shall see in a later chapter – was to reduce Nairne's salary. The latter wrote to Gualterio from Montefiascone that 'I shall be only too happy to leave both the court and life itself whenever God wishes'.[266] Thirty years since he had first been employed by Lord Melfort, he now longed to retire and resume the ex-patriate life that he had once had in France. His son was an officer in the service of Spain, his daughters seemed destined to live permanently in Paris, and he himself no longer retained the same unquestioning loyalty to the Jacobite king that he had maintained for so long. In November 1719, now that James III was back in Italy, Nairne told Gualterio that he (Gualterio, not the king) was 'the only Patron in this country in whom I have complete trust'.[267] From a man who had served as James III's minister in Rome for part of 1718 and much of 1719, this was a significant statement.

Endnotes

1. This refers to Charles Booth (*maggiordomo*), Roger Strickland (groom of the bedchamber), Dr Lawrence Wood (physician) and Lord Edward Drummond (gentleman of the bedchamber) (Corp, *The Jacobites at Urbino*, pp. 62–3).

2. This refers to Dominic Sheldon (vice-chamberlain), Lord Edward Drummond, who had returned to the court, Lord Clermont (*maggiordomo*) and Charles Booth (assistant to the *maggiordomo*, who had also returned) (Corp, *The Jacobites at Urbino*, p. 66).

3. The other senior servants were Sir William Ellis (controller of the Household, and treasurer) and James Delattre (equerry). Their salaries were, respectively, 159*l* 14*s* 06*d* and 117*l* 12*s* 10*d*, whereas Nairne's was 205*l* 03*s* 02*d* (Corp, *The Jacobites at Urbino*, pp. 152–3).

4. Corp, *The Jacobites at Urbino*, p. 55.

5. BL. Add MSS 20312, f.228, Nairne to Bianchini, 25 March 1718.

6. BL. Add MSS 31261, f.200, Nairne to Gualterio, 18 August 1718; BL. Add MSS 20298, f.59, Nairne to Gualterio, 21 August 1718.

7. BL. Add MSS 20298, f.65, Nairne to Gualterio, undated. Gualterio's reply is dated 1 September 1717 (BL. Add MSS 20300, f.371).

8. BL. Add MSS 20298, f.18, Nairne to Gualterio, 17 January 1718.

9. Nairne's letters of 1717–19 to Gualterio are in BL. Add MSS 20298, 31260 and 31261. Gualterio's letters of 1717–19 to Nairne are in Bod. Carte MSS 257 and 258. The drafts of Gualterio's letters are in BL. Add MSS 20300, 20301 and 20302.

10. BL. Add MSS 31260, f.82, Nairne to Gualterio, 18 July 1717.

11. BL. Add MSS 31260, f.95, Nairne to Gualterio, 1 August 1717.

12. BL. Add MSS 31261, ff.27, 46, Nairne to Gualterio, 30 January and 20 February 1718.

13. BL. Add MSS 31261, f.78, Nairne to Gualterio, 24 March 1718.

14. BL. Add MSS 31261, f.161, Nairne to Gualterio, 17 July 1718. But see also BL. Add MSS 31261, f.125, Nairne to Gualterio, 19 June 1718: 'Les chaleurs commencent a etre fort violentes ici.'

15. BL. Add MSS 20298, f.45, Nairne to Gualterio, undated (early August 1718).

16. Corp, *The Jacobites at Urbino*, Chapter 7.

17. HMC *Stuart* V, p. 267, Mar to Nicolini, 9 December 1717.

18. BL. Add MSS 312361, f.50, Nairne to Gualterio, 24 February 1718.

19. HMC *Stuart* VI, p. 93, St Andrews to Nairne, 6 March 1718.

20. BL. Add MSS 31261, f.56, Nairne to Gualterio, 6 March 1718.

21. BL. Add MSS 31261, f.31, Nairne to Gualterio, 3 February 1718.

22. BL. Add MSS 31261, f.70, Nairne to Gualterio, 20 March 1718.
23. HMC *Stuart* VI, p. 389, Paterson to Mar, 28 April 1718.
24. BL. Add MSS 20298, f.35, Nairne to Gualterio, 7 July 1718.
25. BL. Add MSS 20298, f.47, Nairne to Gualterio, 7 August 1718.
26. HMC *Stuart* VII, p. 384, Nairne to Paterson, 13 October 1718. Lady Nithsdale had recently joined her husband at the court. William Erskine and John Graham were both Scottish pensioners. Francis Panton was on the Grand Tour with Lord Linton, who was probably one of the two lords. See also HMC *Stuart* VII, p. 367, Nairne to Paterson, 9 October 1718: 'I carried Mr Erskine to the Benediction last night, where he heard [Innocenza Magnani] for the first time and after Salut he made his visit to [see her] at the grate' of her convent.
27. HMC *Stuart* VII, p. 365, Nairne to Mar, 8 October 1718.
28. Halloran, *The Scots College Paris*, p. 211.
29. Nairne lent 100 *livres* to Lord Winton in 1700 (Diary, 1 June 1700), and obtained a pass for him from the French government in 1707 (Diary, 31 March and 4 April 1707).
30. HMC *Stuart* V, p. 487, Mar to Panmure, 17 February 1718.
31. SCA. BL 2/210/1, Nairne to T. Innes, 16 April 1716.
32. Corp, *The Jacobites at Urbino*, p. 73.
33. Ibid. p. 57.
34. Halloran, *The Scots College Paris*, p. 211. Nairne had also met the 2nd Duke of Perth, then Lord Drummond, on his return from Rome in 1691, when Drummond was travelling with Hay's father: see p. 47.
35. Corp, *The Jacobites at Urbino*, p. 44.
36. The king's new Irish confessor, Father Brown, also spoke Italian. For Nairne's high opinion of him, see BL. Add MSS 31260, ff.95, 204, Nairne to Gualterio, 1 August, 8 November 1717.
37. BL. Add MSS 20298, f.35, Nairne to Gualterio, 7 July 1718.
38. BL. Add MSS 20298, f.47, Nairne to Gualterio, 7 August 1718.
39. BL. Add MSS 20298, f.35, Nairne to Gualterio, 7 July 1718.
40. BL. Add MSS 20298, f.28, Nairne to Gualterio, undated (10 April 1718).
41. BL. Add MSS 20298, f.67, Nairne to Gualterio, undated (end of August 1718).
42. BL. Add MSS 20298, f.35, Nairne to Gualterio, 7 July 1718. Nairne also established very good relations with Don Francesco Soanti, the guardarobba of the palazzo ducale (BL. Add MSS 31260, ff.204, 217, Nairne to Gualterio, 8, 21 November 1717).
43. BL. Add MSS 31260, f.95, Nairne to Gualterio, 1 August 1717.
44. BL. Add MSS 31260, ff.101, 105, Nairne to Gualterio, 5 and 8 August 1717. On this occasion Nairne found Bianchini 'un parfaitem.t honnete homme, et un bon

Prelat qui connoit mieux la science et les astres que les intrigues et la politique'. But Nairne also found him indiscreet and felt that the king should be careful what he said to him (BL. Add MSS 31260, f.113, Nairne to Gualterio, 19 August 1717).

45. BL. Add MSS 31260, ff.127, 195, Nairne to Gualterio, 29 August, 21 October 1717.

46. Corp, *I giacobiti a Urbino*, p. 92.

47. BL. Add MSS 31260, f.195, Nairne to Gualterio, 21 October 1717. Nevertheless he still found Bianchini indiscreet: 'l'humilité du Prelat est tres louable, et je suis persuadé qu'il a les meilleurs intentions du monde, mais je suis convaincu en meme tems que son zele en certains occasions n'est pas toujours accompagné avec toute la prudence et toute la retenuë qu'il seroit a souhaitter' (BL. Add MSS 31260, f.213, Nairne to Gualterio, 18 November 1717). Gualterio replied that 'lors qu'on luy fait le moindre opposition il se pique et il s'emporte d'une estrange maniere' (BL. Add MSS 20301, f.94, Gualterio to Nairne, 24 November 1717).

48. BL. Add MSS 31260, f.227, Nairne to Gualterio, 28 November 1717; BL. Add MSS 20312, f.228, Nairne to Bianchini, 25 March 1718; BL. Add MSS 31261, f.161, Nairne to Gualterio, 17 July 1718.

49. BL. Add MSS 31261, f.185, Nairne to Gualterio, 4 August 1718.

50. BL. add MSS 31261, f.56, Nairne to Gualterio, 6 March 1718. Nairne sent his glasses to be mended in Rome, and received them back ten days later (BL. Add MSS 31261, f.66, 17 March 1717). He had been wearing glasses, perhaps only for reading and writing, since at least 1695 (Diary, 12 December 1695, 15 April 1696).

51. BL. Add MSS 31261, f.127, Nairne to Gualterio, 23 June 1718.

52. SCA. BL 2/222/14, Nairne to T. Innes, 25 June 1718.

53. BL. Add MSS 31261, ff.131, 133, Nairne to Gualterio, 26 and 30 June 1718; BL. Add MSS 20298, f.39, Nairne to Gualterio, undated (10 July 1718). See also HMC *Stuart* VI, p. 580, James III to Vaudémont, 26 June 1718.

54. BL. Add MSS 20298, f.52, Nairne to Gualterio, 11 August 1718.

55. BL. Add MSS 31261, f.133, Nairne to Gualterio, 30 June 1718.

56. BL. Add MSS 31261, f.145, Nairne to Gualterio, 7 July 1718.

57. BL. Add MSS 31261, f.149, Nairne to Gualterio, 10 July 1718.

58. BL. Add MSS 31260, ff.231, 252, 264, Nairne to Gualterio, 2, 19 and 30 December 1717.

59. BL. Add MSS 31261, f.105, Nairne to Gualterio, 24 April 1718.

60. BL. Add MSS 31261, f.227, Nairne to Gualterio, 15 September 1718.

61. ASV. Albani 166, ff.171, 174, 176, three memoranda in the handwriting of Nairne urging the Pope to give James III the extra money which he needed, perhaps as a wedding present, autumn 1718.

62. HMC *Stuart* VII, p. 428, Nairne to Mar, 23 October 1718; BL. Add MSS 20298, f.112, Nairne to Gualterio, 7 January 1719. He probably laid off his servant in May when he wrote that he was 'quite epuisé' and could not 'hold out any longer' with his expenses (SCA. BL 2/222/11, 12, Nairne to T. Innes, 5 and 11 May 1718).

63. Corp, *The Jacobites at Urbino*, p. 49.

64. BL. Add MSS 20298, f.67, Nairne to Gualterio, undated (end of August 1718). In another letter Nairne complained that 'on fait tous les jours les honneurs de la table meme du Roy' to people whose birth was no better than his (BL. Add MSS 20298, f.54, Nairne to Gualterio, undated, mid-August 1718).

65. BL. Add MSS 20298, f.35, Nairne to Gualterio, 7 July 1718. See also HMC *Stuart* VI, p. 427, Ogilvie to Mar, 12 May 1718, which reflects the attitude of Mar and his friends towards Nairne: 'they say he [Ellis] eats and converses with a certain work-creature, that writes some of the King's letters.'

66. HMC *Stuart* VII, p. 384, Nairne to Paterson, 13 October 1718.

67. BL. Add MSS 31260, ff.113, 124, 127, 137, 149, 152, 156, Nairne to Gualterio, 19, 26, 29 August, 5, 13, 16, 20 September 1717. See Corp, *I giacobiti a Urbino*, pp. 62, 106–7.

68. HMC *Stuart* V, p. 574, Nairne to O'Brien, 10 September 1717.

69. BL. Add MSS 31260, f.184, Nairne to Gualterio, 14 October 1717; Corp, *The Jacobites at Urbino*, pp. 54–5. For Nairne's daughter Marie and the Countess of Peterborough, see p. 486, note 38.

70. Corp, *The Jacobites at Urbino*, pp. 60–3.

71. BL. Add MSS 31260, f.101, Nairne to Gualterio, 5 August 1717.

72. BL. Add MSS 38851, f.109, James III to Dillon, 30 July 1717.

73. BL. Add MSS 20298, f.8, Nairne to Gualterio, 30 July 1717.

74. Bod. Carte MSS 257, f.124, Gualterio to Nairne, 4 August 1717.

75. Bod. Carte MSS 257, f.139, Gualterio to Nairne, 11 August 1717.

76. BL. Add MSS 20300, f.335, Gualterio to Nairne, 14 August 1717.

77. BL. Add MSS 31260, f.113, Nairne to Gualterio, 19 August 1717.

78. BL. Add MSS 20300, f.354, Gualterio to Nairne, 25 August 1717.

79. BL. Add MSS 31260, f.127, Nairne to Gualterio, 29 August 1717.

80. SCA. BL 2/217/2, Nairne to T. Innes, 6 November 1717.

81. BL. Add MSS 31260, ff.137, 156, 164, 180, Nairne to Gualterio, 5, 20, 25 September, 10 October 1717; BL. Add MSS 20300, f.447, Gualterio to Nairne, 22 September 1717.

82. BL. Add MSS 31260, ff.191, 202, Nairne to Gualterio, 17 and 24 October 1717.

83. See BL. Add MSS 31260, ff.204, 207, Nairne to Gualterio, 8 and 11 November 1717.

84. BL. Add MSS 31260, f.195, Nairne to Gualterio, 21 October 1717.

85. HMC *Stuart* V, p. 204, Southesk to Paterson, 13 November 1717.

86. SCA. BL 2/217/2, Nairne to T. Innes, 6 November 1717; BL. Add MSS 31260, f.204, Nairne to Gualterio, 8 November 1717. Creagh left Paris separately in the middle of November (HMC *Stuart* V, p. 188, Gordon to Mar, 9 November 1717).

87. BL. Add MSS 31260, ff.207, 213, 222 Nairne to Gualterio, 11, 18 and 23 November 1717.

88. SCA. BL 2/217/2, Nairne to T. Innes, 6 November 1717.

89. Corp, *The Jacobites at Urbino*, pp. 64–5.

90. HMC *Stuart* VI, p. 102, James III to Ormonde, 7 March 1718.

91. BL. Add MSS 31260, f.233, Nairne to Gualterio, 2 December 1717. The miniature, which had been painted at Bar-le-Duc nearly four years previously, was taken to Rome by Lord Edward Drummond. Nairne commented that 'je suis honteux du petit portrait', and explained that 'c'est une copie de la derniere qui a été faite de cette sorte, et je n'en ay point d'autre, car du reste ce n'est plus en effet mon portrait'. See p. 218 and p. 270, note 21.

92. BL. Add MSS 31260, f.260, Nairne to Gualterio, 26 December 1717.

93. Corp, *The Jacobites at Urbino*, pp. 87–91.

94. BL. Add MSS 31260, f.248, Nairne to Gualterio, 16 December 1717.

95. BL. Add MSS 31261, f.27, Nairne to Gualterio, 30 January 1718. See also the undated note describing the package for the queen: BL. Add MSS 20300, f.466.

96. HMC *Stuart* VII, p. 1, Mar to Dillon, 1 July 1718.

97. BL. Add MSS 31261, f.64, Nairne to Gualterio, 13 March 1718. See also BL. Add MSS 31261, ff.37, 44, Nairne to Gualterio, 13 and 20 January 1718.

98. BL. Add MSS 31261, f.78, Nairne to Gualterio, 24 March 1718.

99. BL. Add MSS 31261, f.80, Nairne to Gualterio, 27 March 1718.

100. BL. Add MSS 31260, f.195, Nairne to Gualterio, 21 October 1717; BL. Add MSS 31261, f.8, Nairne to Gualterio, 7 January 1718.

101. BL. Add MSS 31261, f.37, Nairne to Gualterio, 13 February 1718.

102. BL. Add MSS 31261, f.89, Nairne to Gualterio, 3 April 1718.

103. BL. Add MSS 31261, f.50, Nairne to Gualterio, 24 February 1718. See also SCA. BL 2/222/10, Nairne to T. Innes, 22 February 1718.

104. Corp, *The Jacobites at Urbino*, p. 79.

105. BL. Add MSS 38851, f.120, Nairne to Carrara, 24 March 1718; BL. Add MSS 39923, f.36, Nairne to Carrara, 24 December 1718.

106. Corp, *A Court in Exile*, p. 326.

107. HMC *Stuart* VI, p. 162, Mar to Stewart, 17 March 1718.

108. Corp, *A Court in Exile*, p. 326, note 68.

109. BL. Add MSS 20298, f.22, Nairne to Gualterio, 24 March 1718.

110. BL. Add MSS 20298, f.26, undated postscript for Nairne to Gualterio, 24 March 1718.

111. BL. Add MSS 20301, f.366, Gualterio to Nairne, 13 April 1718: 'Vous en avez agi Mr tres prudement. Il ne faut iamais taché la verité. Mais il faut l'insinuer avec discretion ... On ne peut pas douter les bonnes intentions de nostre maistre. On scait sa fidelité pour la Religion. Ses paroles ont peu estre mal menagees et elles se sont en effect. Comme il a une droiture infinie et une tres grande capacité il le reconnoistra sans faute.'

112. SCA. BL 2/222/11, Nairne to T. Innes, 5 May 1718.

113. SCA. BL 2/222/12, Nairne to T. Innes, 11 May 1718, with postscript of 12 May.

114. HMC *Stuart* VI, p. 30, James III to Mar, 12 March 1718.

115. BL. Add MSS 31260, f.101, Nairne to Gualterio, 5 August 1717.

116. Corp, *The Jacobites at Urbino*, pp. 91–103.

117. BL. Add MSS 20298, ff.64, 78, Nairne to Gualterio, 26 August 1718, undated (early September 1718).

118. BL. Add MSS 20298, f.35, Nairne to Gualterio, 7 July 1718; BL. Add MSS 31261, f.149, Nairne to Gualterio, 10 July 1718. In the second of these letters Nairne dismissed the *palazzo apostolico* at Albano, which would later be given to James III for his *villeggiature*, as 'impratticable' as a permanent residence 'pour la famille du Roy'. (See p. 84, note 32 for his visit to Albano in 1690).

119. BL. Add MSS 31261, f.155, Nairne to Gualterio, 14 July 1718.

120. BL. Add MSS 20298, f.76, Nairne to Gualterio, 11 September 1718.

121. BL. Add MSS 20298, f.88, Nairne to Gualterio, 2 October 1718.

122. BL. Add MSS 20298, f.35, Nairne to Gualterio, 7 July 1718.

123. BL. Add MSS 20298, f.47, Nairne to Gualterio, 7 August 1718.

124. For example, Mar persuaded the king to defend his valet, a heretic apostate and 'un malheureux debauché', against the Inquisition, and Nairne was obliged to try to enrol the support of Gualterio, which gave Nairne 'une vraye douleur' (Corp, *The Jacobites at Urbino*, p. 57 and p. 176, note 70).

125. For example, the king alienated the Duke of Parma by refusing to address him as 'Altesse' ('Celsitudo'), because the King of France did not address him like that, despite the fact that both the Emperor and the King of Spain gave him that honour. Nairne commented to Gualterio that this was politically unwise 'dans la conjoncture presente ou la prudence veut qu'on menage jusqu'au moindres Princes' (BL. Add MSS 20298, f.154, Nairne to Gualterio, 13 June 1718).

126. BL. Add MSS 31261, f.258, Nairne to Gualterio, 20 October 1718.

127. BL. Add MSS 20298, f.41, Nairne to Gualterio, 30 July 1718.

128. BL. Add MSS 20298, f.35, Nairne to Gualterio, 7 July 1718.

129. BL. Add MSS 20298, f.41, Nairne to Gualterio, 30 July 1718. See also BL. Add MSS 20298, f.71, undated (end of August 1718): 'sans excepter personne je ne

compte pas avoir ... un veritable et sincère ami de coeur et d'inclination au monde comme V. E..'

130. Corp, *The Jacobites at Urbino*, pp. 96, 104–5.

131. Murray had been very ill during August and had only recently recovered (BL. Add MSS 31261, ff.200, 201, 205, 211, 227, Nairne to Gualterio, 18, 21, 27 August, 1, 15 September 1718). If he had died at Urbino during the summer of 1718 the history of the Stuart court in exile, and Nairne's life in particular, would have been very different.

132. BL. Add MSS 20298, f.78, Nairne to Gualterio, undated (mid to late September 1718).

133. BL. Add MSS 20298, f.88, Nairne to Gualterio, 2 October 1718.

134. BL. Add MSS 31261, f.244, Nairne to Gualterio, 6 October 1718. Nairne, who normally ate at the second table with Father Brown and Dr Maghie, had by now revised his earlier favourable opinion (see above, note 36): 'Le P. Br ... est un pauvre genie, et un peu flatteur ... Je n'admire pas plus la capacité du medecin du corps ... que celle du medecin de l'ame' (BL. Add MSS 20298, f.88, Nairne to Gualterio, 2 October 1718).

135. Although Nairne was not invited to attend the king's wedding he had been charged by James III with obtaining the bed in which the latter intended to sleep with his bride. It was to be in the French style ('a la françoise') with 'deux bons matelas de bonne laine d'Ang[leter]re'. Nairne asked Gualterio to have the bed made in Rome, and gave him the precise dimensions required (BL. Add MSS 31261, f.178, Nairne to Gualterio, 28 July 1718; BL. Add MSS 31259, f.203, 'memoire pour un lit', enclosed in the letter of 28 July; BL. Add MSS 31261, f.189, Nairne to Gualterio, 7 August 1718).

136. BL. Add MSS 31261, f.251, Nairne to Gualterio, 16 October 1718; HMC *Stuart* VII, p. 394, Nairne to Paterson, 16 October 1718.

137. BL. Add MSS 31261, f.258, Nairne to Gualterio, 20 October 1718.

138. BL. Add MSS 31261, f.256, Nairne to Gualterio, 20 October 1718; Corp, *The Jacobites at Urbino*, p. 106.

139. HMC *Stuart* VII, p. 399, James III to Nairne, 18 October 1718.

140. See pp. 17-19. The pension was increased from 300 to 400 *livres* in 1687.

141. BL. Add MSS 20298, f.118, Nairne to Gualterio, 21 January 1719.

142. HMC *Stuart* V, p. 204, Southesk to Paterson, 13 November 1717.

143. BL. Add MSS 20298, f.131, Nairne's memoire for Clement XI, June 1719: 'un Couvent Anglois de Chanoinesses Regulieres de St Augustin a Paris, ou [Marie] et sa soeur [Françoise] ont eté elevées et sont toujours demeurées depuis la mort de leur mere.' See also pp. 224–5.

144. See p. 246.

145. SCA. BL 2/222/11, Nairne to T. Innes, 5 May 1718. See also SCA. BL 2/222/12, Nairne to T. Innes, 11 March 1718: 'I am quite epuisé and know not how to hold out any longer wth my childrens expenses.'

146. BL. Add MSS 31261, f.72, Nairne to Gualterio, 20 March 1718.

147. For Nairne's salary, see BL. Egerton MSS 2517 (1709); RA. SP 8/92 (1715); RA. SP 9/30 (1716); RA. SP Box 3/89 (1717); and p. 382, note 118.

148. BL. Add MSS 31261, f.87, Nairne to Gualterio, 3 April 1718. It should be added that Nairne was now being paid in Bologna *livres* which were worth less than the *livres tournois* which he had to pay in France.

149. BL. Add MSS 31261, f.133, Nairne to Gualterio, 30 June 1718: 'Je sçais seulement qu'à Paris mon fils m'a couté bien d'avantage par an, en Maistres, en entretien, et en tout.'

150. SCA. BL 2/222/10, Nairne to T. Innes, 22 February 1718; BL. Add MSS 31261, f.72, Nairne to Gualterio, 20 March 1718.

151. SCA. BL 2/222/11, Nairne to T. Innes, 5 May 1718.

152. SCA. BL 2/222/13/2, Nairne to T. Innes, 14 May 1718. Apparently Louis was not actually 'vicious' and his father wrote: 'God preserve him allways so' (SCA. BL 2/222/14, Nairne to T. Innes, 25 June 1718).

153. BL. Add MSS 31261, f.72, Nairne to Gualterio, 20 March 1718. See also BL. Add MSS 20298, f.22, Nairne to Gualterio, 24 March 1718.

154. Tommaso Del Bene was *maestro di camera* at the Tuscan court from March 1700 until March 1719 when he became *maggiordomo maggiore*.

155. BL. Add MSS 31261, f.87, Nairne to Gualterio, 3 April 1718.

156. BL. Add MSS 31261, ff.87, 62, Nairne to Gualterio, 3 and 10 April 1718; BL. Add MSS 20298, ff.27, 28, Nairne to Gualterio, 4 April 1718 and undated (April 1718).

157. BL. Add MSS 20298, f.31, Nairne to Gualterio, 21 April 1718.

158. BL. Add MSS 31261, f.11, Nairne to Gualterio, 1 May 1718; BL. Add MSS 20298, f.57, Nairne to Gualterio, undated (end of April or early May 1718).

159. SCA. BL 2/222/11, Nairne to T. Innes, 5 May 1718.

160. BL. Add MSS 31261, ff.78, 89, 62, 105, 101, 109, 111, 24 March, 3 April, undated (10 April), 24, 27, 28 April, 1 May 1718; BL. Add MSS 20298, ff.28, 31, Nairne to Gualterio, undated (10 April), 21 April 1718; BL. Add MSS 20298, f.30, Davia to Nairne, 14 April 1718; HMC *Stuart* VI, p. 404, Marelli to Nairne, 4 May 1718.

161. SCA. BL 2/222/12/12, Nairne to T. Innes, 11 May 1718, with postscript of 12 May.

162. BL. Add MSS 31261, f.115, Nairne to Gualterio, 3 June 1718. This visit took place while the Duke of Mar was in Rome.

163. BL. Add MSS 31261, f.127, Nairne to Gualterio, 23 June 1718.

164. SCA. BL 2/222/12, Nairne to T. Innes, 11 May 1718.

165. BL. Add MSS 31261, f.127, Nairne to Gualterio, 23 June 1718.

166. SCA. BL 2/222/12, Nairne to T. Innes, 11 May 1718, with postscript of 12 May.

167. SCA. BL 2/222/13/1 and 2, Nairne to T. Innes, both of 14 May 1718.

168. SCA. BL 2/222/14, Nairne to T. Innes, 25 June 1718; BL. Add MSS 31261, ff.133, 164, Nairne to Gualterio, 30 June and 21 July 1718; BL. Add MSS 20298, f.41, Nairne to Gualterio, 30 July 1718. Louis stayed in Florence for four or five days (BL. Add MSS 31261, f.185, Nairne to Gualterio, 4 August 1718) and was well treated by the duca di Salviati and Tommaso Del Bene. He was also given an audience by the Grand Duke (BL. add MSS 31261, f.193, Nairne to Gualterio, 11 August 1718). Nairne wrote to thank the duca di Salviati and told Louis to write to the duke's son, the marchese di Salviati (BL. Add MSS 20298, f.54, Nairne to Gualterio, undated but mid-August 1718). For their replies, see HMC *Stuart* VII, p. 185, duca di Salviati to Nairne, 20 August 1718; and HMC *Stuart* VII, p. 186, marchese di Salviati to Louis Nairne, 20 August 1718.

169. BL. Add MSS 31261, f.133, Nairne to Gualterio, 30 June 1718.

170. BL. Add MSS 31261, f.193, Nairne to Gualterio, 11 August 1718.

171. BL. Add MSS 20298, f.33, Nairne to Gualterio, 1 July 1718.

172. BL. Add MSS 20298, f.35, Nairne to Gualterio, 7 July 1718.

173. BL. Add MSS 20298, f.47, Nairne to Gualterio, 7 August 1718.

174. BL. Add MSS 20298, f.67, Nairne to Gualterio, undated (end of August 1718).

175. BL. Add MSS 20298, f.73, Nairne to Gualterio, 3 September 1718.

176. BL. Add MSS 20298, ff.47, 54, 71, 76, 78, 84, Nairne to Gualterio, 7 August, undated but mid-August, undated but late August, 11 September, undated but late September, 29 September 1718; BL. Add MSS 31261, ff.201, 219, Nairne to Gualterio, 21 August, 7 September 1718.

177. Louis had started his secondary education at the English Benedictine monastery at Douai, but had been moved to the English Jesuit college at Saint-Omer in 1715 when he was sixteen years old. See pp. 225–8, 230, and 245–6'.

178. BL. Add MSS 31261, f.247 and 20298, f.90, Nairne to Gualterio, 9 October 1718.

179. BL. Add MSS 20298, f.54, Nairne to Gualterio, (mid-August 1718).

180. BL. Add MSS 20298, ff.35, 39, 47, 54, 64, Nairne to Gualterio, 7 July, undated but July, 7 August, undated but mid-August, 26 August 1718. Nairne also wanted his son to be given a 'comanderie de St Etienne', the Tuscan order of chivalry (BL. Add MSS 31261, f.133, Nairne to Gualterio, 30 June 1718; BL. Add MSS 20298, ff.47, 59, Nairne to Gualterio, 7, 21 August 1718), but Gualterio advised him that it was too early to think of that (BL. Add MSS 20298, f.71, Nairne to Gualterio, undated but end of August 1718). On 3 September Nairne noted that his son had behaved 'assés bien' so far (BL. Add MSS 20298, f.73, to Gualterio).

181. At first Nairne believed that the Grand Duke would only pay 266 *scudi* each year, and that he would need 300 to cover the costs of the college (BL. Add MSS

20298, f.35, Nairne to Gualterio, 7 July 1718). He was relieved to discover that the Grand Duke had actually promised 400 *scudi* each year (BL. Add MSS 20298, f.54, Nairne to Gualterio, undated but mid-August 1718).

182. BL. Add MSS 20298, f.39, Nairne to Gualterio, undated (early July 1718).

183. BL. Add MSS 20298, f.52, Nairne to Gualterio, 11 August 1718; BL. Add MSS 31261, f.193, Nairne to Gualterio, 11 August 1718.

184. BL. Add MSS 20298, f.64, Nairne to Gualterio, 26 August 1718.

185. BL. Add MSS 20298, f.54, Nairne to Gualterio, undated (August 1718).

186. BL. Add MSS 31261, f.201, Nairne to Gualterio, 21 August 1718; BL. Add MSS 20298, ff.64, 67, 71, 73, 76, Nairne to Gualterio, 26 August, undated (late August), undated (late August), 3 and 11 September 1718.

187. BL. Add MSS 31261, f.251, Nairne to Gualterio, 16 October 1718.

188. BL. Add MSS 31261, f.201, Nairne to Gualterio, 21 August 1718.

189. BL. Add MSS 20298, f.54, Nairne to Gualterio, undated (mid-August 1718).

190. BL. Add MSS 31261, f.247 and BL. Add MSS 20298, f.90, Nairne to Gualterio, 9 October 1718.

191. BL. Add MSS 20298, f.80, Nairne to Gualterio, undated (mid-September 1718).

192. BL. Add MSS 20298, f.92, Nairne to Gualterio, 9 October 1718.

193. BL. Add MSS 31261, f.234, Nairne to Gualterio, 22 September 1718.

194. BL. Add MSS 20298, f.80, Nairne to Gualterio, undated (late September 1718).

195. BL. Add MSS 31261, f.260, Nairne to Gualterio, 29 September 1718 (wrongly dated October).

196. BL. Add MSS 20298, f.84, Nairne to Gualterio, 29 September 1718.

197. BL. Add MSS 31255, f.169, James III to Gualterio, 4 October 1718.

198. BL. Add MSS 20298, f.88, Nairne to Gualterio, 2 October 1718. Nairne made the same point in a letter of 27 December (BL. Add MSS 20298, f.101, to Gualterio).

199. BL. Add MSS 31261, f.244, Nairne to Gualterio, 6 October 1718.

200. BL. Add MSS 31261, f.247, and BL. Add MSS 20298, f.90, Nairne to Gualterio, 9 October 1718.

201. BL. Add MSS 20298, f.92, Nairne to Gualterio, 9 October 1718.

202. See notes 190 and 200. There are two copies of Nairne's letter in Gualterio's papers, one of which Nairne wrote for Gualterio to send to the Grand Duke, but which Gualterio kept.

203. BL. Add MSS 31261, ff.249, 251, Nairne to Gualterio, 13 and 16 October 1718; Bod. Carte MSS 258, f.219, Gualterio to Nairne, 15 October 1718.

204. BL. Add MSS 31261, f.249, Nairne to Gualterio, 13 October 1718.

205. BL. Add MSS 31261, f.272, Nairne to Gualterio, 12 November 1718.

206. BL. Add MSS 31261, f.275, Nairne to Gualterio, 16 November 1718.

207. BL. Add MSS 20298, f.101, Nairne to Gualterio, 27 December 1718.

208. BL. Add MSS 20298, f.94, Nairne to Gualterio, 23 November 1718.
209. BL. Add MSS 20298, f.96, Nairne to Gualterio, 30 November 1718.
210. BL. Add MSS 31261, f.251, Nairne to Gualterio, 16 October 1718. Nairne repaid the sum in November (BL. Add MSS 31261, f.272, Nairne to Gualterio, 12 November 1718; BL. Add MSS 20298, f.100, Nairne to Gualterio, undated but November 1718). He had asked Gualterio to send his son to Rome in a letter of 29 October (BL. Add MSS 31261, f.262).
211. Bod. Carte MSS 258, f.219, Gualterio to Nairne, 15 October 1718.
212. BL. Add MSS 31261, ff.264, 266, Nairne to Gualterio, 1 and 4 November 1718. At first Nairne allowed his son to share with him the apartment he had been given in the Palazzo Gualterio (BL. Add MSS 31261, f.270, Nairne to Gualterio, 9 November 1718) but when the king arrived Nairne was obliged to vacate that apartment for Hay and his wife (BL. Add MSS 31261, f.275, Nairne to Gualterio, 16 November 1718) so he had to find lodgings for himself as well as his son.
213. BL. Add MSS 20298, f.94, Nairne to Gualterio, 23 November 1718.
214. BL. Add MSS 31261, f.284, Nairne to Gualterio, 26 November 1718.
215. BL. Add MSS 20298, f.116, Nairne to Gualterio, 14 January 1719.
216. BL. Add MSS 20298, f.118, Nairne to Gualterio, 21 January 1719. Despite having to stop the music lessons, Nairne was able to take his son to the opera. On 11 January, for example, he told Gualterio that he would take Louis to see *Astianatte* by Francesco Gasparini at the Aliberti in the box of the cardinal's nephew (BL. Add MSS. 31261, f.311). For the identity of the opera, see Corp, *The Jacobites at Urbino*, p. 114.
217. BL. Add MSS 31261, f.258, Nairne to Gualterio, 20 October 1718.
218. BL. Add MSS 20298, f.98, Nairne to Gualterio, undated (late November or early December 1718).
219. BL. Add MSS 20298, f.96, Nairne to Gualterio, 30 November 1718.
220. BL. Add MSS 31261, f.290, Nairne to Gualterio, 7 December 1718.
221. BL. Add MSS 31261, f.284, Nairne to Gualterio, 26 November 1718.
222. BL. Add MSS 20298, f.98, Nairne to Gualterio, undated (late November or early December 1718).
223. BL. Add MSS 20298, f.101, Nairne to Gualterio, 27 December 1718.
224. BL. Add MSS 31261, f.305, Nairne to Gualterio, 5 January 1719.
225. BL. Add MSS 20298, f.110, Nairne to Gualterio, undated but 5 January 1719.
226. BL. Add MSS 20298, f.112, Nairne to Gualterio, 7 January 1719.
227. BL. Add MSS 20298, f.114, Nairne to Gualterio, 12 January 1719.
228. BL. Add MSS 20298, f.160, Nairne to Gualterio, undated (January 1719).
229. BL. Add MSS 20298, f.116, Nairne to Gualterio, 14 January 1719.
230. BL. Add MSS 20298, f.118, Nairne to Gualterio, 21 January 1719.

231. BL. Add MSS 31261, f.321, Nairne to Gualterio, 1 February 1719.

232. RA. SP 42/18, 'Directions for Sir William Ellis when His Majesty parted from Rome', [2] February 1719, in the handwriting of Nairne, signed by James III.

233. BL. Add MSS 20298, f.121, Nairne to Gualterio, 2 March 1719.

234. Bod. Carte MSS 258, ff.327, 330, Gualterio to Nairne, 4, 11 February 1719; BL. Add MSS 20298, ff.119, 157, Nairne to Gualterio, 9 February, undated but 11 February 1719; BL. Add MSS 31261, f.326, Nairne to Gualterio, 15 February 1719.

235. BL. Add MSS 20298, f.121, Nairne to Gualterio, 2 March 1719.

236. BL. Add MSS 20298, f.123, Nairne to Gualterio, 16 March 1719; Bod. Carte MSS 258, f.340, Gualterio to Nairne, 16 March 1719; RA. SP 43/6, Nairne to James III, 25 March 1719.

237. Archivio General de Simancas (hereafter AGS.) Secretaria de Guerra, Legajo 2564-1-25 and 2656-15-11, March 1719; BL. Add MSS 31261, f.329, Nairne to Gualterio, 22 March 1719; BL. Add MSS 20298, f.125, Nairne to Gualterio, 3 June 1719; Bod. Carte MSS 258, f.346, Gualterio to Nairne, 3 June 1719.

238. RA. SP 43/71, Nairne to James III, 25 April 1719.

239. RA. SP 43/65, Nairne to James III, 22 April 1719.

240. BL. Add MSS 20298, f.141, Nairne to Gualterio, undated (15 October 1719).

241. RA. SP 44/38, Nairne to James III, 12 August 1719; BL. Add MSS 20298, ff./136, 141, Nairne to Gualterio, 24 September, undated but 15 October 1719; Bod. Carte MSS 258, f.392, Gualterio to Nairne, 17 October 1719.

242. BL. Add MSS 20298, f.136, Nairne to Gualterio, 24 September 1719. See also BL. Add MSS 31261, f.355, Nairne to Gualterio, 1 October 1719; BL. Add MSS 20298, f.141, Nairne to Gualterio, undated (15 October 1719); Bod. Carte MSS 258, f.392, Gualterio to Nairne, 17 October 1719.

243. BL. Add MSS 20298, f.148, Nairne to Gualterio, 4 November 1719.

244. BL. Add MSS 20298, f.114, Nairne to Gualterio, 12 January 1719.

245. Ibid.

246. BL. Add MSS 20298, f.160, Nairne to Gualterio, undated (January 1719).

247. BL. Add MSS 20298, f.127, Nairne to Gualterio, 12 June 1719.

248. BL. Add MSS 20298, f.131, F.Nairne to Nairne, 18 April 1719.

249. BL. Add MSS 20298, f.131, F.Nairne to Nairne, 24 April 1719.

250. BL. Add MSS 20298, f.131, M.Nairne to Nairne, 1 May 1719.

251. The convent was known as Notre Dame de Sion, and its nuns included members of the following Jacobite families which Nairne had known at Saint-Germain: Biddulph, Conquest, Hales, Howard, Leyburne, Martinash, Molyneux, Perkins, Stafford and Waldegrave (Corp, *A Court in Exile*, p. 149). The superior was Anne Tyldesley (1698–1720) and she was succeeded by Anne Frances Throckmorton (1720–1728). According to Françoise (see note 254), 'Mlle Trocmorton porta

son habit de Religieuse a l'autel, la fille de Milord Falconbridge [*sic*: Viscount Fauconberg] porta la couronne et une autre Dlle Angloise de qualité son cierge, deux petites Dlles habillés en anges alloient toujours au devant d'elle, et toutes les autres la suivoient'.

252. The daughters of the 1st and 2nd Dukes of Powis were Anne, Viscountess Carington and Lady Mary Herbert respectively. Lady Dillon's daughter was Catherine (who later became a Carmelite nun, and eventually the superior of the convent at Saint-Denis). Dorothy Sheldon was the daughter of Dominic Sheldon's brother Ralph. The other ladies present included a daughter of Lady Tuke, who was herself the sister of Dominic Sheldon, Ralph Sheldon and Lady Dillon; and Christian, Dowager Countess of Bute who was accompanied by her son John (who later joined the Stuart court in Rome).

253. BL. Add MSS 20298, f.131, Southcott to Nairne, 7 May, and L. Innes to Nairne, 9 May 1719. For Nairne's high opinion of Southcott, whom he said he knew well in Paris, see BL. Add MSS 31261, f.119, to Gualterio, 9 June 1718.

254. BL. Add MSS 20298, f.131, F.Nairne to Nairne, 9 May 1719.

255. BL. Add MSS 20298, f.127, Nairne to Gualterio, 12 June 1719.

256. BL. Add MSS 20298, f.129, Nairne to Gualterio, 22 June 1719.

257. Bod. Carte MSS 258, f.350, Gualterio to Nairne, 22 June 1719. It is not clear what happened to Nairne's memoire. In this letter Gualterio told Nairne that he would present it to the Pope and try to arrange an audience. But on 24 September, over three months later, Nairne asked Gualterio if he had yet handed the memoire to the Pope (BL. Add MSS 20298, f.136).

258. BL. Add MSS 20298, f.131, Nairne's memoire for the Pope, with 'extraits de quelques lettres ecrittes de Paris au Chev.r Nairne au sujet de sa fille la Religieuse', undated but June 1719.

259. RA. SP 44/6, Nairne to James III, 20 June 1719.

260. RA. SP 44/38, Nairne to James III, 12 August 1719.

261. BL. Add MSS 20298, f.135, Nairne to Gualterio, 14 August 1719.

262. According to Alfred de Compigny, Nairne continued to receive 'la pension de 400 livres' until his death. See Compigny, *Les Entretiens de Cambrai*, p. 62.

263. BL. Add MSS 20298, f.136, Nairne to Gualterio, 24 September 1719.

264. In January 1719 Nairne described his *rente sur l'hôtel de ville* as 'une bagatelle de rente de peu de chose' (BL. Add MSS 20298, f.114, to Gualterio, 12 January 1719). In October 1719, he said that he had only '100 livres par mois a St Germain que j'avois laissé là pour mes filles, et qui est en grand danger d'etre retranché (BL. Add MSS 31261, f.254, to Gualterio, 18 October 1719). In November 1719, William Dicconson, the king's treasurer at Saint-Germain, told James III that the regent had decided that new investments at the *hôtel de ville* in Paris would involve

contracts worth one million *livres* each. As the king only had 600,000 *livres* to invest Dicconson asked if the remaining 400,000 *livres* might be made up with money from Lord Dillon, Lewis Innes, John Ingleton, Sir William Ellis, himself, and Nairne if the latter's old *rente* had not been 'disposed of' (RA. SP 45/90, Dicconson to James III, 13 November 1719). James III replied at the beginning of December that he agreed to this suggestion, and mentioned Dillon, Innes, Ingleton, Ellis and Dicconson himself, but not Nairne (RA. SP 45/104, James III to Dicconson, 4 December 1719). As the file copy is in Nairne's handwriting this implies that Nairne's *rente* had indeed already been 'disposed of' by that time. For the receipt of 1100 *livres* from the sale of the *rente*, see RA. SP 46/13 and 138, Dicconson to Nairne, 19 February and 13 May 1720.

265. BL. Add MSS 20298, f.148, Nairne to Gualterio, 4 November 1719.
266. BL. Add MSS 31261, f.254, Nairne to Gualterio, 18 October 1719.
267. BL. Add MSS 20298, f.148, Nairne to Gualterio, 4 November 1719.

Jacobite Minister at Rome, 1718–1719

From October to November 1718, while Cardinal Gualterio was at his country estate at Corgnolo, Nairne was accredited to the papal court as James III's minister at Rome. His mission then lapsed when the king himself arrived in the city. In February 1719, however, while Gualterio was still in the country, James left Rome and travelled to Spain, hoping to join a Spanish fleet sailing to invade England. Nairne's accreditation as Jacobite minister was therefore renewed, and he continued to hold that post until, the invasion attempt having failed, James III returned to the Papal States at the end of August.

On 22 October 1718 Nairne received a letter from James III, then in Bologna, ordering him to leave Urbino and go immediately to Rome. Princess Clementina and her mother had been arrested on the Emperor's orders at Innsbruck, and Nairne was instructed to see the Pope, the papal secretary of state (Cardinal Paulucci), the Pope's three nephews (Cardinal Albani, Don Carlo Albani and Don Alessandro Albano), the pro-Jacobite cardinals (Imperiali and Sacripanti), and the Spanish ambassador (Cardinal Aquaviva). 'In fine', the king told him, 'your business is to make all the clamour and noise you can and to move heaven and earth for remedy and in speaking of it to call everything by its own name'. In practice this meant persuading the Pope to send a formal protest to the Emperor, demanding the release of the princess. To this end James provided Nairne with a letter which he had written to the Pope, and which Nairne was told 'you must deliver with your own hand'.[1] The king's letter begged 'your Holiness to listen favourably to the bearer, who is not unknown to you'.[2]

Having seen Don Carlo Albani, who was at Urbino, Nairne set out on the morning of 24 October, taking with him one of the footmen, and travelled down the Via Flaminia to Rome as fast as he could.[3] He carried the king's letter to the Pope, and another one from Don Carlo to Cardinal

Albani his brother. At Foligno he stopped off to see Cardinal Imperiali and obtained from him a letter of support to Cardinal Paulucci. At Soriano (the Albani estate near Viterbo) he saw Cardinal Albani and obtained another letter to Paulucci and one to Don Alessandro Albani, who was looking after the family's interests in Rome. He finally reached the Porta del Popolo 'an hour after midnight' on 27 October, and went straight to the Palazzo Gualterio on the Corso, where an apartment was prepared for him.[4]

Nairne was not optimistic that he would achieve very much, commenting in a letter to Mar that 'I dare say the Pope neither will nor can refuse me to write as strongly as he can, but I am afraid George's threatenings will have more weight at Vienna than the Pope's, suppose he should have the courage to threaten as well as exhort, which I doubt much'.[5] This, of course, was the problem. It was one thing to persuade the Pope to protest to the Emperor, it was quite another to persuade the latter to release the princess. Nevertheless on 28 October Nairne went to see Cardinal Paulucci and was given an audience at the Quirinale by the Pope, who was 'very gracious' and 'kept me above an hour'. Nairne gave the Pope the letter from James III, and then launched into a condemnation of what the Emperor had done:

> I was going on, according to my orders, to represent the thing in the odious colours it naturally deserves, without mincing the matter, when the Pope took me by the hand and stopped me, bidding me let him speak first, that I might know what were his sentiments and his true concern for your Majesty, before you had sent me to him.

The Pope then told Nairne that what the Emperor had done was 'unjustifiable' and that he would 'write a strong letter in his own hand to the Emperor and would send it by an express'. In relating this to James III, Nairne added that the Pope 'seemed to be in a very good humour', and 'talked of Urbino'.[6] All seemed well, and Nairne had apparently succeeded in obtaining what the king wanted. James wrote back to say that he approved of all that Nairne had 'said and done', and hoped that 'the pope has already writ as he promised'.[7]

Nairne spent the next few days seeing as many influential people as he could, and then reported to the king:

> I called things by their names and have not spared representing the fact and the aggravating circumstances in their natural colours ... and have encouraged and excited all others to exclaim against the action, which, as far as I hear, all Rome does.

But he remained pessimistic, commenting that 'I am afraid the Emperor will laugh at all that and go on still with the measures he has taken with George'.[8]

On 2 November, the Pope summoned Nairne to see him again at the Quirinale, and explained that he had not actually written to the Emperor, but hoped to do so in 'a day or two', after he had spoken to the Imperial ambassador. Nairne urged him to write as promised without further delay, but 'could not move him to alter his resolution', and confided to the king his suspicion that the Pope was insincere and was 'afraid and in awe of the Emperor'.[9] He told Gualterio that the more he dealt with the papal court, the less he understood it; that people, all of them apparently trustworthy, made promises, then failed to carry them out and sometimes actually did the opposite. Even if the Pope were to write to the Emperor, he said, he very much doubted if that would secure the release of Princess Clementina.[10]

The Pope's letter to the Emperor was finally despatched on 7 November, a full five days after Nairne's second audience, and the latter wrote that 'I see nothing more for me to do but sit quiet'.[11] The king, however, told Nairne that so long as the princess was 'detained' at Innsbruck 'it is our business' to go on making 'all the noise we can'.[12] Nairne, of course, found this very embarrassing and wrote frankly to the king on 8 November:

> As for making all the noise I can here and teasing the Pope etc, about this affair, though I be naturally the unfittest person in the world for either one or t'other, yet as far as I could judge it to be your intention and interest, I have done it hitherto, but to rail or be too importune I thought would not be altogether so proper, but I encourage and excite others to exclaim as much as I can, and, as far as I can learn, the Emperor is sufficiently cried out against in Rome even by Germans themselves, if that can move him to make amends for the unworthy step he has made, but it is from England and not from hence that he'll take his measures. However, we must hope still.[13]

Nairne must have been very worried about continuing to 'make noise' in Rome because he sent another letter to the king on the following day with a similar message:

> I shall continue, as you order me, to make all the noise I can here, for I suppose you mean what noise is proper and decent for a person, employed immediately by you, whose business it is to convince people by reason that the usage is cruel, unjust, dishonourable and not excusable on any management whatever that politicians

pretend the Emperor was obliged to have for his ally, but for me to rail, exclaim and speak disrespectfully would irritate and do rather harm than good, but underhand I encourage others to do it because that cannot be supposed to be done by your immediate directions.

As Nairne continued to point out, 'it is not the noise in Rome that will have any decisive influence on the Vienna counsels'.[14] And in fact the Pope's letter achieved nothing, because the Emperor determined that he would continue to keep Clementina and her mother under house arrest at Innsbruck.

Even if Nairne had not been instructed to go on making all the 'noise' he could in Rome he would not have returned to Urbino, because James III had decided to move his court to Rome. Indeed, the letter ordering Nairne to go to Rome had announced that the king would 'come back no more ... to Urbino',[15] and by 10 November all the household servants and nearly all the pensioners – apart from the ones at Bologna and Ferrara – had arrived in Rome.[16] The household servants were lodged either in the Palazzo Gualterio with Nairne or in the surrounding area. Because the cardinal was still in the country he told Nairne that 'the king should make use of his palace and coaches as entirely his own'.[17]

The king, however, was still in Bologna, and Nairne was afraid that the Emperor might send a message to the Pope ordering him not to allow James to live in Rome. He therefore urged the king to leave Bologna and come to Rome as quickly as he could, before that could happen. He also argued that the king should give up any idea of living at Castel Gandolfo, because the *palazzo apostolico* there could easily be attacked from the coast, and that James should therefore definitely spend the winter in Rome. The king was persuaded by Nairne's arguments and arrived in Rome with John Hay on 14 November, followed shortly afterwards by Hay's wife Marjory, James Murray and the Duke of Mar, now accompanied by his wife (who had just joined him from England).[18] They all moved into the Palazzo Gualterio, and Nairne found himself obliged to give up the apartment he had been occupying with his son, so that it could be given to John and Marjory Hay. He told Gualterio that 'I preferred to take a room in town rather than making one of Y. E.'s people move out'.[19]

The arrival of the king and his favourites not only brought to an end Nairne's mission to the papal court, it also made him effectively redundant as the secretary dealing with the Roman correspondence. He kept in touch with Gualterio, now in his palazzo at Orvieto, and wrote to the latter that 'for the moment while the King himself is here my letters and negotiations are no longer useful, and when Y. E. arrives (which I hope will be soon) I shall have the pleasure to receive orders from each of you and to carry them out'.[20]

Gualterio, however, could not return to Rome until the Jacobite court had vacated his palazzo on the Corso, and Nairne was now given the task of finding a building somewhere in Rome into which James III and his courtiers could move. He did this with Francesco Bianchini, with whom he had established good relations at Urbino, and whom he now described as 'truly zealous and a sincere well-wisher of the King's and ready to give himself any trouble to serve him'.[21]

It was agreed that the *Camera Apostolica* would pay the rent of whichever building was selected, so Bianchini drew up a list of the palazzi which were available, from which he and Nairne selected as a temporary residence the Palazzo Cibo on the west side of the Piazza dei Santi Apostoli, opposite the Palazzo Colonna. Nairne told the king that 'it stands in the Piazza Santi Apostoli in a very fine situation and looks noble without, but it has no garden'.[22] There was a very 'fine appartement' for the king and 'there is a good deal of lodging in it' for the household servants.[23] On 19 November, Nairne told Gualterio that he hoped that the court would be able to move into the palazzo for about six weeks or two months until a more permanent or better residence could be found, which would enable the cardinal to return to Rome.[24]

At this point Monsignor Cibo, the owner of the palazzo, changed his mind and said he was not willing to let James III occupy the building.[25] Nairne and Bianchini therefore had to start again, and this time they selected a palazzo in the same piazza, but at the north end. It belonged to the marchese Giovanni Battista Muti, contained plenty of accommodation, and – an important point – also had its own garden. Nairne wrote that 'on espere que le Palais de Muti quoique de peu d'apparence aura beaucoup de commodité'.[26]

Nairne originally hoped that the palazzo would be available before Christmas, thus allowing Gualterio to return to Rome before 'the festivities',[27] but it soon became clear that nothing would ever be done that quickly in Rome,[28] so Nairne suggested that the king should look elsewhere to enable Gualterio to return. However he was overruled:

My feeling was that the King should propose to take the palazzo occupied by the Cardinal de la Tremoille, who had thought to use it for Christmas. This would suit H. M. better than having to wait so long for the Muti one, but I was not supported in this, and H. M. was advised to take the latter.[29]

Various building works had to be carried out in the palazzo of marchese Muti and these, as Nairne remarked at the end of December, 'move forward like everything in this country – *piano*'.[30] They continued throughout January,[31] and it was not until the beginning of February that Nairne could report to Gualterio that they were nearly finished.[32] By then some of the Jacobite courtiers had already begun to move out of the Palazzo Gualterio into their new accommodation, and finally, on 11 February, Nairne told the cardinal that his palazzo was empty and he could at last return to Rome whenever he wanted.[33]

Although, therefore, Nairne had some misgivings about it, it was he who had been responsible for selecting the building which, renamed the Palazzo del Re, was to become the permanent residence of the Stuart court in exile throughout most of the eighteenth century. The Palazzo del Re was not, and is not, one of the more impressive palazzi in Rome, but it must be remembered that the largest ones often contained shops on the ground floor, and normally contained apartments which were rented out to other people. The great advantage of the Palazzo del Re, apart from having its own private garden, was that it was completely self-contained, occupied exclusively by the Jacobites themselves. It was also conveniently close to the Pope and the papal court at the Quirinale.

Apart from selecting the building to be occupied by the court, and keeping Gualterio informed about the progress of the building works, Nairne had little to do between the arrival of the king on 14 November and the latter's departure on 8 February. He had made a brief visit with the king in 1717, but this was the first time that he had lived in Rome for an extended period since he had been in the city with Lord Melfort in 1689–91. On that occasion he had kept a detailed diary which recorded whom he met and where he went, and in particular which churches he attended, and it is unfortunate that no such information has survived for 1718–19. We may speculate, however, that he went regularly, probably every day, to one or more of the churches he had then frequented, and in particular to the church of the Santi Apostoli, situated immediately beside the Palazzo del Re. He was already on good terms with some of the English and Scottish priests in the city, all of whom he now met, as well as Melfort's son Lord William Drummond, known as the Abbé Melfort. He also saw Father Louis Sabran, who had been the rector of the English Jesuit college at Saint-Omer when his son Louis had been a boarder there, and was now also living in Rome.[34]

Not surprisingly Nairne began to take advantage of the rich musical life in Rome, and he mentions in his letters some concerts given by the Principessa di Piombino[35] and at the English College.[36] On 7 January 1719, the three opera houses of Rome opened for the new carnival season, with new works by Francesco Gasparini, Alessandro Scarlatti and Giovanni Bononcini, and Nairne went to them all, probably more than once.[37]

Much of Nairne's time, however, was taken up with worrying about his son Louis and, since he now had to find his own accommodation in Rome,[38] the deterioration of his finances. He told Gualterio on 5 January that he hid from the king the fact that he was in debt out of 'discretion',[39] but complained that the king gave to Hay, Murray and Mar, 'the new and favoured advisers in the household', all the money that they wanted.[40] In another letter he wrote that 'my only remedy is to cut back all that I can in my personal expenses, ... and to maintain the discretion and silence towards the king that I am resolved to keep'. But he increasingly resented 'the comfortable and contented state in which I see the new favourites, to whom everything is granted'. He tried to suppress these thoughts as unworthy of 'a Christian' and 'a decent man', but admitted that, 'being neither blind nor insensitive I confess to my shame that I am often pained by it'.[41]

Shortly after this, at the beginning of February, Nairne looked back over the thirty years of his career, and commented very frankly on what he regarded as James III's lack of appreciation or gratitude for all the political work he had done, and on his sense of resentment towards the new favourites:

> I have worked in these matters for 30 years, though in a lower rank, but I find that being a confidant of princes is more of a burden and cause for anxiety than a pleasure, and that such confidence has always given me more work and fatigue than any other

advantages. Moreover one tends to regard certain confidences as marks of favour and subsequently discover to one's chagrin that one was mistaken, and when we are weak, as I am, this is painful. We still have our self-respect and flatter ourselves too easily, when we have served without reproach for many years, that some reward is merited, rather than seeing it being granted to those who have only worked for an hour and have not felt the heat and fatigue of working all day. However when the master finds it fitting to give recent arrivals as much or more than to those already in his service, he is the master and can do as he pleases, and as long as one receives the salary that was agreed, one must not grumble. This is a lesson from the Bible that I must try to follow and God give me the grace to learn from it.[42]

Shortly before Nairne wrote this, when the Emperor had still not released Princess Clementina, a plan was hatched whereby Charles Wogan and some other officers of Dillon's regiment would go to Innsbruck with a view to helping Clementina escape from her house arrest. In a letter of 8 January, Nairne told Gualterio about the plan, and suggested that he delay his return to Rome so that no one would suspect him of knowing about Wogan's mission.[43] Then, after Wogan had left, Nairne told Gualterio that he (Gualterio) was the only person to be let into the secret, and that Nairne regarded it as so sensitive that, exceptionally, he did not even dare keep a copy of his own letter.[44] In thanking him, Gualterio wrote that 'when matters are between you and me only, H. M. can be assured that secrecy will be guaranteed'.[45]

There was an even greater secret, however, which Nairne was instructed not to pass on to Gualterio.[46] War had broken out between Spain and the Emperor, the ally of George I, and the Spanish government was fitting out a fleet with which to invade England. James III had been invited to join the Spanish fleet, and he was preparing to make a sudden departure from Rome without giving anyone, not even the Pope, advance warning. The only people let into the secret were the king's three favourites (Hay, Murray and Mar), and the Duke of Perth, John Paterson and Nairne.

It was nearly eleven years since one of the European powers had prepared a fleet to invade Great Britain and restore James III, and there was naturally considerable optimism that at last the Jacobite exile was about to come to an end. The Spanish fleet was to carry an army made up of both Spanish and Irish regiments, under the command of the popular Duke of Ormonde, who had previously been commander-in-chief of the British forces at the end of the War of the Spanish Succession. We now know that the invasion attempt was doomed to fail, but at the time James III did not expect ever to return to Rome, and Nairne had every reason to assume that his long service at the exiled court was about to come to an end.

The plan was that James III and John Hay would leave Rome on 8 February and board a ship at Nettuno. They would then sail to Spain, join the Duke of Ormonde at Corunna, and sail directly to England. On the previous day, the 7th, the Dukes of Mar and Perth, with John Paterson disguised as the king, would leave Rome and travel north overland in order eventually to join the king in England. The Jacobites in Rome, meanwhile, both the household servants in the Palazzo del Re and the Scottish pensioners in the surrounding area, would remain where they were until news of the successful restoration had been received, when they also would all leave and return to England or Scotland, either to serve the king or recover their estates. Nairne, who had no desire to return to Scotland and wished to retire, would be the only Jacobite left behind in Rome. He would serve as the king's minister or diplomatic representative at the papal court, in collaboration with Gualterio as Cardinal Protector of England, until James III could send an ambassador from England to replace him. At that time Nairne would retire on a pension, and return to live in France.

The instructions which James drew up before his departure made this very clear. Murray was appointed acting secretary of state to replace Mar, with proxy power 'to solemnize the King's marriage with the Princess' if Wogan was able to rescue her from Innsbruck.[47] The household servants were placed under the authority of Sir William Ellis, who substituted for Hay as *maggiordomo*. As treasurer, Ellis would continue to receive the monthly papal pension, which he would use to pay all the salaries and pensions, but he was ordered 'to follow Mr Murrays directions whether in money matters or others'.[48] Nairne was no longer to be paid by Ellis, and was now to receive his salary out of the income from the king's investments in the *luoghi di monti*, to be given him by Gualterio.[49] This meant that when James III had been restored to his thrones, and the papal pension was no longer needed, Nairne would still have a guaranteed income on which to live and represent the king in Rome.

At a time when he was so worried about his son and younger daughter, Nairne must have been delighted by this development, particularly as the king made him a baronet to give him greater status.[50] He was happy to work with Gualterio, and had no wish to undermine the latter's authority, as he emphasized to the cardinal:

> God knows that I have only accepted this honest position with the intention of always putting myself entirely under the dependency and protection of Y. E.. I have been persuaded and still remain so that I am not displeasing to you, and that you would believe me incapable of ever having so much as thought in any way to diminish the superior authority of Y. E., which you hold with such dignity.[51]

> Y. E. knows me well, and that I never intrude in matters unless I am asked to do so. As long as I can live here quietly and decently under Y. E.'s protection and honourably retain this recent mark of recognition and satisfaction for my long service given to me by H. M., remaining with some sort of status and not merely as a private individual, a servant who has been dismissed and disgraced, that is all I ask for.[52]

Despite his optimism that James III would soon be restored, and that he himself could look forward to an honourable retirement, Nairne was actually in a very vulnerable position. If by any chance the Spanish fleet was unable to invade Engtland and restore the king, and if James was therefore obliged to return to Rome, then Nairne would no longer have anything to do. He would not be needed as the Jacobite minister to the papal court. Nor would there be any Roman correspondence for him to conduct, for the simple reason that the king would himself be in Rome, and able to meet and converse with Gualterio and the other cardinals. In that event Nairne would either become, as he feared, 'a private individual and a servant who has been dismissed and disgraced'. Or, if the king wanted to keep him, he would have to be demoted to the rank of under-secretary, no longer responsible directly to the king but rather to the secretary of state – as he had been before December 1713. Nairne's whole future was dependent on the success of the Spanish expedition.

Before he left Rome, James gave Nairne a 'lettre de créance', dated 7 February, which was addressed to the Pope. It described Nairne as 'our oldest and faithful subject Sir David Nairne, Secretary of the Closet, and member of our Privy Council', and asked the Pope to regard him 'as one of our longest serving and most loyal and devoted Catholic subjects in whom Your Holiness can have total confidence, and honour him with a favourable audience and with complete trust in what he will have the honour to say to you on our behalf'. In the absence of Gualterio, Nairne was to be James III's 'confidential envoy to the Pope without any official position'.[53]

Nairne's main task was to see the Pope and present this letter, once it was known publicly that the king had left Rome, and to apologize that James had left without informing the Pope and taking a formal farewell. He did this on 9 February and was relieved when the Pope gave him a friendly reception and made a point of not asking him why the king had left so suddenly or where he was going.[54] He told James that 'I said nothing but a short compliment and referred to the letter I gave him'.[55]

Once this had been done, there were several specific things that Nairne was to achieve from the Pope. He was to persuade the latter to continue to put pressure on the Emperor to release Princess Clementina, and to look after the princess if she should arrive in Rome when James was still away. He was to persuade the Pope to allow the Jacobite court to continue to occupy the Palazzo del Re, even though the king was no longer present. He was to ask the Pope to find a way of giving Gualterio some financial recompense for having accommodated the court in his palazzo, perhaps by giving him an abbey. He was to recommend to the Pope several Jacobites and all the people in the Papal States who had been particularly helpful since his arrival at Pesaro. And in particular he was to ask the Pope to confer princely status on the Salviati family.[56] It was understood that Nairne would at all times work in concert with Gualterio, particularly when the latter returned to Rome,[57] and that he would inform Murray (as acting secretary of state) of everything that he did. Then, once he had done all that was required of him, he would wait for news that James had been restored, after which Murray and the court would depart, leaving him to remain in Rome as the English diplomatic agent.

Nairne had four further audiences with the Pope (on 23 February, 3 March, at the end of March, and on 17 April), during which the latter agreed to look after Princess Clementina if she arrived in Rome and to let the Jacobite court continue to occupy the Palazzo del Re, and said he would consider the other requests.[58] Nairne told the king that 'at all times' he spoke 'with advice and concert according to my directions', and that 'to avoid mistakes in nice points [i.e. in Italian], I writt down the very words

I intended to speak, and had them considerd and approvd before hand, and stuck exactly to them.'[59] By the beginning of April Nairne's mission at the papal court had been accomplished.

Nairne had no difficulty in working with Gualterio, although the latter 'seemd to be a little shy and uneasy in the beginning' when he discovered that he had not been let into the secret of James III's departure.[60] But Nairne assured Gualterio that 'I shall always be governed by the opinions of Y. E., whose protection and friendship mean everything to me in the decision I have made in present circumstances to remain here.'[61] And he told the king that he hoped to behave towards Gualterio 'with such deference and circumspection, and cordiality that he having allways been the best of friends to me and professing still to be the same I am confident I shall make him very easy for I am sure I love him.'[62] Given the very friendly relations between the two men, and all that the cardinal was doing to help provide for Nairne's children, there was never any doubt that the two men would continue to work closely together.

Nairne's relations with the arrogant Murray, on the other hand, were likely to be strained, and he warned Gualterio to confine all personal comments to their secret correspondence as their official letters would now have to be shown to Murray.[63]

The situation was complicated when the Duke of Mar and the Duke of Perth unexpectedly returned to Rome in March, having been arrested by the Imperial authorities as they were travelling through the Duchy of Milan. They remained at the court until the middle of April, and during that time Mar and Murray had a major row about the management of the court and the king's correspondence.[64] Nairne told Gualterio, who had gone away temporarily to Orvieto, that Mar had behaved towards him 'very decently', though Nairne did all he could to remain neutral so that he could 'live here quietly and decently under the protection of Y. E.'.[65]

In the middle of March, the news reached Rome that James III had arrived safely in Spain, and would be able to make his way to join the invasion fleet at Corunna.[66] Nairne therefore began to send a letter to the king every Saturday, using Cardinal Aquaviva's diplomatic bag, and starting on 18 March. He told the king that he was 'overjoyd with the expectations' of the restoration and that 'he fancys himself ten years younger than he

Figure 12. *James Murray, Earl of Dunbar*, 1719 (101.6 × 76.2 cm),
by Francesco Trevisani (Scone Palace)
This was painted while James III was in Spain, leaving Murray in charge of the Stuart
Court in Rome.

was and dos not dispair to see his master yet before he dys in the place
he wishes him, or at least to be of some use and service to him where his
master thought fitt to leave him intrusted'. He added:

> When ever I shall find it becoming me and expected of me to begin a more regular
> and fuller correspondence with the King or his chief Agent when he has joynd him,
> I shall not spare my labour to give all the necessary informations in conformity to
> my Instructions. Till then I meddle no further than I am directed and I hope what
> ever my other faults may be neither the King nor any of his chief servants shall ever
> find me defective either in modesty prudence or zeal for peace and union which last
> I allways look upon to be important for the good of the King's service wch is already
> and allways shall be while I live my chiefest view in this world.[67]

For the time being Murray was the king's chief agent in Rome, and Nairne
would not have a 'fuller correspondence' with the king until the court had
left Rome.

Nairne's weekly letters informed the king of everything that he himself
had done for him in Rome, as well as the people he met (notably the three
Albani brothers, various cardinals and Francesco Bianchini), but he made
no attempt to write about more general issues, leaving this to Murray as
acting secretary of state or, as he put it, 'being persuaded that the King is
perfectly informd from better hands of all that has past here in relation to
his affaires since his departure'.[68] When Mar returned to Rome Nairne told
the king that he knew Mar and Murray both wrote 'so fully that I would be
troubling the King with needless repetitions, for me to write of any business', and he assured James that he did nothing, 'nor shall ... while they are
upon the place', without their 'knowledge and directions'.[69]

Nairne knew that his letters would take a long time to reach James III,
and by April he was hoping that the king would receive them in England
rather than in Spain.[70] On 8 April, he wished that 'the Alleluias and rejoyc-
ings of tomorrow [Easter Sunday] may soon be followd by those which all
good men have been longing for these thirty years, and that after sitting
or rather wandering and weeping so long *super flumina Babylonis* we may
now at last see the happy day'.[71] He remained equally optimistic on 15 April,
once again assuming that Murray would have kept the king fully informed,
but this time looking forward to when Murray and the court would have
left Rome to join the king in England:

When it shall please God to give the hopd-for success to the King's affairs, as he'l then be able to put N. in a way to serve him creditably here, so N. will be in a condition also then to serve him more effectually than he can at present, eclat would be foly, caracter is not essentiall, but a decency and conveniency to a certain degree is absolutly necessary in this place for ones masters sake and the good of the service.[72]

And so the weeks went by, with Nairne longing to receive the news that James III had landed in England and been successfully restored to his thrones, and looking forward to Murray's departure. Although his letters to the king tell us whom he met and with whom he corresponded, we know very little about his other activities during these weeks. In March he complained of 'a bit of gout which continues to make me unwilling to walk',[73] and in April he recorded in one of his letters that 'I have such sore eyes today that it is with some difficulty I have writt this'.[74] There is no reason to doubt that he passed many hours in the various churches that he liked, and especially in the church of the Santi Apostoli beside the Palazzo del Re whenever he found it difficult to work. By chance, one letter has survived which gives us a little insight into his private life at this time. It is interesting because, at a time when his son had joined the Spanish army, and when France and Spain were at war, the letter was written to Nairne by one of his French friends in Rome.

The letter, dated 4 May, was written by a man named Bourrier, perhaps a member of the French embassy. It is an invitation to Nairne and Robert Creagh (Murray's chief clerk) to 'take the air at our vineyard', something which Nairne had apparently said he would like to do. Bourrier tells Nairne that he would collect him in his carriage at two o'clock that afternoon, and that they could pass the rest of the day together:

We could spend some time there together playing billiards, playing chess, and bocce, or tric trac; and I could have the pleasure of your conversation for a little longer, without fearing that I am disturbing you or interrupting your work.[75]

Here, then, we find evidence of Nairne enjoying exactly the same recreations (with the exception of cards) that are mentioned in his diary when he was previously at Rome and when he was at Saint-Germain-en-Laye.

It was easier for Nairne to spend an afternoon in this way because Murray had been steadily marginalizing him. Shortly before he received this invitation Nairne had written to the king that 'Mr Murray is so capable so active and so diligent that while he is here there is little left for me either to do or say, so I look upon the most part of the exercise of my employment in this place as suspended as long as another dos so willingly and heartily alone all that is needful'. Whether or not Nairne was sincere in complimenting Murray like this is debatable, particularly as he added:

> For my part I still am (as the King knows I allways was) so afraid of meddling further than he has a mind I should, that I had rather be a cypher in my proper imployment, than either be officious, or uneasy to any body.[76]

While Nairne and the other Jacobites were waiting in Rome for news of the king's restoration, disaster had struck the Spanish fleet. It had sailed from Cadiz, intending to collect the king at Corunna, but had run into a terrible storm off Cape Finistere. After twelve days of battering some ships had been sunk, and others had returned to port unfit to make the journey to England. When James III arrived at Corunna on 17 April, he was given the appalling news. He withdrew to Lugo in Galicia for three long months, hoping that something might yet be achieved by a diversionary force sent to Scotland.[77] Nairne wrote on 29 April, just before the news reached Rome, that the delay in hearing anything positive 'makes us all very unquiet and uneasy, but there being nothing as yet that is bad except the delay, we hope still from post to post to have something that is good'.[78] It was shortly after he wrote this that the news finally reached Rome that the Spanish invasion attempt had had to be cancelled. For Nairne, this was a personal as well as a political catastrophe.

It was at this moment that Charles Wogan brought off a spectacular coup and managed to rescue Princess Clementina from Innsbruck. She arrived at Bologna during the first week of May, and Murray and his sister went to meet her, accompanied by Lawrence Mayes, the Agent of the English Catholic Clergy in Rome. On 9 May, using the power given him by the king, Murray had a proxy marriage ceremony performed by Mayes, after which he brought Clementina, now given the title of the Queen of England, to Rome. She arrived on 16 May and was lodged by the Pope in the Ursuline convent.[79] Nairne, extremely worried about his own future, lamented to Gualterio that he was not permitted by Murray to see the queen, and that he was 'neither consulted nor called'.[80] Murray, by contrast, now had the added prestige of having married the queen by proxy, and of being able to control (in fact deny) access by the Jacobites to their new queen.

There remained the possibility that the diversionary force sent to Scotland might succeed in raising the northern kingdom against George I and his Whig government, so James III remained in Spain hoping that he would not need to return to Rome. But Nairne no longer believed that there would be a restoration, and realized that Murray and the court would not therefore be able to leave. He wrote to Gualterio on 12 June that 'I am no longer useful to seve the King', and begged the cardinal 'never to withdraw his protection from a creature who for several years now has been so intimately and respectfully loyal'. He described himself as 'old, useless and a bad courtier'.[81]

The Stuart Papers have preserved Nairne's weekly letters to the king from 18 March to 29 April inclusive, but there is then a gap of six weeks. Either Nairne stopped writing, or his letters were mislaid and never reached the king in Spain: the latter is more likely. There are then two letters of 17 and 20 June, followed by another gap of seven weeks until August. The letters of June were written before the news reached Rome of the defeat of the diversionary force at Glenshiel in Scotland. The letters of August were written after they arrived, and when it was known that James III would definitely have to leave Spain and return to Rome. Both sets of letters reveal how Nairne's attitude changed in response to the failure of the Spanish plans.

The letter of 17 June acknowledged the receipt of the first letter that Nairne had received from the king since the latter's departure from Rome. 'The only particular orders your Ma.ty is pleasd to honour me with being to follow the Cardinals in every thing', he wrote, 'I can assure your Ma.ty that they shall be most cheerfully and punctually obeyd'. He then told the king that he did all he could to work in harmony with Murray:

> For I love peace and live as retirdly as I possibly can, I wait on the Card.l [Gualterio] from time to time to ask if he has any orders for me, and what letters I receive of

news or other things I communicat regularly to his Em.ce and to Mr Murray which last shews them to the Queen when there is any thing worth her knowledge. I see also Card. Aq[uaviva] some time who is extreme civil to me.[82]

In the letter of 20 June, he told the king that he had not been allowed by Murray to meet the queen, but that he had been able to see her from a distance 'in the croud' and that he had been 'charmed at all times with her gracious and obliging behaviour'. He then begged James 'to be continued still in some share of your royal favour and protection and with Gods providence in all things to depend upon in this world for my own support in my old age'.[83] Anticipating that the king would no longer need him as his diplomatic agent in Rome, he was in effect asking to be allowed to retire on a pension.

The two letters of 12 and 19 August are very different. For one thing they are enormously long – so long, indeed, that it is hard to believe that the king actually read them! What is particularly striking about them, however, is that, for the first time in letters to the king, they contain the kind of criticisms and expressions of discontent which Nairne had previously restricted to his secret letters to Gualterio. They indicate the extent to which Nairne was feeling worried about his future.

He had just had his first audience with the queen in her convent – three months after her arrival in Rome – and had been 'charmd with her gracious and gaining conversation'. So he went to see Murray to thank him for having arranged the audience 'unaskd which I supposd to have been an effect of his advice or insinuation'.[84] Nairne then gave the following account of their conversation:

> he told me I might have seen her sooner if I had askd it and spoke to him but I told him I did not think it proper for such an useless person, as I saw I was to her Ma.ty, to ask any such thing; that I was unwilling to be troublesom or uneasy to any body, and that I pretended to no distinction but just to make my Court as all the rest of yr Ma.ties subjects do, but I could not but tell him at the same time, that I thought it impossible for any body to have an audience of the Queen and not be ready to give his life (if it was necessary) to serve her and that it was enough for her to give but a gracious audience to gain the hearts of any one she gave it to, wch popularity certainly could not but be both hers and yr Ma.ties service. He told me indeed as to me that I was too nice and ceremonious, and that as I was imployd in yr Ma.ties affaires my case was different from others.

This prompted Nairne to make the following reflections to the king:

> As to this last I confess I thought so my self in the beginning, but afterward finding
> such a continuation of reservedness and discouragement I was easily rebufed, and so
> at last took the party which I thought would be lik'd best, for peaces sake. Nor would
> I for the same reason so much as take notice to Mr Mur. that I had some reason to
> think I was at least neglected, if not distrusted.

He explained that he had made no complaints because he wanted to keep
the peace, and that he had chosen 'rather to be passive and patient as far
as decency and honour' would allow. But nevertheless he could not help
noticing that he was treated by Murray with 'reserve', and that this had
begun to influence Cardinal Gualterio:

> I must say that the Card.l is extreme civil and obliging, and ready to do me any
> kindness upon all occasions and assures me his friendship for me is not changd in
> the least, tho I cannot without being blind but perceive that his confidence in many
> things is not the same it was formerly when he saw I had the honour to be intirely
> trusted by your Ma.ty which he has perhaps some grounds given him to doubt of at
> present for reasons which I shall not penetrat into.

Nairne then referred to the fact that the failure of the Spanish expedition had undermined his position as James III's diplomatic representative
at the papal court, because Murray had not left Rome. 'All I ambition', he
explained, 'is to live in quiet and to have leave to continue with decency to
render your Ma.ty any little service I can in the station you have been pleasd
to leave me in in this place'. This brought him at last to his main complaint:

> Perhaps I might be of a litle more use in it than I am, if I were a litle more authorisd
> and less dependant, and had not to writhe against all the present appearances which
> can give litle or no notion to this court of my being thoroughly trusted and employd
> by Yr Ma.ty when they see and know very well that I meddle with nothing, so if I
> should take upon me to act more than I do in the lessening and disadvantagous cir-
> cumstances I am in at present, I could not expect to act with any sort of success with
> persons prevented with all the aparent presumptions of my having litle or no credit.

For the moment, and as long as Murray remained in Rome, Nairne
wrote that 'I have nothing to say or do'. He would not try to 'interfere' in
Murray's 'employment, since I chuse rather to lessen my own than make

any body uneasy'. But he hoped that when the king returned to Rome he might let Nairne continue to liaise with Gualterio rather than be demoted, and that in the event of a future restoration he might still be employed as James's agent in Rome:

> When things change as they must some way or other before it be long (and I pray God it be for the better for your Ma.ties affairs) if then your Ma.ty thinks me capable to serve you here in a more active and less limited and eclipsed capacity, I hope in God I am not so disagreeable to you nor so destitute of prudence or experience but that I may perform my duty as well as another, and even please and serve Cardinal Gualterio himself as well as your Ma.ty a great deal better than I can do now, for 'tis plain that his respect for yr Ma.ty is such, that wherever he sees your Ma.tys trust and confidence is placed, there he chiefly dos and allways will shew his.[85]

In the letter of 19 August, Nairne informed the king that he had been told by his friends in France (Lewis Innes and William Dicconson) that Lord Middleton 'was very ill of a feavor and in danger'. Comparing Middleton with both Mar and Murray, he commented that 'I may boldly say without disparagement to any, that your Ma.ty never had nor can have a more dissinterested servant of more true honour, merit and loyalty'. The same, of course, could have been said about Nairne himself, who now indicated to the king that he would really like to retire:

> I have been much out of order all this week and obliged to take phisick, and have not yet quite recoverd my strength, which is not very surprizing at my age, in which it is more reasonable I should hereafter expect and prepare my self for frequent infirmitys and the last natural consequence of them, than flatter my self either with perfect health or long life. Placida senectus would no doubt be more agreable to nature than labor et color, but Gods will is allways the best and to that I hope I am and allways shall be resignd.'[86]

Shortly before Nairne wrote this letter, James III and John Hay embarked from Vinaros (between Tarragona and Valencia) to return to Italy. Everything that Nairne had most feared had come about, and he was now in suspense, waiting to see how he would be treated by the king. Would he be retained as the secretary of the closet, or would he be allowed to retire, or would he be demoted? The one positive development was that he now had an admiration for the queen, who had recently forced a reluctant Murray to let her meet her husband's Jacobite servants and courtiers.[87] The queen was also regularly visited by Cardinals Gualterio and Aquaviva. Nairne recorded in August that the latter

> has now for two sundays consecutively invited her to see the great concours of coaches in Piazza Navona which is all coverd with water all the sundays of this month, and in some parts comes up to the horses bellys, the Queen was seated in a balcony under a canapy very richly furnishd with red damasc and gold fringes, where her Ma.ty made a very glorious appearance, and drew the chief attention of all the spectators ... She had Card. Aquaviva that waited upon her, and receivd her there ..., and there was a noble entertainment of all sorts of rifraichissements, the Card.l being a person that dos every thing very nobly. I had the pleasure to go in a coach of purpose to see the shew from the piazza and was truly delighted with it.[88]

At the end of August 1719, the news reached Rome that James III, accompanied by John Hay, had landed at Leghorn and would be returning to Rome. Arrangements were immediately made for his proxy marriage to Clementina to be formally solemnized, and Gualterio and the Pope decided that the king should be met by his wife on his way south at the hill-top town of Montefiascone, where the bishop, Sebastiano Bonaventura, was an old friend from Urbino.

Murray, as head of the court in the absence of the king, had to decide whom he would allow to accompany him and the queen to Montefiascone, to attend and witness the marriage. Apart from some grooms and the coachman, he only invited three men and three women. They were Charles Wogan (who had rescued Clementina from Innsbruck), Sir John O'Brien (Wogan's superior officer in Dillon's regiment), Father John Brown (the king's confessor), Murray's own sister Marjory Hay, and two chambermaids (one of whom was Nairne's cousin Mary Fitzgerald, who had recently joined her husband at the court).[89] Nairne himself was not included.[90] Nor were any of the Scottish lords and ladies, and there was not a single Englishman in the party.

The king and queen met at Montefiascone on 1 September, and were married by Bonaventura at midnight in the private chapel of his palazzo opposite the cathedral. The marriage contract was formally witnessed by Hay, Murray, Wogan, O'Brien, Brown and the local vicar-general. The couple then remained at Montefiascone for two months until 28 October.[91]

Although Nairne was not present at the ceremony, the king needed him in order to conduct his correspondence with Gualterio and the papal court. A messenger was therefore sent to Rome summoning him to go to Montefiascone as quickly as possible. Nairne arrived there on 3 September and sent a letter to Gualterio apologizing for having left the city without taking his leave.[92] Two weeks later he recorded how pleased he was to have escaped from 'the great heats' in Rome: 'I myself was so inexpressibly exhausted in Rome, but the air here has helped me to recover a little.'[93]

Unfortunately for Nairne, it was not only the king who needed his secretarial services, because Murray, as acting secretary of state, had not brought his clerk, Robert Creagh, to Montefiascone. Nairne therefore found himself – for the first time since 1713 – having to work for the secretary of state as well as the king. It was the one thing he had been trying to avoid.

During September, Nairne persuaded the king to live in Rome rather than elsewhere,[94] and then corresponded with Gualterio about having the royal apartments in the Palazzo del Re fully furnished and decorated.[95] The Stuart Papers, however, show that Nairne was now obliged to write letters for and under the dictation of Murray.[96] And the letters which Murray forced him to send were such that he must have felt deeply humiliated, because they were very offensive. In particular, they rudely told some of the Jacobites in Rome that they were not welcome to visit the king and queen at Montefiascone.[97]

While James III had been away in Spain, Murray had succeeded in alienating all the Jacobites in Rome (the Scottish pensioners as well as the household servants) by his excessive arrogance and rudeness,[98] and the pensioners in particular now wanted to bring their grievances to the attention of the king. Nairne, who as minister to the papal court had ceased to be a regular member of the Jacobite court, and who had expected to remain in Rome after a restoration, had deliberately distanced himself from all the problems created by Murray. In March, when Mar had returned temporarily to Rome and had had a major row with Murray, Nairne told the king that all he wanted was 'peace and union'[99] and that he had kept out of 'a certain tracasserie'.[100] In April he assured the king that 'as for family affairs, I do not meddle'.[101] In June he was more specific:

> I love peace and live as retirdly as I possibly can ... As for visits to our people in town I make none, and if there be any disgusts among them, I thank God I have no hand in them, and am far from encouraging them either directly or indirectly.[102]

Nairne hoped that these comments would prevent his getting involved in the recriminations which were bound to come to a head when the king returned. In August he warned James that there were 'indiscreet factions divisions or discontents' among the Jacobites in Rome, and assured him that 'I have kept myself free [from them] hitherto', and that 'with the help of God I shall allways continue to do [so]'.[103] Although he was living in the Palazzo del Re, and both he and Murray had apartments on the first floor of the building,[104] he told the king that he had 'been so little abroad' that he had not seen Murray for several days.[105] But if Nairne thought that he would be able to avoid being drawn into the 'factious divisions' at the court he was to be sorely disappointed. He was brought down because he made the tactical mistake of forwarding a letter to the king from Lord Pitsligo, one of the Scottish pensioners who was also one of Murray's strongest critics.

By the middle of June, Murray had become so overbearing and rude to the Jacobites in the Palazzo del Re, including even the Duchess of Mar, that Pitsligo decided to send a letter of complaint to James III in Spain:

> I think it absolutely for your Mat.'s honour and interest to acquaint you that the person in whose hands you left your affairs has managed them in the manner least agreeable in the world to your people here and I am afraid to the inhabitants who know anything of them ... it was observed very soon after your Mat. left Rome, that Mr Murray put on more airs than before.

Pitsligo told the king that Murray had prevented the Scottish lords and gentlemen from being properly introduced to the queen, and had refused to allow them to wait on her, monopolizing her himself. Even the Duchess of Mar and Lady Nithsdale were kept away as much as possible. Pitsligo added one more damning complaint: that Murray was repeatedly rude to the duchess in public.[106]

Having written this letter, Pitsligo had to ensure that it was sent to the king. But the only people corresponding with James were Murray and Nairne, which meant that Pitsligo had to persuade the latter to forward his letter to Spain. In his own letter of 20 June, Nairne told the king that he was enclosing a 'letter ... from My Lord Pitsligo who brought it me last night and told me only it was about some privat affairs of his own, and that he would be glad it should come streight into your own hands'. Whether or not Nairne was aware of what the letter contained cannot be said, though he assured the king that 'I inquird no further only assurd him I should forward it with care'.[107] Either way it was this letter which was to cause Nairne to be demoted at Montefiascone.

The rude letters which Murray forced Nairne to send to Rome provoked Pitsligo to ask Nairne if he had ever sent on to the king the private letter which he had written in June. Nairne showed Pitsligo's letter to the king, who pretended he had never received the earlier one,[108] and instructed Nairne to tell Pitsligo that he 'might when you [Pitsligo] think fitt aquaint him with the contents of it'.[109] As Pitsligo had kept a copy he then transcribed it and sent it to Montefiascone, hoping to make the king realize how badly Murray had been behaving.[110] James III, however, was very angry when he read (or re-read) the letter, completely supported Murray, and ordered Pitsligo to make sure he had left Rome before he (the king) returned. James's letter, in the handwriting of Nairne, was dated 30 September,[111] and it seems that the latter, as Pitsligo's go-between, was now regarded with suspicion as having taken sides against the king's favourite.

Feeling both humiliated and isolated at Montefiascone, Nairne was looking forward to seeing Cardinal Gualterio, whom the king had invited to visit.[112] He wrote to the cardinal on 1 October, one day after sending the letter for the king to Pitsligo, that 'I am looking forward to having the honour of speaking to Y. E. about my own little affairs, and other confidential matters, when I have the pleasure of seeing him here'.[113] Apart from the problems of his children, this referred primarily to the awkward position in which he now found himself because of Pitsligo. As we shall see, it also referred to the question of his salary.

On 9 October, while Gualterio was still at Montefiascone, Nairne received a long letter of explanation from Pitsligo, which he immediately showed to the king.[114] He could hardly have refused to do so, but it provoked James III and Murray to punish him for what they regarded as his disloyalty in taking the side of the Scottish pensioners against the favourite.[115] On the following day, the 10th, the king wrote a letter to Gualterio informing him that he was demoting Nairne, who would become Murray's under-secretary and no longer responsible for conducting the king's Roman correspondence. The letter has not survived among Gualterio's papers, but a letter from Murray to the cardinal records the fact that they made Nairne convey the message of his own demotion:

> I have reason to believe that in this letter to Y. E. the King has gone into some detail and I therefore take the liberty to beg Y. E. most humbly not to communicate the contents to Mr Nairne even though he has brought the message to you.[116]

On the following day Gualterio left Montefiascone and went to Orvieto, and Nairne wrote to tell him how sorry he was that he had left. He added:

> As for myself I am able to let some rather disagreeable things pass so as not to upset anyone, but it does not mean that I do not feel them keenly.[117]

Nairne remained at Montefiascone for another two weeks, during which he was told that his salary would now be reduced. In Lorraine and at Avignon, he had been paid in French *livres* and had received 205*l*. 3*s*. 2*d*. each month.[118] At Urbino he had been paid the same amount, but now in Bologna *livres* which were worth less. (One Bologna *livre* was worth 0.83 of a French *livre*).[119] In February 1719 his salary had been increased to 40 *scudi*, the equivalent of 240 Bologna *livres*, to be paid by Gualterio out of the *luoghi di monti* in Rome which James III had inherited from Queen Mary of Modena.[120] In fact the king's *luoghi di monti* did not yield enough money to pay this amount,[121] and anyway Gualterio did not have a procuration to allow him to draw any money from them.[122] As a result Gualterio had to pay Nairne out of his own pocket, and by September (when he gave Nairne that month's money in advance) he had given him his salary for eight months, amounting to 320 *scudi*.[123] Gualterio told the king that there was absolutely no need to repay him the money he had given Nairne,[124] and when he came to Montefiascone at the beginning of October the king told him that he would now start paying Nairne himself.[125] It was then that the king reduced Nairne's salary by a half, from 240 to 120 *livres* each month. As Nairne put it in one of his secret letters to Gualterio, he was now to get '20 *scudi* each month from Sir William Ellis, instead of the 40 I was receiving from Y. E.'[126]

For Nairne, the weeks that he spent at Montefiascone were deeply depressing, and his feelings of dissatisfaction were increased because the king made no apparent effort to maintain good relations with the Pope and his nephews. After all, as Nairne pointed out to Gualterio, the king was dependent on them 'for a part of his maintenance and lodging':

> instead of preserving the affection of those who are attached to us, and trying to win over new friends, I am sorry to see that some have become disgusted, have become cooler in their attentions and are thinking of leaving. I am not close enough to the King to tell him what I see, as he does not ask me, but I cannot hide my distress from Y. E.. I hope with all my heart that you can soften such blows, patch things up with certain people, and forestall the results of this discontent which can never be good for H. M.'s service.[127]

The problem, as Cardinal Albani put it, was that James III was 'led by two boys', his favourites John Hay and James Murray, and accepted uncritically the advice that they gave him.[128] Murray, in particular, was a disastrous choice as secretary of state because he was both arrogant and rude, especially to the queen but also to Cardinal Aquaviva.[129] In October, for example, James III wrote a letter to Don Alessandro Albani which provoked the following commentary from Nairne:

> I hope I am fortunate enough still to be sufficiently in Y. E.'s good graces to dare to convey to him my private thoughts on the secret letter sent by the King to Don Alessandro. In my opinion, the letter was rather too strongly worded, and it risked much to send such a letter hoping for the discretion of D. Al.. It was not at all obliging towards H[is] H[oliness] nor in my view fit to be seen by him both because of the little affection D. Al. has for H. M. and because of the sensitivity he must feel where his own family is concerned ... He is bound to be shocked to see the Court and his uncle's conduct treated with arrogance and disdain. I cannot see any good for the King in this, unless the Pope and his family are people who have definitely to be treated with disdain to get anything from them. But in the state in which the King is, uncertain of any solid help from any other quarter, unsure even of being able to stay in Rome, it would seem to me that a little more patience and restraint would have been more appropriate than writing things which could irritate. That, between ourselves, is my feeling, of which I only said one thing to the King when I was copying it, which was that I found it rather strong, but without insisting or explaining my reasons.'[130]

This was merely one example of what Nairne now had to witness on a daily basis:

> I see many things that I am not courtier and hypocritical enough to approve, but prudence dictates that I submit to higher authority. As long as I live I will be second to none in true zeal for the service of H. M. ... despite all the skill others have had in gaining his good graces.[131]

In other letters to Gualterio, he worried that the king would suffer politically[132] and wished that the favourites would show 'the submission that they should'. But the situation was

> so delicate that I avoid as far as possible getting involved, especially having such small influence and perhaps having let it be known too widely that I cannot approve all that I see, thus making myself somewhat suspect.

So he had to maintain '*un respectueux silence*' and try to continue working as well as he could:

> and when I am no longer here others younger than me will be able to serve him better and in a manner more to his liking and I shall be delighted. But despite my age I dare say this because it is known and can be seen that I have until now played my part in all the tiring work, without sparing myself and with God's help having survived thus far, but that this cannot last much longer, in the nature of things. In any case when it pleases God that everything comes to an end, I pray that the Lord gives me the grace to be able to say with as much truth and confidence towards Him as I believe I can say truthfully towards the King, *fidem servani cursum consummavi* (I have kept the faith and finished my course).[133]

Nairne left Montefiascone on 21 October and travelled slowly back to Rome, where he arrived on the 26th.[134] The king and queen, accompanied by the Hays and Murray, then arrived on 1 November and moved into their newly prepared apartments in the Palazzo del Re.[135] By the beginning of November Nairne had still not received his October salary, either because the king had forgotten to tell Sir William Ellis that he, rather than Gualterio, should now pay Nairne, or simply because the king and Murray wanted to punish Nairne for transmitting Pitsligo's letters. On 4 November, when all the household servants and the pensioners had received their October money, Nairne sent the following letter to Gualterio, who had now also returned to Rome:

depuis le payment que V. E. eut la bonté de m'ordonner, je n'ay pas touché un sols du Roy et on ne m'en parle seulem.t pas quoique on paye la famille ici actuellement, et je suis resolû de n'en pas ouvrir la bouche, et d'attendre avec patience ce qu'il plaira a S. M. d'en ordonner, au reste je serai bien trompé et agreablement si après avoir attendu tant que je pourrai je n'ay pas l'honneur d'etre le seul ici de la famille qui serai retranché et reduit de 40 a 20 Ecus par mois. Je souhaitte que je me trompe.[136]

Now that Nairne and Gualterio were both in Rome, and also because Nairne had been demoted back to the rank of under-secretary, the correspondence between the two men, came to an end. The letter quoted immediately above was in fact the last of the regular letters that Nairne sent to Gualterio. He was presumably given his October money at some point during November, but the available documents do not let us know when that was.[137]

By the end of 1719, Nairne was sixty-four and a half years old, an age at which anyone in his position might reasonably have wanted to retire. And given that there was no longer any Roman correspondence for him to conduct he should have been allowed to do so. Moreover there were other people who might now have been employed as Murray's under-secretary. It reflects very badly on both James III and his favourites that they would not let Nairne leave the court in Rome and return to live with his daughters in Paris, as he was longing to do. Of course Nairne could simply have resigned his position and left, but he was too loyal to do that and was totally dependent on the salary that he was receiving from the king. Unless James was willing to convert that salary into a pension, then Nairne was completely trapped, and the king and his favourites took an unscrupulous advantage of this. After more than thirty years loyal service to both James II and James III, as well as to their first three secretaries of state (Melfort, Caryll and Middleton) it was particularly cruel to demote him, to make him work for Murray, a much younger man who was disliked by most of the members of the court,[138] and actually to reduce his salary. Finally, it was politically inept because the community of exiled Jacobites in both Italy and France was discouraged from joining a court where a popular and highly regarded servant could be treated in such a way.[139] The excessive favouritism showed by the king to the Hays and Murray would have serious implications for the future of the exiled court, and the treatment of Nairne, following that of Charles Booth and Lord Clermont at Urbino, and that of Lewis Innes at Saint-Germain, was an indication of what was to come.

Endnotes

1. HMC *Stuart* VII, p. 399, James III to Nairne, 18 October 1718. See also ibid. pp. 417 and 421, James III to Nairne, 21 and 22 October 1718 for his further instructions.
2. Ibid. p. 408, James III to Clement XI, 19 October 1718.
3. He travelled in 'the Duke of Mar's French chair', and did not leave Urbino until the morning because 'in those hills without moonshine it was not thought safe'. He left Urbino via Fossombrone rather than the more direct route via Aqualagna which he felt was 'too dangerous in a French chair'. He had fallen badly on that road when he had first arrived at Urbino the previous year, and commented that 'burnt bairns fire dread' (ibid. p. 428, Nairne to Mar, 23 October 1718).
4. Ibid. p. 457, Nairne to James III, 29 October 1718. This very long letter has been published and is only very briefly summarized here. It gives all the details of Nairne's journey, and of his conversations with Imperiali and Albani *en route*, and with Paulucci and various other people shortly after his arrival in Rome.
5. Ibid. p. 428, Nairne to Mar, 23 October 1718.
6. Ibid. p. 457, Nairne to James III, 29 October 1718.
7. Ibid. p. 491, James III to Nairne, 3 November 1718.
8. Ibid. p. 484, Nairne to James III, 2 November 1718.
9. Ibid. See also BL. Add MSS 31261, f.264, Nairne to Gualterio, 1 November 1718, with postscript of 2 November.
10. BL. Add MSS 31261, f.272, Nairne to Gualterio, 12 November 1718. See also HMC *Stuart* VII, p. 495, Nairne to Mar, 5 November 1718: 'I continue very incredulous and desponding of any good success from this step of the Pope's, though it was proper for the King to ask it and the Pope's duty to grant it.'
11. HMC *Stuart* VII, p. 495, Nairne to Mar, 5 November 1718.
12. Ibid. p. 491, James III to Nairne, 3 November 1718.
13. Ibid. p. 502, Nairne to James III, 8 November 1718.
14. Ibid. p. 513, Nairne to James III, 9 November 1718. See also BL. Add MSS 31261, f.270, Nairne to Gualterio, 9 November 1718: 'Il [le Roy] me dit de continuer de faire tout le bruit que je pourrai sur cette affaire, cela m'embarasse car le bruit

n'est pas mon caractere, et je ne suis pas persuadé que ce soit ni du service du Roy ni convenable a moy de criailler contre l'Empereur.' He was afraid that if he did as instructed he would lose his reputation as an 'homme moderé'.

15. HMC *Stuart* VII, p. 399 James III to Nairne, 18 October 1718.

16. Corp, *The Jacobites at Urbino*, pp. 108–10.

17. HMC *Stuart* VII, p. 463, Nairne to Mar, 29 October 1718.

18. Corp, *The Jacobites at Urbino*, pp. 110–12.

19. BL. Add MSS 31261, f.275, Nairne to Gualterio, 16 November 1718. Since his arrival in Rome Nairne had been invited to eat most of his meals with Gualterio's private secretary (Cavaliere Lucci) who lived near the Palazzo Gualterio and had remained in Rome (BL. Add MSS 31261, f.262, Nairne to Gualterio, 29 October 1718; HMC *Stuart* VII, p. 484, Nairne to James III, 2 November 1718; and BL. Add MSS 31261, f.266, Nairne to Gualterio, 4 November 1718: 'aimant a etre retiré j'ay pris ce parti plutôt que de m'engager avec d'autres companies dans des auberges'). He presumably continued to do this. At the time Lucci was hoping to leave the service of Cardinal Gualterio and obtain a post at the Stuart court (HMC *Stuart* VII, p. 388, 'Minutes of the King's Order to be sent to Mr Nairne', 14 October 1718; BL. Add MSS 20298, f.101, Nairne to Gualterio, 27 December 1718). See also note 59.

20. BL. Add MSS 31261, f.279, Nairne to Gualterio, 19 November 1718.

21. HMC *Stuart* VII, p. 484, Nairne to James III, 2 November 1718.

22. Ibid.; and p. 490, Nairne to Mar, 2 November 1718.

23. Ibid. p. 495, Nairne to Mar, 5 November 1718. See also BL. Add MSS 31261, f.275, Nairne to Gualterio, 16 November 1718.

24. BL. Add MSS 31261, ff.279 and 282, Nairne to Gualterio, 19 and 22 November 1718.

25. BL. Add MSS 31261, ff.284 and 286, Nairne to Gualterio, 26 and 30 November 1718.

26. BL. Add MSS 31261, f.294, Nairne to Gualterio, 14 December 1718.

27. BL. Add MSS 31261, f.290, Nairne to Gualterio, 7 December 1718.

28. BL. Add MSS 31261, f.292, Nairne to Gualterio, 13 December 1718.

29. BL. Add MSS 20298, f.101, Nairne to Gualterio, 27 December 1718.

30. BL. Add MSS 20298, f.103, Nairne to Gualterio. See also BL. Add MSS 31261, ff.303 and 307, Nairne to Gualterio, 4 and 7 January 1719.

31. BL. Add MSS 31261, ff.309, 314 and 319, Nairne to Gualterio, 8, 18 and 28 January 1719.

32. BL. Add MSS 31261, f.321, Nairne to Gualterio, 1 February 1719.

33. BL. Add MSS 31261, f.324, Nairne to Gualterio, 11 February 1719. See also Corp, *The Jacobites at Urbino*, pp. 117–21.

34. HMC *Stuart* VII pp. 457 and 513, Nairne to James III, 29 October and 9 November 1718. The priests with whom Nairne was on good terms included Lord Richard Howard (known as *abate* Howard), Lawrence Mayes, William Stuart and the rector of the English College (WDA. Epist Var 6/no.58, Nairne to Mayes, 3 September 1717).
35. BL. Add MSS 31261, f.282, Nairne to Gualterio, 22 November 1718.
36. BL. Add MSS 31261, ff.300 and 303, Nairne to Gualterio, 28 December 1718 and 4 January 1719.
37. BL. Add MSS 20298, f.160, Nairne to Gualterio, undated (January 1719). For the operas, see Corp, *The Jacobites at Urbino*, p. 114. For seeing Gasparini's *Astianatte* twice at the Aliberti, see BL. Add MSS 31261, f.311, Nairne to Gualterio, 11 January 1719.
38. Corp, *The Jacobites at Urbino*, pp. 113–14.
39. BL. Add MSS 31261, f.305, Nairne to Gualterio, 5 January 1719.
40. BL. Add MSS 20298, f.110, Nairne to Gualterio, undated but 5 January 1719.
41. BL. Add MSS 20298, f.112, Nairne to Gualterio, 7 January 1719.
42. BL. Add MSS 20298, f.155, Nairne to Gualterio, undated (early February 1719).
43. BL. Add MSS 31261, f.309, Nairne to Gualterio, 8 January 1719.
44. BL. Add MSS 31261, f.315, Nairne to Gualterio, 21 January 1719.
45. Bod. Carte MSS 258, f.321, Gualterio to Nairne, 24 January 1719.
46. BL. Add MSS 31261, f.326, Nairne to Gualterio, 15 February 1719.
47. Bod. Carte MSS 208, f.321, 'Power given to Mr Murray when the King parted for Spain to open letters and to solemnize the Kings marriage with the Princess', 2 February 1719.
48. Corp, *The Jacobites at Urbino*, pp. 122–6.
49. BL. Add MSS 31255, f.178, James III to Gualterio, 7 February 1719: 'Vous luy donnerés s'il vous plait 40 Ecus Romains par mois, a commencer par ce mois de Fevrier sur les monte de pieté.'
50. RA. SP 43/9, Salviati to Nairne, 26 March 1719: 'Je viens d'apprendre seulement que le Roy en partant de Rome vous a donné des nouvelles marques de son estime et de sa justice en vous declarant Chevalier Baronet d'Angleterre.' See also RA. SP 43/81, Sempill to Nairne, 8 May 1719: [He congratulates him on his recent honour and on] the choice he [the king] has made of you to reside at Rome ... I hope you'll thereby have occasion to render such services as will soon procure us the satisfaction to see you joyn his Majesty with greater marks of distinction than those lately conferd upon you.'
51. BL. Add MSS 20298, f.121, Nairne to Gualterio, 2 March 1719.
52. BL. Add MSS 20298, f.124, Nairne to Gualterio, 18 March 1719.
53. ASV. Albani 167, f.19, James III to Clement XI, 7 February 1719.

54. BL. Add MSS 20298, f.119, Nairne to Gualterio, 9 February 1719.
55. RA. SP 42/97, Nairne to James III, 18 March 1719.
56. Corp, *The Jacobites at Urbino*, pp. 126–8. Apart from the Salviati family, the people whom Nairne recommended to the Pope included Lord Richard Howard, Lord William Drummond, Eustachio Buglioni, John Ingleton, Thaddeus Connell, Charles Booth, Lawrence Mayes and William Stuart (ASV. Albani 167, f.25, Nairne to Clement XI, undated but February 1719). Between 1717 and 1719 Nairne attempted repeatedly to obtain benefices in France for Ingleton and Connell, and also to persuade the Pope to pay for the education of Booth's sons at the English Jesuit college at Saint-Omer. He was unsuccessful, as he also was in his efforts to obtain a canonicat for William Dicconson's brother. See particularly BL. Add MSS 31260, f.90, Nairne to Gualterio, 27 July 1717; BL. Add MSS 20298, f.28, Nairne to Gualterio, undated (April 1718); BL. Add MSS 31261, f.115, Nairne to Gualterio, 3 June 1718; RA. SP 44/66, Nairne to James III, 19 August 1719 for Ingleton, Connell and Dicconson, and eight letters to Gualterio from 1 August 1717 to 30 January 1718 for Booth's sons.
57. BL. Add MSS 31255, f.178, James III to Gualterio, 7 February 1719: 'J'ay laissé entre les mains de Nairne une espece de lettre de créance pour luy au Pape ... je vous recommende ce vieux et fidele domestique qui vous rendra compte de luy meme.'
58. The Pope eventually agreed to confer princely status on the Salviati family in June (BL. Add MSS 20298, f.125, Nairne to Gualterio, 3 June 1719).
59. RA. SP 42/97, Nairne to James III, 18 March 1719. The 'copie[s] de de que je dis au Pape dans l'audience que j'eus de S. S. le ... 23 fevrier 1719' and 'le ... 3 mars 1719', written in Italian, are in RA SP 42/57 and 72. See also 'Memoria di Mr Nairne a Sa Sainteté' and 'Altra Memoria del Mr Nairne', both undated and in French, in BL. Add MSS 20313, ff.40 and 78. For his last audience with the Pope, see RA. SP 43/65, Nairne to James III, 22 April 1719. When James III left for Spain he gave a warrant to Cavaliere Lucci appointing him to be his 'agent' (Bod. Carte MSS 208, f.320, 'Brevet d'agent pour M. le Chev. Lucci', 4 February 1719, in the handwriting of Nairne). See also note 19.
60. RA. SP 43/6, Nairne to James III, 25 March 1719.
61. BL. Add MSS 20298, f.119, Nairne to Gualterio, 9 February 1719. See also BL. Add MSS 20298, f.157, Nairne to Gualterio, undated but 11 February 1719 in which he told Gualterio that 'je viverai et mourrai le plus devouée de ses creatures'.
62. RA. SP 42/97, Nairne to James III, 18 March 1719. See also RA. SP 43/6, Nairne to James III, 25 March 1718 in which Nairne said he would make it 'one of his chiefest studys to increase rather than lessen his [Gualterio's] authority' in Rome.
63. BL. Add MSS 20298, f.119, Nairne to Gualterio, 9 February 1719.
64. Corp, *The Jacobites at Urbino*, p. 129.

65. BL. Add MSS 20298, f.124, Nairne to Gualterio, 18 March 1719.
66. Corp, *The Jacobites at Urbino*, p. 129.
67. RA. SP 43/6, Nairne to James III, 25 March 1719.
68. RA. SP 42/97, Nairne to James III, 18 March 1719.
69. RA. SP 43/6, Nairne to James III, 25 March 1719.
70. RA. SP 43/22, Nairne to James III, 1 April 1719.
71. RA. SP 43/36, Nairne to James III, 8 April 1719.
72. RA. SP 43/51, Nairne to James III, 15 April 1719.
73. BL. Add MSS 31261, f.329, Nairne to Gualterio, 22 March 1719.
74. RA. SP 43/36, Nairne to James III, 8 April 1719.
75. RA. SP 43/80, Bourrier to Nairne, 4 May 1719.
76. RA. SP 43/65, Nairne to James III, 23 April 1719.
77. Corp, *The Jacobites at Urbino*, p. 130.
78. RA. SP 43/79, Nairne to James III, 29 April 1719.
79. Corp, *The Jacobites at Urbino*, p. 131.
80. BL. Add MSS 20298, f.125, Nairne to Gualterio, 3 June 1719.
81. BL. Add MSS 20298, f.127, Nairne to Gualterio, 12 June 1719. See also BL. Add MSS 20298, f.129, Nairne to Gualterio, 22 June 1719: 'J'espere meme qu'avec le tems V. E. connoitra mieux peut etre qu'Elle ne fait presentement que mon respectueux attachement pour Elle est a l'eppreuve de tout et que quoique vieux et tres mauvais courtisan ne pouvant ni feindre ni flatter ni me contraindre autrement qu'en me taisant me retirant et me soumettant lorsque je crois que la prudence et la modestie le demandent je scais toujours ce que je dois a mes superieurs et a mes bienfaiteurs.'
82. RA. SP 43/117, Nairne to James III, 17 June 1719.
83. RA. SP 44/6, Nairne to James III, 20 June 1719. The docket of this letter is at RA. SP 43/125.
84. The audience had probably really been arranged by Cardinal Gualterio, who (as Nairne recorded) had seen the queen earlier that day.
85. RA. SP 44/38, Nairne to James III, 12 August 1719.
86. RA. SP 44/66, Nairne to James III, 19 August 1719.
87. Corp, *The Jacobites at Urbino*, p. 135.
88. RA. SP 44/38, Nairne to James III, 12 August 1719.
89. Mary Fitzgerald, who was married to the king's barber (Gerard Fitzgerald), was allowed to join her husband in Rome in February 1719 (Corp, *The Jacobites at Urbino*, p. 126). Clementina had six German servants but none of them was allowed to attend her wedding (ibid. p. 136).
90. It is possible that Nairne was among the small group of people invited to meet the king at Montefiascone (Corp, *The Jacobites at Urbino*, p. 137), but he did not witness the marriage, and the letter in note 92 suggests that he was not included.

91. Corp, *The Jacobites at Urbino*, pp. 137–8.

92. BL. Add MSS 31261, f.333, Nairne to Gualterio, 3 September 1719.

93. BL. Add MSS 31261, f.344, Nairne to Gualterio, 16 September 1719.

94. Corp, *The Jacobites at Urbino*, p. 140.

95. BL. Add MSS 31261, ff.339, 344 and 347, Nairne to Gualterio, 12, 16 and 19 September 1719.

96. RA. SP 44/112, Nairne to Dicconson, 12 September 1719; RA. SP 44/125, 126 and 127, Nairne to Nithsdale, Clepham and McKenzie, 16 September 1719; RA. SP 44/139, Nairne to Pitsligo, 23 September 1719. See also BL. Add MSS 20298, f.148, Nairne to Gualterio, 4 November 1719: 'J'ay eu beaucoup a travailler aujourdhuy tant avec le Roy et dans son cabinet que pour son service.'

97. Corp, *The Jacobites at Urbino*, pp. 140–2.

98. Ibid. pp. 128–36.

99. RA. SP 43/6, Nairne to James III, 25 March 1719.

100. RA. SP 43/22, Nairne to James III, 1 April 1719.

101. RA. SP 43/51, Nairne to James III, 15 April 1719.

102. RA. SP 43/117, Nairne to James III, 17 June 1719.

103. RA. SP 44/38, Nairne to James III, 12 August 1719.

104. Corp, *The Stuarts in Italy*, p. 135.

105. RA. SP 44/66, Nairne to James III, 19 August 1719.

106. Corp, *The Jacobites at Urbino*, pp. 131–2.

107. RA. SP 44/6, Nairne to James III, 20 June 1719.

108. The fact that Nairne's letter is among the Stuart Papers is evidence that the king did receive both it and its enclosure. Moreover the docket of the letter is in RA. SP 43/125, whereas the letter itself is at RA. SP 44/6.

109. RA. SP 44/139, Nairne to Pitsligo, 23 September 1719.

110. Corp, *The Jacobites at Urbino*, p. 142.

111. Ibid.

112. BL. Add MSS 31261, ff.347 and 351, Nairne to Gualterio, 19 and 23 September 1719.

113. BL. Add MSS 31261, f.335, Nairne to Gualterio, 1 October 1719.

114. Tayler, Henrietta, *The Jacobite Court at Rome in 1719* (Edinburgh, 1938), p. 84, Nairne to Pitsligo, 10 October 1719.

115. For Pitsligo's two letters to Nairne of 24 and 26 October 1719, and Nairne's reply of 2 November (dictated by Murray) referring to Pitsligo's 'mistakes', see Ibid. pp. 89–91 and 92–3.

116. BL. Add MSS 31262, f.9, Murray to Gualterio, 10 October 1719.

117. BL. Add MSS 20298, f.143, Nairne to Gualterio, 11 October 1719.

118. See the lists of the salaries and pensions of the king's household in RA. SP 8/92 (1715), RA. SP 9/30 (1716), and RA. SP Box 3/89 (1717). See also p. 342, note 147.

119. Corp, *The Jacobites at Urbino*, p. 170.
120. BL. Add MSS 31255, f.178, James III to Gualterio, 7 February 1719.
121. RA. SP 44/38, Nairne to James III, 12 August 1719. Nairne also told the king that 40 *scudi* was not really enough: 'I have been obliged not only to spend all the allowance your Ma.ty was pleasd to appoint me, but also to run considerably in debt to maintain myself with a servant here with some decency.' Nairne now employed a valet who was from Orvieto (BL. Add MSS 20298, f.146, Nairne to Gualterio, 16 October 1719), but had previously employed Joseph Martinash, whose mother had been the wet nurse of Princess Louise Marie at Saint-Germain (RA. SP 43/512, Nairne to James III, 15 April 1719; BL. Add MSS 31261, f.331, Nairne to Gualterio, 11 August 1719), and whose three sisters were nuns in the English Augustinian convent in Paris (RA. SP Box 3/89, a list of salaries and pensions, 1717).
122. RA. SP 44/66, Nairne to James III, 19 August 1719. Gualterio drew up a model of a procuration to be sent to the king, and suggested that it be made out in Nairne's name. The latter told the king:

> having told him that I did not doubt but your Ma.ty had rather charge him than any other with the trust of receiving these smal rents, if you knew it would be agreable to him, he answered me that he believed it would be proper and convenient to have the procuration filld in my name giving for reason that he may happen to be absent from this and perhaps for a considerable time ... Whether his declining this be only modesty, and to make a compliment to me to whom it may be of some credit and honour whereas to him in his rank it can be none, or whether he really will be glad to avoid it, is what I cannot decide.

By the time he received the procuration James was already in Italy.
123. BL. Add MSS 31261, ff.333 and 347, Nairne to Gualterio, 3 and 19 September 1719.
124. BL. Add MSS 31261, f.353, Nairne to Gualterio, 27 September 1719.
125. Bod. Carte MSS 258, f.392, Gualterio to Nairne, 17 October 1719. Nairne had hoped that he would continue to be paid by Gualterio, now that the king was back and could give instructions regarding his *luoghi di monti*, and had even asked the cardinal to advance him his money for October in the middle of that month (BL. Add MSS 20298, f.141, Nairne to Gualterio, undated but 15 October 1719).
126. BL. Add MSS 31261, f.254 [*sic*], Nairne to Gualterio, 18 October 1719.
127. BL. Add MSS 20298, f.143, Nairne to Gualterio, 11 October 1719.
128. Corp, *The Jacobites at Urbino*, p. 200. Cardinal Albani's opinion was recorded by Lord Richard Howard.
129. Ibid.

130. BL. Add MSS 20298, f.153, Nairne to Gualterio, undated (mid-October 1719).
131. Ibid.
132. BL. Add MSS 20298, f.1241, Nairne to Gualterio, undated but 15 October 1719.
133. BL. Add MSS 31261, f.254 [*sic*], Nairne to Gualterio, 18 October 1719. Gualterio replied on 24 October 1719:

> Votre moderation est toujours louable Monsieur, mais je trairois la verite si je ne vous confirmois encore qu'il me paroit toujours par des marques aussy certaines que reiterees que vous avez toute la part aux bonnes graces et a la confience de SM. Ainsy vous devez estre en repos la dessus.
>
> Pour ce qui est de petites affaires de la Cour, je ne doute pas que tout se calmera a l'arrivee du Roy qui assurement a des tendres sentiments de bonte pour ses ... [?] ... et qui estime les seigneurs qui l'ont suivi.

(Bod. Carte MSS 258, f.394).

134. BL. Add MSS 31261, f.357, Nairne to Gualterio, 28 October 1719. Shortly before he left Montefiascone Nairne probably enjoyed the singing of the celebrated castrato Pascolino Tiepoli, including in a new oratorio by Alessandro Scarlatti, specially composed for the king and queen and performed by four soloists. The libretto of the oratorio was by Cardinal Benedetto Pamphili, and had originally been set by Giovanni Lorenzo Lulier in 1687. It was performed in the *Seminario* of Montefiascone and entitled 'Maria Maddalena de' pazzi. Oratorio a quattro voci fatta cantare da Monsignor Sebastiano Pompilio Bonaventura Viscovo di Montefiascone, e Corneto alla presanza delle reali maestà di Giacomo Terzo re della Gran Bretagna, e Maria Clementina Sobieschi di lui regia consorte' (http://en.wikipedia.org/wiki/Benedetto_Pamphili, accessed 2 july 2016). For Pascolino Tiepoli, see RA. SP 45/71, James III to Sheldon, 26 October 1719: 'Pascolini is ... here, who is a great resource in this melancholy place.'
135. BL. Add MSS 31261, f.359, Nairne to Gualterio, 1 November 1719.
136. BL. Add MSS 20298, f.1487, Nairne to Gualterio, 4 November 1719.
137. Until he was paid he had to borrow money from Belloni, the king's banker, and live on credit (BL. Add MSS 20298, f.148, Nairne to Gualterio, 4 November 1719).
138. It was not only the members of the court who disliked Murray, because the queen 'despised him' (Corp, *The Jacobites at Urbino*, p. 200).
139. Corp, *The Stuarts in Italy*, pp. 131, 141.

CHAPTER 8

Under-Secretary at Rome and Bologna, 1719–1729

The seven years which followed Nairne's return from Montefiascone to Rome continued to be a period of major disappointment, both politically and personally. The prospects of a Stuart restoration, to which he had devoted the last thirty years of his life, now seemed more remote than ever. And instead of the retirement which he had anticipated and longed for, he found himself obliged to go on working indefinitely in the Jacobite secretariat. Moreover, by the time he celebrated his sixty-fifth birthday in August 1720, he had been demoted to become little more than chief clerk. He retained both his title as secretary of the closet and his restored salary of 205*l*. 03*s*. 02*d*. (at that time the highest paid to anyone at the court),[1] but he was now subordinate to James Murray and excluded from the king's secret correspondence. In a private letter of 9 July 1720, he described himself as 'old and useless', and asked his friend (a Scottish priest) to remember him in his prayers because 'I want them very much'.[2]

Apart from Nairne himself, James III's secretariat consisted of Murray, the acting secretary of state, and Francis Kennedy who had returned with the king from Spain and was appointed under-secretary. In January 1721, these men were joined by Thomas Sheridan who arrived from Saint-Germain and became joint under-secretary. Nairne disliked Murray but he seems to have enjoyed perfectly cordial relations with Sheridan, whereas Kennedy, though a much younger man, seems to have become a friend. Robert Creagh, whom Nairne had known at Saint-Germain and Urbino, and who had served as Murray's under-secretary while the king was in Spain, now became private secretary to Queen Clementina.[3] He too seems to have had cordial relations with Nairne. The latter had always tried to remain as detached as possible from court rivalries and factions. But as the Palazzo del Re became more polarized in the years after 1720, so Nairne inevitably became associated with the majority of the courtiers who disliked and opposed the king's favourites. The situation was eased a little when Murray left the court in February 1721, but he was replaced as acting secretary of state by John Hay, so the atmosphere in the secretariat was not improved.[4]

Nairne's principal task now was simply taking dictation, copying letters and other papers, and preparing drafts of the king's routine correspondence. In a letter of August 1722, he wrote that 'I have had the honour to serve the king to the best of my understanding and with all the zeal I was capable of as long as he was pleasd to trust and imploy me'. Those days, however, were now over, and he added that he no longer dealt with 'news or politics': 'I meddle no more in business which I am now too old and unfitt for.'[5] A few years later, when a correspondent in Paris sent him a Jacobite cypher, he replied that 'I ... have not dealt in things of that kind or any thing relating to politicks these severall years'.[6] By 1726, when he was nearly seventy-one years old, he claimed that he had even lost much of his interest in politics, explaining in another of his letters that 'I have a Paris [Gazette] sent me every post, wch is all the gazette I see ... I never was much curious of news, and now less than ever so I am very easy upon that head.'[7]

Under these circumstances, Nairne was anxious to avoid giving the impression that he was trying to involve himself again in the secret business of the court. He scrupulously avoided political subjects in his private correspondence, and explained to his friends in Paris that he always showed their letters to the king.[8] One of them noted with regret that 'Sir D. Nairne shows all his letters to the King, and so mentions nothing but the business ordered'.[9]

During the early 1720s, however, the king still employed Nairne to negotiate on his behalf with Gualterio and the other cardinals. As much of this work was conducted orally, with Nairne receiving his instructions directly from the king and reporting back when he returned to the court, it is not possible to know exactly what business he transacted, but a few documents have survived which indicate the kind of things with which he was entrusted. In November 1720, for example, he was sent to speak to the cardinal in charge of the Datary.[10] In the following month he negotiated with both Cardinal Paulucci (the Secretary of State) and Cardinal Annibale Albani concerning the ceremonial to be adopted, and the people to be invited, for the birth of Prince Charles.[11] As these conversations were probably conducted in Italian,

Figure 13. *Queen Clementina and Prince Charles,* 1721 (167.6 × 116.8 cm),
by Girolamo Pesci (Stanford Hall)
It was Nairne who negotiated the ceremonial to be adopted,
and the people to be invited, for the birth of the prince.

Nairne was at that time still the only person in the secretariat capable of speaking to the cardinals.[12]

Gualterio, the Cardinal Protector of England, could speak and read French, so Murray and Hay were increasingly able to negotiate and correspond with him.[13] Nairne, who had once been on such intimate terms with Gualterio during 1717–19, admitted that 'I can not brag that I have much credit [with him] ever since the King left me intrusted here when he went to Spain.'[14] Nevertheless the two men seem to have corresponded from time to time,[15] and in June 1722 James III sent Nairne to discuss with Gualterio how and when he (Nairne) should present the compliments of the king and queen to the newly elected Grand Master of the Order of Malta.[16] Someone had to do this sort of thing, and Nairne probably did it very well, but the really important political work of the secretariat was meanwhile being conducted by Hay, Kennedy and Sheridan.

One typical task entrusted to Nairne was receiving and responding to the many Christmas and New Year greetings which the king received every December and January. During one winter, for example, Nairne had to write fifty-nine of these 'bonnes festes', all within a fairly short time.[17] The work was socially and even politically necessary, but of course it was in no sense secret or confidential.[18]

One of the people to whom Nairne had to send 'bonnes festes' for the king was Cavaliere Pietro Paolo Carrara, the Gonfalonier at Fano, with whom he (Nairne) had become particularly friendly when the court was at Urbino. Nairne himself corresponded with Carrara,[19] and some of his letters have survived. Carrara was a poet who had already published some of his work, and in 1720 he sent Nairne some new poems in manuscript, which the latter then showed to Cardinal Pamphili. Early in 1721 Carrara had these poems printed and sent fifteen of the copies to Nairne, asking him to give them to the king and queen, to keep one for himself and to distribute the other twelve to influential people in Rome. Nairne wrote back in February to say that the king and queen sent their thanks for their copies, and he added:

> I have already distributed some of the twelve that you did me the honour of sending, and it pleased me to see that they are very much admired by connoisseurs. I had already shown them to Cardinal Pamphilij in manuscript, and as you know he

is a poet and a good judge, and I have just given a printed copy to Mr St Urbin, the agent here of the Duke of Lorraine, who was enchanted by them and said he would send them to his Court.[20]

Apart from illustrating his friendship with Carrara, this letter indicates that Nairne continued to meet and socialize with the cardinals and other important members of Roman society whom he had met during previous years.

Another of Nairne's letters to Carrara may be quoted here because of the light it sheds on his habitual modesty. Nairne, who had been fluent in French as well as his native English for well over forty years, who wrote both languages extremely well, and who was now able to read, write and converse in Italian, wrote to Carrara in December 1724:

> Nothing could be more obliging and polite than the letter you have done me the honour of writing to me ... But the style of it is too elegant for me to reply properly, for I am only able to stammer in the very few languages that I know. So that to compare my bad French with the subtlety and perfection of language with which you write would be ridiculously bold. Let us just say, Monsieur, that I thank you most humbly for the honour you have done me by remembering at this time a servant who is of absolutely no use to you.[21]

Within the Jacobite court itself, it is hard to know with whom Nairne had especially good relations, because the surviving documents are unhelpful. Most of his friends at the court had either died or been left behind at Saint-Germain-en-Laye. Those who had accompanied the king to Italy had become dissatisfied at Urbino and returned to France in 1717 and 1718. What little evidence we have suggests that Nairne enjoyed good or even friendly relations with Sir William Ellis (the king's cofferer) and with James Delattre (the king's equerry), both of whom had lived at Saint-Germain. Among the Scottish pensioners who had joined the court at Avignon in 1716 he seems to have been on good terms with Charles Fleming (first cousin once removed of the 1st Duke of Perth), who had visited Saint-Germain in 1706 and 1707. Perhaps there were others, but the available documents do not reveal their names.[22]

After his arrival in Rome, however, Nairne became particularly friendly with four British clergymen already resident in the city, two of them English and two of them Scottish. The first was Lord Richard Howard, known as the *abate* Howard, younger brother of the 8th and 9th Dukes of Norfolk, and a canon of St Peter's. Howard and Nairne shared a love of music, and when the former died in the summer of 1723 the latter wrote to ask if the Duke would let him keep his brother's harpsichord as a souvenir of their friendship. John Ingleton, who had been both under-preceptor and confessor to James III, wrote from Paris to a mutual friend:

> Sir David Nairne has several times writ to me concerning a harpsical that belonged to your deceasd friend; supposing I had some correspondence with the Duke of Norfolk or his Brother, which I have not in the least. Pray mention Sir David's desire of this harpsical to one of them. He was so much the Abbot's friend that I am perswaded the Duke would make him a present of it, and he well deservs this favour from us.[23]

At that time the Duke of Norfolk was in prison in London following the failure of the Atterbury Plot,[24] so it was felt more prudent to have no correspondence with him. Nairne therefore had Howard's harpsichord transported to his apartment in the Palazzo del Re and kept it there as a permanent loan.[25]

Another of Nairne's friends was Father William Clark, the Rector of the Scots College in Rome,[26] who was appointed confessor to King Philip V of Spain in 1726.[27] Just as Nairne had been particularly friendly with the secular priests (such as Lewis and Thomas Innes) attached to the Scots College in Paris and those (such as John Ingleton) attached to the court at Saint-Germain, so now Nairne found his closest friends among the secular British clergy in Rome. During the early 1720s he developed particularly warm relations with Father Lawrence Mayes and Father William Stuart, respectively the Agents of the English and Scottish Catholic clergy in Rome.[28] In one of his letters Nairne specified that 'Ecclesiastical matters ... are not of my sphere'.[29] Nevertheless only one month later we find him asking James III to recommend both Mayes and Stuart to be given additional money from the Datary, and hoping that the king 'will pardon to me who is not naturally guilty of overmeddling'.[30] It appears that the recommendation was unsuccessful, because over a year later Stuart wrote on behalf of himself and Mayes to thank Nairne 'for your charitable office in having laid our humble petition once more before the King' for additional money from the Datary.[31] Nairne was clearly willing to risk royal displeasure in order to help his friends. Similarly one of his letters records that he spoke to the cardinal in charge of the Datary on his own initiative to obtain a clerical benefice for one of the sons of Cavaliere Carrara.[32]

All the friends mentioned so far were men, and indeed there were hardly any women at the Stuart court between 1716 and 1719. This changed, however, when James III married Clementina Sobieska at Montefiascone. The king was not willing to give his new wife a separate household, but he could not deny her a small group of personal servants, including two chambermaids and various necessary women and washerwomen. Most of these servants were the wives of men already employed by the king. They had been left behind at Saint-Germain but were now allowed to come to Rome. The most important was the senior chambermaid, Mrs Mary Fitzgerald (née Gordon), whose husband Gerald Fitzgerald was one of the king's *valets de chambre*. Because Mary Fitzgerald was one of Nairne's cousins, through her he was drawn into the immediate entourage of the queen, whom he greatly admired for her beauty and her piety. This link was then strengthened when Mary's sister Isabella Gordon was also appointed chambermaid to the queen, and Mary's brother Alexander Gordon was appointed to be the queen's personal servant.[33]

The queen, however, needed female servants of a higher status than chambermaids, so the king appointed Marjory Hay, the wife of his favourite John Hay, to be her lady of the bedchamber, and Lady Misset (whose husband had helped Clementina escape from Innsbruck) to be her bedchamber woman. As the queen strongly disliked Marjory Hay and her husband she turned increasingly to Lady Misset and her chambermaids for companionship and support. Nairne also disliked the Hays and was living by himself without his two daughters, whom he had left behind in Paris. He now turned to his younger cousins for friendship, and this strengthened still further the link between him and the people at court who admired the queen and disliked the king's favourites. It was thus increasingly hard for Nairne to remain detached from the growing court rivalries.

These rivalries were increased after the birth of Prince Charles at the end of 1720, when Lady Misset was placed in charge of the little baby at the request of the queen but against the wishes of the Hays. After a few months, John and Marjory Hay persuaded the king to change his mind and dismiss Lady Misset, who was then replaced by the woman (Lois

Hughes) who had been the prince's wet nurse.[34] This of course was no more than a temporary arrangement, but the queen was very displeased. Meanwhile the king looked around for someone who could bring up the child for several years until he could be handed over to men. In March 1722, he settled on Dorothy Sheldon, the daughter of one of his equerries at Saint-Germain, and someone whom Nairne had known for many years. As Dorothy Sheldon was also a friend of Nairne's daughters,[35] her arrival had the effect of associating him even more closely, whether he liked it or not, with the queen's faction at court.

Apart from his work for the king in the secretariat, and his increasing involvement in the growing polarization of the court, we know virtually nothing about Nairne's life in Rome during these years. He did not eat at the gentlemen's table, and instead of being given his 'diet' was given an 'allowance of forty sols a day'[36] with which he had to 'buy [his] own bread and wine'.[37] But did he take an active interest in Roman antiquities? Did he attend the opera each carnival season? And if so did he prefer the Venetian works of Vivaldi or the new 'galant' style from Naples? We do not even know what he read. We do, however, know a little about the small apartment which he occupied on the first floor of the Palazzo del Re. His rooms were situated in the south-east palazzetto, and looked out both at the back of the adjacent Palazzo Muti and along the via del Vaccaro.[38] There were three, the first of which was described in inventories as his antechamber or *stanza di passaggio*. The second was referred to as his 'first room' or *gabinetto*, and the last as his bedchamber or *camera*. The *stanza di passaggio* was occupied by his servant, and contained a bed, a table, a *cassabanco* and a *credenza*. The *gabinetto* was used by Nairne for music parties and for entertaining his friends. It contained two harpsichords, one of which had belonged to Lord Richard Howard, and a *violone*. There were several tables, seven chairs without arms, some 'green and mixt hangings' for the walls and two 'linnen rideaux to ye windows'. There were also some unspecified portraits. The *camera* was used for working as well as sleeping. In addition to a 'green bed and bolstore pillow' and two 'Indian covers and green counterpane', there was the essential 'close stool and cover'. The walls were covered with red and yellow hangings, and there were probably some family portraits. Nairne had an 'ecritoire' and a 'repository for papers' – including all his papers which are now in the Bodleian Library, and the private papers of the Duke of Ormonde which the latter had entrusted to him when he left the court in 1717.[39] As there were also five chairs and a table in the room we may assume that Nairne sometimes entertained or ate or conducted business in his bedchamber.[40]

It was from this room that Nairne corresponded with his daughters in Paris. By the beginning of 1722 Françoise was twenty-eight years old and still unmarried. Her sister Marie was twenty-one and had taken the habit as a novice three years previously at the English Augustinian convent. Nairne, by selling his *rente* at the Hôtel de Ville, had raised the money to grant her the necessary dowry to become a nun,[41] but then at the last moment, in May 1720, and to her father's 'trouble and concern', Marie had changed her mind and decided that she did not want to become a nun after all.[42] So the two sisters continued to live as *pensionnaires* in the convent, and Nairne gave them both his annual French pension of 400 *livres* and the dividend from his new investments at the Hôtel de Ville. He also sent money to them from Rome,[43] but this was not enough to maintain the two young ladies properly or provide dowries in the event of their receiving offers of marriage. Nairne wrote to a friend on 16 March 1722:

> Hitherto the poor girls have made what shift they could, so I hope Providence will continue to provide for them, and move some good friend or other to do something for them, especially if their conduct continue to be without reproche, as I thank God it has been hitherto.[44]

It was shortly after this, in June 1722, that a good friend did indeed do something. This friend, who would eventually become Nairne's son-in-law, was the Chevalier Andrew Ramsay.

By 1722 Ramsay had made a considerable reputation for himself in Paris as the author of *Essai philosophique sur le gouvernement civil*, and was employed as tutor to the son of the Regent's *premier gentilhomme de la chambre*, the comte de Sassenage. He was in close contact with Lewis and Thomas Innes at the Collège des Ecossais, and through them he was introduced to Françoise and Marie Nairne. In June 1722, he decided to do what he could to help. Without any prompting from Nairne, he sent a letter to James III in which he suggested to the king that he (James III) might ask Cardinal de Rohan, the chief almoner of France, to give the sisters a pension. He added that he would personally hand the letter to Rohan, and use his own credit in Paris to urge its acceptance. The king agreed to do this[45] and Ramsay carried out his promise.[46] Much to Nairne's surprise and delight the approach succeeded, and Rohan then granted a generous annual pension of 1000 *livres*, to be paid quarterly.[47] Nairne wrote to thank the king on 29 August for 'his charitable recommendation of them to Card.l de Rohan'. He added, characteristically:

> if his Ma.ty had not been graciously pleasd to recommend my poor girls at the solicitation of others I should not have had the boldness to have askd it myself.[48]

The question arises as to why Ramsay behaved in such a generous way to Nairne's daughters. The answer might perhaps be found in a letter which Nairne wrote several years later in March 1735, when Ramsay asked to be allowed to marry his younger daughter Marie. Nairne then commented that 'Mr Ramsay resolves to show the same friendship to the youngest he designd formerly for the eldest'. That, he added, was 'fourteen years ago', which would imply that Ramsay had proposed to Françoise in 1721,[49] one year before he obtained the pension. She must have declined his offer but remained on terms of friendship with him.

The pension of 1,000 *livres* from the French clergy obtained from Cardinal de Rohan was soon supplemented by another of 600 *livres* from the French court, this time thanks to the influence of Marie-Christine, duchesse de Gramont (1672–1748), a daughter of the duc de Noailles whose family lived at Saint-Germain-en-Laye. The evidence comes from a letter of thanks to James III from both Françoise and Marie Nairne, who wrote that they had only received the second pension because they were known to be under the king's protection.[50] It might be added that the duchesse de Gramont was personally acquainted with Andrew Ramsay.

The first of these two pensions coincided with an important turning-point in Nairne's career. In the summer of 1722, James III left Rome to visit Bagni di Lucca, where Queen Clementina had gone a few weeks earlier with Marjory Hay, Mary Fitzgerald and Isabella Gordon.[51] In previous years the king would have taken Nairne with him on such a trip, but this time Nairne was left behind in Rome with very little to do. On 29 August, three and a half weeks after the king's departure, Nairne asked to be allowed to retire and live with his daughters, who now had their own pension. His letter, in which he described himself as a 'useless and insignificant ... old fellow', was addressed to John Hay, who was with the king:

> what ever my other faults have been (which I hope his Ma.ty is so good as to pardon) I think in point of fidelity I have nothing to reproche myself; so if he be satisfyd wth my past services, and be but graciously pleasd to look upon me still as one of his old faithfull servants, and continue me his bounty and countenance as such for the short time I have to live, tis all the recompence and comfort I ask, for I promise you Sir I have not the least ambition to meddle in business. I have scribled enough these 33 years past, and being now enterd in my 68 I find I am not able to undergo much toyl or fatigue, and therefore if I outlive this winter I own to you in confidence that I should be glad the King (to whom you see I am of very little or no use at all here), would give me leave in the next spring to go and end my old days with my daughters and joyn my prayers with theirs for his prosperity and happy restoration. If with the help of your good offices I can obtain this great favour of his Ma.ty to grant me this honourable retreat with the continuation of my allowance in Rome to be remitted to me either privately or in what manner so ever he pleases I shall be obliged to you as long as I live, and as old as I am if in any thing that is not of too great fatigue and for my age I can be serviceable either to the King or you in France in case it be thought fitt to put me to the tryal, I hope I shall allways be found an honest man to the last, and neither unworthy of the continuation of his Ma.ty's favour nor of your friendship. Mine is not worth offering you ... You shall never find me a false friend.[52]

The surviving documentary evidence does not reveal how this letter was received, or to what extent – if at all – Hay tried to persuade the king to let Nairne retire. All we can say is that the latter remained in the Jacobite secretariat in Rome, then Bologna, for another six years, so we must assume that his request was rejected. But it should be added that both the king and Hay had more important things on their minds at this time. Nairne's letter coincided with the failure of the Atterbury Plot, the arrest of the leading Jacobites in England, and the cancellation of James III's secret plans to leave Lucca and sail from Genoa to England. It also coincided with the total collapse of the relations between the queen and both John and Marjory Hay. It was only a few weeks after he received Nairne's letter that John Hay sent an insulting letter to the queen in which he referred to rumours that his own wife was her husband's mistress. In the tense atmosphere which followed, when Clementina complained to the king and showed him this letter, Hay was replaced as *maggiordomo*, and James tried to appease his wife by taking her on a tour of Tuscany and the major cities of the northern part of the Papal States (including Bologna and Urbino). By the time the king and queen returned to Rome at the end of October[53] Nairne's request had presumably been set aside.

In the absence of evidence to the contrary, Nairne's life during 1723 seems to have been relatively uneventful. In May he received the news that his son Louis had been promoted to the rank of captain in the Spanish army.[54] Then, in September, he received the alarming news that his daughter Françoise was dangerously ill in Paris with a 'dystemper'.[55] She did not recover until the end of December, by which time she was described as 'much thinner and slender' than she had previously been.[56]

The other significant development of 1723 which concerned Nairne indirectly was the growing tension within the secretariat. No longer involved with the management of the household as *maggiordomo*, Hay now concentrated all his energies on conducting the king's correspondence as acting secretary of state. He completely alienated his under-secretary, Francis Kennedy, who told people that he regarded Hay as his enemy and said he would like to escape the court and return to Scotland.[57] As Nairne regarded Kennedy as a friend, this development increased his own desire to retire and live in France.

The tension was eased when Hay was sent on a mission by the king to consult the leading Jacobites in France, and to recruit a preceptor for the three-year-old Prince of Wales. The man selected was Nairne's friend, though they had not yet met, Andrew Ramsay.

Nairne and Ramsay had been corresponding since at least 1722, and probably since 1721, and the former had made a point of showing the latter's letters to the king. He commented on one occasion that 'he [Ramsay] expresses his duty to the King in so zealous a manner, that I thought it would be an injustice done him if I should keep it up'.[58] By 1723 James III, no doubt partly influenced by Nairne, had decided that Ramsay might be the best person to employ as his son's preceptor.[59] The prince was still only two years old, but the king was informed that Ramsay was now available because no longer employed by the comte de Sassenage.[60] James therefore hoped that he might be persuaded to join the court in Rome shortly after the prince's third birthday. To show his high regard for Ramsay James asked Cardinal de Rohan to give him a pension on an abbey at Villeneuve-les-Avignon which he believed – wrongly – was about to become vacant,[61] and he backed up this request by giving Ramsay a 'déclaration de noblesse' in May.[62]

That summer saw the publication in Paris of Ramsay's *Histoire de la vie de Fénelon*,[63] who had served as preceptor to the sons of the Dauphin, and this biography reinforced James III's desire to employ Ramsay as preceptor to his own son. In September 1723, the king asked the Regent to give Ramsay a pension on another abbey,[64] and he sent Hay to Paris with the specific aim of persuading Ramsay to come to Rome.[65] Hay's mission was a success, and when he returned to Rome in January 1724 he brought Ramsay with him.[66] When Nairne heard the news he was reported to be absolutely overjoyed.[67]

For the first few weeks both the king and Hay seem to have been pleased with Ramsay,[68] but it was not long before the latter began to speak out against the king's favourites and what he regarded as their mismanagement of the court and the lack of a separate household for the queen. The fact was that Ramsay, although a Jacobite, was not a political exile and not financially dependent on the king, unlike all the other courtiers, so he was prepared to say what others only thought. At the beginning of April, James III made it clear that 'Ramsay is not to be anyways concernd in writing or politics',[69] and then a few weeks later Ramsay had a furious argument with both Hay and Thomas Forster, the new *maggiordomo*. We do not know the precise details of the dispute, but swords were drawn, Ramsay was slightly wounded by Forster, and the latter was only saved from being killed by the timely arrival of other people.[70] It was against this background that Ramsay met Nairne and that the two men became firm friends.[71]

During that summer of 1724, James III withdrew his confidence from his leading advisers in Paris – the so-called Triumvirate of the Duke of Mar, Lord Lansdowne and Lord Dillon.[72] As these men were all on good terms with Ramsay and associated with the group in Rome which supported Queen Clementina against the Hays, so Nairne found himself gradually identified more and more with Ramsay and the opposition at court. We have no details, but a letter written by Nairne in February of the following year refers to the fact that the king had become 'displeased with me'.[73] Given that Nairne worked so loyally in the secretariat, this must presumably be

Figure 14. *John Hay, Earl of Inverness*, 1724 (96.5 × 76.2 cm),
by Francesco Trevisani (collection of the Earl of Kinnoul)
In 1723 Antonio David started work on a portrait of John Hay, but before he
could finish it Hay was sent on a mission to Paris. Deprived of his sitter, David's
likeness was judged by a group of courtiers to be unrecognizable, so the painter
destroyed it. When Hay returned to Rome in 1724, the commission to paint his
portrait was then given to Trevisani.

a reference to the growing friction between the queen's servants and the king's favourites.

From September to November, the court moved to the Palazzo Apostolico at Albano while the Palazzo del Re was refurbished and made more suitable to be a permanent residence for the exiled king.[74] It is not clear if Ramsay accompanied Nairne and the other courtiers to Albano, or whether he remained in Rome where, as a celebrated man of letters, he had been welcomed by society.[75] It was during this period, however, that Ramsay decided that he would leave the court and return to join the Triumvirate in Paris.[76]

In a letter dated 24 October, Ramsay informed Cardinal de Polignac that the king now treated him 'brusquely', and that 'those who are in vogue these days will never agree with my way of thinking. My simplicity and rectitude betray me frequently and will always do so.'[77] Presumably he was referring to his opinions on the upbringing of the Prince of Wales in particular, and on the treatment of the queen in general, though perhaps also on the king's treatment of Nairne. At any rate he decided to speak his mind to the king, who then commented in a letter:

> Ramsay is an odd body. He exposed himself strangely here to myself and others, but as yet I will be charitable enough to think him a madd man.[78]

On 17 November, about the time that the court returned from Albano to Rome, Ramsay left Rome for Paris.[79]

For Nairne the whole episode was most unfortunate, as it undoubtedly made him suspect in the eyes of the king. Nevertheless he and Ramsay remained firm friends, and the abbé Foucquet wrote to Ramsay from Rome to say that all the latter's books were being sent back for him to Paris by Nairne: 'He left my room sorely affected, but a real friend to us. He sends his greetings.'[80] Shortly after his arrival in Paris Ramsay again proposed marriage to Françoise Nairne, presumably having obtained her father's permission in Rome. This second proposal was also declined.[81] A few weeks later Nairne wrote to a mutual friend in Paris:

> pray give my kind service [to Mr Ramsay]. He knows that my writing regularly to him in his and my present circumstances could be of no service to him, so I follow his example and write but seldom but he shall always find me incapable of ingratitude.[82]

Françoise Nairne's decision to reject Ramsay's second marriage proposal encouraged her father to ask the king if he might invite his two
daughters to look after him in Rome. In a letter of February 1725, he wrote
to John Hay:

> Upon your last advice to me I have given over all thoughts of attempting any more
> to have leave to go and end my old days in quiet with my poor daughters in France,
> especially upon your assuring me that the King is not now displeased with me, but
> if I could by your means have his Ma.tys leave to bring my daughters here to live
> wth me and take care of me it would be the greatest of comforts to me. We should
> be able to live here comfortably and retirdly together upon what they and I have
> without their being troublesome in the least to the King or pretending to anything
> whatsoever at Court, for I thank God they are far from having the least ambition of
> being of a meddling busy intriguing character. When you are at leisure I hope you'l
> give me some comfortable hopes upon this affair.[83]

We do not know how Nairne's request was received, as Hay's reply was
probably delivered orally. The fact that Nairne's daughters remained in
France strongly suggests that the king was not prepared to let them come
to Rome. However, there is a letter written to Hay five months later by
Lewis Innes which states that the king *did* give his consent:

> give me leave to joine with honest Sr Da. Nairne in returning most hearty thanks
> to your L.sp for the great kyndness you have shewn him of late, of wch he is most
> sensible, especially in procuring for him the Kings consent for his sending for his
> daughters to live with him at Rome; he thinks that will be such a comfort to him in
> his old age, that he longs for it beyond what I could have imagind. I wish both he
> and they may find their account in it. All that I can say is that his daughters, wherever
> they have been, have gaind everybodie's friendship and esteem by their prudent and
> discreet behaviour.[84]

Despite this, Nairne's daughters remained in France, so we must assume
that the king changed his mind. And in July 1725, the very month in which
this letter was written, the animosities at the court were greatly increased
by a new crisis within the secretariat which might well have made the king
change his mind.

In March 1725, Queen Clementina had given birth to her second child,
Prince Henry, Duke of York. To celebrate the birth, James III had given

John Hay a peerage as Earl of Inverness and had confirmed his appointment as secretary of state.[85] This greatly strengthened the latter's position at court, and displeased the queen who still had to tolerate Mrs Hay, now Lady Inverness, as her only lady of the bedchamber. Then, in July, the king decided to appoint men to look after the four year old Prince of Wales. James Murray was to return as governor of the prince, with a peerage as Earl of Dunbar. Sheridan was to become under-governor, and consequently leave the secretariat, where he was to be replaced by James Edgar. Handing over the young prince to men when he was still only four years old was bitterly opposed by the queen, by Dorothy Sheldon and of course by Nairne's cousins Mary Fitzgerald and Isabella Gordon. The court as a whole was divided, with most people (including Nairne) opposed to the planned changes.[86]

It was at this moment, in July 1725, that Francis Kennedy, a friend of both Nairne and Ramsay, decided he could no longer work for Lord Inverness. He spoke to the king in 'a violent manner' and asked to be allowed to leave the court and go to France. The king agreed to the first request, but told him if he wanted to keep his salary he had to stay in Italy, so he went to live in Siena.[87] He was not replaced in the secretariat, which meant that Nairne was needed to do more of the routine work and could not be allowed to retire. In the following month, August, Nairne celebrated his seventieth birthday. Perhaps we might imagine him inviting his friends and cousins to pass a summer evening in the *gabinetto* of his apartment in the south-east palazzetto of the Palazzo del Re.

Lord Dunbar returned to the court in September and the prince was immediately entrusted to his and Sheridan's care. What followed has often been described by Jacobite historians. At the beginning of November Dorothy Sheldon was openly rude to the king, who then dismissed her. Six days later, the king and the queen had a furious argument in front of their servants, and four days after that (on the 15th) the queen left the court and took refuge in the Convent of Santa Cecilia in Trastevere. There she was joined by Mary Fitzgerald and Isabella Gordon, and a little later by Dorothy Sheldon. The scandal caused by this separation divided opinion within Roman society,[88] as well as within the Jacobite community in Italy and France. In France, of course, Ramsay's opinion carried great weight as the only person at Paris or Saint-Germain who had served at the court in Rome.[89] Nairne probably tried to keep his opinions to himself, but his dislike of both Inverness and Dunbar was well known, and there is a letter written a little later by James III in which the king admits that "tis true I have not of a long time been pleased with Nairn [sic] for some particulars".[90]

The shock of the queen's departure from the court must have caused Nairne, who remembered how different things had been at Saint-Germain, very considerable anxiety. In the middle of February 1726, he had another attack of gout, which was particularly bad for two weeks,[91] and did not subside until the middle of March. He then wrote to a friend:

> I have been troubled with the gout since the 15th of last month, but thank God I am now much better and can go abroad to mass. Infirmitys are what I must expect will now increase dayly with me at my age. I pray God give me grace to profit of them for the good of my soul ... I judge of others by my self, and consequently conceive very easily what a comfort it would be for them if after so much labour they could enjoy a quiet retreat in their old age.

This letter also contains a comment which seems to imply that he had been ordered, either by the king or by Inverness, to have no communication with Ramsay. Nairne asked Thomas Innes to 'give my service to ... Mr Ramsay': 'I intended to have writt to the last by this post to answer his last to me, but I am in a doubt yet whether I can or not.'[92]

During the spring and summer of 1726 the queen remained in the convent with Dorothy Sheldon and Nairne's two cousins, while he himself continued reluctantly to work in the secretariat.[93] In April he was told that his two daughters had been at Compigny and that they had returned to Paris 'in perfect health ... The eldest is more lusty and healthy than when shee went to the Country.'[94] In May and June Nairne went with the court to Albano,[95] and after his return to Rome some letters record that he sent 'a packet of silk handkerchifs' to his daughters.[96]

Perhaps prompted by this kindness, but more likely by their father's expressed desire to see them again, Françoise Nairne decided in September to write directly to the king. She begged him to allow her to come and live with her father in Rome, as she had wanted to do for a long time, 'to help and care for an elderly father'.[97] In a second letter, she informed

Figure 15. *Queen Clementina*, 1727 (43 × 32 cm), by Antonio David
(photo courtesy of Sotheby's)
This portrait, which belonged to David Nairne, was painted when the queen was living
in the convent of Santa Cecilia in Trastevere with Nairne's cousins Mary Fitzgerald
and Isabella Gordon. It measures 43 × 32 cm, and shows the book held by the queen
to be above the table, whereas the other known copies all measure approximately
73 × 61 cm and show the book with its spine resting on the table.

Inverness that her father knew nothing about her writing to the king, and
asked him to support her request that either she or her sister Marie might
be allowed to look after their old father.[98] These two letters reached Rome
at the precise moment that James III decided to go for several months to
Bologna, taking with him nearly all the members of the court, including
Nairne. If, then, Françoise ever received a reply it would certainly have
been in the negative. With the queen and her ladies still in the convent,
the king had no desire to introduce people whom he must have regarded
as potential troublemakers into his reduced court at Bologna.

In September 1726, when James III left for Bologna, the servants employed at the Stuart court in Rome were divided into three groups. Those who had joined the queen in the convent of Santa Cecilia in Trastevere, including Nairne's cousins Mary Fitzgerald and Isabella Gordon, were now to be paid by the queen instead of the king and left behind with their mistress in Rome. A small group of the king's servants was also to be left in Rome to look after the Palazzo del Re. All the rest, including Nairne, were to go with the king.[99]

The courtiers set out in various groups between 27 September and 2 October. Nairne himself left Rome on 1 October accompanied by Charles Fleming and several others whose names were not recorded. They travelled via Florence[100] and arrived at Bologna on the 10th after a journey of nine days. The king had selected the Palazzo Fantuzzi to be his own residence, and the adjacent Palazzo Ranuzzi-Cospi to be occupied by the two princes, with a newly constructed arch to permit communication between the two buildings. While the palazzi were being prepared and the arch was being built the king moved temporarily into the Casa Belloni, where he had already stayed during his three previous visits to Bologna.[101]

Nairne was not given accommodation with the king in the Casa Belloni, a clear indication of his reduced importance in the secretariat. Instead he was given an apartment in the Palazzo Monti, not far from the Casa Belloni but 'a good mile from' the Palazzo Fantuzzi.[102] He shared the apartment with his friend Father Lawrence Mayes, who not only acted as the king's chaplain but had also been appointed preceptor to Prince Charles and 'gos twice a day to teach him his christian Doctrine'.[103] Once the Palazzo Fantuzzi was ready, the king moved into his new apartment, leaving the princes in the Casa Belloni until the Palazzo Ranuzzi-Cospi and the arch were also prepared. As both Nairne and Mayes were to be given rooms with the princes in the Ranuzzi-Cospi rather than with James III in the Fantuzzi, they remained in their temporary accommodation for several weeks after the king had moved. During this period, Nairne was obliged to travel across town whenever the king wanted to see him, a great contrast to what he had experienced at Rome and in all the buildings previously occupied by the court. On 6 November, Mayes told a friend that he and Nairne 'live in a distracted manner forc'd to runn hither and thither as being yet unsettled'.[104] That same day Nairne himself wrote that, 'after several goings and comings', he had 'just came from the King between one and two of night which is near a mile from this'.[105]

Under these circumstances it is hardly surprising that Nairne wished that the court had not moved. Six days after his arrival, he wrote that 'hitherto I am not much fond of Bologna' and 'still regrett Rome'.[106] It was the same in November: 'neither [Mayes] nor I are much fond of this place we still regrett Rome';[107] and 'both of us had rather be in Rome ... than where we are'.[108] It was not until 23 November, more than a month after the king had moved into the Palazzo Fantuzzi, that the Palazzo Ranuzzi-Cospi was ready, and this inconvenient arrangement came to an end.[109] Nairne wrote from his new accommodation in the Ranuzzi-Cospi on 18 December:

> for my part I have a chimny here, and make allways a good fire so I have not sufferd much of the cold hitherto. [Mayes] is well lodged too and has allways a good fire and wants for nothing here. He has dinner and supper and eats wth a Countess [probably Lady Nithsdale, governess of Prince Henry], and I have only a dinner alone and buy my own bread and wine as I did at Rome.

He was not complaining. He would be 'very well satisfyd wth that', he added, 'if everything els went well'.[110] But everything else did not at all meet with Nairne's approval. The court was dominated by Lord and Lady Inverness, and by Lord Dunbar, there seemed no prospect of any reconciliation between the king and the queen, and what had originally been intended to be an extended *villeggiatura* at Bologna was becoming a permanent arrangement.[111]

Nairne wanted news of the queen but was not allowed to correspond with Mary Fitzgerald or Isabella Gordon,[112] so he asked his friend William Stuart to send him what information he could get.[113] He commented in January 1727 that 'the late unfortunat disunion and our leaving Rome ... have had no good effect', and added: 'I pray God direct his Ma.ty for the best, and give him good Council'.[114] So long as Lord Inverness remained secretary of state, however, Nairne doubted that the king *would* get 'good Councill'.

Nairne himself suffered in the secretariat at the hands of Lord Inverness, commenting in April 1727 that 'I am neither usefull nor agreable nor well used'.[115] His duties remained what they had been in Rome: drafting, copying, translating and taking dictation.[116] However he now also had to deal with the new postal arrangements resulting from the division of the court. Instead of most Jacobite correspondence going directly to and fro between Rome and Paris in the king's packet, it was now necessary to have additional deliveries between Rome and Bologna, and to synchronize the arrival of the post from Rome with the departure of the post for Paris. James III gave orders that the Jacobites in Rome and Paris should not use his bag for sending their private letters to each other via Bologna, but Nairne arranged for an exception to be made for his Scottish friends, William Stuart in Rome and the priests at the Collège des Ecossais in Paris.[117]

It is Nairne's own letters to Stuart and to Thomas Innes in Paris which provide us with most of the information about this period of his life. In one of them he told Stuart that he regarded him as 'the best friend I have' in Rome,[118] and their correspondence bears witness both to their shared sense of humour and to their affection for Mayes, an Englishman from Yorkshire whom they referred to as the Archbishop of York.[119] In a letter of November 1726 Nairne wrote to Stuart, whom he always called Don Guglielmo and referred to as the Archbishop of St Andrews,[120] about the imminent promotion of new cardinals by the Pope:

> 'You tell us nothing of ... any Roman news nor politicks nor whether you have securd a Cap for yourself in the approching promotion. I should be very glad to see the A.Bp of York at his return to Rome waiting in your antichamber to make his complim.t of congratulation to your Em.ce upon the justice done by the holy see to his worthy metropolitan the great A.Bp of St Andrews in borgo. We have seen more ex.ry things happen in this good Popes time.'[121]

Nairne's correspondence with Thomas Innes at the Collège des Ecossais in Paris[122] tended to be rather more serious and to concentrate on two subjects about which he (Nairne) felt very strongly. The first was the Catholic mission in Scotland; the second concerned his two daughters Françoise and Marie.

The Catholics in Scotland had since 1694 been governed by a vicar apostolic whose remit covered the entire kingdom.[123] The first man to hold the post (Thomas Nicolson) had been succeeded in October 1718 by James Gordon, who had studied at the Collège des Ecossais in Paris between 1679 and 1692 and whom Nairne had known for many years.[124]

Like his predecessor, Gordon was ordained a bishop *in partibus* so that, although only a vicar apostolic in Scotland, he was nevertheless able to perform episcopal duties.[125]

In April 1720, Pope Clement XI appointed John Wallace, another of Nairne's old friends from the Collège des Ecossais, to be coadjutor vicar apostolic for all of Scotland.[126] Like Gordon, the new coadjutor was also ordained a bishop *in partibus*, so that Scotland now had one vicar apostolic but two Catholic bishops. This was the background to Nairne's involvement with the mission while he was in Bologna.

In the autumn of 1726, Bishop Gordon suggested that the Catholic church in Scotland should be divided into two districts, to be called lowland and highland. He proposed that he and Bishop Wallace should continue to be vicar apostolic and coadjutor for the lowland district and that a new man should be appointed vicar apostolic for the highland district and ordained a bishop *in partibus*. The man selected was Alexander John Grant, who had studied and been ordained a priest at the Scots College in Rome before returning to Scotland. If the proposal were accepted, then Scotland would gain a third Catholic bishop as well as a second vicar apostolic.[127]

Bishop Gordon's proposal received strong support from Lewis Innes and the Collège des Ecossais in Paris and was then submitted to James III in Bologna. The king agreed, so Nairne was instructed to draft two letters of recommendation, one for the Pope and one for Giuseppe Sacripanti, the Cardinal Protector of Scotland. The matter was bound to be referred to the Congregation of Propaganda Fide, so the king himself wrote to Cardinal Gualterio 'as being his Ma.tys Minister' to lobby support for the idea in Rome.[128]

Nairne told Stuart, the agent of the Scottish Catholic clergy in Rome, that 'I hope the affaire of our new highland Bishop will go well',[129] but he was worried about the attitude of the Pope. Benedict XIII was displeased with James III for leaving Rome and was still siding with Queen Clementina in her dispute with her husband, so he might not be willing to agree. Moreover, as an ex-Dominican he was also known to favour the appointment of regular rather than secular priests, so he might not accept the nomination of Alexander Grant. Nairne wrote that 'I hope ... that the Pope will not ... thwart the Congregation ... with imposing a Regular over the head of the British Clergy'.[130]

The question became more delicate in December 1726 when Grant travelled to Paris and made it known that he intended to continue to Rome in order to support both the proposal and his own candidature. Thomas Innes agreed that Grant should do this, whereas both Nairne and Stuart were strongly opposed. Nairne wrote to the latter on Christmas day:

> I cannot imagine what they propose to themselves by sending that man to Rome it would look as if they had mony to throw away in travelling or that they are not so poor as they peep. You have done very well to tell them to expect no mony in Rome, and it would be ridiculous after this great new favour granted them wch they were so impatient for, I mean of getting a 3d bishop to have this 3d bishop appear here immediately to come and bag a 3d pension. I wonder they are not ashamd to be so importune beggars and never content. I cannot help being in the spleen against them.[131]

By the beginning of January 1727, the Congregation of Propaganda Fide had accepted the proposal to divide Scotland into two districts, each under its own vicar apostolic, but no decision had yet been taken about the candidature of Alexander Grant. Nairne and Stuart maintained their opposition to his coming to Rome, but agreed that if nevertheless he insisted on coming then the Jesuits, who were lobbying for the appointment of a regular priest, should be informed in advance and told that Grant was trying to show 'that he be obedient to Rome and dos not fear to shew himself in it'.[132]

A few days after this letter was written, Cardinal Sacripanti died in Rome and it became necessary for the Pope to appoint a new Cardinal Protector for Scotland. James III wrote to Benedict XIII to recommend Cardinal Gianantonio Davia for the post,[133] but the Pope gave it instead to Cardinal Alessandro Falconieri, without even consulting the king.[134] This naturally made Nairne and his friends worried lest Benedict should do the same and appoint someone other than Grant to be the vicar apostolic for the new highland district. Nairne wrote to Thomas Innes in Paris to try to persuade him to stop Grant's coming to Rome:

> Mr Stuart ... is afraid your new recommended phisitian his coming forward to these parts may have no good effect, he has consulted wise men of the bestwellwishers to the company who disapprove of it, so unless you have very strong reasons for persisting in encouraging him to that expensive journey I humbly think you should have regard to Don Guglielmo's advice in that matter.

But it was now the new development in Rome which concerned him even more:

What Mr Stuart writes me, (and I do not doubt to you also) of the Popes having declard a new Protector for Scotland without so much as acquainting the K. to have his concurrance and consent at least, is very disoblidging, and shows that the good old man has no more that regard he had formerly for his Ma.ty. I am heartily sorry for this bad understanding.... He has not been managed as he might have been.... This step his hol. has made freightens good Don Guglielmo least he should also reject his Ma.ties recommendation as to Mr Grant affaire and with reason for every body knows his partiality for Regulars.[135]

In February, the Congregation of Propaganda Fide decided unanimously in favour of Grant's appointment but, as Nairne put it, 'yet dare not so much as propose him at this time to his hol: because they are morally sure he'l tell them I'l have a Religious'. Nairne therefore redoubled his efforts to prevent Grant's travelling to Rome. In a very long letter of 25 February he tried to persuade Thomas Innes to withdraw his support and tell Grant that he should return to Scotland rather than 'to throw away a good deal of a poor missions mony to come to Rome against the opinion of all the best friends and wellwishers of the mission there'. But Nairne's objection was not just financial. 'Besides', he added, 'is it decent for him to appear in Rome to solicit himself to be made a Bishop? ... Dos he think he'l have more credit with the Pope than the Congregation?'[136]

Despite the opposition of both Nairne and Stuart, Grant left Paris during February and made his way to Rome. It was while he was *en route* that the Congregation of Propaganda Fide took 'courage and ... resolvd to venture to propose him to the Pope', so that, as Nairne supposed, the 'affaire will be either granted or refused before Grant can be upon the place'.[137]

In fact, the affair moved much more slowly than Nairne expected. Grant arrived in Rome, stayed there a few weeks and left with nothing decided. 'God be thanked', Nairne commented, 'there is no other harm happened but that the good man has lost his labour and spent a little mony, which I am sorry for, but if the main thing go well, as I hope in God still it may, we must have patience for the rest'.[138] It was not until 23 July that Pope Benedict XIII gave his approval to the division of Scotland into two districts, and not until 16 September that Grant was eventually appointed to be both the first vicar apostolic of the highland district and a titular bishop *in partibus*. The conclusion, however, was a complete anti-climax. Grant died in Scotland three days after his appointment, so he was never ordained a bishop, and no successor was appointed until nearly three and a half years later, in February 1731.[139]

The episode revealed how much Nairne still cared about the country that he was brought up in but which he had left over fifty years previously. His involvement in this affair is perhaps also an indication of how detached he had become from his routine work in the secretariat. When, however, he had failed to prevent Grant's journey to Rome, Nairne showed his usual humility and sent a letter of apology to Thomas Innes for arguing against him:

> I am sorry my rash judgement in relation to Mr Grant journey (wch I ought not to have condemnd of imprudence with so much freedom as I did) has given you the trouble to explain all that matter to me ... You might have very justly told me without more ado that it was not my business to meddle in these matters, much less to judge of a church man whom I did not know. But you have had the goodness to pardon my indiscreet zeal because you knew my intentions were good. I was in such fear and concern least his coming should spoile a thing which Mr Stuart and I thought was put in a good way and not without some pains to both and which had been so earnestly pressd for, for a long time, by Bp G[ordon] for the good of his mission, that I was really peevish and vexd to see you all venture to send a man forward here to risk to spoil it against the reiterated advices of good Mr Stuart ... that I could not forbear hinting to you my reflections upon that affaire. But ... you acted as men (as you say very well) having your reasons (wch you were best judge of) for not opposing his coming forward, when he was come your length. So I have nothing more to say but to beg you pardon for having said so much against a thing, the reasons of which you saw, and I did not.[140]

It was during these months when he was corresponding about the mission to Scotland that Nairne was also becoming increasingly worried about his children. In the case of his son Louis, it was the latter's prospects of promotion in the Spanish army which concerned him. When he heard the news that Father William Clark had been appointed confessor to King Philip V of Spain, he confided to Stuart that 'if he be a good friend and countryman I hope he'l recommend my son to some pension or advancem.t', and added that 'I intend at least to write to try him.'[141] Nairne did write to him,[142] but there is no evidence in Louis Nairne's Spanish service record that his letter had any effect.[143] By April 1727, Nairne was more concerned with his son's physical safety, because war had broken out between Spain and Great Britain. He commented in a letter to Thomas Innes that 'I hope … your brother [Lewis] will not forget his poor godson in his good prayers for I reckon his life to be in a very precarious way, while the siege of Gibraltar lasts'.[144] The siege had begun in February and was not called off until the middle of June but, despite the terrible conditions faced by the Spanish troops, Louis Nairne himself came to no harm.[145]

Nairne was worried about his daughters' futures, as well as his own. By 1726, when he went to Bologna, Françoise Nairne was thirty-two years old, and her sister Marie was twenty-five. They were both still living in rented rooms at the English Augustinian convent in the rue des fossés Saint-Victor, where their accommodation cost them 300 *livres* a year.[146] On top of that, they had to pay for their food, but Nairne was confident that they were financially secure, mainly because they had an overall annual income of at least 2,200 *livres*,[147] but also because they had been befriended by the duchesse de Gramont.[148] What worried him, however, was their prospects, because neither of them was married and he was not able to provide either of them with a substantial dowry. Separated from them as he had been for over ten years, he was also prevented from talking to them and could only give advice by letter.

Nairne was still hoping to be allowed to retire from the court in Italy and to return to France. To that end he was living as frugally as possible and regularly sending money to Paris to be invested there. His aim seems to have been to let his daughters keep both his French pension and the *rentes* from his investments at the Hôtel de Ville. In January 1727, for example, he asked Alexander Smith, the procurator of the Collège des Ecossais, to buy some 'actions' for him,[149] and in a letter of February he referred to 'the project in hand' to create an additional 'little fund' by buying three more 'actions … to the value of the 400 Rom[an] crowns for wch I bid him buy one'. As he informed Thomas Innes, his daughters were unaware 'that I have a farthing but my salary'[150] and knew 'nothing of my having that little fund wch I am now endeavouring to remitt and settle there'.[151] His hope was to be able to live with and be looked after by his unmarried daughters without having to reduce the money he was giving them. He confided to Thomas Innes in February 1727 that 'I am sure if the D.sse [de Gramont] pleasd she has credit enough with her brother [the duc de Noailles] to get

a lodging for them in St Germains for nothing, where I might go and live
with them when I get leave to go to them, (wch I still hope my old age and
inutility here will obtain at last before this year be at an end)'.[152]

This plan, however, was called into question while Nairne was at
Bologna because Françoise told her father that she wanted to become a
nun and live permanently in one of the Paris convents. In December 1726,
Nairne told William Stuart that 'you would be surprizd to read the touching
letters of piety she writes to me upon that subject almost every post'. Nairne
did not want his daughter to become a nun, and was unwilling to pay the
money to provide her with the necessary dowry to enter a convent but, as
he put it in one of his other letters, he would in all other matters 'willingly
oblige my poor girls if it were possible'.[153] Françoise Nairne wanted to join
the *Couvent des Filles du Saint-Sacrement* in the Faubourg Saint-Germain,
a Benedictine house also known as the *couvent de l'adoration perpetuelle
du Saint-Sacrement*.[154] In January 1727, Nairne asked Thomas Innes to try
to persuade her to change her mind:

> I hope yr brother will have desird you to speak in privat with my youngest daugh-
> ter [Marie] about the state of the monastry where her sister [Françoise] is so bent
> on being a nun, after wch let me beg of you to do all you can to shew this last the
> imprudence of it, and I wish you could perswad her not to think at all of changing
> her state. I am persuaded she is in a way of salvation in the virtuous way she lives, *e
> chi sta bene non si muove*.[155]

While awaiting Thomas Innes' response, Nairne wrote again in February:
'When you see my daughters I shall be glad of it that you may inquire into
the reasons and motives of the eldest professing so much to let her be a
nun, and give me your opinion upon that matter.'[156]

Before Nairne could post this letter to Paris he received 'a very long
touching letter from Fanny upon her vocation'. But he also received one
from Alexander Smith in which the latter said he had spoken to Françoise
'about her vocation' and confirmed that she would definitely need a large
dowry. Nairne added a postscript in which he said that he did not understand why his daughter wanted to become a nun ('her vocation ... puz-
zels me very much') but emphasized that he would not pay the necessary
money:

if she must have a dote as she says, that decides all for she cannot expect that having 2 other children I am in a condition to furnish to her alone such a dote besides her pension and therefore that alone should answer all her scruples since no body is obliged to impossibilitys.[157]

When he received this letter, Thomas Innes went to see both of Nairne's daughters to discuss the question, but failed to dissuade Françoise: 'she is much inclined to a Religious life', he wrote, 'and as far as I can judge, on very solid motives; in case that shee had your consent and the moyen to compass it'. Innes was clearly impressed by the way Françoise spoke. 'Shee is of very good sense', he added, 'and a dutiful child and therefore will do nothing but in concert with you.' If Nairne could not provide the necessary dowry, then perhaps the duchesse de Gramont might be prepared to help, and here Innes was able to give some encouraging news: 'The Dsse Marechale de Gramont is now to take a lodging adjourning that Convent where your Daughter is, who will therefore have more occasion to lay her case before her'.[158]

This letter from Thomas Innes persuaded Nairne to consider letting his daughter become a nun, though he remained adamant that he would not himself pay for her dowry:

As to my eldest daughter, you'l have known before now that I have bid her consult your brother and Mr Southcoat[159] about her resolution and shew them her reasons, and mine, and if they condemne me to submitt, I shall oppose her no more, but then she must look for a portion for herself, for I cannot in justice or prudence take the only sure bread I have for my self and my other children, and give it away to a convent for her alone ... And therefore if her friend the D.sse (who I doubt not will be altogether for making nuns) has a mind to forward the work, and to give her or get her a portion towards it good and well.

Nairne, unhappy and even lonely in Bologna, was clearly very upset at the prospect that his elder daughter, who was perhaps his favourite, would no longer be able to live with him when he was finally able to escape from the Stuart court in Italy. He wrote that 'I had rather my poor Fany livd a saint, and led a vertuous good devout woman with her sister and me than have her venture into a convent at her age, and with her tender health'. Separated from both his daughters and his friends, however, he knew he could not really control the situation: 'since I have now left the decision of that affaire to others, I'l say no more of it, but resigne myself to Providence'.[160]

During the spring and summer of 1727, Lewis Innes and Southcott presumably spoke to Françoise, discussed her vocation, and concluded that she should be allowed to become a nun – but unfortunately there is a gap in the documentation at this point. It seems clear, however, that all of Nairne's old friends in Paris supported his daughter. In July John Ingleton informed Lawrence Mayes that 'Sir David's ... eldest daughter ... is a person of great merit' and that both he and Lewis Innes had supported her in her 'resolution'.[161] A few days later Françoise herself wrote to James III to ask his permission for her sister Marie to travel to Italy to look after her father. The letter suggests that Nairne's formal agreement had nearly but not quite been obtained:

> God who has His designs for mankind has inspired in me the wish to become a nun and this desire has made me decide to try to obtain my father's permission to live for a certain time by the rule, to be sure that my health will allow me to undertake that which will deprive me of the happiness of seeing your Majesty ... My sister, Sire, is as keenly and respectfully devoted as I am. Her modesty dictates her silence and the permission she is hoping for from your Majesty will not make her in any way dependent on you. Her only wish is to come and do her duty to her father, who deserves this proof of his children's love. She will be so delighted when your Majesty permits her to pay court to him'.[162]

In the absence of any more documentation, we cannot know if Nairne eventually decided to pay the money for his daughter's dowry, or if – much more likely – the money was provided by the duchesse de Gramont. At any rate, on 17 May of the following year, 1728, Françoise Nairne became a postulant at the *Couvent des Filles du Saint-Sacrement* in Paris, attended by her father's old friends from the Collège des Ecossais and from the Stuart court at Saint-Germain.[163]

Although Nairne's correspondence with his friends in Rome and Paris tells us about these family matters, it provides very little information about his daily life in Bologna. A letter from Sir William Ellis in Rome to the *maggiordomo* at the court in Bologna, however, records that in February 1727, at precisely the time that he was worried about the Scottish mission and his daughter's desire to become a nun, some of Nairne's possessions were stolen from his room in the Palazzo Ranuzzi-Cospi by a locally recruited Italian undersweeper.[164] Apart from this inconvenience we can only speculate about how Nairne occupied his free time. He had left both his harpsichords and his *violone* in Rome, so perhaps he bought or hired other instruments to play while he was at Bologna. We might also assume that he attended some of the operas performed for James III in 1726 and 1727, notably Orlandini's *La fedeltà coronata* at the Teatro Malvezzi, featuring the two celebrated *castrati* Antonio Bernacchi and the young Farinelli.[165]

Apart from his friendship with Lawrence Mayes, Nairne was probably now a relatively isolated figure at the Stuart court. He was significantly older than most of the other Jacobites in Bologna, and no longer had the companionship of his female cousins. He seems, however, to have been on friendly terms with Charles Fleming whom he had known at Saint-Germain and with whom he had travelled from Rome. Fleming was preparing to leave the court and return to Scotland, and it seems that Nairne used his contacts at the Collège des Ecossais (where Fleming had been educated)[166] to have money transferred for him from Flanders to Paris.[167]

Nairne also renewed contact with another old friend. This was Sir Joseph Ronchi, who had been a gentleman usher of the king's privy chamber at both Whitehall and Saint-Germain. Ronchi, whose real name was Giuseppe and who once told Nairne that 'I do like as little to be an Italian as possible, but I cannot help it',[168] had been created a baronet in 1715 while James III was in Lorraine.[169] He had then returned to his family home in Bologna. In one of his letters Nairne asked Alexander Smith at the Collège des Ecossais to provide him with information for Ronchi about the latter's investments 'upon the hotel de ville' in Paris.[170]

The spring and summer of 1727 brought an improvement to Nairne's position at the Stuart court. Like most of the other Jacobites in Italy, he longed for a reconciliation between the king and the queen, and the return of the latter to the court. The queen, however, had made it clear that she would never do this so long as Lord and Lady Inverness remained with the king, and unless she were to be given her own separate household.[171] Nairne was therefore delighted and relieved when Inverness and his wife finally agreed to leave. Three days after their departure on 5 April, he wrote to Thomas Innes:

I suppose your brother will have heard before now that at last My Lord and Lady Inverness have thought fitt to retire from Court, they parted Saturday last and are gone to live at Pistoia or Pisa. I pray God this unexpected removall of a favorite ministre may produce soon a happy reunion between the King and Queen, which is what all honest and good men have been wishing and praying for this long while, and which I hope we shall now have the satisfaction to see soon.[172]

Now that Inverness had left the court, Nairne hoped that he too might be allowed to retire. The king decided to appoint Sir John Graeme to be his new secretary of state, and until the latter's arrival at the end of May,[173] Nairne knew that he could not be spared. Once Graeme had settled in, however, he hoped that he would be allowed to leave. He wrote on 8 April:

if I can get leave to retire, with assurance of the continuation of my pension, it is all the grace and favour I would desire of his Ma.ty. I wish this new change may facilitat this retreat of mine, which I have had but too just reasons to desire for this several years past, and the more I grow old and unfitt either for Courts or business, the more I think it hard upon me to oblige me to stay against my inclination ... We shall see between this and the latter season of this year what new alterations may happen and accordingly I shall take my measures. In all wch I trust and resigne my self to Divine Providence.'[174]

During the interval between the departure of Inverness and the arrival of Graeme the court at Bologna received two important visitors. The first was the Duke of Liria, who joined the court from 29 April to 4 May on his way from Madrid to take up his post as Spanish ambassador at St Petersburg. Nairne had known Liria (the eldest son of the Duke of Berwick) at Saint-Germain, and both of them had been in the entourage of James III in Scotland in 1716. On 30 April, the king invested Liria as a Knight of the Order of the Garter in his apartment at the Palazzo Fantuzzi, and the ceremony would certainly have been attended by Nairne and all the other more senior members of the court.[175]

On the same day, 30 April, the Duke of Beaufort arrived in Bologna, where he stayed for three nights in an *albergo* on his way from Rome and Venice back to France. On his last evening he entertained the Jacobites with a *serenata* and generous refreshments,[176] and we may also assume that Nairne was among the people present.

During June James III finally agreed to grant his wife her own separate household, so the way was cleared for the return of Queen Clementina. This meant that the court would be expanded and enhanced with the employment of some ladies of the bedchamber and some gentlemen in attendance on the queen.[177] It also meant the return of Nairne's two cousins, Mary Fitzgerald and Isabella Gordon. There was only one minor disappointment from his point of view. The king decided to rent the Villa Alamandini outside Bologna for his summer *villeggiatura* so that he could welcome his wife there when she arrived from Rome, and Nairne was not included among the people invited to be there with him.[178]

The queen was expected to arrive in the middle of July, but at the beginning of the month the news reached Bologna that King George I had died at Osnabrück. James III hastily left on the 5th and travelled *incognito* to Lorraine, hoping that the time for his long-delayed restoration had finally arrived.[179] He took with him both his secretary of state (Sir John Graeme) and his under-secretary (James Edgar) and seven other servants,[180] leaving Nairne at Bologna with all the other members of the court. Queen Clementina arrived on 13 July, but she decided to lead a solitary life at the Villa Alamandini rather than go into Bologna,[181] and it was not until three months later, on 13 October, that she moved to the Palazzo Fantuzzi and brought her household servants with her.[182] It was while James III was in Lorraine and Queen Clementina was at the Villa Alamandini that Françoise Nairne sent her letter to the king asking him to allow her sister Marie to look after their father in Bologna.[183]

The king, meanwhile, had been disappointed in his hopes for a restoration, and moved in August from Lorraine to Avignon, whither he invited some more members of the court to join him. His plan was that the queen should join him in Avignon with all her servants during the autumn, to be followed by the two princes and their servants during the spring of 1728.[184] We do not know how James III responded to the request for Marie Nairne to join her father, but when Nairne himself asked to be allowed to join the king in Avignon the latter sent an abrupt message to Lord Dunbar: 'Tell Nairn [*sic*] that he must have patience to come with the gros baggage next spring.'[185]

So Nairne remained in Bologna[186] and his daughter Marie remained in Paris with her sister. Meanwhile Queen Clementina refused to leave her children and join her husband in Avignon because she knew that the French court had not agreed to her going there,[187] and James himself came under pressure from Versailles to return to Italy. In October, Nairne's old friend Lewis Innes sent a frank letter to the king complaining of the way he (Nairne) was being treated. James III had persistently refused to let Nairne retire, had not agreed to let either Françoise or Marie come to look after him, had left him behind in Bologna and, apparently, had even withdrawn from him the board wages of 40 *sols* a day for food which he had been given when he no longer ate at one of the king's tables. Innes' letter has not survived, because James III burned it, but we do have the latter's reply. The king reassured Innes:

> Nairn [*sic*] stays in Italy till my children come here. I am far from having any objection to his Daughters going to him either there or here, the moment it is no expense to me.[188]

And a week later James sent an instruction to Bologna that 'Sir David Nairn [*sic*]' should be given 'what was actually granted when [he] had not [his] dyet'.[189]

It now seemed to be agreed that Marie Nairne should be allowed to join her father. It was uncertain, however, whether she would find him in Bologna or Avignon, but in December the king gave way to French pressure and returned to Italy. He arrived back in Bologna on 7 January 1728[190] and was reunited with Queen Clementina, so the entire court was finally brought together in the Palazzo Fantuzzi and the Palazzo Ranuzzi-Cospi. Nairne, therefore, remained in Bologna and continued to carry out his clerical duties in the secretariat, now under the supervision of Sir John Graeme.[191]

It was the death of his old friend Cardinal Gualterio in April 1728 which finally opened the way for Nairne to be allowed to retire. James III decided to employ Gualterio's private secretary, Mathurin Jacquin, who was already privy to Jacobite secrets, as Nairne's successor. When Graeme then announced that he would like to retire and return to France, the king decided to reorganize the secretariat. The post of secretary of state would be abolished; James Edgar, the under-secretary, would be promoted to become the king's private secretary; and Jacquin would handle political correspondence as Edgar's clerk or under-secretary.[192]

On 17 May 1728, Françoise Nairne, as already mentioned, became a postulant at the *Couvent des Filles du Saint-Sacrement* in Paris. On the following day, her sister Marie set out to join her father in Bologna.[193] She passed through Turin in June[194] and presumably arrived later that same month. It is not clear where she lived, but she probably joined her father in his apartment in the Palazzo Ranuzzi-Cospi.[195] Nairne's entire future, however, depended on whether or not the king would continue to pay his pension now that he was no longer employed. Once more Lewis Innes intervened to help him. He wrote to James III on 2 August:

> I cannot but humbly and earnestly recommend to your Majesty the case of an old faithfull servant Sr David Nairne, that in his old age he may not want bread, but that if your Majesty hath no further use for him, his pension may be continued to him.[196]

The king replied that 'tis true I have not of a long time been pleased with Nairn [*sic*] for some particulars, but that won't hinder me from continuing to pay his pension'.[197]

Nairne's final months in Bologna are not documented, so we can do no more than speculate how he might have passed his time in the city. His financial future was secure and he had the company of his daughter Marie, now twenty-seven years old, as well as his cousins Mary and Isabella (respectively forty and thirty-nine).[198] He presumably waited on the king and queen in their apartments from time to time, and otherwise occupied himself with his devotions, with reading and with music. Perhaps he attended some of the operas performed for James III,[199] though perhaps he preferred to save the money he would have spent on tickets so that he could transmit it to Paris to augment his 'little fund' there. In any event, liberated at last from his thankless work in the secretariat, and looked after by his daughter Marie, we may assume that the autumn and winter of 1728–9 brought Nairne both repose and some happiness.

Endnotes

1. Corp, *The Stuarts in Italy*, p. 357.
2. SCA. BL 2/228/18, Nairne to Carnegy, 9 July 1720.
3. Corp, *The Jacobites at Urbino*, p. 123; Corp, *The Stuarts in Italy*, p. 133. It might be added that Dempster had died at Saint-Germain in June 1720. Nairne had recommended Monnot to the king in a letter of 17 June 1719 (RA. SP 43/117), after which Monnot was employed by James III at Saint-Germain, principally to handle negotiations concerning his investments in Paris (see, e.g., RA. SP 46/57, James III to Dicconson, 14 April 1720; RA. SP 52/151A, Monnot to Nairne, 29 March 1721; RA. SP 91/99, Monnot to Inverness, 11 March 1726). See p. 463, note 66 and p. 470, note 168.
4. For the secretariat, see Corp, *The Stuarts in Italy*, p. 128 and p. 357.
5. RA. SP 61/145, Nairne to Hay, 29 August 1722.
6. SCA. BL 2/289/6, Nairne to T. Innes, 13 March 1726.
7. SCA. BL 2/289/7, Nairne to Whiteford, 10 July 1726.
8. WDA. PSP no.487, Nairne to Ingleton, 16 March 1722.
9. WDA. Epist Var 7/no. 44, Ingleton to Mayes, 10 February 1721.
10. BL. Add MSS 38851, f.126, Nairne to Carrara, 13 November 1720.
11. BL. Add MSS 31262, ff.65, 69, 37 [*sic*], Murray to Gualterio, 4, 7 and after 18 December 1720.
12. Sheridan, who joined the court in January 1721, had lived in Rome and could speak Italian (HMC *Stuart* V, p. 586, note by Anne Oglethorpe, 4 October 1717).
13. Their letters to Gualterio are preserved in BL. Add MSS 20303, and 31262 to 31266.
14. WDA. PSP no. 477, Nairne to Ingleton, 23 February 1722.
15. BL. Add MSS 20298, f.152, Nairne to Gualterio, 30 January 1720; BL. Add MSS 31265, f.14, Nairne to Gualterio, March 1721; BL. Add MSS 31264, f.141, Hay to Gualterio, 17 April 1724.
16. BL. Add MSS 20303, f.150, Hay to Gualterio, June 1722. Antonio Manoel de Vilhena was elected *Capo d'Ordine* (Grand Master of the Order of Malta) on 19 June 1722.
17. RA. SP 89/4, 59, minutes by Nairne on the 'Bonnes festes', December 1725 to January 1726.
18. Examples of these 'bonnes festes' letters can be seen in Bibl. Univ d'Urbino: Fondo del Comune, busta 212, fasc I, pp. 83, 81, 77, 75, 73, Nairne to the Gonfalonier and Priors of Urbino, 30 December 1719, 25 December 1720, 27 December 1721, 6 January 1723, 23 December 1723; and BL. Add MSS 39923, ff.37, 41, 46, Nairne to Carrara, 18 December 1720, 23 December 1722, 24 December 1723.

19. BL. Add MSS 39923, ff.37, 47, Nairne to Carrara, 18 December 1720; 30 December 1724. Nairne also corresponded with Eustachio Buglioni, but the latter did not often reply, so they soon lost touch (BL. Add MSS 39923, ff.46, 47, 48, Nairne to Carrara, 24 and 30 December 1724, 17 March 1725).

20. BL. Add MSS 39923, f.38, Nairne to Carrara, 15 February 1721. These and other poems were eventually published as *Poesie in vario metro ed in tomi divise, offerte alla Sacra Maestà di Giacomo III, re della Gran Bretagna* (Fano, 1754).

21. BL. Add MSS 39923, f.47, Nairne to Carrara, 30 December 1724.

22. See, however, SCA. BL 2/294/12, Stewart to Lady Bute, 26 September 1726. This letter, which John Stewart sent to his mother is, in the handwriting of Nairne, though signed by Stewart himself. This might suggest that Nairne and Stewart were on friendly terms.

23. WDA. Epist Var 8/no. 39, Ingleton to Mayes, 20 September 1723.

24. Cruickshanks, Eveline and Erskine-Hill, Howard, *The Atterbury Plot* (Basingstoke, 2004), pp. 166–7.

25. WDA. Epist Var 10/no. 87, Ingleton to Mayes, 25 May 1733.

26. BL. Add MSS 38851, f.126, Nairne to Carrara, 13 November 1720. Although he was the rector of the Scots College, Father Clark was an English Jesuit. See A. Bellenger, *English and Welsh Priests, 1558–1800* (Downside Abbey, 1984), p. 48.

27. SCA. BL 2/289/11 and 13, Nairne to Stuart, 2 and 13 November 1726.

28. For Stuart, see SCA. BL 2/228/17, Nairne to T. Innes, 21 May 1720; SCA. BL 2/228/18, Nairne to Carnegy, 9 July 1720. For Mayes, see RA. SP 61/156, Nairne to Hay, 1 September 1722.

29. WDA. PSP no. 527, Nairne to Ingleton, 2 August 1722.

30. RA. SP 61/169, Nairne to Hay, 5 September 1722.

31. SCA. BL 2/257/15, Stuart to T. Innes, 11 October 1723.

32. BL. Add MSS 38851, f.126, Nairne to Carrara, 13 November 1720.

33. For the queen's servants, see Corp, *The Stuarts in Italy*, pp. 132–4.

34. Ibid. pp. 142–3.

35. BL. Add MSS 20298, f.131, Françoise Nairne to Nairne, 9 Maty 1719.

36. RA. SP 103/29 and 153, Ellis to Inverness, 5 and 19 February 1727.

37. SCA. BL 2/289/17, Nairne to Stuart, 18 December 1726.

38. Corp, *The Stuarts in Italy*, p. 135.

39. RA. SP 79/1, Inverness to Hamilton, 23 June 1725.

40. RA. SP 98/131, 'Inventory of goods in the King's Palace at Rome', October 1726; RA. SP 106/79, 'An Inventory of the King's palaces at Rome', April 1727.

41. See Chapter 6, pp. 246–7.

42. SCA. BL 2/228/17, Nairne to T. Innes, 21 May 1720.

43. SCA. BL 2/306/5, Nairne to T. Innes, 25 February 1727. When this letter was written the dividend was 200 *livres* per annum.

44. WDA. PSP no. 487, Nairne to Ingleton, 16 March 1722.
45. RA. SP 60/102, Françoise and Marie Nairne to James III, undated but received 1 July 1722.
46. RA. SP 61/70, Ramsay to James III, 1 August 1722.
47. SCA. BL 2/306/5, Nairne to T. Innes, 25 February 1727.
48. RA. SP 61/145, Nairne to Hay, 29 August 1722.
49. RA. SP 178/83, Nairne to James III, 7 March 1735.
50. RA. SP 66/38, Françoise and Marie Nairne to James III, undated but received 11 February 1723. For the amount of the pension, see SCA. BL 2/306/5, Nairne to T. Innes, 25 February 1727.
51. Corp, *The Stuarts in Italy*, p. 146.
52. RA. SP 61/145, Nairne to Hay, 29 August 1722.
53. Corp, *The Stuarts in Italy*, pp. 22–4, 147–8.
54. AGS. Secretaria de Guerra, Legajo 2656-15-11, May 1723. Nairne had asked his daughters to lobby in Paris to obtain this promotion for their brother. See WDA. PSP no.527, Nairne to Ingleton, 2 August 1722.
55. SCA. BL 2/252/7, T. Innes to Stuart, 20 September 1723; RA. SP Box 1/28, 29, Stuart to Nairne, 4 and 11 October 1723; SCA. BL 2/257/15, Stuart to T. Innes, 11 October 1723; RA. SP Box 1/31, Stuart to Nairne, 25 October 1723; SCA. BL 2/252/9, T. Innes to Stuart, 25 October 1723.
56. SCA. BL 2/252/16, T. Innes to Stuart, 27 December 1723. Also SCA. BL 2/269/2, Stuart to T. Innes, 18 January 1724.
57. Corp, *The Stuarts in Italy*, p. 150.
58. RA. SP 61/97, Nairne to Hay, 12 August 1722. See also RA. SP 61/145, Nairne to Hay, 29 August 1722: 'I send you here a third letter I have had from him which you'l be pleasd to shew to the King.'
59. Henderson, G. D., *Chevalier Ramsay* (London, 1952), p. 92, James III to Lansdowne, 11 April 1723.
60. Ibid. p. 65.
61. Ibid. p. 89, James III to Southcott, April 1723.
62. RA. SP Misc 21, p. 13. Ramsay's *déclaration* is omitted from Ruvigny, *The Jacobite Peerage*.
63. It was published in London the same year in translation as the *Life of Fénelon*.
64. Paris, Archives Diplomatiques (hereafter Arch. Dipl), Rome 650, f.37, Tencin to Orléans, 7 September 1723. The abbey of Saint-André at Villeneuve-les-Avignon belonged to a relation of the marchese di Cavaglià whose brother (Paolo Francesco Gonteri) was the Archbishop of Avignon. When that relation did not die, as expected, the king asked the regent to give Ramsay a pension on the abbey of Signy, worth 2000 *livres per annum*. The pension was eventually settled on

Ramsay in August 1725. (I am grateful to Bernard Homery for giving me both this reference and the additional information).

65. He also sounded out Fleury (Arch. Dipl, Rome 188, ff.112, 113, Gualterio Fleury, 3 October and 16 November 1723) and informed Lansdowne on 13 November 1723 (Henderson, *Chevalier Ramsay*, p. 66). (I am grateful to Bernard Homery for giving me the reference in the Archives Diplomatiques).

66. SCA. BL 2/264/1, T. Innes to Stuart, 3 January 1724. Innes commented that Ramsay is 'a man of excellent parts, but as yet of a much better and more generous heart and soul, the most ready that ever I knew to do service to every body and do it wt pleasure. But [Nairne] who knows him wtout having ever seen him, will make you acquaint both wt his caracter and person.'

67. SCA. BL 2/269/1, Stuart to T. Innes, 4 January 1724.

68. Henderson, *Chevalier Ramsay*, pp. 96–7, 101.

69. Corp, *The Stuarts in Italy*, p. 152.

70. Ibid. p. 153.

71. For their friendship, see SCA. BL 2/266/12, Nairne to T. Innes, 14 March 1724; and RA. SP 79/47, Mar to Nairne, 15 January 1725.

72. Corp, *The Stuarts in Italy*, p. 153.

73. RA. SP 80/107, Nairne to Hay, February 1725.

74. Corp, *The Stuarts in Italy*, pp. 54–5.

75. For example, he became a close friend of François Foucquet, who was himself a friend of Cardinal Gualterio (Corp, *The Stuarts in Italy*, p. 153).

76. Corp, *The Stuarts in Italy*, p. 154.

77. Arch. Dipl, Rome 658, f.642, Ramsay to Polignac, 24 October 1724. (I am grateful to Bernard Homery for giving me this reference).

78. Corp, *The Stuarts in Italy*, p. 154.

79. SCA. BL 2/270/12, Stuart to T. Innes, 20 November 1724.

80. BAV. Fondo Borgia Lat MS 565, f.333, Foucquet to Ramsay, 20 November 1725.

81. RA. SP 80/107, Nairne to Hay, February 1725. After rejecting Ramsay's second proposal Françoise and Marie Nairne apparently left Paris and went to live at Compigny for fifteen months (SCA. BL 2/306/5, Nairne to T. Innes, 25 February 1727).

82. SCA. BL 2/277/9, Nairne to T. Innes, 21 March 1725.

83. RA. SP 80/107, Nairne to Hay, February 1725. It is sad to record that Nairne was reduced to humbling himself before Hay with the following preamble:

> I was twice to wait on you this morning but was told you was not up ... Since you have been so kind as to encourage my confiding to you all my domestick concerns, I hope you'l excuse the continuation of this trouble I give you, and

allow me to hope the continuation of your friendship and good advice as long
as I do nothing to deserve your depriving me of either.

84. RA. SP 84/149, L. Innes to Inverness, 29 July 1725. When this letter was writtren
     Nairne's daughters were living at Compigny (see above, note 81).

85. James III had actually given John Hay a peerage as Earl of Inverness in October
     1718, but the title was not used between January 1719 and March 1725. The king
     intended to recognise the title again in September 1724, but deferred doing so
     because Marjory Hay went to England at that time. She did not return to Rome
     until March 1725 (Corp, *The Stuarts in Italy*, pp. 129, 159–60).

86. Corp, *The Stuarts in Italy*, pp. 157–8, 161–3.

87. Ibid. p. 161.

88. Ibid. pp. 163–5.

89. Ibid. pp. 167–9.

90. RA. SP 119/60, James III to L. Innes, 19 August 1728. It is clear from the queen's
     letters to her father that she shared Nairne's low opinion of Inverness and Dunbar.
     In November 1725 she described them as having 'ny honeur ny religion ny Con-
     siense', and in January 1726 as being both 'arrogants' and 'insolents'. (I am grateful
     to Dr Aneta Markuszewska for giving me these extracts from Queen Clementina's
     letters, preserved in the Nacyjanalnyj Gistarycznyj Archiu Bietarasu in Minsk,
     reference f.694, o.12, rkps 358, 359 and 360).

91. SCA. BL 2/293/5, Stuart to T. Innes, 28 February 1726.

92. SCA. BL 2/289/6, Nairne to T. Innes, 13 March 1726. Nairne added a postscript
     to this letter on the following day: 'This morning I have writt a line to Mr Ramsay
     wch I send here along with this.' He asked Innes to deliver the letter as he did
     not want to be seen to be sending a separate envelope addressed to Ramsay.

93. See RA. SP Misc 16, James III to Benedict XIII, 17 August 1726, in the handwrit-
     ing of Nairne.

94. SCA. BL 2/286/16, T. Innes to Stuart, 29 April 1726. In a letter of 25 February
     1727 Nairne referred to the '15 months when they [his daughters] were in the
     country' (SCA. BL 2/306/5, Nairne to T. Innes: see above, notes 81 and 84).

95. SCA. BL 2/293/15, Stuart to T. Innes, 11 June 1726; Corp, *The Stuarts in Italy*,
     p. 170.

96. SCA. BL 2/294/4, 5, 6, Stuart to T. Innes, 25 July, 31 July, 8 August 1726. The
     packet was sent to Nairne's old friend Christophe-Alexandre Pajot de Villers,
     who was asked to give it to Françoise Nairne.

97. RA. SP 97/18, Françoise Nairne to James III, 9 September 1726.

98. RA. SP 97/19, Françoise Nairne to Inverness, 9 September 1726.

99. Corp, *The Stuarts in Italy*, pp. 176–8.

100. SCA. BL 2/289/18, Nairne to Stuart, 23 October 1726.

101. Corp, *The Stuarts in Italy*, pp. 178–9.
102. SCA. BL 2/289/10, Nairne to Stuart, 16 October 1726; SCA. BL 2/289/2, Mayes to Stuart, 2 November 1726.
103. SCA. BL 2/289/11, Nairne to Stuart, 2 November 1726.
104. SCA. BL 2/289/3, Mayes to Stuart, 6 November 1726.
105. SCA. BL 2/289/12, Nairne to Stuart, 6 November 1726.
106. SCA. BL 2/289/10, Nairne to Stuart, 16 October 1726.
107. SCA. BL 2/289/11, Nairne to Stuart, 2 November 1726.
108. SCA. BL 2/289/13, Nairne to Stuart, 13 November 1726.
109. Corp, *The Stuarts in Italy*, p. 179; SCA. BL 2/289/3/2, Mayes to Stuart, 16 November 1726; SCA. BL 2/289/16, Nairne to Stuart, 11 December 1726.
110. SCA. BL 2/289/17, Nairne to Stuart, 18 December 1726. In a letter of 6 November, Nairne referred to the 'little collation and drink of health' which he and Mayes had together each night before going to bed (SCA. BL 2/289/12, Nairne to Stuart).
111. Corp, *The Stuarts in Italy*, pp. 172, 182. Because Nairne assumed that the court would not remain at Bologna for very long he arranged 'to leave his whole salary to be paid' in Rome (RA. SP 98/4, Ellis to Inverness, 12 October 1726). In February, when there seemed no immediate prospect of a return to Rome, he asked to have it paid in Bologna (RA. SP 103/153, Ellis to Inverness, 19 February 1727; RA. SP 104/55, minute by Ellis on Marsi to Ellis, 26 February 1727; RA. SP 104/98, Ellis to Inverness, 5 March 1727; RA. SP 102/87/5, Ellis to Forster, 5 March 1727).
112. SCA. BL 2/289/14, Nairne to Ellis, 20 November 1726.
113. SCA. BL 2/289/13, Nairne to Stuart, 13 November 1726.
114. SCA. BL 2/306/4, Nairne to T. Innes, 14 January 1727.
115. SCA. BL 2/306/6, Nairne to T. Innes, 8 April 1727.
116. Nairne had previously been responsible for keeping the entry book of the king's letters, but it was now taken away from him and looked after by Lord Inverness (SCA. BL 2/289/15, Nairne to Stuart, 10 November 1726).
117. SCA. BL 2/289/10, 18, 12, 13, 15, Nairne to Stuart, 16, 23 October, 6, 13, 20 November 1726; SCA. BL 289/14, Nairne to Ellis, 20 November 1726; SCA. BL 2/306/4, Nairne to T. Innes, 14 January 1727.
118. SCA. BL 2/289/16, Nairne to Stuart, 11 December 1726. See also SCA. BL 2/306/4, Nairne to T. Innes, 14 January 1727: 'good Mr Stuart is all heart and zeal, he is both active and prudent ... he tells you his thoughts freely.'
119. SCA. BL 2/289/12, Nairne to Stuart, 6 November 1726. Nairne also wrote in this letter: 'I shewd your last letter ... to the King and to My Lord who were together and they laughd heartily at your reproching your Yorkshire friend with York justice.'
120. SCA. BL 2/289/15, Nairne to Stuart, 20 November 1726.

121. SCA. BL 2/289/13, Nairne to Stuart, 13 November 1726.

122. Nairne corresponded with four people at the Collège des Ecossais: Lewis Innes (the former principal), Charles Whiteford (the principal), Thomas Innes (the prefect of studies), and Alexander Smith (the procurator) (SCA. BL 2/306/4, Nairne to T. Innes, 14 January 1727). In one of his letters he commented that 'Mr Smith … is too sparing in writing to me', whereas 'good Mr Whiteford … allways favours me with a line every post' (SCA. BL 2/306/5, Nairne to T. Innes, 25 February 1727). None of the letters sent to Nairne has survived, and of Nairne's own letters we only have a small selection of the ones he sent each week to Thomas Innes.

123. Nairne took a particular interest in the Scottish mission. When in 1694 he heard that the Pope was considering appointing a bishop or a vicar apostolic for Scotland he wrote that he was 'glad of it wth all my soul' (SCA. BL 1/181/4, DN to Leslie, 5 April 1694. See also SCA. BL 1/181/5, DN to Leslie, 12 April 1694).

124. On 11 April 1701, for example, Nairne had presented Gordon to John Caryll (Diary. See also 11 June 1701, 11 September and 21 October 1702, 15 September 1704).

125. Halloran, *The Scots College Paris*, pp. 73–4, 210. Gordon had been ordained a bishop at Montefiascone in April 1706, and had since then been the coadjutor to Nicolson, the vicar apostolic. See also Nairne's diary, 15 October 1705.

126. Ibid. pp. 72, 211. John Wallace, who like Nairne was from Fife, had studied at the Collège des Ecossais from about 1687 to 1706. Also like Nairne, he had converted to Catholicism, though in his case having previously been an Episcopalian clergyman. In June 1719, Nairne had written to James III that 'the Scottish mission requires a coadjutor', and had recommended James Carnegy (RA. SP 44/6).

127. <http://www.catholic-hierarchy.org/bishop/bgranta.html> (accessed on 12 April 2014).

128. SCA. BL 2/289/12, Nairne to Stuart, 6 November 1726. Although Nairne drafted the letter to the Pope, it was translated into Latin for him by Mayes (SCA. BL 2/289/13, Nairne to Stuart, 13 November 1726). For the file copy in Nairne's handwriting, see RA. SP Misc 16, James III to Benedict XIII, 8 November 1726.

129. SCA. BL 2/289/15, Nairne to Stuart, 20 November 1726.

130. SCA. BL 2/289/17, Nairne to Stuart, 18 December 1726.

131. SCA. BL 2/289/19, Nairne to Stuart, 25 December 1726.

132. SCA. BL 2/306/2, Nairne to Stuart, 1 January 1727. In most of Nairne's correspondence Grant is referred to by his code name, which was Geddes. See, e.g., SCA. BL 2/306/3, Nairne to Stuart, 8 January 1727: 'I hope Geddes will follow yr advice and not come forward.'

133. RA. SP Misc 16, James III to Benedict XIII, 8 January 1727, in the handwriting of Nairne.
134. Corp, *The Stuarts in Italy*, p. 31.
135. SCA. BL 2/306/4, Nairne to T. Innes, 14 January 1727.
136. SCA. BL 2/306/5, Nairne to T. Innes, 25 February 1727.
137. Ibid. postscript.
138. SCA. BL 2/306/6, Nairne to T. Innes, 8 April 1727.
139. <http://www.catholic-hierarchy.org/bishop/bgranta.html> (accessed on 12 April 2014).
140. SCA. BL 2/306/6, Nairne to T. Innes, 8 April 1727. Nairne added the following comments concerning Grant himself:

> As for Mr Grant himself I do now respect him very much upon the character you now give me of him, and I am heartily glad I was mistaken in him when I thought him too willfull and positive for a young missioner, and not docile and obedient enough to his elders and superiours advices, for I was informd that it was even sore against Bp Gordons will too, that he came away from his post, but Mr Stuart confirms now to me that he has found him a very pious good man and a man of parts and tractable, wch I am edifyd with. I was in hopes to have seen him here in his return, and I should have been very glad of it, and would have shewd him all the kindness I could and Mr Mayes the same, but I find he durst not venture to pass here least he might have been known here. So I wish him a good journy and shall be glad to hear of his safe return to you.

141. SCA. BL 2/289/11, Nairne to Stuart, 2 November 1726. Nairne also wrote: 'I never would have thought that he had sufficient merit to supply that post. I hope at least he'l do all the service he can in it for the King.'
142. SCA. BL 2/289/13, Nairne to Stuart, 13 November 1726: 'I wish F. Clark in his new post may do something for the King and something also for my son. I have put him in mind of both.'
143. AGS. Secretaria de Guerra, legajo 2656-15-11, and legajo 2559, vi, 9.
144. SCA. BL 2/306/6, Nairne to T. Innes, 8 April 1727. Nairne added characteristically: 'God almighty preserve him if it be his holy will.' See also Nairne's list of his children at the back of NLS. MS 14266 in which he recorded that his son Louis had 'une compagnie dans le Reg.t ... d'Anvers, dans lequel il a servi au siege de Gibraltar'.
145. The Anglo-Spanish war which resulted from the siege was not terminated until the Treaty of El Pardo in 1728, followed by the Treaty of Seville in 1729.
146. SCA. BL 2/306/5, Nairne to T. Innes, 25 February 1727.

147. Ibid. Their own two pensions amounted to 1,600 *livres*, on top of which they had 400 *livres* from their father's French pension and another 200 *livres* from the *rentes* from his investments at the Hôtel de Ville de Paris.

148. This comment needs to be qualified because in February 1727 Nairne was shocked to discover that his daughters had been overspending and falling into debt. Françoise wrote to him:

> voila 15 jours que je suis sans argent, et si Mad. de Gramont par son credit ne m'avoit fait avancer un quartier de notre pension de mil livres je ne scais ce que nous aurions fait, mais aussi nous n'en receverons plus que dans 5 mois, ce qui me fait trembler, mais j'abandonne tout a la providence. Je suis faché de vous entretenir sur un si triste sujet, consolons nous dans la pauvreté de notre Seig.r et reposons nous dans son sein. Je suis tranquille et contente en contant sur la providence au jour le jour.

(Françoise Nairne to Nairne, February 1727, quoted in SCA. BL 2/306/5, Nairne to T. Innes, 25 February 1727). Nairne complained to Thomas Innes:

> they have no sort of management, and tis vain for me to be labouring and denying my self every thing in order to settle some thing to make them easy, if they have no economy on their side ... if I were with them I am very sure I would manage their little stock so as that they would not be reduced to these extremitys. I am loath to chide them too severely, but I should be glad you made them understand that they are far from being so good managers as they should be, and as I expected they would be.

Nairne asked Innes to give them enough money to prevent their being 'absolutely in want' until 'they be payd their pensions or get some help from the D.sse or from els where', and promised to repay him from the money he had in Paris (SCA. BL 2/306/5, Nairne to T. Innes, 25 February 1727).

149. SCA. BL 2/306/4, Nairne to T. Innes, 14 January 1727.

150. SCA. BL 2/306/5, Nairne to T. Innes, 25 February 1727.

151. SCA. BL 2/306/6, Nairne to T. Innes, 8 April 1727.

152. SCA. BL 2/306/5, Nairne to T. Innes, 25 February 1727.

153. In December 1726, Nairne received letters from both Françoise and Marie informing him that 'an intimat friend of theirs', a nun named Marie-Marguerite Le Pelletier de Saint-Fargeau, had been nominated by Louis XV 'to an abbaye worth ... 15000*l* a year'. His daughters told him, however, that their friend was unable to pay the '500*l* to pay the expedition of the bulls', so they asked him to contact Cardinal de Polignac and the cardinal in charge of the Datary and ask

them for 'a gratis or a diminution ... of the Bulls' (SCA. BL 1/289/16, Nairne to Struart, 11 December 1726). Shortly afterwards Nairne received another letter from Françoise enclosing two letters that she had herself written to the two cardinals, and asking him to forward them to Rome. He wrote to Stuart to request his help and commented: 'I should never [have] had the boldness to do [that] my self, but to comply with my poor daughter who has this so much at heart, I have done what she desires, and have writt 2 letters to accompany hers to the aboves.d Card.ls' (SCA. BL 2/289/19, Nairne to Stuart, 25 December 1726). Stuart and Nairne then discussed in their correspondence who would be the best French person in Rome to approach the cardinals and hand to them the four letters, but were advised that 'there is no hopes of a gratis or a diminution' and that Madame de Saint-Fargeau would have 'to get credit upon her abbaye for the expense of the Bulls' (SCA. BL 2/306/2, Nairne to Stuart, 1 January 1727). Nairne told Stuart in January that 'I am afraid both my daughter and I have writt in vain to Card.l Polignac and Card.l Dataire' (SCA. BL 2/306/3, Nairne to Stuart, 8 January 1727), and he added in a letter to Thomas Innes that it 'seems strange to me' that Madame de Saint-Fargeau should be unwilling to pay 500 *livres* for an abbey worth 15,000 *livres* a year. The point, however, was that Nairne had been prepared to help his daughters in a matter of which he did not really approve:

> She is an intimat friend of my daughters who commend her virtue and merit to the skys ... tis a pitty the good nun should be kept out of it for want of such a small sum. I therefore bid my daughters discourse with Mr Smith and you about it, and if any body can be found to lend her that sum upon good security I wish it could be done for my daughters sake ... When we can do a kindness to a person that deserves it, I think it is both a pleasure and a duty to do it, besides that I hope that that abesse owing such an obligation to my daughters, she will not be ungratefull to them hereafter.'

(SCA. BL 2/306/5, Nairne to T. Innes, 25 February 1727). Marie-Marguerite Le Pelletier de Saint Fargeau had been a nun in the Prieuré Royal de Haute-Bruyère at Saint-Rémy l'Honoré (Yvelines), and then the abbess of the convent of Le Parc-aux-Dames en Valois from 1723 to 1724. She had resigned from the latter because of the convent's poverty.

154. The *Couvent des Filles du Saint-Sacrement* had been opened in 1659 in what is now 18–24 rue Cassette. The nuns took a vow to dedicate themselves to the *adoration perpetuelle du Saint-Sacrement*. The convent was closed in 1793 during the Terror, and the buildings were then sold and demolished in 1796. Nairne and

his wife had joined the Confraternity of the Saint-Sacrament at Saint-Germain in 1702 (see p. 114).

155. SCA. BL 2/306/4, Nairne to T. Innes, 14 January 1727.
156. SCA. BL 2/306/5, Nairne to T. Innes, 25 February 1727.
157. Ibid. postscript.
158. SCA. BL 2/303/13, T. Innes to Nairne, 17 March 1727.
159. Abbot Thomas Southcott was the president of the English Benedictines.
160. SCA. BL 2/306/6, Nairne to T. Innes, 8 April 1727.
161. WDA. Epist Var 9/no.56, Ingleton to Mayes, 14 July 1727.
162. RA. SP 108/108, F.Nairne to James III, 21 July 1727.
163. WDA. Epist Var 9/no.70, Ingleton to Mayes, 17 May 1728: 'Pray give my kind service to Sir David Nairne. I am going this afternoon to the cloathing of his eldest daughter.' Nairne wrote of Françoise in the list of his children at the back of NLS. MS 14266 that 'elle est Religieuse Benedictine de l'adoration perpetuelle du St Sacrement rue Cassette ou elle a pris l'habit le 17 May 1728'.
164. RA. SP 102/87/3, Ellis to Forster, 26 February 1727: 'I was sorry to hear of Sr D. Nairne's loss, but it is well his watch escaped, if ye boy had lighted on that, Sr David would hardly, in all probability have got it so easily back again as he did at Albano ... Mr Macarty disowns ye having recommended him [the undersweeper]'.
165. Corp, *The Stuarts in Italy*, pp. 91–2.
166. Halloran, *The Scots College Paris*, p. 211.
167. SCA. BL 2/306/5 and 6, Nairne to T. Innes, 25 February and 8 April 1727. Nairne deliberately omitted the name of 'my friend here', but it is difficult to think who that might have been other than Charles Fleming who was planning to return to Scotland via Paris.
168. RA. SP 52/74, Ronchi to Nairne, 1 March 1721.
169. Ruvigny, *The Jacobite Peerage*, p. 160. Ronchi was made a baronet on 24 July 1715, but he was not given a warrant until James III was in Bologna on 5 October 1722. However, the warrant was not entered into the book of entries and warrants until June 1756 (RA. SP Misc 19, p. 149).
170. SCA. BL 2/306/5, Nairne to T. Innes, 25 February 1727.
171. Corp, *The Stuarts in Italy*, pp. 156, 165–7.
172. SCA. 2/306/6, Nairne to T. Innes, 8 April 1727.
173. Corp, *The Stuarts in Italy*, p. 184.
174. SCA. BL 2/306/6, Nairne to T. Innes, 8 April 1727.
175. Corp, *The Stuarts in Italy*, p. 186. The king's apartment in the Palazzo Fantuzzi consisted of five rooms *enfilade*: a guard chamber (*salone*), a presence chamber (*camera delle udienze*), a privy chamber (*anticamera*), a bedchamber (*camera da letto e alcove*), and a closet (*camera*). Behind the alcove of the bedchamber there

were two *toelette*. The plan of the apartment and a description of the contents of each room, based on an inventory of 1730, can be found in Giuseppe Marinelli, 'Il palazzo Belloni di via de' Gombruti e i soggiorni dei reali Stuart', pp. 287–9.

176. Corp, *The Stuarts in Italy*, p. 186.

177. Ibid. pp. 187–90.

178. SCA. BL 2/305/16, Mayes to Stuart, 7 June 1727.

179. Corp, *The Stuarts in Italy*, p. 187.

180. Ibid. p. 193. He also recalled Inverness from Pistoia to join him in Lorraine.

181. Ibid. p. 193.

182. Ibid. p. 194.

183. See above, p. 414. Françoise enclosed her letter to the king in one to Sir John Graeme of the same date. She probably sent both letters to Bologna, in which case they would have had to be forwarded to Lorraine and Avignon (RA. SP 108/109, 21 July 1727).

184. Corp, *The Stuarts in Italy*, p. 194.

185. RA. SP 111/71, James III to Dunbar, 16 October 1727.

186. RA. SP 110/125, Graeme to Nairne, 29 September 1727.

187. Corp, *The Stuarts in Italy*, pp. 194–5.

188. RA. SP 111/131, James III to L. Innes, 25 October 1727.

189. RA. SP 112/28, James III to Ellis, 9 November 1727. See also RA. SP 112/86, Ellis to James III, 2 December 1727.

190. Corp, *The Stuarts in Italy*, p. 195.

191. See, e.g., BL. Add MSS 20661, pp. 120 and 31, Prince Charles to L.Gualterio, 4 January 1728, and James III to L.Gualterio, 4 February 1728, both of them in the handwriting of Nairne.

192. Corp, *The Stuarts in Italy*, p. 199.

193. WDA. Epist Var 9/no. 70, Ingleton to Mayes, 17 May 1728.

194. NA. SP 92/33/Part 1/f.45, Allen to Newcastle, 16 June 1728: 'This week one Mrs Nairne a Daughter of a Secretary of the Pretenders past thro' this place [Turin] in her way to Bologna.'

195. James III wrote of Jacquin: 'Je ne propose pas de luy donner ny logement ny cuisine ny a manger, mais au lieu de cela de luy donner pour le moins en acquit le valeur de tout ce que le feü Cardinal luy donnois en details' (BL. Add MSS 20661, p. 39, James III to L.Gualterio, 24 September 1728). Nairne therefore continued to occupy his apartment in the Palazzo Ranuzzi-Cospi.

196. RA. SP 118/137, L. Innes to James III, 2 August 1728.

197. RA. SP 119/60, James III to L. Innes, 19 August 1728.

198. ASVR. Santi Apostoli vol. 65, p. 91, *Stati d'Anime* for 1735.

199. Corp, *The Stuarts in Italy*, p. 94.

CHAPTER 9

Retirement at Rome and Paris, 1729–1740

At the beginning of 1729, James III decided that the time had come for him, the queen and all the court to return to Rome. James himself left Bologna with Dunbar and most of his servants on 30 January and reached Rome on 6 February. Prince Charles left on 22 April with his servants and arrived at the end of that month. Finally the queen and Prince Henry, accompanied by all the remaining members of the court, left Bologna on 18 May and arrived in Rome on 5 June.[1]

Nairne and his daughter Marie remained with the queen and eventually returned to Rome with her and their cousins Mary and Isabella. Although he was now retired, it seems that Nairne was instructed to deal with any of the king's correspondence which arrived in Bologna before the queen's departure. For example, he forwarded to Rome a letter from Lady Sophia Bulkeley to the king. A note of 16 April in Edgar's letter book records: 'Returnd her Lady Sophia Bukleys ... letter layd before the King, and desird him [Nairne] to make proper compliments in HM's name in return.'[2]

Nairne was still hoping to be allowed to leave the court and return to France, so he wrote to Dunbar on 9 March and asked him to obtain the king's permission. James himself replied on the 16th:

> Lord Dunbar gave me your letter of the 9th and explained to me what you desired. I have no difficulty in allowing you to go into France, where I shall continue to you what I now give you as long as I am able, not doubting but you will behave yourself there in such a manner as to deserve the continuance of my protection, and of those marks of it wch I shall be always desirous to show you and yours.[3]

Despite this, however, Nairne knew that he would first have to return to Rome. This was partly because he had left most of his possessions, including his papers and his two harpsichords, in the Palazzo del Re,[4] and no doubt also because he wanted his daughter to see the city before they returned to Paris. Above all he could not consider departing from the court for ever without seeing the king once more and formally taking his leave. And so Nairne left Bologna in the entourage of the queen on 18 May. They travelled via Fano, where the queen stayed in the palazzo of Nairne's friend Pietro Paolo Carrara and visited the tomb of her confessor Father John Brown.[5] They reached the Palazzo del Re on 5 June.

There is a letter of 29 August 1729 in which John Ingleton wrote from Paris to Lawrence Mayes in Rome that 'I hear Sir David will soon be moving this way'.[6] Ingleton had presumably been told that the king had given his permission for Nairne to return to France, but in fact the latter did not leave Rome – and not for another four years! There are no documents which explain this. Might the king have changed his mind and told Nairne to remain in Rome? Might Marie have persuaded her father to postpone their departure? One possibility is that Nairne fell ill and was unable to make the long and hazardous journey. He was now, in the summer of 1729, seventy-four years old. We know that he was ill at the beginning of the year,[7] and there is a letter of March 1730 in which Thomas Innes in Paris wrote to William Stuart in Rome that he was glad to know that Nairne had recovered from his illness.[8] But the letter makes no mention of for how long Nairne had been ill or from what he had suffered. And anyway this would not explain why he remained in Rome for another three years, until 1733.

If it is frustrating for a biographer to remain unaware of the reasons for such a long delay, it is also disappointing that no information has yet come to light to tell us where Nairne and his daughter lived in Rome. His apartment in the Palazzo del Re had now been given to Thomas Forster,[9] and in a letter of May 1730 Nairne explained that he did not live elsewhere in the building, 'where [he wrote] I go but very seldom just to appear and make my Court'.[10] The annual *stati d'anime* of all the parishes in Rome, preserved in the Archivio Storico Vicariato di Roma, would probably tell us where he lived, but the extensive researches of Brinsley Ford, who studied the annual returns of the parishes favoured both by the Jacobites and the visiting Grand Tourists, found no mention of his name.[11] It is possible that he lived at the Scots College in Rome opposite the Palazzo Barberini, but for the time being we have to accept this additional gap in our knowledge of his life.

In fact, very few documents concerning Nairne have survived from his last four years in Rome. He continued to see both William Stuart and Lawrence Mayes, and subsequent letters show that his other friends at court included James Edgar (secretary), Thomas Forster (*maggiordomo*), James Delattre (equerry), Dr Robert Wright (physician), John Stewart (gentleman of Prince Charles), John O'Brien (equerry of Prince Charles), and Henry Fitzmaurice (pensioner).[12] He was closest, however, to his cousins Mary Fitzgerald and Isabella Gordon. On 30 January 1730, his small family circle was increased when Isabella was married in the church of Santi Apostoli to Pietro Marsi, the paymaster, who had joined the court at Bologna in 1726.[13] She was forty-one years old and her husband (who originated from near Lodi in Lombardy) was several years older.[14]

Three months later Nairne wrote to his friend Thomas Innes in Paris that,

> all my ambition [is] to see my poor children settled before I dy and to end my old days in a quiet retreat at Paris near my old friends, and if it please God to grant me this consolation before I dy I shall think my self much happier than if I were the greatest favorite at our Court, of which I have had a long enough experience to convince me that a privat life with a very moderat fortune, and the pleasure of enjoying the company of a few select friends of merite and vertue is infinitly preferable to it, in all respects, both for ones happiness in this world and in the next.[15]

He was particularly concerned to find a suitable husband for his daughter Marie, who by 1730 was twenty-nine years old. Her sister Françoise was now happy with her new life as a postulant in the *Couvent des Filles du Saint-Sacrement* in Paris. On 4 March 1731, she finally took her vows to become a nun with the name *Mère de la Misericorde*.[16] Her brother Louis was still serving in the Spanish army. Since seeing action at the siege of Gibraltar his regiment had been based at Ceuta, and it then participated in the reconquest of Oran from the Ottoman protectorate of Algiers in June and July 1732.[17] However he had still gained no promotion beyond the rank of captain.[18]

There is a letter written by Thomas Innes in Paris on 15 September 1730 in which he commented that,

> I am very sorry to hear that worthy Sir David meets with trouble and affliction when he had least reason to expect it, there never having been a more kind and indulgent

Father than he who all along hath been indifferent about himself in order to be more beneficial to his children.[19]

As this letter was sent to Rome it seems likely that the 'trouble and affliction' referred to was caused by Marie rather than by Françoise in Paris or by Louis in north Africa. If so, we have no information about the problem. We do know, however, that in 1732 Nairne was suddenly confronted with a serious problem when Dr Robert Wright proposed marriage to his daughter Marie. Wright was a friend and was Scottish, but he had no money beyond his salary.[20] More important than this was the fact that Wright was a Protestant,[21] and he had no intention of leaving Rome, so the marriage would have meant Nairne's not seeing his daughter again once he himself returned to Paris. Our only information about Wright's marriage proposal comes from a letter that Nairne wrote the following year, in July 1733:

> I ... hope that God allmighty will give me the comfort before I dy to see this poor girle of mine well provided for in France and by his means, and out of the danger I was threatened with last year of seeing her marryd miserably and against her father's will to a heretick phisitian in Rome. This danger wch cost tears both to the nun and me is now God be thanked out of doors.[22]

Apart from this family crisis, Nairne's life in Rome during these years was probably uneventful. He continued to play the harpsichord,[23] he now had enough free time to read whatever he wanted, including Thomas Innes' celebrated history of Scotland, entitled *A Critical Essay on the Ancient Inhabitants of the Northern Parts of Britain or Scotland*, first published in 1729,[24] and he regularly attended mass and other services.[25] As already noted, he rarely went to the Palazzo del Re, and when he did go there he went 'without meddling with any thing or asking questions of any body, for a Court to me at my age and in my present circumstances is quite the reverse of my inclination'.[26] He did, however, express an interest in the conclave following the death of Pope Benedict XIII. Cardinal Davia had succeeded Cardinal Gualterio as the Protector of England, and Nairne wrote that,

> Card.l Davia is now very much talkd of. I believe he would make a very good Pope, and be a true friend to the King, and I have reason to believe too that he wishes me well.[27]

In the event, Cardinal Corsini was elected as Pope Clement XII.

During these years, Nairne continued to correspond with his friends at the Collège des Ecossais in Paris,[28] and to send them more money so that they could buy additional *actions* to increase his income when he and Marie eventually left Rome.[29] At one point the *Trésor Royal* stopped paying him his dividend – for reasons which are not recorded – but an appeal to Jean-Jacques Amelot, the *intendant des finances*, ensured that the money was eventually paid.[30] This was just as well, because in 1733 the value of the *actions* collapsed from 3,000 *livres* to 1,800 *livres*, and then again to 1,230 *livres*. He wrote philosophically in August of that year:

> We must be content in that, as in every thing els with what God pleases. After all, the fall of the actions is no loss to us who do not intend to sell them at least at present ... provided ... the rent continue still to be punctually payd every semester at the present rate the actioners will have no reason to repent their having placed their mony upon that fund.[31]

By the time Nairne wrote this he had at last decided – or obtained the permission of the king – to return to France. The following year, by which time he was living in Paris, he wrote that

> le Roy de la G. B. daujourdhuy, (dans le service de qui, et du feu Roy son Pere, j'ay l'honneur d'avoir passé plus de 46 ans) [*sic*: 1689–1733 = 44 ans] scait que c'est a cause de mon grand age et de mes infirmités, qu'il eut la bonté de m'accorder l'année derniere sa permission de me retirer de sa Cour a Rome (ou je ne lui étois plus utile a rien) pour venir finir mes jours en repos en France.[32]

Nairne originally decided that he and Marie would leave Rome in May,[33] but then changed his mind and decided to leave at the beginning of September when 'the great heats may be over to begin our journey to Paris'.[34] He planned to travel via Florence, Bologna and Turin, then over the Mont Cenis pass to Lyon, and then thence to Paris. Presumably he decided to sell many of his possessions before setting out, including one of his harpsichords, but we know that he took with him his diary (which is now in the National Library of Scotland), his papers (which are now in the Bodleian Library) and the relic of the True Cross which had been given him by the Superior General of the Jesuits in 1691.[35] His other harpsichord, by contrast, was to travel by sea, probably from Civita Vecchia to Marseille, and thence up the river Rhone and by canal to the river Seine.[36] His framed oil portraits would presumably have gone with the harpsichord.

The delay in setting out was to prove very beneficial to Nairne himself, and even more to his daughter Marie, because in July James III at last showed his appreciation of Nairne's long and faithful services. The latter asked if part of his pension might be transferred to his daughter, so that she could go on receiving it after his death. James agreed that 50 *livres* of Nairne's monthly pension should be given to Marie, leaving Nairne himself with 155*l* 3*s* 2*d*. The latter wrote on 15 July that,

> his Ma.ty has consented to my putting 600*l* of my pension in my daughters name which is a greater favour than I expected to obtain. She is now actually upon the list of his pensioners for that sum, and has had already a months payment, and I carryd her Saturday last to the King who receivd her very graciously, and told her in my presence that *he was very glad to do any thing he could for her in consideration of her fathers services, and that if he did not do more for her, it was only because he could not, and that we might allways reckon upon his protection etc.*[37]

Nairne also asked the king if he would be willing to advance part of the pension to cover the costs of the expensive journey he and his daughter were about to undertake. To his surprise James agreed and, as Nairne put it, 'granted me the advance I askd, without requiring any security in case of my death'.[38] In August, the king gave Nairne 350 *livres*, the equivalent of 'seven months advance here of my daughter's pension'.[39]

Nairne was exceptionally grateful to the king and immediately wrote to tell his friends in Paris of 'his Ma.tys great goodness for my daughter and me'. He also asked Lewis Innes to write to the king to tell him that 'we are both of us (as we really are) penetrated with this ex[traordina]ry goodness of his'.[40] Innes agreed to do this,[41] and the king replied that 'I shall always be desirous to be as kind to him as my circumstances will allow'.[42] Nairne himself wrote to Thomas Innes:

> I thank both your brother and you for the goodness you have to shew so much satisfaction for what his Maty has been so graciously pleasd to do for my daughter and me. I look upon the cordiall congratulations you make me upon this occasion and upon what your brother has writt to the King on this subject as new proofs of your reall friendship for me of which I never doubted, and I hope never shall be forgetfull.[43]

Nairne spent July and the first half of August making the preparations for his journey. Having planned his route, the most important thing to do – as all Grand Tourists were well aware – was to ensure that he had enough letters of credit to supplement the money that he carried with him. He obtained one from Belloni for an unspecified sum, though it was probably the advance he had been given by the king, which could be used in Turin,[44] and then another which could be drawn on 'Messrs Chalmette pere et fils at Lyons' for 711 *livres*.[45] Before Nairne left Rome Thomas Innes sent him a second 'letter of credit on Lyons' for an unspecified sum. Thanking him, Nairne wrote that 'I hope in God I shall not want to make use of it; but tis good upon such great journeys as this is to take all the precautions one can in case of accidents'.[46]

By the middle of August, everything was ready, and James III wrote to Lewis Innes in Paris that 'I believe you will soon have Nairn [*sic*] with you, he holds out very well for his age'.[47] The plan was that Nairne and his daughter Marie would leave Rome on 1 September, accompanied by John, 4th Lord Bellew who in 1731 had married Lady Anne Maxwell (daughter of the Earl and Countess of Nithsdale)[48] and who was travelling with her back to Paris. But then Nairne fell ill and their departure had to be postponed. He wrote on the planned departure day:

> I thank God my health is pretty good again, but I continue weak yet. So I am not allowd to part from hence before next week, but I am going on preparing still every thing for the journey.[49]

When he eventually set out with Marie and the Bellews, probably on 8 September, the king gave him five books to be given to John Ingleton[50] and a 'little box of relicts' for the marquise de Mézières.[51] James commented that 'he [Nairne] ventured fair in undertaking such a journey in his weak condition'.[52] The fact that he left Rome under these difficult circumstances seems clear evidence of how keen Nairne was to get away from the Jacobite court and return to his old friends in France.

Nairne's party would have travelled by coach and stayed each night in an inn, carrying passports obtained from the duc de Saint-Aignan, the French ambassador in Rome. They had reached Florence by 27 September, whence Baron von Stosch noted that 'je trouve icy logé en compagne de My

L. Bellew ... Sir David Nairn [*sic*]'.[53] A week later, Stosch recorded that 'Sir David Nairn [*sic*] ... [qui] étoit venu a Florence avec Myl et Myladi Bellew, a continué sa route vers Boulogne avec la meme compagnie'.[54] And so Nairne found himself back in Bologna, where he had lived from 1726 to 1729.

No further documents have come to light describing Nairne's journey back to France. When he had left Rome nearly forty-two years earlier, in 1691, he had travelled via Loreto, Bologna, Modena and Florence, before going by sea from Leghorn to Marseille.[55] This time he was returning by exactly the same route that he had taken with the king when they had first come to Italy at the beginning of 1717.[56] From Bologna the Nairnes and the Bellews travelled via Parma, Piacenza and Alessandria to Turin, and thence via Rivoli and Susa to the Col du Mont Cenis, which in October must have been so much less hazardous than when he had crossed it in early February. From there they travelled west via Chambéry to Lyon, and then up through France to Auxerre. We do not know if Nairne needed to use either of the letters of credit that he carried to be presented to the bankers in Lyon. Nor do we know when and where he and his daughter separated from Lord and Lady Bellew. But at some point on their route, perhaps at Sens on the river Yonne, Nairne left them to continue their journey to Paris, while he and Marie went to stay on their family estate at Compigny. We may assume that Nairne himself had found the long journey particularly exhausting, so a long stay at Compigny offered him the possibility of recovering his health before going on to meet his old friends and his daughter Françoise in Paris. It also gave him the opportunity, for the first time, to see his wife's grave in the parish church.

Nairne and Marie remained at Compigny for about a month and a half, from the end of October until the middle of December.[57] While he was recuperating there, his daughter Françoise was critically ill (we are not told with what) at her convent in Paris, a development that Marie chose not to tell him about for fear of worrying him and delaying his recovery. Eventually, when they were well rested, they continued their journey to Paris and went straight to the Collège des Ecossais,[58] where his friends had agreed to lend him a room. This was convenient, because Marie was able to return to the English Augustinian convent in the next-door building, where she knew most of the nuns, and where she also found Lady Bellew,[59] whose husband had gone to England 'to settle his concerns'.[60] On 21 December, Nairne wrote to tell James Edgar of his safe arrival:

> I arrivd here only ten to 12 days ago and have not got a lodging yet ... I am come safe
> to Paris and am in very good health thank God and much better than I could well
> have expected after such a long journey at my age ... [Marie is] very well, tho the
> Nun [Françoise] was at deaths door while I was upon the road, wch her sister hid
> from me so that I knew nothing of it till all was over, and had the comfort to find
> her perfectly recovered at my arrivall.[61]

Nairne had finally returned to live in the city which he had left in
January 1689 when he had first been employed by Lord Melfort at the
recently arrived Stuart court. And he was at the Collège des Ecossais with
his old friends Charles Whiteford and Thomas Innes, and especially Lewis
Innes, the man who had originally recommended him to Melfort. He visited John Ingleton at the English seminary to give him the five books from
the king,[62] and sent away the box of relics to be delivered to the marquise
de Mézières.[63] And then, it seems, he had a relapse and fell ill for several
weeks until the following spring.[64] But he had at last escaped from the
exiled court, he was reunited with both his daughters as well as his other
old friends in Paris[65] and Saint-Germain,[66] he could start looking for a
permanent lodging, and above all could start to live the quiet retired life
for which he had longed for so many years.

***

Sir David Nairne passed the last six years of his life in Paris, with no doubt
the occasional visit – though none is actually documented – to Saint-
Germain-en-Laye and to Compigny. He rented all or part of the Hôtel de
Ponac on the Quai des Théatins (now known as the Quai Voltaire).[67] His
new home, which he shared with Marie, looked straight across the river
Seine towards the *grande galérie* of the Louvre, with the Louvre itself on
the right and the Château des Tuileries on the left. With a very short walk
across the Pont Royal he was able to take full advantage of the Jardin des
Tuileries. Yet whether he actually did so is uncertain. In August 1734, he
told James Edgar that,

> when I would see my best old friends Mr Inese and Dr Ingleton I cannot go far
> without a coach; by wch you may see I am upon my last leggs; and indeed tis time,
> since I enter next month in my eighty.[68]

By the time Nairne wrote this letter, Marie had fallen dangerously ill
and was in the hands of some Parisian doctors:

The poor girle is but in a bad way of health, she's mightily chang'd, she has been blooded thrice of late, wh.of twice in the foot, for a stitch in her side, a palpitation in her heart and a bad dry coff. The Phisitians advise milk and change of air, so I reckon to send her to the country some time next month: all my disease at present is weakness and old age, but otherwise I am well enough to hold out perhaps longer than my poor daughter, which is very poor comfort to me. In fine we are both of us in Gods hands, his holy will be done.[69]

A few weeks later, Nairne noted that 'my daughter is still in a very doutfull state of health', and that her doctors had failed to bring about any improvement:

The milk dos not agree so well with her as we wish, yet the phisitians continue it, and tis resolved she should go to the country near about Paris but tis not fixd yet where, only she is too weak to go far off. She has herself a great deal of patience and courage but for my part I confess I am afraid of the worst.[70]

By January he could report that Marie was 'something better, and we have good hopes that the milk and the country air in the spring will recover her'.[71] Finally, by March 1735, she was 'in a convalescent way'.[72] By then, however, Nairne himself had had a bad bout of illness. 'I began this year', he wrote in January 1735,

with a violent coillick that lasted 24 hours, after which I was much out of order for 5 or 6 days and obliged to keep at home, now I am better and I believe I shall take phisick to morrow, but I cannot expect otherwise at my age than to be frequently indisposd amplius labor et dolor being the point I am now fully reached to.'[73]

Feeling that his own life was now drawing to a close, Nairne took a renewed interest in his surviving relations in Scotland, and particularly his brother Samuel's widow Margaret. He sent her some money, and Thomas Innes, who forwarded it for him to a priest in Edinburgh, commented that 'Sr David is being mighty zealous of her good'.[74] He was more concerned, however, about his son Louis, whom he had not seen since the beginning of 1719, and who continued to cause problems for his family.

At the end of August 1733, Louis had written from Barcelona to inform his father that his regiment was being transferred to the service of the Infante Charles, youngest son of Philip V of Spain, who had recently succeeded his maternal uncle as Duke of Parma.[75] This means that Louis returned to Italy at precisely the moment that Nairne left Rome and returned to France.[76] Nairne sent a message to tell his son that 'I am come safe to Paris',[77] but received nothing in reply. He therefore asked Edgar to contact Colonel Hervey, an Irish officer already in the service of Parma, to try to get news of his son.[78] Hervey sent what news he could, but Louis Nairne could not be persuaded to write to his father. Nairne thanked Edgar at the end of August 1734 for letting him know of 'my sons being in Parme and very well':

> I could not believe that they would have put a good old Waloon Regiment of 2 battail-lons in a garison, when the armys in the field, but since Coll. Hervey writes it from Plaisance he cannot but know it, being so near Parme. I have the satisfaction at least that my son has been there all this while out of harms way, but his having been at the same time out of the way of preferment I am sure is no small mortification to him.
>
> Now that I know where a letter will find him I write the inclosed to him, wch I beg of you to forward either to Mr Hervey or directly to himself as you think most proper. I make him such heavy reproches of his long silence that I hope he'l be ashamed of it, and that I shall have letters henceforth from him more frequently.[79]

Louis obviously resented his father's 'heavy reproches' because he continued to refuse to send him a letter. All he would do was to send a reply to Hervey, which was forwarded to Paris via Edgar in Rome. Nairne thanked the latter in September:

> I thank you Sir for having sent me my sons answer to Mr Hervey, which was a sat-isfaction both to his sister and me to see his hand and know at least that he is alive besides that he makes me hope I shall have a letter from him in a post or two.[80]

But no letter came, despite the fact that Colonel Hervey sent Louis three letters urging him to write to his father, and 'some of ye officers of his Regiment' spoke to him 'upon ye same subject'.[81] In January 1735, Nairne wrote that 'there must be something very extraordinary that is the cause of this long obstinat silence of my sons so contrary to his own interest'. He wanted to know, as perhaps any father would, about 'his health, the circumstances of his affaires, his way of living, what character he has in his corps, whether he be easy beloved and esteemed in it and in any apparent proximity of being advanced in it, and in what state his company is'. But he knew nothing, so he asked Edgar to help him:

I am in the dark as to all this as well as to his present sentiments in relation to his father and his sisters whom it is not likely he could have neglected to the degree he has done above this 10 month past without some motive or other.

It is in vain for me to write any more to him till I know in what disposition of mind he is. So I beg of you Dr Sir to use your endeavours to get me what possible knowledge you can of what relates to this son of mine who in the total ignorance I am in at present of all that concerns him is in a manner a lost son to me. You'l do me a particular pleasure as well as to both my daughters.[82]

The months went by, and Louis still refused to contact his father,[83] despite the fact that Colonel Hervey again pressed him to do so.[84] William Stuart commented in Rome that 'it looks very odd that Sir Davids sone makes noe return to his fathers letters after soe long a time'.[85] Eventually Nairne gave up and accepted that he would not hear from his son. He wrote to Edgar:

By your last I find you have done all you could by Mr Herveys means to procure me a letter from my son, but all in vain so I must have patience ... tell him to give himself no further trouble upon that score. His last to you (wch you sent me) gives my daughter and me the satisfaction at least to know my son is alive.[86]

Nairne had other worries at this time, because his friends at the Collège des Ecossais had become embroiled in the controversy over Jansenism. They had already been accused by the clergy of the highland mission of encouraging and even teaching Jansenism,[87] but in June 1733 the two vicars apostolic (Bishop James Gordon of the lowland district, and Bishop Hugh MacDonald of the highland district)[88] wrote to Pope Clement XII and to the Cardinal Protector of Scotland, Domenico Riviera, repeating this accusation and calling for Thomas Innes in particular to be dismissed. These two letters, with another one to Riviera from seven missionary priests in Scotland, were taken to Rome to be considered by the Congregation of Propaganda Fide.[89] When Nairne heard about the three letters he told Thomas Innes that 'I have lost all my good opinion of the bulk of them and even of their 2 leaders, especially the youngest [Bishop Hugh MacDonald] who must be a very pert young domineering gentleman'. In his opinion they were persecuting 'the most solid and most pieux of their brethren'.[90] But he warned Innes that even William Stuart was hostile to Jansenism: 'on the point of the Constitution his sentiments differ from yours and mine.'[91]

In fact, the letters did not reach the Congregation of Propaganda Fide because, knowing their contents, a member of the Scots College in Rome kept them unopened and refused to pass them on. At the beginning of 1736, two of the missionary priests travelled to Rome to complain, and Cardinal Riviera demanded that the letters should be handed over. As a result the Congregation ruled that all missionary priests in Scotland should be forced to sign the formulary accepting the papal bull *Unigenitus* against Jansenism, and that the accusations against the Collège des Ecossais should be fully investigated.[92]

Because Nairne was now in Paris and in regular contact with Thomas Innes and his other friends at the college his opinions on these developments have not survived in the available documents. Nevertheless we may assume that he was seriously troubled by them, particularly when the acting papal nuncio in Paris (Niccolò Lercari) reported in March 1737 that the college was teaching pure Jansenism.[93] One person who testified against the college was Lord William Drummond, a son of the 1st Duke of Melfort and known as the Abbé Melfort,[94] whom Nairne had known since he (Drummond) was born. Although there are no surviving letters recording Nairne's opinion, there is one from Andrew Ramsay denouncing what he describes as a malicious and unwarranted attack on his friends in the college, and this probably reflects what he and Nairne both thought.[95]

Despite all this, there were more positive developments during Nairne's first two years back in Paris. In 1734 James III revived the project to have his father beatified, as the first step towards his eventual canonization.[96] He instructed Lewis Innes that he, Ingleton, Dicconson and Nairne should all testify what they knew about James II's saintly life at Saint-Germain during the 1690s.[97] All four men[98] gave written depositions to the archbishop of Paris in July 1734, after which they were summoned to appear before a special commission appointed by the archbishop to discuss their evidence.[99] Nairne, 'the last of the four principall witnesses', appeared before the tribunal in July and again at the beginning of August.[100] Of the four men, he was probably the one who had had the most intimate relationship with James II, and by chance his own copy of his 'Attestation of the Chevalier Nairne concerning what he knows of the virtues and the Saintly life of the late King James II of Great Britain' has survived. It is dated 3 July 1734 and provides the best account we have of the daily life of the exiled king.

Nairne began his 'attestation' with a general introduction, (which was written while his daughter Marie was seriously ill):

> It was believed, despite my being nearly 79 years old, that I could remember some details of that Prince's life. This is why I have just learnt that I will shortly be interviewed, along with other former officers of H. M.'s household, that we may each give true testimony to his life and manners. At the same time I was asked to commit to paper my memories, to ensure greater accuracy.
>
> That is therefore what I shall do, with all the frankness of which I am capable, as as if I were in God's presence, before whom I will soon appear. Not blessed with an excellent memory (which has never been good and is worse than ever now) I shall not be able to show my dedication on this occasion as much as I would wish ... But despite my small powers I shall obey as faithfully as I can the orders I have been given.

Nairne then described the king's 'paternal affection', his regular attendance at religious offices in the chapel royal, the parish church and elsewhere, his charity, his tolerant attitude towards all Protestants, his 'spiritual retreats' to various houses in Paris and La Trappe, and his piety. The attestation also gave details both of the king's final illness and death and of the miraculous cures associated with him. 'Nevertheless', Nairne commented, 'I am only attesting to facts here, not concerning myself with any discussion of what is or is not miraculous.' Nairne signed the paper 'having this morning received a summons to appear ... at the Archbishop's Palace to be sworn in before the Judges who have been delegated to examine the witnesses named in the case for the late King of England James II of happy memory, and to receive their deposition.'[101]

The case for James II's beatification was sent to Rome in January 1735, after which Lewis Innes sent the king's Papers of Devotion and his correspondence with Rancé from the archives of the Collège des Ecossais as further evidence. However the project eventually came to nothing, one reason for which was the decision, following the death of Queen Clementina in January 1735, to concentrate on *her* saintly life and on the miraculous cures which followed *her* death rather than on those which had taken place over thirty years previously.[102] When he heard the news of Clementina's death, Nairne wrote of 'the generall affliction which we have all had for the death of our dear late Queen', whom he described as 'the best of mistresses'.[103]

During 1734, Nairne also renewed his friendship with Andrew Ramsay, who had been at the court in Rome ten years earlier and who had befriended both his daughters. Since then he had made a considerable reputation as an international scholar. Following the publication of *Les Voyages de Cyrus* in 1727 he had been invited to visit England where he had been elected a Fellow of the Royal Society in December 1729 and a Doctor of Civil Law by the University of Oxford in April 1730. Having returned to France he was appointed by the duc de Bouillon in December 1730 to be the governor of his only son, known as the prince de Turenne.[104] Because the duc de Bouillon was married to Queen Clementina's sister Marie-Charlotte, Ramsay was therefore the governor of the first cousin of Prince Charles and Prince Henry Stuart.

In addition to his duties as governor, Ramsay had been asked to write a biography of the duc de Bouillon's great-great-uncle, the maréchal vicomte de Turenne. James II had served with Turenne when he was Duke of York during the 1650s, the period of the first Stuart exile, and had described his experiences in his memoirs, which were kept in the Collège des Ecossais. It is unlikely that Ramsay would have been granted access to those memoirs, but the Bouillon family had been given two copies of the part which covered the 1650s, which was all that he needed to use.[105] Ramsay, however, wanted to reproduce in its entirety one of the Bouillon copies as an appendix to his book, and felt he needed to have it authenticated, so he approached Nairne and asked him to do this for him. Nairne's certificate is dated 24 December 1734. It states that this French translation of James II's memoirs had been made in the winter of 1695–6 and given to Cardinal de Bouillon, having been 'reviewed and corrected by the aforementioned King James, translated on his orders ... to be used in the biography of the Vicomte de Turenne'. Although written by Nairne the certificate was signed by Lewis Innes, Charles Whiteford, Thomas Innes, George Innes and Alexander Smith, his friends at the Collège des Ecossais who were responsible for preserving the original manuscript.[106] When the book was about to be published in 1735, Lewis Innes wrote to explain the situation to James III:

> Mr Ramsay ... is now governor to the D. of Bouillons only son: he has gott good credit amongst the French, and is just upon publishing the Life of the famous Marechall de Turenne, which he has wrote from Originall Memoires of that familly. And as to 4 or 5 years of that great man's life, Mr Ramsay makes mainly use of the authentick abstracts he has of the Originall Memoirs of the late King your Majesties father of Blessed memory, who made 4 Campagnes with Mr de Turenne, and wrote in his own hand all that past during that time.

Innes made no mention of Nairne's attestation, but explained that James II allowed a copy of his memoirs to be given to the Bouillon family, and that that was what Ramsay had used.[107] When the book was published shortly afterwards it included both James II's memoirs and Nairne's certificate as one of the appendices.[108]

There is no doubt that Nairne and Ramsay would have met each other in Paris anyway, but the publication of the biography of Turenne brought the two men together and probably resulted in Ramsay's visiting the Nairnes at the Hôtel de Ponac. During his visits in the winter of 1734–5, Ramsay would also have met Marie, whom he had known during the 1720s but who was now dangerously ill. It must have been during one of these visits that Ramsay decided that, if Marie recovered, he would propose marriage to her. On 7 March 1735, the day when Nairne wrote that 'my daughter is in a convalescent way',[109] he sent the following letter to James III:

> By a singular Providence my journey to France has procur'd me a very comfortable establishment for my daughter. Mr Ramsay resolves to show the same friendship to the youngest he designd formerly for the eldest. His circumstances were not such fourteen years ago as they are now, being very much alterd to the better. So I cannot in my daughters and my present circumstances, expect a more advantageous settlement for her. I therefore humbly beg your Ma.ties Royall consent to this mariage, and do assure your Ma.ty that the principal motive that has determind me to consent to it, is the Chevalier de Ramsays constant fidelity and attachement to your Ma.ties service, of which I have had incontestable proofs since my coming into this Country.[110]

Nairne was well aware that Ramsay, whose monthly salary from the duc de Bouillon was 1,000 *livres*[111] and who had an additional income from the publication of his books, might have made a much better marriage if he had chosen to do so. Nairne, therefore, asked the king if he would give Ramsay a baronetcy:

> But Sir as all my daughters fortune consists in pensions on funds that may fail, and consequently cannot amount to such a portion as Mr Ramsay (considering the generall esteem and advantageous condition in which he now is) might reasonably expect, it would make up what is wanting to the portion both to his satisfaction and mine, if your Ma.ty would be graciously pleased to bestow on him the title of Knight Baronet. I durst not venture to ask this favour of your Ma.ty on account of my own services, tho' never so long or faithfully performed, since in that I did but

what was my duty, but considering that Mr Ramsay has not only been allways a most faithfull subject, but that he may also be one day an usefull servant to your Majesty in this Country, that consideration (I say) has mainly encouraged me to make this proposal; which is humbly submitted to your Majesties Royall pleasure, with all the profound respect that is due.[112]

Nairne's request was then backed up by Lewis Innes, who wrote to the king on the same day:

I know not whether your Majesty will think fit to grant the tittle Sir David desires for Mr Ramsay, but I find it is mightily desird and expected to make up what is wanting in the marriage portion, and therefor I cannot but wish your Majesty found no inconvenience in granting it. Mr Ramsay hath indeed on all occasions behaved with great zeall and fidelity in every thing that related to your Majesties service.[113]

By 1735, James III was reluctant to grant peerages or baronetcies, partly because they could be seen as empty or meaningless titles, partly because granting a title to one Jacobite would provoke requests from other Jacobites who were equally deserving.[114] Ramsay, however, though a Jacobite, was an ex-patriate rather than an exile and was employed by the Bouillon family. James therefore decided that he would grant the baronetcy, but only if the duchesse de Bouillon would make the request.[115] Fortunately for Nairne, the duchesse agreed. The warrant was backdated to 23 March[116] and sent to the duchesse, who gave it to Ramsay in May. Both Ramsay and Marie Nairne sent their thanks to the king on 22 May, and the former sent with his letter a copy of his newly published biography of Turenne.[117] Nairne then sent the following letter to thank the king:

The honour your Maty has been pleas'd to conferr upon my son in law, and consequently on my daughter, is so sensible a consolation to me in my old age, (not so much for the sake of the honours, as for the new proof this gives me of the continuation of your Ma.ties great goodness for me and my family) that I cannot dispense my self from reiterating my most humble thanks to your Ma.ty, conjointly with the brides and bridegroom's, for the publick mark you have given to the world of your honouring their mariage with your Royall approbation, and doing both them and me the justice to be persuaded of our untainted loyalty, and unalterable attachement to your Ma.tys service. Sentiments which I hope all mine will carry to their grave with them, as I reckon to do very soon my self. May the Allmighty reward your Ma.ty (as I still hope he will do in his own good time) with a happy restoration in this world, and a Crown of glory in the next.[118]

Sir Andrew Ramsay and Marie Nairne were married on 7 June 1735 'à une heure du matin dans la chappelle de Mad. de Sassenage par le Vicaire de St Sulpice'.[119] He was forty-nine years old and she was thirty-four. It was the refusal of Marie's brother Louis to write to his family in Paris, even after being told about this marriage, which made Nairne finally give up trying to get news from his son.[120]

One more year passed during which Nairne had no news of his son. Then, in May 1736, by which time his regiment was in Naples, Louis decided to visit Paris and asked Edgar in Rome if his father was still alive. When the latter had assured him that he was indeed still living in Paris,[121] Louis Nairne set out and arrived in the French capital during September,[122] intending to stay with his father in the Hôtel de Ponac for several months. Nairne informed Edgar at the beginning of October that 'the prolongation of congé he [Louis] ask'd is granted, which my son was informd of three weeks ago, by the Spanish minister here, who was good at his and Sr Andrew Ramsays desire as to write about it himself to the court of Naples'.[123]

Louis Nairne remained in Paris for six months, from September 1736 to March 1737, but it is not clear if amicable relations were restored between father and son, despite the mediation of Sir Andrew and Lady Ramsay. Nairne described his son as a 'tal Spaniard' whose 'slow motions have tried [people's] patience',[124] and Ramsay referred to 'his Spanish lethargy and indolence'. But Ramsay explained: 'His heart is good, but he is subject to mencoly and that distemper produces very often appearances where the heart has no show.'[125] The visit is important in the life of Sir David Nairne for two main reasons. The first concerns the family estate at Compigny; the second sheds light on the family's connection with Freemasonry.

Since 1698, when his father-in-law Louis had died, the estate at Compigny had been owned jointly by Nairne's wife Marie Elisabeth and her brother, Jean-Louis.[126] After the death of Marie-Elisabeth in 1715, her one-sixth share had then been inherited by Louis, who received 50 per cent, and by Françoise and Marie, who each received 25 per cent of what she had owned. As Jean-Louis de Compigny was a priest and would therefore have no legitimate children, it seemed very likely that when he died his share would then pass either to his brother or to Nairne's three children. However, while the Stuart court was at Bologna, Jean-Louis announced in

1727 that he had obtained a dispensation to leave holy orders in order to get married. The ceremony took place on 2 July 1727 and his wife (Marie-Anne Le Chapelier de la Rivière) bore him a son (also called Jean-Louis) in January 1729. Two more sons and five daughters followed between 1730 and 1742, which meant that Nairne's son and two daughters acquired a new family of little first cousins, and that Nairne himself, when he returned to France and stayed at Compigny, had the opportunity to get to know some of his new nephews and nieces.[127]

Louis Nairne's visit to Paris provided the occasion for the family to discuss the future of their shares of the Compigny estate. As Françoise was now a nun and had renounced her worldly possessions, and Louis was unlikely to return to France, it seemed sensible that the Nairnes' share of the Compigny estate should now be vested exclusively in Lady Ramsay, giving her the one-sixth previously owned by her mother. The evidence suggests that during his visit Louis agreed to transfer his share to his sister. The matter took a long time to be resolved, but in July 1737, by which time Louis was back in Naples, Ramsay enclosed 'a letter for my Brother in Law Captain Nairne' in one for James Edgar. 'It contains', he explained, 'the coppy of a procuration which he might get transcrib'd and legaliz'd in the place he is.'[128] Edgar forwarded the letter to Louis in Naples,[129] and eventually a formal legal agreement was signed between Louis and his sister Marie. It was dated 10 February 1738:

> Maître Claude Linotte, lawyer at the Parlement, residing on the quai Malaquais in Paris, in the name of and holding the power of attorney for Mr Louis de Nairne, captain in the Antwerp regiment, in the service of the King of the Two Sicilies, and residing in Naples, heir in half share to his late mother lady Elisabeth de Compigny, at her death the spouse of Mr David de Nairne, baronet, and baron of Saint-Ford [*sic*: Sandford] in Scotland, proprietor of one sixth part of the land at Compigny in Champagne, near Bray-sur-Seine, in the judicial area of Meaux. The aforementioned Sieur Linotte, provided with a special procuration, to the effect which follows, that the aformentioned sieur Louis de Nairne, who was received by Mr Devant junior, Chancellor of the consulate of France in Naples, which sieur Linotte, in his name, yielded and gave up to Lady Marie de Nairne, sister of the donor, spouse of sire Michel de Ramsay, chevalier, baronet of Scotland, residing in the house of M. le comte de Ponac, quai des Théatins, that portion of the property at Compigny belonging to the aforementioned Mr de Nairne, in consideration of the essential services rendered to him by the said lady, his sister.[130]

It is not surprising that the Ramsays should have employed a lawyer who lived on the Quai Malaquais, which was (and is) the extension of the Quai des Théatins towards the east on the left bank of the Seine.[131] The agreement was important for Lady Ramsay because she would make frequent visits to her relations at Compigny in later years. But for us the interest of this document lies in the fact that it refers to 'Lady Marie de Nairne ... spouse of sire Michel de Ramsay ... residing in the house of M. le comte de Ponac, quai des Théatins'. In other words, when the Ramsays were in Paris they lived with Sir David Nairne.[132] And this is of relevance to the history of Freemasonry.

It must have been shortly after the arrival of Louis Nairne in September 1736 that Ramsay, the *Grand Orateur* of the Grande Loge de France, composed his celebrated 'Discours de M. le chevalier de Ramsay prononcé à la loge de Saint-Jean le 26 Xbre'.[133] It would be surprising if Ramsay had not discussed its contents with his wife or his father-in-law or his brother-in-law. On the day after Ramsay pronounced his 'Discours' the Earl of Derwentwater, who had returned from Rome to Paris a few weeks before Louis Nairne, was elected the *Grand Maître* of the Grande Loge.[134] Derwentwater must have known Sir David Nairne while they were both in Rome at the Stuart court between 1729 and 1733, and it is perfectly possible that Derwentwater would have visited both Ramsay and Nairne at the Hôtel de Ponac while Ramsay was at work on his 'Discours'.

At the end of January 1737, Louis Nairne decided that he would leave Paris at the beginning of March.[135] So Lewis Innes wrote to ask James III to recommend him for promotion in the Neapolitan army:

> Captain Nairne who is now returning to his Regiment wher he hath served about 20 years as an officer, and allways (as I am informd) without the least reproache: he wants now, after so long service, to be advanced, and in order to that most humbly beggs your Majesties recommendation, which I hope you will not refuse to the son of an old faithfull servant, and at the most humble request of another old servant.[136]

Louis Nairne travelled via Avignon and Marseille, but as he only left Avignon for Marseille on 2 April he probably did not leave Paris until at least the middle of March.[137] It was only a few days later, on 20 and 22 March, that Ramsay sent his well-known letters in defence of Freemasonry to

Cardinal Fleury. While Louis was in Avignon he would have met one of his brother-in-law's friends, the comte de Tressan, who sent a poem to Ramsay in honour of the 'illustre' Lord Derwentwater. On 24 March, Ramsay delivered the second and very much longer version of his 'Discours', which included the poem just sent him from Avignon, this time 'à la Réception des Francs-maçons'.[138]

Louis arrived in Rome in April 1737, presumably with messages to the king from both his father and brother-in-law. On 9 May, he attended a meeting of the Jacobite Masonic Lodge in Rome,[139] which implies that he must have been received as a Freemason while he was in Paris. As his reception must surely have been sponsored by Ramsay, we may therefore take this as evidence that the latter did indeed discuss the contents of his 'Discours' with his family at the Hôtel de Ponac. Six days after this meeting of the Jacobite Lodge, during which time Louis Nairne spoke again to James III, the latter wrote back to Lewis Innes that 'I have recommended Cap.n Nairne in strong terms to the Duke of Berwick, and I did it with pleasure on your account, and that of his old Father'.[140] Louis then remained at the court in Rome for another month, before travelling south to see Berwick, who was the Spanish ambassador in Naples.[141] From Paris, Nairne thanked both the king for his recommendation and Edgar for 'all the civilitys you and my other friends in Rome have been pleasd to show him while he was there'.[142]

Louis Nairne remained in Naples from May to December 1737 'to solicit his preferment at the Court',[143] but failed to secure a promotion. He then rejoined his regiment which by then had been posted to Sicily.[144] Whether or not the Duke of Berwick would have been willing or able to secure him a promotion we cannot say, because he (Berwick) died at the beginning of June 1738. But Louis Nairne had still not been promoted by that time.

The developments in Paris during and after Louis Nairne's visit inevitably raise the question of whether or not Sir David himself was ever initiated as a Freemason. Throughout his career he had been closely linked with Jacobite families which are known to have had masonic links, such as the Drummonds of Melfort and Perth, the Middletons and the Sheldons,[145] yet no evidence has emerged (even in his private diary) to show that Nairne was himself a Freemason. He had left Rome before the surviving minute book of the masonic lodge there was opened, and his name is never mentioned in connection with the Grande Loge de France during the 1730s. Yet whether or not he was himself a mason he must have been familiar with the tenets of the Craft because Ramsay composed and delivered both versions of his 'Discours', as well as his letters to Fleury, while residing with him at the Hôtel de Ponac.

Although the Ramsays lived with Nairne in Paris for most of the year, they also went to the Bouillon estate at Pontoise for extended visits every summer and autumn.[146] In July 1736, Marie had a miscarriage,[147] but she was pregnant again the following year and in September 1737 Ramsay wrote from Pontoise that 'my wife ... is gone to Paris to ly in'.[148] She gave birth on 12 October to a son who was named Jacques. Six days later Ramsay wrote that 'my wife recovers every day, [and] the child promises good health'.[149] He also assured James III of his own loyalty and said that his son would be brought up with the same sentiments.[150]

The Ramsays seem to have had a very happy marriage, and this must have been a great consolation to Nairne during the last years of his life. In August 1738, by which time she was pregnant again, Marie wrote from Pontoise that 'God had given me' her 'dear Ramsay ... as a father, brother, and husband'.[151] On another occasion she described his relationship with her as being 'like that of a father, a brother, a friend, and a spiritual guide'.[152] In November 1738, Ramsay told a friend that Marie was in her eighth month of pregnancy and was expecting to give birth to their second child in January. Their son Jacques, he added, was by then 'a hefty strong child'.[153] In January 1739 Marie gave birth to another child, this time a healthy girl, who was baptized Marie Catherine Joseph. A few months later Ramsay wrote to a friend:

> I must say, God has given me a help meet for me. Our internal union is yet greater than our conjugal bond, and all the temporal succours I find in her society are far inferiour to the spiritual comforts her virtues and example give me.[154]

Ramsay also benefited from the financial generosity of his father-in-law.[155] Nairne and his daughter continued to receive their monthly pensions of 155l. 3s. 2d. and 50 livres from James III in Rome. At first they were sent as letters of credit by William Stuart,[156] but in June 1737, Stuart was assassinated.[157] When he heard the news, Nairne wrote to Edgar:

> I am sensibly afflicted by poor Don Guglielmo's melancholy death, which is a very great loss to our poor Scots mission. I lose also a very good friend in him. He was so good as to take the trouble every month to receive Madame de Ramsay's monthly pension and mine and take a bill from Belloni for it and send it me in a line inclosed in your pacquet to Mr Waters. I must desire you to propose to Mr Marsy in My Lady Ramsays name and mine to be so good as to do the same favour the deceasd was pleasd to do us, for doing whereof the inclosed note signed by my daughter and me will be his warant. You'l please to give it him with our humble service to himself and to his spouse and sister in law.[158]

Thereafter the letters of credit were sent each month by Pietro Marsi, who was married to Nairne's cousin Isabella.[159]

The amount of the pensions actually varied from month to month, because their combined value of 205*l*. 3*s*. 2*d*. had been computed in Rome to become 41 *scudi* and 3 *baiocchi*, and it was that amount which was sent in letters of credit to Paris. As the exchange rate varied, so the value of the combined pensions also varied. In 1734 and 1735, the amount in Paris fluctuated between 227 *livres* and 255 *livres*.[160] During 1738 and 1739, the letters of credit yielded much less, fluctuating between 196*l*. 16*s*. and 213*l*. 7*s*..[161]

Of these monthly amounts, Nairne gave 125 *livres* of his own pension to his daughter, keeping only a very small amount for himself. One reason for this was because the duc de Bouillon was in debt and had stopped paying Ramsay his pension.[162] Lady Ramsay explained in a letter to James III:

> He [Sir David Nairne] helped me daily by his economies, he spent nothing on himself so that he could give money to his children. He passed on to me fifteen hundred livres a year out of the pension that Y. M. had the goodness to pay him. Mon.r de Ramsay has a modest income, apart from the generous gifts given him by S. A. M. le Comte d'Evreux, and he receives nothing from M. le Duc de Bouillon for educating M. le prince de Turenne. The finances of the father are in such a bad state that he cannot follow his naturally generous instincts.[163]

In another letter Ramsay himself explained that Nairne gave them an additional 500 *livres* each year out of the money from his investments, making 'near two thousand livres' each year.[164]

Apart from the pleasure of knowing that his daughter Marie was happily married, the delight he no doubt obtained from his two little grandchildren, and the satisfaction of occasionally seeing Françoise at her convent, Nairne lived a very quiet life at the Hôtel de Ponac. Ramsay even stated that 'he [Nairne] passed the last six years of his life in continual prayer, abnegation and solitude'.[165] In November 1737 Ramsay reported to James Edgar in Rome that 'Sir David decreases at every moment. I am affrayd for his life if he catch a second cold for the one he has had already brought him very low.'[166]

Nairne probably continued to play his harpsichord in his apartment, but given his age and declining strength, and also his frugal life style, it is perhaps unlikely that he would have attended the Académie Royale de Musique at the Palais Royal on the other side of the Seine. All the *tragédies-lyriques* of Lully, and several of the those of Campra and Destouches, were still in the repertory between 1733 and 1739, and it was precisely those years which witnessed the phenomenal success of the first five operas of Rameau.[167] There is no evidence, however, that Nairne attended any of their performances.

Several of his friends and colleagues at the old Stuart court were still living in Paris and Saint-Germain-en-Laye, such as the Duchess of Melfort, Lady Middleton, Charles Booth, William Dicconson, Lord Edward Drummond and Lord Clermont (now 3rd Earl of Middleton),[168] and he might well have seen them, but most of his closest friends died during these years. They included Lewis Innes in February 1738, Charles Whiteford in December 1738, John Ingleton in January 1739, and Christophe-Alexandre Pajot de Villers in December 1739.[169]

Meanwhile, Nairne kept in touch with his old friends at the Stuart court in Rome, and even corresponded with Lord Dunbar as well as Edgar. He also paid a debt to Dr Wright in 1736 for medical treatment he had received before he returned to France.[170] But it was his cousins Mary and Isabella whom he missed the most,[171] and when Queen Clementina died he was worried about their future, writing to Edgar:

> I ... desire you'l make my compliments and condoleances to Mrs Fitzgerald and Mrs Marsy ... As I allways had an esteem and concern for them I should be glad to know how they are provided for.[172]

He must have been pleased that they retained both their lodgings and their salaries (converted into pensions) at the Palazzo del Re.[173]

When his son Louis returned to Rome from Paris in 1737 Nairne asked Edgar to give his 'respects to ... the two sisters whom I condemne to treat you and my son with a dish of tea and a song'.[174] And subsequent correspondence shows that he kept in touch with his two cousins,[175] asking Marsi on one occasion 'd'embrasser pour moy les deux cheres soeurs'.[176] But after Louis' visit to Paris, he hardly had any further contact with his son, and never saw him again.

There is an extensive correspondence between Nairne and Ramsay in Paris and Edgar in Rome concerning Louis' refusal to reply to letters and contact his father and sister.[177] Edgar tried to contact Louis on their behalf but received no acknowledgement,[178] and eventually sent a threatening letter in October 1737:

> Tho I have writ to you thrice without receiving the pleasure of an answer from you, I cannot however for this once but write you this to let you know that yr sister my Lady Ramsay was on the 12th of this month safely deliverd of a son. Yr Father Sir David is in great concern that he does not hear from you or of you, so if you think fit to answer this letter, and to give me yr address, I shall acquaint yr friends of it. But if you do not, you'll give me leave to tell you that it shall be the last I shall write to you, and that if yr friends send any letter for you, I shall return it to them, and desire them to find out some other way of conveing it to you.[179]

This at last drew a brief apology from Louis Nairne, who tried to justify himself by explaining that the reason he did not write to his father and sister was because he had no news to give them.[180] Edgar forwarded this letter to Ramsay[181] who replied that 'the news of his sons being alive revivd him [Nairne] very much'.[182] And so it went on, with Edgar forwarding letters to Louis Nairne in Sicily,[183] and asking him 'to at least acknowledge the receipt of what I writ to him'.[184] On the rare occasions when Louis did have news to send his father, he merely enclosed it in a short letter to Edgar rather than addressing it to his father personally.[185] Then, as if to add insult to injury, Louis began a correspondence with Edgar to secure James III's influence 'to procure a matrimonial dispense for a cap.n in the Regiment a friend of his to marry his cousin german'.[186] Nairne commented in December 1738:

I am sorry my son should have given you the trouble of a second letter about other peoples concerns, he who is so backward in writing about his own affairs that he has given no account of them to Sir Andrew nor me this twelve month past. However the goodness you have had to send me both his letters has made me profit of the trouble he has given you, by giving me the satisfaction to see at least under his own hand that he is yet alive, for which we are all obliged to you, and I hope we shall be obliged to you yet more next post in receiving by your means letters from himself if he be as good as his word.[187]

By the time Nairne wrote this letter, he was eighty-three and a half years old and his life was drawing to a close. He must have assumed that the Stuart restoration he had worked for ever since 1689 was unlikely to be achieved in his own lifetime, but did he remain optimistic that James III or one of his sons would eventually recover their thrones? We cannot say. Perhaps his strong belief in Providence as well as in the righteousness of the Stuart cause convinced him that a restoration was still a possibility. It is interesting to note that, through conviction or merely good manners, he concluded this letter to Edgar with the following:

Sir Andrew as well as my daughters ... join with me to wish you a very merry Christmas and the next in England, with many happy new years after that.[188]

By 1739, Nairne was increasingly frail and rarely left the Hôtel de Ponac. Ramsay told a mutual friend in July of that year that 'Sir David is pretty well for his age',[189] but when he celebrated his eighty-fourth birthday the following month, it was clear that his life was drawing to a close. By the beginning of January 1740, the end was near, and Ramsay wrote to Edgar in Rome to warn him of 'Sir David's decaying state of health'.[190]

At some point, perhaps in 1739 though perhaps earlier, Nairne drew up his last will and testament. It seems that he left nearly all his investments and his possessions, including his papers and portraits, to his daughter Marie. He also settled a small income of 150 *livres* each year on his sister-in-law Margaret in Scotland.[191] His daughter Françoise and his son Louis probably received something as well, but we cannot say because the will has not yet been discovered. In any event Louis was to succeed to his father's baronetcy.

Sir David Nairne died on 15 January 1740 and his body was buried in the 'Couvent des filles du St Sacrement rue Cassette', where his daughter

Françoise was a nun.[192] Nine days later, Ramsay wrote to inform James III in Rome and Louis Nairne in Sicily.[193] Meanwhile Marie wrote to tell her aunt in Scotland.[194] She also wrote a letter to James III in which she described her father as 'one of the most ancient and I dare say one of his most faithful subjects'.[195] The king replied to Ramsay shortly afterwards:

> I have received your letter in which you inform me of ye death of Sr David Nairn [*sic*] whom I regret with reason having lost in him a faithfull old servant whom I have known ever since I was a child, and in whom I had so much confidence when he was in a condition to assisting me. I shall never forget his services, and be allways glad to shew his daughter and you on all proper occasions the memory I retain of them.[196]

Nairne would undoubtedly have been very pleased if he had been able to read this tribute, but a letter that Ramsay wrote in March 1740 contains a more appropriate epitaph:

> My wife lost lately old Sir David, or rather we have gain'd an advocate in heaven, for he was truly an upright, pure, detach'd soul.[197]

Endnotes

1. Corp, *The Stuarts in Italy*, pp. 33, 94, 206–8.
2. RA. SP 123/89, Edgar to Nairne, 16 April 1729.
3. RA. SP 125/177, James III to Nairne, 16 March 1729.
4. RA. SP 106/79, 'an inventory of the Kings palaces at Rome', April 1727.
5. Corp, *I giacobiti a Urbino*, p. 181. Father John Brown, an Irish Dominican, had been confessor to Queen Clementina from 1719 to 1727, when he left the court because of ill health. He died in 1728 and was buried in the church of San Domenico in Fano.
6. WDA. Epist Var 9/no. 97, Ingleton to Mayes, 29 August 1729: 'My kind service to ... Sir David, who I hear will soon be moving this way.'
7. SCA. BL 2/324/13, Mayes to Stuart, 16 February 1729.
8. SCA. BL 2/328/12, T. Innes to Stuart, 30 March 1730.
9. Corp, *The Stuarts in Italy*, p. 209.
10. SCA. BL 2/329/3, Nairne to T. Innes, 3 May 1730.

11. Ingamells, John, *A Dictionary of British and Irish Travellers in Italy, 1701–1800*, compiled from the Brinsley Ford Archive (New Haven and London: Yale University Press, 1997).

12. These were the people in Rome to whom he asked to be remembered in his letters to Edgar from Paris: RA. SP 166/194, 21 December 1733; RA. SP 171/144, 23 August 1734; RA. SP 181/51, 18 July 1735.

13. ASVR. Santi Apostoli, vol. 23, Matrimoni, 1727–1781, p. 12; Corp, *The Stuarts in Italy*, p. 185.

14. Marsi's age, as recorded in the annual *stati d'anime*, varied so much each year that it is impossible to establish when he was born (ASVR. Santi Apostoli, vols 65–77).

15. SCA. 2/329/3, Nairne to T. Innes, 3 May 1730.

16. The list of Nairne's children in the back of NLS. MS 14266: 'Elle ... a fait profession sous le nom de Mere de la Misericorde le 4 Mars 1731 qui etoit le 4e Dim latere du Caresme.'

17. Same reference: 'il a servi au siege de Gibraltar, à Ceuta, [et] a la prise d'Oran.'

18. AGS. Secretaria de Guerra, Legajo 2559, vi, 9.

19. SCA. BL 2/328/14, T. Innes to Stuart, 15 September 1730.

20. Corp, *The Stuarts in Italy*, p. 357. Dr Wright's monthly salary was 100 *livres*, whereas Nairne's pension was 205*l* 3*s* 2*d*.

21. His father, also called Robert Wright, had been 'Minister of the Gospel at Culross' in Fife (RA. SP Box 1/343, Dr Wright's will, 9 March 1752, contained in RA. SP 330/137, Wright to Edgar, 5 April 1752).

22. SCA. BL 3/6/8, Nairne to T. Innes, 22 July 1733.

23. WDA. Epist Var 10/no.87, Ingleton to Mayes, 25 May 1733. Unfortunately we have no evidence concerning Nairne's musical taste at this time. Did he prefer the suites that he had known at Saint-Germain, such as those by Françoise Couperin, or Italian works which he had encountered in Rome or Bologna? We cannot say.

24. SCA. BL 2/329/3, Nairne to T. Innes, 3 May 1730; RA. SP 136/114, Edgar to T. Innes, 10 May 1730. In 1716 Nairne had encouraged Innes to write the book (SCA. BL 2/210/10, 11, Nairne to T. Innes, 1, 20 October 1716). And in 1717 he had asked Cardinal Gualterio to arrange for research to be done for Innes in the papal archives in Rome and Avignon (BL. Add MSS 31260, f.234, Nairne to Gualterio, 9 December 1717; BL. Add MSS 31261, f.111, Nairne to Gualterio, 1 May 1718).

25. There are no specific references to support this statement. We do not know if Nairne continued to attend Bona Morte services, or if he continued to spend time before the Blessed Sacrament as a member of the Confraternity of the Blessed Sacrament. He probably did, but we have no evidence.

26. SCA. BL 2/329/3, Nairne to T. Innes, 3 May 1730.
27. SCA. BL 2/329/3, Nairne to T. Innes, 3 May 1730.
28. Some of Nairne's letters to Thomas Innes have survived and are quoted here. They refer to his correspondence with Lewis Innes, James Carnegie, Alexander Smith and Charles Whiteford. In one letter he wrote: 'I'm afraid good Mr Whiteford is not pleasd I have not writt to him of a long time, so I'l write a line to him, tho I have nothing to say' (SCA. BL 3/6/6, Nairne to T. Innes, 15 July 1733).
29. SCA. 2/330/2 and 5, Stuart to Carnegy, 9 March and 13 April 1730; SCA. BL 2/329/3, Nairne to T. Innes, 3 May 1730. James Carnegy had succeeded Alexander Smith as the procurator of the Collège des Ecossais in 1729 (Halloran, *Scots College Paris*, p. 20).
30. SCA. BL 2/329/4 and 5, Smith to L. Innes, 12 June and June 1730. Nairne did however lose 300 *livres* in legal fees.
31. SCA. BL 3/6/9, Nairne to T. Innes, 19 August 1733. See also SCA. BL 3/6/6 and 10, Nairne to T. Innes, 15 July and 1 September 1733.
32. Bod. Carte MSS 208, f.368, 'Attestation du Chevalier Nairne', 3 July 1734.
33. SCA. BL 3/5/6, T. Innes to Stuart, 18 May 1733.
34. SCA. BL 3/6/8, Nairne to T. Innes, 22 July 1733.
35. See above, p. 46.
36. WDA. Epist Var 10/no. 87, Ingleton to Mayes, 25 May 1733: 'The occasion of giving you this trouble is a letter I have from Sir David Nairne concerning a harpsical which belongd to Canon Howard, and which Sir David has had in possession these ten years. At his request I writ to you upon this subject in 1723, and your answer was so favourable that he presumes or hopes he may keep the harpsical without paying for it. If so, he intends when he returns to France to transport it by water. Your answer to him or to me will decide this little affaire.'
37. SCA. BL 3/6/6, Nairne to T. Innes, 15 July 1733.
38. SCA. BL 3/6/6, Nairne to T. Innes, 15 July 1733.
39. SCA. BL 3/6/9, Nairne to T. Innes, 19 August 1733.
40. SCA. BL 3/6/6, Nairne to T. Innes, 15 July 1733.
41. SCA. BL 3/6/8, Nairne to T. Innes, 22 July 1733; RA. SP 163/127, L. Innes to James III, 27 July 1733.
42. RA. SP 164/10, James III to L. Innes, 12 August 1733.
43. SCA. BL 3/6/9, Nairne to T. Innes, 19 August 1733.
44. SCA. BL 3/6/6, Nairne to T. Innes, 15 July 1733.
45. SCA. BL 3/6/8, Nairne to T. Innes, 22 July 1733. The letter of credit at Lyon was sent him by the Bishop of Fimbore [?]. The latter sent 'a bill of credit on a banquier here in Rome for 120 Roman Crowns with another at the bottom of that upon Messrs Chalmette pere et fils at Lyons to pay me to the value of sd

120 Crowns, 711 livres French in case I should not have made use of the credit in Rome'. Nairne told Thomas Innes that 'this bill I have receivd with a very kind letter the Bp has writt to the nun [Françoise] ... So I have hitherto all reason to look upon him as a sincere effectuall friend'. I have not been able to identify this bishop, though he might have been Michael Macdonagh, Bishop of Kilmore.

46. SCA. BL 3/6/10, Nairne to T. Innes, 1 September 1733. Nairne had asked Alexander Smith at the Collège des Ecossais to call in a debt for him: 'I hope he'l see to recover the 298 livres from Mr Cornette wch would be a very seasonable help to me at present' (SCA. BL 3/6/9, Nairne to T. Innes, 19 August 1733).

47. RA. SP 164/10, James III to L. Innes, 12 August 1733.

48. Lord Bellew had married Lady Anne Maxwell at Lucca in September 1731 (Maxwell Stuart, *Lady Nithsdale and the Jacobites*, p. 150). The couple lived at Pistoia until February 1732, since when they had been in Rome (NA. SP 98/32/ff.275, 343, Stosch to Newcastle, 13 October 1731 and 23 February 1732).

49. SCA. BL 3/6/10, Nairne to T. Innes, 1 September 1733. See also SCA. BL 3/5/15, T. Innes to Stuart, 24 August 1733: 'S David I suppose will be parted before this can reach you.'

50. RA. SP 165/213, James III to Ingleton, 28 October 1733.

51. RA. SP 173/107, Nairne to Edgar, 20 September 1734.

52. RA. SP 165/213, James III to Ingleton, 28 October 1733.

53. NA. SP 98/32/f.575, Stosch to Newcastle, 27 September 1733. Stosch described Nairne as 'le Tresorier du Pretendant' and informed the British government that he was 'passer secretement en Angleterre'. This letter provides a good example of (1) the unreliability of Stosch as a source for the activities of the individual servants at the Stuart court, and (2) his habit of pretending that he had access to the secrets of the court.

54. NA. SP 98/32/f.577, Stosch to Newcastle, 3 October 1733.

55. See above, pp. 46–7.

56. See above, pp. 255–9.

57. RA. SP 166/111, Ingleton to James III, 30 November 1733: 'Sir David Nairne has made a long stay in the country, nor do I hear that he is yet arrived in Paris.' See also RA. SP 165/213, James III to Ingleton, 28 October 1733: 'I hope old Nairn [*sic*] is well with you by this time.'

58. SCA. BL 3/6/8, Nairne to T. Innes, 22 July 1733: 'I reckon to come straight to the Colledge and to have the pleasure of waiting on your brother and you as two of the first and best old friends I have in that country.'

59. RA. SP 166/194, Nairne to Edgar, 21 December 1733. Nairne also wrote that Mrs Mary Plowden 'is our next neighbour here at the English monastry'.

60. RA. SP 167/5, J. P. Stafford to Edgar, 22 December 1733. John Paul Stafford, the brother of Mary Plowden, had joined the court at Bologna in 1728 to become

under-governor of Prince Henry, but had left the court and returned to Paris in 1730 (Corp, *The Stuarts in Italy*, pp. 197, 311, 364). Lady Bellew joined her husband in London in 1734, and died in childbirth the following year (Maxwell Stuart, *Lady Nithsdale and the Jacobites*, pp. 153–4).

61. RA. SP 166/194, Nairne to Edgar, 21 December 1733. See also RA. SP 167/119, Edgar to Nairne, 13 January 1734.

62. RA. SP 166/194, Nairne to Edgar, 21 December 1733: 'I have seen ... Dr Ingleton, who is much troubled with the gravall but is otherwise very well ... I deliverd to him the books ... and ... the Doctor is extremely pleased with them. My Ld Strafford lodges with him at the English Seminary.'

63. RA. SP 173/107, Nairne to Edgar, 20 September 1734: 'One of my first cares after my arrivall in Paris last year was to perform the commission his Ma.ty charged me with, of having the little box of relicts safely deliverd to Mad. de Mezieres. I was not acquaint with the Lady and I found she lived at such a vast distance that I did not think it necessary to carry the box to her myself. So I chusd rather to charge Mr Waters with it. Accordingly in December last being then lodged in the Scotch Colledge I writt a note to Mr Waters and sent a servant of the Colledge with it and the box, and prayd Mr Waters to send it with all safety to Madame de Mezieres and let her know it was sent to her by the King.'

64. RA. SP 169/3, James III to L. Innes, 17 March 1734: 'I am glad Nairn [*sic*] is recoverd of his late illness.'

65. Nairne's friends in Paris included Andrew Ramsay and Christophe-Alexandre Pajot de Villers. He went to see the latter shortly after his arrival in Paris (RA. SP 166/194, Nairne to Edgar, 21 December 1733). They had remained in contact, and on one occasion Cardinal Fleury had used Pajot de Villers and Nairne as a means of knowing the opinion of James III on a minor matter (RA. SP 143/2, Pajot de Villers to Nairne, 13 February 1731).

66. Nairne's friends at Saint-Germain included Charles Booth, William Dicconson and Etienne du Mirail de Monnot. The Duchess of Melfort and the Countess of Middleton, the widows of the secretaries of state whom Nairne had served, were also still living in the château, as were Lord Edward Drummond and the 3rd Earl of Middleton (previously Lord Clermont) who had returned to France from Urbino.

67. SCA. BL 3/31/4, G. Innes to Paterson, 16 January 1737: 'his address is a Mr Le Chevallier de Nairne a l'hotel de Ponac Quai des Theatins proche les Theatins a Paris.' The hôtel belonged to Philogène Alexis-François, come de Ponac, also known as Ponnat, whose family came from the Dauphiné. Born in 1709, the comte de Ponac had been a *page de la Grande Ecurie* at Versailles since 1726. The Quai des Théatins stretched from the rue des Saints-Pères to the rue de Beaune, and the Théatins themselves occupied a building on the site of what are now

numbers 15 to 21bis, with the entrance to their church the present number 16. Nairne's home was possibly at number 7, in a building which had been divided up in 1733 after the death of its owner (<http://fr.wikipedia.org/wiki/Quai-Voltaire>, accessed on 23 July 2016). The mother house of the Théatins was the church of Sant'Andrea della Valle in Rome, which Nairne had often attended. Nairne's new home was not far from the rue Cassette, where Françoise was a nun in the *Couvent des Filles du Saint-Sacrement*.

68. RA. SP 171/144, Nairne to Edgar, 23 August 1734.
69. RA. SP 171/144, Nairne to Edgar, 23 August 1734.
70. RA. SP 173/107, Nairne to Edgar, 20 September 1734.
71. RA. SP 176/173, Nairne to Edgar, 10 January 1735.
72. RA. SP 178/82, Nairne to Edgar, 7 March 1735.
73. RA. SP 176/173, Nairne to Edgar, 10 January 1735.
74. SCA. BL 3/11/13, T. Innes to Grant, 4 December 1734.
75. RA. SP 166/194, Nairne to Edgar, 21 December 1733.
76. In the list of his children at the back of NLS 14266, Nairne noted that Louis had been in Italy 'depuis la fin de 1733'. See also RA. SP 167/119, Edgar to Nairne, 13 January 1734.
77. RA. SP 166/194, Nairne to Edgar, 21 December 1733.
78. RA. SP 171/144, Nairne to Edgar, 23 August 1734. Hervey was described in 1728 as 'an Irish man and Capt of Horse in the Duke of Parma's service' (NA/. SP 92/33/Part 1/f.83, Allen to Newcastle, 31 July 1728). By 1734 he had been promoted to the rank of colonel.
79. RA. SP 172/185, Nairne to Edgar, 30 August 1734.
80. RA. SP 173/107, Nairne to Edgar, 20 September 1734.
81. RA. SP 175/101, Edgar to Nairne, 1 December 1734.
82. RA. SP 176/173, Nairne to Edgar, 10 January 1735.
83. RA. SP 178/82, Nairne to Edgar, 7 March 1735.
84. RA. SP 180/46 and 123, Edgar to Nairne, 15 and 29 June 1735.
85. SCA. BL 3/20/8, Stuart to G. Innes, 14 July 1735.
86. RA. SP 181/51, Nairne to Edgar, 18 July 1735.
87. Halloran, *The Scots College Paris*, p. 108.
88. Hugh MacDonald had been appointed in February 1731 after a gap of three and a half years since the death of Alexander Grant in 1727: see p. 410.
89. Halloran, *The Scots College Paris*, pp. 109–14.
90. SCA. BL 3/6/10, Nairne to T. Innes, 1 September 1733.
91. SCA. BL 3/6/7, DN to T. Innes, 19 July 1733:

> Tho our friend Mr Stuart be one of the best of men and a true clergyman yet on the point of the Constitution his sentiments differ from yours and mine,

so when you write on this subject I think you need not open your mind too much to him, not but that he has all the value and respect for your brother and you that you desire and is far from approving at the violence and persecution on that point, but he is afraid the mission whose maintenance depends upon Rome may be ruind if the missioners be not all obedient to Rome in what they make now a Regle de foy, but more of this when we meet.

92. Halloran, *The Scots College Paris*, pp. 117–18.

93. Ibid. pp. 133–4.

94. Ibid. p. 137.

95. SCA. BL 3/65/13, Ramsay to unidentified (Lord William Drummond?), 1 February 1740.

96. Corp, *The Stuarts in Italy*, p. 220.

97. RA. SP 168/85, James III to L. Innes, 10 February 1734. The submission was co-ordinated by Abbot Thomas Southcott, President of the English Benedictines (Corp, 'James II and David Nairne', p. 1407, note 137).

98. Written depositions were subsequently presented by Charles Booth and George Rattray (Corp, 'James II and David Nairne', p. 1408, note 140).

99. RA. SP 171/185, L. Innes to James III, 26 July 1734.

100. RA. SP 172/76, L. Innes to James III, 9 August 1734.

101. Bod. Carte MSS 208, f.368, 'Attestation du Chevalier Nairne touchant ce qu'il scait des vertus et de la vie Ste du feu Roy de la G. B. Jacques 2d', 3 July 1734.

102. Corp, 'James II and David Nairne', p. 1408; Corp, *The Stuarts in Italy*, pp. 220–3.

103. RA. SP 178/83, Nairne to James III, 7 March 1735.

104. Charles Godefroy de la Tour d'Auvergne (1706–1771) succeeded his father as duc de Bouillon in 1730. He had been married to Queen Clementina's sister Marie-Charlotte since 1724. Their son Godefroy Charles Henri had been born in 1728. In addition to prince de Turenne, the boy was also known as the duc de Château-Thierry and the comte d'Evreux, although he did not succeed his great-uncle to the latter title until 1753. He succeeded his father as duc de Bouillon in 1771 and died in 1792. For Ramsay's appointment, see Bibliothèque de Sedan, Fonds Gourjault, Carton 174/9. The Hôtel de Bouillon, where Ramsay was employed, was situated on the Quai Malaquais, very close to the Quai des Théatins (which was actually its extension towards the west). It is possible that it was Ramsay who had recommended the Hôtel de Ponac to Nairne as a possible residence, or that Nairne chose that location because of its proximity to the Hôtel de Bouillon.

105. Both copies were given to Turenne's nephew, the Cardinal de Bouillon, the first in January 1696, and the second in January 1705. The latter is now in BL. Add MSS 70522 (Corp, 'James II and David Nairne', p. 1394, note 52).

106. University of Indiana at Bloomington, Lilly Library, miscellaneous MSS 1652–1660, James II , certificate by Nairne dated 24 December 1734, and attached to 'Memoires du duc d'York' with a 'Preface du Cardinal de Bouillon' dated at Rome, 16 February 1715.

107. RA. SP 178/77, L. Innes to James III, 7 March 1735.

108. The memoirs and the certificate were published in volume II of Ramsay, A. M. De, *Histoire de Henri de la Tour d'Auvergne, Vicomte de Turenne* (Paris, 1735). The 'Memoirs du Duc d'Yorck' were the third of three 'Preuves' provided as appendices (pp. iii–cl), with Nairne's 'Certificat des Supérieurs du College des Ecossois à Paris' reproduced on p.cl. The memoirs and the certificate were published for the second time in *The Memoirs of James II: His Campaigns as Duke of York*, translated and edited by A. Lytton Sells (London, 1962), which includes a facsimile of Nairne's certificate opposite p. 120.

109. See above, p. 442.

110. RA. SP 178/83, Nairne to James III, 7 March 1735.

111. The duc de Bouillon did not actually give Ramsay a salary, but instead promised to build for Ramsay 'un pavillon [à Pontoise] isolé à la campagne, entouré d'un parc; il ajoutait à ce don une rente de 12000 livres, pour l'entretien de la propriété, et le droit de chasse dans tous les environs' (Compigny, *Les Entretiens de Cambrai*, p. 59). Mathieu Marais stated incorrectly that Ramsay had '3000 livres de pension' (*Journal et Mémoires de Mathieu Marais, sur la Régence et le Règne de Louis XV (1715–1737)*, ed. M. de Lescure, 4 vols (Paris, 1863–8), vol. 4, p. 193, a letter dated 30 December 1730.

112. RA. SP 178/83, Nairne to James III, 7 March 1735.

113. RA. SP 178/77, L. Innes to James III, 7 March 1735.

114. Corp, *The Stuarts in Italy*, pp. 371–2.

115. RA. SP 178/173, James III to L. Innes, 29 March 1735:

> Mr Ramsay, whose marriage with Miss Nairn [*sic*] will soon be concluded if it only sticks at my giving him a Warrant of Knight Baronet. For Lord Dumbar has already writ to her Father that the Warrant shall be sent, if Mr Ramsay gets the Dutchess of Bouillon to ask it of me, for granting it at the Dutchess's desire for her sons Governour, makes it a particular case, and no general precident, and I shall be very glad of an occasion of doing what is agreable to both parties concernd.

The king wrote to Inverness that,

> it is an odd story you write to Edgar about a certain person's courtship. It is true he was made a Knight Baronet, and the Duchesse de Bouillon desired it; but it is true that I contrived she should desire it, being desirous to grant the favour in that shape

(Henderson, *Chevalier Ramsay*, p. 181, no date given, presumably March 1735). For Edgar's letter of 30 March informing Nairne, see RA. SP 176/102, Edgar's letter book, in which he listed the letter but did not keep a copy).

116. RA. SP Misc, p. 22, 'Warrant for Andrew Ramsay to be made a Baronet to please the Duchesse de Bouillon', 23 March 1735.

117. RA. SP 179/104 and 106, Ramsay and M.Nairne to James III, 22 May 1735.

118. RA. SP 179/185, Nairne to James III, undated, but received 6 June 1735.

119. The list of children at the back of NLS. MS 14266. Madame de Sassenage was Marie-Thérèse d'Albert de Luynes (1673–1743), daughter of Charles Honoré d'Albert, duc de Luynes and widow of René Berenger, comte de Sassenage (1672–1730). Ramsay had been the tutor of her son Charles François Bérenger, comte de Sassenage (1704–1762). For Edgar's letter of 15 June 1735 congratulating Nairne on the marriage of his daughter, see RA. SP 180/46. The *Gazette* of 10 July 1735 reported that 'M. de Ramsay auteur de l'Histoire de Turenne qui a épousé, il y a un mois environ Melle de Nairne, d[emois]elle écossaise a obtenu du Chevalier de Saint-Georges [i.e. James III] le titre héréditaire de chevalier baronet d'Angleterre, ce qui donne à Mme son épouse celui de Milady', quoted in Chevalier, Pierre, *Les Ducs sous l'Acacia, 1725–1743* (Geneva, 1964), p. 259. In 1929 Alfred de Compigny recorded that he had 'de ce temps [1735] une ravissante miniature qui représente Marie de Nairne ... Les traits sont reguliers, la bouche une tantinet sensuelle, les yeux vifs et intelligents' (*Les Entretiens de Cambrai*, p. 61). The present location of this miniature is unknown.

120. See above, p. 444.

121. RA. SP 187/79, Edgar to L. Nairne, 19 May 1736; RA. SP 187/94, 188/114 and 189/33, Edgar to Nairne, 23 May, 4 July and 15 August 1736.

122. RA. SP 189/138, Edgar to Nairne, 12 September 1736.

123. RA. SP 190/3, Nairne to Edgar, 1 October 1736.

124. RA. SP 195/97, Nairne to Edgar, 15 April 1737.

125. RA. SP 202/42, Ramsay to Edgar, 18 November 1737.

126. See above, p. 104.

127. Compigny des Bordes, *Les Entretiens de Cambrai*, pp. 60–1.

128. RA. SP 199/68, Ramsay to Edgar, 15 July 1737.

129. RA. SP 199/124, Edgar to Nairne, 24 July 1737; RA. SP 199/162, Edgar to L. Nairne, 2 August 1737; RA. SP 199/188, Edgar to Ramsay, 8 August 1737.

130. Archives Départementales de la Seine-et-Marne, Baillage de Provins B.636, 10 February 1738.

131. Claude Linotte (1686–1768) had become an adviser to the duc de Bouillon in 1726 and 'tuteur onéraire' to the prince de Turenne in 1730, at the same time as Ramsay had become the prince's governor. Linotte probably lived in the Hôtel de Bouillon on the Quai Malaquais. See Velde, François R., 'The Case of the Undying Debt', *Federal Reserve Bank of Chicago, Working Paper Series 2009–12*,

33pp, at p. 6 (reprinted in the *Financial History Review*, vol. 17, no. 2, October 2010, pp. 185–209).

132. This is confirmed by a letter from Lady Ramsay to James III of 25 January 1740 in which she wrote that she had 'la consolation de vivre avec un pere tendre que j'aimois' (RA. SP 220/28).

133. Négrier, Patrick, *Textes fondateurs de la Tradition maçonnique, 1390–1760* (Paris, 1995), pp. 311–17.

134. Corp, *The Stuarts in Italy*, p. 331.

135. RA. SP 193/134, Nairne to Edgar, 28 January 1737.

136. RA. SP 194/126, L. Innes to James III, 6 March 1737.

137. RA. SP 195/97, Nairne to Edgar, 15 April 1737.

138. Corp, *A Court in Exile*, pp. 341–2. Ramsay remained in Paris until May, when he went to Pontoise with the prince de Turenne (Bod. Carte MSS 226, p. 326, Ramsay to Carte, 20 May 1737). While he was there, he wrote his letter of 16 April 1737 to the marquis de Caumont, in which he explained that there were 'trois sortes de confrères' in Freemasonry, and discussed the aims of Lord Derwentwater as Grand Master (London, Wellcome Library, MS 5744/10). For the second version of Ramsay's 'Discours', see Négrier, *Textes fondateurs de la Tradition maçonnique*, pp. 324–32. The poem is printed on p. 325.

139. Hughan, William James, *The Jacobite Lodge in Rome, 1735–1737* (Torquay, 1910), p. 51.

140. RA. SP 196/92, James III to L. Innes, 15 May 1737.

141. RA. SP 197/19, Nairne to Edgar, 27 May 1737: 'He tells me he reckond to set out the 13 or 14 at furthest to joyn his Regiment in Naples.'

142. RA. SP 197/94, Nairne to Edgar, 3 June 1737.

143. RA. SP 199/15, Nairne to Edgar, 8 July 1737.

144. RA. SP 203/10, Edgar to Ramsay, 12 December 1737.

145. Corp, Edward, 'Lord Burlington's Clandestine Support for the Stuart Court at Saint-Germain-en-Laye', pp. 7–26, in Corp, Edward, ed., *Lord Burlington – the Man and His Politics: Questions of Loyalty* (Lampeter, 1998), at p. 20.

146. This comment is based on the locations from which Ramsay wrote his letters, particularly the ones to Francis Kennedy in the Kennedy Papers.

147. RA. SP 189/33, Edgar to Nairne, 15 August 1736: 'I am very glad My Lady Ramsay is so well after ye misfortune happened to her.'

148. Kennedy Papers, Ramsay to Kennedy, 25 September 1737.

149. RA. SP 202/42, Ramsay to Edgar, 18 November 1737.

150. RA. SP 202/2, L. Nairne to Edgar, 8 November 1737.

151. Kennedy Papers, Ramsay to Kennedy, 5 August 1738.

152. RA. SP 250/77, Edgar to G. Innes, 6 June 1743.

153. Kennedy Papers, Ramsay to Kennedy, 29 November 1738.
154. Kennedy Papers, Ramsay to Kennedy, 9 June 1739.
155. In a letter of 25 September 1737, he told a friend that he was short of money (Kennedy Papers, Ramsay to Kennedy).
156. RA. SP 169/3, James III to L. Innes, 17 March 1734; SCA. BL 3/13/5, Stuart to Carnegy, 9 September 1734; SCA. BL 3/13/6, 8 and 10, Stuart to G. Innes, 23 September, 10 October and 9 December 1734; SCA. BL 3/26/1, Stuart to G. Innes, 5 January 1736.
157. SCA. BL 3/29/4, Edgar to L. Innes, 19 June 1737: 'Don Guglielmo Stewart is dead! barbarously murtherd last Friday afternoon in his room by a young French man of Rochel [La Rochelle] about 18 years of age, who had been instructed by him, and abjured Hugonotisme the Friday before.' He was hit on the head with a candlestick which fractured his skull, and was then stabbed with his own pen knife two or three times and robbed of his money and possessions. There is a similar description in Valesio, Francesco, *Diario di Roma, VI, 1737–1742*, ed. Scana, Gaetano (Milano, 1979), p. 52, 14 June 1737; and another in the 'Pilgrim Book, 1733–1771' of the Venerable English College, Rome, Libri 292, p. 17. See also RA. SP 199/35, Edgar to L. Innes, 10 July 1737.
158. RA. SP 199/15, Nairne to Edgar, 8 July 1737.
159. In a letter of 20 January 1738 Nairne explained to Marsi that he intended to pay him the same overall annual fee which he had previously given to William Stuart:

> Votre lettre de change Monsieur du 2 de ce mois ... pour la pension de Madame de Ramsay et la mienne pour le courant mois m'a agreablement surprise car je ne l'attendois que dans huit jours au plutot. Je vous remercie de votre puntualité a me l'avoir envoyé si promptement. Vous devez avoir receu votre colombat tout des premiers car je vous l'envoyai le lundi 30 xbre mais vous m'offenséz de proposér de me payer une bagatelle comme celle là. Je vous prie de ne me plus parler de la sorte car c'est la moindre chose que vous me puissiez permettre de vous envoyer tous les ans une aussi petite etraine que celle la. (RA. SP 204/56)

160. SCA. BL 3/13/11, Stuart to G. Innes, 16 December 1734; SCA. BL 3/19/1, 7 and 11, Stuart to G. Innes, 5 January, 10 February and 9 March 1735; SCA. BL 3/20/1 and 5, Stuart to G. Innes, 5 May and 9 June 1735. For the payment of the pensions in Rome, see RA. SP 176/89 for August to December 1734, and RA. SP 184/161 for 1735.
161. RA. SP 204/119; 205/138 and 161; 206/109; 207/62 and 132; 208/103; 209/30 and 161; 210/124; 211/81; 212/71 and 118; 215/5; 219/109.

162. By 1730 the duc de Bouillon had debts of 6 million *livres*, as against 2.8 million *livres* of free assets. He sold the Vicomté de Turenne to King Louis XV in 1738 for 4.2 million *livres* (Velde, 'The Case of the Undying Debt', p. 6).

163. RA. SP 220/28, Lady Ramsay to James III, 25 January 1740. For Ramsay's expenses, see Bibliothèque de Sedan, Fonds Gourjault, Carton 174/120, 'quittances de M. de Ramsay, gouverneur de M. le prince de Turenne', 1730–41. (I owe this reference to Bernard Homery).

164. Kennedy Papers, Ramsay to Kennedy, 15 March 1740.

165. Ibid.

166. RA. SP 202/42, Ramsay to Edgar, 18 November 1737.

167. Prod'homme, J. G., *L'Opéra (1669–1925)*, (Paris, 1925), pp. 65–77.

168. Other Jacobites whom Nairne might have met during these years included Etienne du Mirail de Monnot (who died in June 1735), Nicholas Dempster's widow Philippa, John Paterson (Mar's under-secretary at Urbino) and John Paul Stafford (Prince Henry's under-governor in Rome).

169. For the death of Lewis Innes see RA. SP 206/9, T. Innes to James III, 7 April 1738, and for that of Charles Whiteford see Halloran, *The Scots College Paris*, p. 209. For the death of John Ingleton see RA. SP. 213/84, Dicconson to Edgar, 1 February 1739. For that of Christophe-Alexandre Pajot de Villers, see RA. SP 219/129, Edgar to Dufort, 7 January 1740. It should also be mentioned that there is a 'Copie du testament de Mr George Crouley, fait à Paris ce 21 février 1735' in the handwriting of David Nairne. It is in the archives of the Irish College in Rome: Arch. Coll. Hib., Lib. XXVI/no.101/f.142, and names executors for the establishment of a foundation to benefit any Irish students by the same name during their studies. George Crouley was probably a son of Sir Miles and Lady Crouly [*sic*] who were naturalized in France in 1695 (HMC *Stuart* I, pp. 94, 105). Anne, Lady Crouly was a sister of the Duchess of Perth, and on one occasion Nairne recorded that 'I writt ... a certificat on a Placet of Widow Crolie' (Diary, 28 June 1704). See also his Diary for 28 January 1706 where he mentions the murder of 'master Croly'.

170. SCA. BL 3/26/2, Stuart to G. Innes, 12 January 1736. See also RA. SP 210/52, Nairne to Marsi, 20 October 1738: 'Je vous prie Monsieur de retenir sur le premier argent que vous recevréz de la pension de Madame de Ramsay ou de la mienne, *trente polles* que vous payeréz s'il vous plait a Mr Wright Medecin du Roy a qui Me de Ramsay doit la dite somme.'

171. RA. SP 171/144, Nairne to Edgar, 23 August 1734; RA. SP 176/173, Nairne to Edgar, 10 January 1735.

172. RA. SP 178/82, Nairne to Edgar, 7 March 1735.

173. Corp, *The Stuarts in Italy*, p. 309. See also RA. SP 181/51, DN to Edgar, Paris, 18 July 1735: 'tell Mrs Fitzgerald that I receivd with pleasure her kind letter upon

my daughters settlement and I showd it to both the new marryd couple who
desire to be rememberd kindly both to her and her sister, and you'l assure Mr
Marsi also of my daughters compliments and mine.'

174. RA. SP 181/51, Nairne to Edgar, 15 April 1737.
175. For example, RA. SP 204/56, Nairne to Marsi, 20 January 1738.
176. RA. SP 205/138, Nairne to Marsi, 24 March 1738.
177. RA. SP 197/94, 198/64 and 199/15, Nairne to Edgar, 3 June, 29 June and 8 July
     1737; RA. SP 199/124 and 200/164, Edgar to Nairne, 24 July and 19 September
     1737.
178. See RA. SP 199/162, Edgar to L.Nairne, 2 August 1737; and RA. SP 200/154,
     Edgar to L.Nairne, 17 September 1737: 'This is the third letter I have writ to you
     and have been obliged to trouble my friends with forwarding them, because I
     don't know where you are, nor yr address. You'l do me a pleasure if in return to
     this you let me know how I may forward any letter that comes to my hands for
     you.'
179. RA. SP 201/138, Edgar to L. Nairne, 31 October 1737. See also RA. SP 250/77,
     Edgar to G. Innes, 6 June 1743:

> If Sir Lewis Nairn does not write of his own accord to his sister, there is no
> method I believe can be tried that will engage him to write to her, or upon his
> own affairs. I remember two or three years ago, I sent some letters to him from
> France. I writ to him alongst with them, and pressed him as much as possible
> to send me his answers. I know these letters were deliverd into his own hands,
> but he never writ to me in return. In my third letter I think to him, I urged him
> in strong terms to write, and told him unless he answerd that letter, I should
> never more write to him.

180. RA. SP 202/2, L. Nairne to Edgar, 8 November 1737.
181. RA. SP 202/23, Edgar to Nairne, 14 November 1737.
182. RA. SP 202/42, Ramsay to Edgar, 18 November 1737.
183. RA. SP 203/88, Edgar to L. Nairne, 27 December 1737; RA. SP 209/63, Edgar
     to Nairne, 15 September 1738: RA. SP 214/120, Ramsay to Edgar, 15 March 1739.
184. RA. SP 205/168, Edgar to Nairne, 3 April 1738.
185. RA. SP 209/155, Edgar to L.Nairne, 4 October 1738. But see RA. SP 209/168,
     Edgar to Nairne, 8 October 1738 for an exception: 'I recd last week a letter from
     yr son, wch I cannot but send you here inclosed, that you may know he is well,
     in case the letter he mentions to have sent you by Marseilles should not have
     reached you.'
186. RA. SP 211/64, Edgar to Nairne, 27 November 1738. See also RA. SP 209/155,
     Edgar to L. Nairne, 4 October 1738; and RA. SP 209/168, Edgar to Nairne, 8
     October 1738.

187. RA. SP 211/157, Nairne to Edgar, 15 December 1738.

188. Ibid.

189. SCA. BL 3/57/6, Ramsay to G. Innes, 23 July 1739.

190. RA. SP 220/53, Edgar to Ramsay, 28 January 1740. Edgar thanked Ramsay for his letter of 4 January, and added: 'I ... am very sorry for Sir David's decaying state of health.'

191. SCA. BL 3/64/3, G. Innes to Fife, 22 January 1740:

> By S. D's last will there is settled upon his sister during life 150*l* a year wch I shall pay her regularly at 75*l* for each semest, and ye same rate will be due to her daugh.r Sr David's niece a compleat year after her mothers death. T'is absolutely necessary she be told yt as her rent depends on an action I can only pay her according as the action rent goes; so yt if it should diminish by taxes or otherwise, t'is what I can't help.

192. Kennedy Papers, Lady Ramsay to Kennedy, 6 June 1743.

193. RA. SP 220/28, Lady Ramsay to James III, 25 January 1740; RA. SP 220/115, Edgar to Ramsay, 11 February 1740.

194. She wrote on 22 and 30 January, and both letters were forwarded from the Collège des Ecossais by George Innes (SCA. BL 3/64/3, to Fife, 22 January 1740; and SCA. BL 3/62/2, to Burnet, 30 January 1740).

195. RA. SP 220/28, Lady Ramsay to James III, 25 January 1740.

196. RA. SP 220/95, James III to Ramsay, 6 February 1740. See also RA. SP 220/115, Edgar to Ramsay, 11 February 1740: 'I have recd yours of ye 24th Jan.ry. I condole with you and my Lady Ramsay very sincerely on ye loss you have sustained by good Sir David Nairn's death; I shall forward carefully yr letter to yr Brother in Law.'

197. Kennedy Papers, Ramsay to Kennedy, 15 March 1740.

CHAPTER 10

A Jacobite Legacy

After Nairne's death, his legacy lived on during the eighteenth century and beyond. In the short term, of course, this was because he had three children and two grandchildren. In the longer term, however, it was because he had gathered a large collection of papers which his daughter Marie gave to the Collège des Ecossais and which were to assume a significance for historians many years after he himself had been forgotten. This final chapter will examine the last years of Nairne's ex-patriate family in Europe.

During the spring of 1740, the Ramsays left the Hôtel de Ponac and moved to the Hôtel de Bouillon on the adjacent Quai Malaquais.[1] There, in June 1740, their son Jacques fell ill and died of an 'abcess in the lungs'.[2] This was a bitter blow, coming as it did only five months after Sir David's death. Ramsay wrote in July that he now hoped to retire to live at Pontoise in two or three years' time,[3] and admitted in December that 'I am sometimes whole weeks without working three hours'.[4] Then, in March 1741, the Ramsays left Paris and went to live permanently at Pontoise earlier than expected. He explained that 'the great losses I have suffered by my father in laws death ... together with the excessive dearth of everything here' (caused by the War of the Austrian Succession) obliged them to move.[5] Sir Andrew and Lady Ramsay then lived at Pontoise with their little daughter Marie Catherine from the spring of 1741 until the autumn of 1742.

For much of the time Ramsay was very ill[6] and was no longer able to devote any time to the education of the prince de Turenne. The one positive development, as he wrote in April 1741, was that 'the *pavillon* which the duke of Bouillon has given us for life is now a building [i.e. being built]'.[7] During that summer the duke agreed to release Ramsay and pension him off.[8] The latter wrote to his friend Francis Kennedy in July:

> The Duke of Bouillon has settled on my head for life a pension of a thousand crowns, and in case of my death fifteen hundred livres on my wife's head. God grant it to be well payd. If he finish the *pavillon* promisd me at Pontoise this with my new pension

from the Comte d'Evreux of a thousand crowns will make about three hundred pounds revenue in all or the Equivalent.[9]

In the summer of 1742, Ramsay decided 'for my health's sake to take a trip this autumn and pass the winter with the oldest ... friend I have in France the Bishop of Boulogne sur mer en picardie'. The bishop (Augustin César d'Hervilly de Devise) had been a canon of Cambrai Cathedral when Fénelon had been the archbishop there and, as Ramsay explained, 'we were educated together in his house for many years'.[10] Having borrowed over 1,000 *livres* from Kennedy, who was in Scotland,[11] Ramsay left Marie and their daughter in Paris during October (probably at the convent with Françoise) and travelled up to the coast.[12] When he arrived at Boulogne, however, he discovered that his friend had just died and been buried.[13] He returned in November to be told that the duc de Bouillon's debts were now so great that he could no longer deliver what he had promised, and that all work on the *pavillon* at Pontoise had had to be cancelled. In failing health, and needing a substitute for the sea air of Boulogne, he decided to leave Pontoise and move to Saint-Germain-en-Laye, where Marie had been born and brought up, and where there was still a large Jacobite community. Ramsay wrote on 16 December:

> I have taken a house for six years very compact, proper, neat, and solitary. The air of the place is fine, subtle and very proper to hindering my blood from thickning of stagnation. The forest is spatious, the royal Gardens and Terrasses are beautifull and fine. I hope to enjoy here peace, Liberty and Independence from the Great.[14]

Less than five months later, on 6 May 1743, Ramsay died at Saint-Germain, leaving Marie a widow with her four-year-old daughter. He was buried in the parish church,[15] but Marie arranged for his heart to be removed and presented to the 'Convent of the Sisters of the Holy Sacrament rue Cassette as was his wish and to be placed beside my father's grave which lies there'.[16] Marie, a widow of forty-two years of age, then returned two weeks later to Saint-Germain 'where I intend to make my home'.[17]

Lady Ramsay lived at Saint-Germain for the next fourteen years, until 1757. In October 1743, when her daughter was four years old, she wrote that 'my little girl is very well, and is making marvelous progress'.[18] We then hear no more of little Marie Catherine until December 1748, by which time she was nearly ten years old, when Lady Ramsay recorded that the education of her daughter was difficult because she was young for her age and 'extremely bright, unruly, and mischievous'.[19] A letter of January 1749 is much more positive,[20] but thereafter we are given very little information about her.[21] In February 1751, by which time Marie Catherine was twelve years old, her mother wrote that 'my daughter … went to spend a fortnight with my only sister, a nun at the convent of the Perpetual Adoration in Paris, who loves the child dearly'.[22] And at the end of that year she wrote how very pleased she was with her daughter's progress.[23] Then, in January 1753, when she reached her fourteenth birthday, Marie Catherine was sent to complete her education as a boarder at the convent of English Benedictine nuns at Pontoise.[24]

Meanwhile Lady Ramsay's relations with her brother Louis remained during the 1740s and 1750s the same as they had been during the previous decade. After the death of her son Jacques in 1740 Edgar wrote to Ramsay from Rome:

> I am sorry your Brother in Law does not write to you, but I don't see any help for it, he is certainly very inexcusable for this neglect.[25]

Another letter from Edgar, this time in June 1743 after the death of Ramsay himself, echos the same sentiments:

> If Sir Lewis Nairne does not write of his own accord to his sister, there is no method I believe can be tried that will engage him to write to her, or upon his own affairs … I have no hopes that Sir Lewis can be prevailed upon to write by any means, or by any arguments [that] can be used.[26]

Five and a half years later, when he intended to visit Rome and needed assistance, Sir Louis eventually sent a letter to Edgar giving information about himself. This was passed on to Dr Robert Wright, Marie's former suitor, who copied it and sent it on to Saint-Germain.[27] Then, in the spring of 1752, Sir Louis decided to pay a second (and final) visit to France and actually stayed with his sister.[28] Thereafter he relapsed again into silence,[29] so that Lady Ramsay wrote to Edgar in December 1756 that 'mon frere … me laisse toujours dans l'ignorance de ses nouvelles et de son avancement'.[30]

During these years, Lady Ramsay considered making a visit to see her relations in Scotland, whom she had never met. She wrote to Kennedy in

February 1742 that she would like 'to take one day a trip to London and Scotland, the native soil of my ancestors',[31] and again in August 1749 that she would like to visit Scotland with her daughter.[32] In fact she never went, in part no doubt because she lacked the necessary money, and passed the rest of her life in France.

Although Lady Ramsay never met her Scottish relations,[33] she did visit her uncle and cousins at Compigny, where she owned one sixth of the family estate. In December 1748, for example, she wrote that she had recently returned to Saint-Germain from Compigny, where she had stayed for longer than she intended, having slipped and fallen on a parquet floor.[34] In another letter, this time of December 1751, she told Kennedy that 'I spent a part of the summer in the country, where business matters kept me until the Autumn'.[35] The best description of these visits was provided in the 1920s by Antoine de Compigny, who was descended from one of her cousins:

> Marie de Nairne [*sic*] came many times to stay at Compigny ... where her uncle, Jean-Louis, was the joint owner, as she was. Even in the last years of her life she loved to be in the peaceful Champagne countryside, where in the early morning the houses built of white stone look like wrinkled ancestors. Her cousins: Jean-Louis de Compigny [born in 1729], who became a soldier but died young; Marie-Catherine [born in 1730] who would go to school at Saint-Cyr [in 1739]; Claude-François [born in 1731] ... Anne-Thérèse [born in 1734], struck down by death before she was ten; Claude-Barthélemy [born in 1742], and the beautiful Marie-Anne [born in 1741], ... all gave to Marie de Nairne, when she came to Compigny, the impression that she was a member of a fine family that loved her.[36]

Lady Ramsay's own daughter Marie Catherine had been born in 1739, so was approximately the same age as the younger of her many cousins, and we may suppose that she visited Compigny with her mother.

Lady Ramsay had known most of the Jacobites at Saint-Germain since she was a child, though none of the available documents tells us with whom she was particularly friendly. We may assume that her father's links with the Drummond and Middleton families, both of them Scottish, would have made her a welcome addition to their circle, notably with Lord Edward Drummond (son of the 1st Duke of Perth) and his wife Elizabeth (daughter of the 2nd Earl of Middleton). When the latter's brother John (the 3rd Earl, previously Lord Clermont) died in 1746 his apartment in the château-vieux was given to Lady Derwentwater, whom Lady Ramsay had known for several years in Rome.[37] She was probably included in the small party of Jacobites who were entertained with Lady Derwentwater at Louveciennes by Prince Charles in the summer of 1747.[38]

By the early 1750s, when she was in her fifties, there is evidence that Lady Ramsay's health was not good. She wrote in February 1754 that she had a serious problem with the white of her left eye,[39] and added in December of that year that she had developed gout in her knees and hands.[40] But what particularly worried her during these years was a shortage of money, and in particular the fear that if she were to die her daughter would be left without any income.

Lady Ramsay had three regular pensions, of which the largest was the one she received from James III. Its theoretical value was 50 *livres per mensem* or 600 *livres per annum*, sent as letters of credit from Rome by Pietro Marsi, though the exchange rate affected the precise sum that she received.[41] She had inherited the pension of 400 *livres per annum*, which her father had received for over fifty years from the French crown.[42] Her third pension brought her 300 *livres per annum*, and was her share of the one which the duchesse de Gramont had obtained for her and her sister in 1723.[43]

As we have seen, the duc de Bouillon had promised in July 1741 that in the event of Ramsay's death his widow would be given a pension of 1500 *livres per annum*.[44] In fact, the pension was never paid, because of Bouillon's considerable debts. In November 1747, however, the comte d'Evreux persuaded his nephew to give Lady Ramsay an annual pension of 500 *livres* for the education of her daughter Marie Catherine.[45] With this new fourth pension, therefore, her income was increased from 1,300 *livres* to 1,800 *livres per annum*, and she used the first 500 *livres* to repay about half the money that her husband had borrowed from Francis Kennedy.[46]

Unfortunately for Lady Ramsay, the duc de Bouillon then had second thoughts and suddenly stopped paying the pension after only a year and a half, in July 1749.[47] She obviously had to retrench her planned expenses, but, with Marie Catherine now a boarder at Pontoise, she asked the princesse de Turenne, the wife of her late husband's former pupil, to intervene with her father-in-law to have the payment of the pension resumed. The princesse eventually agreed, but only on condition that the request would be supported by James III. Lady Ramsay therefore wrote to Edgar in March 1756, explaining the situation and asking for the king's support, adding that she was not only 'the widow of a loyal supporter whom he honoured with his kindness', but also 'I am the daughter of a longtime servant who had the honour to grow old in your service, and who was treated with trust and kindness by Your Majesty'. She enclosed a copy of the *placet* she intended to present to the duc de Bouillon, in which she described herself as 'the daughter of Sir David Nairne, Secretary of the Closet of the Monarch who is the brother-in-law of H. H., and who lost by his faith and by his loyalty to his King, both his property and his homeland'.[48]

The relations between James III and the duc de Bouillon had been strained for several years,[49] so Edgar sent Lady Ramsay a negative reply in April, stating that the king 'is sorry on your account he cannot recommend you as you desire to the Duke of Bouillon, for if he could have done it, he would have been glad of that occasion to give you a mark of the regard and consideration he has for you'.[50] Lady Ramsay therefore asked James III instead to approach Cardinal de Tavannes, the *Grand Aumonier de France*, and ask him to agree to extend the pension of 300 *livres per annum* to her daughter *en survivance*: 'the supplicant ... would wish that after her death the same Favour might be continued to her daughter, and to have the assurance now that this will be the case.'[51] It is unlikely that the king agreed to do this, but his reply has apparently not survived.

It was the failure of these two requests, and particularly the attempt to recover her Bouillon pension, which persuaded Lady Ramsay that she would have to take her daughter out of the convent at Pontoise and move from Saint-Germain-en-Laye to live in a cheaper place. In 1757, she settled on Sens, partly because it was only twelve miles from Compigny, and partly because there was a small Jacobite community already living there.[52] But the move was to have a tragic consequence. She wrote in June 1759:

> For financial reasons of which my beloved child was the main object I decided ... to leave St Germain to come and live here in the town of Sens. But alas, a short time after, a terrible outbreak of smallpox took my darling child from me. It was the 26th of September last yeat [1758] that I suffered this loss ... I am now but an isolated being on this Earth, I have lost all that was dear to me, and my days now are days of tears.[53]

Marie Christine was only eighteen years old when she died.

Lady Ramsay considered returning to live at Saint-Germain, but in fact she remained at Sens, where the cheaper cost of living enabled her to pay off her remaining debt to Francis Kennedy.[54] In addition, the British victories against the French in the Seven Years' War had made life uncomfortable for the remaining Jacobites at Saint-Germain,[55] so she felt safer in relative provincial obscurity at Sens. She commented in December 1759 that 'I only go from time to time to Paris to spend time with my sister who is a nun, and my sole consolation in this world since I lost my Angel'.[56]

At the beginning of 1761, Lady Ramsay celebrated her sixtieth birthday. She now suffered from problems with both her eyes and she had regular attacks of gout,[57] but was able to visit her uncle and cousins at Compigny where, she reminded Kennedy, 'I have relatives on my mother's side, an uncle who has children'.[58] She was conscious, however, that her own family – the family of Sir David Nairne – had no future. She wrote in February 1761:

> all will be ended, so to speak, after my death. Having but one brother and one sister, the former only one year older than me and unmarried, an officer in the troops of the King of Naples, and my sister who is a Nun in Paris and several years older than me.'[59]

Lady Ramsay never again saw her brother, who continued to disappoint her by failing to send her any news.[60] In December 1767, Andrew Lumisden wrote from the Stuart court in Rome to tell her that Sir Louis Nairne had recently died at Bari – probably in November of that year.[61] The date of the death of her sister Françoise is at present unknown, but it was probably during the late 1760s, or possibly the early 1770s. She would have been eighty years old in 1774.

Lady Ramsay now had to consider what she should do with the possessions she had inherited from her father, of which the most important were the relic of the true cross, various Stuart and family portraits, and a collection of family papers including her father's diary. In 1771 she decided to present the relic to the parish church of Compigny, and at about the same time she determined to bequeath everything else to a young Scottish gentleman whom she had met at Sancerre.

The relic of the true cross had been given to David Nairne by the General of the Jesuits on 28 August 1691.[62] Lady Ramsay had it authenticated at Sens before presenting it to the church, presumably by showing people the entry in her father's diary which referred to it. The relic itself was preserved in a reliquary, which was in turn preserved in a box measuring 16.5 × 15.5 centimetres, on which she had the following inscription engraved on copper:

> In this box lies a glass Cross which holds a Relic in chased silver containing a Piece of the True Cross of our Saviour brought here from Rome. The relic, verified and certified by M. l'abbé d'Hesselin, Vicar-General and Dean of Sens, is enclosed in the base of the Cross sealed with the stamp of His Excellency M. le Cardinal de Luynes. This relic was given to the Church of Compigny by Lady Ramsay daughter of Baron de Nairne [sic], and of Elisabeth de Compigny in 1771.[63]

The relic escaped the destructions caused by the French Revolution and was still in the church in the early 1920s when it was photographed by Antoine de Compigny. The photograph, which he published in 1924, shows the reliquary being held by a certain Madame Rondeau, who can be seen standing beside her young son Roger, who holds the box with the copper inscription.[64] Roger Rondeau, who subsequently became the *maire* of Compigny, noted in 1981:

> The reliquary in the Church of Compigny given by Lady Ramsay in 1771 was taken from Compigny and deposited with the Dean of Sergines who was then to deposit it at Sens. We have never found any trace of this reliquary at Sens.[65]

Its present whereabouts, if it has survived, are still unknown.

During the 1760s, while she was living at Sens, Lady Ramsay had become acquainted with the family of Lord Nairne, who was living in another small Jacobite community further south at Sancerre. Lord Nairne was in no way related to Sir David Nairne, despite sharing the same family surname, but Lady Ramsay convinced herself that they *were* related, and thus she created a new family for herself to replace the ones she had lost in France and had never seen in Scotland. It was a member of this new family to whom she decided to bequeath her portraits and her father's diary.

The second Baron Nairne was a Jacobite and had narrowly avoided having to go into exile with James III in 1716. He had been created Jacobite Earl Nairne in 1721 and had died in Scotland in 1726. His eldest son John had then succeeded as third Baron Nairne and second Jacobite Earl Nairne. The latter had been actively involved in the Jacobite rising of 1745–6, after which he had escaped to France and been attainted for high treason. He settled at Sancerre with two of his sons (Henry and Thomas), and several other Scots,[66] and at some point in the late 1760s Lady Ramsay left Sens and went to join them there. She was with them in 1770 when Lord Nairne died and the titles passed to his eldest surviving son, also called John, who thus became the attainted 4th Baron and the Jacobite 3rd Earl Nairne.[67]

The new Lord Nairne visited Sancerre, but had not been involved in the Jacobite rising so was still able to live in Scotland, where he could not however assume the family titles. It was he, as head of his family, whom Lady Ramsay designated as her heir. She was particularly friendly with his younger brother Henry, and when the latter left Sancerre[68] she decided to return to Sens. It was there that she drew up her testament on 8 November 1775. Apart from various small legacies to her servants, and a portrait of Archbishop Fenelon which she bequeathed to Cardinal de Luynes (the Archbishop of Sens), she left everything to John Nairne. The four items which she regarded as the most valuable are the only ones which were actually specified in the will:

> To Mr John Nairne, Scottish gentleman ... her Relation ... The Portrait of King James III of England [Figure 9], that of Princess Sobieska [*sic*] who died in the odour of sanctity [Figure 15], that of Mr Nairne her Father [Figure 6], and that of M. De Ramsay her Husband, the last in pastel, with their frames, all estimated by the testator to be worth a hundred and fifty livres.[69]

Although we cannot know all the other things she bequeathed to John Nairne, we can nevertheless identify two of them: the portrait of her mother Marie-Elisabeth, [Figure 3] David Nairne's wife; and her father's diary covering the years from his birth in 1655 up to his return from the Franco-Jacobite attempted invasion of Scotland in 1708.

After the death of Lady Ramsay in July 1776,[70] the portraits of David Nairne and Marie-Elisabeth Nairne, respectively by Alexis-Simon Belle and François de Troy,[71] were sent to Scotland, where they can still be seen today. They passed by descent from John Nairne to his son and then his grandson, and then to a cousin whose daughter married the 4th Marquess of Lansdowne. By that time, in 1867, the real identities of the sitters had been forgotten, and the paintings were described as portraits of the 2nd Earl Nairne and of the mother-in-law of one of the 2nd Earl's brothers – neither of whom was ever in France at the right time to be painted by Belle or Troy. The two portraits are now at Meikleour House, and were eventually given their correct identifications by the present author in the 1990s.[72]

The portrait of James III was the bust copy of his 1717 portrait given to David Nairne by Antonio David in March 1718. It measured 44 × 33 cm. The one of Queen Clementina was a copy of David's portrait of 1727 showing her in the convent of Santa Cecilia with a breviary beside her crown. It measured 43 × 32 cm.[73] Both of these portraits were also eventually inherited by the 4th Marquess of Lansdowne, but at some point thereafter they were sold to Caroline Henrietta (née Stuart of Blantyre), the wife of the 7th Earl of Seafield. They were subsequently sold in 2011 and are at present in private collections.[74] The pastel portrait of Ramsay, on the other hand, has definitely not survived. It was by Rosalba Carriera and was described by Lady Ramsay in one of her letters as 'un médiocre [medium-sized] pastel bien resemblant.'[75]

The fate of David Nairne's diary was different, because it was given away by John Nairne to Andrew Lumisden in 1777, only one year after Lady Ramsay's death.[76] At that time, Lumisden was living in Paris, having previously served as James III's last private secretary.[77] It was there that he met John Nairne, who had presumably come to France to see the members of his family at Sancerre and supervise the transfer to Scotland of his inheritance. John Nairne might have realized from the contents of the diary that his family was in no way related to that of Sir David Nairne. Or perhaps he believed that Lumisden was a more suitable person to keep the diary of a man who had also served for many years as one of James III's secretaries. Whatever the reason, the diary came into the possession of Lumisden, who then took it with him when he was given a free pardon to return to Scotland.

Thereafter the diary was inherited after Lumisden's death by his sister Isabella who was married to Sir Robert Strange. Isabella left it to her daughter, who in turn left it to a niece. The latter's daughter-in-law, by then a widow, deposited it on loan in the National Library of Scotland in 1948, and thereby ensured its survival. It is still in the National Library, which received it as a gift from the next generation of the family in 1969.[78]

Until the 1990s, the existence of the diary remained unknown to most historians of the period.[79] It was then realized that it provided not only an account of the life of David Nairne himself, but also the only surviving account giving details of the life of the exiled Stuart court at Saint-Germain-en-Laye, thus enabling historians to understand both the workings of the court itself, and also the many personal factors behind the politics of the court.[80] Moreover, the diary contained significant new information about the last years of King James II and revealed, what no one appears to have suspected, that David Nairne had been entrusted with assembling the king's papers and writing his first biography.[81]

At the end of this volume in the National Library of Scotland, David Nairne wrote that 'the following years of my life [are] in another Tome of my Journal'. That second volume has unfortunately disappeared without trace. It cannot have been inherited by John Nairne and given to Andrew Lumisden, because the latter only refers to receiving the first volume.[82] It must, therefore, have been destroyed or deposited elsewhere, and we can only speculate what might have happened to it. It is very unlikely that it would have been destroyed either by David Nairne himself or by his daughter. The most likely explanation of its disappearance is that it was deposited in the Collège des Ecossais in Paris and destroyed during the French Revolution.

The vulnerability of such documents can be shown if we turn our attention to Lady Ramsay's share of the Compigny estate. This was inherited by her surviving nephews Claude-François and Claude-Barthélemy, and we may assume that they would also have kept some of her family papers, particularly those relating to the estate. When Antoine de Compigny was researching his family background during the early 1920s, he discovered that there was a collection of such papers in London:

> Mme Marry [sic] Elliott, of London, descendant of the Compigny family, had many family papers. I asked her to do some research, and received from her the draft of a letter written by Marie de Nairne, dated 1771, but unfortunately incomplete.

These family papers might also have contained letters from Sir David Nairne to his Compigny relations, written from Saint-Germain, Lorraine, Avignon or Italy, but they also seem to have been lost without trace. Compigny explained: 'Mme Elliott died ... without having been able to give me a photograph of the fragment.'[83] Under these circumstances it was particularly fortunate that Lady Ramsay had deposited her father's papers in the Collège des Ecossais, because many of them were then taken back to Engtland and have been safely preserved until the present day.

Endnotes

1. West Sussex County Record Office, Goodwood MSS 112, f.316. (I am grateful to Bernard Homery for this reference). Ramsay wrote on 6 December 1740 that 'I hide my self and my little family in this left of the nook' (Kennedy Papers, to Kennedy).

2. Kennedy Papers, Ramsay to Kennedy, 15 July 1740. See also RA. SP 225/130, Edgar to Ramsay, 11 August 1740.

3. Kennedy Papers, Ramsay to Kennedy, 15 July 1740.

4. Kennedy Papers, Ramsay to Kennedy, 6 December 1740.

5. Kennedy Papers, Ramsay to Kennedy, 13 March 1741. See also his letter to Kennedy of 25 December 1741 in which he explained that high taxation and the high prices in Paris caused by the scarcity of food obliged him to live a very retired life in the country (Kennedy Papers).

6. Kennedy Papers, Ramsay to Kennedy, 6 December 1740; Lady Ramsay to Kennedy, 23 February 1742; and Ramsay to Kennedy, 18 August 1742.

7. Kennedy Papers, Ramsay to Kennedy, 24 April 1741. For the *pavillon*, see p. 466, note 111.

8. Henderson, *Chevalier Ramsay*, p. 192.

9. Kennedy Papers, Ramsay to Kennedy, 18 July 1741.

10. Kennedy Papers, Ramsay to Kennedy, 18 August 1742.

11. Kennedy Papers, Lady Ramsay to Kennedy, 22 October 1747. On 2 May 1749, Lady Ramsay informed Kennedy that she was still a long way from being able to repay the debt. She sent him an unspecified amount on 14 August 1752, and wrote on 13 June 1759 that she had twice sent him 300 *livres*. She repaid the remaining amount on 6 December 1759 (Kennedy Papers).

12. Kennedy Papers, Ramsay to Kennedy, 10 October 1742.

13. Kennedy Papers, Ramsay to Kennedy, 22 October 1742.

14. Kennedy Papers, Ramsay to Kennedy, 16 December 1742.

15. Ramsay's burial the following day, 7 May, was recorded in the parish register of Saint-Germain, and the relevant page is reproduced in Corp, Edward and Sanson, Jacqueline, *La Cour des Stuarts à Saint-Germain-en-Laye au temps de Louis XIV*, (Paris, 1992), p. 216.

16. Kennedy Papers, Lady Ramsay to Kennedy, 6 June 1743.

17. Kennedy Papers, Lady Ramsay to Kennedy, 15 June 1743.

18. Kennedy Papers, Lady Ramsay to Kennedy, 2 October 1743. See also same reference, Lady Ramsay to Kennedy, 4 December 1743.

19. Kennedy Papers, Lady Ramsay to Kennedy, 12 December 1748.

20. RA. SP 296/142, Edgar to Lady Ramsay, 30 January 1749.

21. In the summers of both 1749 and 1750, she was very ill (Kennedy Papers, Lady Ramsay to Kennedy, 15 June 1749 and 1 July 1750).

22. Kennedy Papers, Lady Ramsay to Kennedy, 18 February 1751.

23. Kennedy Papers, Lady Ramsay to Kennedy, 21 December 1751.

24. Compigny, *Les Entretiens de Cambrai* p. 62.

25. RA. SP 225/130, Edgar to Ramsay, 11 August 1740. Sir Louis Nairne did apparently send a letter to his sister in April 1741 (RA. SP 232/3, Edgar to Ramsay, 13 April 1741), but in 1742 his continued silence caused the Ramsays to wonder if he was dead (RA. SP 240/107, Edgar to Ramsay, 8 March 1742).

26. RA. SP 250/77, Edgar to G.Innes, 6 June 1743.

27. RA. SP 296/142, Edgar to Lady Ramsay, 28 January 1749. Dr Wright had remained on friendly terms with Marie. In 1737, for example, Ramsay wrote to Edgar: '[give] my compliments to good Dr Wright, [and] tell him that my wife recovers pretty well. As she has writ to him lately I shall not trouble him with a letter' (RA. SP 202/42, Ramsay to Edgar, 18 November 1737).

28. RA. SP 331/37, Lady Ramsay to Edgar, 23 April 1752. In this letter she explains that her brother had been negligent about writing to Edgar, but that he intended to do so that day. She adds that he would soon rejoin his 'corps'. In the same letter Lady Ramsay informed Edgar that Dr Wright, 'mon ancien ami', was visiting France, though he would not be coming to Paris. Wright had intended to visit his nephew in the south of France, but instead went by ship from Genoa to Cadiz when he discovered that his nephew was now in Lisbon (RA. SP 330/137, Wright to Edgar, 5 April 1752). Given the dangers that such a journey involved, Wright had drawn up his will before setting out from Rome in March. His will, dated 9 March 1752, is in RA. SP Box 1/343.

29. See, e.g., RA. SP 353/57, Lady Ramsay to Edgar, 5 January 1755.

30. RA. SP 367/56, Lady Ramsay to Edgar, 19 December 1756. But see RA. SP Box 2/459, Lady Ramsay to Edgar, undated, in which she thanked him for having

procured 'des nouvelles de mon frere, et a lui faire vaincre sa paresse, vous avez mieux reussi que je n'aurois esperé, puisque voila deux lettres que vous m'en procuré en assez peu de tems, il me fait esperer par sa derniere qu'il me donnera plus souvent de ses nouvelles que par le passè.' It is impossible to determine when this letter might have been written.

31. Kennedy Papers, Lady Ramsay to Kennedy, 23 February 1742.

32. Kennedy Papers, Lady Ramsay to Kennedy, 13 August 1749.

33. She had of course met Mrs Mary Fitzgerald and her sister Isabella Gordon (later Mrs Marsi) while she was in Rome. As a child she had also met the children of Mary Nairne, another cousin who had lived at Saint-Germain and married an Irishman named Cornelius Collins. (Mary died before her husband, who died at Saint-Germain on 31 December 1706: Nairne's diary, and the Saint-Germain parish registers). See pp. 122–3.

34. Kennedy Papers, Lady Ramsay to Kennedy, 12 December 1748. See also her letter to him of 30 January 1749, in which she wrote that she was gradually recovering from her fall (same reference).

35. Kennedy Papers, Lady Ramsay to Kennedy, 21 December 1751.

36. Compigny, *Les Entretiens de Cambrai*, pp. 60–1. This list of cousins omits Catherine-Victoire (born in 1732) and a previous Marie-Anne (1736–1739). Compigny explained that Sir David Nairne's wife was 'une de mes arrière-grand'tantes' (ibid. p. 17) and 'la nièce d'Antoine de Compigny, mon ancêtre direct à la neuvième génération' (ibid. p. 60).

37. Corp, *A Court in Exile*, p. 344; and *The Stuarts in Italy*, p. 244.

38. Corp, *A Court in Exile*, p. 344, note 37. Prince Charles visited the château of the Princesse de Conti at Louveciennes in June 1747 and invited Lady Derwentwater and her family to visit the Machine de Marly with him. During the previous year Marie had represented the Dowager Countess of Peterborough at the baptism of the daughter of a Jacobite named George Leslie (Saint-Germain parish registers, 16 November 1746). Lady Peterborough was the celebrated opera singer Anastasia Robinson, who sang in most of Handel's operas in London until her retirement in 1724.

39. Kennedy Papers, Lady Ramsay to Kennedy, 6 February 1754.

40. Kennedy Papers, Lady Ramsay to Kennedy, 24 December 1754.

41. See above, Chapter 9, p. 334. The three months of July to September 1746, for example, yielded 153*l* 15*s* (RA. SP 277/104, Lady Ramsay to Edgar, 8 October 1746). For entries in the Stuart accounts, see RA. SP 236/59, 247/53, 254/137, 259/133; 280/3, 309/156, 315/3, 331/58, 370/35, and Box 3/69.

42. Compigny, *Les Entretiens de Cambrai*, p. 62: 'Fleury continuait à Marie de Nairne [*sic*] la pension de 400 livres dont jouissait son père'.

43. See above, p. 394.
44. See above, pp. 473–4.
45. RA. SP 362/16, Lady Ramsay to Edgar, 28 March 1756.
46. Kennedy Papers, Lady Ramsay to Kennedy, 22 October 1747. See above, note 11.
47. Kennedy Papers, Lady Ramsay to Kennedy, 21 December 1751 and 14 August 1752.
48. RA. SP 362/16, Lady Ramsay to Edgar, 28 March 1756.
49. F. McLynn, *Prince Charles Edward Stuart* (London, 1988), pp. 105, 488.
50. RA. SP 362/67, Edgar to Lady Ramsay, 20 April 1756.
51. RA. SP Box 2/461, Lady Ramsay to James III, undated (1756).
52. The Jacobite community at Sens included Sir William Hay, whom she had known at the Stuart court in Rome (Corp, Edward, 'The Scottish Community at Saint-Germain-en-Laye after the Departure of the Stuart Court', in Macinnes, A. I., German, K., and Graham, L., *Living with Jacobitism, 1690–1788: The Three Kingdoms and Beyond* (London, 2014), pp. 27–38 (37)). See also Kennedy Papers, Lady Ramsay to Kennedy, 6 December 1759. The Jacobites were protected by the Archbishop of Sens, Paul d'Albert de Luynes, who had been nominated a cardinal by James III in 1754 (Corp, Edward, 'Maintaining Honour during a Period of Extended Exile: The Nomination of Cardinals by James III in Rome', *Zwischen Schande und Ehre. Errinerungsbrüche und die Kontinuität des Hauses*, eds. Wrede, Martin, und Carl, Horst, (Verlag Philipp von Zabern, Mainz am Rhein, 2007), pp. 157–69 (166)).
53. Kennedy Papers, Lady Ramsay to Kennedy, 13 June 1759.
54. Kennedy Papers, Lady Ramsay to Kennedy, 6 December 1759. In fact Kennedy returned the money to her (Kennedy Papers, Lady Ramsay to Kennedy, 22 April 1760).
55. See, e.g., RA. SP 369/20, Mary Plowden to James III, 27 February 1757: 'our present situation in France is terrible, as your Majesty may immagine. God send us peace.'
56. Kennedy Papers, Lady Ramsay to Kennedy, 6 December 1759.
57. Kennedy Papers, Lady Ramsay to Kennedy, 13 June and 6 December 1759.
58. Her uncle, Jean-Louis de Compigny, did not die until 1769.
59. Kennedy Papers, Lady Ramsay to Kennedy, 12 February 1761.
60. NLS. MS 14261, pp. 13, 30, Lumisden to Lady Ramsay, 27 January and 24 February 1767; and p. 31, Lumisden to Erskine, 28 February 1767.
61. NLS. MS 14261, p. 117, Lumisden to Lady Ramsay, 8 December 1767.
62. See above, p. 46.
63. Compigny, *Au déclin de l'Ancien Régime*, p. 27. The words engraved on the box are also reproduced, with slight differences of spelling, in the section on Compigny

in *Inscriptions de l'Ancien Diocèse de Sens*, vol. 2, p. 169: 'Sacristie. Inscription sur cuivre gravée sur un reliquaire. Ce reliquaire consiste en une croix en filigrane d'argent, et l'inscription est gravée sur une plaque de cuivre appliquée sur la boëte qui renferme ce reliquaire.' See also Compigny, *Les Entretiens de Cambrai*, p. 46.

64. Compigny, *Au déclin de l'Ancien Régime*, opposite p. 48.

65. Manuscript notes by Roger Rondeau, 30 March 1981, sent to the author by the *mairie* of Compigny, 28 January 1993. Roger Rondeau was the *maire* of Compigny from 1953 to 1983.

66. For the Jacobites at Sancerre, see Corp. 'The Scottish Community at Saint-Germain-en-Laye after the Departure of the Stuart Court', p. 218, note 97).

67. NLS. MS 14262, pp. 101, 100, Lumisden to J. Nairne, 8 August and 20 September 1770.

68. Henry Nairne died in Scotland in 1816 ('Pedigree of the Most Honourable Emily Jane Mercer-Elphinstone de Flahault, Marchioness Dowager of Lansdowne, in relation to her Claim to the Title, Honour and Dignity of Baroness Nairne in the Peerage of Scotland', undated but after 1870, a copy of which was kindly given to the author by the late Peter Drummond Murray, Slains Pursuivant).

69. Archives Départementales de l'Yonne 40.B.43, Baillage de Sens vol. 328, f.17, Testament de Lady Ramsay, 8 November 1775.

70. See note 69. The testament of Lady Ramsay was registered on 10 July 1776. Her *acte de décès* is conserved with another copy of her testament in Archives Départementales de l'Yonne, Baillage d'Auxerre, 3.E.70140 (I am grateful to Bernard Homery for this reference).

71. They were painted in 1714 and 1701. See above, p. 218 and p. 121.

72. The two portraits are at Meikleour House. For the re-identification of the portrait of David Nairne, see Corp, *La Cour des Stuarts à Saint-Germain-en-Laye au temps de Louis XIV*, p. 166. For an explanation of the re-identification, see 'James FitzJames, 1st Duke of Berwick: a New Identification for a Portrait by Hyacinthe Rigaud, *Apollo*, London, vol. CXLI, n°.400, June 1995, pp. 53–60 (59, note 24).

73. See above, pp. 300–1, for the portrait of James III. For the portrait of Queen Clementina, see Corp, *The King over the Water*, pp. 63, 67; and *The Stuarts in Italy*, pp. 117–18.

74. The portraits were bequeathed by the Countess of Seafield to her nephew Major William Baird of Lennoxlove, whose family sold them at Sotheby's, London on 14 April 2011, lots 200 and 201. Both copies are considerably smaller than the original versions painted by Antonio David. At the time of writing (2016) the portrait of James III is owned by the Weiss Gallery in London.

75. Kennedy Papers, Lady Ramsay to Kennedy, 6 December 1759. This was one of three portraits of Sir Andrew Ramsay, none of which has survived. The others were a miniature made for a bracelet and an oil on canvas by an unidentified young Scottish painter showing Ramsay with a 'bonnet sur l'oreil'. The latter was copied by another unidentified artist who showed Ramsay with a wig (as in the pastel) rather than with the 'bonnet' (Kennedy Papers, Lady Ramsay to Kennedy, 6 December 1759, 22 April 1760, and 12 February 1761).

76. A note by Lumisden at the beginning of NLS. MS 14266: 'This original journal of Sir David Nairne, under secretary of state to King Jamers the vii and his son, from the year 1655 till the month of May 1708, was given by his daughter Lady Ramsay, to Captain John Nairne, who gave it to me, May the 21 1777.'

77. NLS. MS 14263, letters to Andrew Lumisden, 1753–92; Corp, *The Stuarts in Italy*, pp. 304, 341–5, 349–52.

78. The diary belonged to Isabella, Lady Strange, then to her daughter Isabella Katherina Strange and to the latter's niece, Isabella Trotter (née Strange), who left it to her son Alexander Trotter, who loaned it to the National Library of Scotland in 1948. The latter's daughter, Mrs Gundred Beck, gave it to the library in 1969 (Ian Cunningham, Keeper of Manuscripts at the National Library of Scotland, to the author, 27 November 1992).

79. It was used in particular by Paul Hopkins and Daniel Szechi.

80. Corp, *La Cour des Stuarts à Saint-Germain-en-Laye au temps de Louis XIV*; and *A Court in Exile*.

81. Edward Corp, 'James II and David Nairne', pp. 1383–411.

82. NLS. MS 14265, catalogue of Andrew Lumisden's library, written in his own hand, c.1800, at f.109: 'Nairne, Sir David ... His original journal ... 1755–1708. MS fol.'

83. Compigny, *Les Entretiens de Cambrai*, pp. 45–6. She was only fifty-five years old and died of breast cancer at Westminster Hospital in January 1925. Despite Compigny's description of her as 'Mme Elliott', she was actually a spinster who had lived near Guildford in Surrey. (This information about Miss Mary Elliot is taken from a certified copy of her entry in the Register of Deaths in the District of St George, Hanover Square, given at the General Register Office, 12 July 1994). Efforts to trace the descendants of her brother, who then lived nearby at Cranleigh, have so far proved unsuccessful.

The Nairne Papers

If it were not for Sir David Nairne, we would know virtually nothing about either the politics or the social life of the Stuart court at Saint-Germain. If it were not for Nairne – the only senior member of the court to serve the exiled kings from 1689 until the late 1720s, in France, Lorraine and Italy – we would know very much less about the evolution of the court following the Jacobite rising of 1715–16. It is thanks to the chance survival of so many of his own papers, as well as much of his official and private correspondence, that the history of the exiled court has now been written.

In 1775, one year before Lady Ramsay's death at Sens, a book was published in London entitled *Original Papers containing the Secret History of Great Britain*. The book was edited in two volumes by James Macpherson and carried the following Advertisement:

> These volumes contain the papers of the family of Stuart and those of the house of Brunswick Lunenburgh. The first consist of the collection of Mr Nairne, who was under-secretary, from the Revolution to the end of 1713, to the ministers of King James the Second, and to those of his son ... Mr Nairne's papers came into the possession of Mr Carte, some time before his death ... The ORIGINALS are now in the hands of the bookseller.

The papers of Sir David Nairne were originally deposited in the Collège des Ecossais, to join the many papers already left there by both James II and James III. It is not known exactly when this was done, but they covered the years from 1689 to 1720. It is possible that the earlier papers were deposited in the college when Nairne left Saint-Germain in 1712, or when he went to Scotland in 1716. It is also possible that Nairne kept all the earlier papers with him and brought the entire collection back from Rome when he eventually returned to live in Paris. We do not know. The first reference

to the papers is to be found in a letter of 16 November 1741 from James
Edgar to Thomas Innes:

> As to the 12 or 13 vol. little and big of Entrys etc found in Sir David Nairn's custody
> after his death, HM knew nothing that Sir David had carryd away such books from
> hence with him, and He takes yr and Mr George [Innes]'s recovering of ym and plac-
> ing ym with his papers in yr College as a great mark of yr attention towards him, of
> wch he is very sensible. HM thinks it needless you should be at the pains to send
> him a particular Inventory of all these volumes containes, but at yr leisure will be
> glad to know *en gros* of what nature these entries, commissions, letters etc are of.[1]

In fact, there were more than '12 or 13' volumes, perhaps because the
others were already in the college, and an inventory was indeed subsequently made and sent to Rome. As the papers were virtually all of an
official nature, and thus formed an integral part of the political archives of
the exiled court, the king sent instructions that they should be kept with
his own papers in the Collège des Ecossais:

> I have recd yours of the 11th xber, and have had the honor to lay it, and the inventory
> of Sir David Nairn's Entry books etc inclosed in it, before the King, upon which HM.
> directs me to tell you as by what appears to him, he wants no further information
> on the matter. All he has to say upon it at present is to desire you would keep these
> entry books in yr College with his other papers, but H. M. remarking what you
> say of several letters and memoires found in these books and especially in the 10th
> vol. wch concern Sir David's, and his children's affairs, HM thinks these should be
> returned to his daughter, it being HM's intention that nothing but what relates to
> his own affairs should be kept among his papers.[2]

Although the inventory has not survived, we know that the entire
collection could be divided into four categories of papers,[3] of which the
first contained the file copies of the letters sent by the three secretaries of
state whom Nairne served at Saint-Germain:

- Lord Melfort: one folio volume of letters to the French ministers, 1691–4
  (c.300 pages).
- Lord Caryll: two folio volumes of letters to Rome and Spain, 1694–1711,
  'with a chasm from 1707 to 1710' (c.400 pages in each).

– Lord Middleton: four quarto volumes of letters to England and Spain, 1693–1703 (300–400 pages each).
: two entry books, 1693–5, and 1700–12 with gaps from 1700 to 1703 and from 1708 to 1709 (104 and 238 pages).
: another entry book containing letters described as 'some by E. Mid and most by DN', 1709–13 (70 pages).

The second category contained loose papers collected by Nairne during the course of his career from 1689 to 1720, and bound up into two folio and four quarto volumes. The spines of the folios were stamped: 'DN I. De 1689 à 1701', and 'DN II. De 1701 à 1719'. Those of the quartos were stamped: 'DN I', 'DN II', 'DN III' and 'DN IV', of which the first two contained papers from 1689 to 1701, and the third and fourth from 1701 to 1720.

The third category contained Nairne's correspondence with Cardinal Gualterio from 1713 to 1719: both the entry books of letters he sent,[5] and four quarto volumes of the letters he received.

The fourth and last category, as we have seen, contained 'letters and memoires ... wch concern Sir David's, and his children's affairs', which were 'returned to his daughter'. It is possible that the second volume of Nairne's diary, beginning in 1708, had also been deposited in the college, and that its political contents were of a sufficiently political nature for it to be retained, because Innes was instructed that 'what relates to his [the king's] own affairs should be kept with his papers'.

The family papers which were returned to Lady Ramsay have not survived, and we have no way of knowing when they were destroyed. The other three categories of papers, however, were kept in the Collège des Ecossais, and it was some of these which were published by James Macpherson in 1775 in his *Original Papers*. One year before Lady Ramsay's death, therefore, her father's name suddenly became familiar to everyone in Great Britain and elsewhere who took an interest in the history of the United Kingdom since the Glorious Revolution. We need to consider how Macpherson acquired what subsequent generations have referred to as the 'Nairne Papers'.

In January 1740, shortly after Nairne's death, the Jacobite historian Thomas Carte was given permission by James III to examine and make extracts from 'The Life of King James II', which had been written by

David Nairne covering the years up to 1678 and completed by William Dicconson.[6] He returned to the college in October 1741 to examine the original memoirs of James II on which 'The Life' had been based.[7] It seems that Carte took advantage of his second visit to the college library to remove about half of Nairne's papers. This cannot have been done with the agreement of the senior members of the college, so there can be no doubt that the volumes of papers were actually stolen.[8] Carte then took them back to England, where it seems that he made no use of them,[9] and when he died in 1754 they were inherited by his widow, who gave them to her second husband, Nicholas Jernegan. It was he who made them available to James Macpherson.[10] Either Carte or Jernegan, but more probably Macpherson, undid the volumes of loose papers, rearranged their contents and then rebound them, because those volumes are not in their original form. It is clear that many papers were destroyed and that others were removed to the wrong volumes, while at least one paper from a later period was added.

There were in total eleven volumes which Carte had taken from the Collège des Ecossais, only two of which were folios (presumably more difficult to remove). The division of the papers and their final destiny was as follows:

> Category 1. The three folio volumes of letters from Lord Melfort and Lord Caryll, and the four quarto volumes of letters from Lord Middleton all remained in the college. Carte, however, removed the three entry books of Lord Middleton.
>
> Category 2. Carte took both folios and all four quartos of loose papers collected by Nairne. These were the ones which were rearranged and rebound.
>
> Category 3. The entry books of Nairne's letters to Gualterio remained in the college. So too did the two quarto volumes of Gualterio's letters to Nairne of 1713–15, but Carte took the quarto volumes of Gualterio's letters to Nairne of 1716–19.
>
> Category 4. Carte did not take the second volume of Nairne's diary – that is, if it had been deposited in the college in the first place.

When he was preparing the *Original Papers* for publication, Macpherson also visited the College des Ecossais and was permitted to make some additional extracts from 'The Life of King James II'. He also saw some of the Nairne Papers which had remained in the college library, notably the two folio volumes of letters of Lord Caryll, from which he also copied various extracts.[11] He then provided the following introduction to the first volume of his book:

> The late Mr Thomas Carte ... had been extremely industrious in collecting materials ... Having obtained an order from Rome for inspecting such papers, belonging to the family of Stuart, as LAY OPEN in the Scotch college at Paris, he spent several months in that place, ... collecting notes ... But his most valuable acquisition was the papers of Mr Nairne, who had served as under-secretary to three successive ministers of King James, during his exile in France, from the Revolution to the year 1701. Upon the death of that prince, Nairne continued in the service of his son; and his collection contains an almost uninterrupted series of the correspondences and secret negociations of the family of Stuart, down to the year 1719.
>
> It is needless to explain minutely, why papers of such value lay so long neglected and almost unknown. They are jumbled together in such a mass of confusion, that a great deal of time and industry, and, it may even be said, a very considerable knowledge of the period to which they relate, were absolutely necessary, to give them the importance they deserve. They were placed in the Editor's hands, as materials for the history of this country ...
>
> How Nairne's collection came into the possession of Carte is as unimportant in itself, as it is imperfectly known. Several papers, particularly the letters of lord Caryll, which compleat the chain of the secret correspondence with Britain, are in the Scotch college, and have passed through the Editor's hands.[12]

In both volumes of the *Original Papers*, Macpherson included specific references in the margins to the particular volumes of the Nairne Papers from which he had taken each document. Readers of the book, and future historians who consulted it, were therefore constantly reminded of the name of the man who had originally collected the documents. At the end of the second volume, Macpherson also provided a detailed description of the two folio volumes and the nine quarto volumes which he had consulted and which had been removed from the Collège des Ecossais.[13] It was two years after the publication of Macpherson's *Original Papers*, and possibly prompted by it, that John Nairne gave the first volume of Sir David Nairne's diary to Andrew Lumisden which, as we have seen, ended up in the National Library of Scotland. One year after that, in 1778, Nicholas Jernegan gave all eleven volumes of the 'Nairne Papers' to the Bodleian Library as part of the Carte Manuscripts.[14] As a result the papers became available to any future historians who wished to consult them and who were granted access to the library. Meanwhile the diary remained in private hands, completely unknown except to a small group of family and friends.

While the eleven volumes of Nairne Papers were thus safely resting on the shelves of the Bodleian Library in Oxford, the remaining volumes of Nairne's papers and all the archives of the Stuart court at Saint-Germain were still in the Collège des Ecossais in Paris, vulnerable to the political upheavals which were beginning to overtake France. In the early 1790s, during the chaos of the French Revolution, the Collège des Ecossais was invaded by the Paris mob and its contents violated.[15] Nearly all the papers of James II and James III, and all the remaining papers of Sir David Nairne, were then confiscated by the revolutionary government and destroyed.[16] From an historical point of view this was a complete disaster, which made it impossible for nineteenth- and twentieth-century historians to carry out comprehensive research into the political and social life of the exiled court in France. Apart from various anecdotes and legends, repeated from book to book and generally misleading, the only solid evidence for the politics of the court was therefore to be found in Macpherson's published *Original Papers*, and in the Nairne Papers in the Bodleian for those who wished to check Macpherson's transcriptions, translations and selections.[17] Whether published or in manuscript, the Nairne Papers thus assumed a position of primordial importance in all books and articles on the subject of Jacobitism in British history from 1689 to 1714. This was particularly the case during the debate on the Camaret Bay Letter, and on whether or not the future Duke of Marlborough had betrayed a military secret to the Jacobite court, which was carried on in the pages of *The English Historical Review* and elsewhere between 1894 and 1933.[18]

Although David Nairne's name was frequently cited in these debates in connection with his papers, very little was known about the man himself. What had he done before 1689, and why was he originally employed by Lord Melfort? What had he done after 1714, when Macpherson's published selection came to an end, or after 1719 when the correspondence from Cardinal Gualterio abruptly terminated? The first of these questions could finally be answered when Nairne's diary was loaned by its private owners to the National Library of Scotland in 1948. The second would be answered when the archives of the Stuart court in Italy (covering the period from 1716 onwards), and many of the archives of the Collège des Ecossais, both of which narrowly escaped destruction during the Napoleonic wars, were eventually made available for research. They had been brought to England and Scotland for safety in the first half of the nineteenth century and preserved with the Royal Archives at Windsor and the Scottish Catholic Archives in Edinburgh.[19] It was the survival of these sources, together with the Nairne Papers and Nairne's private diary, which made possible the present biography.

One other source, however, needs to be mentioned. Cardinal Gualterio assembled an enormous collection of papers, covering all periods and aspects of his long career, and his archives were preserved by successive generations of his family after his death in 1728. The collection included all the letters that he received from James III and members of the Jacobite court, including the many from David Nairne, and they were sold to the British Museum by marchese Filippo Antonio Gualterio in 1854 and 1880.[20] For a study of the life and career of Nairne, these acquisitions were of the greatest importance, as they covered the years when Nairne was at his most influential. The letters received by Gualterio from Nairne from 1713 to 1719 replaced Nairne's own entry books, which had remained at the Collège des Ecossais and been destroyed during the French Revolution. The file copies of Gualterio's letters to Nairne from 1713 to 1715 replaced the original letters destroyed during the Revolution, while the ones he sent from 1716 to 1719 complemented the originals in the Bodleian Library which Carte had stolen.

It was the survival of all these papers – the Nairne Papers in the Bodleian Library, his private diary in the National Library of Scotland, the Stuart Papers at Windsor Castle, the correspondence of the Collège des Ecossais in the Scottish Catholic Archives, and the papers of Cardinal Gualterio in the British Library – which caused the legacy left by Sir David Nairne to become so important to historians of the late seventeenth and early eighteenth centuries. A biography of Sir David Nairne necessarily concentrates on the activities of one man, but it helps us to understand the conditions faced by a British ex-patriate in France and by the many British and Irish exiles who served James II and James III in France and Italy after the Glorious Revolution.

Endnotes

1. RA. SP 238/50, Edgar to T. Innes, Rome, 16 November 1741.
2. RA. SP 239/39, Edgar to T. Innes, Rome, 4 January 1742.
3. Corp, 'An Inventory of the Archives of the Stuart Court at Saint-Germain-en-Laye, 1689–1718', pp. 145–6.
4. See ibid., p. 144, for the return of some of Melfort's papers to the court in 1694. There were originally at least three volumes of Melfort's letters in the court archives. In 1703, when Nairne succeeded Lindsay as Middleton's under-secretary, he found 'only 3 entry books, viz one of Memorials and 2 of letters' in Middleton's closet (Nairne's diary, 11 June 1703).
5. See the note by Nairne on Middleton to Berry, 14 December 1713: 'the roman correspondence being my separate province I kept entrys of all my letters to Rome in a book apart from that time' (Bod. Carte MSS 212, f.62).
6. McRoberts, G., 'The Scottish Catholic Archives, 1560–1978', The Innes Review vol. XXVIII/2, autumn 1977, p. 82.
7. Ibid. p. 83.
8. Halloran, The Scots College Paris, p. 184. See also the comment on Carte MSS. 180 in the Bodleian Library manuscript 'Calendar of the Carte Papers' by E. Edward, volume 75: 'hitherto I have failed to find in Carte's MS correspondence any account of, or clue to, the manner in which Nairne's papers passed into his hands.'
9. Macpherson argued, rather implausibly, that 'Carte was not apprized of the treasure which had fallen into his hands' (Original Papers, volume I, introduction, p. 11).
10. See Edward Edwards' manuscript 'Calendar of the Carte Papers' (1877–83) in the Bodleian Library, and Madan, F. A., A Summary Catalogue of Western Manuscripts in the Bodleian Library at Oxford, vol. III (Oxford, 1895), pp. 113–56.
11. Macpherson's marginal references mention at least one of the two folio volumes of Carte's letters.
12. Macpherson, Original Papers, vol 1, pp. 5–7.
13. Ibid. vol. 2, pp. 667–80. Macpherson gave each quarto volume a number, as follows:

I to IV	DN I to DN IV
V	Lettr et Memo du Cardinal Gualterio 1716 et 1717
VI	Lettr et Memo du Cardinal Gualterio 1718 et 1719
VII to IX	Lord Middleton's entry books

14. The two folio volumes became Carte MSS 181 and 180 [*sic*], and the four quarto volumes became Carte MSS 208, 209, 210 and 211. The letters from Cardinal Gualterio became Carte MSS 257 and 258. The entry books of Lord Middleton became, respectively, Carte MSS 256, 238 and 212 [*sic*].

15. McRoberts, 'The Scottish Catholic Archives', p. 88, Gordon to Lumisden, 2 September 1792: 'Will you believe that, since 13 August the Scots College has been twice filled with armed banditti.'

16. Ibid. pp. 90–2. The papers were confiscated and never returned. Some other papers had previously been taken to Saint-Omer in 1793, where they were also destroyed (ibid. p. 89). See also Halloran, *The Scots College Paris*, p. 187.

17. See the comment on Carte MS 180 in the Bodleian Library's manuscript 'Calendar of the Carte Papers' by E. Edwards, volume 75: 'the well known printed collection of State Papers of this period by James Macpherson, which owed some of its important contents to these Nairne volumes, prints very few of the documents textually; and scarcely one of them, other than the English papers, in the original language. He always translates; almost always he selects and abridges.'

18. See pp. 57–8.

19. For the Stuart Papers, see Tayler, *The Stuart Papers at Windsor*, pp. 1–36; and Gain, M. F., 'The Stuart Papers at Windsor', *Royal Stuart Paper* XVII, 1981. For the correspondence of the Collège des Ecossais, see McRoberts, 'The Scottish Catholic Archives', pp. 92, 99.

20. The Gualterio Papers are now in the British Library.

List of Manuscript Sources

Aberdeen
    Scottish Catholic Archives: BL 1/122, 124, 130, 140, 153, 154, 166, 181
        BL 2/207, 210, 217, 222, 228, 252, 257, 264, 266, 269, 270, 277, 286, 289, 293, 294, 303, 305, 306, 324, 328, 329
        BL. 3/5, 6, 11, 13, 19, 20, 26, 29, 31, 57, 62, 64, 65
        CA. 1/9
Auxerre
    Archives Départementales de l'Yonne: 2.E.115, 3.E.70140, 40.B.43
Avignon
    Bibliothèque de la Ville d'Avignon: MS 1725, 3188
Bloomington
    University of Indiana, Lilly Library: Misc MSS 1652–1660
Bologna
    Archivio di Stato: Assunteria di Magistrati, Affari Diversi 118/19
    Biblioteca Universitaria: MS 20, 770/88
Dublin
    Trinity College Library: MS 3529
Edinburgh
    National Library of Scotland: MS 14261, 14262, 14263, 14265, 14266, 14269
Leeds
    Leeds University, Brotherton Library: MS Dep 1984/2/5
London
    British Library: Add MSS 10118, 20292, 20298, 20300, 20301, 20302, 20303, 20311, 20312, 20313, 20577, 20661, 31254, 31255, 31257, 31259, 31260, 31261, 31262, 31263, 31264, 31265, 31266, 37660, 38851, 39923, 40733, 61254, 70522
        Egerton MSS 2517
        Lansdowne MSS 1163
    National Archives: SP 92/32, 33
        SP 98/32
    Westminster Diocesan Archives: Epist Var 5, 6, 7, 9, 10
        PSP
    Wellcome Library: MS 5744
Melun
    Archives Départementales de la la Seine-et-Marne: B.636

Nancy
  Archives Départementales de Meurthe-et-Moselle: 4.F.14
Oxford
  Bodleian Library: Carte MSS 180, 181, 208, 209, 210, 211, 212, 226, 238, 257, 258
  Rawlinson MSS C.987, D.21
Paris
  Archives Diplomatiques: Correspondance Politique Angleterre 211
    Correspondence Politique Rome 188, 650, 658
  Bibliothèque Nationale de France: MSS Fd Fr Pièces Originales 2088
Rome
  Archivio Storico Vicariato di Roma: Santi Apostoli 23, \ 65, 66, 67, 68, 69, 70,
    71, 72, 73, 74, 75, 76, 77
  Irish College: Lib XXVI
  Scots College: Vol. 3 (Leslie Papers)
  Venerable English College: Libri 292
    Membrane M. 405
    Scritture 11/12, 17/2
Saint-Germain-en-Laye
  Eglise Paroissiale: Martyrologue
Simancas
  Archivio General: Secretaria de Guerra, Legajo 2559.vi, 2564.1, 2656.15
Somerset, England
  Private Collection: Kennedy Papers
Urbino
  Biblioteca Universitaria: Fondo del Comune, b.212
Vatican
  Archivio Segreto Vaticano: Fondo Albani 166, 167
    Segretario di Stato Inghilterra 25
  Biblioteca Apostolica Vaticana: Fondo Borgia Lat MS 565
    Vaticani Latini 14937
Windsor
  Royal Archives: SP 1, 3, 8, 9, 41, 42, 43, 44, 45, 46, 52, 60, 61, 66, 71, 72, 79, 80,
    84, 89, 97, 98, 102, 103, 104, 106, 108, 110, 111, 112, 118, 119, 123, 125, 136, 143,
    164, 165, 166, 167, 168, 169, 171, 172, 173, 175, 176, 178, 179, 180, 181, 184, 187,
    189, 190, 193, 194, 195, 196, 197, 198, 199, 200, 201, 202, 203, 204, 205, 206,
    207, 208, 209, 210, 211, 212, 213, 214, 215, 219, 220, 225, 232, 236, 238, 239, 240,
    247, 248, 250, 254, 277, 280, 296, 309, 315, 330, 331, 353, 362, 367, 369, 370
  SP Add 1
  SP Box 1, 2, 3
  SP Misc 7, 16, 18, 19, 21, 22

Index

Studies in the History and Culture of Scotland

Valentina Bold, General Editor
University of Edinburgh

This series presents a new reading of Scottish culture, establishing how Scots, and non-Scots, experience this devolved nation. Within the context of a rapidly changing United Kingdom and Europe, Scotland is engaged in an ongoing process of self-definition. The series will deal with this process as well as with cultural phenomena, from debates about the relative value of Gaelic-based, Scots and Anglicised culture, to period-specific definitions of Scottish identity. Orally transmitted culture – from traditional narratives to songs, customs, beliefs and material culture – will be a key consideration, along with the reconstruction of historical periods in cultural texts (visual and musical as well as historical). Taken as a whole, the series will go some way towards achieving a new understanding of a country with potential for development into parallel treatments of locally based cultural phenomena. The series welcomes monographs as well as collected papers.